Handbook of Research on Technological Developments for Cultural Heritage and eTourism Applications

João M. F. Rodrigues
University of Algarve, Portugal

Célia M. Q. Ramos
University of Algarve, Portugal

Pedro J. S. Cardoso
University of Algarve, Portugal

Cláudia Henriques
University of Algarve, Portugal

A volume in the Advances in Hospitality, Tourism, and the Services Industry (AHTSI) Book Series

IGI Global
DISSEMINATOR OF KNOWLEDGE

Published in the United States of America by
IGI Global
Business Science Reference (an imprint of IGI Global)
701 E. Chocolate Avenue
Hershey PA, USA 17033
Tel: 717-533-8845
Fax: 717-533-8661
E-mail: cust@igi-global.com
Web site: http://www.igi-global.com

Library of Congress Cataloging-in-Publication Data

Names: Rodrigues, Joao M. F., 1971-
Title: Handbook of research on technological developments for cultural heritage and eTourism applications / Joao M. F. Rodrigues, Celia M. Q. Ramos, Pedro J. S. Cardoso, and Claudia Henriques, Editors.
Description: Hershey PA : Business Science Reference, [2018]
Identifiers: LCCN 2017012413| ISBN 9781522529279 (hardcover) | ISBN 9781522529286 (ebook)
Subjects: LCSH: Tourism--Computer network resources. | Culture and tourism--Computer network resources. | Heritage tourism--Computer network resources.
Classification: LCC G156.5.I5 .T43 2018 | DDC 910.285--dc23 LC record available at https://lccn.loc.gov/2017012413

This book is published in the IGI Global book series Advances in Hospitality, Tourism, and the Services Industry (AHTSI) (ISSN: 2475-6547; eISSN: 2475-6555)

British Cataloguing in Publication Data
A Cataloguing in Publication record for this book is available from the British Library.

All work contributed to this book is new, previously-unpublished material. The views expressed in this book are those of the authors, but not necessarily of the publisher.

For electronic access to this publication, please contact: eresources@igi-global.com.

Advances in Hospitality, Tourism, and the Services Industry (AHTSI) Book Series

ISSN:2475-6547
EISSN:2475-6555

Mission

Globally, the hospitality, travel, tourism, and services industries generate a significant percentage of revenue and represent a large portion of the business world. Even in tough economic times, these industries thrive as individuals continue to spend on leisure and recreation activities as well as services.

The Advances in Hospitality, Tourism, and the Services Industry (AHTSI) book series offers diverse publications relating to the management, promotion, and profitability of the leisure, recreation, and services industries. Highlighting current research pertaining to various topics within the realm of hospitality, travel, tourism, and services management, the titles found within the AHTSI book series are pertinent to the research and professional needs of managers, business practitioners, researchers, and upper-level students studying in the field.

Coverage

- Destination Marketing and Management
- Tourism and the Environment
- Food and Beverage Management
- Cruise Marketing and Sales
- Sustainable Tourism
- Service Design
- Service Management
- Health and Wellness Tourism
- Leisure & Business Travel
- Casino Management

IGI Global is currently accepting manuscripts for publication within this series. To submit a proposal for a volume in this series, please contact our Acquisition Editors at Acquisitions@igi-global.com or visit: http://www.igi-global.com/publish/.

The Advances in Hospitality, Tourism, and the Services Industry (AHTSI) Book Series (ISSN 2475-6547) is published by IGI Global, 701 E. Chocolate Avenue, Hershey, PA 17033-1240, USA, www.igi-global.com. This series is composed of titles available for purchase individually; each title is edited to be contextually exclusive from any other title within the series. For pricing and ordering information please visit http://www.igi-global.com/book-series/advances-hospitality-tourism-services-industry/121014. Postmaster: Send all address changes to above address.

Titles in this Series

For a list of additional titles in this series, please visit: www.igi-global.com/book-series

Tourism and Opportunities for Economic Development in Asia
Patricia Ordóñez de Pablos (University of Oviedo, Spain) and Zeyar Myo Aung (Ministry of Hotels and Tourism, Myanmar)
Business Science Reference • copyright 2017 • 341pp • H/C (ISBN: 9781522520788) • US $205.00 (our price)

Handbook of Research on Strategic Alliances and Value Co-Creation in the Service Industry
Shai Rozenes (Afeka Tel-Aviv Academic College of Engineering, Israel) and Yuval Cohen (Afeka Tel-Aviv Academic College of Engineering, Israel)
Business Science Reference • copyright 2017 • 507pp • H/C (ISBN: 9781522520849) • US $235.00 (our price)

Driving Tourism through Creative Destinations and Activities
Alžbeta Kiráľová (University College of Business in Prague, Czech Republic)
Business Science Reference • copyright 2017 • 375pp • H/C (ISBN: 9781522520160) • US $200.00 (our price)

Handbook of Research on Holistic Optimization Techniques in the Hospitality, Tourism, and Travel Industry
Pandian Vasant (Universiti Teknologi PETRONAS, Malaysia) and Kalaivanthan M. (Rasa Sayang Resort and Spa, Malaysia & Golden Sands Resort, Malaysia)
Business Science Reference • copyright 2017 • 515pp • H/C (ISBN: 9781522510543) • US $235.00 (our price)

Opportunities and Challenges for Tourism and Hospitality in the BRIC Nations
Mohinder Chand Dhiman (Kurukshetra University, India)
Business Science Reference • copyright 2017 • 426pp • H/C (ISBN: 9781522507086) • US $205.00 (our price)

Strategic Place Branding Methodologies and Theory for Tourist Attraction
Ahmet Bayraktar (Bozok University, Turkey) and Can Uslay (Rutgers University, USA)
Business Science Reference • copyright 2017 • 394pp • H/C (ISBN: 9781522505792) • US $205.00 (our price)

Global Place Branding Campaigns across Cities, Regions, and Nations
Ahmet Bayraktar (Bozok University, Turkey) and Can Uslay (Rutgers University, USA)
Business Science Reference • copyright 2017 • 368pp • H/C (ISBN: 9781522505761) • US $205.00 (our price)

Global Dynamics in Travel, Tourism, and Hospitality
Nikolaos Pappas (The University of West London, UK) and Ilenia Bregoli (University of Lincoln, UK)
Business Science Reference • copyright 2016 • 372pp • H/C (ISBN: 9781522502012) • US $205.00 (our price)

IGI Global
DISSEMINATOR OF KNOWLEDGE

701 East Chocolate Avenue, Hershey, PA 17033, USA
Tel: 717-533-8845 x100 • Fax: 717-533-8661
E-Mail: cust@igi-global.com • www.igi-global.com

Editorial Advisory Board

List of Contributors

Table of Contents

Detailed Table of Contents

Information and Communication Technologies (ICT) have established a growing and deeper interconnection alliance with the tourism sector. Few solutions have contributed to the dissemination of cultural and religious heritage of the regions, as a means of promoting it, making known and enriching the culture of its visitors and residents. The development of an intelligent application that allows the dissemination of cultural and religious heritage can bring new experiences and sensations for tourists and for residents in general, and for those with accessibility problems in particular. The present chapter proposes a methodological framework for the development of a recommendation system associated with the Religious Tourism Experience Model (RTEM), with the objective of identifying and selecting consumer preferences for the dissemination of cultural heritage in general, and religious heritage in particular.

With the constant development of digital means of entertainment – that are easily made available to people and, in most cases, can be used anywhere – nowadays, a visit to a museum have to surround publics with unexpected and interactive experiences, in order to capture their attention and make them want to go to these places, in addition to continue to communicate their collections and promote society education. In this regard, it was discussed in this chapter the actual panorama of interactive technologies used in museums exhibitions worldwide, and there are discussed how these institutions are designing digital installations and utilizing virtual media to enhance the visitors' experience, promoting positive relations between them and their publics. The main conclusion and reflection of the chapter is based on how this new era of technology is allowing increasing physical, cognitive and sensory accessibility, and transforms this kind of experience for disabled publics.

Technological advances have had an impact on many industries as well as the tourism industry. Augmented reality applications, one of the emerging new technologies in recent years, have also started to be used in our daily lives. Augmented Reality (AR) is a technology that allows its users to see the real world together with an additional virtual world that is added in real time to the same field of view. The augmented reality applications contribute to the enrichment of tourists' tourism experiences, especially during their visit and result in augmented satisfaction levels. Furthermore, it is one of the effective tools that can be used against the wear and tear of cultural heritage sites caused by overcrowding. In this chapter, the application fields of the augmented reality in the field of tourism have been discussed under the subtitles. As a result of our study, recommendations for the development of AR applications both for the literature and real-life application have been presented.

The acquisition, digital representation and interaction of cultural heritage (CH) assets is of high interest for an accurate documentation of our cultural legacy. Detailed studies demand more information on the assets apart from the mere visual appearance or even shape of objects. In this regards, some research works can be found that combine shape with other kind of data, such as radiometric (e.g., IR, thermal radiation, etc.) or semantic information, leading to multi-Dimensional (mD) virtual objects. In this chapter, we review the state of the art of different techniques to deal with mD acquisition of CH tangible assets. We also discuss some representation (e.g., visual, sonic, etc.) and interaction approaches to enhance the value of CH by means of the technologies of virtual reality (VR) and augmented reality (AR), considering also the application of these techniques to tourism. Finally, we also point out some current needs and technological barriers that need to be tackled by the research community regarding the acquisition and dissemination of heritage.

The Mobile Five Senses Augmented Reality System for Museums (M5SAR) project aims to development an Augmented Reality mobile system for museums. Museums are amazing places, where it is important to sensorial augment as much as possible the visits, permitting to see, ear, touch, smell, and taste all the interesting objects there exist. Also fundamental is that visitors with different profiles (child, adult, expert, etc.) can have different experiences when visiting the same object. In the M5SAR system, the visitor uses its smartphone to select the object(s) to explore, and the user interface adapts on-the-fly to the object(s) and user's profile. Simultaneously, when integrated, a paired hardware device allows the extension of the augmented reality system to the human five senses, complementing the visual and auditory information about the objects. This chapter presents the initial framework to develop a five senses mobile adaptive museum system.

This chapter focuses on an Interactive Guide of the Portuguese Way of St. James (Camino de Santiago) created by using an Augmented Reality application. This application was developed specifically for the section of the Portuguese Route to Santiago that crosses the municipality of Barcelos (Northwest of Portugal). The Guide has the geo-information needed for the Pilgrim, in the passage by the municipality of Barcelos to Santiago, and can be accessed through a smartphone. The pilgrim will have at his or her disposal a set of interactive geo-information about Barcelos. At the level of interactivity with the user, each of these points of interest in the Guide will be signaled by a portrait done by a painter from Barcelos (monuments) and universal graphic icons (other geo-information).

Accurate modeling/reconstruction and visualization of real environments, particularly archaeological sites, is both a major challenge and a crucial task. This work will address the entire process of the virtual reconstruction of archaeological sites, since the construction of the virtual model until its visualization. The chapter begins with an introduction to the process of virtual reconstruction of archaeological sites, where the several stages that should take place to obtain a faithful virtual representation of an archaeological site and its artifacts are identified. Moreover, each stage is characterized and its main methods and techniques are identified, in dedicated sections. The authors' contribution for the state of the art will be highlighted in each stage. The chapter ends with the authors' vision about future trends for this field and unveils what could be their contributions to this vision.

This chapter offers an in-depth analysis of archaeological sites and the value they represent to the field of cultural tourism. Specifically, this chapter discusses the suitable means of studying and managing archaeological sites, which represent tangible examples of cultural tourism. Managed properly, such sites may attract a larger number of visitors and thereby contribute to the region's socioeconomic development. In order to illustrate this line of research, this analysis will focus on one archaeological site in particular, namely the Archaeological Park of Segóbriga in the province of Cuenca, Spain. More specifically, the chapter reviews survey data collected over several years by related public institutions. The findings lend support to several measures that may improve the management of such sites in the context of cultural tourism. The most important of these is the dissemination and promotion of information about the site through WOM and eWOM.

The accessibility of monuments and archaeological sites by disabled persons and persons with restricted mobility in general, constitutes a social, financial and political demand. The project "PROSPELASIS" attempted to counter this problem by focusing on creating a methodology for facing monuments' accessibility and perceptibility problems for people with disabilities and testing its application at Byzantine monuments of Thessaloniki. In six major monuments included in UNESCO's World Heritage List,

The trend of information and communication technologies (ICT) employment to enhance transactions and to deliver better experience to visitors of mass events has been growing increasingly popular over the years. The emergence of "smart tourism" agenda which highlights new, more sustainable ways of business management, experience enhancement and destination management also creates new opportunities for ICT employment in mass event. Thus, this chapter discusses existing ICT holding potential for smart approach employment on mass events. An additional case of Exit festival was used as an exploratory evidence to support the main idea of the chapter. Based on comprehensive literary review and additional information on visitors' familiarity with ICT gained from the Exit festival, recommendations for mass event managers are presented.

Creative tourism has been a proficuous ground for the implementation of ICT's (Information and Communications Technology) strategies and the so-called creative industries. New cultural mediators are changing tourism consumption. Postmodern consumers have brought new perceptions to cocreation processes through user-generated content, eWOM (Electronic Word of Mouth), peer-to-peer exchange, collaborative economy, SoLoMo (social-local-mobile) tourists, among others. Booktubers and music fans/consumers in Chile constitute examples of diverse consumption through virtual and physical mediation, as capital construction enables social practices. In this exploratory study, the authors discuss how creative experiences are being consumed through cultural mediation made possible by technological developments. The creative tourism network website is analysed in the light of postmodern cultural mediation and capital construction.

This study aims at measuring the image of the tourism brand "España Verde" by using the social media platform Facebook. The ever-increasing competition within the tourism industry makes it vital for destinations to address their target group by tailored marketing measures. Furthermore social media channels are changing the interaction between Destination Management Organizations (DMOs) and

analysis of the online community's reviews from the TripAdvisor website. The study indicates that (1) connectedness to death suggests the existence of spirituality needed by people, at the same time indicating understanding of mortality; (2) social connections developed as a result of visiting Trunyan cemetery not only bring self-awareness and awareness of others, revolving around intrapersonal communication about spirituality and interpersonal communication among members of the online community, but also illustrate the development of dark tourism and conceptualise the role of tourists in building authentic experience as the essence of a death site's brand image.

This chapter aims to expose the current situation of the adoption of cloud computing in companies in general and in enterprises of the tourism sector in particular. For this, a review of the literature has been carried out to establish the conceptual framework of technology and of the new economic model that underlies its adoption. Cloud computing is one of the technologies less known to many organizations and especially users, as it is a new technology based on the Internet, through which information is stored on servers, is provided as a service and on clients' demand. Therefore, the main theories of adoption that have been used to explain the different adoption models are presented, as well as, the different solutions that are being used in the tourist industry.

Cultural content and cultural assets are increasingly seen as invaluable drivers for education, entertainment, tourism, knowledge, and shared memory initiatives. As such, cultural information, as stored in cultural institutions such as museums, archives, and specialized libraries is increasingly demanded by several actors, from public policy, tourism, app developers and software companies, schools and the citizen at large. To satisfy the needs of such a large spectrum of consumers and end users, the information must be format independent, multi-lingual, multi-purpose, and make use of standards, norms and national and international recommendations. In this is paper we describe our past and current efforts to develop cultural information systems that can satisfy those requirements and those of the specialized public, such as scientists and curators. We describe an inventory and content management system and the conceptual and architectural choices that were made to allow its evolution, standards' compliance and multi-purpose use.

Foreword

Culture matters in sustainable economic development. A symbiotic relationship between culture and tourism should ensure that powerful drivers such as the economy, creativity, innovation, knowledge, take full advantage of the and information and communication technologies (ICTs). ICTs are established as a critical factor for sustainable competitiveness. Technology supports tangible and intangible cultural heritage to play an important role in enhancing authenticity and conservation efforts. It can reinforce engagement with prospective and actual visitors, support community values and identity as well as stakeholder participation.

A range of technologies have been used historically to support tourism (Buhalis, 2003; Egger & Buhalis, 2008; Buhalis & Law, 2008). Technology has supported consumers and the tourism demand, such as enabling tourists to plan visits to destinations more easily and allowing a progressive enrichment of tourists' experiences and knowledge. This has resulted in higher satisfaction levels among these travelers as well as in their engagement through social media and contribution to the image of the destination (Leung et al., 2013; Fotis et al., 2011; Williams et al., 2017; Hays et al., 2012; Neuhofer et al., 2014). ICTs have highlighted tourists, residents, and professionals' roles, enabling a better understanding of how their part in planning, managing, and marketing processes can produce top-quality, long-lasting tourism products.

ICT applications are widely used industry, tourism boards, and regional tourism associations. ICTs are also now applied in cultural and culture-related institutions (e.g., museums, libraries, and archives). This has resulted in significant outputs that have facilitated building the cultural identity and image of host countries, places, and attractions and have enhanced the communication of relevant content. The ever-increasing competition within the travel, tourism, cultural, and creative sectors has made it vital for destinations to address their target groups' needs by redefining marketing policies through these technologies.

Given the increased, widespread impact of new technologies on cultural tourism (Tscheu & Buhalis, 2016), this book seeks to offer a comprehensive discussion of research trends in the study of contemporary ICT systems and applications in cultural heritage and tourism. The chapters enclosed were written by international experts on the design, evaluation, implementation, and use of innovative technologies in this field. This volume's contents combine the different perspectives of cultural tourism management and technological uses in this industry and examine the role of ICTs in enhancing the value of heritage. Each chapter, therefore, connects technological developments with cultural heritage, linking and exploring the relationships between four main topics: (a) ICTs, (b) cultural heritage, (c) eTourism, and (d) tourism and assistive technologies and accessibility.

In this context, this book presents germane discussions exploring the use of ICTs such as augmented reality, multi-dimensional virtual objects, virtual reality, and a mobile system to accurately model and/or reconstruct and visualize real environments. Other applications covered are Wi-Fi information systems, building information modelling, mobile instant messaging, GISs, online community reviews, cloud computing, social media, recommendation systems, intelligent interfaces, and marketing intelligence. Further chapters discuss gamification, tangible user interfaces, 3D printing, beacons, multi-touch, and mobile and cloud computing.

Overall, this volume highlights how ICTs can be adapted to enhance cultural attractions or facilities, including not only monuments, archaeological sites, and museums but also cultural and gastronomic or cultural and religious routes, among other tourism attractions. To highlight the varied ways that cultural heritage can be interconnected with ICTs, many types of tourism are explored, namely, heritage, religious, dark, gastronomic, smart, and rural tourism. Finally, the enclosed chapters highlight the importance of companies such as hotels and restaurants to the travel and tourism industry, as well as emphasizing the role of management boards.

Cultural tourism is a growing tourism segment and experts now recognize its deep interconnection with ICTs. By enhancing the value of regional culture and history, these technologies help their preservation and dissemination, as well as promoting accessibility and reducing social and physical barriers.

Dimitrios Buhalis
Bournemouth University, UK

Dimitrios Buhalis *is Head of Department Tourism and Hospitality, Director of the eTourism Lab and Deputy Director of the International Centre for Tourism and Hospitality Research, at Bournemouth University in England. He is a Strategic Management and Marketing expert with specialisation in Information Communication Technology applications in the Tourism, Travel, Hospitality and Leisure industries. His research area is cutting across a number of disciplines and is looking into adoption of innovations for creating value for both consumers and organisations. Current research focus includes Smart Tourism, SoCoMo Marketing (Social media Context and Mobile Marketing), Augmented Reality, Experience management and Personalisation, Reputation and Social Media Strategies, Accessible and Special Diet (Alergens) Tourism. Close collaboration with industry, governments and international organisations from around the world ensures that results have relevance and impact in the real world whilst constantly pushing the boundaries of knowledge and academic excellence. Dimitrios is also the immediate past President of the International Federation for Information Technologies in Travel and Tourism (IFITT). Dimitrios is researching, lecturing, advising and facilitating progress in organisations globally, whilst his books and publications are studied widely by both students and professionals around the world. He is frequently delivering keynote presentations, speeches, seminars and workshops in both academic and professional conferences globally.*

REFERENCES

Boes, K., Buhalis, D., & Inversini, A. (2016). Smart tourism destinations: Ecosystems for tourism destination competitiveness. *International Journal of Tourism Cities*, *2*(2), 108–124. doi:10.1108/IJTC-12-2015-0032

Buhalis, D. (2003). *eTourism: Information technology for strategic tourism management*. Pearson.

Buhalis, D., & Law, R. (2008). Progress in tourism management: Twenty years on and 10 years after the internet: The state of eTourism research. *Tourism Management*, *29*(4), 609–623. doi:10.1016/j.tourman.2008.01.005

Egger, R., & Buhalis, D. (2008). *eTourism Case studies: Management & Marketing issues in eTourism*. Butterworth Heinemann Oxford.

Fotis, J., Buhalis, D., & Rossides, N. (2011). Social media impact on holiday travel: The case of the Russian and the FSU markets. *International Journal of Online Marketing*, *1*(4), 1–19. doi:10.4018/ijom.2011100101

Hays, S., Page, S., & Buhalis, D. (2012). Social media as a destination marketing tool: Its use by national tourism organisations. *Current Issues in Tourism*, *16*(3), 211–239. doi:10.1080/13683500.2012.662215

Leung, D., Law, R., van Hoof, H., & Buhalis, D. (2013). Social Media in Tourism and Hospitality: A Literature Review. *Journal of Travel & Tourism Marketing*, *30*(1-2), 1–2, 3–22. doi:10.1080/10548408.2013.750919

Neuhofer, B., Buhalis, D., & Ladkin, A. (2014). A Typology of Technology-Enhanced Tourism Experiences. *International Journal of Tourism Research*, *16*(4), 340–350. doi:10.1002/jtr.1958

Tscheu, F., & Buhalis, D. (2016). Augmented Reality at Cultural Heritage sites. In A. Inversini & R. Schegg (Eds.), *Information and Communication Technologies in Tourism 2016 ENTER* (pp. 607–619). Springer. doi:10.1007/978-3-319-28231-2_44

Williams, N., Inversini, A., Buhalis, D., & Ferdinand, N. (2017). Destination eWOM drivers and characteristics. *Annals of Tourism Research*, *64*, 87–101. doi:10.1016/j.annals.2017.02.007

Preface

INTRODUCTION

Computational devices capable of connecting to the Internet, such as personal computers, smartphones or tablets, are currently available to almost everyone. Those computational devices are used in the most ordinary activities, including recreation, education or travelling, bringing information, culture and visiting experiences to a different level, while possibly helping in the accessibility improvement as well as in the info-exclusion mitigation. Upstream to the referred activities are the Information and Communications Technologies (ICT), often used as an extended synonym for Information Technologies. ICT is a more extensive term that stresses the role of unified communications, enterprise software, middleware, storage, and audio-visual systems, which enable users to access, store, transmit, and manipulate information.

On the other hand, touristic experiences, and in particular Cultural Tourism experiences, can only be understood in a dynamic and evolutionary framework, considering the complexity of the culture conceptualization as well as its role in a sustainable development. Therefore, culture can be considered as a key tourism resource, which contributes and inspires millions of tourists to travel and visit new destinations, several times a year. Cultural Tourism can be a considerable strength for the promotion and safeguarding of the tangible and intangible heritage it relies on, if it is managed and developed in a sustainable manner, while promoting and encouraging the development of creative activities associated to this heritage and the enhancement of the destination profile.

Marrying ICT and Cultural Tourism experiences concepts will enhance touristic destination profiles, providing innovation through the interconnection between culture, knowledge and technologies. The correct conjugation of those will also grant an enduring sustainable development. The profile enhancement creates a main drive for the development of a region where the authenticity, conservation, community, cultural values, and stakeholder's participation play the main role.

This reflection leads us to the Cultural Heritage perspective which should be understood as an expression of the ways of living developed by a community and passed on from generation to generation, including customs, practices, places, objects, artistic expressions, and values. Cultural Heritage is also often expressed as either tangible culture, which includes e.g., buildings, monuments, landscapes, books, works of art, and artefacts, or intangible culture, which includes e.g., folklore, dance, traditions, language, and knowledge. Nevertheless, it can also include natural heritage, such as culturally significant landscapes and biodiversity. In this context, the main assumption is that Cultural Heritage should consider the cultural values of the heritage, processes, community concerns, and administrative practices, conjugated in a way that contributes to a participation in socio-economic benefits for the stakeholders.

Therefore, considering the importance of culture in a sustainable development, it is relevant the role of ICT promoting a balanced approach between the needs, to potentiate the growth of cultural tourism market and better tourism experiences on one side, and the preservation of artifacts, historical sites, and local traditions on the other. A memorable cultural tourism experience should be based on uniqueness, authenticity and differentiation. Having in mind a growing emphasis on creativity, the basis to a more future-oriented creative tourism that values culture, contemporary creativity, technological platforms and contents, innovation, and networks is achievable, financing not only public but also private partnerships.

Associated with the Cultural Heritage experiences, is the eTourism ("electronic travel" or "electronic tourism") which can be defined as the analysis, design, implementation and application of IT and e-commerce solutions in the travel and tourism industry, as well as the analysis of the respective economic processes and market structures and customer relationship management.

Handbook of Research on Technological Developments for Cultural Heritage and eTourism Applications addresses the contemporary ICT technology applied to the disclosure of cultural and natural heritage, including tangible and intangible culture. In parallel, the book aims to reflect on the contemporary ICT relationship between tourism and history, based on the touristic use of the human cultural heritage. Likewise, the book addresses the interconnection with the called smart destinations, as the innovative tourist destination built on an infrastructure of state-of-the-art technology, which guarantees the sustainable development of tourist areas, facilitates the visitor's interaction with the surroundings, increasing the quality of the experience at the destination, but also in the improvements on residents' quality of life. The integration of this technology as special cases of smart cities, will also be an important point of interest.

Essentially, this book unites and explores the relations between three main topics: (a) Information and Communications Technology, (b) Cultural Heritage, and (c) eTourism. The objective of the book is to bring together a comprehensive collection of research trends on contemporary ICT systems and application in Cultural Heritage and Tourism from a set of international experts on the design, evaluation, implementation and use of innovative technologies on the field. In summary, the book emphasizes the connection between contemporary information and communications technologies with cultural heritage and tourism and eTourism.

Policy makers, academicians, researchers, advanced-level students, technology developers or simple curious, that are interested in the new trends in ICT systems and application to Cultural Heritage and Tourism are the target Audience. The book focuses on several different systems and applications, from mobile to "desktop" (three-dimensional) interfaces based on different natural interactions, to augmented reality solutions, and educational applications. Applications dedicate to different ways/types of accessibilities and applications where the Internet-of-Things is the interconnection of uniquely identifiable embedded computing devices, are also presented. All these, are centered in the main subject of Cultural Heritage and eTourism. All actors in this huge area will find this text useful in furthering their research exposure to pertinent topics and assisting in furthering their own research efforts in this field.

ORGANIZATION OF BOOK

The book is organized as follows:

Chapter 1 proposes a methodological framework for the development of a recommendation system associated with the Religious Tourism Experience Model, with the objective of identifying and selecting consumer preferences for the dissemination of cultural heritage in general, and religious heritage in particular.

Chapter 2 discusses the actual panorama of interactive technologies used in museums exhibitions and how these institutions are designing digital installations and utilizing virtual media to enhance the visitors' experience.

In Chapter 3, the authors present a concept of augmented reality, the different aspects of it from other similar concepts, the infrastructure requirements, and analyze the applications examples in the tourism industry in the world especially within the content of destination marketing.

Chapter 4 reviews the state of the art of different techniques to deal with multi-dimensional acquisition of cultural heritage tangible assets. The authors also discuss some representation (e.g., visual, sonic, etc.) and interaction approaches to enhance the value of cultural heritage by means of the technologies of virtual reality and augmented reality, considering also the application of these techniques to tourism. Finally, they also point out some current needs and technological barriers that need to be tackled by the research community regarding the acquisition and dissemination of heritage.

Chapter 5 presents a framework to develop a mobile five human senses augmented reality museum system. This is to be used as a guide in cultural, historical and museum events, complementing or replacing the traditional orientation given by tour guides, directional signs, or maps. The system consists of a smartphone/phablet application and a hardware device to be integrated with smartphones/phablets, in order to explore the five human senses: sight, hearing, touch, smell, and taste.

Chapter 6 focuses on an Interactive Guide of the Portuguese Way of St. James (Camino de Santiago) created by using an Augmented Reality application. The Guide has the geo-information needed for the Pilgrim, in the passage by the municipality of Barcelos to Santiago, and can be accessed through a smartphone.

In Chapter 7, the authors begin with an introduction to the process of virtual reconstruction of archaeological sites, where the several stages that should take place to obtain a faithful virtual representation of an archaeological site and its artifacts are identified. Moreover, each stage is characterized and its main methods and techniques are identified. The chapter ends with the authors' vision about future trends for this field and unveils what could be their contributions to this vision.

Chapter 8 offers an in-depth analysis of archaeological sites and the value they represent to the field of cultural tourism. Specifically, it discusses the suitable means of studying and managing archaeological sites. In order to illustrate this line of research, this analysis will focus on one archaeological site in particular, namely the Archaeological Park of Segóbriga in the province of Cuenca, Spain.

In Chapter 9, the authors mention the problem associated to the accessibility of monuments and archaeological sites by disabled persons and persons with restricted mobility in general, which constitutes a social, financial and political demand. To overcome this problem, the authors presents the project "PROSPELASIS" to counter this challenge by focusing on creating a methodology for facing monuments' accessibility and perceptibility problems for people with disabilities and testing its application at Byzantine monuments of Thessaloniki.

Chapter 10 presents an approach for the preservation and exploration of the archaeological-historical information using the most modern methods of building information modelling together with virtual and augmented reality adapted to archaeology. This three-dimensional model is used to virtually reconstruct the Milreu archeological site, bringing this ancient Roman villa to life again, and supports the virtual reality platform and augmented reality for mobile devices.

Chapter 11 presents an essay involving the relations between the tourist appropriation of an historical architectural attraction – namely Jesuitic Mission of São Miguel – Brazil (legacy of the Guaraní Jesuit Missions - South America) – and the use of digital technology tools.

Chapter 12 discusses the information and communication technology potential to implement a smart approach on mass events. A known music festival was used as an exploratory evidence to support the main idea of the chapter, allowing to present some recommendations for mass event managers.

In Chapter 13, the authors present an exploratory study with the discussion of how creative experiences are being consumed through cultural mediation made possible by technological developments. In addition, the study is complemented with analysis of the creative tourism network website in the light of postmodern cultural mediation and capital construction.

Chapter 14 aims at measuring the image of the tourism brand "España Verde" by using the social media platform Facebook. The ever-increasing competition within the tourism industry makes it vital for destinations to address their target group by tailored marketing measures. Furthermore, social media channels are changing the interaction between Destination Management Organizations and customers. With the aim of exploring España Verde's image, a three components approach: cognitive, affective and conative was applied. Related to the measurement of the cognitive component, the study also focuses on España Verde's touristic potential ranging from a rich and diverse culture as well as a unique natural heritage to a suitable infrastructure for touristic purposes.

In Chapter 15, the cultural tourism consumers are analyzed in a way to understand their decision making process, when use the mobile instant messaging as a communication channel to choice a restaurant, in a social media platform. To achieve the objective was conducted a questionnaire to identify which channels are most used by consumers, when they intend to receive gastronomic recommendations. In the study, the conclusions identified that the channel use is determined by its instantaneousness and permanent information availability and due to a lack of knowledge about the area where the users is.

Chapter 16 analyzes the relationship between mycological tourism and Geographic Information Systems as a tool for tourism planning in rural areas. All this from a participatory approach in which traditional ecological knowledge serves as a source of information and a point of reference to guide policies for economic restructuring of rural areas.

Chapter 17 presents an essay that aims to explain the phenomenon and effect on tourism of the Balinese cemetery in the village of Trunyan, where the dead are not buried. It is a narrative enquiry combined with critical theory largely grounded in the scholarship of dark tourism and communication theory, coupled with content analysis of the online community's reviews from the TripAdvisor website.

In Chapter 18, the adoption of cloud computing in companies in general and in enterprises of the tourism sector in particular is addressed. The chapter includes a literature review to establish the conceptual framework of the technology and of the new economic model that underlies its adoption.

Chapter 19 describes some of the major issues around the cultural semantic web, including issues and range of choices institutions are facing to make data available on the web. Also introduced was Index Rerum, an inventory system based on an object-oriented model, as an example of managing collections and publishing data using the linked open data principles.

Last but not the least, for the book conclusion, one of the main topics that should always be in the center of any technological development and/or travel, the ecological footprint. In this case the minimization of energy consumption and the use of renewable energy. Chapter 20 describes the challenges involved in developing of a decision support platform to help hoteliers monitor their energy consumption, identify which points are consuming more than expected, decide which investments are more cost effective, and manage their equipment in an optimum way. In this sense, the chapter covers several research fields, including internet of things networks, smart grids, renewable energy, and energy efficiency.

As a final point, it is important to reinforce, that the major contribution of the book, it is the "book as a whole". The "all" is bigger than the sum of the "parts", once the sum of the chapters created a book expected to interest to everyone that works or studies ICT applied to Cultural Heritage and Tourism. Nevertheless, each chapter brings to its respective sub-area the state of the art, showing applications, most of them not yet developed, except by the authors.

João M. F. Rodrigues
University of Algarve, Portugal

Célia M. Q. Ramos
University of Algarve, Portugal

Pedro J. S. Cardoso
University of Algarve, Portugal

Cláudia Henriques
University of Algarve, Portugal

Acknowledgment

The editors would like to acknowledge the help of all the people involved in this project. We especially would like to express our gratitude to the chapter authors' and to the colleagues Ana Mafé Garcia, Ana Renda, António Cunha, Arsénio Reis, Cristiano Cabrita, Cristina Moreira, Delia Garijo, Fernando Perna, Francisco Munoz Lleiva, Gorete Dinis, Isabel Sofia Brito, Janet Hernandez, José Álvarez García, José Figueiredo Santos, Mª Mercedes Rojas Gracia, Muhammad Islam, Özgür Külcü, Pedro Garcês, Raul Guerreiro, Roberto Lam, Silvia Fernandes, Susana Gastal, Tuğçe Ozansoy Çadırcı, Vitor Filipe, Vitor Roque, who took part in the review process.

The editors would also like to acknowledge their research centers, LARSyS (Laboratory of Robotics and Engineering System – FCT: UID/EEA/50009/2013), ISR-Lisbon (Institute for Systems and Robotics, CIAC-UAlg (Center for Research in Communication Sciences and Arts), CEFAGE (Center for Advanced Studies in Management and Economics of the Universidade de Évora - CPEst-C/EGE/UI4007/2013) and CIEO - UAlg (Centre for Spatial and Organizational Dynamics).

Chapter 1
Religious Tourism Experience Model (RTEM): A Recommendation Model for Dissemination of Cultural and Religious Heritage

Célia M. Q. Ramos
University of Algarve, Portugal

Cláudia Henriques
University of Algarve, Portugal

João M. F. Rodrigues
University of Algarve, Portugal

ABSTRACT

Information and Communication Technologies (ICT) have established a growing and deeper interconnection alliance with the tourism sector. Few solutions have contributed to the dissemination of cultural and religious heritage of the regions, as a means of promoting it, making known and enriching the culture of its visitors and residents. The development of an intelligent application that allows the dissemination of cultural and religious heritage can bring new experiences and sensations for tourists and for residents in general, and for those with accessibility problems in particular. The present chapter proposes a methodological framework for the development of a recommendation system associated with the Religious Tourism Experience Model (RTEM), with the objective of identifying and selecting consumer preferences for the dissemination of cultural heritage in general, and religious heritage in particular.

DOI: 10.4018/978-1-5225-2927-9.ch001

INTRODUCTION

At present, cultural consumption has become increasingly important, constituting a way of experiencing tourist experiences that are different from the daily routine of individuals (Urry, 2002). Richards (1996) and Russo and Borg (2002), have shown that cultural tourism is the main source of income for tourism (Urry, 2002).

Al Subhi, Bell and Lashmar (2015) point out that technologies are needed to enhance / increase the experiences of visitors so as to increase revenues and increase audiences (new visitors). They further note that the cultural heritage sector recognizes the value of presenting different content and different styles of personalization for different types of people (Falk, 2009), and that services can be customized to the different needs and preferences of children, parents and teachers.

In addition, Al Subhi et al. (2015) note that the existing literature on heritage and mobile technology is virtually focused on museums, and that there is a large gap in the use of devices, furniture and technology in large heritage sites such as monuments. Most studies have been carried out on tourist towns, and little attention has been given to integrated solutions for heritage sites and technology that enhance the socio-economic benefits of regions and cities. Lastly, it is beneficial to consider user-centered solutions that allow for a substantial collection of information by non-professional users, in order to create experiences and different values for visitors seeking a cultural aspect.

The structuring of cultural (religious) products for tourist purposes should be based on knowledge of trends in consumer behavior and major tourist market niches. At the same time, it should be "to facilitate knowledge and assist in co-designing sustainable tourism development" (Center for Tourism, Innovation and Culture [TIC], 2015).

The acquisition of knowledge of religious heritage by tourists, residents, and in particular those who have access difficulties (i.e., physical and mental disabilities) is enhanced when it is associated with technological innovations, especially once it is possible to offer new experiences and sensations to all visitors, including ones who have accessibility problems. One of the most important features is the possibility for a tourist to have access to the same information, regardless of their physical limitations. Another relevant potentiality is to reduce the negative impacts of tourism by reducing overcrowding of visitors attempting to access threatened or protected places.

ICT is excellent for contributing to the communication and acquisition of the cultural heritage of a region (Inversini & Cantoni, 2011) and for allowing the development of innovative solutions that meet the interests of economic and touristic partners. In parallel (Falk, 2009), the cultural heritage sector recognizes the value of presenting different content and different styles for different types of people where services can be tailored to the different needs and preferences of children, parents and teachers.

An innovative solution to meet this need is the development of a pioneering mobile smart application to disseminate tourism, cultural and religious heritage content in order to improve the tourist experience, as well as residents' learning.

The development of applications for mobile devices applied to the tourism sector is not new, since there are several prototypes developed in the academic world that combine tourism with Artificial Intelligence (AI) in a recommendation system to the tourist.

In this chapter the authors proposes a framework for the development of a recommendation system in order to identify and select consumer preferences, which can be classified according to the target market, forms of recommendation, use of knowledge or algorithms implementation, with the aim of promoting contents associated with heritage, cultural and religious tourism: The Religious Tourism Experience Model (RTEM).

The chapter is organized as follows: in the next section, Background, describes religious tourism and religious itineraries that potentiate the cultural tourism experience valorization, followed by the contributions that ICT makes to tourism activity, taking in consideration the recommendation systems that have been developed through research carried out in the academic community, and in terms of developing commercial applications applied to tourism activity. This section also identifies some gaps and challenges that these kinds of systems have to overcome. The next section presents the framework proposed by the authors, RTEM, associated with the development of a recommendation system for the Religious Tourism Experience Model, including the definition of the methodology needed to build the system, and consequently the explanation of each part of the technological architecture. The following section suggests future directions in research and ways that the proposed technological model can be improved. Finally, some conclusions are presented about the recommendation system and technological architecture presented in this chapter.

BACKGROUND

Religious Tourism and Religious Heritage Itineraries: A Cultural Tourism Experience

According to UNESCO's 2001 Universal Declaration on Cultural Diversity, culture can be seen as "the set of distinctive spiritual, material, intellectual and emotional features of a society or a social group that encompasses art and literature, lifestyles, ways of living together, value systems, traditions and beliefs" (UNESCO, 2001). UNWTO/UNESCO's (2015) World Conference on "Tourism and Culture: Building a New Partnership" recognizes culture as: "A key tourism asset, inspiring millions of tourists to visit new destinations each year. Sustainably managed, tourism can be a considerable force for the promotion and safeguarding of the tangible and intangible heritage it relies on, while encouraging the development of arts, crafts and other creative activities".

Religion, as part of culture, is linked with various elements of people's lives (Poria, Butler, & Airey, 2003; Nyaupane, Timothy, & Poudel, 2015). "Religion as a cultural system" (Geertz, 2004), as "a system of symbols" (Geertz, 2004: 91), is associated with a "the religious perspective". This perspective "is a particular way of looking at life, a particular manner of construing the world, as when we speak of an historical perspective, a scientific perspective, an aesthetic perspective, a common-sense perspective, or even the bizarre perspective embodied in dreams and in hallucinations" (Geertz, 2004: 101).

Regarding the relationship between religion and tourism, it could be better understood in a historical context. As Rot, Mikinac and Bogdan (2014) underlines, it is "clearly visible in a deeper insight into the historical context of tourism, especially if religion is viewed as one of the oldest motives of human migration a fundamental need to travel". Recently, the "Conference on Religious Heritage and Tourism: How to increase religious heritage tourism in a changing society" (UNWTO, 2016), highlights the importance of tourism, and namely religious heritage tourism as "an international phenomenon, involving thousands of people of different nationalities from around the world". The conference discussed how religious heritage sites enrich the attractiveness of destinations and how they drive international tourism and economic growth. The main questions in discussion were: "How can we further develop the social and economic impact of religious heritage tourism?; How can we further develop religious heritage sites as tourist destinations?; From which good practices can we learn to bring religious heritage tourism forward?".

Religious tourism is associated with a complex and wide spectrum of definitions. Following UNWTO (2011: xv), this type of tourism is "spiritually inclined or favorably disposed towards the values of different cultures and is sensitive towards, and cognizant of, differences, has an important role to play in creating social solidarity at various levels, and hence is crucial in the maintenance of existing social structures and creation of organization and structure where none existed before."

Religious tourism definitions vary from the visitation of a particular "holy" destination, to individual or group travel: with the core motive of experiencing religious forms, or the products they induce, like art, culture, traditions and architecture (SIGA, 2012: 2).

However, religion could be the primary motivation for traveling to a destination, but it could also be combined with other tourist motivations (linked to other kind of attractions). "According to UNWTO estimates, 300 to 330 million tourists visit the world's key religious sites every year, with approximately 600 million national and international religious voyages in the world, 40% of which take place in Europe. Being key tourism destinations, religious heritage sites not only drive international tourism and economic growth, but also provide important meeting grounds for visitors and host communities, making vital contributions to tolerance, respect and mutual understanding between different cultures." (UNWTO, 2014).

As other types of tourism, religious tourism has positive and negative impacts. For instance, the concentration of many visitors (pilgrims, cultural and religious tourists) into a limited area on the occasion of particular religious events can cause a secularization of the phenomenon, a weakening of beliefs in the sacred and divine and a general limitation of the social role of religious institutions (Timothy & Olsen, 2006: 12-13). Consequently, planning and management are determinants in order to value the places and induce positive impacts in local communities.

"Itineraries, understood as opportunities for integrated marketing of culture, economy and tourism, are increasingly preferred to places. An itinerary enables the tourist to access the "ancient palimpsest", the unique text, written and rewritten over the course of time, that is the landscape-system, to decode it and to interpret it, to grasp its environmental, historic and cultural meaning, to experience it profoundly even in terms of its economic aspects (Scazzosi, 1999: 10; in Rizzo, Rizzo & Trono, 2013: 62). Itineraries (whether they are based on food-and-wine, nature, culture or religion) enable a linear enjoyment of the landscape in terms of its physical components and historic layers, together with its underlying system of signs and its distinctive economic resources. They favor short production chains in integrated economic activities such as agriculture, handicrafts and accommodation. They bring together various factors of cultural interest (gastronomy, handicrafts, folklore, architecture) and environmental interest, providing an opportunity for regional development. This type of journey has considerable implications in terms of planning the tourist sector and other economic activities: it promotes tourist marketing activities, facilitates the creation of a network of alliances between rural areas, and produces income and employment." (Rizzo et al., 2013: 62).

Creating a cultural itinerary means implementing public policies that safeguard it and promote it. The recognition on the institutional level (regional and/or European) of routes of historic, artistic, religious and naturalistic interest represents the validation of a new model of cultural tourism involving exciting journeys that go beyond traditional circuits, making it possible to rediscover the most authentic cultural roots in the sharing of a common heritage. However, it is also a powerful expression of interest in a new model that creates regional development. (Rizzo et al., 2013: 62).

Itineraries linked to religious tourism or local religious heritage could be seen as a "depositary and representative" of local qualities, cultures, identities and landscapes that it itself has partly contributed toward forging over the course of time (Rizzo et al., 2013: 62).

Linked with a tourist cultural (religious) experience, the itinerary involves "everything a tourist goes through at a destination as experience" (Bosangit, Hibbert, & McCabe, 2015:1), considering behavior and perception, cognition and emotions; either expressed or implied (Oh, Fiore & Jeoung, 2007; Skavronskaya et al., 2017). According to Lin and Kuo (2016), the nature and range of tourist experiences offered by a destination determines the destination's value and in turn, customer satisfaction, loyalty to the destination and intention to return. Therefore, customer experience understanding and management are essential for tourism professionals.

A tourist experience (Pine & Gilmore, 1999; Richards & Wilson, 2006), once it is associated with a thematic, leads, in a religious tourism context, to a "thematic analysis led to the identification of both secular and more spiritual experiences. The two dominant experiences revealed by visitors' feedback are getting an educational experience and having a good time".

Customer experience is partly revealed by the stories customers tell (McGregor & Holmes, 1999), and narrative approaches have been widely used to gain insights into experiential consumption (Thompson & Arnold, 1998). The rise of online social networks, tourist blogs and platforms such as TripAdvisor or Facebook has made customer stories increasingly available online. These online stories provide a new and valuable pool of data for researchers in tourism to analyze. Customer experiences revealed through online customer feedback need to be taken into account by tourism marketing managers as they are known to influence future visitors' decisions to travel to a destination (Cerutti & Piva, 2016; Skavronskaya et al., 2017).

The ICT inserted into the religious tourism environment can contribute, promote and divulgate the cultural heritage of a region and at the same potentiate the acquisition of knowledge about the residents' value and identity. One of the most appropriate solutions is to develop a recommendation system to show the religious heritage to the cultural tourist, in general, and in particular to the religious tourist and to the residents.

RECOMMENDATION SYSTEMS APPLIED TO TOURISM ACTIVITY

Recommendation Systems (Fesenmaier, Wöber, & Werthner, 2006; Gavalas, Konstantopoulos, Mastakas, & Pantziou 2014; Staab et al., 2002) are terms used in the area of information systems to achieve the goal of identifying and selecting consumer preferences. Other names for this type of application may appear in the scientific community: "Collective intelligence" (Xiang & Gretzel, 2010), "Business intelligence" (Burke & Hiltbrand, 2011), "Intelligent environments" (Blohm & Leimeister, 2013), "Smart user-centered interfaces" (Xu, Weber, & Buhalis, 2013), "Smart technology" (Neuhofer, Buhalis, & Ladkin, 2015).

To develop smart environments for tourists, recommendation systems need to include: Intelligent user-centered interface that integrates usability and accessibility features, supports the behavior and learning and decision-making process of consumers and integrates assistive technologies to provide users with accessibility problems, since this interaction can affect the decision-making processes of tourists and residents.

These kinds of information systems can work by using demographic data (Lam, Vu, Le, & Duong, 2008), where recommendations are presented according to the personal characteristics of the user, by request of evaluations (Roine, 2010) and presentation of suggestions according to the evaluations, by cold-start (Roine, 2010) ("fast learners, trusted users, tagging"), by itinerary (pre-defined travel plan (Roine, 2010), artistic or cultural value (Ardissono et al., 2001; Kabassi, 2010), by price (Huang & Bian, 2009) and by geographical position (Roine, 2010).

The recommendations can appear by taking into consideration methods based on: Probabilistic models (Lillegraven & Wolden, 2010), Bayesian models (Roine, 2010, Huang & Bin, 2009, Hsu, Lin, & Ho, 2012), Case Based Reasoning (Coyle & Cunningham, 2003; Anacleto, Figueiredo, Almeida, & Novais, 2014), Association Rules (Schiaffino & Amandi, 2009), K-means clusters (Kops, 2013), Ontologies (Anacleto et al., 2014), Decision trees (Anacleto et al., 2014), Genetic Algorithms (Zheng, Liao, & Qin, 2017), among others.

Also, different approaches can be considered (Burke, 1999; Lu, Wu, Mao, Wang & Zhang, 2015) to develop these systems, such as: Content-based filtering, Collaborative filtering, Knowledge-based, Computational Intelligence (Bayesian networks, clustering, genetic algorithm, neural networks and fuzzy logic), Social networks based or based on context.

New applications are emerging every day to recommend tourists to visit certain cultural sites or Points-of-Interest (POI), which enhance and benefit tourism (Herlocker, Konstan, & Riedl, 2000): the recommendation of a particular site justifies its cultural importance and enhances its value as justify-motivation, the more knowledge a user acquires, the more involvement he / she will generate since he / she can use his / her own knowledge and personal skills in the decision-making process. The potentialities and gaps of the system are transparent to the user which leads to a rapid acceptance by the user (acceptor), who finally, through the clarification and acquisition of knowledge, studies the gaps and potential of the sites and learns to value them.

In this context, the development of applications for mobile devices associated with tourism has aroused the interest of several entities in the professional and scientific community, which has fostered the emergence of several applications that do not contemplate the intelligence component and which have the objective of presenting personalized information in accordance with the category of the tourist, but not in terms of identifying intelligence associated with consumer behaviors.

The development of applications for mobile devices' recommendation systems applied to tourism is not recent, even in the scientific environment and commercial world, there are several prototypes developed to support activity undertaken during a trip.

RECOMMENDATION SYSTEMS IN THE SCIENTIFIC COMMUNITY

In the scientific community, recommendation systems can be based on different approaches as presented earlier (Lu et al., 2015). Table 1 presents the works that were evidenced in the review of literature on tourism recommendation systems, developed in the last fifteen years; however, the list of the works is not limited to the table.

Schmidt-Belz et al. (2002) developed a system called CRUMPET (Creation of User-friendly Mobile Services Customized for Tourism) with customization, context-sensitive features, ease of iteration and

Table 1. Tourism recommendation systems in the scientific community

	Personalization	Context Awareness	Location Based	Itinerary	Highlights
CRUMPET (Schmidt-Belz, Nick, Poslad & Zipf, 2002)	X	X	X		
MTSR (Roine, 2010)		X	X	X	Interactive map
CARS (Adomavicius & Tuzhilin, 2011)	X (by consumption segment)	X	X		Include the weather, temperature and user's emotional state
ITAS (Hsu, Lin, & Ho, 2012)				X	Considers the purchasing decision process and the model EBM (Blackwell, Miniard & Engel, 2001)
MyTourGuide (Husain, Dih, Yen & Jothi, 2012)	X		X	X	Considers the scores awarded by others.
TourExp (Buján et al., 2013)	X	X	X	X	Ubique computacion
George (Kops, 2013)	X (by consumption segment)		X		Consider usability and content design concepts
PSiS Mobile (Anacleto et al., 2014)	X	x	X	X	Battery saving Stores all user moves
WHACY (Adukaite, 2015)			X	X	Game to informally educate and facilitate sustainable tourism

Source: Author's elaboration.

mediation of services. The objective of this project was to implement, test and validate personalized services for tourists, based on technology that integrated the systems based on the location and presentation of personalized information for the user.

The interests of users were modeled according to the domain of taxonomy. The taxonomy of services related to tourism, which consist of a set of concepts and attributes that describe the service, as well as the interest of the user is seen as a function that maps these concepts and attributes according to the probability of the user's interest in that service.

Yu and Chang (2009) presented a prototype application of a recommendation system and development for an object-oriented database, defined by an entity association model that was transformed into a relational model, which aggregated information on landscapes, restaurants and accommodation. The system presented the recommendation of an itinerary to the tourist based on the tourist location.

Garcia, Arbelaitz, Linaza, Vansteenwegen and Souffriau (2010) developed a Personalized Electronic Tourist Guide (PET) for local attractions and the public transport system through the presentation of an intelligent and personalized itinerary. This was presented in three phases: recommendation, creation of the itinerary and personalization of the itinerary. The PET system uses an Operations Research algorithm to generate custom itineraries for tourists, which could be configured. The calculated itinerary was aimed at maximizing customer satisfaction, taking into account the times of public transport and the POIs that the tourist would like to visit. It was initialized with data from the city of San Sebastian in Spain.

Roine (2010) introduced the Mobile Tourism Service Recommender (MTSR), which was an application developed for Smartphones with an Android operating system. The MTSR's information was presented on an interactive map where the user could zoom and move the map, context-sensitive and location-based (which can be based on person-oriented Location-based system (LBS) or device-oriented LBS), where the user can search for POIs, complete travel itineraries or evaluate where they have been. This system considered the Bayesian reasoning model to perform. The recommendations were based on the demographic data: age, gender, occupation, type of vacation, nationality and budget. The calculations were made by the "client", where they considered several matrices constituted by Boolean variables to increase the speed of calculations. On the client side this architecture has as limitations the fact that the calculations are carried out on the customer side, which shortens the battery very quickly and consequently increases the time needed to make an order and receive a response.

In applications whose content is context-sensitive, Kabassi (2010) states that it is necessary to take into account the personal context that includes the user's current location, previously visited POIs and personal preferences so that it is possible to identify characteristics that are likely to be in accordance with preferences of the tourist.

Adomavicius and Tuzhilin (2011) have developed the Context-Aware Recommender System (CARS) with the assumption that the application should be able to reach and "touch" consumers anytime and anywhere in order to present them with real-time products that contribute to their experience, for which it is necessary to include data mining concepts (for example, to identify changes in the preferences, marital status, births of children), e-commerce personalization (in order to create a contextual consumer profile for each purchase and a comparison is made between each profile so that it is possible to predict consumer behavior in each specific context and in each consumer segment) (Palmisano, Tuzhilin & Gorgoglione, 2008), time, place and weather, mobile devices with ubiquitous links to location systems (to identify nearby objects, people around them and possible changes in these elements, should also include date, season, temperature and, if possible, the emotional state of the user), databases (to store all consumer data), extraction of information that takes into account the characteristics associated with context, marketing and management (each consumer can adopt different strategies in the process and may prefer different products according to the context in which they are found).

Another concept referred to by Adomavicius and Tuzhilin (2011) in terms of context, is a context taxonomy in order to classify it in terms of representation (structural attributes and stored in the database that do not change significantly) or interaction (consumer attributes that may change according to the context in which it is inserted). The CARS system takes into account the user's context; a rating is assigned to each triple attribute combination (User × Item × Context = Rating) instead of considering only the user and item (Attribute) attribute pair, creating a multidimensional model associated with the recommendations (cube).

Hsu et al. (2012) developed an intelligent recommendation system that integrated the EBM model (Engel-Blackwell-Miniard (Blackwell, Miniard, & Engel, 2001)), Bayesian networks and Google Maps to recommend itineraries and tourist attractions through an interactive interface using Google Maps (ITAS - Intelligent Tourist Attractions System). The developed system had as its objective the ability to minimize the cost to the user in the process of information search and to recommend attractions to tourists according to their preferences. The EBM model involves six phases in the purchasing decision process: recognition of the need / problem, search for information, evaluation of alternatives, purchase decision, purchase and post-purchase evaluation.

Husain et al. (2012) developed a MyTourGuide recommendation system that allowed the exchange of information between tourists and tourism companies for business-to-business (B2B) and business-to-consumer (B2C) contexts. Its objective was to overcome the problem of travelers facing a high range of information on the Internet that does not meet their preferences. The MyTourGuide system made recommendations based on location, traveler preferences and scores assigned by tourist communities. To get recommendations, tourists had to enter information such as the destination to visit, their preferences and the money they had available. The suggested itinerary could be changed to suit the traveler. At the same time, tourists could share their experiences and memories in a module called e-album, which provided features for uploading photos, and could access a blog to share experiences. It also included a module that allowed electronic payment for paying for business transactions.

Buján et al. (2013) report that few papers analyze the information context while taking into account human mobility and the notion of context that includes the requirements associated with the domain of tourism and ubiquitous computing. The solution they envisage considers a TourExp information system where tourists and tourism professionals (travel agencies, hotels, among others) can publish their information, and as a result the system recommends places to visit. The data model considered is based on ontology, since the authors note that it is the most suitable for contextual information management. In terms of contextual information, the following have to be considered: information about the user and his / her profile on social networks (human factors); Historical information on where the traveler is, on infrastructure and on weather (environmental factors); Information about the user's interactivity with the application and access mode (system factors).

Kops (2013) developed a recommendation system (George) tailored for the city of Berlin, which recommended tourist services, by gaining market knowledge by identifying coherent user segments in order to obtain new, improved services and to improve knowledge and the tourist experience. The George system was developed taking into account the identification of market segments, and the concepts of usability and content design. The recommendations were made according to the segments that were based on analysis of clusters and from which four segments resulted: versatility (new experiences and new cultures), business, family visits and for pleasure.

Anacleto et al. (2014) developed a recommendation system called PSiS Mobile (Personalized Sightseeing Planning System), whose purpose was to recommend and support the planning of trips for tourists during their vacations in the city of Porto, Portugal, provides recommendations on POI to visit based on the preferences of tourists. In parallel, the system keeps track of all the movements of the tourists and tasks that are executed in order to remind the user of how the trip was made. The PSiS system recommends POI based on user preferences in its current context and is connected to the online weather service (WorldWeatherOnline) to receive the weather forecast, and according to the time of day (to know if the POI is closed), provide a map to the traveler to help guide him / her, and give directions from wherever he / she is to the POI. The authors consider that the system is intended to be a travel diary, where it is possible to know the time that was spent at each place, the photos they took, the feedback that they left and characteristics that allow the tourist to do a posteriori analysis of their trip. Currently, one of the major challenges in mobile devices is the capacity of the battery and in this sense, the PSiS system is designed to only be connected in a timely manner (smart client) in order to reduce network traffic; in parallel there is a temporary database on the device that allows access to the data. In order for the GPS to consume less battery, they have developed an algorithm that allows the adjustment and updating of the GPS in order to minimize the load consumption.

Garau (2014) presents a pilot application that recommends customized ways of promoting cultural tourism in Castello (Cagliari, Italy), extolling the benefits of using augmented reality associated with tourist sites, providing a "smart decision-making" environment for informing and involving tourists and the residents in the tourist town. The author considers that the application not only adds value to tourism, but also allows local administrators and professionals to define the cultural sites that city values the most. This application was part of the application project of the city of Cagliari to the title of European Capital of Culture of 2019.

Adukaite (2015) has evaluated WHACY (World Heritage Awareness Campaign for Youth in Southern African Development Community) using a gaming platform that aims to informally educate about heritage and sustainable tourism in South Africa, and which, on the other hand, also intends to complement formal curriculum plans and teaching activities of teachers in the community of higher education students. The author also points out that ICT has a great potential for education (Cantoni, Kalbaska & Inversini, 2009) and for facilitating sustainable tourism through raising awareness, promotion and guidance for residents and tourists (Schieder, Adukaite, & Cantoni, 2014)

In summary, in order to develop intelligent environments for tourists, the recommendation systems need to include an intelligent user-centered interface that integrates usability and accessibility features to support users' behavior and learning processes, while at the same time integrating assistive technologies for users with accessibility problems, since this interaction may affect the decision-making processes of tourists and residents.

RECOMMENDATION SYSTEMS IN COMMERCIAL TERMS

In parallel to the scientific community, the professional players in the tourism sectors realized the potential of the use of technologies in supporting tourism activity; consequently, the development of tourism recommendation systems also followed the same idea or were quickly developed by trading partners and adopted or bought by companies operating in activities related to tourism. Table 2 presents the commercial applications, which were evidenced in the Play store on the Internet; the list of works is not limited to those that were analyzed.

The applications presented above are the most relevant for the work considered in the present study and were evidenced in the search conducted on the Internet, which will be explained in detail below:

- App Ammergau – Travel Alps (2017) is for the Alps region and features an offline map of the region, slideshows, cultural events, gastronomic specialties and ideas about sports activities. It allows for interaction with the application and uses gamification concepts to interactively inform the destination through memory games, videos and other multimedia resources.
    - Easy Go App (2017) allows for the selection of itineraries classified in "areas" or "themes", where the user can view several photos to help to decide on a choice as well as to have access to actual comments made by other tourists. It also offers individual travel suggestions based on the user's travel style and previous travel taste history. The website is not intended for a specific region or location.
- App Smart Tourism Taiwan (2017) is for Taiwan Island, it is composed of a set of intelligent features for tourism that intelligently personalizes the suggestion of places and tourist activities to support the process of planning the trip.

Table 2. Tourism recommendation systems in Play Store

APP	Information	Concepts	Highlights
Ammergau Alps - Travel	Region, Cultural events	Gamification	Individual travel tips taking into account the user's travel style and history. Offline map of the Region
Easy Go	Comments, Photos, Suggestions.		
Smart Tourism Taiwan	Sites and activities	Personalization	Intelligent customization associated to location recommendation
TripAdvisor	Hotels, entertainment, restaurants.	Possibilita as avaliações, vídeos, fotografias e opiniões dos viajantes.	Helps to plan a trip, makes it easier to find lower airplanes fares. It allows location by GPS and recommends to the traveler the options located near an address.
TripIt		Synchronize travel plans with Google Calendar or Outlook	Allows sharing photos and travel plans. Allows the access to routes even in offline mode. Automatically create itineraries if the user use Gmail or Google Apps.
Tripoto Travel App: Plan Trips	Photos, Maps, Budgets, Opinions, Flights, trains and other transport.	Geo-tag	It allows access to accommodation information as well as booking made through links to other partners (Expedia, Airbnb or booking.com). Allows the planning and sharing of travel itineraries.
Visit Dubai	Events, Attractions, Promotions, Etiquette.		Allows the user to customize their own itinerary. Places to explore based on user location and time of day.
Driving Mode (Google)	Associated with Maps for Android, it will allow you to predict the destination where you are traveling, taking into account your location and history, to indicate the route, the duration of the route and the weather.		

Source: Author's elaboration.

- TripAdvisor App (2017) is not intended for a specific location. It helps to plan a trip, facilitates the search for more airborne tasks, including information on hotels, amusement, restaurants, among other services. TripAdvisor provides unbiased reviews, articles, recommendations and opinions on hotels. It allows the user to view the location on GPS and recommends options located near where the user is or according to an indicated address. App TripIt (2017) allows the user to create itineraries automatically. If the user is connected to Gmail or Google Apps, he / she can have access to itineraries even in offline mode as well as access to directions and maps for a particular destination. It allows synchronization of travel plans with Google Calendar or Outlook and allows sharing of photos and travel plans.
    - Tripoto Travel App: Plan Trips (2017) allows planning and sharing of travel itineraries between users and querying of thematic itineraries, including travel to remote locations. It allows the sharing of photos, maps, budgets and opinions about places visited, which may have an associated geo-tag. It allows access to up-to-date information on flights, trains and other transport. In the case of hotels, it allows access to accommodation information as well as booking made through links to other partners (Expedia, Airbnb or Booking.com). App Visit Dubai (2017) is aimed at travelers to the city of Dubai. It features the suggestion of places to explore based on the location of the user, the time and their interests. It integrates a set of information about events, attractions and promotions, culture and etiquette and allows the user to customize their own itinerary.

In addition to these applications, Google intends to present the Driving Mode functionality (2017) associated with Maps for Android that will allow prediction of the destination to which a user is headed, taking into account their location and history, with the purpose of indicating the route to the intended destination, the duration of the route and the weather. The application will present personalized information according to each user, but will only be associated with the route made in geographic terms.

In summary, none of the above applications mention the use of assistive technologies in their development, nor the combination of intelligence associated with different presentations of content taking into account the type of user. The intelligence associated with business models to obtain economic advantages for local tourism partners was also not mentioned.

RECOMMENDATION SYSTEMS GAPS AND CHALLENGES

The recommendation systems are fundamental to defining marketing strategies for the destinations and regions or in order to identify the segments of the consumers who have specific interests, actions and characteristics.

There are several ways to define the characteristics (variables) to be used in the segmentation of consumers, however Kotler and Armstrong (2010) propose four categories of variables, which should be considered and are analyzed in Table 3.

The recommendation systems already developed have previously tried to segment users into categories such as "cultural", "sun and beach" and "nature" (Ricci, 2002) or by classifications into "families", "business", "simple travelers" (Wang, 2012), with the aim of presenting personalized recommendations.

However, these systems have failed to present recommendations associated with POIs and did not reach the objectives of the concepts associated with marketing intelligence (Büchner & Mulvenna, 1998), which include the identification of similar segments among users and their specific preferences within the group with a view to gaining insight into creating new services or improving existing ones to increase user satisfaction.

An information system that includes marketing intelligence concepts will bring benefits to a tourist destination, once it contributes to enhancing the user experience and adding value to the trip through the recommendation of restaurants and POIs, among others and in accordance with consumer preferences, offers tailor-made services and makes possible the improvement of services and products available to

Table 3. Categories used in the segmentation of consumers

Categories	Description	Variable Type
Demographic	Divide the market into different groups, based on the demographic characteristics.	Age, gender, occupation, nationality, income, education, date of birth and language.
Geographic	Divide the market in different territorial units.	Residence (city, region and country), climate, geographical location (latitude and longitude).
Psychograhic	Divide the market into different groups based on social class, lifestyle or personal style.	Benefits, attitudes. Values, characteristics of the personality. Reason for travel. Trip type Device type. Type of accommodation.
Behavioral	Divide the market based on the knowledge of the consumer, the attitude, use or response to a product.	Occasion, benefits, user status, loyalty status, attitude towards a product. Emotional state.

Source: Adapted from Kotler and Armstrong (2010).

tourists in the region, taking into consideration the personal information, or in another cases the segment information, as presented in Figure 1, as a way of increasing its success.

On other side, there are technological challenges such as battery capacity of mobile devices and the need to include assistive technologies, to treat all the persons as equal with or without limitations.

Additional challenges, in terms of the creation of a system with intelligence, involves: offering different content presentations that take into account the type of user; offering the business stakeholder intelligent models in order to obtain economic advantages for the local tourist partners; permitting the development of consumer intelligence models to identify trends and new patterns of consumption; and contributing to the improvement of marketing intelligence models to recommend the POI, service or other information, in the place where the visitor is, taking into account their interests, the context awareness, the right place and at the right time.

RELIGIOUS TOURISM EXPERIENCE MODEL (RTEM)

The development of a recommendation system that allows the dissemination of cultural and religious heritage, which helps to find information and acquire knowledge about cultural heritage, can bring new experiences and sensations to tourists and residents, in general and to those who have accessibility problems, in particular.

The intelligent recommendation system aims to contribute to the promotion of new tourism experiences associated with religious tourism, in order to contribute to the acquisition of additional knowledge about the cultural, spiritual and religious heritage of a region through interaction with an interface presented on a personal mobile device as a way of encouraging a personal and spiritual experience when visiting the religious heritage associated with a religious or thematic itinerary (Ramos, Henriques, & Lanquar, 2016).

According to Engelberger (1982), for there to be innovation it is necessary to: satisfy the needs of consumers, achieve benefits for organizations and have appropriate technology to develop an innovative product that meet the three pillars presented. In the context of cultural and religious tourism, an intelligent tourism recommendation system will allow tourists and the local population to meet their cultural needs in an educational and entertainment environment in order to add value to their experience,

Figure 1. Marketing Intelligence associated with the recommendation systems
Source: Author's elaboration.

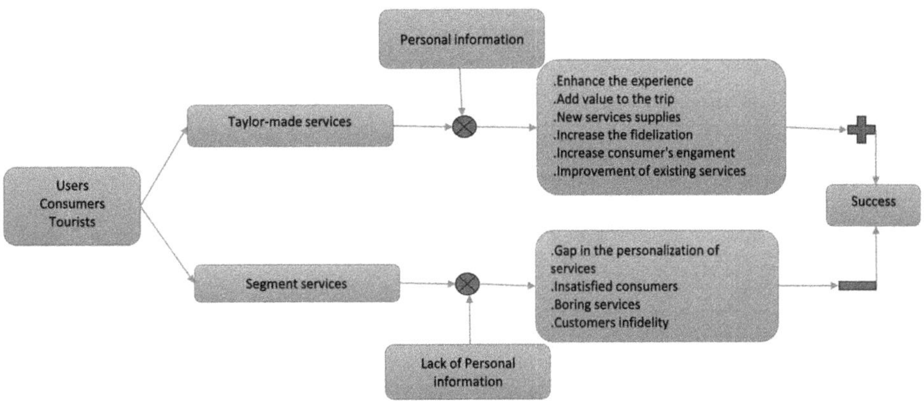

and at the same time will allow for the sharing and dissemination of heritage in order to increase the number of visitors, thereby contributing in economic terms to the region as well as increased valuation of the visited heritage, and lastly, identifying the full range of technology that can be integrated into a technological architecture, to develop a model of religious tourism experience that can contribute to leveraging the development of a smart destination, contributing to its sustainability and improving the living conditions of residents and visitors.

In analyzing technology relevant to creating a cultural and religious experiences tourism model, it is essential to consider those designated by smart technology that are characterized by features that adapt to different circumstances, people or places.

The authors' proposed *Religious Tourism Experience Model* (RTEM) allows tourists, residents and the religious community to have access to three different experiences: tourism, cultural and technological, providing residents and visitors with a wealth of experience, as well as defining and creating a cultural identity for the region, as presented in Figure 2.

The RTEM intends to contribute in three different dimensions to the associated experience of a person who visits a POI: When a tourist/resident visits a specific heritage element, he/she can have a (a) touristic experience, enjoying the heritage that contributes to adding value to the trip; a (b) cultural experience, where they acquire knowledge about a patrimonial element and increase the cultural knowledge; and a

Figure 2. Religious Tourism Experience Model (RTEM)
Source: Author's elaboration.

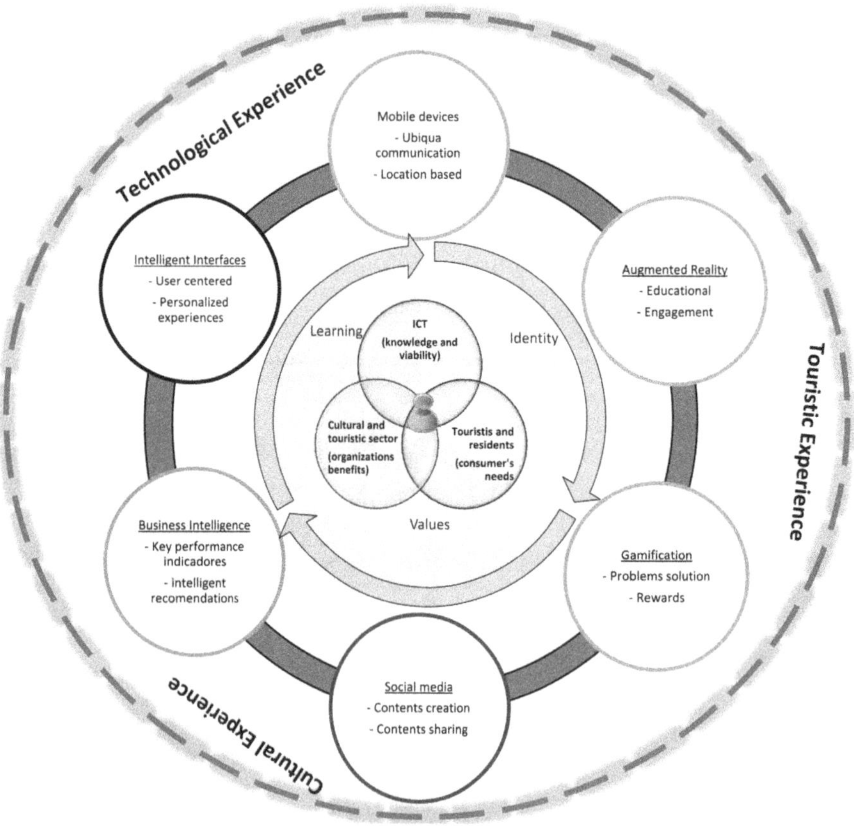

(c) technological experience, once the user can interact with the technological application while having fun, and sharing their opinion and comments on e.g. social media.

As presented in Figure 2, to develop a technological application that contributes to a touristic experience subdivided in the above three dimensions, it is necessary to consider technologies associated with the concept of "smart technology". According to Neuhofer et al. (2015, p. 243), the term "intelligent and smart" technology has several functionalities that can be adapted to various circumstances, persons or places. This includes location-based systems (Gavalas et al., 2014; Pendrana, 2014; Yovcheva, Buhalis, Gatzidis, & van Elzakker, 2014), social networks (Ahmedi, Rrmoku, Sylejmani, & Shabani, 2017; Margaris, Vassilakis, & Georgiadis, 2017; Munar & Jacobsen, 2013), user-centered design (Bower, Howe, McCredie, Robinson, & Grover, 2014; Chen, 2014; Gavalas et al., 2014; Yovcheva et al., 2014); augmented reality (Bower et al., 2014; Buhalis & Amaranggana, 2013; Chen, 2014; Garau, 2014; Yovcheva et al., 2014; Ramos et al., 2016), gamification (Buhalis & Amaranggana, 2013; Fino, Martín-Gutiérrez, Fernández, & Davara, 2013; Mortara et al., 2014; Xu, 2011; Xu et al., 2013), mobile technologies (Gavalas et al., 2014), business intelligence systems for tourists (Burke & Hiltbrand, 2011; Gretzel, 2011), real-time navigation systems (Yamamoto, & Fujita, 2017) and Internet-based technologies, among others.

As shown in Figure 2, in the center of the model there are three environments represented that are provided by the RTEM, which allows tourism consumers to enjoy religious tourism experiences, which have a cultural and touristic component, and at the same time the technological experience via the utilization of several technologies that are integrated and linked into one technological platform which presents recommendations based on several characteristics. In the technologies presented in Figure 2, and discussed above, there are some that stand out and should be enlightening, such as:

1. **Mobile Devices:** These permit ubiquitous consumer communication and allow users to have access to information based on their location.
2. **AR:** This allows a better understanding of the real world and permits the integration of virtual elements that complement religious resources.
3. **Gamification:** Gaming mechanics solve problems, making it possible to measure and evaluate the reputation or performance of a product or destination.
4. **Social Media:** With the user-generated content and sharing tools associated with gamification, this has become a tool used to define new business models strategically.
5. **Business Intelligence:** Tools can be used to analyze the information collected in social gaming associated with AR and to enhance the discovery of new consumption patterns of tourists and residents.
6. **Intelligent Interfaces (Human-Computer Interaction):** These are the key to increasing the value of religious tourism experiences, since interfaces offer personalized information according to each consumer.

A recommendation system developed with the technology presented above is essential for creating a tourist experience application that takes into consideration the characteristics of the consumer/tourist, such as: preferences, age, and segment and which will: allow tourists / users to obtain additional information about the cultural, spiritual and religious heritage of a region, add value to the trip, increase the affective involvement of tourists, contribute to acquiring knowledge about the tangible and intangible heritage and enhance their personal and spiritual experience.

RTEM DESIGN CONSIDERATIONS

The methodology considered to develop an intelligent recommendation system takes into consideration the implementation of a technological architecture, which will play an important role in a religious tourism experience environment. RTEM can be divided into three phases (as presented in Figure 3): (1) planning and definition of content associated with cultural and religious heritage, (2) planning and implementation of the recommendation system and (3) testing and validation of the intelligent recommendation system to verify if the objectives are achieved.

1. **First Phase:** Harvesting the information about places that should be shared with the public can be divided into three steps:
    a. Research of primary sources;
    b. Research of secondary sources;
    c. Definition of the structure of the contents to be disclosed.
2. **Second Phase:** Implementing the recommendation system associated to the RTEM can be structured into three steps:
    a. Analysis of technology relevant to include in the model;
    b. Technology Architecture Design;
    c. Development of an Intelligent Recommendation System.
3. **Third Phase:** Testing and validating the intelligent recommendation system can be divided into three steps:
    a. Analysis of the Technology Acceptance Models to be used (Davis, 1989);
    b. Application of surveys to users / tourists;
    c. Analysis and evaluation of results.

To develop a recommendation system with the aim of creating a touristic experience, with the assumptions presented above, it is important to consider all the emergent technology discussed earlier and identified in Figure 2, and how these technologies are integrated into one platform that constitutes the intelligent recommendation system's technological architecture associated with the RTEM.

Recommendation System Technological Architecture Associated to the RTEM

The technological architecture to make the development possible of an intelligent recommendation system to communicate the culture associated to a region (in general terms, and in particular associated to the tangible and intangible religious heritage) should consider a platform support on the web, with tools considered in the cloud. Figure 4 represents the technological architecture that will be subdivided in parts and explained in detail in Figures 5 to 9. Figure 4 presents the proposed technological architecture to develop a recommendation system, which supports the tourists and residents in educational, cultural, enjoyment and evasion terms, using the concepts associated with economy of experience proposed by Pine and Guilmore (1999). In the center the environment provided by the Internet is represented, which integrates the concepts of cloud computing, both in terms of application development and in terms of web information systems.

Figure 3. Methodology used to develop the intelligent recommendation system associated with RTEM
Source: Author's elaboration.

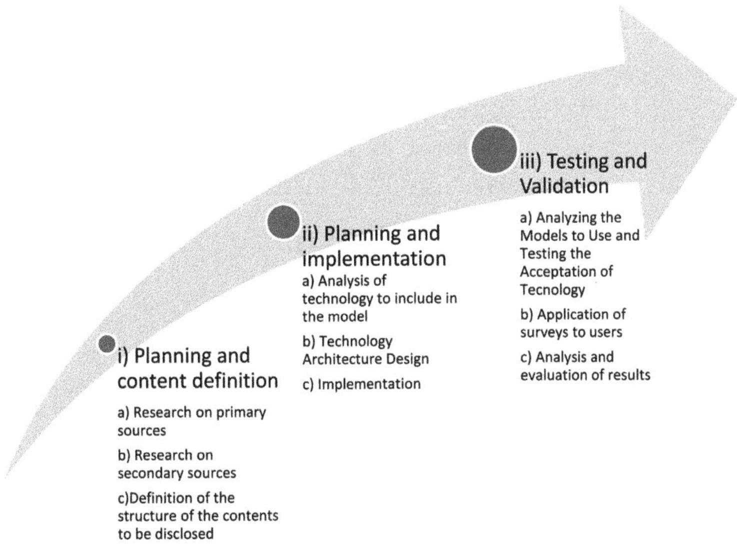

Figure 4. Technological architecture associated with RTEM
Source: Author's elaboration.

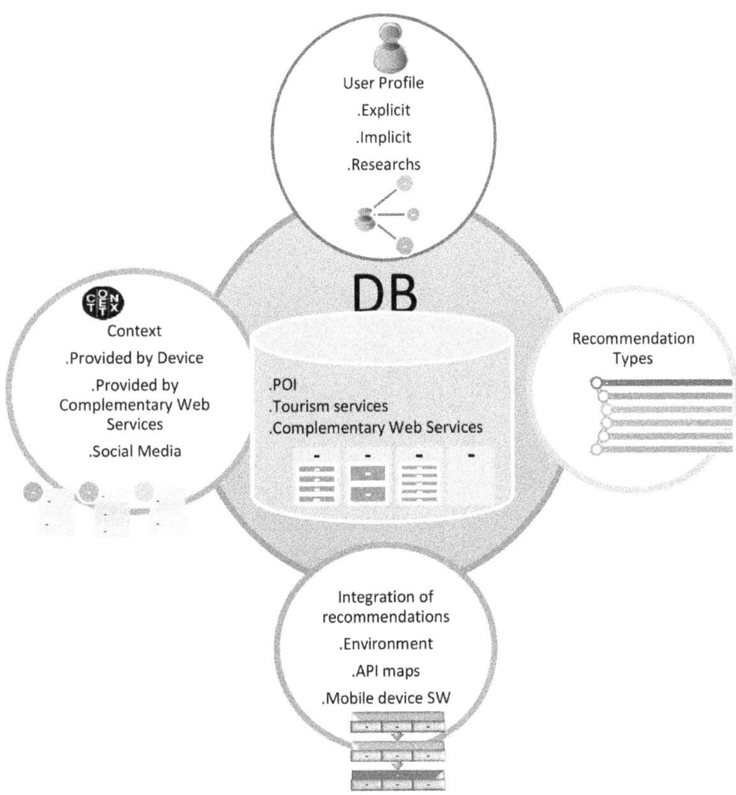

Figure 5. Example of information categories associated to touristic sector (module of the technological architecture RTEM, see Figure 4)
Source: Author's elaboration.

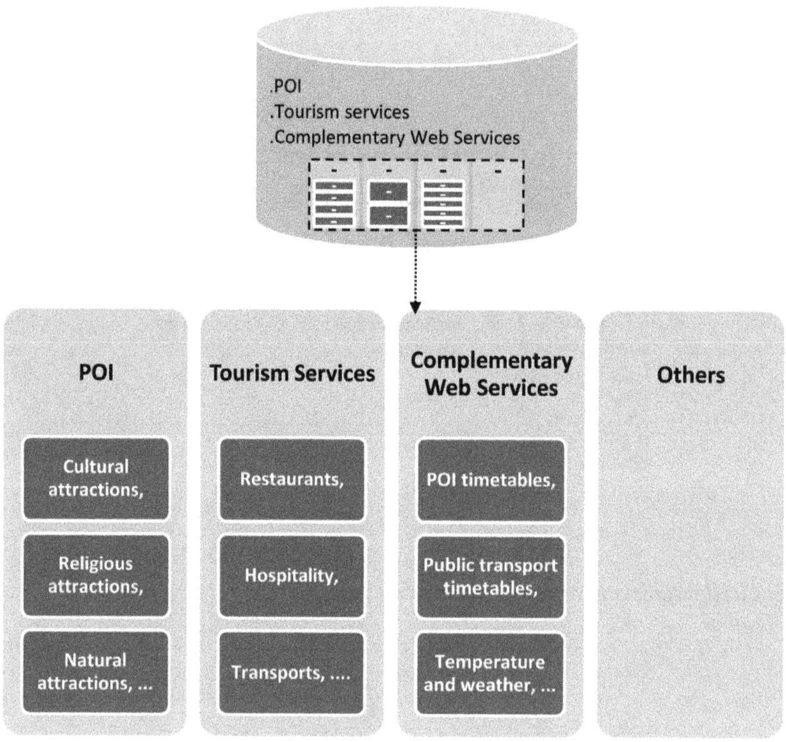

Figure 6. User's profile information to be included in the system (module of the technological architecture RTEM, see Figure 4)
Source: Author's elaboration.

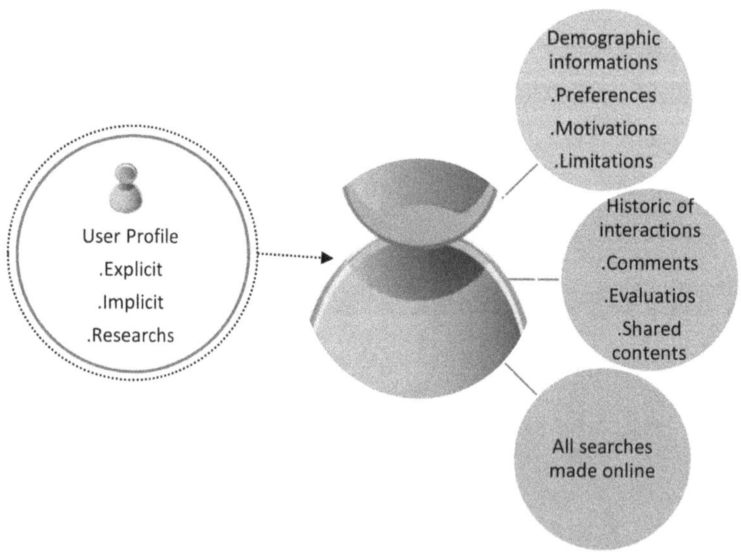

Figure 7. Recommendation types considered in the system (module of the technological architecture RTEM, see Figure 4)
Source: Author's elaboration.

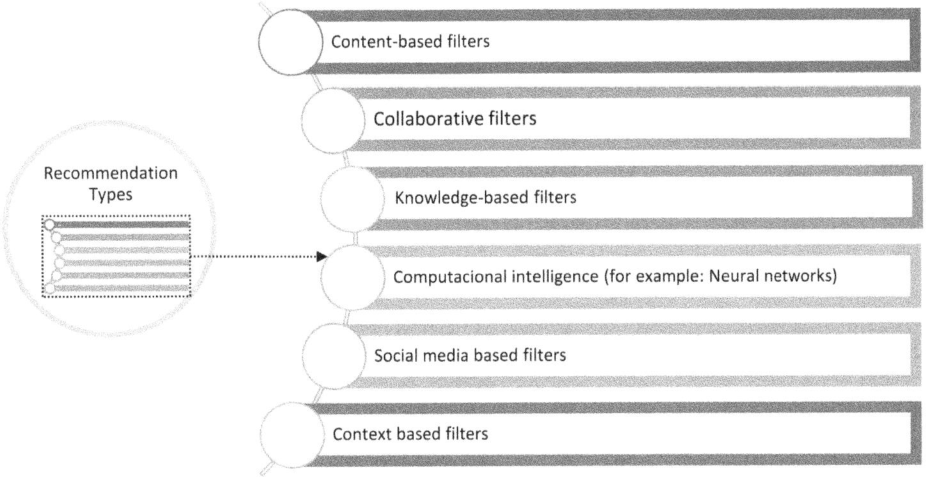

Figure 8. Integration of the recommendations in the system (module of the technological architecture RTEM, see Figure 4)
Source: Author's elaboration.

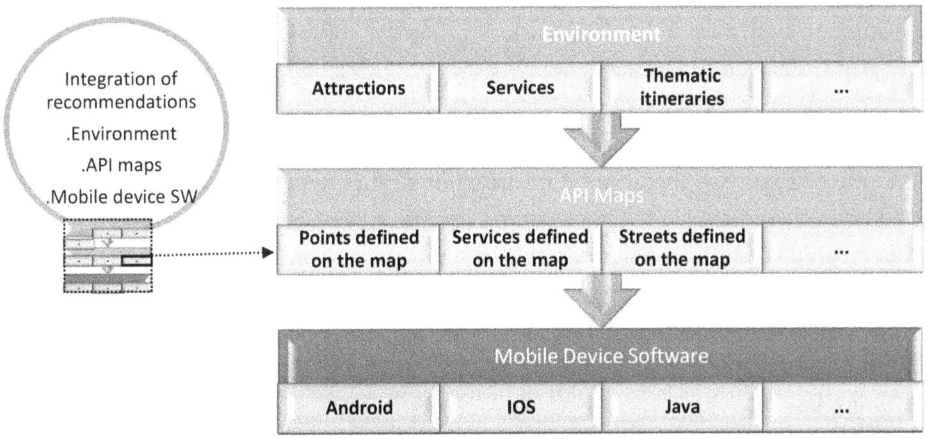

The web information systems are essential to the information management, concretized in robust databases, to store, update and communicate the information associated to all the different categories that coexist in tourism, such as: points of interest, touristic services available, the auxiliary services on the web and information useful to consumers. In parallel, it is necessary to store information about the profile, context and recommendations associated to the user, as presented in Figure 5.

At the top of Figure 4, all characteristics associated with the users are represented, which is also called the user's profile, which includes several types of information associated with the consumer that is essential for enabling the development of an intelligent system whose recommendations are personalized and that take into account the person and not the segment. Only in this way will it be possible to personalize contents, recommendations or enhance the user's involvement, as presented in Figure 6.

Figure 9. Context information considered in the system (module of the technological architecture RTEM, see Figure 4)
Source: Author's elaboration.

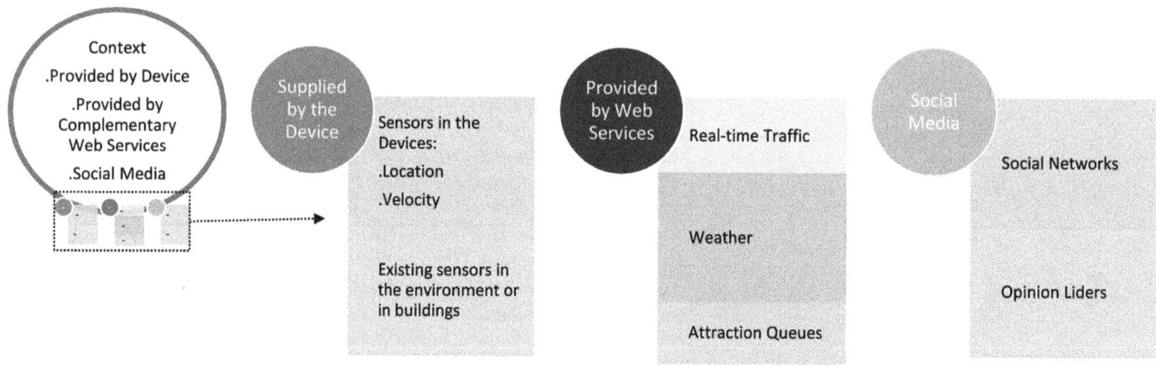

On the right side of Figure 4, several types of recommendations are represented, which can coexist in the platform to produce intelligent recommendations personalized in accordance with the characteristics of the user. The recommendations can filtered by content-based, collaborative, knowledge-based, social-media based and context-based information and can also integrate computational intelligence approaches: neural networks and genetic algorithm, among others, as presented in Figure 7.

On the bottom of Figure 4, some of the different Application Programming Interfaces (API) are presented, which should be integrated in the system. These APIs exist in applications associated with the physical environment, such as in a thematic park or itinerary; some map applications, which include the streets and the points defined in the maps, are associated with a specific software device that should be considered in the system as a way of developing a responsive technological architecture, as represented in Figure 8.

On the left side of Figure 4, the context information that is necessary to develop an intelligent recommendation system is represented. This system presents a notification to the user in accordance with their profile, but also takes in to consideration the context, place and time where the tourist is inserted. To define the context of the user is necessary to store and manage the information in real time about the location, the used device, the speed at which it travels, the temperature and weather of the place where it is, opinions' shared in social media about the attractions and POIs, queues, sensors, among others, as presented in Figure 9.

The technological architectural presented above will permit the development of an intelligent recommendation system that engages consumers, expands tourism experiences and presents technological innovations that match the individual tourist's motivations. Meanwhile, we also intend to include the concepts of encoding and communicating between objects via the Internet (i.e., the Internet of Things), which enables participation in integrated networks in the areas of knowledge and intelligent systems allows the development of sustainability indicators using business intelligence tools and contributes to the advance of the building of Smart cities and regions.

FUTURE RESEARCH DIRECTIONS

The development of a recommendation system to a region can contribute to the development and sustainability of the same. However, this presents some challenges and limitations that need to be overcome: privacy concerns of tourists and residents, selection of the right databases and economic interests.

One challenge is concern with data privacy, it is necessary to acquire data by third parties through social media and gamification in order to make it possible to recommend POI in accordance with all the data associated with the user.

Another challenge has to do with the size of databases (Big Data), as this aspect enables the management, storage, processing and dissemination of information, which increases exponentially when data collection occurs at high speeds in association with attractions, accessibility, amenities and ancillary services—representing a large volume of data that increases every day.

The main component that contributes to the success or failure of an intelligent application to support decision processes during traveling is mobile technology. This component is of great importance, since it is through it that the user interacts with the application; it must be built with the most current functionalities possible, knowing that every day new features appear. It must present functionalities and content according to the profile and preferences of the user, which depends not only on algorithms and business intelligence techniques associated with the data, but also on interactions with the interface. It also requires additional storage capacity, battery capacity and the need to develop several versions of responsive, intelligent and user-friendly interfaces adapted to each type of operating system and mobile device. On the other hand, it is also necessary to consider the mechanisms necessary for the payment of commercial transactions to be considered safe by the user. Mobile technology, although not one of the most worrying challenges, such as the one below, will be one that is continually presenting the need for updates and adaptations to emerging mobile technologies in society, to overcome the gap in the use of devices and to integrated solutions for heritage sites and technology that enhance the socio-economic benefits of regions and cities and contributes to communicating and sharing heritage and cultural knowledge.

The final issue is related to the need to establish public-private partnerships that are essential when developing technological solutions with the characteristics listed above.

Each challenge has to be overcome in order to mitigate any inconvenience to individual consumers, in particular, and to contribute to the joint creation of innovative solutions that meet the interests of all.

CONCLUSION

In this chapter a methodological framework, RTEM, is proposed for the development of a recommendation system with the objective of identifying and selecting consumer preferences for the dissemination of cultural heritage, in general, and in particular, religious heritage.

Cultural and religious tourism has attracted tourists seeking to meet their needs to acquire knowledge and new experiences, taking into account their interests, the context awareness, the right place and at the right time. Tourist experiences can combine entertainment, education, aesthetics and avoidance.

The recommendation systems are a type of information system that achieves the goal of identifying and selecting consumers in order to develop intelligent environments. They need to include an intelligent user-centered interface that integrates usability and accessibility features to support users' behavior and learning process, while at the same time integrating assistive technologies to provide users with accessibility problems, since this interaction may affect the decision-making process of tourists and residents.

In the applications developed in commercial terms, the use of assistive technologies was not detected, and neither was the combination of intelligence associated with different presentations of content that takes the type of user into account. The intelligence associated with business models in order to obtain economic advantages for local tourism partners was also not mentioned. Also, concepts associated with the definition of consumer intelligence models are not mentioned, but they have an essential role in identifying trends and new patterns of consumption, taking into consideration technology acceptance as a way to define consumer behavior.

There are some technological challenges in the development of these systems, such as: battery capacity of mobile devices and the need to include assistive technologies in order to treat all the persons as equal with or without limitations. The technological solutions must consider functionalities that allow the adaptation to different places, people and situations (Smart / Intelligent), that presents personalized information according to the characteristics of the user: profile, preferences and place where he / she is, among others. In addition, it should contribute to the development of marketing intelligence models that recommend POI, service or other information, near the place where the visitor is, taking into account their interests and delivering the information at the right time. Finally, it should integrate with innovative urban solutions aimed at structuring supply and enhancement, that is, integration into Smart Cities.

ACKNOWLEDGMENT

This work was supported by the Portuguese Foundation for Science and Technology (FCT), project LARSyS (UID/EEA/50009/2013), CIAC and CEFAGE (PEst-C/EGE/UI4007/2013).

REFERENCES

Adomavicius, G., & Tuzhilin, A. (2011). Context-aware recommender systems. In Recommender systems handbook (pp. 217-253). Springer US. doi:10.1007/978-0-387-85820-3_7

Adukaite, A. (2015). Technology Enhanced Learning in Tourism. Teachers' and Students' Perspectives in South Africa. In M. Fuchs, W. Hopken, Z. Xiang, & A. Mariussen (Eds.), *Enter 2015 PhD Workshop, Research Proposals*, (pp. 41-47). Academic Press.

Ahmedi, L., Rrmoku, K., Sylejmani, K., & Shabani, D. (2017). A bimodal social network analysis to recommend points of interest to tourists. *Social Network Analysis and Mining*, *7*(1), 14. doi:10.1007/s13278-017-0431-8

Al Subhi, N., Bell, D., & Lashmar, P. (2015). Location based modelling for Heritage Mobile Applications. *UKAIS Conference 2015.*

Anacleto, R., Figueiredo, L., Almeida, A., & Novais, P. (2014). Mobile application to provide personalized sightseeing tours. *Journal of Network and Computer Applications*, *41*, 56–64. doi:10.1016/j.jnca.2013.10.005

APP Ammergau – Travel Alps. (2017). *Ammergau Alps - Travel*. Retrieved: January 12, 2017, from https://play.google.com/store/apps/details?id=de.ammergau.en

APP Easy Go. (2017). *Easy Go*. Retrieved: January 12, 2017, from https://play.google.com/store/apps/details?id=com.cnc.easygo&hl=pt_PT

APP Smart Tourism Taiwan. (2017). *Smart Tourism Taiwan*. Retrieved: January 12, 2017, from https://play.google.com/store/apps/details?id=tw.org.iii.ari.smarttourism

APP TripIt. (2017). *TripIt: Travel Organizer*. Retrieved: January 12, 2017, from https://play.google.com/store/apps/details?id=com.tripit

APP Visit Dubai. (2017). *Visit Dubai*. Retrieved: January 12, 2017, from http://www.visitdubai.com/en/travel-planning/travel-tools/get-the-app

Ardissono, L., Felfernig, A., Friedrich, G., Jannach, D., Schäfer, R., & Zanker, M. (2001). Intelligent interfaces for distributed web-based product and service configuration. In Web Intelligence: Research and Development (pp. 184-188). Springer Berlin Heidelberg. doi:10.1007/3-540-45490-X_21

Blackwell, R. D., Miniard, P. W., & Engel, J. F. (2001). *Consumer behavior* (9th ed.). Fort Worth, TX: Harcourt College Publishers.

Blohm, I., & Leimeister, J. M. (2013). Gamification. *Business & Information Systems Engineering*, *5*(4), 275–278. doi:10.1007/s12599-013-0273-5

Bosangit, B., Hibbert, S., & McCabe, S. (2015). If I was going to die I should at least be having fun: Travel blogs, meaning and tourist experience. *Annals of Tourism Research*, *55*, 1–14. doi:10.1016/j.annals.2015.08.001

Bower, M., Howe, C., McCredie, N., Robinson, A., & Grover, D. (2014). Augmented Reality in education–cases, places and potentials. *Educational Media International*, *51*(1), 1–15. doi:10.1080/09523987.2014.889400

Büchner, A. G., & Mulvenna, M. D. (1998). Discovering internet marketing intelligence through online analytical web usage mining. *SIGMOD Record*, *27*(4), 54–61. doi:10.1145/306101.306124

Buhalis, D., & Amaranggana, A. (2013). Smart tourism destinations. In Z. Xiang & L. Tussyadiah (Eds.), *Information and Communication Technologies in Tourism 2014* (pp. 553–564). Springer International Publishing. doi:10.1007/978-3-319-03973-2_40

Buján, D., Martín, D., Torices, O., López-de-Ipiña, D., Lamsfus, C., Abaitua, J., & Alzua-Sorzabal, A. (2013). Context management platform for tourism applications. *Sensors (Basel, Switzerland)*, *13*(7), 8060–8078. doi:10.3390/s130708060 PMID:23797739

Burke, M., & Hiltbrand, T. (2011). How gamification will change business intelligence. *Business Intelligence Journal*, *16*(2), 8–16.

Burke, R. (1999). Integrating knowledge-based and collaborative-filtering recommender systems. *Proceedings of the Workshop on AI and Electronic Commerce*, 69-72.

Cantoni, L., Kalbaska, N., & Inversini, A. (2009). E-learning in tourism and hospitality: A map. *Journal of Hospitality, Leisure, Sports and Tourism Education (Pre-2012), 8*(2), 148.

Cerutti, S., & Piva, E. (2016). The role of tourists' feedback in the enhancement of religious tourism destination. *International Journal of Religious Tourism and Pilgrimage*, *4*(3), 6–16.

Chen, W. (2014). Historical Oslo on a handheld device–a mobile augmented reality application. *Procedia Computer Science*, *35*, 979–985. doi:10.1016/j.procs.2014.08.180

Coyle, L., & Cunningham, P. (2003). Exploiting re-ranking information in a case-based personal travel assistant. *Proceedings of the 5th International Conference on Case-based Reasoning*, 11-13.

Davis, F. D. (1989). Perceived usefulness, perceived ease of use and user acceptance of information technology. *Management Information Systems Quarterly*, *13*(3), 319–339. doi:10.2307/249008

Driving Mode functionality. (2017). *Google Maps será capaz de descobrir sozinho para onde o utilizador vai.* Retrieved: January 12, 2017, from http://exameinformatica.sapo.pt/noticias/software/2016-01-13-Google-Maps-sera-capaz-de-descobrir-sozinho-para-onde-o-utilizador-vai?utm_source=newsletter&utm_medium=mail&utm_campaign=newsletter&utm_content=2016-01-14

Engelberger, J. F. (1982). Robotics in practice: Future capabilities. *Electronic Servicing & Technology Magazine.*

Falk, J. (2009). *Identity and the museum visit experience*. Walnut Creek, CA: Left Coast Press.

Fesenmaier, D. R., Wöber, K. W., & Werthner, H. (Eds.). (2006). *Destination recommendation systems: Behavioral foundations and applications*. Cambridge, UK: CAB International. doi:10.1079/9780851990231.0000

Fino, E. R., Martín-Gutiérrez, J., Fernández, M. D. M., & Davara, E. A. (2013). Interactive Tourist Guide: Connecting Web 2.0, Augmented Reality and QR Codes. *Procedia Computer Science*, *25*, 338–344. doi:10.1016/j.procs.2013.11.040

Garau, C. (2014). From territory to smartphone: Smart fruition of cultural heritage for dynamic tourism development. *Planning Practice and Research*, *29*(3), 238–255. doi:10.1080/02697459.2014.929837

Garcia, A., Arbelaitz, O., Linaza, M. T., Vansteenwegen, P., & Souffriau, W. (2010). Personalized tourist route generation. In *International Conference on Web Engineering* (pp. 486-497). Springer Berlin Heidelberg.

Gavalas, D., Konstantopoulos, C., Mastakas, K., & Pantziou, G. (2014). Mobile recommender systems in tourism. *Journal of Network and Computer Applications*, *39*, 319–333. doi:10.1016/j.jnca.2013.04.006

Geertz, C. (2004). Religion as a cultural system. In *The interpretation of cultures: selected essays* (pp. 87–125). Fontana Press.

Gretzel, U. (2011). Intelligent systems in tourism: A social science perspective. *Annals of Tourism Research, 38*(3), 757–779. doi:10.1016/j.annals.2011.04.014

Herlocker, J. L., Konstan, J. A., & Riedl, J. (2000). Explaining collaborative filtering recommendations. In *Proceedings of the 2000 ACM conference on Computer supported cooperative work* (pp. 241-250). ACM.

Hsu, F. M., Lin, Y. T., & Ho, T. K. (2012). Design and implementation of an intelligent recommendation system for tourist attractions: The integration of EBM model, Bayesian network and Google Maps. *Expert Systems with Applications, 39*(3), 3257–3264. doi:10.1016/j.eswa.2011.09.013

Huang, Y., & Bian, L. (2009). A Bayesian network and analytic hierarchy process based personalized recommendations for tourist attractions over the Internet. *Expert Systems with Applications, 36*(1), 933–943. doi:10.1016/j.eswa.2007.10.019

Husain, W., Dih, L. Y., Yen, H. F., & Jothi, N. (2012). MyTourGuide. com: a framework of a location-based services for tourism industry. In *Computer & Information Science (ICCIS), 2012 International Conference* (*Vol. 1*, pp. 184-189). IEEE.

Inversini, A., & Cantoni, L. (2011). Towards online content classification in understanding tourism destinations information competition and reputation. *International Journal of Internet Marketing and Advertising, 6*(3), 282–299. doi:10.1504/IJIMA.2011.038240

Kabassi, K. (2010). Personalizing recommendations for tourists. *Telematics and Informatics, 27*(1), 51–66. doi:10.1016/j.tele.2009.05.003

Kops, L. (2013). *Improving a travel recommender service by segmentation and personalization* (Master's degree dissertation). University of Twente.

Kotler, P., & Armstrong, G. (2010). *Principles of marketing*. Pearson Education.

Lam, X. N., Vu, T., Le, T. D., & Duong, A. D. (2008). Addressing cold-start problem in recommendation systems. In *Proceedings of the 2nd international conference on Ubiquitous information management and communication* (pp. 208-211). ACM.

Lillegraven, T. N., & Wolden, A. C. (2010). *Design of a bayesian recommender system for tourists presenting a solution to the cold-start user problem* (Master's degree dissertation). Institutt for datateknikk og informasjonsvitenskap, Trondheim.

Lin, C. H., & Kuo, B. Z. L. (2016). The behavioral consequences of tourist experience. *Tourism Management Perspectives, 18*, 84–91. doi:10.1016/j.tmp.2015.12.017

Lu, J., Wu, D., Mao, M., Wang, W., & Zhang, G. (2015). Recommender system application developments: A survey. *Decision Support Systems, 74*, 12–32. doi:10.1016/j.dss.2015.03.008

Margaris, D., Vassilakis, C., & Georgiadis, P. (2017). Knowledge-Based Leisure Time Recommendations in Social Networks. In *Current Trends on Knowledge-Based Systems* (pp. 23–48). Springer International Publishing. doi:10.1007/978-3-319-51905-0_2

McGregor, I., & Holmes, J. G. (1999). How storytelling shapes memory and impressions of relationship events over time. *Journal of Personality and Social Psychology*, *76*(3), 403–419. doi:10.1037/0022-3514.76.3.403

Mortara, M., Catalano, C. E., Bellotti, F., Fiucci, G., Houry-Panchetti, M., & Petridis, P. (2014). Learning cultural heritage by serious games. *Journal of Cultural Heritage*, *15*(3), 318–325. doi:10.1016/j.culher.2013.04.004

Munar, A. M., & Jacobsen, J. K. S. (2013). Trust and involvement in tourism social media and web-based travel information sources. *Scandinavian Journal of Hospitality and Tourism*, *13*(1), 1–19. doi:10.1080/15022250.2013.764511

Neuhofer, B., Buhalis, D., & Ladkin, A. (2015). Smart technologies for personalized experiences: A case study in the hospitality domain. *Electronic Markets*, *25*(3), 243–254. doi:10.1007/s12525-015-0182-1

Nyaupane, G. P., Timothy, D. J., & Poudel, S. (2015). Understanding Tourists in Religious Destinations: A Social Distance Perspective. *Tourism Management*, *48*, 343–353. doi:10.1016/j.tourman.2014.12.009

Oh, H., Fiore, A. M., & Jeoung, M. (2007). Measuring Experience Economy Concepts: Tourism Applications. *Journal of Travel Research*, *46*(2), 119–132. doi:10.1177/0047287507304039

Palmisano, C., Tuzhilin, A., & Gorgoglione, M. (2008). Using context to improve predictive modeling of customers in personalization applications. *IEEE Transactions on Knowledge and Data Engineering*, *20*(11), 1535–1549. doi:10.1109/TKDE.2008.110

Pendrana, M. (2014). Location-based services and tourism: Possible implications for destination. *Current Issues in Tourism*, *17*(9), 753–762. doi:10.1080/13683500.2013.868411

Pine, J., & Gilmore, J. (1999). *The experience economy*. Boston: Harvard Business School Press.

Poria, Y., Butler, R., & Airey, D. (2003). The core of heritage tourism. *Annals of Tourism Research*, *30*(1), 238–254. doi:10.1016/S0160-7383(02)00064-6

Ramos, C., Henriques, C., & Lanquar, R. (2016). Augmented Reality for Smart Tourism in Religious Heritage Itineraries: Tourism Experiences in the Technological Age. In J. Rodrigues, P. Cardoso, J. Monteiro, & M. Figueiredo (Eds.), *Handbook of Research on Human-Computer Interfaces, Developments, and Applications* (pp. 250–278). Hershey, PA: IGI Global. doi:10.4018/978-1-5225-0435-1.ch010

Ricci, F. (2002). Travel recommender systems. *IEEE Intelligent Systems*, *17*(6), 55–57.

Richards, G. (1996). *Cultural tourism in Europe*. Wallingford: CAB International.

Richards, G., & Wilson, J. (2006). Developing creativity in tourist experiences: A solution to the serial reproduction of culture?. *Tourism Management*, *27*(6), 1408–141. doi:10.1016/j.tourman.2005.06.002

Rizzo, L. S., Rizzo, R. G., & Trono, A. (2013). Religious Itineraries as the Driving Forces behind Sustainable Local Development in the Veneto? Towards a Proposal for Promoting an Unusual and Often "Subliminal" Form of Heritage: Sanctuaries and Minor Churches. *Almatourism-Journal of Tourism, Culture and Territorial Development*, *4*(7), 59–92.

Røine, P. C. (2010). *Tourist application for android. Specialisation project. Department of Computer and Information Science, Norwegian University of Science and Technology*. NTNU.

Rot, E., Mikinac, K., & Bogdan, S. (2014). General Characteristics of Religious Tourism in Croatia. *UTMS Journal of Economics*, *5*(1), 79–87.

Russo, A. P., & Borg, J. (2002). Planning considerations for cultural tourism: A case study of four European cities. *Tourism Management*, *23*(6), 631–637. doi:10.1016/S0261-5177(02)00027-4

Schiaffino, S., & Amandi, A. (2009). Building an expert travel agent as a software agent. *Expert Systems with Applications*, *36*(2), 1291–1299. doi:10.1016/j.eswa.2007.11.032

Schieder, T., Adukaite, A., & Cantoni, L. (2014). Mobile Apps Devoted to UNESCO World Heritage Sites: A Map. In Z. Xiang & I. Tussyadiah (Eds.), *Information and Communication Technologies in Tourism 2014* (pp. 17–31). Springer.

Schmidt-Belz, B., Nick, A., Poslad, S., & Zipf, A. (2002). Personalized and location-based mobile tourism services. *Workshop on "Mobile Tourism Support Systems" in conjunction with Mobile HCI.*

SIGA. (2012). *Diverse Beliefs: Tourism of Faith Religious tourism gains ground.* FICCI and YES BANK Ltd. Retrieved January 26, 2017, from http://ficci.in/spdocument/20207/diverse-beliefs-tourism-of-faith.pdf

Skavronskaya, L., Scott, N., Moyle, B., Le, D., Hadinejad, A., Zhang, R., Gardiner, A., Coghlan, A. & Shakeela, A. (2017). Cognitive psychology and tourism research: state of the art. *Tourism Review, 72*(2).

Staab, S., Werthner, H., Ricci, F., Zipf, A., Gretzel, U., Fesenmaier, D. R., & Knoblock, C. (2002). Intelligent systems for tourism. *IEEE Intelligent Systems*, *17*(6), 53–64. doi:10.1109/MIS.2002.1134362

Thompson, C. J., & Arnould, E. J. (1998). Narrative analysis of a marketing relationship: The consumers perspective. *Psychology and Marketing*, *15*(3), 195–214. doi:10.1002/(SICI)1520-6793(199805)15:3<195::AID-MAR1>3.0.CO;2-5

TIC. (2015). *Centre for Tourism, Innovation and Culture (TIC)*. Retrieved January 26, 2017, from http://www.sdu.dk/en/Om_SDU/Institutter_centre/C_Tik.aspx

Timothy, D. J., & Olsen, D. H. (Eds.). (2006). *Tourism, Religion and Spiritual Journeys*. London: Routledge.

TripAdvisor APP. (2017). *TripAdvisor.* Retrieved: January 12, 2017, from https://play.google.com/store/apps/details?id=com.tripadvisor.tripadvisor&hl=pt_PT

Tripoto Travel App. Plan Trips. (2017). *Tripoto Travel App: Plan Trips*. Retrieved: January 12, 2017, from https://play.google.com/store/apps/details?id=com.tripoto

UNESCO. (2001). *UNESCO Universal Declaration on Cultural Diversity a vision a conceptual platform a pool of ideas for implementation a new paradigma*. UNESCO. Retrieved January 26, 2017, from http://unesdoc.unesco.org/images/0012/001271/127162e.pdf

UNWTO. (2011). *Religious Tourism in Asia and the Pacific*. Retrieved January 26, 2017, from http://cf.cdn.unwto.org/sites/all/files/pdf/110325_religious_tourism_excerpt.pdf

UNWTO. (2014). *Tourism can protect and promote religious heritage.* Press Release. Retrieved January 26, 2017, from http://media.unwto.org/press-release/2014-12-10/tourism-can-protect-and-promote-religious-heritage

UNWTO. (2016). *Conference on Religious Heritage and Tourism: How to increase religious heritage tourism in a changing society.* Cultural Heritage Agency of the Netherlands and UNWTO. Retrieved January 26, 2017, from http://europe.unwto.org/event/conference-religious-heritage-and-tourism-how-increase-religious-heritage-tourism-changing-soc

UNWTO/UNESCO. (2015). *World Conference on Tourism and Culture, Building and Partnership, Siem Reip* – 2015. Author.

Urry, J. (2002). *The tourist gaze.* London: Sage Publications.

Wang, P. (2012). A Personalized Collaborative Recommendation Approach Based on Clustering of Customers. In D. Yang (Ed.), *International Conference on Applied Physics and Industrial Engineering 2012, Pt B* (Vol. 24, pp. 812-816). doi:10.1016/j.phpro.2012.02.121

Xiang, Z., & Gretzel, U. (2010). Role of social media in online travel information search. *Tourism Management, 31*(2), 179–188. doi:10.1016/j.tourman.2009.02.016

Xu, F., Weber, J., & Buhalis, D. (2013). Gamification in tourism. In *Information and Communication Technologies in Tourism 2014* (pp. 525–537). New York, NY: Springer International Publishing. doi:10.1007/978-3-319-03973-2_38

Xu, Y. (2011). Literature review on web application gamification and analytics. Honolulu, HI: Academic Press.

Yamamoto, K., & Fujita, S. (2017). A Dynamic Real-Time Navigation System for Urban Tourists. In *Planning Support Science for Smarter Urban Futures* (pp. 167–184). Springer International Publishing. doi:10.1007/978-3-319-57819-4_10

Yovcheva, Z., Buhalis, D., Gatzidis, C., & van Elzakker, C. P. (2014). Empirical Evaluation of Smartphone Augmented Reality Browsers in an Urban Tourism Destination Context. *International Journal of Mobile Human Computer Interaction, 6*(2), 10–31. doi:10.4018/ijmhci.2014040102

Yu, C. C., & Chang, H. P. (2009). Personalized location-based recommendation services for tour planning in mobile tourism applications. In *International Conference on Electronic Commerce and Web Technologies* (pp. 38-49). Springer Berlin Heidelberg. doi:10.1007/978-3-642-03964-5_5

Zheng, W., Liao, Z., & Qin, J. (2017). Using a four-step heuristic algorithm to design personalized day tour route within a tourist attraction. *Tourism Management, 62*, 335–349. doi:10.1016/j.tourman.2017.05.006

KEY TERMS AND DEFINITIONS

Augmented Reality: This facilitates a better understanding of the real world and permits the integration of virtual elements that help to complement real resources.

Business Intelligence: This results from information systems that combine data with analytical tools in order to provide information relevant to decision making, while seeking to improve the quality and availability of this information to decision makers.

Consumer Behavior: This is the focus of studies of consumers and the processes they employ to choose, use (i.e., consume), and dispose of products and services.

Cultural Heritage: This comprises physical artifacts and intangible attributes of a place or society that are inherited from past generations. Tangible heritage includes buildings, monuments, landscapes, books, works of art, and artifacts. Intangible heritage includes folklore, traditions, language, and knowledge.

Gamification: Gaming mechanics can be used to solve problems in nongaming environments, such as in a business, making it possible to measure and evaluate the reputation or performance consumers associate with products and destinations.

Intelligent Interface: This is any human-computer interface that can predict what users want to do and present information based on this prediction. The key idea is that this interface is more intuitive and helpful in a way that presents information to users in an appropriate context that is more adequate to their needs.

Social Media: These aggregates of online communications channels can be considered tools that can be used to define new business models strategically, taking into consideration analyses of community user-generated content and information shared with other members of these online communities.

Tourism Experience: This is a set of activities in which individuals engage on their personal terms, such as pleasant and memorable places, allowing each tourist to build his or her own travel experiences so that these satisfy a wide range of personal needs, from pleasure to a search for meaning.

Chapter 2
Interactive Technologies in Museums:
How Digital Installations and Media Are Enhancing the Visitors' Experience

Roberto Ivo Fernandes Vaz
University of Porto, Portugal

Paula Odete Fernandes
Polytechnic Institute of Bragança, Portugal

Ana Cecília Rocha Veiga
Federal University of Minas Gerais, Brazil

ABSTRACT

With the constant development of digital means of entertainment – that are easily made available to people and, in most cases, can be used anywhere – nowadays, a visit to a museum have to surround publics with unexpected and interactive experiences, in order to capture their attention and make them want to go to these places, in addition to continue to communicate their collections and promote society education. In this regard, it was discussed in this chapter the actual panorama of interactive technologies used in museums exhibitions worldwide, and there are discussed how these institutions are designing digital installations and utilizing virtual media to enhance the visitors' experience, promoting positive relations between them and their publics. The main conclusion and reflection of the chapter is based on how this new era of technology is allowing increasing physical, cognitive and sensory accessibility, and transforms this kind of experience for disabled publics.

DOI: 10.4018/978-1-5225-2927-9.ch002

INTRODUCTION

Because one lives in an era where people spend the most part of their time in front of screens and connected to the internet, museum professionals have to think about how to make collections and exhibitions still relevant nowadays, and how to compete with all the available entertainment ways and technological developments, in order to capture the visitor's attention and encourage their visit to these spaces.

Once this chapter focuses on exploiting digital ways of interactivity in museums, it is crucial, first of all, to understand their role in contemporary: "A Museum is a non-profit, permanent institution in the service of society and its development, open to the public, which acquires, conserves, researches, communicates and exhibits the tangible and intangible heritage of humanity and its environment for the purposes of education, study and enjoyment" (Desvallées & Mairesse, 2010, p. 57). Based on this professional definition, widely recognized and disseminated by ICOM – International Council of Museums – since 2007, it is clear that museums must provide to society the access to education, offering moments of study and leisure, in order to cooperate for its development, committing itself to safeguard and communicate their collections to the public (Desvallées & Mairesse, 2010).

As institutions are increasingly interested in providing outstanding informal learning experiences, there has been an effort to meet the visitor's aspirations, through the adaptation of innovative technology to communicate and encourage the visit to these spaces (Chelini, 2012). As pointed out by Sree Sreenivasan – the Metropolitan Museum of Art's chief digital officer, until June of 2016 – on an interview to Gilbert (2016), museums no longer need to compete with each other, because they are losing their visitors to the omnipresent technologies, games and social media consumed by the modern society; instead, those institutions have to find out ways to embrace the fact that smartphones, tablets, smartwatches and other digital devices are everywhere, and take advantage of the fact that people use them no matter when or where: "People ask me what our biggest competition is (…) It's not the Guggenheim; it's not the Museum of Natural History. It's Netflix. It's Candy Crush" (p. 32) and most recently, Pokémon Go (McCluskey, 2016). Taking these facts into account, it is self-explained why museums are committed, more than ever, in providing new scenarios of interaction and contact with their exhibitions.

On the other hand, it is important to make clear that the use of digital resources would not even be an option to communicate and to interact with the exhibitions if their use offers no contribution to what is being presented: in some cases, technological solutions are seen as essential for facilitating the reproduction of stories and intangible processes, like sound recordings, music, videos and other non-physical heritage; in other instances, they contribute to expand information about what cannot be exposed, like no longer existing artefacts and places, giving access to reconstructions and digital replicas (Chanda, 2013).

About the exhibition of physical samples, the use of digital resources proves to be beneficial because it enables visitors to have a better understanding of objects and ideas – since it allows offering complementary information in a more attractive way for visitors, without overloading the exhibitions environment with excess of information – and allows to increase accessibility and enable opportunities for disabled persons (Freeman et al., 2016; Israel, 2011).

However, professionals should be aware that technology must be used as a medium and not as an end, according to Israel (2011), McMullan (2015) and Olesen (2016), where, ideally, the museum themes should be harmoniously combined with digital content to communicate effectively the exhibitions and, at the same time, provide an incredible experience to visitors while using them: "given the increased emphasis on user experience, it is no longer sufficient to ensure that a system is merely usable" (O'Brien & Toms, 2008, p. 939).

Taking these considerations into account, this chapter aims to make a contribution to better understand the actual panorama of interactive technologies that museums are embracing to communicate their exhibitions, and to explore how the use of these digital installations and media are enhancing the experience of visiting these spaces, transforming the relations between them and their publics. Thus, they are discussed the virtual museum and online collections, the role of interactive kiosks and multi-touch surfaces to amplify exhibitions, interactive projections for immersive experiences, mobile applications and five types of emerging technologies. For each one, they will be addressed at least four projects currently implemented in museums all around the world and, at the end of the chapter, it is made a reflection about the use of technology to increase accessibility in museums and discussed examples of installations designed for enhancing the experience of disabled publics.

THE VIRTUAL MUSEUM: ONLINE COMMUNICATION, COLLABORATION AND SOCIAL MEDIA

According to Holdgaard (2011), there is no well-defined conceptualization for virtual museum: online museum, electronic museum, hyper museum, digital museum, cyber museum, web museum, among others, are the many possible names for the virtual museum. Regardless of the nomenclature, this is a database made digitally available over the internet, and can be distinguished in three main variants, with focus on content, communication and collaboration, that can also be fully connected with the museum's own museographic tools (Geser & Niccolucci, 2012; Holdgaard, 2011).

The museum's web site provides not only information support, but also contents generated by visitors through posted photos and videos, wikis and discussions, blogs, microblogs, collective subtitles, social bookmarking, tagging, integration and sharing of information via social media platforms, like Facebook, Twitter, Instagram, Pinterest, among others (Geser & Niccolucci, 2012; Johnson, Becker, Estrada & Freeman, 2015). Actually, there is a trend toward a preference, by users, of interactive, and not only passive, virtual relations (Carvalho & Raposo, 2014). The user, therefore, actively influences the construction of museum knowledge, structuring a new paradigm for the museum-visitor relationship. The museum's presence on the internet, in our days, may represent its very subsistence, since the lack of virtual communication may result in invisibility to many potential visitors.

Over the last two decades, the boom of web sites and social media associated to museums raised the question of whether those virtual spaces will, one day, take the place of the physical museum. It has been debated, actually, since the early days of photography. It is believed that the virtual museum will never eliminate the longing for physical matter that is present in all of us. On the contrary, from virtuality it can foretaste the knowledge of reality, and thus have a greater longing for a broader knowledge of it. Virtuality may, ultimately, work as a bridge toward reality or its amplification (Veiga, 2013).

The Louvre Museum is an example of that kind of bridge. It is possible, through the tools available at the museum's web site, to: download the maps of the museum; take an interactive, virtual tour through each one of the museum's floors; take a virtual tour through the museum's rooms, with 360° controllable images and 3D exploration; have access to mini-sites of specific works of art, as well as quick documentaries at the "eye-openers" section; have access to a huge database of works, with catalog information about them; schedule visits to researcher-only areas, such as technical reserves and fragile collections (Louvre, 2016). In recent queries, one found out that the Louvre's web site has broadened the acquisition of knowledge about the archives and the institution, optimizing visitation time through previous planning and maximizing one's own experience with the real collections.

As an example of amplification of real-life experience, it can highlight the Google Art Project, which made available virtual tours to many art works in museums around the world, with the possibility of unusual approaches. That tool allows the detailed observation, even more than in a real-life visit, of the painting's surface, creating the possibility of technical and esthetical studies that would not be possible only with the direct observation of the work in the museum (Cultural Institute, 2013).

The project VanGo Yourself joins virtual exhibits, creation of contents, interactivity and the use of social media. The proposal consists in recreating, with friends, scenes portrayed in famous works of art. The visitor selects the work from various criteria, such as the number of persons portrayed or by choosing a specific museum. As soon as the photo is generated, the user uploads it to the web site, where the image is then twinned with the original and shared on social media (VanGo Yourself, 2016.).

The Art Detective portal is free-to-use online networks where anyone can help public art collections across the United Kingdom enhance painting information, uncovering attributions and solve mysteries through public discussions. Participants can post or answer questions related to various aspects of the work under analysis: artist, theme, date of execution, technique, support, description, among others. Since its debut in 2014, over 100 discussions have been initiated, bringing forth about 40 new findings (Art UK, 2016).

It has been realized that a solid and quality virtual museum isn't merely a repository of photographs of artefacts of the collection, but the ultimate challenge is to create virtual environments that are concerned with the narrative and relational aspects of the digital exhibition, that promotes collaboration between public and museum experts, social interaction and sharing, as well as foment knowledge dissemination. From this point, it will be analysed and discussed digital installations and technologies that are being used in-situ by museums, all over the world.

FROM INTERACTIVE KIOSKS TO MULTI-TOUCH SURFACES: AMPLIFYING THE EXHIBITION

A kiosk is defined, according to the Oxford Dictionary, as a fixed terminal that uses a computational system to provide information, incorporating one or more interactive display screens. The content configuration can be done according to the purpose that it intends to serve in the institution in which it is inserted, and the navigation trough the content is usually done by touching the screen (with just one finger) and, in most cases, it can be used only by one person at a time (Kidd, Ntalla & Lyons, 2011).

Taking into account the presence of these terminals in several museums, Hall (2013) conducted a study where it is concluded that, in most cases, these terminals were not designed in a way to allow visitors to have an interesting interaction: since the large volume of information that can be accessed in a kiosk (such as text, images, video and some games) is not suitable for group use and doesn't allow a good experience of interaction, the social activity during the visit is limited; and this constitutes a problem, as "we often visit museums with others – whether friends, family, peers or colleagues – and even when we visit a museum alone we are sensitive to the behavior of others" (Heath & Vom Lehn, 2010, p. 266). This fact is also corroborated by Kidd et al. (2011), pointing out that the greatest criticism about the use of interactive kiosks to communicate museum exhibitions is exactly the limitation of the social experience during the visit.

Opposite to the case of interactive kiosks, multi-touch screens provide a greater openness to social sharing, because these interfaces facilitate the access to information to a larger number of people, simultaneously: multi-touch interfaces are input devices that identify two or more simultaneous touches providing opportunities to several users to interact with an application at the same time (EDUCAUSE, 2008). Beyond this, due the dimensions of the area to touch – corresponding, normally, to a big screen – and the interface design characteristics, the harmonious integration of these surfaces into the space narrative of the exhibitions constitutes, by itself, an immediate invitation to visitors to interact with this interfaces (Kidd et al., 2011).

One of the most mediatic multi-touch projects is located in Gallery One at Cleveland Museum of Art, a space near the entrance of the museum, where more than 4100 objects from the most important museum's in the world are displayed, on the *40-foot Collection Wall* installation. This surface, arranged as an enormous interactive wall, can be used by several visitors, simultaneously, to navigate through the collection. When an image is touched, the screen enlarges it and gives extra details about the object and where it is located, allowing visitors to personalize and share their own tours – according to its favourite's ones – in order to discover some pieces that are in exhibition inside other galleries of the Museum (Bernstein, 2013; Cleveland Museum of Art, 2013).

After a huge renovation, at the end of 2014, the Cooper Hewitt Smithsonian Design Museum reopened with new digital installations to enhance the public's experience. Several multi-touch high definition tables were used as a medium to communicate, interactively, the Museum themes, in which visitors can explore pieces of the collection – *Collection Browser* area, learn about the history and architectural details of the building – *Mansion History*, and understand the relationship between donors and objects in the collection – *People Browser* area (Chan & Cope, 2015; Cooper Hewitt, 2016). According to Cooper Hewitt (2016), it is possible to note that allowing the socialization during the visit was a core aspect of the Museum intentions, since the tables have various dimensions and the largest ones are described as to allow up to six visitors to interact with them, at the same time.

At the Los Angeles Museum of the Holocaust, visitors can interact with *The Memory Pool*, a multi-touch interface where information emerge on the surface of a table, as objects floating in a pool full of water, showing photographs of people in their daily lives before the Holocaust, like socializing with friends, playing sports, going to school, celebrating weddings, etc. When an image is touched, the information regarding to these moment is load and visitors could get to know more about that moment. On the other hand, if there is no interaction with some of the pictures, the images fade away, representing the loss of these memories (Potion, 2010).

As a last example of this section, the *Science Storms* exhibition, opened in 2010 at the Chicago Museum of Science and Industry, visitors can explore scientific principles behind natural phenomena, like tornados, tsunamis, lightning, and others (Lord & Piacente, 2014). In one of that interfaces, a touch screen is used to create and control, in real time, an authentic experience about the influence of water on fire: during the interaction with this installation it is possible to manipulate a real flame, by varying the gas flow rate and adjusting the water that is being sprayed (Museum of Science and Industry, 2016). With this, public can experiment and learn more about scientific phenomena by controlling, by their own, some of the variables that affect what they are seeing.

CREATING IMMERSIVE EXPERIENCES THROUGH INTERACTIVE PROJECTIONS

In addition to increasing the engagement of audiences, some projects are being developed to integrate scenarios of new incredible experiences of immersion in museums' spaces, transforming the paradigms of information visualization and interaction with exhibitions.

The installation *Pure Land: Inside the Mogao Grottoes at Dunhuang* is one of these cases, described by Julian Raby – director of the Arthur M. Sackler Gallery and Freerer Gallery of Art, Smithsonian Institution – as an exhibition experience of the future (Smithsonian Institution, 2012), in which visitors can actually feel like if they had been transported to another place: while people are standing inside a panoramic enclosure that shows one cave of Mogao Grottoes – an UNESCO World Heritage Site – they "engage in a surrogate true-to-life experience of being inside this cave temple and seeing its magnificent Buddhist wall paintings at one-to-one scale" (Kenderdine, 2013, p. 204). The installation, first shown to public at City University of Hong Kong, integrates high-resolution digital photography's and tridimensional architectural models of the archeological space, combining them into a 360-degree visualization projection system, allowing visitors to navigate through the virtual space and also to interact with 3D animated objects, revealing key details when people uses digital glasses to better inspect the cave's walls (Kenderdine, 2013).

The *Connected Worlds* exhibition at the New York Hall of Science is, according to Holmes (2015), the largest installation ever created that uses projections. It aims to help visitors understand the interconnectivity and balance of a natural ecosystem, in which the interaction with the digital environment is made by using gestures and body movements, constantly tracked by 12 Kinects and an infrared system. The biosphere environment combines six ecosystems that form an interconnected world, so the changes introduced into a virtual organism impacts the system as a whole, regardless of whether they were personal or collective. In addition, visitors can use physical objects to setup the path of a virtual waterfall, and understand the effects that this cause. In an interview to Holmes (2015), the creators of the project said that the children's immersion into the virtual world facilitates and aids their learning: children of a wide range of ages make really impressive interpretations and also associate it to concepts they had been discussing in class.

In addition to promoting the exploration of distant places and enhance education through the interaction with virtual scenarios, some museums are using projection technologies to present art exhibitions. It is the case of *Pipilotti Rist: Pixel Forest* at the New Museum, where the artist' work explores physical and psychological experiences of the living world, through the presentation of textures, forms, lights and sounds, in immersive environments (New Museum, 2016). Described as being radiant with colour, projections on the floor, walls and ceilings expand video images everywhere, and to improve the visitors' experience, the space was embedded with steps, pillows and beds (Smith, 2016).

Contrary to this exhibition, where visitors' interaction with the digital world doesn't provoke a direct effect in what is being presented, the *Immersion Room* at the Cooper Hewitt Smithsonian Design Museum was designed to do so. Allowing public to browse the most important collection of wallcoverings in North America on a multi-touch table (Chan & Cope, 2015), the high-resolution digitized wallpapers are projected at full-scale on the walls around, and some can even be experienced accompanied by comments of their designers. Besides this, visitors can sketch their own designers and see them projected on the walls, in real time (Cooper Hewitt, 2016).

The last project presented in this section belongs to Museum Victoria and was built as a solution to the same difficulty that most museums face: due the lack of space, only a fraction of their collections can be displayed to public. The *mARChive* interface consists in a 360-degree three-dimensional stereoscopic interactive visualization environment that allows the navigation through more than eighty thousand digital records of objects of the Museum, grouped in eighteen themes, projected all around the surrounding walls. Using a tablet to browse and select images, and 3D glasses to visualize them, the immersive cinematic experience is augmented by the possibility of examine the high resolution images, at one to one scale, with descriptions of the objects (Kenderdine & Hart, 2014). This project constitutes a new way of organizing and thinking about how pieces that aren't in exhibition can be digitally accessed, and how they can be communicated to the public in an interactive scenario.

As seen, interactive projections are being used by museums to transform spatial environment, allowing visitors to interact with them using their body gestures, imagination and making decisions, contributing to improve education while providing new experiences of immersion inside their spaces.

MOBILE APPLICATIONS: AUGMENTED EXHIBITIONS, MUSEUM TOURS, AND GAMING EXPERIENCES

Portable devices like smartphones, tablets and smartwatches became ubiquitous and, in addition to allowing connections to the Internet, also include built-in cameras and sensors that enable the interpretation of the real world, which can contribute, in some cases, to stimulate new interactions with collections and museum spaces (Freeman et al., 2016; Johnson, Adams & Witchey, 2011).

In fact, most part of visitors bring their own devices when visiting museums and, as result, these institutions are embracing and taking advantage of this reality by producing applications (apps), since "they can meet those visitors in their comfort zones to not only fulfil information needs, but also encourage enhanced exploration, interpretation and sharing … heighten visitor experiences by providing more comprehensive materials, including multiple critical interpretations, stories and contextual information" (Freeman et al., 2016, p. 16).

According to McMulla (2015), successful museum apps are those who create engagement with museum themes and invite public to move within the space, in a way that learning can be complemented with enjoyment, instead of requiring constant attention to what is happening on the digital world. As an example, the San Francisco Museum of Modern Art designed the *SFMOMA* app to encourage visitors to explore the museum with their eyes on the physical exhibition and art, instead of having to look and being concentrate on their phone screens, as they listen to unique descriptions while moving through the museum (SFMOMA, 2016). Based on a virtual map created by Apple for the museum, the app implementation goal was to use visitor's phone's location-aware technology to triangulate its position and combine immersive audio storytelling that adjusts its contents – like perspectives, reflections and responses to artworks, and point-to-point direction to locations in the building – accordingly to their walking (Chun, 2016; SFMOMA, 2016).

On the other hand, the *Second Canvas* app by Museo del Prado was created to let visitors explore with extra detail 14 masterpieces from the permanent collection, in images with giga-pixel resolution, which means a level of detail practically invisible to the naked eye. Additional information about the layers of paintings can be exposed by using super-zoom, ultraviolet, infrared and x-ray vision functions, only experienced before by the curators and restorers of the museum, and the app allows to share cropped images of the pieces directly via Facebook and Twitter (Mad Pixel Factory, 2014; Williams, 2014). In an interview to Williams (2014), the deputy director of the Museo del Prado – Gabriele Finaldi – says this app aims to change the way people experience artworks, providing a deeper level of understanding while using smartphones and tablets to discover the paintings: with the app you can discover every centimetre of the work of art in your own time on your iPad, leading to a profounder understanding of how it was created and each element the artist included.).

Some museums, like the Royal Ontario Museum allow visitors to experience the past by using augmented reality. Through the *SopifyROM* app it is possible to add skins to dinosaur skeletons, give life to extinct animals, restore destroyed objects to their original form, decipher antique languages and see objects in its original setting (Czikk, 2013). The app also allows x-ray views of some pieces and to scan QR codes scattered throughout the museum, which give visitors extra information about the artefacts in exhibition, in the form of video, audio, text and interactive graphics (Oliveira, 2013).

In an effort of trying to reduce the distance between visitors and museum professionals, the Brooklyn Museum designed the *ASK* app, that allows onsite visitors to ask questions and have conversations with experts, in real time, and get responses about the works of art in the museum, with the facility of capturing images and sending photographs directly to them, which helps to give context to the question being asked (Browne, 2014). After measuring the impact of ASK, Shelley Bernstein – the Deputy Director of Digital Initiatives and Chief Experience Officer at the Barnes Foundation – concludes that the conversations via the app are a success for deeper engagement and understanding of the works, and the use rate and depth of interaction achieved was never so high on Brooklyn Museum previous projects, like comment kiosks, mobile tagging and QR Codes (Bernstein, 2015).

As the last project of this section it is mentioned the *Capture the Museum* app from the National Museum of Scotland, the first physical team game developed for a museum in which visitors, with their own smartphones, explore galleries of the museum to solve exhibit-related puzzles and scan into territories using their device's camera, in order to beat the other team. With duration of 30 minutes, the game can accommodate up to 50 players at the time and a map shows in real time which team is winning the challenges concerning to the different galleries of the museum. Gamification was the surprise element when designing the app, since visitors didn't expect to find nothing like this in such an august institution and, by introducing technology to encourage visitors to learn more about history, it was expected that the app could appeal to new audiences (National Museums Scotland, 2013).

EMERGING TECHNOLOGIES

The *New Media Consortium Horizon Report Series* are recognized all around the world for the longest-running exploration of emerging technology trends in museums. On the *2016 Museum Edition*, the expert panel identified some categories of emerging technologies that they believe will be widespread use in museums over the next five years (Freeman et al., 2016). Based on this work and research of recent projects being developed in museums, this section will explore five types of emerging technologies that are changing interaction and opening new scenarios of exhibitions' communication, providing, as well, examples of their implementation in museological institutions.

3D-Printing and Scanning Technologies

According to Hancock (2015), 3D-scanning and printing technology provide myriad possibilities to increase engagement and depth understand of museum pieces, because visitors "can feel and look at objects previously only view under glass" (p. 33), which provides sensory information that allows to feel and experience the exhibit in new and direct ways.

Currently, there are three main uses of 3D-printing by museums, pointed out by Professor Daniel Short, from the Environmental Science Department at Robert Morris University: for hands-on studies and educational purposes by scanning and replication of original pieces, for educational exhibits about 3D-printing (including Maker Faire and Fab Labs) and for restoration of damaged artefacts and exhibits (Schuster, 2015).

Some museums, like The Art Institute of Chicago are using 3D-technologies, in this case, to allow visitors to hold and touch tridimensional replicas of selected objects from the collection (which were scanned, 3D-modeled and printed at a 1:1 scale when possible) with the aim of creating multi-sensory tours for adults with Alzheimer's and low vision, where discussions and learning about the original works of art are promoted (Association of Art Museum Directors, 2015). Despite the three dimensional printed representation of objects not being perfect in most cases, the original ones remain preserved and safe from close contact (Hancock, 2015; Neumüller, Reichinger, Rist, & Kern, 2014).

Another example of using those technologies in museums is the *Ancient Lives, New Discoveries* exhibition from the British Museum and the Samsung Digital Discovery Center, in which visitors, after handling three replicas from the collection, could recreate, design and 3D-print their own Egyptian amulets, while discovering the different themes associated with each. As complement of the experience, participants were able to animate an Egyptian river scene and 3D-print their models, with the help of a professional 3D artist (Biggs, 2014).

At the Metropolitan Museum of Art, some activities were developed to educate and encourage visitors to explore 3D-technologies to construct replicas of artefacts in exhibition in the museum, by taking pictures of the objects from all sides (using the *123D Catch* free program). In turn, if a visitor is not comfortable with using these technologies, the museum provides models available online, in an effort to enhance the experience. After this, the sculptures can be 3D-printed and visitors can take them home (Undeen, 2013).

To finish, another project using three dimensional technologies to extend museum objects besides their physical spaces is the *Smithsonian X 3D*, from Smithsonian Institution, which offer pieces from its collection that have been digitalized and placed online, with the aim to make museum collections and scientific specimens more widely available and contribute to improve education all around the world (Clough, 2014; Smithsonian Institution, 2016): lectures can now download data from a new Smithsonian website and generate precise replicas for students to inspect using a relatively inexpensive 3D printer" (Clough, 2014). With this project, even students from the other side of the world can get to know the physical objects and engage with them.

Virtual Reality

When the subject is virtual reality, there are being current debates about it at the most important world-wide institutions, since it is expected to be the next digital trend on entertainment, gaming, tourism, culture and information industries, among others.

In fact, the conceptualization of virtual reality is not so recent and some works in the past were developed in museums:

In 1992, Apple Computer's Virtual Museum was one of the first documented implementations, which consisted of a demonstration disc for Apple's QuickTimeVR (Freeman et al., 2016, p. 42).

However, the high costs associated to virtual reality were an obstacle to museums in general, until the recent development of devices, such as HTC Vive, Samsung Gear VR and Oculus Rift, that, by the fact of being powerful, user-friendly and low-cost, started to become commercially available (Adams, 2016; Jung, tom Dieck, Lee & Chung, 2016).

Virtual reality refers to computer-generated environments that replicate places, presence of people and objects, or fictional worlds, allowing realistic sensory experiences by the full immersion in a digital environment (Adams, 2016; Freeman et al., 2016; Jung et al., 2016). Virtual reality differs from augmented reality, since the first offers the user digital immersive environments where they have the ability to move around and interact with them, opposite to augmented reality, that allows to add digital information to images and real-life contexts (Adams, 2016; Guerra, Pinto & Beato, 2015).

Taking these nuances into account, Adams (2016) clarifies that 360-degree cameras cannot be considered virtual reality: despite users can look around within an immersive visual experience, they can't navigate through the environment, neither interact with anything in them, not controlling the experience as a whole.

The Natural History Museum exhibited the *First Life* virtual reality experience, to allow visitors to explore the world's ancient oceans – using Samsung Gear VR headsets – and interact with sea creatures that existed 500 million years ago, three-dimensionally reconstructed based on the Museum's research about those extinct specimens. The 15-minute adventure is narrated by the nature commentator Sir David Attenborough, transporting visitors to non-existing places and providing a new scenario of experiencing the museum's collection (Natural History Museum, 2015).

At the British Museum, visitors were able to explore a *Bronze Age* site and interact in their historic context with 3D scans of objects from this period (belonging to the museum's collection), with Samsung Gear VR headsets put on to look around and using a touchpad to navigate within the environment. This exhibition enabled the testing of how virtual reality can be applied to enhance the family audience's understanding of a historic collection, and the results showed that feedback received reveals enthusiasm and confirms the positive impact of this experience on learning about the museum's pieces made available (Rae & Edwards, 2016).

In addition to allowing new discoveries about real objects from the collection, a project is using virtual reality to expose inaccessible heritage. The Museum of Stolen Art is a virtual space dedicated to display artworks that have been stolen by criminals, during wars or dubious historical agreements, that cannot be viewed in any exhibition from any museum in the world. Available as a smartphone app, virtual reality is employed to allow "visitors" to navigate virtual galleries, look at works and activate and read pop-up didactic texts, completed with audio tours to contextualize rotating exhibitions (April, 2016).

At the Salvador Dalí Museum, visitors can experience multiple interactions and feel what it is like to be inside a painting, at the *Disney and Dalí: Architects of the Imagination* exhibition, created by a partnership between the museum and Disney. According to Nofuente (2016), the *Disney and Dalí* experience provide a multi-sensory three-dimensional environment of moving image and soundscapes, while views are moving in the picture itself as other visuals from Dalí's works like elephants, birds, ants, using Oculus

Rift headsets as mediators of the surrealist's creations. The author refers that projects like this one, built using virtual reality, are being developed in museums once they offer new and innovative scenarios of communicating the collections, with the expectation of bringing even more foot traffic back to museums.

Beacons for Location Intelligence

According to Freeman et al. (2016), location intelligence is a digital strategy to the mapping of positioning and its association with data. Providing location-based services, it can be used to deliver specific information in response to visitor's surroundings and enable in-depth analytics on their behaviours, contributing to the promotion of formal and informal learning in museums space.

As seen before, triggering content on mobile devices is something that some museums are familiar with, allowing the use of mobile applications to interact with exhibitions through QR Codes or NFC tags disposed near objects in exhibition, for instance. However, beacons enable automatic content delivery to nearby smart devices via Bluetooth, functioning as wireless tools that can be installed anywhere – since the chosen location has no barriers like walls, vitrines and objects – and are almost invisible. This reality enhances the interconnection between objects and digital devices, playing a significant role in advancing the "internet of things" concept (Bernstein, 2015; Nilsson, Blackwell, Hogsden & Scruton, 2016).

In a collaboration between the University of Kansas and the Spencer Museum of Art, a mobile app using iBeacon technology was developed to encourage a deeper engagement with the collection and enhance onsite visitors' experience. The devices were placed strategically throughout the museum and, when someone is near, the app alerts with a pop-up message that there are items of interest approaching, offering additional images, video and text about the objects of the collection (Association of Art Museum Directors, 2015).

The Australian Maritime Museum uses a Beacon solution to monitor the visitor's behaviour inside the museum spaces, to better manage exhibit space and public engagement. Given that this project is not to visitors interact directly with the exhibition, there was no necessity of requiring them to download a specific app. Instead, the solution adopted was by attaching a Beacon as a key ring that it's given to visitors when they use the storage locker service of the museum. While moving inside the museum, iPods paced throughout the museum detects the Beacons and send live data via Wi-Fi to an online dashboard, where staff can access the information (Nomad Agency, 2016).

The University of Cambridge Museums consortium designed a mobile game named *Ghosts!* that use the beacons placed through the gallery spaces and across the eight museums that compose the consortium, to lead visitors through the different museums. The narrative unfolds while walking, so the app pop-up on the screen of the visitor' mobile device some 'ghosts' that are lost and need help finding their way back to their home artefacts – each one equipped with its own Beacon – while feedback about the directions is constantly being provided (Nilsson et al., 2016). From the designers' perspective, the great advantage of using Beacon technology to develop games for museums is "the ability to create an ongoing dialogue between objects (or their digital representation in a mobile app) and visitors where the communication between the two is constantly changing according to how visitors move through, and around, gallery spaces" (p. 135), without the need for expansive technical infrastructure.

To finish this section, it is referred the experiments across different departments at the Metropolitan Museum of Art with location-aware content delivery through Beacons. Positive aspects pointed out about the use of this technology are the potential in informing and alerting visitors about locations of special exhibitions, about current tours and events happening near to them, and the learning value that can be achieved by providing supplementary audio and video content for communicate the objects. Nevertheless, efficacy issues such as temperature changes and human traffic were reported, since these phenomena affect the signal of each Beacon device (Doljenkova, 2015).

Wearable Technology

Taking into account the growing trend of wearable devices, such as smartwatches from Apple, Samsung, Sony and Pebble, bracelets from Jawbone, Nike and Fitbit, and Google Glass, among others, museums are exploring the potential of these technologies in their spaces because they allow new scenarios of storytelling and interaction.

Wearable technology refers to computer-based devices that take the form of a portable and lightweight accessory that can be worn by users, and can integrate tools to track social media interactions, movement, vital signs, perform productive tasks like check emails, etc (Johnson, Becker, Estrada & Freeman, 2015).

The exhibition *Body Metrics* at the Tech Museum of Innovation allow visitors to explore and understand their body metrics, using a wearable Sensor Kit that measures and displays their activity level, tension, mental focus, talkativeness, attitude and the number of people nearby, in real time. The aim of the exhibition is to let visitors learn more about how some activities affect their physical and mental wellbeing, by exploring the metrics collected by the kit: a smartphone is worn around the neck to explore the surrounding environment, a NeuroSky wireless headset measures brainwaves and a Somaxis EXG sensor is worn on the skin to register muscle tension and heart rate (Tech Museum Of Innovation, 2014).

According to Corine (2014), the San Francisco de Young Museum was the first to offer a tour where visitors could wear Google Glass to see digital content and learn more about the artworks, on the *Keith Haring: The Political Line* exhibition. This wearable was chosen because of being a non-intrusive solution for augmenting the exhibition and being a light-weight device, so visitors can walk around the gallery and immerse themselves into the exhibition: when approaching an artwork, visual and audio content about the artist' life and work is presented automatically – trough Beacon technology embedded at the museum space – eliminating the necessity of interaction with the wearable device. Augmented reality effects are provided as well, so hidden details not easily visible can be observed as the explanation about the pieces occurs (Corine, 2014; Gąsiorek, 2015).

Most recently, the Oscar de la Renta Retrospective exhibition at the same museum (de Young) designed a mobile app that integrates a smartwatch to acts as an invisible tour guide, delivering additional interpretative information in real time, so visitors can always be concentrated in the art itself, without needing to look to the screen of a device: anyone with an Apple Watch can go "through the museum and hear recordings about the nearest display when alerted by a vibration on their wrist… Tap the watch and Andre Leon Talley or de la Renta himself will discuss the influences behind the piece" (Kelly, 2016, para. 3).

As a last example, it is mentioned that the Design Museum is working on designing the *Fear and Love: reactions to a Complex World* exhibition that aims to track visitor's vital signals to interact with installations by manipulating their biometrics with breathing exercises. Smartglasses are embodied with sensors to measure heart rate, breathing and brain waves, and the data is processed by an oversized belt that allows influencing the digital art that is being presented. For instance, a green square covers or reveals the image of a rose depending on how stressed a visitor is; the calmer he/she is, the less a busy crowd is displayed and according to his/her breathe, the rope being pulled in two directions, in a video, becomes more or less tense, as organic signs are being measured (Charara, 2016).

Tangible User Interfaces

The beginnings of the concept of tangible user interfaces dates back to 1993, when the publication of *Back to the Real World*, which warned that the digital environment of computers and augmented reality did not constitute natural habitats for humans, so it was evident the need to develop practices that allow a more balance interaction between the real world and the virtual one, in which the physical dimensions were enriched by digital elements (Shaer & Hornecker, 2010).

Two years passed till Fitzmaurice, Ishii and Buxton (1995) introduced the term *Graspable User Interface*, where tangible blocks – *bricks* – were used to manipulate digital objects, making it possible, among other actions, to control the position of the digital material and make use of both hands at the same time. These authors highlight that space-multiplexed input, contrary to time-multiplexed input, provide a new way of human-computer interaction, since a specific transducer can be associated to a unique function, which occupies its own space and allows any of these points to be accessible at any time to the user, and to be handled simultaneously.

Based on these works, the conceptual model of *Tangible User Interfaces* was proposed as a combination of the architecture of ubiquitous computing system with the conceptual model of augmented reality and physical computing, turning the world into an interface. To this end, there are three key concepts: "coupling of bits and atoms" to the allocation of digital data to tangible objects, which gain expression when they come into contact with the "interactive surfaces" – solid interfaces adapted to the coexistence of both worlds. Finally, the "ambient media" includes elements that discretely allow influence human perception, including changes in sound, light and air movement (Ishii & Ullmer, 1997).

With this, tangible objects simultaneously allow the representation and manipulation of digital content, opening space to the inclusion of this concept in many aspects of daily life, in which they have proving to be effective, such as in the educational and learning areas, new scenarios of information visualization, problem solving and planning, entertainment and games, music and performances, social communication Shaer and Hornecker (2010), amongst others, and for museum exhibitions, which constitutes this chapter main focus.

At the Lille Natural History Museum, visitors can discover the collection of more than one thousand mineral samples of the collection – that cannot be in exhibition due to lack of space, while ensuring their conservation – by manipulating tangible disks on a surface, which represent atoms. Each one of these is associated to geological samples made of that particle and it is possible to combine various elements, on a horizontal interface, to form more complex atoms aggregation. At the same time, a vertical screen shows images and textual information about the rocks (Dalbavie, 2014). The author points out that the *Tangible Lille* installation is available for use by one or more visitors at the same time, promoting collaborative learning and a high level of personalization, since three modes (scientific, simples and game) allow access to several layers of information about the minerals.

Another example of using this technology in museums exhibitions is the *SynFlo* exhibit, a project developed for The Tech Museum Of Innovation, that utilizes physical objects with integrated displays and laboratory objects, with which visitors can interact to explore bio-design activity: when manipulating real lab items, it is possible to add virtual plasmid or toxins to the previous gene selected and observe the results of these reactions in the active tangible tokens (Okerlund et al., 2016). The authors suggest that the combination of gestural interaction with active tangible tokens in exhibitions foster visitor's involvement and provide more serious context to the activity.

Belongings is an interactive tangible table top display developed to explore the intangible cultural heritage and the belongings as a cultural knowledge, using replicas of unearthed Musqueam objects, as well as other elements used by the community nowadays. During the exhibition *c̓əsnaʔəm: the city before the city*, through the installation, visitors could learn about ancient knowledge, culture and technology, by interacting with the material objects, which according to Muntean et al. (2015) encouraged interactions between visitors, the sharing of information and informal discussion about the themes explored. This project was a partnership between the Museum of Vancouver, the Museum of Anthropology, the Musqueam Indian Band and the University of Waterloo.

The *Diplomacy and Sèvres Porcelain, Prestige and the French art of living in the 18th century* exhibition included a tangible user interface dedicated to the exploration of the artefacts at the Louvre DNP Museum Lab –a museum created by collaboration between the Louvre Museum and Dai Nippon Printing. Visitors were provided with a set of physical miniatures of some of the objects in exhibition which, when placed in a specific area, allowed to visualize and manipulate a three-dimensional virtual representation of the objects, providing access to extra details and complementary information (Musée du Louvre & Dai Nippon Printing, 2010). Also at the Louvre DNP Museum Lab, the exhibition *El Niño Azul, Goya and Spanish Painting in the Louvre* had a space dedicated to understanding the factors related to painting, through an installation named *The painting, a material object*. Visitors could handle eight physical elements that allowed to virtually act in the different layers of the work, in order to get to know the various stages of its creation and the alterations in the original work caused by weather, humidity, heat and light exposure (Musée du Louvre & Dai Nippon Printing, 2012).

To end this section, it points out that the major potential of this technology is that tangible objects can be handled, revealing new scenarios of interaction and communication of exhibitions. According to Classen (2007), in most cases the artefacts in museums can only be looked at, ignoring one of the major human senses that allow interaction with the world: the touch. The possibility of being able to establish physical contact with the exhibits has the advantage of complementing some sensory aspects that vision cannot grasp by itself, such as weight, texture, shape, materials and hardness of the objects (Classen, 2007; Damala et al., 2016; Morgan, 2012).

ACCESSIBLE INSTALLATIONS FOR DISABLED PUBLICS

The International Classification of Functioning, Disability and Health defines disability as an umbrella term for impairments, action limits and participation restrictions (World Health Organization, 2016), and estimates that over a billion people worldwide (about 15% of the world's population) have some form of disability. Taking this data into account, it is understood that museums, as cultural institutions in the service of society and its development, have the responsibility of improving accessibility of their exhibitions, facilities and create programs for disabled populations.

According to Freeman et al. (2016), "developments in technology have the potential to increase access and enable opportunities for disabled persons" (p. 26), allowing these members of the public having more inclusive available ways to understand and interact with exhibitions, contributing to a better experience while visiting museums.

As an example of using technology to reintegrate touch and other non-retinal senses into a museum space, an accessible exhibitor based on tangible user interfaces was developed for MM Gerdau – Mines and Metal Museum, allowing visitors the handling of four geological samples of the collection. When interacting with the exhibits, the interface presents augmented information about the pieces and, at the same time, voiceovers provide to blind and other visual impaired visitors the same information to those that don't have disability, plus a detailed description about the shapes, textures and roughness of which geological sample, for an easy identification. In order to increase learning during the exhibition, whenever two pieces were handled at the same time, the presenting themes relates to a comparison of the pieces (Vaz, Fernandes & Veiga, 2016). This project received a prize on museums education practices, by Ibermuseus Program, so an accessible circuit of interactive exhibitors based on this one will be developed in order to enhance the visitors experience and provide a larger access to samples of the MM Gerdau's collection (Ibermuseus, 2016).

Other museums, like the North Carolina Museum of Natural Sciences, are designing mobile apps to provide an enhanced experience for visitors with some kinds of disabilities. By providing audio feedback through map features and integrating a high contrast option, individuals with visual impairments can move inside the museum and zoom information for high-resolution text, so they can learn more about the museum's exhibits while moving. Also, for people with hearing impaired and autism, the app includes descriptions with photos and captions for videos, which proved to be a robust solution to enhance the experience of those persons while visiting the museum (Institute of Museum and Library, 2015). At the Canadian Museum of Human Rights, the app includes an interactive map that tells where visitors are and guide them to a specific destination and, by using iBeacons, voices of museum staff members describe each gallery and provides highlights of exhibits and architecture, so blind visitors or with low vision can appreciate the exhibition. As well, the app was designed to assist deaf or hard of hearing publics, including additional sign-language content for several exhibits (Murphy, 2015).

Technologies like 3D printing and scanning are expected to bring visitors closer to exhibits, paintings and artworks – that cannot be directly touched – as a multi-sensorial form of experiencing culture for all visitors (Bernardo, 2016), providing, as well, "a great benefit for the accessibility of cultural heritage, especially for persons with learning difficulties, for children, the elderly, for blind or visual impaired visitors" (Neumüller et al., 2014, p. 119). The *Hoy toca el Prado* exhibition at the Prado Museum carried out three dimensional copies of six representative works, which could be touched by visitors with visual disabilities, in order to allow them to recreate painting mentally by feeling and understanding their space, depth and perspective (Museo del Prado, 2015).

As seen until now, technology can be beneficial to visitors with blindness or deafness, opening new possibilities to understand exhibitions that previously were inaccessible to them. However, people with physical disability can also enjoy the museum collections, even if they cannot go to those places: "since 2014, "telepresence" robots have been able to lead people with disabilities into every nook and cranny of a museum" (Bernardo, 2016, para. 15). The San Francisco de Young Museum allows people with disabilities to see the art in high resolution, plus enabling interaction in real time with guides and other people in the museum. Through microphone, screen, camera and speakers embedded on an ambulatory device known as Bearn, comments or questions from the visitor can be responded, allowing an independent and interactive experience (Fine Arts Museums of San Francisco, 2015).

To end this chapter, it is pointed out that some of technologies that are used to enhance the non-disabled public' experience can improve, as well, the disabled visitors' experience, coexisting simultaneously and contributing for a more interesting and accessible visit to museums.

CONCLUSION

This chapter aimed to make a contribution in the discussion of the appliance of digital technologies to enhance the visitor's experience, as well as provide practical examples of their use in real museum contexts, rather than approaching technology from the point of view of conservation of museological objects, logistics, maintenance or learning curve of professionals.

As seen, nowadays a visit to a museum must respond to visitors' high expectations for the ease of gathering interactive information about the exhibitions, at the same time that have to be effective on communicating a good message to their publics. It is important to make clear that museum artefacts and themes themselves should always be the focus, no matter what technology is being used to increase the public's experience. Instead of detracts visitor's attention from real objects and museological themes, those technologies must be properly designed to provide unique and exciting moments – that will be part of the visitor's memories in the future – as well as to ensure a magnificent and effective mixture between entertainment and education, conveying solid information and making sure that it reaches people.

The presence of museums in the virtual world enable engagement and interaction with users outside their physical barriers, involving online visitors on collaborative activities plus promoting discussions about diverse themes, at the same time as they facilitate sharing on social media, constituting, in some cases, global public spheres for deliberation that boost creativity and knowledge dissemination.

Installations like multi-touch surfaces allow the condensation of information in a restricted space –amplifying the exhibition without overloading the physical space – and promote scenarios of social living, sharing and collaboration.

In turn, interactive projections can create immersive learning experiences throughout the spatial environment, and it is common that visitors can interact with the installations by using their body gestures. Also, virtual reality – that is expected to introduce and replicate new multisensory contexts related to heritage, in the future – gives visitors the opportunity of experiencing exhibitions on a full immersion mode, in which visitors can feel like they had been transported to a whole new world.

Mobile applications are being used to augment information concerning to exhibits, to create gaming experiences, to establish dialogues between visitors and museum staff, as well as to help to create tours or facilitating navigation throughout museums. The emerging Beacon technology as proven to be effective on helping to shape a visit and for the presentation of specific content when it is supposed to happen, creating precise connections between collections communication and publics.

Due the desire to explore the authentic artefacts of a collection in person, tangible user interfaces can combine them with digital content, ensuring that details and other education content are being communicated to visitors at the same time as they handle the objects. Furthermore, when pieces of the museum cannot be directly touched (because there are associated questions of conservation, damaging, stealing, among others), digitalization and 3D printing play an important role, since they allow the direct contact with copies of pieces in exhibition which, otherwise, would be absolutely inaccessible. Additionally, the digitalized content can allow the building of partnerships and collaborations between museums and other institutions, like schools, for instance, increasing the easier access to objects to other publics that cannot come to these institutions.

Lastly, wearable technologies are presented as being non-intrusive and light-weight solutions that can augment the people's experience while visiting museums, since they allow the constant attention on the exhibition, instead of having to look to a screen, as well as they represent a new opportunity for designers on creating completely new interactive experiences.

The final main goal of this chapter was to highlight the role of technology in helping to promote physical, cognitive, sensory, in short, cultural accessibility of museums exhibitions, supporting, on one hand, the dissemination of information about the exhibits and, on the other, contributing for an inclusive museum that are committed to providing outstanding learning experiences and enhancing the disabled visitors' experience.

As future work, and once during the study wasn't found a solid guide of rules about when to use and in which objects should be or not used technology in a museum context, it could be very interesting conduct a research regarding these questions, in order to provide easy and assertive guidelines for those who already work with technologies in museums and for other persons that relate to this area.

REFERENCES

Adams, E. (2016). *Most Virtual Reality Is Not Virtual Reality. Here's Why* [online article]. Retrieved December 5, 2016, from http://gearpatrol.com/2016/07/18/virtual-reality-vs-360-video/

April, Q. (2016). *Virtual Absence and Presence in the Museum of Stolen Art* [online article]. Retrieved December 5, 2016, from http://www.artpractical.com/column/locating-technology-the-museum-of-stolen-art/

Art, U. K. (2016). *Welcome to Art Detective* [website]. Retrieved December 21, 2016, from http://www.artuk.org/artdetective/

Association of Art Museum Directors. (2015). *Next Practices in Digital and Technology* [online book]. Retrieved December 4, 2016, from https://aamd.org/sites/default/files/document/Next Practices in Digital and Tech.pdf

Bernardo, Á. (2016). *Museums that are Accessible Thanks to Technology* [online article]. Retrieved December 19, 2016, from https://www.bbvaopenmind.com/en/museums-that-are-accessible-thanks-to-technology/

Bernstein, F. (2013). Technology That Serves to Enhance, Not Distract. *The New York Times*. Retrieved from http://www.nytimes.com/2013/03/21/arts/artsspecial/at-cleveland-museum-of-art-the-ipad-enhances.html?hpw&_r=0

Bernstein, S. (2015). *Measuring Success* [online article]. Retrieved November 30, 2016, from https://www.brooklynmuseum.org/community/blogosphere/2015/08/19/measuring-success/

Bernstein, S. (2015). *The Realities of Installing iBeacon to Scale* [online article]. Retrieved November 29, 2016, from https://www.brooklynmuseum.org/community/blogosphere/2015/02/04/the-realities-of-installing-ibeacon-to-scale/

Biggs, K. (2014). *Mummies, mobiles and 3D printing* [online article]. Retrieved December 4, 2016, from https://blog.britishmuseum.org/2014/05/30/mummies-mobiles-and-3D-printing/

Browne, J. (2014). *Simply ASK* [online article]. Retrieved November 30, 2016, from https://www.brooklynmuseum.org/community/blogosphere/2014/10/06/simply-ask/

Carvalho, J., & Raposo, R. (2014). A adoção de media sociais como estratégias comunicacionais por museus: aplicações e tendências. In B. Passarelli, A. M. da Silva, & F. Ramos (Eds.), E-Infocomunicação: Estratégias e Aplicações (4th ed.; pp. 329–348). São Paulo: Senac.

Chan, S., & Cope, A. (2015). Strategies against Architecture: Interactive Media and Transformative Technology at the Cooper Hewitt, Smithsonian Design Museum. *Curator*, *58*(3), 352–368. doi:10.1111/cura.12118

Chanda, S. (2013). The special visitor: Each and every one of us. *ICOFOM Study Series*, (42), 83–96. Retrieved from http://network.icom.museum/fileadmin/user_upload/minisites/icofom/pdf/ISS_42__2013_Rio_red.pdf

Charara, S. (2016). *Hussein Chalayan has turned emotion sensing into a thing of beauty: Biometric wearables at the Design Museum's new Fear and Love exhibition* [online article]. Retrieved December 7, 2016, from http://www.wareable.com/wearable-tech/hussein-chalayan-emotions-design-museum-3603

Chelini, M. (2012). Novas tecnologias para...novas (?) expografias. *Revista Museologia & Interdisciplinaridade, 1*(2), 59–71. Retrieved from http://seer.bce.unb.br/index.php/museologia/article/view/7904

Chun, R. (2016). *The SFMOMA's New App Will Forever Change How You Enjoy Museums* [online article]. Retrieved October 29, 2016, from https://www.wired.com/2016/05/sfmoma-audio-tour-app/

Classen, C. (2007). Museum manners: The sensory life of the early museum. *Journal of Social History*, *40*(4), 895–914. doi:10.1353/jsh.2007.0089

Cleveland Museum of Art. (2013). *About Gallery One*. Retrieved from http://www.clevelandart.org/gallery-one/about

Clough, G. W. (2014). *How Will 3-D Printing Change the Smithsonian?* [online article]. Retrieved December 5, 2016, from http://www.smithsonianmag.com/smithsonian-institution/how-will-3d-printing-change-the-smithsonian-180949426/?no-ist

Corine, B. (2014). *GuidiGO new storytelling platform enhances Keith Haring exhibition at the de Young Museum through Google Glass* [online article]. Retrieved September 10, 2016, from http://blog.guidigo.com/blog/guidigo-new-storytelling-platform-enhances-keith-haring-exhibition-at-the-de-young-museum-through-google-glass/

Cultural Institute. (2013). *Google Art Project: Toda a Arte do Mundo na Ponta dos Seus Dedos* [online article]. Retrieved December 21, 2016, from https://www.google.com/intl/pt-BR/culturalinstitute/about/artproject/

Czikk, J. (2013). *New ScopifyROM App Gives Royal Ontario Museum Visitors an Augmented Experience* [online article]. Retrieved September 15, 2016, from http://www.betakit.com/new-scopifyrom-app-gives-royal-ontario-museum-visitors-an-augmented-experience/

Dalbavie, J. (2014). La table interactive du musée d'Histoire Naturelle de Lille. *La Lettre de l'OCIM*, (152). 10.4000/ocim.1339

Damala, A., Van der Vaart, M., Clarke, L., Hornecker, E., Avram, G., Hub, K., & Ruthven, I. (2016). Evaluating tangible and multisensory museum visiting experiences: Lessons learned from the meSch project. *MW2016: Museums and the Web 2016*. Retrieved from http://mw2016.museumsandtheweb.com/paper/evaluating-tangible-and-multisensory-museum-visiting-experiences-lessons-learned-from-the-mesch-project/

Desvallées, A., & Mairesse, F. (2010). Key Concepts of Museology. Paris: Armand Colin. Retrieved from http://icom.museum/fileadmin/user_upload/pdf/Key_Concepts_of_Museology/Museologie_Anglais_BD.pdf

Doljenkova, V. (2015). *Beacons: Exploring Location-Based Technology in Museums* [online article]. Retrieved December 6, 2016, from http://www.metmuseum.org/about-the-museum/museum-departments/office-of-the-director/digital-media-department/digital-underground/2015/beacons

du Louvre, M., & Printing, D. N. (2010). *Diplomacy and Sèvres Porcelain, Prestige and the French art of living in the 18th century* [press release]. Retrieved October 5, 2016, from http://www.museumlab.eu/press/pdf/Louvre-DNPMuseumLab_7_PressRelease_EN.pdf

du Louvre, M., & Printing, D. N. (2012). *El niño azul, Goya and Spanish Painting in the Louvre: Louvre-DNP Museum Lab Ninth presentation in Tokyo* [press release]. Retrieved September 14, 2016, from http://www.museumlab.eu/press/pdf/Louvre-DNPMuseumLab_9_PressRelease_EN.pdf

EDUCAUSE. (2008). 7 Things You Should Know About Multi-Touch Interfaces. *EDUCAUSE Learning Inititative (ELI)*. Retrieved from http://www.educause.edu/ELI/7ThingsYouShouldKnowAboutMulti/162960

Fine Arts Museums of San Francisco. (2015). *FAMSF Improves Museum Access with Beam Device* [online article]. Retrieved December 15, 2016, from https://www.famsf.org/about/technology/beam

Fitzmaurice, G. W., Ishii, H., & Buxton, W. A. S. (1995). Bricks: Laying the Foundations for Graspable User Interfaces. In *Proceedings of the SIGCHI Conference on Human Factors in Computing Systems* (pp. 442–449). New York: ACM Press/Addison-Wesley Publishing Co. http://doi.org/ doi:10.1145/223904.223964

Freeman, A., Adams Becker, S., Cummins, M., McKelroy, E., Giesinger, C., & Yuhnke, B. (2016). *NMC Horizon Report: 2016 Museum Edition*. Austin, TX: The New Media Consortium. doi:10.1111/j.2151-6952.2010.00064.x

Gąsiorek, A. (2015). *Beacon-Enabled Google Glass at Museums: "It's Not Some Distant Future. It's Already Happening"* [online article]. Retrieved December 2, 2016, from https://kontakt.io/blog/beacon-enabled-google-glass-at-museums/

Geser, G., & Niccolucci, F. (2012). Virtual museums, digital reference collections and e-science environments. *Uncommon Culture, 3*(5/6), 12–37. Retrieved from http://firstmonday.org/ojs/index.php/UC/article/view/4714

Gilbert, S. (2016). Please turn on your phone in the museum: Cultural institutions learn to love selfies and social media. *Atlantic (Boston, Mass.), 3*, 32–33.

Guerra, J., Pinto, M., & Beato, C. (2015). Virtual Reality-Shows A new vision for tourism and heritage. *European Scientific Journal, 11*(9), 49–54.

Hall, S. (2013). *Creating strong cross media concepts for museum exhibitions*. Umeå Universitet. Retrieved from http://umu.diva-portal.org/smash/record.jsf?pid=diva2:630513

Hancock, M. (2015). Museums and 3D Printing: More Than a Workshop Novelty, Connecting to Collections and the Classroom. *Bulletin of the Association for Information Science and Technology, 42*(1), 32–35. doi:10.1002/BUL2.2015.1720420110

Heath, C., & Vom Lehn, D. (2010). Interactivity and Collaboration: new forms of participation in museums, galleries and science centres. In Museums in a digital age (pp. 266–280). JOUR, Routledge.

Hewitt, C. (2016). *The New Cooper Hewitt Experience* [website]. Retrieved November 1, 2016, from http://www.cooperhewitt.org/new-experience/

Holdgaard, N. (2011). The Use of Social Media in the Danish Museum Landscape. In Trant & D. Bearman (Eds.), *Museums and the Web 2011: Proceedings*. Toronto: Archives & Museum Informatics. Retrieved from http://www.museumsandtheweb.com/mw2011/papers/the_use_of_social_media_in_the_danish_museum_1

Holmes, K. (2015). *The Environment Is Your Playground in an Interactive 3D Ecosystem* [online article]. Retrieved October 15, 2016, from http://thecreatorsproject.vice.com/blog/the-environment-is-your-playground-in-an-interactive-3d-ecosystem

Ibermuseus. (2016). *Anunciamos os resultados do 7º Prêmio de Educação e Museus* [press release]. Retrieved December 20, 2016, from http://www.ibermuseus.org/acao-educativa/conheca-os-projetos-vencedores-do-7o-premio-ibero-americano-de-educacao-e-museus/

Institute of Museum and Library. (2015). *Opening the World of Museums and Libraries to Visually Impaired Visitors* [online article]. Retrieved December 19, 2016, from https://www.imls.gov/news-events/project-profiles/opening-world-museums-and-libraries-visually-impaired-visitors

Ishii, H., & Ullmer, B. (1997). Tangible Bits: Towards Seamless Interfaces Between People, Bits and Atoms. In *Proceedings of the ACM SIGCHI Conference on Human Factors in Computing Systems* (pp. 234–241). New York: ACM. doi:10.1145/258549.258715

Israel, K. (2011). *Informação e tecnologia nos museus interativos do contemporâneo*. Universidade de São Paulo. Retrieved from http://www.usp.br/celacc/ojs/index.php/blacc/article/view/285

Johnson, L., Adams, S., & Witchey, H. (2011). *The NMC Horizon Report: 2011 Museum Edition*. Retrieved from http://www.nmc.org/pdf/2011-horizon-report-museum.pdf

Johnson, L., Becker, S., Estrada, V., & Freeman, A. (2015). *NMC Horizon Report: 2015 Higher Education Edition*. Austin, TX: The New Me; http://doi.org/ISBN

Jung, T., tom Dieck, M. C., Lee, H., & Chung, N. (2016). Effects of Virtual Reality and Augmented Reality on Visitor Experiences in Museum. In A. Inversini & R. Schegg (Eds.), *Information and Communication Technologies in Tourism 2016: Proceedings of the International Conference* (pp. 621–635). Cham: Springer International Publishing. doi:10.1007/978-3-319-28231-2_45

Kelly, H. (2016). *This museum wants the Apple Watch to be your tour guide* [online article]. Retrieved December 7, 2016, from http://money.cnn.com/2016/03/31/technology/apple-watch-de-young-museum/

Kenderdine, S. (2013). Pure Land: Inhabiting the Mogao Caves at Dunhuang. *Curator: The Museum Journal*, *56*(2), 199–218. doi:10.1111/cura.12020

Kenderdine, S., & Hart, T. (2014). *mARChive: Sculpting Museum Victoria' s Collections* [online article]. Retrieved November 29, 2016, from http://mw2014.museumsandtheweb.com/paper/marchive-sculpting-museum-victorias-collections/

Kidd, J., Ntalla, I., & Lyons, W. (2011). Multi-touch interfaces in museum spaces: reporting preliminary findings on the nature of interaction. *Proceedings of the International Conference Re-Thinking Technology in Museums 2011: Emerging Experiences*. Retrieved from http://www.idc.ul.ie/techmuseums11/paper/paper1.pdf

Lord, B., & Piacente, M. (2014). *Manual of Museum Exhibitions*. Rowman & Littlefield.

Louvre. (2016). *Louvre Website* [website]. Retrieved December 21, 2016, from http://www.louvre.fr/en/homepage

Mad Pixel Factory. (2014). *Second Canvas: The Second Screen for Art*. Retrieved November 30, 2016, from http://www.secondcanvas.net/

McCluskey, M. (2016). *Holocaust Museum Asks Guests to Stop Playing Pokémon Go There*. Retrieved November 17, 2016, from http://search.ebscohost.com/login.aspx?direct=true&site=eds-live&db=heh&AN=116804468

McMullan, T. (2015). *Shake up the gallery: how iPads are changing the way we visit museums* [online article]. Retrieved October 15, 2016, from http://www.alphr.com/apple/1001182/shake-up-the-gallery-how-ipads-are-changing-the-way-we-visit-museums

Morgan, J. (2012). The multisensory museum. *Glasnik Etnografskog Instituta*, *60*(1), 65–77. doi:10.2298/GEI1201065M

Muntean, R., Hennessy, K., Antle, A., Rowley, S., Wilson, J., Matkin, B., … Wakkary, R. (2015). ʔeləw̓k̓w – Belongings: A Tangible Interface for Intangible Cultural Heritage. In Electronic Visualisation and the Arts (EVA 2015) (pp. 360–366). doi:<ALIGNMENT.qj></ALIGNMENT>10.14236/ewic/eva2015.41

Murphy, A. (2015). *Accessibility in museums: creating a barrier-free cultural landscape* [online article]. Retrieved December 5, 2016, from http://advisor.museumsandheritage.com/features/accessibility-in-museums-creating-a-barrier-free-cultural-landscape/

Museo del Prado. (2015). *Hoy toca el Prado* [online article]. Retrieved September 10, 2016, from https://www.museodelprado.es/actualidad/exposicion/hoy-toca-el-prado/29c8c453-ac66-4102-88bd-e6e1d5036ffa

Museum, N. (2016). *Pipilotti Rist: Pixel Forest.* Retrieved November 29, 2016, from http://www.newmuseum.org/exhibitions/view/pipilotti-rist-pixel-forest

Museum of Science and Industry. (2016). *Exhibit Science Storms: Wonder Is All Natural* [website]. Retrieved November 22, 2016, from http://www.msichicago.org/explore/whats-here/exhibits/science-storms/the-exhibit/fire/fire-and-water/

National Museums Scotland. (2013). *National Museums Scotland looks to grab new audiences with digital game of territories* [press release]. Retrieved December 1, 2016, from http://www.capturethemuseum.com/press/

Natural History Museum. (2015). *Explore virtual reality with David Attenborough's First Life* [online article]. Retrieved December 5, 2016, from http://www.nhm.ac.uk/about-us/news/2015/june/dive-back-in-time-with-david-attenborough-s-first-life.html

Neumüller, M., Reichinger, A., Rist, F., & Kern, C. (2014). 3D Printing for Cultural Heritage: Preservation, Accessibility, Research and Education. In M. Ioannides & E. Quak (Eds.), 3D Research Challenges in Cultural Heritage: A Roadmap in Digital Heritage Preservation (pp. 119–134). Berlin: Springer Berlin Heidelberg. doi:<ALIGNMENT.qj></ALIGNMENT>10.1007/978-3-662-44630-0_9

Nilsson, T., Blackwell, A., Hogsden, C., & Scruton, D. (2016). Ghosts! A Location-Based Bluetooth LE Mobile Game for Museum Exploration. In L. Joyce & B. Quinn (Eds.), Mapping the Digital: Cultures and Territories of Play (pp. 129–138). Oxford, UK: Inter-Disciplinary Press. Retrieved from http://arxiv.org/abs/1607.05654

Nofuente, K. (2016). *Virtual Reality and The Future of Museum Tours: Using Oculus Rift to Dream with Disney and Dalí* [online article]. Retrieved December 1, 2016, from http://www.techtimes.com/articles/127404/20160127/virtual-reality-future-museum-tours-using-oculus-rift-dream-with-disney-dali.htm

Nomad Agency. (2016). *Beacon Analytics at Maritime Museum* [online article]. Retrieved December 6, 2016, from http://www.nomadagency.com.au/portfolio-item/beacon-analytics-at-maritime-museum/

OBrien, H. L., & Toms, E. G. (2008). What is user engagement? A conceptual framework for defining user engagement with technology. *Journal of the American Society for Information Science and Technology*, *59*(6), 938–955. doi:10.1002/asi.20801

Okerlund, J., Segreto, E., Grote, C., Westendorf, L., Scholze, A., Littrell, R., & Shaer, O. (2016). SynFlo: A Tangible Museum Exhibit for Exploring Bio - Design. *Proceedings of the TEI '16: Tenth International Conference on Tangible, Embedded, and Embodied Interaction*, 141–149. doi:10.1145/2839462.2839488

Olesen, A. R. (2016). For the sake of technology? The role of technology views in funding and designing digital museum communication. *Museum Management and Curatorship, 31*(3), 283–298. 10.1080/09647775.2016.1163643

Oliveira, M. (2013). *Royal Ontario Museum ScopifyROM App Adds Interactivity to Exhibits* [online article]. Retrieved November 30, 2016, from http://www.huffingtonpost.ca/2013/10/02/royal-ontario-museum-app_n_4031715.html

Potion. (2010). *Memory Pool*. Retrieved from http://www.potiondesign.com/project/memorypool/

Rae, J., & Edwards, L. (2016). Virtual reality at the British Museum: What is the value of virtual reality environments for learning by children and young people, schools, and families?. *MW2016: Museums and the Web 2016*. Retrieved from http://mw2016.museumsandtheweb.com/paper/virtual-reality-at-the-british-museum-what-is-the-value-of-virtual-reality-environments-for-learning-by-children-and-young-people-schools-and-families/

Schuster, E. (2015). *How do you envision 3D printing finding a place in science centers and museums? Do you already use or have plans for 3D printing?* [online article]. Retrieved December 4, 2016, from http://www.astc.org/astc-dimensions/how-do-you-envision-3d-printing-finding-a-place-in-science-centers-and-museums-do-you-already-use-or-have-plans-for-3d-printing/

SFMOMA. (2016). *The New SFMOMA Announces Transformed Digital Strategy: Supported by Bloomberg Philanthropies, SFMOMA Puts Mobile at the Forefront*. Press release, San Francisco Museum of Modern Art. Retrieved from https://s3-us-west-2.amazonaws.com/sfmomamedia/media/press-releases/downloads/SFMOMA_Digital_Engagement_Press_Release_5_2_2016.pdf

Shaer, O., & Hornecker, E. (2010). Tangible User Interfaces: Past, Present, and Future Directions. *Foundations and Trends in Human-Computer Interaction*, *3*(1–2), 1–137. doi:10.1561/1100000026

Smith, R. (2016). *"Pipilotti Rist: Pixel Forest," Deep in the Wilds of Video* [Art & Design Article [online]]. Retrieved November 29, 2016, from http://www.nytimes.com/2016/10/28/arts/design/pipilotti-rist-pixel-forest-deep-in-the-wilds-of-video.html

Smithsonian Institution. (2012). *New Technology Resurrects Ancient Chinese Cave at Smithsonian's Sackler Gallery: "Pure Land" Digital Installation Brings Buddhist Treasures to Washington, D.C.* [press release]. Retrieved November 28, 2016, from http://www.asia.si.edu/press/2012/sackler-25-digital-cave-release.asp

Smithsonian Institution. (2016). *Smithsonian Releases High-Resolution 3-D Model of Apollo 11 Command Module to Explore and Print* [online article]. Retrieved December 5, 2016, from http://newsdesk.si.edu/releases/smithsonian-releases-high-resolution-3-d-model-apollo-11-command-module-explore-and-print

Tech Museum of Innovation. (2014). *Body Metrics* [website]. Retrieved December 7, 2016, from https://www.thetech.org/plan-your-visit/galleries/bodymetrics

Undeen, D. (2013). *3D Scanning, Hacking, and Printing in Art Museums, for the Masses* [online article]. Retrieved November 4, 2016, from http://www.metmuseum.org/about-the-museum/museum-departments/office-of-the-director/digital-media-department/digital-underground/posts/2013/3d-printing

VanGo Yourself. (2016). *Recreate Artworks with Your Friends* [website]. Retrieved December 21, 2016, from http://vangoyourself.com/

Vaz, R., Fernandes, P., & Veiga, A. (2016). Proposal of a Tangible User Interface to Enhance Accessibility in Geological Exhibitions and the Experience of Museum Visitors. *Procedia Computer Science, 100*, 832–839.

Veiga, A. (2013). *Gestão de Projetos de Museus e Exposições*. Belo Horizonte: C/Arte.

Williams, R. (2014). *Second canvas: the art of apps* [online article]. Retrieved November 30, 2016, from http://www.telegraph.co.uk/technology/apple/10804445/Second-canvas-the-art-of-apps.html

World Health Organization. (2016). *Disability and health* [online article]. Retrieved December 5, 2016, from http://www.who.int/mediacentre/factsheets/fs352/en/

KEY TERMS AND DEFINITIONS

Augmented Reality: A technological way to access digital information integrated in the user's environment, in real time, using, normally, apps designed for mobile devices.

Fab Lab: The abbreviation of *Fabrication Laboratory*, a program started in the Media Lab at Massachusetts Institute of Technology (MIT) that intends to offer workshops of digital fabrication, so that products can be built by anyone interested on the theme.

Kinect: The name of a device for motion sensing created by Microsoft, originally as a game controller, that is used in numerous projects to allow recognize gestures and movements.

Maker Faire: Events related to innovation and experimentation across the spectrum of science, engineering, art, performance and craft, where people can design and create things on publicly-accessible places.

NFC: The abbreviation of *Near Field Communication*, a wireless technology to data transfer in close proximity, without the need for an external connection, like the internet.

QR Code: The abbreviation of *Quick Response Code*, a two-dimensional barcode that can be read by some digital devices, by using a camera, and points to information about the object to which is attached.

Social Media: Computer-mediated technologies that are used for sharing, creating and visualize information, via online virtual communities and networks.

Chapter 3
Augmented Reality:
Applications and Implications for Tourism

Erkan Özdemir
Uludağ University, Turkey

Serkan Kılıç
Uludağ University, Turkey

ABSTRACT

Technological advances have had an impact on many industries as well as the tourism industry. Augmented reality applications, one of the emerging new technologies in recent years, have also started to be used in our daily lives. Augmented Reality (AR) is a technology that allows its users to see the real world together with an additional virtual world that is added in real time to the same field of view. The augmented reality applications contribute to the enrichment of tourists' tourism experiences, especially during their visit and result in augmented satisfaction levels. Furthermore, it is one of the effective tools that can be used against the wear and tear of cultural heritage sites caused by overcrowding. In this chapter, the application fields of the augmented reality in the field of tourism have been discussed under the subtitles. As a result of our study, recommendations for the development of AR applications both for the literature and real-life application have been presented.

INTRODUCTION

Today, as it is the case in many industries, there has been an intense competition in the tourism industry as well. In the face of this competition, the organizations in the tourism industry have used new technologies to stay competitive and develop marketing campaigns in various forms (Jung & Han, 2014). One of the techniques developed in this challenging competition is Augmented Reality (AR) applications. The AR technology is a new technology that can offer many opportunities that are difficult to be presented and met by the other technologies (Alkhamisi & Monowar, 2013).

In recent years, there have been many augmented reality applications used in different industries in the world. The augmented reality applications are used in many fields such as industry and military,

DOI: 10.4018/978-1-5225-2927-9.ch003

training and education, travel and tourism, medicine and health care, and retail and marketing (Martínez, Skournetou, Hyppölä, Laukkanen, & Heikkilä, 2014). The tourism industry is also one of the industries where augmented reality applications have a comprehensive area of implementation. The tourism industry is an area in which especially the AR applications have higher potential of use. The availability of the AR applications, especially in mobile devices, causes these applications in the tourism industry to become even more widespread.

Today, the question of protecting cultural heritage has become very important. In addition to natural degradation, due to the negative effects caused by development activities and overcrowding, inheritance conservation efforts are vital in ensuring the sustainability of heritage sites. Just at this point, the advances in digital technologies such as virtual reality (VR) and augmented reality (AR) are the applications that can be valuable in preserving the heritage. These technologies will minimize the impact of overcrowding in the threatened heritage sites, but at the same time they will increase the overall experience of the visitors (Ab Aziz & Siang, 2014). The purpose of this kind of synergy between reality and virtual is to develop and consolidate the place-based economic development, culture, quality and the integration of local resources by preserving their historical identities. The tourism products are developed to include more cultural offerings among the various participating institutional actors, with a balanced dose of competition, co-operation and coordination (Garau, 2014). Augmented reality applications in the tourism industry are dealt with within the scope of smart tourism (Buhalis & Amaranggana, 2013; Koo, Shin, Kim, Kim, & Chung, 2013).

The aim of this chapter is to explicate the concept of augmented reality, the different aspects of it from other similar concepts, the infrastructure requirements, and analyze the applications examples in the tourism industry in the world especially within the content of destination marketing. Hence, in the background section, firstly the relationship between the concept of augmented reality and virtual reality, and the hardware and software infrastructure of the augmented reality is discussed. Afterwards, augmented reality applications in the tourism industry are discussed together with relevant examples. In the conclusion section, technical and social problems of the augmented reality applications are discussed and proposed solutions are presented.

BACKGROUND SECTION

Augmented Reality

AR is a combination of real-object and computer-generated data where the virtual object has been collated with the real world. This means that it is visible to the user that the virtual field and the real object co-exist in the same place (Azuma, 1997). The AR technology proposes that the real and virtual objects coexist in the same place (Linaza, Gutierrez, & García, 2014, p.498). Today, especially the rapid development of the latest generation of mobile devices now allows anyone with a computer or just a smartphone to be able to make connections in real time and get information from the virtual world as a result of augmented reality through the overlap of information layers (Garau, 2014). The rapid development in the use of smartphones and mobile applications create new ways of connecting with the visitors in many sectors as well as in the tourism industry (Kennedy-Eden & Gretzel, 2012).

Although a virtual environment is used in augmented reality applications created by computer graphics, the main playground is the real environment. Computer graphics perform the function of adding real information to the necessary information (Kim & Kim, 2014). With the AR, the marketers can take the physical world and combine it with the digital world. In this way, it is possible for consumers and brands to make more connections with the product before, during and after the purchase of a product (Çeltek, 2016). Thanks to the augmented reality that allows the digital content to be placed in our real-world images, the user can view the real world enhanced with additional 3D graphics by their field of view using the camera of a smartphone or a tablet. This technology can be used in many areas of the tourism industry, including the reconstruction of historical monuments, the reconstruction of monuments and the recreation of historical sites (Richards, 2014). The space between reality and virtual reality, which allows the real and virtual elements to be combined at various levels, is called mixed reality (Schmalstieg & Höllerer, 2016, p. 28). The mixed reality is the presentation of real and virtual objects within a single display (Milgram & Kishino, 1994).

Principally, in contrast to the virtual reality (VR) used before or after the tour, the augmented reality (AR) increases the experience of tourists, especially on-trip (Tian, Xu, & Fu, 2013). The augmented reality applications can also be a useful instrument for having an experience in the destination before, during, or after the sightseeing tourism experience. The AR can also be considered as *a complementary product* that helps the tourism experience with additional level of knowledge. Unlike the virtual reality, users can see the actual destination in their surroundings in the augmented reality (Pedrana, 2014). Augmented reality completes the sightseeing experiences of the tourists. Due to the lack of control over the dynamic and diverse environment in which these experiences take place, the issues and factors that need to be taken into account in augmenting the sightseeing tourism experience are fundamentally different from the factors that determine the VR environment. Therefore, for an authentic augmented tourism experience, it is important to provide high degree association between the virtual and physical objects in the augmented reality applications (Yovcheva, Buhalis, & Gatzidis, 2013a).

Augmented Reality Technology

Augmented reality applications should be designed for the users with little computer knowledge who wish to enjoy the digital content of a cultural heritage through a device. For this reason, the application should have the following qualities; intuitive to use (the user should be able to use the application without reading any manual), real time (the application should be able to respond to user actions in real time) cross-platform (the application should be able to be used in different mobile platforms as well), fault tolerant (the application should be able to correctly handle errors such as loss of connectivity from external modules or noise images from the camera). The main functional requirements for the AR application are described below (Vecchio et al., 2015, pp. 53-54) In general, except for those mentioned here, for other AR applications it is possible to have a different set of requirements.

- **Objects' Detection:** The user should be able to easily use the camera on his or her mobile device to frame a cultural entity and obtain the associated content associated with the digital content. The application should be able to detect objects in the target.
- **Overlapping of the Actual Images With the Digital Content:** After an object was defined, the application should be able to retrieve all relevant digital content and present all the information to the user by placing the virtual content on top of the actual view from which it was acquired.

- **Managing Huge Amounts of Data:** The application should be able to handle large amounts of data in many different formats, such as texts, images, videos, and sounds associated with a particular cultural entity.
- **Offline Mode:** The application should also continue to function if the connection is weak or not available.

In the AR design, there are two main software challenges related to the recognition of the environment and the creation of virtual content. The advances in VR technology provide a positive contribution to the creation of virtual content.

However, virtual content can be created using a 3D modeling software as well. The AR researchers have mainly focused on recognition of the environment. This is conventionally accomplished by using computer vision algorithms or positioning based systems. The pointer-based algorithms were widely used in the past. It was because they provided a robust and fast recognition process (Martínez et al., 2014).

Until recently, special design equipment that was not feasible in terms of scale and cost was needed for the AR applications. However, the development of mobile devices, together with the progression of location and visualization technologies, all the components required by the AR applications can be integrated into smartphones at a low price (Linaza et al., 2014). In 2008-2009, the first commercial AR scanners for smartphones were introduced onto the market. These AR scanners were based on GPS tracking instead of computer images, as it was still not enough computing power for image recognition. With the rapid development of smartphones and the expansion of tablets, the number of computer vision-based AR applications has also begun to increase rapidly (Martínez et al., 2014). The fact that the existing smartphones and tablets of today are equipped with fast processors and embedded sensors makes them suitable for both indoor and outdoor AR applications (Fiore, Mainetti, Manco, & Marra, 2014).

There are three main components required in most of the AR applications. The first component is *a camera* used to capture the real environment (but GPS or non-3D positioning of virtual items can avoid using the camera in some vision systems). Depending on the requirements of the remaining equipment, virtually any rack type camera (e.g. USB cameras, internal cameras, IP cameras, industrial cameras) can be used for AR applications. The video obtained with the virtual information needs to be processed by the second component, *the computing unit*. The final component is *a device* that displays the ultimate augmented information. In addition to these three components, other equipment (e.g. GPS, human motion sensors, accelerometers, gyroscopes, etc.) can be included in the system designed to serve a specific purpose (Martínez et al., 2014).

One of the most important issues in AR applications is pose estimation, in which virtual objects are registered in the real world (captured by a smartphone camera). At this point, marker-based, markerless and location-based tracking are used. The design of the markers can be a bar code, symbol or company / product logo. The use of these markers may limit the interaction. It is because this marker may be restricted by a series of photographs or objects. Moreover, these markers need to be created and distributed in advance for widespread use. In markerless AR technology, on the other hand, points, segments, lines, contours, or a combination of these different features are used as geometric key factors. For a location-based AR, the location of the objects on the smartphone's screen is calculated using the user's location and the user's direction. The AR applications reveal the orientation of the compass (by the compass), the direction of the phone with the accelerometer (by accelerometer), and the location of all the points of interest with GPS or Wi-Fi. Compared to the object-based (marker-based, markerless) approach, the location-based AR applications do not require much computation in the smartphone processor. Most of AR applications used in tourism today are location-based (Tian et al., 2013).

The traditional AR display process consists of the steps of image capture, image analysis, object recognition, object monitor, calculate virtual information and image combination. In the mobile AR applications where a location-based tracking technique is used, on the other hand, the display process consists of the steps of image capture, getting the direction of the sensor and the image combination (Hui, Hung, Chien, Tsai, & Shie, 2014).

Mobile augmented reality (MAR) has emerged as the most popular and most convenient form of augmented reality, especially because of the proliferation of mobile devices (Vert & Vasiu, 2014). In addition to built-in cameras, sensors, computing resources, improvements in cloud technology today contribute to the use of augmented reality in mobile devices (Huang, Hui, Peylo, & Chatzopoulos, 2013). Cloud services are a new trend in the field of AR that can lead to a new standard in AR computing. The use of cloud services is attractive. Since most of the calculations are done remotely, it also allows for the use of powerful computer vision algorithms as well as low hardware requirements. However, the cloud technology also brings with it certain disadvantages, such as the need for continuous internet connection and a constant bandwidth for the targeted cloud service (Martínez et al., 2014).

Augmented reality applications are used on many mobile platforms such as iPhone, Windows Phone, and Android smartphone (Hui et al., 2014). Mobile augmented reality can be implemented in a variety of practical everyday applications ranging from information acquisition and navigation to tourism, entertainment and social interaction. The targets for which augmented reality can be applied to vary from surrounding places, buildings, areas, or other static destinations to activities, people, or other dynamic or abstract goals (Olsson, Lagerstam, Kärkkäinen, & Väänänen-Vainio-Mattila, 2013).

The use of AR technology has many advantages. Among the few of these advantages include; highly specialized hardware is not required, devices can be operated in open and closed areas, presentation quality can be adapted to the device used, full interaction is supported and more information can be accessed (Deliyiannis & Papaioannou, 2014). However, there are some difficulties in the design of AR scanners in the field of tourism. For instance, the fact that the city tourists visit has many objects, that each object contains a considerable amount of information, that each video is visually heterogeneous and dynamic, that tourists are in a foreign environment, and that they have different information needs than city dwellers (Yovcheva, Buhalis, Gatzidis, & van Elzakker, 2014).

AUGMENTED REALITY APPLICATIONS IN THE TOURISM INDUSTRY

Destination, which is one of the important issues in tourism, can be defined as the mix of tourism products offering integrated experiences. Experience is the essence of the tourism industry (Neuhofer, Buhalis, & Ladkin, 2014). Augmented reality applications do not replace traditional modes of tourism, but it helps these modes of tourism (Richards, 2014). Developments in mobile and wireless technologies have led to the emergence of new applications in the tourism industry as well as in many other areas. For instance, mobile travel guides, location-based information applications, annotation and bookmarking, and mobile social networks are some of these areas. In recent years, augmented reality applications have also been added to them. These applications enable the tourists to enjoy uninterrupted and have access to multimedia-rich travel-related information anywhere. At the same time, mobile positioning capabilities can be adapted to the needs and desires of tourists, making it easier to filter the travel information (Kourouthanassis, Boletsis, Bardaki, & Chasanidou, 2015).

One of the areas where the AR applications are used most commonly today is the publishing industry. Many magazines with different target audiences have developed AR applications. This new generation of advertising applications can be applied to the tourism catalogs, brochures, pamphlets, flyers and any other type of paper-based promotion. Hotels, casinos, theme parks, as well as special events or virtual roller-coaster trips use the AR technology to create a better sense and impression of what the customer buys. In fact, the AR technology has a tremendous power to persuade customers, allowing them to successfully market products and services in the tourism industry (Buhalis & Yovcheva, 2014). In this section, the augmented reality applications in the tourism industry and examples of use are covered in separate headings.

Augmented Reality Applications for Cultural Heritage

Augmented reality applications are one of the promising technologies that augment the users' cultural heritage visit experience with the digital content developed for the cultural heritage. Augmented reality technology allows visitors to present digital images together with real images (Vecchio et al., 2015). If it is included in the tourism AR application developed, the AR technology, which includes information about people in cultural heritage sites and buildings, allows users to switch between the historical periods and see the different aspects of the city over time. The combination of additional information and real scenes improves people's sense of reality and existence in a particular place (Chang, Hou, Pan, Sung, and Chang, 2015).

With the AR applications, tourists can establish a direct link between the current real object and the virtual object in the past, thanks to a superimposition of the old images of the cultural entity (Fiore, et al., 2014). Recreation of ancient temples and historical buildings can be realized with the AR applications. The first cultural heritage site that has benefit from the restructuring of an ancient temple with the augmented reality is the Olympia in Greece, where the ArcheoGuide AR system was developed (Buhalis & Yovcheva, 2014).

Augmented reality applications have a great potential to increase and spread the value of cultural heritage. It is because the AR applications do not take the place of reality; they improve the content of existing cultural heritage. It is a useful technology for improving and getting to know the heritage because of the ability to add elements to the actual appearance of an object and present its different versions (Fino, Martín-Gutiérrez, Fernández, & Davara, 2013). Ab Aziz and Siang (2014), who proposed the technological combination of VR-AR as a conceptual model, stated that it could be a holistic solution for the protection of the UNESCO world heritage site in Melaka, Malaysia. These technologies provide both protection for these heritage sites and can be used as a marketing and educational tool.

AR applications have an important role in the dissemination of cultural heritage. The benefits provided by Valtolia and his colleagues (2005, p. 219) in the dissemination of cultural heritage of virtual reality can be articulated for AR applications as well. AR applications do not only make a site more easily accessible, but also have the capacity to carry cultural content attractive to the user. AR applications also provide the opportunity to tell an engaging story to the people around the users. In this sense, AR applications can lead users to explore the cultural heritage more willingly. In the event that the results of user experiences are positive, users will make positive word of mouth advertisements of the cultural heritage AR applications. Therefore, all of these, as a result, will be visited by the users more often in the areas of cultural heritage. However, successfully developed AR applications at this point will be one of the critical success factors.

Augmented Reality Applications for Urban Cultural Tourism

Today, new urban culture tourism has emerged that aims to improve user experience. The territory as a whole has taken on the role of a complex "museum". The regions that can be expressed as museums have evolved into synergistic promotions over time, with virtual "physical objects" (Museums, archaeological sites and parks, cultural places and institutions such as archives, libraries and monumental complexes) (Garau, 2014).

There are studies carried out in different parts of the world in the sense of urban cultural tourism. For instance, Hui et al. (2014) devised a mobile augmented reality application on the Yilan hot spring in their study. This application consisted of two parts as the map module and the AR module. In the map module application, the graphical location search of the users' hot spring of Yilan was combined with the Google Maps. The AR module, on the other hand, transfers the virtual technology information to the screen of reality. Both the map module and the AR module allow users to receive relevant information. Garau (2014), on the other hand, piloted the AR application, which could be downloaded to smartphones or PC tablets, in Castello, one of the four historic districts of Cagliari (Italy). The Castello region is essentially a region of historical and cultural landmarks that have been intensively occupied and that have remained unchanged since the medieval period of Pisan.

The AR applications are also used in the architectural field and are particularly useful in the development of urban tourism areas. The AR applications can help managers and planners to make the most appropriate decisions by making in-situ comparisons of alternative scenarios. For instance, the Dutch Institute of Architecture has created a free Urban Augmented Reality (UAR) application that allows the residents and tourists from eight cities in the Netherlands to experience the urban environment in three different time periods, past, present and future. This application is useful for the creation of tourism application areas such as theme parks, holiday centers and attraction centers (Buhalis & Yovcheva, 2014).

Some researchers have also investigated the social aspects of the AR application, which is still an emerging technology. For instance, Yovcheva et al. (2014) found that all tourists had a very positive attitude towards the AR technology, even though they were unfamiliar with the AR applications. It is also another result that the tourists think that this technology will be useful in urban areas that they do not particularly know about. Han et al. (2014), who investigated the needs of tourists for the development of a mobile AR tourism application in urban heritage, conducted their in-depth interviews with international and domestic tourists visiting the city of Dublin. This project, articulated as the Dublin AR Project, comes from the idea of supporting Dublin's brand development to become an 'innovative city' in Europe. As a result of the study, it was found that multi-language functionality, ease of use and the ability to personalize the application were the basic requirements to be taken into account in order to attract tourists and encourage the regular use of the application.

The AR Tourism Navigation and Translation

The tourism industry is largely based on information and technology and technology plays an important role not only in delivering tourism services but also in enhancing the experience of tourists and travelers. The discovery of new places is the main motivation of tourism and navigation is very important in this respect. The AR technology is used to facilitate access of the visitors to the destination overlapping live arrows with virtual arrows indicating the direction which the visitor is required to follow in real time (Martínez et al., 2014).

Augmented reality applications can also be used for the mobile proposal systems. For instance, the AR applications in this area generate location-sensitive personalized routes for selected travel destinations and provide augmented views of the physical points (Gavalas, 2014). The AR applications, one of the ideal technologies to guide tourists in a foreign environment, reduce the mental effort required by the tourists for both pedestrian and vehicle navigation. One of the best-known examples in the world in this regard is the Nearest Tube augmented reality application, which shows the way to the London subway stations from where the users are located (Buhalis & Yovcheva, 2014).

The navigation and exploration of unfamiliar environments is greatly influenced by the lack of clear translation of foreign signs and instructions. The AR applications allow street names, as well as written texts in dining menus, train tariffs or newspaper titles, to be translated in real time into the language preferred by the foreign user (Buhalis & Yovcheva, 2014).

Augmented Reality Applications for Museums

Augmented reality applications such as a built-in camera, can provide real-time information on a site, monument, or even visitors about the buildings they stand before. This, then, allows users to visit monuments, sites, or museums that are known less but equally important. Therefore, with the augmented reality applications, the attractiveness of sites such as museums can be increased (Garau, 2014). Recently, interactive digital storytelling techniques have also been applied to the museums to increase their educational potential. For instance, the Digital Binocular Station (DBS) generates an interactive, dynamic and interesting adventure that will enhance the retention time and return visits by converting the museum's static content to life. The AR applications can stimulate the experiences in the museums by animating the endangered animal species, frayed frescoes, or fragmented cultural artifacts with the AR technology that are impossible (Buhalis & Yovcheva, 2014). Indeed, the AR applications designed for the museums can generate immersive experiences that are impossible, realistic and comprehensive experiences to achieve with traditional tools such as print media. These applications, which can also be used for educational purposes, can increase the interest of tourists as well as the city-dwellers for the historical sites and events (Mäkilä et al., 2013). Thanks to browsers such as Layar, Wikitude and Junaio developed in recent years, the augmented reality applications have begun to become an important communications channel for institutions such as museums that are culture and education-oriented institutions (Casella & Coelho, 2013).

At the present time, when a visitor visits a museum, the visitor is presented with supplementary materials such as audio guides, brochures or books for the visitor to learn about the items displayed in the museum. These disadvantages are that the unavailability of enough materials for all the visitors, the depletion of brochures, obsolete information in the brochures, or expansion of the existing information. In fact, since the museums constantly change their collections, this last disadvantage is quite common. Today, the development of technology enables the display of multimedia content on mobile devices. Moreover, accessibility to the target audience is made even easier with personalized content. For instance, it is much easier for the elderly to listen to oral statements than to read an informative poster (Villarrubia, De Paz, De La Prieta, & Bajo, 2014).

There are projects or studies in different parts of the world regarding the AR applications for museums. For instance, the Futuristic History project of Mäkilä et al. (2013) was launched in Finland in 2013. In this two-year project, the Luostarinmäki Handicrafts Museum dating back to the 18th century and the palace-style mansions of Finland in the Turku region, which was the former capital of Finland and had many historical interesting sites, was presented using the daily life and works of the original residents using the augmented reality solutions. Damala et al. (2012) examined the ARTSENSE Project, an AR application developed for museums and cultural heritage. With the AR application developed for this project, it was aimed to determine the psychological conditions according to the movements of the visitors in the museum and present the additional relevant contents and applications to the visitors.

Villarrubia et al. (2014) developed a mobile AR application for the Salamanca Cathedral (Spain) for end-users that was suitable for the Android and IPhone devices. A Web viewfinder was also designed to monitor the overall performance of the system and analyze the behavior of visitors in the museum. Firstly, after downloading the relevant mobile AR application, the visitor can see the nearby museums by the help of geo-positioning technology. The location system identifies which part of the museum the visitor is in, and after this area is identified, only the potential images of patterns and monuments close to the visitor's location are downloaded. And then, the user focuses on the box she/he wants to receive information from and recognizes the table correctly. When the image is recognized, a menu containing information about the displayed image becomes available to use. This information can be related to an image gallery, a descriptive video or text etc. From the museum management point of view, a different real-time location can be seen using the AR application. Furthermore, the behavior patterns in the museum can be revealed by analyzing the location of the users. For instance, it is also possible to determine in which areas and pictures the visitors have spent more time. As it appears, the augmented reality technology enables museum managers to improve their existing services with virtual content. With the help of this technology, it is possible to create a more customized experience, save on the exhibition space and achieve higher visitor satisfaction. Besides, the augmented reality applications at the same time can be used as tools of product differentiation and branding (Attila & Edit, 2012).

The AR Tourism Guide

Information communication technologies make it easier to visit the sites detailed in the guide without getting lost in the city and provide detailed information about each building turn streets, buildings and history, in other words transforms the city into a place suitable for tourists (Fino et al., 2013). Location-based services, defined as services to which the user belongs, can be used for almost every tourist area. Traditional tourist services, such as tourist guides, can be extensively modified, especially with augmented realistic applications. Increasing the sense of sight, hearing and reality provides a useful tourist guidance service in tourism destinations (Pedrana, 2014). Today, the increasing use of mobile devices has also led to the development of a wide variety of applications. Augmented reality applications that feature voice guidance allow users to save the need for a personalized guide and focus not only on what they see and hear, but also on enjoying their cultural heritage (Garau, 2014).

Augmented Reality (AR), which combines the virtual knowledge on real scenes, provides good solutions for on-site tour guides. Contrary to the traditional tour guides, AR-based tour guides allow tourists to live intuitive and realistic experiences by overlaying their virtual content into their cultural heritage sites (Seo, Kim & Park, 2010). The mobile guide not only supports the interaction between the visitors and the exhibit, but also strengthens the interaction between the visitors and the context behind the exhibits (e.g. being aware of historical and social perspectives while watching the heritage site) (Chang et al., 2015). Consequently, they get a deeper visit experience about the daily cultural heritage of the past.

One successful example is an AR application developed by the Saint Petersburg Clearwater Bureau, which offers a high-level 3D experience for potential tourists. The experience, called Two Treasures 3D Tour, offers a virtual tour guide that can be viewed from a video camera. The experience includes a virtual tour guide and presents the world famous beaches and museums to potential consumers with a convincing and interactive preview (Buhalis & Yovcheva, 2014). With the AR applications, users can obtain the data open to the public and prepare personalized tours based on user interests / preferences. Applications such as personal translators, virtual guides, voyeur vacation and games can also be used with devices that have the AR application. GeoTravel application and Layar Reality Browser are the applications that can be used in this regard (Ganapathy, 2013).

Chang et al. (2015) investigated the impact of the mobile phone augmented reality application in Taiwan to increase the sense of place for the heritage sites (Sense of Place for Heritage Places). As a result of the study, it was found regarding the factors contributing to the formation of Sense of Place that all of the participants in the AR guidance responded positively in terms of place affection and place interest. It was also found that the group receiving the AR guidance responded more positively than the groups without audio guidance and no-guidance groups.

Augmented Reality Applications in Tourism Education

Today, thanks to the mass spread of new information and communication technologies (ICT), they also play an important role in the new media education. This new media promotes communication and feedback and enriches interactivity and teaching practices. The AR, one of the newest technologies, offers new ways to attract and educate students in an effective and attractive way. In particular, the absence of a laboratory or room limitation greatly expands the field of application. In this sense, it can be used as an augmented reality media to teach history and tourism. The mobile devices with the AR technology can present interesting information to students in real space-time. Students with a mobile device can learn more effectively with the multimedia content including AR (Kysela & Štorková, 2015).

The learning experience in cultural heritage areas is one of the most important topics that visitors need in their cultural heritage sites visits. It is because the visitors want to learn the history hidden in the cultural heritage. However, this need cannot be met sufficiently by the traditional media. Augmented reality is an alternative to existing technologies used to facilitate the learning experience in cultural heritage sites (Pendit, 2014). Apart from the traditional tourist information channels, the AR can offer tourists the opportunity to learn what they want. While this provides flexibility and mobility for tourists, it at the same time enables the tourists to learn only what they are interested in. With the mobile AR applications, historical sites, actions taking place in these areas, audio recordings, interpretations, and many visual and audio presentations such as archive photographs of these places can be shown to the visitors (Kysela & Štorková, 2015). For instance, Jiménez Fernández-Palacios et al. (2015) studied the AR application, which was called the ARCube System, which focused on archaeological objects and used the 3D target in this focus. Thanks to this application, archaeological discoveries can be visualized in 3D. This visualization is an application that can particularly be useful in tourism education.

The AR applications also play an important role for users to have a satisfying learning experience. Indeed, Gonzàlez et al. (2012), who worked on an e-learning project based on AR applications to teach cultural heritage, found that participants in the survey perceived the AR applications as a meaningful and very useful experience for their training and professional future.

Tourism AR Games

The tourism industry can benefit greatly from the gaming items. Applications and games can be developed to increase the knowledge of tourists about tourist attractions. For example, for big tourist cities, interactive games where tourists will have information about the city can be used (Linaza et al., 2014). With a range of entertainment functions included in the smartphones, users can enhance the edutainment experience of cultural resources (Lee, Lee, & Ham, 2013). Tourists usually want to visit the historic buildings, unique landscapes, mysterious locations, specific or thematic Points of Interest (PoIs). Location-based games can be used as a way to experience these PoIs (Linaza et al., 2014). The AR games promote the physical activity using the real world locations and objects as part of an immersive gameplay. The location-based AR games are motivating and engaging for tourists. One of the interesting examples is the TimeWarp game. In this open-air AR game, tourists travel through the city of Cologne in Germany doing "jumping" through time portals and experience different historic and future events. Tourists describe these experiences as fun, novel and realistic (Buhalis & Yovcheva, 2014).

When exploring an urban destination or cultural heritage site, it is an amusing game experience to educate tourists with amusing attractions, the aim of locally based mobile augmented reality games, which is an innovative way of attracting tourists to interactive playgrounds is to provide an entertaining gaming experience with the use of location-based storytelling, personalized features and social interaction. As a result, a higher engagement level can be achieved by the destination for the users (Weber, 2014). Linza et al. (2013) examined the ExCORA, a mobile experience aimed at bringing the general public together with the Urgull Mountain in San Sebastian, Spain, in relation to the AR games in tourism. It is a game where the players travel in the real world and visit important places while watching a treasure game on mobile devices. This game is intended to encourage the visitor to visit and explore the natural environment and is also intended to train the visitors who may visit the mountain.

In location based AR games, the player location and context of playing are important. However, the issue of how the location-based AR games will be designed in the context of tourism is still not handled much by the game designers (Weber, 2014).

The AR Applications for Hotels and Restaurants

In a search for "Augmented Reality" in the Android Market or the iTunes App Store, it appears that a significant portion of the results are in travel and tourism. The AR applications have become an important tool to help tourists learn about nearby ATMs and restaurants, the nearest metro stop and places of interest. When the camera of a smartphone with an AR application is directed to a restaurant, not just the location but also other information and images uploaded onto the application related to the restaurant may be seen on the screen (Tian et al., 2013). For example, in the AR application generated for the Inamo restaurant in London, the customers who use this application can interact with the table they are on. Customers can choose their own desktop theme, order from the multimedia-rich menu or view a live video feed from the kitchen. Hotels are also very suitable venues for the development of AR applications. One of the best-known examples in this regard was developed by Holiday Inn. In this hotel AR application, by using their smart devices, the guests can be virtually seen Olympic and Paralympic athletes as if they were in the reception, the saloon, or in their hotel rooms (Buhalis & Yovcheva, 2014).

CONCLUSION

In recent years, the use of information communication technologies has increased rapidly as people learn new technologies more quickly and comfortably (Fino et al., 2013). It is possible to say that this increase will continue in terms of tourism industry as well. It is because it was evidenced by the results of Buhalis and Wagner's (2013) study on the question of the future of online destinations involving fifty participants, consisting of academics, students and tourism professionals. In their study, they concluded that future usage of mobile applications, reviewing websites, one stop shops, social media and knowledge categories would increase.

It is possible to say that the adoption of AR applications in the tourism industry has two major problem areas from technical and social point of view. From a technical point of view, most AR applications in the tourism industry are based on location-based, in other words GPS locations. For this reason, the fact that databases such as Google maps are incomplete, incorrect, or out of date can cause the AR application to not work or place the graphics correctly. On the smartphones, GPS accuracy is currently about 10 meters, depending on various factors such as the number of GPS satellites available. This accuracy may not be sufficient for historic sites where many interesting objects or ruins are tightly connected. Besides, high buildings, mountains and other obstacles can obstruct the view of GPS satellites. The problem of losing the GPS signal can be compensated by the Wi-Fi supported by the smartphone. Nowadays, however, this may be quite expensive or unusable for data on international circulation. Other major problems encountered by the existing tourism AR applications are the rapid depletion of the battery in case the smartphone is used for the AR application and the potential to create accidents while using the AR applications (Tian et al., 2013). Moreover, the mobile applications based on the AR technology are still not available in all mobile phone operating systems (Kounavis, Kasimati, & Zamani, 2012).

From a social perspective, the non-use and non-adoption of AR applications in the tourism industry by visitors can be considered as another problem area. However, the previous research shows that the potential for adoption of the AR applications in the tourism industry is quite high. For example, the study results of Yovcheva et al. (2014) showed that participants could understand and use the AR applications without prior AR experience. Given the initial attitudes and reactions of the participants in the study, it appeared that the AR applications provided a suitable visualization paradigm for rapid information acquisition in a foreign environment. Lee et al. (2013) found that mobile AR applications had a significant impact on the satisfaction of tourists when they were used in heritage sites, educational and entertainment experiences. Although the educational experience had a positive effect on tourism satisfaction, the influence of entertainment experience on tourist satisfaction was the greatest. Kourouthanassis et al. (2015), on the other hand, investigated the reactions of tourists to mobile augmented reality (MAR) travel guides in Greece. As a result of the study, it was stated that mobile AR applications were sufficient to provide valuable and effective services, but it was very important to investigate the expectations and needs of potential users for a broad social acceptance of such applications.

In their study to promote a mobile AR acceptance model in the context of urban heritage tourism, Tom Dieck and Jung (2015) created five focus groups of tourists visiting Dublin and experiencing the mobile AR application experience. As a result of thematic analysis, information quality, system quality, costs of use, recommendations, personal innovativeness, risk, and facilitating conditions dimensions were found to be necessary dimensions in the AR acceptance research. As a result of the study, it was found that these dimensions affected the perceived ease of use and perceived usefulness of the AR applications.

In their study in which they investigated the AR users' destination intentions in the tourism industry, Chung et al. (2015) found that attitudes of tourists towards the AR increased their potential visit to a real-heritage destination. In particular, three factors such as personal, stimulus (visual appeal), and situational factor (facilitating conditions) are important elements (game-changers) for the success of AR applications in the tourism industry. Also, since technology also includes very powerful visual elements such as visual appeal, the AR applications should be compatible with the true environment of the heritage destination. Therefore, positive attitudes towards the AR need to be developed in order to achieve wide-ranging AR use. At this point, tourism operators, destination marketing organizations (DMOs), tourism application developers, and tourism marketers should continue to conduct research to determine the aspirations and desires of users until the AR applications are widely adopted. For instance, in one of these studies, Lee et al. (2015) investigated the cultural differences in accepting the mobile augmented reality in South Korea and Ireland. As a result of the study, it was seen that there were differences between the two countries. In South Korea, for instance, which had high power distance, collectivism, and high uncertainty avoidance culture, it was found that there was a stronger dependence on the social effect and hedonic properties of the AR. Furthermore, the strong influence of aesthetic properties of AR apps from the perspective of hedonic knowledge on the perceived enjoyment of users was another result of the study. However, it is possible to say that the development of tourists' experience and effective and useful design of AR technology with the potential of the making this experience unique is still in their early stages (Yovcheva, Buhalis, & Gatzidis, 2012). Therefore, more research should be conducted on the subject of design. For instance, in one of these studies, Yovcheva et al. (2013b) focused on the design of smartphone AR browsers for unfamiliar urban tourism requirements that can be stated as easy and flexible such as access, distinct affordances, privacy and control, reactivity, relevance and reliability should be emphasized in order to provide satisfactory experiences for mobile augmented reality users (Olsson et al., 2013).

In this chapter, the augmented reality applications in the tourism industry were discussed together with the relevant examples. The present study, which has provided subject matter integrity, is stimulating both from theoretical and empirical perspectives. In the future research, the subject can be converted into a text book format by dealing with the subject more comprehensively and with the same integrity. It will also be beneficial to extend the research on the adoption of AR applications developed for the tourism industry in different countries. It is observed that such studies are lacking especially in the developing countries.

REFERENCES

Ab Aziz, K., & Siang, T. G. (2014). Virtual reality and augmented reality combination as a holistic application for heritage preservation in the UNESCO World Heritage Site of Melaka. *International Journal of Social Science and Humanity*, *4*(5), 333–338. doi:10.7763/IJSSH.2014.V4.374

Alkhamisi, A. O., & Monowar, M. M. (2013). Rise of augmented reality: Current and future application areas. *International Journal of Internet and Distributed Systems*, *1*(04), 25–34. doi:10.4236/ijids.2013.14005

Attila, K., & Edit, B. (2012). Beyond reality: The possibilities of augmented reality in cultural and heritage tourism. *2nd International Tourism and Sport Management Conference*, 1-6.

Azuma, R. T. (1997). A Survey of Augmented Reality. *Presence (Cambridge, Mass.)*, *6*(4), 355–385. doi:10.1162/pres.1997.6.4.355

Buhalis, D., & Amaranggana, A. (2013). *Smart tourism destinations. In Information and Communication Technologies in Tourism* (pp. 553–564). Cham: Springer.

Buhalis, D., & Wagner, R. (2013). *E-destinations: Global best practice in tourism technologies and applications. In Information and Communication Technologies in Tourism* (pp. 119–130). Berlin: Springer.

Buhalis, D. & Yovcheva, Z. (2014). *Augmented reality in tourism: 10 best practices.* Academic Press.

Casella, G., & Coelho, M. (2013). Augmented heritage: situating augmented reality mobile apps in cultural heritage communication. *Proceedings of the International Conference on Information Systems and Design of Communication*, 138-140. doi:10.1145/2503859.2503883

Çeltek, E. (2016). *Augmented Reality Advertisements in Tourism Marketing. In Mobile Computing and Wireless Networks: Concepts, Methodologies, Tools, and Applications* (pp. 1082–1102). Hershey, PA: IGI Global.

Chang, Y. L., Hou, H. T., Pan, C. Y., Sung, Y. T., & Chang, K. E. (2015). Apply an Augmented Reality in a Mobile Guidance to Increase Sense of Place for Heritage Places. *Journal of Educational Technology & Society*, *18*(2), 166–178.

Chung, N., Han, H., & Joun, Y. (2015). Tourists intention to visit a destination: The role of augmented reality (AR) application for a heritage site. *Computers in Human Behavior*, *50*, 588–599. doi:10.1016/j.chb.2015.02.068

Damala, A., Stojanovic, N., Schuchert, T., Moragues, J., Cabrera, A., & Gilleade, K. (2012). Adaptive augmented reality for cultural heritage: ARtSENSE project. *Euro-Mediterranean Conference*, 746-755. doi:10.1007/978-3-642-34234-9_79

Deliyiannis, I., & Papaioannou, G. (2014). Augmented Reality For Archaeological Environments On Mobile Devices: A Novel Open Framework. *Mediterranean Archaeology and Archaeometry*, *14*(4), 1–10.

Fino, E. R., Martín-Gutiérrez, J., Fernández, M. D. M., & Davara, E. A. (2013). Interactive tourist guide: Connecting web 2.0, augmented reality and QR codes. *Procedia Computer Science*, *25*, 338–344. doi:10.1016/j.procs.2013.11.040

Fiore, A., Mainetti, L., Manco, L., & Marra, P. (2014). Augmented reality for allowing time navigation in cultural tourism experiences: a case study. *International Conference on Augmented and Virtual Reality*, 296-301. doi:10.1007/978-3-319-13969-2_22

Ganapathy, S. (2013). Design guidelines for mobile augmented reality: User experience. Human Factors in Augmented Reality Environments. In Human Factors in Augmented Reality Environment. Springer.

Garau, C. (2014). From territory to smartphone: Smart fruition of cultural heritage for dynamic tourism development. *Planning Practice and Research, 29*(3), 238–255. doi:10.1080/02697459.2014.929837

Gavalas, D., Konstantopoulos, C., Mastakas, K., & Pantziou, G. (2014). Mobile recommender systems in tourism. *Journal of Network and Computer Applications, 39*, 319–333. doi:10.1016/j.jnca.2013.04.006

Gonzàlez, F., Villarejo, L., Miralbell, O., & Gomis, J. M. (2012). How to use mobile technology and augmented reality to enhance collaborative learning on cultural and natural heritage? An e-learning experience. *New Trends on Global Education Conference*, 1-5.

Han, D., Jung, T., & Gibson, A. (2014). Dublin AR: Implementing Augmented Reality (AR) in Tourism. In Z. Xiang & I. Tussyadiah (Eds.), *Information and Communication Technologies in Tourism* (pp. 511–523). Wien: Springer International Publishing.

Huang, Z., Hui, P., Peylo, C., & Chatzopoulos, D. (2013). *Mobile augmented reality survey: A bottom-up approach.* arXiv preprint arXiv:1309.4413

Hui, L., Hung, F. Y., Chien, Y. L., Tsai, W. T., & Shie, J. J. (2014). Mobile Augmented Reality of Tourism-Yilan Hot Spring. *Ubi-Media Computing and Workshops (UMEDIA), 7th International Conference*, 209-214.

Jiménez Fernández-Palacios, B., Nex, F., Rizzi, A., & Remondino, F. (2015). ARCube—The augmented reality cube for archaeology. *Archaeometry, 57*(S1), 250–262. doi:10.1111/arcm.12120

Jung, T., Chung, N., & Leue, M. C. (2015). The determinants of recommendations to use augmented reality technologies: The case of a Korean theme park. *Tourism Management, 49*, 75–86. doi:10.1016/j.tourman.2015.02.013

Jung, T.H. & Han, D.I. (2014). Augmented Reality (AR) in Urban Heritage Tourism. *e-Review of Tourism Research, 5*, 1-8.

Kennedy-Eden, H., & Gretzel, U. (2012). A taxonomy of mobile applications in tourism. *E-review of Tourism Research, 10*(2), 47–50.

Kim, Y. G., & Kim, W. J. (2014). Implementation of augmented reality system for smartphone advertisements. *International Journal of Multimedia and Ubiquitous Engineering, 9*(2), 385–392. doi:10.14257/ijmue.2014.9.2.39

Koo, C., Shin, S., Kim, K., Kim, C., & Chung, N. (2013). Smart Tourism of the Korea: A Case Study. PACIS, 1-38.

Kounavis, C. D., Kasimati, A. E., & Zamani, E. D. (2012). Enhancing the tourism experience through mobile augmented reality: Challenges and prospects. *International Journal of Engineering Business Management, 4*, 1–6. doi:10.5772/51644

Kourouthanassis, P., Boletsis, C., Bardaki, C., & Chasanidou, D. (2015). Tourists responses to mobile augmented reality travel guides: The role of emotions on adoption behavior. *Pervasive and Mobile Computing*, *18*, 71–87. doi:10.1016/j.pmcj.2014.08.009

Kysela, J., & Štorková, P. (2015). Using augmented reality as a medium for teaching history and tourism. *Procedia: Social and Behavioral Sciences*, *174*, 926–931. doi:10.1016/j.sbspro.2015.01.713

Lee, H., Chung, N. & Jung, T. (2015). Examining the cultural differences in acceptance of mobile augmented reality: Comparison of South Korea and Ireland. *Information and Communication Technologies in Tourism*, 477-491.

Lee, K., Lee, H.R. & Ham, S. (2013). The effects of presence induced by smartphone applications on tourism: Application to cultural heritage attractions. *Information and Communication Technologies in Tourism*, 59-72.

Linaza, M.T., Gutierrez, A. & García, A. (2013). Pervasive augmented reality games to experience tourism destinations. *Information and Communication Technologies in Tourism*, 497-509.

Mäkilä, T., Helle, S., Viinikkala, L., Lehtonen, T., Arimaa, J. P., Heimo, O., & Pönni, V. et al. (2013). The Futuristic History project: recreating history with augmented reality solutions. *Proceedings of NODEM*, 165-170.

Martínez, H., Skournetou, D., Hyppölä, J., Laukkanen, S., & Heikkilä, A. (2014). Drivers and bottlenecks in the adoption of augmented reality applications. *Journal of Multimedia Theory and Application*, *1*, 27–44.

Milgram, P., & Kishino, F. (1994). A taxonomy of mixed reality visual displays. *IEICE Transactions on Information and Systems*, *77*(12), 1321–1329.

Neuhofer, B., Buhalis, D., & Ladkin, A. (2014). A typology of technology enhanced tourism experiences. *International Journal of Tourism Research*, *16*(4), 340–350. doi:10.1002/jtr.1958

Olsson, T., Lagerstam, E., Kärkkäinen, T., & Väänänen-Vainio-Mattila, K. (2013). Expected user experience of mobile augmented reality services: A user study in the context of shopping centres. *Personal and Ubiquitous Computing*, *17*(2), 287–304. doi:10.1007/s00779-011-0494-x

Pedrana, M. (2014). Location-based services and tourism: Possible implications for destination. *Current Issues in Tourism*, *17*(9), 753–762. doi:10.1080/13683500.2013.868411

Pendit, U. C., Zaibon, S. B., & Bakar, J. A. A. (2014). Mobile Augmented Reality for Enjoyable Informal Learning in Cultural Heritage Site. *International Journal of Computers and Applications*, *92*(14), 19–26. doi:10.5120/16077-5286

Richards, G. (2014). *Tourism trends: The convergence of culture and tourism*. Academy for Leisure NHTV University of Applied Sciences. Retrieved January 10, 2017, from https://www.academia.edu/9491857/Tourism_trends_The_convergence_of_culture_and_ tourism

Schmalstieg, D., & Höllerer, T. (2016). *Augmented Reality: Principles and Practice*. Boston: Addison-Wesley Professional. doi:10.1145/2897826.2927365

Seo, B. K., Kim, K., & Park, J. I. (2010, November). Augmented reality-based on-site tour guide: a study in Gyeongbokgung. *Asian Conference on Computer Vision*, 276-285.

Tian, F., Xu, F., & Fu, J. (2013). Augmented reality technology overview for tourism app development. *2013 International Conference on Machine Learning and Cybernetics*, *4*, 1483-1489. doi:10.1109/ICMLC.2013.6890839

Tom Dieck, M. C., & Jung, T. (2015). A theoretical model of mobile augmented reality acceptance in urban heritage tourism. *Current Issues in Tourism*, 1–21. doi:10.1080/13683500.2015.1070801

Valtolina, S., Franzoni, S., Mazzoleni, P., & Bertino, E. (2005). Dissemination of cultural heritage content through virtual reality and multimedia techniques: A case study. *Multimedia Modelling Conference, Proceedings of the 11th International*, 214-221. doi:10.1109/MMMC.2005.36

Vecchio, P., Mele, F., De Paolis, L. T., Epicoco, I., Mancini, M., & Aloisio, G. (2015). Cloud computing and augmented reality for cultural heritage. LNCS, 9254, 51–60. doi:10.1007/978-3-319-22888-4_5

Vert, S., & Vasiu, R. (2014). Relevant aspects for the integration of linked data in mobile augmented reality applications for tourism. *International Conference on Information and Software Technologies*, 334-345. doi:10.1007/978-3-319-11958-8_27

Villarrubia, G., De Paz, J. F., De La Prieta, F., & Bajo, J. (2014). Hybrid indoor location system for museum tourist routes in augmented reality. *Information Fusion (FUSION), 17th International Conference*, 1-8.

Weber, J. (2014). Augmented Reality Gaming: A new Paradigm for Tourist Experience. Information and communication technologies in tourism. *Information and Communication Technologies in Tourism, eProceedings of the ENTER 2014*.

Yovcheva, Z., Buhalis, D. & Gatzidis, C., (2012). Smartphone augmented reality applications for tourism. *e-Review of Tourism Research*, *10*(2), 63-66.

Yovcheva, Z., Buhalis, D., & Gatzidis, C. (2013a). Engineering augmented tourism experiences. In L. Cantoni & Z. Xiang (Eds.), *Information and communication technologies in tourism* (pp. 24–35). Springer Berlin Heidelberg.

Yovcheva, Z., Buhalis, D., Gatzidis, C., & van Elzakker, C. P. (2014). Empirical evaluation of smartphone augmented reality browsers in an urban tourism destination context. *International Journal of Mobile Human Computer Interaction*, *6*(2), 10–31. doi:10.4018/ijmhci.2014040102

Yovcheva, Z., Buhalis, D., Gatzidis, C., & van Elzakker, C. P. J. M. (2013b). Proposing a design framework for smartphone AR browsers used in unfamiliar urban tourism destinations. *Designing Mobile Augmented Reality Workshop*.

KEY TERMS AND DEFINITIONS:

Augmented Reality: Augmented Reality (AR) defined as enhancement of the real environment by computer-generated content allows its users to see the real world together with an additional virtual world added in real time to the same field of view.

Augment Reality in Tourism Industry: The augmented reality applications are used in many fields such as cultural heritage, urban cultural tourism, museums, the AR tourism guide, the AR tourism navigation, tourism education, tourism AR games, hotels and restaurants, and AR translation in the tourism industry.

Cultural Heritage: Cultural heritage is inherited from past generations, is maintained in the present, and for the benefit of future generations, and is the legacy of physical artefacts and intangible attributes of a group or society.

Destination Marketing: Destination marketing is a type of marketing that promotes a destination (town, city, region and country) in order to attract visitors and / or increase the number of visitors.

Mixed Reality: The mixed reality concept relates with the merging of the virtual and the real world with possibly different degrees of merging. The mixed reality is presented together within a single display.

Mobile Augmented Reality: Augmented reality applications that are used on many mobile platforms. Mobile augmented reality (MAR) has emerged as the most popular and most convenient form of augmented reality, especially because of the proliferation of mobile devices.

Virtual Reality: Virtual reality is an artificial environment created with software and presented in a way that makes the user feel that it is in a real environment.

Chapter 4
Multi-Dimensional Acquisition, Representation, and Interaction of Cultural Heritage Tangible Assets:
An Insight on Tourism Applications

Cristina Portalés
Universitat de València, Spain

Sergio Casas
Universitat de València, Spain

Pau Alonso-Monasterio
Universitat Politècnica de València, Spain

María José Viñals
Universitat Politècnica de València

ABSTRACT

The acquisition, digital representation and interaction of cultural heritage (CH) assets is of high interest for an accurate documentation of our cultural legacy. Detailed studies demand more information on the assets apart from the mere visual appearance or even shape of objects. In this regards, some research works can be found that combine shape with other kind of data, such as radiometric (e.g., IR, thermal radiation, etc.) or semantic information, leading to multi-Dimensional (mD) virtual objects. In this chapter, we review the state of the art of different techniques to deal with mD acquisition of CH tangible assets. We also discuss some representation (e.g., visual, sonic, etc.) and interaction approaches to enhance the value of CH by means of the technologies of virtual reality (VR) and augmented reality (AR), considering also the application of these techniques to tourism. Finally, we also point out some current needs and technological barriers that need to be tackled by the research community regarding the acquisition and dissemination of heritage.

DOI: 10.4018/978-1-5225-2927-9.ch004

INTRODUCTION

Cultural Heritage (CH) is a fundamental expression of the richness and diversity of our culture and therefore, its conservation, documentation and dissemination is considered of the utmost importance. Beyond the well-established methods that have been traditionally employed in the field of CH up to the present moment, technological tools have become increasingly popular for the heritage enhancement, tourism experience development and dissemination. This is because they have the ability to engender fascination far beyond a tourist brochure or any other printed material.

The digital documentation and dissemination of CH tangible assets through current technologies usually involves several steps, such as the visual appearance and shape (or three-dimensional, 3D) acquisition of the assets, their virtual reconstruction, storage (e.g. repositories), digital representation or reproduction (mainly visual), and interaction techniques, among others. This chapter focuses on the acquisition, representation and interaction techniques with emphasis in multi-Dimensional (mD) data.

The acquisition step is fundamental, as it deals directly with digitizing the real characteristics of the assets. Thus, it plays an important role in the accurate documentation and safeguard of our cultural legacy. However, not all the acquisition technologies have been exploited in depth so far for the CH sector. In this regards, some research works can be found that combine shape with other kind of data, such as radiometric (e.g. IR, thermal radiation, etc.) or semantic information, leading to the mD virtual objects and opening the avenues for new dissemination and understanding of heritage. One of the aims of this chapter is to provide a review of these acquisition technologies, in order to point out the benefits that they might have for CH and to discuss current needs, technological barriers and/or new trends that might be of interest for the sector.

Additionally, this chapter also aims to give a review on the current representation (not only visual, but also sonic, haptic, etc.) and interaction solutions related to touristic applications, focusing on the technologies of virtual and augmented reality that are increasingly being used in museums, exhibitions, heritage sites, etc., being a vehicle for the access and dissemination of CH to a number of stakeholders and the wide public. Indeed, the dissemination of CH is essential to promote its conservation, so communicating the values and the significance of our heritage, especially to the general public, is a key issue for rising awareness. The thematic interpretation is the main tool to achieve proactive behaviours in general public towards conservation, and it is based upon the following sequence: "Through interpretation, understanding; through understanding, appreciation; through appreciation, protection" (Tilden, 1957, p. 38). The scientific literature regarding the role of new technologies in the dissemination of heritage is extensive. However, there is nothing from the methodological point of view in relation to the specific techniques analysed in this work. Therefore, to evidence this type of applications linked to the dissemination of heritage, various examples developed by the authors are provided through the chapter.

This chapter is organized as follows. In a first section, a review on the state of the art of different available techniques and the related methodologies to deal with mD acquisition for the virtual reconstruction of CH tangible assets are presented and discussed through different examples. In the next section, a review on various visualization and interaction approaches (based on virtual and augmented reality) to enhance the value of CH by means of these virtually reconstructed objects is given. Finally, the discussion section points out some current needs and technological barriers that need to be tackled by the research community in order to further advance on the given topic, which might be relevant for the CH sector, as argumented in the previous sections.

MULTIDIMENSIONAL ACQUISITION OF CH ASSETS

Shape and Visual Appearance

In the last years, the research community has done an intensive work in order to document the shape of CH assets. Different acquisition devices and technologies have been used in order to digitize 3D objects, which are mainly stereo-photogrammetry, laser scanning or structured light-based techniques. Additionally to the 3D shape, textures (RGB values) are usually added to the object's' shape. With the laser scanning technique usually a dense cloud of points is acquired, which might include RGB information combined with cameras (Blais & Beraldin, 2006; Chow & Chan, 2009; Guarnieri, Remondino, & Vettore, 2006; Lerones, Fernández, Gil, Gómez-García-Bermejo, & Casanova, 2010; Navarro et al., 2009; Trinchão Andrade, Mazetto Mendes, de Oliveira Santos Jr, Pereira Bellon, & Silva, 2012; Yastikli, 2007). Laser scanning provides many advantages that make it quite suitable to document the shape of objects (Vidal & Muñoz, 2015). Nevertheless, safety and cost issues may be an important restriction of this technology. On the other hand, the many different approaches provided by structured light techniques (Salvi, Fernandez, Pribanic, & Llado, 2010) bring also high acquisition rates, with the advantage that high resolution images are directly available from the acquisition camera(s). Nevertheless, these techniques are usually dependent on the environment conditions and may be highly demanding in terms of computational cost (depending on the technique). Stereo-photogrammetry, though computationally demanding, has been researched by the photogrammetric community during decades, and robust and accurate algorithms exist nowadays (Cabrelles et al., 2010). Nevertheless, its accuracy is restricted to well-defined targets. Other techniques such as shape from motion or texture gradients, do present some weaknesses (e.g. low accuracy) that make them not suitable for the high fidelity 3D reconstruction of CH assets. Some of the strengths and weaknesses of the different acquisition technologies are depicted in Table 1.

On the other hand, when dealing with archaeological sites, the shape and visual appearance acquisition is usually not fully possible with the use of acquisition devices because most or part of the assets do not exist nowadays. In this sense, additional approaches need to be used, which are mainly based on a rigorous documentation of the past. For instance, in Ercek, Viviers, and Warzée (2010), the relevance of the close collaboration between archaeologists, engineers and computer graphics designers is highlighted, in order to achieve a reliable 3D virtual reconstruction of archaeological sites. Following this, they report the 3D virtual reconstruction of an archaeological site in Itanos, Crete. In Garrido Carretero (2013), the research for the virtual reconstruction of an Andalusian palace is done by surveying the current state of the palace plant and formulating contrasted hypothesis on its elevations. In He, Gao, and Shang (2013), a methodology is proposed for a virtual reconstruction of an archaeological heritage in East Asia, which consists on a combination of an archaeological survey, historical photos, historical archive and artistic paintings.

In (Portalés, Alonso-Monasterio, & Viñals, 2016, 2017), a methodology is developed to reconstruct the Iberian archaeological site "Castellet de Bernabé" that includes on-site observation, comparative research and archaeological interpretation, among others. The team working on this project was multidisciplinary, including archaeologists, engineers and computer graphics designers. The final model of the site and its visual appearance was approved by the archaeologists. Images of the site and its reconstruction are depicted in Figure 1.

Table 1. Comparison of optical range imaging techniques

Technology	Strength	Weakness
Laser scanning	• Relative simplicity. • Performance generally independent of ambient light. • High data acquisition rate.	• Safety constraint associated with the use of laser source. • Limited range and measurement volume. • Missing data in correspondence with occlusions and shadows. • Economic cost.
Structured Light	• High data acquisition rate. • Intermediate measurement volume.	• Safety constraints, if laser-based. • Performance generally dependent of ambient light. • Average computational complexity. • Missing data in correspondence with occlusions and shadows. • Economic cost, if commercial systems.
Stereo-photogrammetry	• Simple and inexpensive. • High accuracy on well-defined targets.	• Computationally demanding. • Sparse data covering. • Limited to well-defined scenes. • Low data acquisition rate.
Time-of-Flight	• Medium to large measurement range. • Good data acquisition rate. • Performance generally independent of ambient light.	• Economic cost. • Accuracy is inferior to triangulation at close ranges.
Interferometry	Sub-micron accuracy in micro-ranges.	• Measurement capability limited to quasi-flat surfaces. • Economic cost. • Limited applicability in industrial environments.
Moiré fringe range contours	• Simple and low cost. • Short ranges.	Limited to the measurement of smooth surfaces.
Shape from focusing	• Simple and inexpensive. • Available sensors for surface inspection and microprofilometry.	• Limited fields of view. • Non-uniform spatial resolution. • Performance affected by ambient light (if passive).
Shape from shadows	• Low cost. • Limited demand for computing power.	Low accuracy.
Texture gradients	Simple and low cost.	Low accuracy.
Shape from shading and stereo-photometry	Simple and low cost.	Low accuracy.

Based on (Sansoni, Trebeschi, & Docchio, 2009).

From a tourism point of view, monuments and cultural assets remains must be reconstructed for public interpretation. Otherwise, visitors need to develop complex mental 3D reconstruction processes in other to make a mental image reproducing the sites. Then, once the volumetry and aspect of the heritage is available in the visitors' mind, they can start to understand the historical sense and relevance and thus to appreciate the heritage. However, without an initial reconstruction of these cultural assets the process is highly time-consuming, leaving little energy to visitors for the heritage interpretation and appreciation.

In the military defence heritage site of Puig-Carassols trench line in Valencia (Spain), some works have been developed for the CH acquisition and reconstruction, using a combination of digital image processing and 3D visualization of graffiti (Palomar-Vazquez, Baselga, Viñals-Blasco, García-Sales, & Sancho-Espinós, 2017). Moreover, in Palomar-Vazquez and Viñals-Blasco (2016), authors explore the

Figure 1. The archaeological site "Castellet de Bernabé", where: (a) and (b) are images of the site; and (c) and (d) are images of its virtual reconstruction.
Source of image (b): Diputación de Valencia.

usefulness of web-based platforms (WebGL) using open source libraries to disseminate 3D reconstruction models through Web navigators of this military trench. To upload the 3D models, processing is required in different degrees of intensity, depending on the site conservation condition and the heritage typology. In this paper, authors work with a relatively well-conserved site, but its typology leads to partially buried structures, which need to be virtually unearthed in order to ease the visitors' mental reconstruction of the site (Figure 2).

Figure 2. The military trench, where: (a) its present appearance; and (b) view of cross section of the tunnel
Source: (Palomar-Vazquez & Viñals-Blasco, 2016).

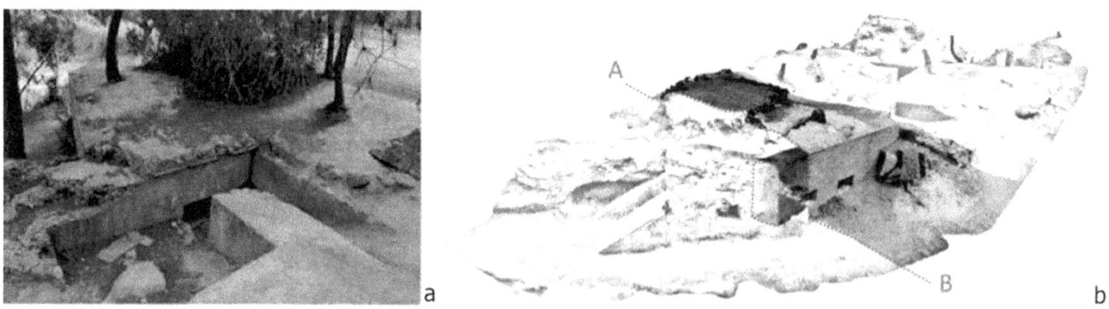

Shape and Mono-Spectral Imaging

Apart from the visual appearance (RGB images), other spectral bands might be also of utmost importance for the documentation of CH. To that end, 3D information is combined with the images acquired with cameras working in specific spectral bands, such as infrared or thermal cameras. Depending on the considered spectral bands, different analysis or studies can be done. In the following lines, some of the most commonly used bands in CH imaging-based analysis are described and examples are given: fluorescence, near-infrared and infrared thermography.

Fluorescence is a member of the ubiquitous luminescence family of processes in which susceptible molecules emit light from electronically excited states. When a surface is exposed to ultraviolet (UV) radiation, the upper layer absorbs and reflects it. Thanks to the fluorescence phenomenon, a part of the absorbed energy is then emitted in the form of radiation in the visible spectral range. For instance, when the technique of UV Fluorescence is applied to an artwork, it allows for investigating the superficial layer, thereby detecting the presence of possible removal or retouchings on the top of ancient varnish, etc. (Cetica, Marras, Materazzi, & Poggi, 2007). In Jensen and Becker (2015) the potential of short-wave UV imaging in archaeology is highlighted, as it reveals information that is not visible to the naked eyed. In Andrew and Eastop (1994) UV is used in combination with infrared in order to examine and document historical textiles for conservation purposes.

Near-Infrared (NIR) imaging is a diagnostic technique that has been used for the analysis of painted surfaces, the pictorial underdrawings, manuscripts (Alexopoulou, Liaros, Panagopoulou, & Kaminari, 2010; Buoso, Ceccato, & Zafiropoulos, 2009), archaeological sites through the use of aerial images (Bearman & Spiro, 1996; Cetica et al., 2007; Verhoeven, 2008), etc. Infrared colour images allow a sharper visualization of the original material and has been used as a non-invasive method for studying coloured material in situ on paintings, manuscripts (Alexopoulou et al., 2010; Buoso et al., 2009) and also in stone and bone tools with pigments on the surface.

Infrared thermography is a technique able to detect and record the infrared radiation emitted by a body in the thermal domain. Measurements are usually carried out by heating the target with a lamp and recording the IR radiation emitted during its cooling. This method is very useful to investigate both historic buildings (structure, walls composition, state of conservation, etc.) and conservation of mural paintings such as frescoes (humidity, salts patina, hidden mortar detachment, etc.) (Bodnar et al., 2012; Imposa, 2010; Lerma, Cabrelles, & Portalés, 2011). Additionally, the monitoring of the emitted infrared radiation at the surface of a sample over time provides information on the structure of the artefact as well as on the thermal properties of the constituting materials. This technique has been applied to the study of library objects, archaeological findings and works of art, enabling detection and characterization of different surface and sub-surface features (Lerma et al., 2011; Mercuri et al., 2011; Pires & Cruz, 2007).

Shape and Multi/Hyperspectral Imaging

Multispectral imaging analysis or imaging spectroscopy is a rather recently developed non-invasive method of investigation. It allows the simultaneous collection of spectral and spatial information of a surface in the visible, near infrared and/or other spectral regions. Primarily used for underdrawing detection in paintings, it has also been successfully applied to the scientific investigation of documents, to the evaluation of conservation treatments and digital imaging for documentation (Arrizabalaga, Gómez-Laserna, Aramendia, Arana, & Madariaga, 2014; Banou, Kaminari, Moutsatsou, Alexopoulou, & Singer, 2010;

Chabries, Booras, & Bearman, 2003; Fischer & Kakoulli, 2006; Martinez, Cupitt, Saunders, & Pillay, 2002; Padoan, Steemers, Klein, Aalderink, & Bruin, 2008). Multispectral imaging has been researched and used extensively also in archaeology (Liang, 2012) during the last century for different purposes. In a recent study on rock art (Ripoll Perelló et al., 2014; Tristán, 2014), hundreds of unknown drawings were discovered thanks to the use of a multispectral camera, which took images from the UV to the NIR band. Researchers of that study recognized that their findings show that many of the works at archaeological sites done so far are not complete, and they will have to re-examine most of them.

Recently, some attempts to combine 3D and multispectral or hyperspectral imaging have arisen, though still the use of these techniques in combination is not widely extended in the CH sector, and thus few examples can be found in the literature. In these works, the 3D shape of the objects is complemented with radiometric information at different spectral bands, and thus providing a more accurate documentation of the CH assets. For instance, in Kim et al. (2012) a device to acquire combined 3D and hyperspectral imaging data between 359 nm and 1003 nm was presented. The system components included a laser scanner to recover 3D information, an imager and a Xenon light source. In Chane, Schütze, Boochs, and Marzani (2013) a method is presented for the in situ study of cultural heritage objects that is tested by digitizing a small canvas with a 3D digitization system and a multispectral camera, while simultaneously tracking the acquisition systems with four cameras. The multispectral camera can acquire seven spectral bands, six in the visible spectrum and one in the near infrared. A shape and hyperspectral imaging acquisition prototype was presented in Granero-Montagud et al. (2013a, 2013b) and Groves, Portalés, and Ribes-Gómez (2014), which allowed the acquisition of hyperspectral data in the ranges 400-700 nm and 900-2500 nm, while the acquisition of 3D cloud of points was performed with structured light techniques. Within this device, they were able to both assess the mechanical and the chemical deterioration of artworks by means of a combination of image-based techniques and classification approaches. In Pamart et al. (2017) a set of image-based documentation techniques are presented for the case of wall painting studies, which includes information about the objects' shape and different spectral bands, among others. The paper shows some ongoing experimentations relying on the assumption that those techniques can be merged through a common pipeline to share their own benefits and create a more complete documentation. In Erenoglu, Akcay, and Erenoglu (2017)a method is presented in order to generate an unmanned aerial system-assisted digital, thermal, and multi-spectral 3D point clouds and orthomosaics in the cultural heritage site. Regarding to the optical system, the set of cameras (three) that they use are able to cover a total of seven spectral bands in the range from 400 mm to 13 μm, though it has to be pointed that two of the bands overlap (green and red channels of two of the cameras).

As it can be seen from the given examples, the number of spectral bands and the spectral ranges can vary depending on the use. A dedicated system that acquires both shape and multi/hyperspectral information and that can be of general use for the CH sector can therefore be difficult to realize.

Shape and Semantics

In recent years, the semantic representation of structured information and knowledge, as well as creating links between the data, has increasingly gained popularity, driven by the Semantic Web technologies (Peña Serna, Schmedt, Ritz, & Stork, 2012). The CH domain is such a knowledge-rich domain that the term "semantics" includes many aspects, such as the object identification, object type, material, aesthetic characteristics, the name of the creator of an object, etc. The review in Vavliakis, Karagiannis, and Mitkas (2012) highlights the importance of semantic information for the analysis of cultural heritage objects and identifies some requirements of semantic management of cultural resources, as collection holders traditionally spend considerable effort on the indexing process of collection objects. They highlight the importance of merging and integration of mD information to uncover new knowledge about artworks and the requirement for easy-to-use tools for making data available in semantic databases. Currently, semantic data is generally acquired in an interactive way. For instance, in Schreiber et al. (2008) a Semantic Web application for multilingual semantic annotation and search in large virtual collections of cultural-heritage objects is described. During the annotation phase, collection metadata and vocabulary is harvest, enriched and aligned. In Peña Serna et al. (2012), cultural heritage objects, such as statues, are manually decomposed in parts and the parts are annotated. This was achieved by using a tool for interactive annotations that allowed the management and the integration of free-text archaeological data and geographic information related to excavations. In Manguinhas et al. (2016) the semantic enrichment technique is studied as a way to improve metadata quality in platforms for accessing digitized CH, such as Europeana (Europeana Collections, 2017). This technique puts objects in context by linking them to relevant entities (people, places, object types, etc.).

The importance of the semantic representation relies on the possibility of extracting new information that remains undisclosed or that is not apparent at a first glance. In this regards, the application of big data and classification technologies to CH can generate a substantial amount of hidden information. Last, but certainly not least, a semantic representation is crucial to provide good storytelling and knowledge for audiences and visitors of CH sites, allowing for a better understanding and appreciation of cultural assets.

REPRESENTATION AND INTERACTION TECHNIQUES

After studying the mD acquisition of CH assets, this section explores the possibilities of Virtual Reality (VR) and Augmented Reality (AR) technologies to represent and interact with the CH acquired/reconstructed content, by means of a set of case studies and recent works found in the literature. Additionally, qualitative comparisons are provided and current limitations and needs are addressed.

Overall, it can be said that while VR substitutes the real world by a synthetic one, AR enriches the real world by means of virtual stimuli, without (completely) replacing the real world. Both technologies have (different) advantages for the representation and interaction of CH assets. On the one hand, VR allows the wide public and other stakeholders to appreciate remote (in space and time) cultural assets; users can access the virtual content from almost anywhere provided that they have Internet connection, which can be very advantageous since users with mobility difficulties or inaccessible sites (private ownership assets, physical difficulties, etc.) can easily reach them. On the other hand, with AR technology, users have to physically visit/access the assets to trigger the related virtual contents, so that in some way users are encouraged to visit such assets, promoting the tourism of the zone. In any case, both technologies are useful to promote tourism and enhance the understanding of heritage: VR recalls memories or triggers new sensations, while AR adds value to existing tourist sites and attractions and encourages visiting a place.

Though VR and AR have a high visual component, other kind of data can be integrated in the virtual or augmented worlds and then be reproduced by computers, thus creating a variety of mD contents that can be reached and managed by end users. Indeed, interaction is in the basis of both VR and AR technologies, as they are defined per se as interactive technologies. The proliferation of affordable sensors (such as Kinect) and displays (such as AR glasses) is opening new avenues for the digital data interaction.

Interaction is no longer restricted to the traditional mouse and keyboard, but opened to many other options that involve a huge range of stimuli: speech, gestural, facial, tactile, etc. Additionally, the increase of the processing capabilities of smartphones and other mobile devices, which additionally integrate cameras and low cost sensors, is leading to an increasing proliferation of VR and AR applications, also in the heritage sector.

Virtual Reality Applications in CH

The term Virtual Reality (VR) refers to the collection of technologies that are able to make people believe they are experiencing a reality in which they are not actually living. VR uses simulation techniques to deceive the human senses so that the perceptual cues that reach the brain are consistent with the belonging of an alternative/simulated reality. These perceptual cues might be mD, but the primary keys are those related to the representation of visual and acoustic information. Interaction is also a key element of VR, since the deceived user needs to interact with the VR world as naturally as possible, and do it in (ideally) the same way as he/she would do it in the real world. This is often the most difficult part of the system and it is usually simplified or limited. Thus, many VR applications are not fully immersive, do not use natural interfaces and, thus, do not provide a full alternative reality. However, it is common to still consider them as VR systems.

With this definition and comments, it comes naturally to think about CH as one of the main areas where VR might be relevant. For instance, as many heritage assets that need to be disseminated do not (partially) exist anymore or are not in their original conditions, they must be recreated with VR techniques for users to be able to experience what was like to e.g. live in a certain place at a certain time. Even when CH assets still exist, it is sometimes interesting to build virtual models and add interactive capabilities in order to analyse them in detail in a non-invasive way, show them in a different fashion or from a different location, or promote cultural tourism. According to Guttentag (2010), planning and management, marketing, entertainment, education, accessibility, and heritage preservation are areas of tourism in which VR may prove particularly valuable. Among the different virtual approaches, virtual tours are one of the most popular productions for dissemination purposes (Bastanlar et al., 2008; Wessels, Ruther, Bhurtha, & Schröeder, 2014). For instance, in Maicas and Viñals (2016), a virtual tour of the Lliria heritage town (Valencia, Spain) named Edeta 360º is presented (Figure 3). The virtual enhancement of the cultural heritage is based on panorama photos following a straightforward procedure with off-the-self equipment and using the freely available software Hugin-2014.0.0 and Easypano Tourweaver

Figure 3. Edeta 360º Virtual Tour, where: (a) Screen about the Iglesia de la Sangre with Bell Tower screen; and (b) same image with an additional pop-up window

7.90®, while keeping the high quality of the final product. The panorama images are part of the virtual resources inside the virtual tour, which contains other kind of multimedia data, such as textual and graphical information about the heritage.

VR techniques allow combining mD information, which is important for CH, since CH assets can be reconstructed, reproduced and interacted by means of different elements/layers/sources of information, depending on the amount and type of data shown to end users. Thus, VR is a very useful technique for archaeological and historical purposes. Multispectral, multi-source information can be combined and visualized provided that the different layers/channels of data are properly synchronized/registered (Simon et al., 2010). This kind of visual techniques is useful to analyse paintings and polychromies (Siotto et al., 2015) in masterpieces or reliques that require non-invasive solutions.

Other multimodal/multisensory and semantic information can be also added, including sound (Christou, Angus, Loscos, Dettori, & Roussou, 2006), haptic (Sreeni, Priyadarshini, Praseedha, & Chaudhuri, 2012), stereoscopic (Bruno et al., 2010; Jiménez Fernández-Palacios, Morabito, & Remondino, 2016) or even olfactive information. CH acoustic reconstruction (Berardi, Iannace, & Maffei, 2016; Debut, Carvalho, Figueiredo, Antunes, & Silva, 2016) is an emerging trend and a good example of this multimodal technology. Haptic information is not always crucial but allows in certain cases to touch fragile objects without risk of damaging them (Bergamasco, Frisoli, & Barbagli, 2002).

VR-based CH applications are often designed to represent tangible assets that have been destroyed or altered. This is the case of archaeological sites that, after reconstructing damaged structures or remains, allow users to acquire knowledge of a whole and realistic vision of some ancient constructions and artifacts, as they were in their original state (Ercek et al., 2010; Guidi, Russo, & Angheleddu, 2014; Rodrigues, Magalhaes, Moura, & Chalmers, 2008). Better yet, the intangible assets associated with these sites/objects, such as stories, battles, dances can also be recreated or simulated by means of VR, adding not only visual but also sonic content accompanied with animations, including recreation of ancient characters. An example of this is shown in (de Heras Ciechomski, Schertenleib, Maïm, & Thalmann, 2005), where crowds of virtual humans are animated for the Roman Odeon of Aphrodisias, which was virtually recreated. An emergent trend in CH is the use of Serious Games (SG) (Anderson et al., 2010) to both recreate and play with tangible assets but also experience intangible assets such as battles or stories. SG can be crucial to engage people into active learning instead of merely being passive spectators (Mortara et al., 2014).

VR techniques have also been used to recreate museums or CH items that do exist but need to be preserved or displayed widely. There are many virtual museum applications (Miguélez Fernández, 2013; Reffat & Nofal, 2013; Styliania, Fotisb, Kostasa, & Petrosa, 2009), which offer the opportunity of exploring a remote site by manipulating (rotate, enlarge, etc.) fragile and precious objects with no risk of damage. Examples of virtual museums are very common, although not all the applications tagged as virtual museums are really VR applications since most of them lack a sense of immersion and natural interaction (like (Wojciechowski, Walczak, White, & Cellary, 2004)).

Regardless of the objective of the system and the data acquisition technique used to gather information to build the CH application, the display and simulation of tangible assets in VR-based CH applications follows basically the same rules as other VR systems. In this regard, older VR-applications used generic graphics libraries (Christou et al., 2006; Gaitatzes, Christopoulos, & Roussou, 2001) such as OpenGL, OpenGL Performer, or Open Scene Graph or specific VR libraries such as CAVElib, but their use has diminished with the maturity of new game development engines. Newer VR-based CH applications are now benefiting from the existence of increasingly complex game development platforms, such as Unreal or Unity (Jiménez Fernández-Palacios et al., 2016), allowing the development of realistic VR applications for CH in shorter time periods, even for non-experts in VR technology. Web deployment (Kiourt, Koutsoudis, & Pavlidis, 2016) can also be considered for some applications where immersion is less important than universal access.

Regarding the reproduced stimuli, there is an increased research work in the area of multisensory museums, and a number of examples is shown in Levent and Pascual-Leone (2014). Another work is presented in Cantoni, Lombardi, Porta, and Setti (2016), where museum's visitors can observe and analyze seven ancient tapestries, illustrating different phases of the battle of Pavia, through 3D reconstructions, virtual simulations, eye interaction and gesture navigation, along with transpositions of the tapestries into tangible images.

Nevertheless, there are certain requirements that CH applications need to emphasize in terms of representation and interaction. The first one is the ability to optimize 3D models that are sometimes obtained with high-resolution devices (the digitalization of existing CH tangible assets tries to obtain a highly detailed model of the scanned object). As the number of polygons increases, so does the complexity of the graphics pipeline calculations. The second one is to choose the appropriate devices for the generation of the perceptual cues. This also influences the interaction paradigm and the role of the user in the CH application. Some applications use VR glasses/helmets such as Oculus Rift (Jiménez Fernández-Palacios et al., 2016), allowing users to walk around a reconstructed CH site. Other applications use more natural interfaces using depth-sensing devices like Kinect or tracking systems like Leap Motion (Webel, Olbrich, Franke, & Keil, 2013). Another common interaction paradigm is to fly over a CH site, or observe it from a distant movable point.

Regarding the display technology, many applications use the CAVE system (Christou et al., 2006; Gaitatzes et al., 2001) in order to provide immersive experiences. Other approaches use big screens (Bruno et al., 2010). More modest approaches include the traditional display with tactile or even standard input devices (keyboard/mouse) (Wojciechowski et al., 2004). Depth cues are also applied using stereoscopic screens, as in Bruno et al. (2010), although recent approaches prefer the use of virtual helmets that already include stereoscopy and motion tracking. Sound is almost always produced in the form of binaural spatially trackable sound (Christou et al., 2006) with headphones or speakers, as the generation of realistic three-dimensional sound is relatively easy to perform.

Augmented Reality Applications in CH

Sometimes, CH reconstruction deals with sites and/or artifacts that are not completely missing, but have suffered alterations through history. In those cases, it is sufficient to reconstruct only some parts, enhancing or augmenting the reality with some kind of new virtual content, so that the heritage can be displayed "as it was" on top of, or complementing, how it is now. Azuma (1997) defines Augmented Reality (AR) as the technology that allows to build systems that simultaneously: (i) combine real and virtual objects; (ii) are interactive in real time and (iii) are registered in 3D. The restriction to include a 3D registration is key, so that the virtual (augmented) information presented to the user is spatially and temporally synchronized with the real information. Interaction is also important, because the user can experience the real world from different points, and the AR system should be able to generate the appropriate virtual content from any location.

AR has a distinctive and special capability in CH and tourism. While VR "extracts" people from the current reality trying to teleport them to a different place and time, AR-based CH applications allow people to perform a mental time travel in situ, and thus making a strong spatial connection with the actual CH location, which can be truly important. Moreover, it has to be pointed out that AR outstands as a very valuable tool when historical events have to be interpreted for visitors. In Gandia Marsh (Valencia, Spain), under the framework of a Visitor Center, it was implemented an AR application to interpret historical events for school-aged audiences (Portalés, Viñals, Alonso-Monasterio, & Morant, 2010), and emerged as a useful application to rise awareness about the heritage to locals. To that end, the shape and visual appearance of ancient tools were reproduced. Additionally, some videos were produced representing historical moments, with actors interpreting various characters. By means of the created AR environment, users were placed inside the narrative shown in the video, wearing or carrying the ancient tools. In this application, sound was also reproduced and tangible interaction was available.

AR representation and content-generation shares many aspects with VR systems, and some of the displays (visual, sonic, tangible, etc.) can be shared. However, AR-based applications often use mobile phones, tablets, cameras, projectors or even mirrors to mix real and virtual information (Portalés Ricart, Giner Martínez, & Sanmartín Piquer, 2005) (Figure 4). All these technologies can be applied to CH. AR-based CH applications use the same techniques as other AR applications, with some particular considerations and restrictions: many CH sites can be visited both outdoors and indoors, so AR needs be applicable for both scenarios. In addition, CH sites cannot usually be altered or modified so the placement of AR-marks or the use of invasive technologies is often forbidden. Therefore, markerless or feature-based AR technology should be the preferred choice, such as in Portalés, Lerma, and Pérez (2009). Indoor AR is also popular to enhance museums, mixing VR and AR systems (Wojciechowski et al., 2004).

Outdoor AR-based CH applications are harder to build since the 3D registration process is more complex due to light interference and noise. Some examples are the works shown in Haugstvedt and Krogstie (2012) and Vlahakis et al. (2002). In the later, three different interaction systems and interaction paradigms are presented to enjoy a time travel to ancient Olympia, Greece.

Mobile AR-based CH applications (using HMD, glasses or mobile devices) represents the most common set-up (Haugstvedt & Krogstie, 2012; Portalés et al., 2009), commonly reproducing sound and visual contents. Mobile phones and tablets are the preferred choice since it is the most affordable and

Figure 4. An AR application showing an ancient building in a modern environment, where: (a) image of the user in the real environment; and (b) an scene of the augmented environment
From (Portalés Ricart et al., 2005).

portable configuration for outdoor use. However, other paradigms, like spatial AR have also been used to project information over real CH items (Ridel et al., 2014).

As with VR applications, different interaction paradigms and multimodal information can also be used, since the non-existing elements of an AR application are virtually reproduced using VR-like techniques. A different approach is shown in the past and present book of the Castellet de Bernabé (Figure 5), where the virtual reconstruction of the site is merged with the existing assets of the site, building augmented images. However, the generated images are static, so they cannot be referred as an AR application.

DISCUSSION AND FUTURE DIRECTIONS

As shown through the previous sections, the mD acquisition, representation and interaction of assets can be relevant for the CH sector, as it might have many benefits. On the one hand, acquiring more information about the assets instead of merely recording their appearance (images) or even the shape (3D data), makes it possible to perform detailed studies on the assets, also allowing scientists to perform inspections non-invasively. For instance, mechanical studies can be done with the shape acquisition of the assets, but if multispectral images are also available, studies related to the chemical deterioration of the assets' surface are possible. On the other hand, and related to the touristic sector, the representation and interaction of cultural assets with mD information, might be essential for their dissemination to the general public, which each time more and more is accostumated to new technologies. In this regards, it has to be pointed out that there is an increased use of the VR and AR technologies in museums, exhibitions, archaeological sites, etc., which is partially due to the interesting capabilities that these technologies bring for interacting with the digitized assets, also being able to reproduce multi-modal stimuli (not only visual, but also sonic, tangible, etc.).

From a tourism-oriented perspective, we can state that the techniques of mD acquisition, representation and interaction applied to the dissemination of heritage can be considered in all the three steps of the tourism management process, namely: (i) the protection and conservation step; (ii) the heritage enhancement step; (iii) finally, the socio-economic revitalization step. The research works cited through

Figure 5. Augmented visualizations for the past and present book of the archaeological site "Castellet de Bernabé", where: (a) an augmented image of the entrance; and (b) an augmented image of the interior of a house showing a grain mill

the paper are a good example of this. These works have been further summarized in Table 2 (in the Appendix), highlighting the following items: the gathered and/or reconstructed dimensions, the outputs and the purpose of the reconstruction. This table has been elaborated with the aim to serve as a reference for the readers when searching for specific works related to the mD acquisition, representation and interaction of CH assets. As the table shows, the dimensions considered here are not all gathered for a single asset (i.e. not all works document all the dimensions), but the kind and number of dimensions depend on the purpose of the reconstruction. Regardless of the different techniques, the important message is that all these mD information sources can be added to the reconstruction of CH assets, enriching the cultural experience and providing insights that go far beyond the human senses. This is of great importance from a human-centered perspective because it allows people to understand and appreciate our cultural heritage deeply, overcoming the limitations of our perception system.

Despite the many different research works and techniques cited in this chapter for the acquisition of CH assets, there are still other issues that are not covered here, such as the documentation of assets including a temporal scale registration, the 3D scanning of transparent objects, the documentation of the interior of the assets, or the automatic generation of semantics for scanned 3D objects. These aspects constitute interesting challenges and future research lines that need to be emphasized in future studies, since they can provide significant benefits and insights to CH applications. At the same time, acquisition techniques that can be at the same time inexpensive, easy to use, accurate, fast, robust and non-invasive should be investigated.

Regarding the tourism applications that can be derived from these techniques of acquisition, representation and interaction, it needs to be pointed out that the development of almost any communication material for visitors and for the general public can be derived from the results obtained through these techniques. Moreover, the registration and reconstruction of the tangible cultural assets can be done from different starting points, as many of the monuments and other cultural assets present varied conservation conditions. Therefore, these techniques are especially relevant for those cases where the assets are in bad conservation conditions – as the case of archaeological sites –, as a starting point for its reconstruction and interpretation. In any case, the focus of the reconstruction/acquisition process is the public, since tourism, especially CH-related tourism, should be consciously leant towards a divulgative human-centered approach.

In the same way, regarding the heritage dissemination issues, it must be acknowledge that it is necessary to delve into how to strengthen the emotional dimension of these applications. Emotional aspects and human factors are of crucial importance when dealing with CH and tourism, since the final goal of this kind of applications is to touch people's emotions so that our cultural patrimony is conserved, remembered, explained, studied, enhanced and (when possible) economically exploited. Some authors like Roussou (2008) have already opened this debate.

CONCLUSION

This chapter presents a variety of dimensions that can be gathered in order to document cultural heritage tangible assets. The most demanded dimension is the shape, also referred as 3D data, usually accompanied with the visual appearance (texture images) of objects. While these dimensions are usually enough to produce digital interactive models of the assets, usually in the form of virtual or augmented reality applications, other studies demand the acquisition of other dimensions. Here, we have reported also the importance of various spectral bands (UV, IR and thermal), the semantics and the gathering of additional data to document the past, in the special case where the assets do not exists nowadays or are in a very bad conservation stage (showing a case study in archaeological sites). Finally, we have shown the different representation (visual, sonic, etc.) and interaction paradigms used for the dissemination of CH assets, highlighting the differences, similarities and possible uses of these techniques, giving an insight for the touristic sector.

The amount of information that can be extracted and learned from these CH assets is huge, and the application of existing and new information technologies to CH can provide great benefits for the society. Therefore, the importance of this topic should be emphasized.

However, it is important to highlight, in relation to the use of these technologies to the dissemination of heritage, that before designing an application, it is necessary to clearly identify the objective pursued and the target audience to be as efficient as possible from the communication point of view. That is, the application must be a means but not an end in itself. Although they are very attractive to the public, their real meaning lays on being part of an interpretative message or theme and of a heritage storytelling. A society that does not remember its heritage and history is bound to live through it again.

REFERENCES

Alexopoulou, A., Liaros, N., Panagopoulou, A., & Kaminari, A. (2010). *False Colour Infrared Imaging as a Tool for the Study of Pigments Used in Ceramics from Areas Within the Mediterranean Basin.* Paper presented at the IIC Congress 2010: “Conservation and the Eastern Mediterranean”, Istanbul, Turkey.

Anderson, E. F., McLoughlin, L., Liarokapis, F., Peters, C., Petridis, P., & De Freitas, S. (2010). Developing serious games for cultural heritage: A state-of-the-art review. *Virtual Reality (Waltham Cross), 14*(4), 255–275. doi:10.1007/s10055-010-0177-3

Andrew, S. R., & Eastop, D. (1994). Using ultra-violet and infra-red techniques in the examination and documentation of historic textiles. *The Conservator, 18*(1), 50–56. doi:10.1080/01410096.1994.9995084

Arrizabalaga, I., Gómez-Laserna, O., Aramendia, J., Arana, G., & Madariaga, J. M. (2014). Applicability of a Diffuse Reflectance Infrared Fourier Transform handheld spectrometer to perform in situ analyses on Cultural Heritage materials. *Spectrochimica Acta, Part A*(129), 259–267.

Azuma, R. T. (1997). A survey of augmented reality. *Presence: Teleoper. Virtual Environ., 6*(4), 355–385. doi:10.1162/pres.1997.6.4.355

Banou, P., Kaminari, A., Moutsatsou, A., Alexopoulou, A., & Singer, B. (2010). *Investigating the Conservation Problems of Oil Paintings on Paper Supports.* Paper presented at the International Symposium “Works of Art and Conservation Science Today”, Thessaloniki, Greece.

Bastanlar, Y., Grammalidis, N., Zabulis, X., Yilmaz, E., Yardimci, Y., & Triantafyllidis, G. (2008). *3D Reconstruction for a Cultural Heritage virtual tour system.* Paper presented at the The International Archives of the Photogrammetry, Remote Sensing and Spatial Information Sciences, Beijing, China.

Bearman, G., & Spiro, I. (1996). Archaeological application of advanced imaging techniques. *Biblical Archaeologist, 59*(1), 56–66. doi:10.2307/3210537

Berardi, U., Iannace, G., & Maffei, L. (2016). Virtual reconstruction of the historical acoustics of the Odeon of Pompeii. *Journal of Cultural Heritage*, *19*, 555–566. doi:10.1016/j.culher.2015.12.004

Bergamasco, M., Frisoli, A., & Barbagli, F. (2002). *Haptics technologies and cultural heritage applications*. Paper presented at the Computer Animation. doi:10.1109/CA.2002.1017503

Blais, F., & Beraldin, J. A. (2006). Recent Developments in 3D Multi-modal Laser Imaging Applied to Cultural Heritage. *Machine Vision and Applications*, *17*(6), 395–409. doi:10.1007/s00138-006-0025-3

Bodnar, J. L., Candoré, J. C., Nicolas, J. L., Szatanik, G., Detalle, V., & Vallet, J. M. (2012). Stimulated infrared thermography applied to help restoring mural paintings. *NDT & E International*, *49*(0), 40–46. doi:10.1016/j.ndteint.2012.03.007

Bruno, F., Bruno, S., De Sensi, G., Luchi, M.-L., Mancuso, S., & Muzzupappa, M. (2010). From 3D reconstruction to virtual reality: A complete methodology for digital archaeological exhibition. *Journal of Cultural Heritage*, *11*(1), 42–49. doi:10.1016/j.culher.2009.02.006

Buoso, M. C., Ceccato, D., & Zafiropoulos, D. (2009). False-Color Infra Red Photography in the Identification of Pigments Used for a Late 13th Century Illuminated Manuscript. *Laboratori Nazionali di Legnaro (LNL) Annual Report, Applied and Interdisciplinary Physics Instrumentation,* 153-154.

Cabrelles, M., Seguí, A. E., Navarro, S., Galcerá, S., Portalés, C., & Lerma, J. L. (2010). *3D Photorealistic modelling of stone monuments by dense image matching*. Paper presented at the International Archives of Photogrammetry, Remote Sensing and Spatial Information Sciences. Commission V Symposium, Newcastle upon Tyne, UK.

Cantoni, V., Lombardi, L., Porta, M., & Setti, A. (2016). Interactive, Tangible and Multi-sensory Technology for a Cultural Heritage Exhibition: The Battle of Pavia. In S. Margenov, G. Angelova, & G. Agre (Eds.), *Innovative Approaches and Solutions in Advanced Intelligent Systems* (pp. 77–94). Cham: Springer International Publishing. doi:10.1007/978-3-319-32207-0_6

Cetica, M., Marras, L., Materazzi, M., & Poggi, P. (2007). Tecniche di imaging multispettrale. In M. Martini, A. Castellano, & E. Sibi-lia (Eds.), Elementi di archeometria. Metodi fisici per i beni culturali (pp. 231–252). Academic Press.

Chabries, D. M., Booras, S. W., & Bearman, G. H. (2003). Imaging the past: Recent applications of multispectral imaging technology to deciphering manuscripts. *Antiquity*, *77*(296), 359–372. doi:10.1017/S0003598X00092346

Chane, C., Schütze, R., Boochs, F., & Marzani, F. (2013). Registration of 3D and Multispectral Data for the Study of Cultural Heritage Surfaces. *Sensors (Basel, Switzerland)*, *13*(1), 1004–1020. doi:10.3390/s130101004 PMID:23322103

Chow, S.-K., & Chan, K.-L. (2009). Reconstruction of photorealistic 3D model of ceramic artefacts for interactive virtual exhibition. *Journal of Cultural Heritage*, *10*(2), 161–173. doi:10.1016/j.culher.2008.08.011

Christou, C., Angus, C., Loscos, C., Dettori, A., & Roussou, M. (2006). A versatile large-scale multi-modal VR system for cultural heritage visualization. *Proceedings of the ACM symposium on Virtual reality software and technology*. doi:10.1145/1180495.1180523

de Heras Ciechomski, P., Schertenleib, S., Maïm, J., & Thalmann, D. (2005). *Reviving the Roman Odeon of Aphrodisias: Dynamic Animation and Variety Control of Crowds in Virtual Heritage*. Retrieved from http://infoscience.epfl.ch/record/99010

Debut, V., Carvalho, M., Figueiredo, E., Antunes, J., & Silva, R. (2016). The sound of bronze: Virtual resurrection of a broken medieval bell. *Journal of Cultural Heritage*, *19*, 544–554. doi:10.1016/j.culher.2015.09.007

Ercek, R., Viviers, D., & Warzée, N. (2010). 3D reconstruction and digitalization of an archeological site, Itanos, Crete. *Virtual Archaeology Review*, *1*(1). 10.4995/var.2010.4794

Erenoglu, R. C., Akcay, O., & Erenoglu, O. (2017). An UAS-assisted multi-sensor approach for 3D modeling and reconstruction of cultural heritage site. *Journal of Cultural Heritage*. doi:10.1016/j.culher.2017.02.007

Europeana Collections. (2017). *Europeana Collections*. Retrieved 03 January, 2017, from http://www.europeana.eu/

Fischer, C., & Kakoulli, I. (2006). Multispectral and hyperspectral imaging technologies in conservation: Current research and potential applications. *Reviews in Conservation*, *7*, 3–16.

Gaitatzes, A., Christopoulos, D., & Roussou, M. (2001). Reviving the past: cultural heritage meets virtual reality. *Proceedings of the 2001 conference on Virtual reality, archeology, and cultural heritage*. doi:10.1145/584993.585011

Garrido Carretero, F. (2013). The virtual reconstruction of the andalusian palace of Onda (Castellón): Architecture and Territory. *Virtual Archaeology Review*, *4*(9). 10.4995/var.2013.4245

Granero-Montagud, L., Portalés, C., Pastor-Carbonell, B., Ribes-Gómez, E., Gutiérrez-Lucas, A., Tornari, V., . . . Dietz, C. (2013a). *Deterioration estimation of paintings by means of combined 3D and hyperspectral data analysis*. Paper presented at the SPIE - Optics for Arts, Architecture, and Archaeology IV. doi:10.1117/12.2020336

Granero-Montagud, L., Portalés, C., Pastor-Carbonell, B., Ribes-Gómez, E., Gutiérrez-Lucas, A., Tornari, V., . . . Dietz, C. (2013b). *SYDDARTA: new methodology for digitization of deterioration estimation in paintings*. Paper presented at the SPIE - Optics for Arts, Architecture, and Archaeology IV. doi:10.1117/12.2020333

Groves, R. M., Portalés, C., & Ribes-Gómez, E. (2014). *Assessment of Mechanical and Chemical Deterioration of Artworks*. Paper presented at the International Conference on Ageing of Materials & Structures (AMS), Delft, The Netherlands.

Guarnieri, A., Remondino, F., & Vettore, A. (2006). Digital photogrammetry and TLS data fusion applied to Cultural Heritage 3D modeling. *International Archives of Photogrammetry, Remote Sensing and Spatial Information Sciences. ISPRS Commission V Symposium.*

Guidi, G., Russo, M., & Angheleddu, D. (2014). 3D Survey and virtual reconstruction of archeological sites. *Digital Applications in Archaeology and Cultural Heritage*, *1*(2), 55–69. doi:10.1016/j.daach.2014.01.001

Guttentag, D. A. (2010). Virtual reality: Applications and implications for tourism. *Tourism Management, 31*(5), 637-651. https://doi.org/10.1016/j.tourman.2009.07.003

Haugstvedt, A.-C., & Krogstie, J. (2012). *Mobile augmented reality for cultural heritage: A technology acceptance study.* Paper presented at the Mixed and Augmented Reality (ISMAR), 2012 IEEE International Symposium on. doi:10.1109/ISMAR.2012.6402563

He, Y., Gao, M., & Shang, J. (2013). A Virtual Reconstruction Methodology for Archaeological Heritage in East Asia – Practical Experience from the Re-relic Program in China. *Virtual Archaeology Review, 4*(9). 10.4995/var.2013.4253

Imposa, S. (2010). Infrared thermography and Georadar techniques applied to the Sala delle Nicchie (Niches Hall) of Palazzo Pitti, Florence (Italy). *Journal of Cultural Heritage, 11*(3), 259–264. doi:10.1016/j.culher.2009.04.005

Jensen, J., & Becker, R. (2015). *Shedding New Light on the Past: The Potential for Short Wave Ultraviolet Photography in Archaeology*. Paper presented at the 80th Annual Meeting of the Society for American Archaeology, San Francisco, CA.

Jiménez Fernández-Palacios, B., Morabito, D., & Remondino, F. (2016). Access to complex reality-based 3D models using virtual reality solutions. *Journal of Cultural Heritage.*

Kim, M. H., Harvey, T. A., Kittle, D. S., Rushmeier, H., Dorsey, J., Prum, R. O., & Brady, D. J. (2012). 3D imaging spectroscopy for measuring hyperspectral patterns on solid objects. *ACM Transactions on Graphics, 31*(4), 1–11. doi:10.1145/2185520.2185534

Kiourt, C., Koutsoudis, A., & Pavlidis, G. (2016). DynaMus: A fully dynamic 3D virtual Museum framework. *Journal of Cultural Heritage, 22*, 984–991. doi:10.1016/j.culher.2016.06.007

Lerma, J. L., Cabrelles, M., & Portalés, C. (2011). Multitemporal thermal analysis to detect moisture on a building façade. *Construction & Building Materials, 25*(5), 2190–2197. doi:10.1016/j.conbuildmat.2010.10.007

Lerones, P. M., Fernández, J. L., Gil, Á. M., Gómez-García-Bermejo, J., & Casanova, E. Z. (2010). A practical approach to making accurate 3D layouts of interesting cultural heritage sites through digital models. *Journal of Cultural Heritage, 11*(1), 1–9. doi:10.1016/j.culher.2009.02.007

Levent, N., & Pascual-Leone, A. (2014). *The multisensory museum: cross-disciplinary perspectives on touch, sound, smell, memory and space*. Rowman & Littlefield.

Liang, H. (2012). Advances in multispectral and hyperspectral imaging for archaeology and art conservation. *Applied Physics. A, Materials Science & Processing, 106*(2), 309–323. doi:10.1007/s00339-011-6689-1

Maicas, J. M., & Viñals, M. J. (2016). Edeta 360º Virtual Tour for visiting the heritage of Lliria (Spain). *Proceedings of the Archaeologica 2.0. 8th International Congres on Archaeology, Computer Graphics, Cultural Heritage and Innovation.*

Manguinhas, H., Freire, N., Isaac, A., Stiller, J., Charles, V., Soroa, A., . . . Alexiev, V. (2016). Exploring Comparative Evaluation of Semantic Enrichment Tools for Cultural Heritage Metadata. In N. Fuhr, L. Kovács, T. Risse & W. Nejdl (Eds.), *Research and Advanced Technology for Digital Libraries: 20th International Conference on Theory and Practice of Digital Libraries, TPDL 2016 Proceedings* (pp. 266-278). Cham: Springer International Publishing. doi:10.1007/978-3-319-43997-6_21

Martinez, K., Cupitt, J., Saunders, D., & Pillay, R. (2002). Ten years of art imaging research. *Proceedings of the IEEE, 90*(1), 28–41. doi:10.1109/5.982403

Mercuri, F., Orazi, N., Zammit, U., Paoloni, S., Marinelli, M., & Valentini, P. P. (2011). *Thermographic analysis of cultural heritage: recent applications and perspectives.* Paper presented at the Matter and Materials in/for Cultural Heritage, Craiova, Romania.

Miguélez Fernández, L. (2013). *Tour virtual por la red de museos de Gijón.* Master, Univeridad de Oviedo.

Mortara, M., Catalano, C. E., Bellotti, F., Fiucci, G., Houry-Panchetti, M., & Petridis, P. (2014). Learning cultural heritage by serious games. *Journal of Cultural Heritage, 15*(3), 318–325. doi:10.1016/j.culher.2013.04.004

Navarro, S., Seguí, A. E., Portalés, C., Lerma, J. L., Akasheh, T., & Haddad, N. (2009). *Integration of tls data and non-metric imagery to improve photo models and recording-a case study on djin block no. 9, petra (jordan).* Paper presented at the Virtual Systems and Multimedia.

Padoan, R., Steemers, T. A. G., Klein, M. E., Aalderink, B. J., & Bruin, G. d. (2008). *Quantitative Hyperspectral Imaging of Historical Documents: Technique and Applications.* Paper presented at the 9th International Conference on NDT of Art, Jerusalem, Israel.

Palomar-Vazquez, J., Baselga, S., Viñals-Blasco, M.-J., García-Sales, C., & Sancho-Espinós, I. (2017). Application of a combination of digital image processing and 3D visualization of graffiti in heritage conservation. *Journal of Archaeological Science: Reports, 12*, 32–42. doi:10.1016/j.jasrep.2017.01.021

Palomar-Vazquez, J., & Viñals-Blasco, M. J. (2016). *Exploring Three-js library possibilities for the dissemination of cultural heritage projects.* doi: 10.4995/var.2016.5834

Pamart, A., Guillon, O., Faraci, S., Gattet, E., Genevois, M., Vallet, J. M., & De Luca, L. (2017). Multispectral photogrammetric data acquisition and processing forwall paintings studies. *Int. Arch. Photogramm. Remote Sens. Spatial Inf. Sci., XLII-2*(W3), 559–566. doi:10.5194/isprs-archives-XLII-2-W3-559-2017

Peña Serna, S., Schmedt, H., Ritz, M., & Stork, A. (2012). *Interactive Semantic Enrichment of 3D Cultural Heritage Collections.* Paper presented at the The 13th International Symposium on Virtual Reality, Archaeology and Cultural Heritage VAST, Brighton, UK.

Pires, J., & Cruz, A. J. (2007). Techniques of thermal analysis applied to the study of cultural heritage. *Journal of Thermal Analysis and Calorimetry, 87*(2), 411–415. doi:10.1007/s10973-004-6775-0

Portalés, C., Alonso-Monasterio, P., & Viñals, M. J. (2016, 5-7 September). *A new methodology for the 3D photorealistic virtual reconstruction of the archaeological site "Castellet de Bernabé" (Llíria, Spain).* Paper presented at the ARQUEOLÓGICA 2.0 - 8° Congreso Internacional, Documentación 3D avanzada, modelado y reconstrucción de objetos patrimoniales, monumentos y sitios, Valencia.

Portalés, C., Alonso-Monasterio, P., & Viñals, M. J. (2017). 3D virtual reconstruction and visualisation of the archaeological site "Castellet de Bernabé" (Llíria, Spain). *Virtual Archeaology Review, 8*(16).

Portalés, C., Lerma, J. L., & Pérez, C. (2009). Photogrammetry and augmented reality for cultural heritage applications. *The Photogrammetric Record, 24*(128), 316–331. doi:10.1111/j.1477-9730.2009.00549.x

Portalés, C., Viñals, M. J., Alonso-Monasterio, P., & Morant, M. (2010). AR-Immersive Cinema at the Aula Natura Visitors Center. *IEEE MultiMedia, 17*(4), 8–15. doi:10.1109/MMUL.2010.72

Portalés Ricart, C., Giner Martínez, F., & Sanmartín Piquer, F. (2005). *Back to the 70's.* Paper presented at the ACM SIGCHI International Conference on Advances in Computer Entertainment Technology, Valencia, Spain.

Reffat, R. M., & Nofal, E. M. (2013). Effective Communication with Cultural heritage using Virtual Technologies. *International Archives of the Photogrammetry. Remote Sensing and Spatial Information Sciences, XL-5*(W2), 519–524.

Ridel, B., Reuter, P., Laviole, J., Mellado, N., Couture, N., & Granier, X. (2014). The Revealing Flashlight: Interactive spatial augmented reality for detail exploration of cultural heritage artifacts. *Journal on Computing and Cultural Heritage, 7*(2), 6. doi:10.1145/2611376

Ripoll Perelló, S., Bayarri, V., Latova, J., Herrera, J. A., Benavides, M., & Tenrero, H. P. (2014). El proyecto de investigación: Elaboración de un Sistema Gestor para la protección, puesta en valor y divulgación de Arte Rupestre y Estaciones Prehistóricas. *Revista Segovia Histórica (SgH)*, 25-40.

Rodrigues, N., Magalhaes, L. G., Moura, J. P., & Chalmers, A. (2008). *Automatic Reconstruction of Virtual Heritage Sites.* Paper presented at the International Symposium on Virtual Reality, Archaeology and Intelligent Cultural Heritage.

Roussou, M. (2008). *The components of engagement in virtual heritage environments.* Paper presented at the New heritage: beyond Verisimilitude. Conference on Cultural heritage and New Media, Hong Kong.

Salvi, J., Fernandez, S., Pribanic, T., & Llado, X. (2010). A state of the art in structured light patterns for surface profilometry. *Pattern Recognition, 43*(8), 2666–2680. doi:10.1016/j.patcog.2010.03.004

Sansoni, G., Trebeschi, M., & Docchio, F. (2009). State-of-The-Art and Applications of 3D Imaging Sensors in Industry, Cultural Heritage, Medicine, and Criminal Investigation. *Sensors (Basel, Switzerland), 9*(1), 568–601. doi:10.3390/s90100568 PMID:22389618

Schreiber, G., Amin, A., Aroyo, L., van Assem, M., de Boer, V., Hardman, L., & Wielinga, B. et al. (2008). Semantic annotation and search of cultural-heritage collections: The MultimediaN E-Culture demonstrator. *Web Semantics: Science, Services, and Agents on the World Wide Web, 6*(4), 243–249. doi:10.1016/j.websem.2008.08.001

Simon, C., Huxhagen, U., Mansouri, A., Heritage, A., Boochs, F., & Marzani, F. (2010). *Integration of high resolution spatial and spectral data acquisition systems to provide complementary datasets for cultural heritage applications.* Paper presented at the IS&T/SPIE Electronic Imaging meeting. doi:10.1117/12.838891

Siotto, E., Dellepiane, M., Callieri, M., Scopigno, R., Gratziu, C., Moscato, A., & Palleschi, V. et al. (2015). A multidisciplinary approach for the study and the virtual reconstruction of the ancient polychromy of Roman sarcophagi. *Journal of Cultural Heritage, 16*(3), 307–314. doi:10.1016/j.culher.2014.05.011

Sreeni, K., Priyadarshini, K., Praseedha, A., & Chaudhuri, S. (2012). *Haptic rendering of cultural heritage objects at different scales.* Paper presented at the International Conference on Human Haptic Sensing and Touch Enabled Computer Applications. doi:10.1007/978-3-642-31401-8_45

Styliania, S., Fotisb, L., Kostasa, K., & Petrosa, P. (2009). Virtual museums, a survey and some issues for consideration. *Journal of Cultural Heritage, 10*(4), 520–528. doi:10.1016/j.culher.2009.03.003

Tilden, F. (1957). Interpreting our heritage (4th ed.). The University of North Carolina Press.

Trinchão Andrade, B., Mazetto Mendes, C., de Oliveira Santos Jr, J., Pereira Bellon, O. R., & Silva, L. (2012). 3D preserving xviii century barroque masterpiece: Challenges and results on the digital preservation of Aleijadinhos sculpture of the Prophet Joel. *Journal of Cultural Heritage, 13*(2), 210–214. doi:10.1016/j.culher.2011.05.003

Tristán, R. M. (2014). *Investigadores revelan el arte rupestre 'invisible' en las cuevas de la meseta (FOTOS).* Retrieved 27 April, 2017, from http://www.huffingtonpost.es/2014/06/15/arte-rupestre-invisible-_n_5492612.html

Vavliakis, K. N., Karagiannis, G. T., & Mitkas, P. A. (2012). *Semantic Web in Cultural Heritage after 2020.* Paper presented at the workshop, "What will the Semantic Web look like 10 years from now?", held in concunction with the 11th International Semantic Web Conference 2012, Boston, MA.

Verhoeven, G. (2008). Imaging the invisible using modified digital still cameras for straightforward and low-cost archaeological near-infrared photography. *Journal of Archaeological Science, 35*(12), 3087–3100. doi:10.1016/j.jas.2008.06.012

Vidal, C., & Muñoz, G. (2015). Métodos avanzados para el análisis y documentación de la arqueología y la arquitectura maya: los "mascarones" de Chiloé y La Blanca. In C. Vidal & G. Muñoz (Eds.), *Artistic Expressions in Maya Architecture: Analysis and Documentation Techniques* (pp. 75–90). Oxford, UK: Archaeopress.

Vlahakis, V., Ioannidis, N., Karigiannis, J., Tsotros, M., Gounaris, M., Stricker, D., & Almeida, L. et al. (2002). Archeoguide: An Augmented Reality Guide for Archaeological Sites. *IEEE Computer Graphics and Applications, 22*(5), 52–60. doi:10.1109/MCG.2002.1028726

Webel, S., Olbrich, M., Franke, T., & Keil, J. (2013). *Immersive experience of current and ancient reconstructed cultural attractions.* Paper presented at the Digital Heritage International Congress (DigitalHeritage). doi:10.1109/DigitalHeritage.2013.6743766

Wessels, S., Ruther, H., Bhurtha, R., & Schröeder, R. (2014). *Design and creation of a 3D Virtual Tour of the world heritage site of Petra, Jordan.* Paper presented at the AfricaGeo.

Wojciechowski, R., Walczak, K., White, M., & Cellary, W. (2004). *Building virtual and augmented reality museum exhibitions.* Paper presented at the ninth international conference on 3D Web technology. doi:10.1145/985040.985060

Yastikli, N. (2007). Documentation of cultural heritage using digital photogrammetry and laser scanning. *Journal of Cultural Heritage*, *8*(4), 423–427. doi:10.1016/j.culher.2007.06.003

KEY TERMS AND DEFINITIONS

Digital Representation of Data: Reproduction of data by means of digital forms, as enabled by computers.

Interaction: A kind of action that occurs as two or more objects have an effect upon one another.

Multi-Dimensional (mD) Data: Data that accounts for three-dimensional information and other kind of data, such as radiometric (e.g. IR, thermal, etc.) or semantic.

Multimodal Technology: A technology that provides several distinct tools for input and output of data, thus allowing multiple modes of interacting with a system.

Tangible Assets: Assets that have a physical form, including buildings, places, monuments, tools, artifacts, etc.

Three-Dimensional (3D) Data: Data that is realized in a three dimensional space, a geometric setting in which three values are required to determine the position of an element.

Virtual Reconstruction: Modeling of structures by means of computational tools.

APPENDIX

Table 2. Classification of the referenced works regarding the considered dimensions or gathered data, the kind of representation (outputs), and the purpose of the reconstruction

Reference	Gathered Data	Outputs	Purpose
(Andrew & Eastop, 1994)	UV and IR photographs	Graphics	Analysis and documentation of historic textiles
(Gaitatzes et al., 2001)	Shape, texture	Virtual reality, immersive systems	Review paper, museum exhibition
(Bergamasco et al., 2002)	Shape	Visual and haptic representations	Enhance visitor's experience at museums
(Vlahakis et al., 2002)	Shape, texture	Mobile augmented reality	Tourism
(Chabries et al., 2003)	Multispectral imaging	Graphics	Deciphering manuscripts
(Wojciechowski et al., 2004)	Shape, RGB photographs	Virtual and augmented reality	Museum exhibitions
(Portalés Ricart et al., 2005)	Shape, texture	Augmented reality	Mix historical and new buildings in a single environment
(Christou et al., 2006)	Shape	Virtual reality in a CAVE system, haptic interface	Museum exhibition
(Guarnieri et al., 2006)	Shape	Synthetic sounds	Development on an approach to simulate sound
(Blais & Beraldin, 2006)	Shape (laser scanning), RGB photographs	Virtual reality	Approach to fuse data
(Fischer & Kakoulli, 2006)	Multispectral and hyperspectral imaging	Virtual reality	Review paper
(Pires & Cruz, 2007)	Thermal imaging	Graphics	Review paper
(Yastikli, 2007)	Shape, RGB photographs	Virtual reality	Review paper on photogrammetry and laser scanning
(Schreiber et al., 2008)	Semantics	Graphics	Semantic search on virtual collections
(Padoan et al., 2008)	Hyperspectral imaging	Graphics	Documentation of historical documents
(Chow & Chan, 2009)	Shape (photogrammetry), RGB photographs	Virtual reality	Interactive virtual exhibition
(Navarro et al., 2009)	Shape (laser scanning), RGB photographs	Virtual reality	Proof of research method
(Portalés et al., 2009)	Shape (laser scanning), RGB photographs	Augmented reality	Visualize a former stage of an architectural asset
(Anderson et al., 2010)	Shape, texture	Virtual reality	Review paper Serious games
(Bruno et al., 2010)	Shape, multimedia data (audio recordings, pictures and movies)	Virtual reality	Develop a methodology for a virtual exhibition system
(Cabrelles et al., 2010)	Shape (photogrammetry), RGB photographs	Virtual reality	Proof of research method
(Simon et al., 2010)	Shape, multispectral images	Virtual reality	Method to register images and 3D models

continued on following page

Table 2. Continued

Reference	Gathered Data	Outputs	Purpose
(Lerma et al., 2011)	RGB, thermal (temporal evolution)	Graphics	Moisture detection
(Liang, 2012)	Multispectral and hyperspectral imaging	Graphics	Review paper: archaeology and art conservation
(Sreeni et al., 2012)	Shape	Graphic and haptic rendering	To provide access of CH to visually impaired people
(Webel et al., 2013)	Shape, texture	Virtual reality	Review paper on different technologies to interact with CH virtual content
(Granero-Montagud et al., 2013a, 2013b; Groves et al., 2014)	Shape (structured light), RGB photographs, hyperspectral images in near IR	Virtual reality	Determination of mechanical and chemical deterioration of artworks
(Mortara et al., 2014)	Shape, texture	Virtual reality	Review paper, series games
(Ridel et al., 2014)	Shape	Spatial augmented reality	Visualize 3D analysis made on the objects
(Siotto et al., 2015)	Shape (laser scanning), RGB photographs, spectral curves (Raman spectroscopy), documentation on the past	Virtual reality	Reconstruction of the ancient colour (original pigments)
(Berardi et al., 2016)	Shape, acoustics	Virtual reality	Expert analysis on acoustics
(Cantoni et al., 2016)	Shape, appearance, acoustics, simulation	3D reconstructions, virtual simulations, eye interaction and gesture navigation	Museum exhibition
(Jiménez Fernández-Palacios et al., 2016)	Shape, RGB photographs	Virtual reality, immersive systems (Oculus Rift)	Methodology to interact with complex CH 3D contents
(Kiourt et al., 2016)	Shape, RGB photographs	Virtual reality	Museum exhibition
(Portalés et al., 2016, 2017)	Shape (surveying & manual editing), RGB photographs, interpretation of the past	Virtual reality (virtual flight, explorer diary, multi-use trail) and augmented visualizations (past & present book)	Enhance user experiences and understanding of the site

Chapter 5
An Initial Framework to Develop a Mobile Five Human Senses Augmented Reality System for Museums

João M. F. Rodrigues
University of Algarve, Portugal

Pedro J. S. Cardoso
University of Algarve, Portugal

Joana Lessa
University of Algarve, Portugal

João André Pereira
University of Algarve, Portugal

João D. P. Sardo
University of Algarve, Portugal

Marco de Freitas
University of Algarve, Portugal

Jorge Semião
University of Algarve, Portugal

Jânio Monteiro
University of Algarve, Portugal & INESC-ID, Portugal

Célia M. Q. Ramos
University of Algarve, Portugal

Roberto Lam
University of Algarve, Portugal

Eduardo Esteves
University of Algarve, Portugal & CCMAR Centre of Marine Sciences, Portugal

Mauro Figueiredo
University of Algarve, Portugal

Alexandra R. Gonçalves
University of Algarve, Portugal

Miguel Gomes
SPIC – Creative Solutions, Portugal

Paulo Bica
SPIC – Creative Solutions, Portugal

DOI: 10.4018/978-1-5225-2927-9.ch005

ABSTRACT

The Mobile Five Senses Augmented Reality System for Museums (M5SAR) project aims to development an Augmented Reality mobile system for museums. Museums are amazing places, where it is important to sensorial augment as much as possible the visits, permitting to see, ear, touch, smell, and taste all the interesting objects there exist. Also fundamental is that visitors with different profiles (child, adult, expert, etc.) can have different experiences when visiting the same object. In the M5SAR system, the visitor uses its smartphone to select the object(s) to explore, and the user interface adapts on-the-fly to the object(s) and user's profile. Simultaneously, when integrated, a paired hardware device allows the extension of the augmented reality system to the human five senses, complementing the visual and auditory information about the objects. This chapter presents the initial framework to develop a five senses mobile adaptive museum system.

INTRODUCTION

The Mobile Five Senses Augmented Reality System for Museums (M5SAR) project aims at the development of an enhanced Augmented Reality (AR) system, to be a guide in cultural, historical and museum events, complementing or replacing the traditional orientation given by tour guides, directional signs, or maps. The system consists of a (i) smartphone/phablet application (APP) and a (ii) hardware device (referenced as HDevice) to be integrated with smartphones/phablets, in order to explore the five human senses: sight, hearing, touch, smell, and taste. Both components, (i) and (ii), can work in stand-alone or integrated fashion.

Nowadays, many personal and context-aware tourism and cultural experiences are constructed based on mobile APPs (Jung, Chung, & Leue, 2015), including the ones that use AR. Those APPs are increasing in number due to the popularity of built-in cameras, global positioning systems, and with the massive availability of Internet connections. On the other hand, most of the present User Interfaces (UI) still traditionally follow a one-size-fits-all model, typically ignoring the needs, abilities, and preferences of individual users. However, past research pointed out that visualization performance could be improved by adapting some of its aspects to the individual user (Steichen, Conati & Carenini, 2014). Conati, Carenini, Toker, and Lallé (2015) state that intelligent adaptive user interfaces (AUI) and/or visualizations, that can adapt on-the-fly to the specific needs and abilities of each individual user, are a long-term research goal. This is due to two main difficulties: (a) the extraction of information about the users' needs and abilities and (b) the implementation of UIs that can adapt/change "themselves" on-the-fly.

Reinecke and Bernstein (2013) refer that a modular UI that allows a flexible composition of various interface elements increases the number of variations of the interface element to the power of the number of adaptable elements. Thus, instead of designing each interface from scratch, a modular user interface approach is possibly a better solution, once it allows achieving many more versions with less design effort. Therefore, the requirement changes to the creation of different designs for all those parts of the interface that are subject to user or cultural preferences. Equal importance should be given to the UI adaptation to users with different impairments. Unfortunately, because of the great variety of existing impairments, it is expectable that manually and, probably, modular designing interfaces, for each one of those impairments, is impractical and not scalable (Gajos, Wobbrock, & Weld, 2008; Rodrigues, Lessa, Gregório, Ramos, & Cardoso, 2016). Nevertheless, the modular and/or adaptive generation of

UIs offers the promise of providing personalized interfaces on-the-fly, although this does not mean that the user will be satisfied with his/her personalized APP. According to Zhao, Lu, Zhang, and Chau (2012), the psychological process behind satisfaction is highly complex and requires a differentiation between transaction-specific satisfaction and cumulative satisfaction. Transaction-specific satisfaction is the judgment of an experienced service encounter at a specific point in time, whereas cumulative satisfaction is the result of "the overall evaluation of all services encountered over time". Augmented reality exacerbates some of the challenges mentioned before because multiple types of augmentation are possible at once, and proactive APPs run the risk of overwhelming users.

Having the above in mind, at least three main challenges arise in the (i) APP implementation, i.e., in the AUI design and implementation: (a) How to harvest the necessary information about the preferences and skills of each user; (b) From the acquired information/data, how to give "intelligence" to the UI implementation so it will adapt on-the-fly to the user's specificities; (c) How to develop the AUI, even a modular UI, without being necessary to develop a huge amount of different (sub-)modules and, at the same time, still optimize the user's experience and the main principles of interaction design.

The traditional AR systems only give sensorial feedbacks to two senses, sight, and hearing. Unlike those, multi-sensorial media focuses on providing immersive communications and enhancing user quality of experience (Yuan, Bi, Muntean & Ghinea, 2015). As mentioned before, the goal of M5SAR is to extend traditional AR to the five senses. With this in mind, this chapter also explores very briefly the implementation of a (ii) hardware device to be integrated with smartphones, allowing the user to feel touch, smell, and taste, therefore expanding the typical experience to all senses. Some existing systems already make use of these concepts, like the Smelling Screen (Matsukura, Yoneda & Ishida, 2013) and the Digital Taste Interface (Ranasinghe, Cheok, Fernando, Nii & Ponnampalam, 2011) which, however, are not portable. The HDevice consists of a compact portable device, adaptable to all smartphones, phablets, and tablets, between 5'' and 10''. The HDevice has its own rechargeable battery and communicates via Bluetooth with the mobile application, from which it receives commands to reproduce different sensation contents at appropriate times, though a series of interactive haptic and multi-sensorial media interfaces, like thermoelectric modules, fans, vibration motors, electronic vaporizers, and fragrance dispersers.

This chapter focus on the initial M5SAR system's framework, namely the APP development with an AUI for a museum application, integrated with gamification concepts (not detailed in this document) and marker-based AR (Cheng, & Tsai, 2013), as well as the hardware device to be integrated with the smartphones to extend AR to the five senses. The main contributions are: (a) the framework for the adaptive on-the-fly card-based UI construction (Adobe, 2016), where the development of the cards has a modular architecture, including the integration with marked-based AR. (b) The framework of the initial (mobile) hardware device to extend the AR to the five senses. In this sense, the chapter is organized as follows. The background and the state-of-the-art are presented in the next section. The following sections introduce the framework to develop the integrated mobile museum system, future research directions, and conclusions.

BACKGROUND

Alvarez-Cortes, Zayas, Uresti, and Zarate (2009) define Intelligent User Interfaces (IUI) as a sub-field of Human-Computer Interaction (HCI), with the goal of improving HCI by the use of new technologies and interaction devices, including the use of Artificial Intelligence (AI) techniques that allow adaptive or intelligent behavior. Akiki, Bandara, and Yu (2014) presented a study about adaptive model-driven UI development systems, where the focus was AUI for mobile application applied to museums, e.g., MNEMOSYNE (Karaman et al., 2016). Schuller (2015) mentioned that what differences future IUIs is the promise to lend them "emotional intelligence": interfaces that "know" and can react appropriately to the satisfaction or anger of their users. The information is thereby increasingly accessed from multiple modalities (Morency, Mihalcea, & Doshi, 2011), in affect recognition and sentiment analysis, thanks to the availability of increasingly large and realistic resources (Schuller, 2015), including deep learning and long-short-term memory architectures (Metallinou et al., 2012), and weakly supervised learning methods. In fact, in the best of all worlds, the system would have sufficient knowledge about a user's culture before he/she first accesses the interface, because the first impression counts (Lindgaard, Fernandes, Dudek, & Brown, 2006). Reinecke and Bernstein (2013) argue that, to appeal to users in expanding markets, a more comprehensive personalization of interfaces to the cultural background is needed. Those authors identify ideas on how to obtain user information in order to subsequently adapt the UI to certain aspects, e.g., by using questionnaires in an initial registration process, through performance tests (Gajos et al. 2008), or by observing the user's interaction (Kralisch, Eisend, & Berendt, 2005). Gajos and Weld (2004) proposed an automatic system for generating UI, a solution based on treating interface adaptation as an optimization problem.

Akiki et al. (2014) present an overview of adaptive model-driven UI development systems, presenting a set of criteria to evaluate the strengths and shortcomings of these systems. In order to approach accessible HCI-designs for mobile devices, the principles of universal design are important to be followed (CEUD, 2016), as well as the guidelines for supporting accessibility (Gnome, 2016). Mobile APPs should move towards completely personalized experiences. Usually, these experiences are built from the aggregation of many individual pieces of content. One way this content could, and is now being presented, is in the form of cards (Babich, 2016). The card-based interaction model is not new and is now spread pretty widely in most of the recent APPs. Experiences are also many times related to gamification which, in this chapter's sense, is the strategy of interaction between people and businesses (museums), based on offering incentives to encourage public engagement with brands in a playful manner. In practice, focused on the recommendation, dissemination, and evaluation, or to attract new customers to the brand, "companies" offer rewards to participants who perform predetermined tasks. The idea involves setting tasks that are in accordance with the company's (in this case museum) objectives, the creation of rules and the application of monitoring systems. The rewards for user interactions can range from virtual incentives such as medals (or "badges") to physical gifts (Negruşa, Toader, Sofică, Tutunea, & Rus, 2015).

This chapter focus also in the implementation of AR. Azuma et al. (2001) defined an AR system as "...supplements the real world with virtual (computer-generated) objects that appear to coexist in the same space as the real world". However, AR can also be defined (depending on the application) as a system that adds information to the environment in order to facilitate HCI in a human environment. The application presented is an AR marker-based, often also called image-based (Cheng et al., 2013). AR-based markers allow adding preset signals (e.g., paintings, statues) easily detectable in the environment and use computer vision techniques to sense them. There are many commercial AR toolkits (SDK) such as Kudan (2016), Catchoom (2016), Wikitude (2016), or Vuforia (2016) and AR content management systems, e.g., Catchoom (2016) or Layar (2016), including open source SDKs, from which probably the most know is the Artoolkit (2016). Each of the above solutions has pros and cons. Some are quite expensive, others consume too much memory (it is important to stress that, the present application will have many markers, at least one for each museum piece), others take too much time to load on the mobile device, etc. Here, the Artoolkit (2016) is briefly compared with an image marker detector developed by the authors, which is based on the ORB binary descriptor (Rublee, Rabaud, Konolige, & Bradski, 2011). A descriptor evaluation can be found in Figat, Kornuta, and Kasprzak (2014).

In terms of museum APPs, almost every known museum has its own, corresponding to a huge amount and variety of applications. For instance, the Wall Street Journal presents an interesting article with their envisage of the best APPs for visiting museums (TWSJ, 2016). The same kind of articles are presented by Information Week, with 10 (fantastic) APPs for museum visits (InformationWeek, 2016), and by The Balance, with some of the fine art museum APPs (Balance, 2016). The use of AR in museums is also not new, including the implementation of head-worn displays (Vainstein, Kuflik, & Lanir, 2016). Vainstein, Kuflik, and Lanir (2016) also discussed the necessary requirements and additional features for useable AR systems in museums. Other AR solutions, nonexclusive for museums, are the Srbija 1914 / Augmented Reality Exhibition at the Historical Museum of Serbia (HMS, 2016), the Invisible Museum from Qualcomm (Qualcomm, 2016), the interactive IPAD Museum catalog from the University of Virginia Art Museum (VAM, 2016), the interactive devices at the Cleveland Museum which includes playing games and social interaction, with face and posture recognition (MWCM, 2016), and the Science Museum - atmosphere gallery (SM, 2016). It is clear to conclude that the development of a museum APP is nothing new; nevertheless, this document will present a framework to develop an APP with different characteristics, which includes AUI and five senses AR.

The second component of the system is a (mobile) multi-sensorial display, which together with the APP, will be able to reproduce different contents for the five human senses. Psychology generally accepts that information will be better perceived if more human senses are used (Kovács, Rozinaj, Murray, Sulema & Rybárová, 2015). Still, most existing multimedia systems in use today focus only on two senses (sight and hearing), being one reason the fact that producing compelling sensations for the other senses is complex. Even though, there has been a series of attempts in the past, but almost none of them seem to be picked up for production.

One technique, which although its limitations is somehow an exception, is the sense of touch through haptic feedback with vibration motors, used for instance in videogames and cellphones (Brewster, Chohan & Brown, 2007). Another interesting technique is the usage of air as a way to stimulate the sense of touch, as the AIREAL solution introduced by Disney Research. Their device uses compressed air to hit the user with an air ring, called a vortex, generating tactile sensations on the skin (Sodhi, Poupyrev, Glisson & Israr, 2013). With the dissemination of Peltier devices, several studies and experiments were conducted on thermoreception. A haptic transmission system for telexistence was developed using the TELESAR V, which was able to detect pressure, vibrations, and temperature on its finger (Kurogi et al., 2013). However, from the point of view of efficiency and energy consumption, the usage of Peltier devices on mobile applications is problematic. Other solutions still exist, such as the virtual reality haptic technology proposed by AxonVR (2016).

The sense of smell reproduction also presents some options, like a flow of air through a scent filter or recipient, vaporizing an aromatized solution, pressurized scented cans, heated or evaporative diffusers, or ultrasonic scent atomization (Yanagida, 2012). One particularly interesting prototype was a wearable olfactory display, which used micro pumps to force a flow of air through an odor filter, releasing it on the user's face (Yamada, Yokoyama, Tanikawa, Hirota & Hirose, 2006). Another peculiar prototype is the Smelling Screen, which combines a display with four fans, rotating at low speed so the user will not perceive the flow of air (Matsukura et al., 2013). For other solutions see e.g. FeelReal (2016) multisensory VR mask. Finally, there is the sense of taste, perhaps the least explored of all senses and probably the hardest to digitally stimulate. In this matter, Ranasinghe et al. (2011) presented a research where two silver electrodes were attached to the user's tongue and pulses applied with different electric properties (like current, frequency, and voltage) seem to produce sour, bitter and salty sensations. Further research demonstrated that combining other influential factors, like temperature, enabled the system to produce a wider variety of results (Ranasinghe, Nakatsu, Nii & Gopalakrishnakone, 2012). Again, other solutions exist; see e.g. the work from Narumi, Kajinami, Nishizaka, Tanikawa, and Hirose (2011).

All the applications that could be related to tourism and cultural activities should obey a minimum of "Accessible Tourism" (EWB, 2016). Tourism experience combines the actions of tourists with a set of memories and emotions related to the visited places, as something "pleasant, engaging, and memorable" (Oh, Fiore, & Jeoung, 2007), and able to satisfy a "wide range of personal needs ranging from pleasure to a search for meaning" (Li, 2000). The consumers/users want to be involved and absorbed into the experience that they are enjoying while having access to simple products (Pine, & Gilmore, 1999). In the above context, the implementation of the present system with its mobile APP, to be successful, depends on the consumers' (museum users) adoption. In this sense, APPs or devices should be validated by a Technology Acceptance Model – TAM (Marangunić & Granić, 2015). The Unified Theory of Acceptance and Use of Technology (UTAUT) is an extension of the TAM (Venkatesh, Morris, Davis, & Davis, 2003), with new improvements in the organizational context and used to investigate the user's intentions when facing a new technology. The UTAUT2 model (Venkatesh, Thong, & Xu, 2012) extends the UTAUT model, by integrating new constructs and relationships to be tailored to the consumer's use context. The UTAUT2 model is adequate, inside the context of the M5SAR project, to study and validate the acceptance of this new technology. Having this in mind, specific surveys will be developed for each segment or group of users, each one with specific characteristics.

FRAMEWORK TO DEVELOP A MOBILE MUSEUM SYSTEM

As previously mentioned, the developed system interfaces with the user through the mobile application installed on the user's smartphone/tablet. This mobile application shows general museum information (e.g., museum's history, map, stores, and collections) and specific information of each museum object. Minimizing as much as possible the network traffic, the mobile application communicates with a "server" each time it needs more contents which, for instance, occurs when the user enters a different section of the museum. The system also integrates a device, HDdevice, that it is lent or rent at the museum's front desk. This device is compatible with different smartphones and tablets.

The mobile application is multiplatform, multilingual and has a modular structure (Reinecke, & Bernstein, 2013) based on UI cards. The development of the UI cards should adapt to the user, by changing the view and the contents or the way they appear. Although the system here presented can adapt itself to more groups of users, at present, four types were considered: child, adult, adult-expert, and family (1+ adult(s) with 1+ child(ren)). How to harvest the necessary information about each user preferences and skills, in order to adapt the UI to the user's specifications, is out of the scope of this chapter.

Other major considerations were contemplated in the APP: (a) deploy the AR module only when the mobile device is in the (almost) vertical position; (b) use of beacons (Estimote, 2016) to detect the approximated user's position in the museum and, in consequence, download any extra contents, if necessary; (c) use gamification principles, i.e., assign "rewards" to the user depending on his/her actions; (d) convert all textual contents to sound contents (audio contents should not disturb other museum users, neither should "silence" the room's ambient sounds); (e) use of adaptive UI and adaptive ("intelligent") navigation, e.g., different (suggestions) paths will be given depending on the objects already seen by the user, as well as its profile; (f) use adaptive luminosity, i.e., the UI luminosity should adapt to the luminosity of the environment and/or piece; and (g) hot/help key available, which appears "spontaneously" each time a user does not know what to do.

This section will detail the most relevant components of the system, as the authors will not go specific over all the elements of the structure (please check the M5SAR project site, for more details). Nevertheless, the four main topics of the framework will be addressed: (a) design consideration, (b) adaptive card implementation, (c) AR and (d) AR device implementation (HDevice). The presented system is being tested in the *Faro Municipal Museum* (located in Faro, Algarve, Portugal). In the future, the user will install a generic museum application in its mobile device, where several museums can be browsed by selecting and downloading the desired contents. Finally, it is also important to stress that the system is being implemented using the Unity development platform (Unity, 2016).

Application Design Considerations

To design the user experience (UX), several objectives were established: the importance to adapt the experience to users' needs, objectives and pace, promoting a pleasurable and ludic experience to engage him/her in the visit; to enrich the visit with an emotional value, which enhances the experience; to educate, giving *in-situ* piece related detailed and clear information; to assist the visitor, with museum map orientation, information on facilities and special needs assistance.

The experience in the museums can be challenging, troubling and overpowering for some visitors, since they have to deal with new information and new situations (Falk, & Dierking, 2013). Pleasurable and ludic aspects help overcome it and therefore are integrated in UX design (Saffer, 2006). The Interaction Design (IxD) approach to emotion here present allows the visitor a subjectivity emotional experience, integrating his/her personal perception and emotional values (Boehner, DePaula, Dourish, & Sengers, 2007), instead of pre-establishing a list of emotions that users should meet. This also meets the purpose of a personalized museum experience. The IxD options outline the APP as: (i) non-obtrusive – layers of information in a window paradigm frame the visitor's surroundings and allow him/her to "navigate" through the exhibition with a non-visually imposing and non-absorbent UI, focusing on the exhibition and not on the UI itself, thus applying the concepts of transparency (Cooper et al., 2014) and flow (Saffer, 2006) to create continuity of experience. (ii) Informative – giving detailed information about collections and pieces, suggesting visit circuits and allowing the visitor to tailor his/her own itinerary, depending on his/her preferences. (iii) Support providing – giving map orientation, guidance, assistance and supporting special needs. (iv) Adaptive – adjust its content to the type of visitor (child, adult, …) and adjust UI visual changes according to each one, taking into account preferences and accessibility issues like sight and physical impairments. (v) Rich, emotional experience provider – fostering and promoting a rich museum experience, enhancing the traditional museum visit also with emotionally driven content created with the convergence of media and languages, in a multisensory designed experience result.

The UI employs the premise previous established in UX, to be user adaptive and convey the perception of easy to use, effective, useful, clever and visually pleasurable. Therefore, the UI adapts to different types of visitors by adjusting visualization of content and layout/graphic adjustments (e.g., size, opacity, contrast, movement). A modular UI approach organizes visual space into chunks of information easily adjusted to the user's needs in number and size. The navigation applies Natural User Interfaces (NUI) strategies, using natural interactions through multi-touch, gestures, movements and also speech (Blake, 2013); and clear contextualized visual support to orientate navigation, comprising users' needs, pace, and digital literacy levels.

The museums are places filled with a visually rich environment: fill with color, forms, textures, etc. The UI layout should not impose itself to the user to avoid competing, for the visitor full attention, with the visual richness of the exhibition pieces. Visual consistency, clarity, and hierarchy applied to UI layout promote order/functionality and pleasure in perception. It responds to a set of attributes that convey museum context and the user experience designed: freshness, elegance, trustworthy, clarity, ludic. So, the graphic language is shaped by: (i) a reduced palette of soft predominantly light and moderated contrast colors in icons and text (suggests freshness, elegance, and clarity; for senior user, contrast is augmented); (ii) reduced number of elements on screen (less elements for senior user and children), organized in a clear structure, promoting a sense of simplicity, associated with a rational/formal attitude (suggests trustworthy) (Blake, 2013); (iii) non-serif typography (suggests clarity, trustworthy) mainly vertical (elegance; for the senior user, semi-bold or bold options considered); (iv) iconic representation use in buttons, easier to identify and understand (minimal and slick shapes for adults; rounded forms for children).

One of the major aspects that contribute to the functionality and aesthetic value is typography. Type legibility and readability, related to light and color contrast are essential to a functional (Bringhurst, 1997) as well as aesthetic UI design, adequate to the visitor segment. Sans-serif fonts promote legibility and readability particularly in small screens (Cooper et al, 2014). Moreover, letter size, weight, line length, leading, number of lines per column are adjusted to visitor type (for seniors and children size is bigger, weight is heavier, contrast is more intense and consequently fewer words per line of text).

When in museum exhibition space and piece identification mode, the UI gives visual continuity of the user's physical surroundings, framing it and enhancing it with AR information presented with a transparent background (applying flow and transparency concepts): when the user points to each major piece, hotspots are visualized on screen; they give access to tagged detailed piece related information in different media (text about author, piece, context; images, audio and video related information; suggested pieces and map location, among other; contents adjusted to visitor type) and to gaming options (quizzes and activities are piece related and adjusted to each visitor type).

Besides the graphic aspects, the APP UI also gives access to piece related audio information, tagged to major pieces. This promotes the emotional experience creating emotional ambiences with high emotional expressivity (Douek, 2013) during the museum visit. The sounds connected to each piece also explore the aspect of spatialization of sound (Begault, 2000), allowing the user to relate spatially to the piece by feeling closer or farther to a particular sound, while being closer or farther to the piece it related to. In big pieces, different parts of the piece would have different sounds, and they would mix into a sound ambience, which would gradually change depending on visitor's position.

Adaptive Card Implementation

In general, a mobile APP has several *views,* many with equal structure and layouts only changing the displayed contents. On the other hand, in a fully adaptive APP there could appear a *view* with a different structure and different contents for each user, leading to an AUI. Regardless of whether or not it is a fully AUI, the layout and structure of a *view* can be used in several "views", e.g., when looking at the products details in a shopping APP, the structure of the *views* are identical only changing the contents to match the product descriptions. Moreover, different users can be grouped such that each group uses the same layout, the same structure, and the same contents.

Given these, if each *view* is built from scratch then there will be repeated information in the application regarding the *view's* structure. Besides, building a *view* from scratch each time it is needed would be extremely inefficient in terms of CPU usage. If a structure of a *view* is to be used in different moments of the execution, why not keep it in memory and simply access it and change the contents according to the *view*'s requirements (creating a modular structure)? Keeping this in mind, the adaptive cards were split into: (i) structure and (ii) contents. The application will create the structure of a *view* and keep it in memory, where it will be used as a *template*. When the display of a *view* is requested, the APP will access this *template* and place the *view*'s contents.

To assemble the (i) cards' structure, a *Template Engine* was designed based on a tree data structure, where each tree's node can be classified as a *content format*, a *cell*, or a *template*. The basic node is the *content format*, forming *cells* when grouped with others. In turn, *cells* can be grouped again into a different *cell* or into a *template*. Therefore, every structure is made up of one or more *cells* and zero or more *templates*. Simpler *templates* can be made and then used/grouped in more complex *templates*, making the engine more efficient. Figure 1 bottom shows a wireframe of a menu *view,* and in the top the wireframe of a *template*; see also (Rodrigues et al., 2017).

Let us further explore these concepts by addressing the example in Figure 1, showing the structure and layout for a *menu template*. The image shows a wireframe of a *view,* where every dashed box represents a node and the number in the top right corner its identifier. As seen, a tree data structure was chosen to store the *view*'s layout since it easily represents our "parent – child" relationship between the (a) *content formats*, (b) *cells*, and (c) *templates*, which are the tree's nodes, as explained next. The *content format* (a) is the most basic node structure and configures the format of the content which can be a text, an image, a button, amongst others. Each content type has its own properties. The example shows four content types: a *button* in node 2, an *image* in node 3, a *spacer* in node 5 and a *text content format* in node 4. Concerning this last one, its properties include the font that should be used for the text (e.g., Arial, Times New Roman, etc.), the text color, the font size, etc. Also note that the *button's content format* contains only the "clicked" behavior (e.g., opening a new *view*) and needs a child to present the user with visual information. This child node can be of any of the mentioned categories.

The *cell* (b), expressed as a (blue) dashed box in node 1, is a node whose sole purpose is to organize its children nodes into a single line that can be oriented horizontally or vertically. A *cell* child can be of any of the three mentioned categories. A *cell* does not relay any new information to the user, being instead used to arrange nodes. In our example, Figure 1 top row, there is a single cell (node 1), that orders nodes 2, 4 and 5 into their respective positions. As a final consideration, node 5 is a *content format,* more specifically a *spacer,* and it can be seen as an invisible image used to give the proper spacing to the *cell* components. Common in both *content formats* and in *cells* are the dimension properties that establishes the size and responsiveness behavior for each node.

A *template* (c) node is a particular node that represents another preexisting template, e.g., it can represent the template menu described above. Often, different structures have common parts between them, making the *template* nodes especially helpful in these situations. This is another point where the template engine can decrease the system resource usage. Instead of creating that common part every single time, it is only created once and its contents changed (here contents represent the actual contents, like the "go back" image in node 3 and the "MUSEUM NAME" text in node 4).

In a tree data structure, there are two terms that must be highlighted: the *root* is the origin node from which all the other nodes must have some sort of relationship; and the *leaf* (or terminal) nodes which are the nodes that have no children (SmartClasses, 2016). When constructing the tree structure of a view two rules can be defined. Firstly, a *leaf* node cannot be a *cell*. As stated above, a *cell*'s goal "is to organize its children nodes". If a *cell* is placed at a *leaf* node then it does not have any child, presenting unnecessary data that needs to be transmitted and treated. Secondly, the root node cannot be a *content format* because a tree structure should represent an organized and well-defined structure of a set of contents. In addition, the root node cannot be a *template* node, if it were then it would be a copy of the referenced template. Therefore, the *root* node can only be a *cell* node. Again, this makes sense, since the sole purpose of a *cell* is to layout its children nodes in an organized manner.

The *Template Engine* uses a depth-first approach when building the templates. In this approach, the engine performs in a recursive manner, starting at the root node and doing the following steps: (1) create the node and define its attributes; (2) for each child process node (executing step 1); and (3) state the parent-child relationships between the nodes.

As mentioned, Figure 1 bottom left shows a template of a *view* that exhibits a *museum information sheet*. In this example, the engine starts in the *root* node by defining that it is a *cell* which is divided vertically. It then goes to the first child (node 6) which, in this case, is the menu *template* detailed in Figure 1 top row (the children are represented by the dashed line). Since this node is a *template,* the engine requests it from memory if it is already instantiated. Assuming it is not, then it proceeds to assemble the menu template. To assemble the menu *template*, the engine starts by creating a horizontal *cell* (a *cell* that is divided horizontally) and defining its size. Next, it goes to the first child, the *button's content format* at node 2 and sets its action (to return to the previous view). Then it creates the *image's content format* (node 3), which comprises the aspect ratio and crop function. After that, it establishes that node 3 is a child of node 2 and node 2 a child of node 1. This finishes the work on the first child of node 1. Afterwards, the engine moves to the second child (node 4), generates the *text's content format*, assigns the correct font formatting and parents it to node 1. Next, node 4 is processed, it is a *spacer* which only contains the dimensions that it should occupy. As expected, the node 4 is set as a child of node 1. This menu template can now be used at any time by any other template that requires it. Following this, the engine now sets this entire (menu) template as a child of the root element for the *museum information sheet* and moves on to the second child (node 7).

The engine work from here on is very similar. Node 7 is a simple *image content format*, node 8 is a *text content format*, node 9 is a *button* that contains a *text* (node 10). The next two nodes (nodes 11 and 12) are a *title* and a *description template*. This template is composed of a vertical *cell* (not indicated in the image) that includes a couple of *text content format,* where the first (node 20) has bold font weight (that can be used as a title), and the second (node 21) has a regular weight (for the body of the text).

Concerning that the *Contents Assembly* (ii) of a *view* should adapt to the different users and different languages, the authors decided to divide the contents in 3 distinct categories: (a) *static contents*, contents that are independent of both the user and the language (e.g., icons); (b) *localized contents*, that are only based on the language (e.g., the "loading" fixed text); (c) *fully adaptive*, contents that change according to the user type (child, expert, …) and the language.

Figure 1. Template for a menu (top) and a museum information sheet (bottom)

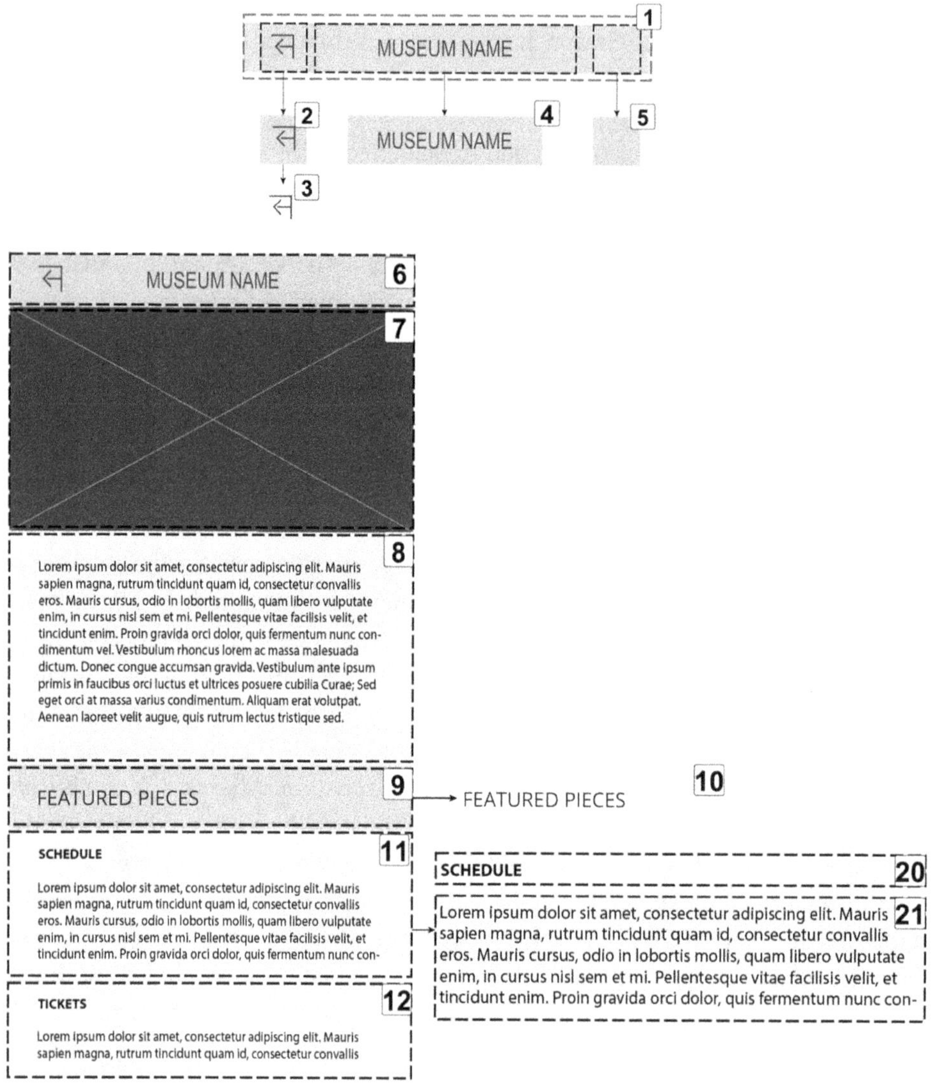

To get the contents for a *view*, the application accesses a database (see next section) which returns the required contents. If contents for two or more *views* are requested, then it is likely that there will be some duplicated information. For example, in Figure 2 both *views* have in common (besides others) a "menu" icon (the three horizontal bars in the top left corner) and a "featured pieces" text. Thus, with memory and CPU optimization in mind, an algorithm was developed to avoid downloading duplicate contents from the server, preserving also network bandwidth. The algorithm produces two separate lists: (a) the contents themselves and (b) a lookup table (LUT) to identify which content belongs to which node in the template (recall that every template is constructed from a tree of nodes).

Figure 2. Two views using the information sheet template shown before

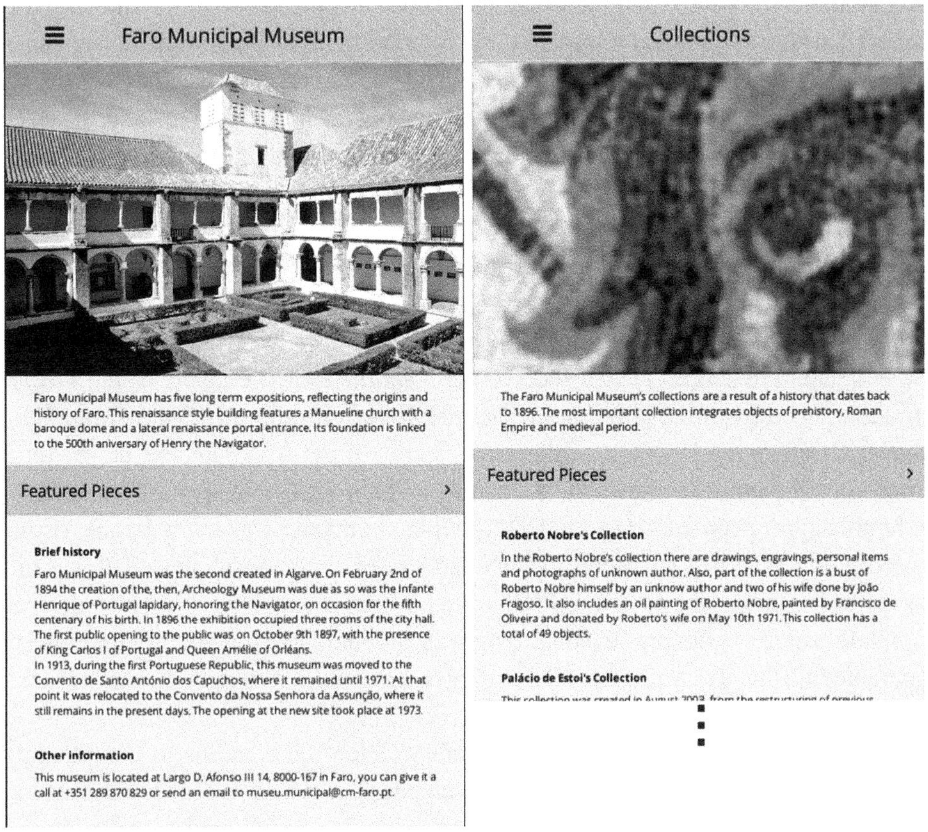

In an application where everything is built from scratch, the structure (template) and contents of a view are closely linked together. With the authors' approach, the contents are not directly coupled to their respective structure but are instead saved in separate tables and linked to their correct location through the lookup table.

Adaptive Card Database

The database (DB) plays a fundamental role in the system, by storing the contents and the harvested user's information. The later information is employed to meet the desired specifications of the user's card-layouts (structure/template) and card-contents. The card-layout implementation in the DB follows the same tree architecture that was presented before and it is subdivided in three major layers: (a) components, (b) formats, and (c) structure.

Basic properties like colors, fonts, outlines, backgrounds, and shadows are defined in the components layer (a). The type of content used in child nodes is indicated by the formats layer (b), through previously created sets of component properties, whether it is a text, an image or a button. Specific properties can also be overridden here if necessary. Finally, the parent-child relationships of the tree architecture are defined in the structure layer (c), node by node, where each node has a unique identifier. Orientation, spacing and other layout and cell information, are also stored here. All these specifications can be aggregated to form templates, so they may be reused when designing a new view, simplifying the process. Regarding the contents for a *view*, they are saved separately from the structure and stored in two lists: (a) the contents (themselves) list and a lookup table to bond them to the template. (b) The content categories, defined by the authors (static contents, localized contents and fully adaptive), are each kept on separate tables, one per category. Concerning the linkage between the contents and the structure, there is a lookup table for each view that associates every node of the used template to an entry in one of the contents table.

Before the App can request a specific *view*, it first needs the template structure and its contents, retrieved in a JSON document format. To support the retrieval of the JSON documents, three individual scripts are running on the server side: (1) the structure JSON generation script, (2) the structure JSON retrieval script, and (3) the content JSON retrieval script. When a new structure template is created, the structure JSON generation script (1) will receive the *template* index, connect to the DB and navigate from table to table, node by node, building up the tree architecture in a JSON format. The script then stores the converted file in the DB with a timestamp, so that if the App detects a newer version for that template, it can simply request the new JSON document. This script runs prior to the App's execution, when a new template has been added to the DB, or when an update was made to an existing template. After the structure template is converted to JSON and stored, it can be requested at any time. For this purpose, the server is running the structure JSON retrieval script (2). This script also determines if that particular template requires other pre-existing templates and includes them in the final assembled JSON to be sent, guaranteeing that every property needed by that template is included, in an organized fashion, inside a single file.

After building the templates, the application needs to fetch the contents to complete the view. To this end, a content JSON retrieval script (3) was developed that returns a (i) set of contents and an (ii) association list. The authors decided to keep this separation to avoid having to process duplicate contents on the mobile device. For each view, the script generates both lists (the set of contents (i) and the association list (ii)) joining the LUT (what contents the view needs) with the contents tables (the contents themselves) resulting in a set of contents (i). The association list (ii) is a list of contents indexes, from list (i), sorted by appearance order of that content in the template. Finally, after carrying out this process on all views, all the resulting lists are merged together, removing duplicate entries on the contents set (i) and updating the association list (ii) to match the final result set. It is important to stress, that this script approach was selected because Unity does not contain an appropriate multi-platform method for accessing a database. This way the application communicates directly with the server, through the retrieval scripts, downloading the necessary information via JSON formats.

Augmented Reality Implementation

In the present application, there is at least one card *view* for each object (paintings, statues, …) in the museum, which appears in the mobile screen when the object is present, i.e., if the object is on the field-of-view of the camera. In this section, the authors focus is on object detection, recognition and tracking, to trigger the card *view* of the object and/or the AR-card associated with the object. It is important to stress that two groups of cards can appear: the ones that occupy the complete screen of the mobile device, and the AR-cards that floats in the mobile screen at the same time we see the scene/object (usually non-overlaying the object).

From the various solutions to use AR (see the Background section), the one chosen for this APP was the usually denominated as "marker-based", which in a simplified way are digital pictures of the original object that work as *templates* – markers. In the present work, objects are photographed in Full HD and stored in the system's database. Resorting to Computer Vision algorithms, the frames captured by the mobile camera and markers are compared. When an object is recognized, the corresponding identifier is triggered and the object's position on the mobile screen is returned. Here, the focus is on a solution with three goals: (a) decrease the time required to download the markers onto the mobile device, (b) perform the marker recognition process in the mobile device, instead of using a server, and (c) try to be as less consuming as possible in terms of power and memory when performing the recognition. To achieve these goals, two options were considered: (A) an implementation developed by the authors, and (B) an already existing multi-platform open source library - ARToolKit (Artoolkit, 2016). The last, is still in active development and with an active community, providing a Unity package.

The authors' marker recognition (object recognition) implementation requires a reliable and fast descriptor since it is projected to run on a mobile device. For that reason, the authors' implementation (A) uses the ORB descriptor (Rublee et al., 2011) for object recognition, as it is a good alternative to other more known descriptors, such as BRIEF, SIFT or SURF (Figat et al., 2014). Although the detailed explanation of the algorithm is available in (Rodrigues et al., 2017), a brief explanation is presented here. It is important to stress that this algorithm is still in development, changes can occur in the near future.

A *Patch* is defined as a parcel of the initial image, of size $N \times M$ pixels (px); e.g. each single square in Figure 3 top, 2nd column. The algorithm works in the following way (system's server side): (i) On the *template* image. (i.1) Compute the ORB descriptor; (i.2) Separate the *template* image in patches, and obtain patches containing keypoints and corresponding descriptors (Rublee et al., 2011); (i.3) Order patches by keypoint/descriptor relevance, and select the K most meaningful extracted patches - those are to be used as *marker patches* ($K \leq 5$; ordered based on the number of keypoints for each patch); (i.4) repeat steps (i.1) to (i.3), using the *template* image resized to 1/2 and to a 1/4 of the original size (resulting in 3 scales; this allows farther and shorter validation distances when targeting the mobile camera onto an object). (i.5) Assemble and order the patches from all different scales, totalizing the number of marker patches per template, r.

(ii) When performing object recognition and tracking (system's client/mobile side): (ii.1) Apply the ORB descriptor to each frame acquired from the mobile camera (Figure 3 top, 3rd column); (ii.2) Choose the *most relevant marker patch* from the 3 scales grouping to test the frame (see step i.5); (ii.3) Select the best classified image template; (ii.4) Using every patch from the correspondent template test the object recognition performing "template-frame" matching; (ii.5) If ratio validation threshold is met then the object is recognized (Figure 3 top, 4th column); (ii.6) Flag if an object is found. Beyond this point the object is only tracked (no recognition tests are performed). (ii.7) Perform object tracking based only on a valid marker patch from the selected *template* (a match between the frame and a single valid marker patch occurs, these steps will continue being performed until the object disappears from the field-of-view of the camera for more than 1 second); (ii.8) If tracking time threshold is reached the recognition process restarts (steps ii.1 to ii.6).

On the other hand, as of May 2016, (B) ARToolKit (2016) started using FREAK as a descriptor for object recognition (Alahi, Ortiz, & Vandergheynst, 2012), and the SURF operator for object tracking (Figat et al., 2014). To create an image recognition application, ARToolKit uses two separate procedures. First, the images (marker templates) must be processed and the FREAK keypoints extracted (it is important to stress that at the time this chapter was written, there are some inconsistencies in ARtoolKit

Figure 3. Top, authors object recognition: left to right: marker template (low res.), original image divided in patches, 3 most relevant patches from the full-size image, the 1/2 and from 1/4 size image, and object matched. Bottom, ARToolKit object detection. Left to right, FREAK descriptor in 2 scales (half and full), and object recognition (all images presented were resized)

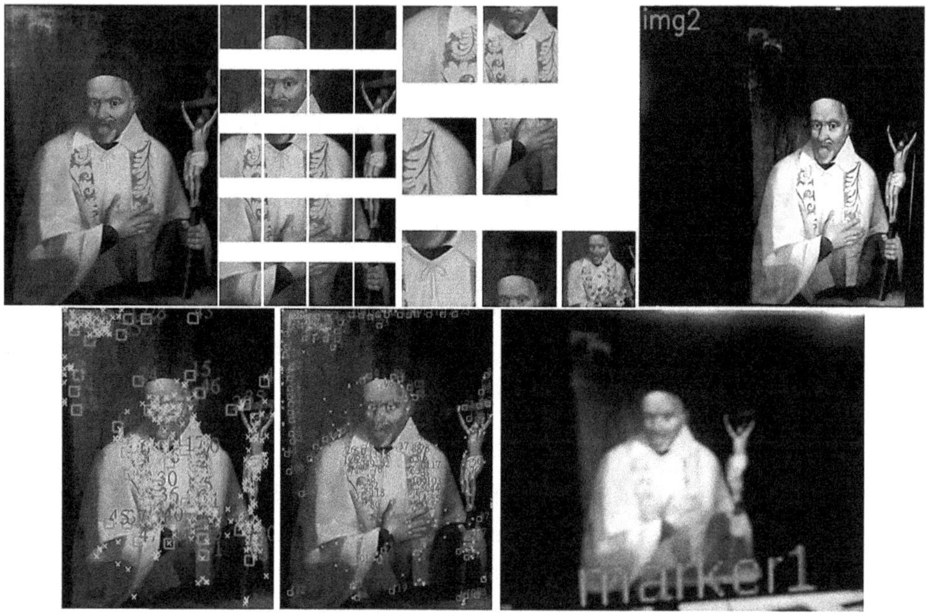

information about which descriptor is used for each procedure). This is an automated process done by a desktop application. For each image scale, it extracts two sets of features, one for tracking and another for recognition. The number of keypoints calculated depends on the image size (in a test image, it calculates around 3.000), however the keypoints kept varies according to the extraction level selected which ranges from a level 0 (in the same image, saved 13 keypoints) to a level 4 (saved 2.754 keypoints). ARToolKit requires that at least 4 keypoints are visible at all time to allow for six degrees of freedom (6DoF), i.e., to allow the marker projection to be invariant to rotations, translations and scale operations. The number of scales results from the dpi (dots per inch) range selected. The ARToolKit feature set generation script defines the number of scales as a result from the difference between the minimum and maximum dpi selected, multiplied by a constant. For example, when reducing the original image from 72 dpi (with 1000×2000 px) to 36 dpi, the resolution will be 1/2 (500×1000 px). In the mentioned example, choosing a minimum dpi value of 36 and a maximum of 72, the generation program returns four different scales (72, 57, 45 and 36). The extracted data is saved into a file and imported to the application. In turn, the application loads the markers onto memory and starts the recognition procedure.

In the present state of development and experimenting, two tests were considered: (a) object recognition at different distances, from 1 to 5 m (meters), and the (b) time necessary to load the templates into mobile memory, to recognize and track the objects. In both approaches (authors and ARToolKit) the tests were performed with the same datasets.

In the first case (a), an extra 1/3 of distractors (templates that should not be detected) were added. Both approaches identified correctly almost all targeted objects at 1m distance with good illumination, substantially decreasing the recognition rate at 5m distance. Another set of tests were also done with different lighting on the objects, so the authors could understand the effects of artificial and natural light exposure. As expected, these results were much worse than the previous. Images still would be detectable up to 1 meter for both solutions, while for farther distances, up to 5 meters, they would either not be detectable or very unstable. In this test, no substantial difference was found between the authors and ARToolKit approaches. The second case (b) tested the load time to memory for 5, 10, 20 and 50 templates and their respective times to recognize and track the objects. Each object-template recognition and tracking was averaged with 50 samples. Regarding the loading of the templates to memory, the authors approach was in average 2 to 4 times faster than ARToolKit. For recognition, it was not possible to obtain the times for ARToolKit. Last but not least, ARToolKit tracking was 20 times faster than the authors' approach (ARToolKit did not work with 50 templates), nevertheless both approaches work in real time (see also section Future Research Direction).

In conclusion, the authors approach shows promising results when compared to ARToolKit, since it can do the recognition and tracking in real time, and is still faster than ARToolKit when loading templates to memory, howbeit this last factor still needs great improvements.

Augmented Reality Device Implementation

The second visible component of the system is the augmented reality device (HDevice), which extends the users' experiences to the five senses. The first challenge was to integrate the visitors' smart devices (tablets/phablets/smartphones) in a compact new device that allows the user to have these five sense experiences. Hence, the device must be portable but flexible enough to adapt itself to the different sizes of the user's smart device. Moreover, the second challenge was to integrate, in a portable and small device, all the hardware needed to allow the five senses experiences. Figure 4 top row shows a sketch of the proposed portable device. The system will consist of two similar hardware parts, placed on each side of the user's device where the mobile application is running, connected in the bottom through adjustable supports.

The device is powered with a rechargeable battery, which gives the module the ability to keep the system running during the museum visiting (the minimum time requirement considered is a couple of hours). As depicted in Figure 4 bottom row, a microcontroller is the core unit of the device. The microcontroller receives instructions from the mobile application and acts accordingly, controlling the remaining hardware of the portable device to grant the five-sense experience to the user. The communication between the device and the mobile application is possible through a wireless connection, using a Bluetooth interface. The communication with the remaining modules, denoted here as physical interfaces, will be wired. These physical interfaces are responsible for creating the stimuli that reproduce three senses: touch, taste, and smell. The remaining senses, sight and hearing (but also touch, although only vibrations), are reproduced in the user's mobile device.

Three techniques are being used for the touch sense: hot/cold touch, vibration and wind. The heat and cold is generated using thermoelectric modules, such as Peltier modules, able to reproduce a certain temperature range, safe for the user, yet still sufficiently noticeable to convey the intended sensation. The heat/cold will be conducted through the metallic handles of the HDevice, thus transmitting the heat/cold sensation to user's hands. The vibration is obtained with two vibration motors, one on each side of the device. This is the same common solution used in every smartphone device, to vibrate during a call, and used in the haptic feedback in gaming. By having two independent motors, it also enables the use on transmitting directions (left, right) to the user and help to navigate in the museum. The wind sensa-

Figure 4. Top, a schematic of the portable device – Hdevice; bottom, block diagram of basic functionalities of the HDevice

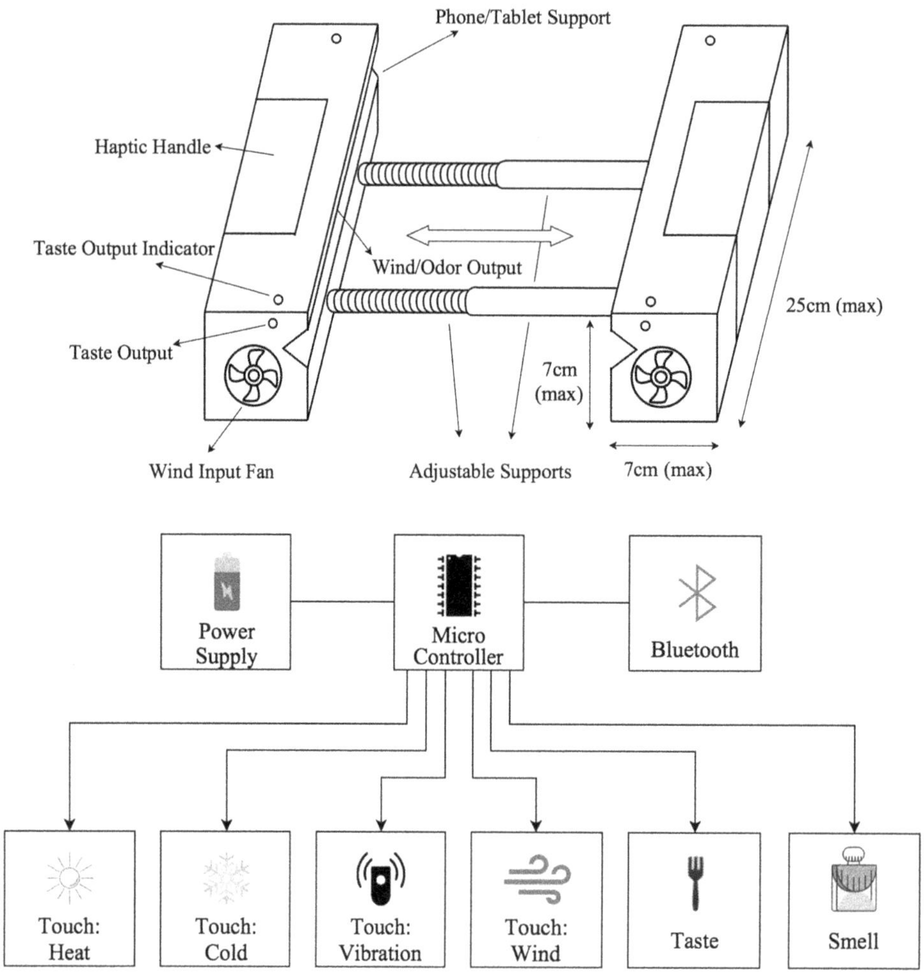

tion is obtained using a ventilation system with four fans, two in each side of the device. As proposed in (Matsukura et al., 2013), the cooperative work of these four fans can cause a sense of wind or a breeze directed to the user's face and, by varying the speed of each one individually, can generate airflow in different directions to the user.

Regarding the taste sense, the solution was to incorporate an electronic vaporizer to give the user the sensation of savoring some food and tasting different flavors. The device is being developed with four electronic vaporizers, two on each side of the HDevice, thus providing four different flavors. In order to guarantee the hygiene of the system, each visitor should receive with the HDevice a disposable tube, that will serve to connect to the outlet of the flavor and at the other end will have a nozzle to savor flavors. For the smell sensation, the first prototype of the device reuses the electronic vaporizer and available fans to help spread the fragrances in the air. This is not a unique solution, as other possibilities were also considered: air circulation per flavored container, fragrance spraying, pressurized spray, and ultrasonic atomization. However, it is important to keep the device with small dimensions, and this option provides a fair smell sensation with a small area and power overhead.

The first prototype of the HDevice is in developing/testing and further details and results will be published in the future (for more details see the M5SAR's website).

FUTURE RESEARCH DIRECTIONS

This chapter presented an initial version of the framework for a mobile prototype that can extent AR to the five senses. This is now an emerging subject, see e.g. AxonAR (2016), and a large amount of systems/solutions are expected to appear in the future. Developing solutions for the touch sense are expected to be easier than other, like the smell. Likewise, extending the AR to the taste will be for certain a huge challenge, even more if the intention is to create mobile devices that can simultaneously augment all five senses.

Different, but also very challenging subject is the full adaptive ("intelligent") UI. This subject has been researched for a few years. Nevertheless, as far as the authors know, still there is not any real adaptive APP in the market. As mentioned in the Introduction section, to harvest the necessary information about each user's preferences and skills is difficult, but with recent Big Data methodologies this starts to be realizable. Then, there is the question on how to give "intelligence" to the UI in order for it to adapt on-the-fly to the user's changes, i.e., how to develop an APP that can "satisfy" the user (Zhao et al., 2012). A final question is how to develop the adaptive UI. Although we present an initial framework to create this adaptive UI others exist, e.g. (Gajos et al., 2008). Finally, the communication between the server and the mobile, in terms of UI card building and AR templates, are being adapted from JSON to FlatBuffers (FlatBuffers, 2017). Initial tests show that this change drastically reduces times related to the marker, UI preparation.

A future emerging trend will be for sure the extension of Augmented Reality to the five senses, and the challenge of creating mobile AR five senses devices that can be applied between other areas to the "Cultural Heritage and eTourism Applications".

CONCLUSION

This chapter presented an initial framework for the development of an architecture capable of producing an adaptive UI (for a museum). The focus was on the creation process of a card-based UI, where the development of the cards has a modular architecture. In addition, a patch-based marker architecture for mobile object recognition with application to AR was also discussed. Finally, it was also presented an initial architecture for a device (HDevice) that can be connected to the user's mobile device to extent the AR to the five senses.

Despite all the modules of the system being yet in an initial stage of development, both AUI and AR marker present satisfactory results. A first prototype of HDevice is now being tested. All the modules of the system were being integrated as the chapter was written. It is important to stress, that more detailed figures and information cannot be shown in the present, once this system is being developed with a commercial company.

For future developments, the authors will focus on how to harvest the necessary information about each user preferences and skills and, from the acquired information/data, how to give "intelligence" to the UI to adapt on-the-fly to the user's changes. In the case of the mobile object recognition system, it is intended to increase the number of real time recognition of different objects on-the-fly, without any necessary connection to a server. Finally, the integration of all elements of the prototype to start real test scenarios in a museum with real persons and apply the UTAUT2 model to validate the technology will be carried out.

ACKNOWLEDGMENT

This work was supported by the Portuguese Foundation for Science and Technology (FCT), project LARSyS (UID/EEA/50009/2013), CEFAGE (PEst-C/EGE/UI4007/2013), CIAC, CIAUD and project M5SAR I&DT nr. 3322 financed by CRESC ALGARVE2020, PORTUGAL2020 and FEDER. We also thank Faro Municipal Museum and the project leader SPIC - Creative Solutions (www.spic.pt).

REFERENCES

Adobe. (2016). *XD Essentials: Card-based user interfaces*. Retrieved: Nov. 16, 2016 from https://goo.gl/gg8qUM

Akiki, P. A., Bandara, A. K., & Yu, Y. (2014). Adaptive model-driven user interface development systems. *ACM Computing Surveys*, *47*(1), 9. doi:10.1145/2597999

Alahi, A., Ortiz, R., & Vandergheynst, P. (2012). *Freak: Fast retina keypoint*. In *IEEE Conference on Computer Vision and Pattern Recognition*, 212 (pp. 510-517). IEEE.

Alvarez-Cortes, V., Zayas, B. E., Uresti, J. A. R., & Zarate, V. H. (2009). *Current Challenges and Applications for Adaptive User Interfaces*. INTECH Open Access Publisher. doi:10.5772/7745

Artoolkit. (2016). *ARtoolKit, The world's most widely used tracking library for augmented reality*. Retrieved: Nov. 16, 2016 from http://artoolkit.org/

Axon, V. R. (2016). *AxonVR*. Retrieved: Dec. 6, 2016 from http://axonvr.com

Azuma, R., Baillot, Y., Behringer, R., Feiner, S., Julier, S., & MacIntyre, B. (2001). Recent advances in augmented reality. *IEEE Computer Graphics and Applications*, *21*(6), 34–47. doi:10.1109/38.963459

Babich, N. (2016). *Designing Card-Based User Interfaces, Smashing Magazine*. Retrieved: Nov. 16, 2016 from https://goo.gl/AM46gT

Balance. (2016). *The balance: Fine Art Museum Apps for Smart Phones*. Retrieved: Nov. 16, 2016 from https://goo.gl/WEsQRN

Begault, D. R. (2000). *3-D sound for Virtual reality and Multimedia*. NASA Center for AeroSpace Information. NASA/TM – 2000-209606.

Blake, J. (2013). *Natural user interface in. Net.* Greenwich, CT: Manning.

Boehner, K., DePaula, R., Dourish, P., & Sengers, P. (2007). How emotion is made and measured. *International Journal of Human-Computer Studies*, *65*(4), 275–291. doi:10.1016/j.ijhcs.2006.11.016

Brewster, S., Chohan, F., & Brown, L. (2007). Tactile feedback for mobile interactions. In *Proceedings of the SIGCHI conference on Human factors in computing systems* (pp. 159-162). San Jose, CA: ACM. doi:10.1145/1240624.1240649

Bringhurst, R. (1997). *The Elements of Typographic Style*. Hartley & Marks.

Catchoom. (2016). Retrieved: Nov. 16, 2016 from http://catchoom.com/

CEUD. (2016). Retrieved: Nov. 16, 2016 from http://goo.gl/fUHPj6

Cheng, K. H., & Tsai, C. C. (2013). Affordances of augmented reality in science learning: Suggestions for future research. *Journal of Science Education and Technology*, *22*(4), 449–462. doi:10.1007/s10956-012-9405-9

Conati, C., Carenini, G., Toker, D., & Lallé, S. (2015). *Towards User-Adaptive Information Visualization*. AAAI.

Cooper, A., Reimann, R., Cronin, D., & Noessel, C. (2014). *About the face: The essentials of interaction design*. Indianapolis: Wiley.

Douek, J. (2013). Music and emotion: A composers perspective. *Frontiers in Systems Neuroscience*, *7*, 82. doi:10.3389/fnsys.2013.00082 PMID:24348344

Estimote. (2016). *Estimote: Create magical experiences in the physical world*. Retrieved: Nov. 16, 2016 from http://estimote.com/

EWB. (2016). *Europe Without Barriers*. Retrieved: Nov. 16, 2016 from http://goo.gl/sqlJrE

Falk, J. H., & Dierking, L. D. (2013). *The Museum Experience Revisited*. Walnut Creek: Left Coast Press.

FeelReal. (2016). Retrieved: Dec. 6, 2016 from http://feelreal.com/

Figat, J., Kornuta, T., & Kasprzak, W. (2014). Performance evaluation of binary descriptors of local features. In *Proceedings International Conference on Computer Vision and Graphics* (pp. 187-194). Springer International Publishing. doi:10.1007/978-3-319-11331-9_23

FlatBuffers. (2017). Retrieved: Jan. 6, 2017 from https://google.github.io/flatbuffers/

Gajos, K., & Weld, D. S. (2004). SUPPLE: automatically generating user interfaces. In *Proceedings of the 9th international conference on Intelligent user interfaces* (pp. 93-100). ACM.

Gajos, K. Z., Wobbrock, J. O., & Weld, D. S. (2008). Improving the performance of motor-impaired users with automatically-generated, ability-based interfaces. In *Proceedings of the SIGCHI conference on Human Factors in Computing Systems* (pp. 1257-1266). ACM. doi:10.1145/1357054.1357250

Gnome. (2016). *User Interface Guidelines for Supporting Accessibility*. Retrieved: Nov. 16, 2016 from https://goo.gl/xGAH6f

HMS. (2016). *Srbija 1914 / Augmented Reality Exhibition at Historical Museum of Serbia, Belgrade*. Retrieved: Nov. 16, 2016 from https://vimeo.com/126699550

InformationWeek. (2016). *InformationWeek:10 Fantastic iPhone, Android Apps For Museum Visits*. Retrieved: Nov. 16, 2016 from https://goo.gl/rYnhm2

Jung, T., Chung, N., & Leue, M. C. (2015). The determinants of recommendations to use augmented reality technologies: The case of a Korean theme park. *Tourism Management*, *49*, 75–86. doi:10.1016/j.tourman.2015.02.013

Karaman, S., Bagdanov, A. D., Landucci, L., DAmico, G., Ferracani, A., Pezzatini, D., & Del Bimbo, A. (2016). Personalized multimedia content delivery on an interactive table by passive observation of museum visitors. *Multimedia Tools and Applications*, *75*(7), 3787–3811. doi:10.1007/s11042-014-2192-y

Kovács, P. T., Rozinaj, G., Murray, N., Sulema, Y., & Rybárová, R. (2015). *Application of immersive technologies for education: state of the art*. Paper presented at the 2015 International Conference on Interactive Mobile Communication Technologies and Learning (IMCL), Thessaloniki, Greece. doi:10.1109/IMCTL.2015.7359604

Kralisch, A., Eisend, M., & Berendt, B. (2005). Impact of culture on website navigation behaviour. *Proceeding of the 11th International Conference on Human-Computer Interaction*.

Kudan. (2016). *Kudan Computer Vision*. Retrieved: Nov. 16, 2016 from https://www.kudan.eu/

Kurogi, T., Nakayama, M., Sato, K., Kamuro, S., Fernando, C. L., Furukawa, M., . . . Tachi, S. (2013). Haptic transmission system to recognize differences in surface textures of objects for telexistence. In 2013 IEEE Virtual Reality (VR) (pp. 137-138). IEEE. doi:10.1109/VR.2013.6549400

Layar. (2016). Retrieved: Nov. 16, 2016 from https://www.layar.com/

Li, Y. (2000). Geographical consciousness and tourism experience. *Annals of Tourism Research*, *27*(4), 863–883. doi:10.1016/S0160-7383(99)00112-7

Lindgaard, G., Fernandes, G., Dudek, C., & Brown, J. (2006). Attention web designers: You have 50 milliseconds to make a good first impression! *Behaviour & Information Technology*, *25*(2), 115–126. doi:10.1080/01449290500330448

Marangunić, N., & Granić, A. (2015). Technology acceptance model: A literature review from 1986 to 2013. *Universal Access in the Information Society*, *14*(1), 81–95. doi:10.1007/s10209-014-0348-1

Matsukura, H., Yoneda, T., & Ishida, H. (2013). Smelling screen: Development and evaluation of an olfactory display system for presenting a virtual odor source. *IEEE Transactions on Visualization and Computer Graphics*, *19*(4), 606–615. doi:10.1109/TVCG.2013.40 PMID:23428445

Metallinou, A., Wollmer, M., Katsamanis, A., Eyben, F., Schuller, B., & Narayanan, S. (2012). Context-sensitive learning for enhanced audiovisual emotion classification. *IEEE Transactions on Affective Computing*, *3*(2), 184–198. doi:10.1109/T-AFFC.2011.40

Morency, L. P., Mihalcea, R., & Doshi, P. (2011). Towards multimodal sentiment analysis: Harvesting opinions from the web. In *Proceedings of the 13th International Conference on Multimodal Interfaces* (pp. 169-176). ACM. doi:10.1145/2070481.2070509

MWCM. (2016). *Multitouch wall Cleveland Museum*. Retrieved: Nov. 16, 2016 from https://goo.gl/kI2oCh

Narumi, T., Kajinami, T., Nishizaka, S., Tanikawa, T., & Hirose, M. (2011). Pseudo-gustatory display system based on cross-modal integration of vision, olfaction and gustation. In *Virtual Reality Conference (VR)*, 2011 *IEEE* (pp. 127-130). IEEE. doi:10.1109/VR.2011.5759450

Negruşa, A. L., Toader, V., Sofică, A., Tutunea, M. F., & Rus, R. V. (2015). Exploring gamification techniques and applications for sustainable tourism. *Sustainability*, *7*(8), 11160–11189. doi:10.3390/su70811160

Oh, H., Fiore, A. M., & Jeoung, M. (2007). Measuring experience economy concepts: Tourism applications. *Journal of Travel Research*, *46*(2), 119–132. doi:10.1177/0047287507304039

Pine, J., & Gilmore, J. (1999). *The experience economy*. Boston: Harvard Business School Press.

Qualcomm. (2016). *Invisible Museum*. Retrieved: Nov. 16, 2016 from https://goo.gl/aS0NKh

Ranasinghe, N., Cheok, A. D., Fernando, O. N. N., Nii, H., & Ponnampalam, G. (2011). Electronic taste stimulation. In *Proceedings of the 13th international conference on Ubiquitous computing* (pp. 561-562). ACM.

Ranasinghe, N., Nakatsu, R., Nii, H., & Gopalakrishnakone, P. (2012). Tongue mounted interface for digitally actuating the sense of taste. In *Wearable Computers (ISWC), 2012 16th International Symposium on* (pp. 80-87). IEEE. doi:10.1109/ISWC.2012.16

Reinecke, K., & Bernstein, A. (2013). Knowing What a User Likes: A Design Science Approach to Interfaces that Automatically Adapt to Culture. *Management Information Systems Quarterly*, *37*(2), 427–453.

Rodrigues, J. M. F., Lessa, J., Gregório, M., Ramos, C., & Cardoso, P. J. S. (2016). *An Initial Framework for a Museum Application for Senior Citizens. In Proceedings Software Development and Technologies for Enhancing Accessibility and Fighting Info-exclusion* (pp. 414–421). ACM. doi:10.1145/3019943.3020002

Rodrigues, J. M. F., Pereira, J. A. R., Sardo, J. D. P., Freitas, M. A. G., Cardoso, P. J. S., Gomes, M., & Bica, P. (2017) Adaptive Card Design UI Implementation for an Augmented Reality Museum Application. *11th Int. Conf. on Universal Access in Human-Computer Interaction, integrated in the 19th Int. Conf. on Human-Computer Interaction*.

Rublee, E., Rabaud, V., Konolige, K., & Bradski, G. (2011). ORB: An efficient alternative to SIFT or SURF. In *Proceedings of the International Conference on Computer Vision* (pp. 2564-2571). IEEE. doi:10.1109/ICCV.2011.6126544

Saffer, D. (2006). *Designing for Interaction: Creating Innovative Applications and Devices*. Berkley, CA: New Riders.

Schuller, B. W. (2015). Modelling User Affect and Sentiment in Intelligent User Interfaces: A Tutorial Overview. In *Proceedings of the 20th International Conference on Intelligent User Interfaces* (pp. 443-446). ACM. doi:10.1145/2678025.2716265

SM. (2016). *Science Museum - atmosphere gallery*. Retrieved: Nov. 16, 2016 from https://vimeo.com/20789653

SmartClasses. (2016). *Smart Classes: Data Structures*. Retrieved: Nov. 16, 2016 from http://btechsmartclass.com/DS/U3_T1.html

Sodhi, R., Poupyrev, I., Glisson, M., & Israr, A. (2013). AIREAL: Interactive tactile experiences in free air. *ACM Transactions on Graphics*, *32*(4), 134. doi:10.1145/2461912.2462007

Steichen, B., Conati, C., & Carenini, G. (2014). Inferring Visualization Task Properties, User Performance, and User Cognitive Abilities from Eye Gaze Data. *ACM Transactions on Interactive Intelligent Systems*, *4*(2), 11. doi:10.1145/2633043

TWSJ. (2016). *The Wall Street Journal: Best Apps for Visiting Museums*. Retrieved: Nov. 16, 2016 from https://goo.gl/cPTyP9

Unity. (2016). *Unity 3D*. Retrieved: Nov. 16, 2016 from https://unity3d.com/pt

Vainstein, N., Kuflik, T., & Lanir, J. (2016). Towards Using Mobile, Head-Worn Displays in Cultural Heritage: User Requirements and a Research Agenda. In *Proceedings of the 21st International Conference on Intelligent User Interfaces* (pp. 327-331). ACM. doi:10.1145/2856767.2856802

VAM. (2016). *Interactive IPAD Museum Catalog*. Retrieved: Nov. 16, 2016 from https://vimeo.com/31821923

Venkatesh, V., Morris, M. G., Davis, G. B., & Davis, F. D. (2003). User acceptance of information technology: Toward a unified view. *Management Information Systems Quarterly*, *25*(3), 425–478.

Venkatesh, V., Thong, J. Y., & Xu, X. (2012). Consumer acceptance and use of information technology: Extending the unified theory of acceptance and use of technology. *Management Information Systems Quarterly*, *36*(1), 157–178.

Vuforia. (2016). *Vuforia*. Retrieved: Nov. 16, 2016 from https://www.vuforia.com/

Wikitude. (2016). *Wikitude, see more*. Retrieved: Nov. 16, 2016 from http://www.wikitude.com/

Yamada, T., Yokoyama, S., Tanikawa, T., Hirota, K., & Hirose, M. (2006). Wearable olfactory display: Using odor in outdoor environment. In *IEEE Virtual Reality Conference (VR 2006)* (pp. 199-206). IEEE. doi:10.1109/VR.2006.147

Yanagida, Y. (2012). A survey of olfactory displays: Making and delivering scents. In Sensors, 2012 IEEE (pp. 1-4). IEEE.

Yuan, Z., Bi, T., Muntean, G. M., & Ghinea, G. (2015). Perceived synchronization of multisemedia services. *IEEE Transactions on Multimedia*, *17*(7), 957–966. doi:10.1109/TMM.2015.2431915

Zhao, L., Lu, Y., Zhang, L., & Chau, P. Y. (2012). Assessing the effects of service quality and justice on customer satisfaction and the continuance intention of mobile value-added services: An empirical test of a multidimensional model. *Decision Support Systems*, *52*(3), 645–656. doi:10.1016/j.dss.2011.10.022

KEY TERMS AND DEFINITIONS

Accessible Tourism: The set of services and facilities that can allow people with specific needs the enjoyment of the holiday and leisure without obstacles and difficulties.

Adaptive User Interfaces: A user interface that adapts to each user, i.e., changes its layout and contents according with the needs of each user.

Augmented Reality: A system that supplements the real world with virtual (computer-generated) objects that appear to coexist in the same space as the real world.

Computer Vision: An interdisciplinary field that deals with how computers can gain high-level understanding from digital images or videos.

Human-Computer Interaction: Researches the design and use of computer technology, focused on the interfaces between humans and computers. Researchers both observe the ways in which humans interact with computers and design technologies that let humans interact with computers in novel ways.

Interaction Design: The practice of designing interactive digital products, environments, systems, and service.

Multi-Sensorial Display: An output device that conveys information for multiple sensory systems.

Chapter 6
Applying an Augmented Reality Tool to the Camino de Santiago in Portugal

Miguel Nuno Pereira
Minho University, Portugal

Miguel Pazos Otón
University of Santiago de Compostela, Spain

José Cotos
University of Santiago de Compostela, Spain

Paula Cristina Remoaldo
Minho University, Portugal

ABSTRACT

This chapter focuses on an Interactive Guide of the Portuguese Way of St. James (Camino de Santiago) created by using an Augmented Reality application. This application was developed specifically for the section of the Portuguese Route to Santiago that crosses the municipality of Barcelos (Northwest of Portugal). The Guide has the geo-information needed for the Pilgrim, in the passage by the municipality of Barcelos to Santiago, and can be accessed through a smartphone. The pilgrim will have at his or her disposal a set of interactive geo-information about Barcelos. At the level of interactivity with the user, each of these points of interest in the Guide will be signaled by a portrait done by a painter from Barcelos (monuments) and universal graphic icons (other geo-information).

INTRODUCTION

In global world where speed and availability of information are increasingly important values, new technologies play a key role. This scenario is due to the significant growth in the number of inventions that have emerged throughout our most recent history, from the invention of the telephone, radio, tele-

DOI: 10.4018/978-1-5225-2927-9.ch006

vision to the Internet. Information must become a global asset of rapid spread and low cost of access. Geographic information is a particular case that is worth studying.

The new trends present a perfect integration between geographic information and virtual reality. In its turn, the usage of Virtual Reality in tourism is also currently increasing (Butler, 2016; Graham, 2016). Presently, the usage of geographic information tools that use Virtual Reality have become more common, more specifically one of its variations - the Augmented Reality (Milgram et al., 1994; Azuma, 1997; Ajanki et al., 2010; Charara, 2016).

Tourism and its value chain, as well as the territories themselves, undergo constant changes as a result of the technological advances, some of them being perceived in real time. According to recent data from the World Tourism Organization (UNWTO, 2014), approximately 60% of current tourists consult and decide their holiday destinations through the Internet, of which around 40% make their reservations via the Internet. These facts lead us to conclude that an important change in the habits of the tourists has happened. Increasingly, travel agencies (intermediaries in the tourism value chain) are losing importance, since the tourist directly book their flight through the reservation center of an airline and their accommodation through the reservation center of any hotel chain. Thus, we are in a new era, the one that Manuel Castells (2002) calls "informationalism", which in turn, originates to what he also calls a new form of capitalism, "informational capitalism."

However, in a postmodern and transforming society, where technology and distance communication prevails, the concept of travel has also undergone transformations. Therefore, the journey began to be made by many from the Internet, in real time, often transcending geographical boundaries, social distances and the very concept of physical travel (Dennis & Urry, 2009).

Based on these assumptions, we chose to develop a research between 2010 and 2014 focused on the following objectives: to explore the topic of Augmented Reality and its importance in territorial marketing, promotion, dissemination and access to tourism; and create a guide for mobile devices. The latter is an interactive guide with Augmented Reality, which supports the pilgrim during his or her visit to the municipality of Barcelos.

The intention was to relate the tools and new technologies accessible to individuals and institutions with the availability, sharing and usage of tourism information. Also demonstrate how to promote a territory, using new technologies in a simple and objective way, trying to attract new tourists and new investments, and contributing to improve the quality of the visit. It's a matter of integrating and making available to the citizen and institutions all the tourist information of a territory in an interactive and accessible way.

The selected territory corresponded to the municipality of Barcelos located in the Northwest of Continental Portugal. It's a territory linked to the Jacobean Pilgrimages, from the beginnings of the Middle Ages. The Legend of the Rooster is the ultimate exponent of this secular connection. The Portuguese Way of Santiago crosses the municipality of Barcelos in a direction of south to north, in an extension of 32 kilometers. It is estimated that about 17,500 pilgrims pass through Barcelos every year, and in Holy Years they can exceed 25,000 pilgrims (Barcelos Tourist Office, 2014).

In order to reach the objectives considered, after collecting the data and the field work carried out including meetings with all stakeholders and agents of the territory, a Geographic Information System applied to municipal tourism planning and management was created and also an interactive guide on The Portuguese Way of Santiago in Barcelos.

This application was the first author application made in Portugal about the Portuguese Way of Santiago in Barcelos. Worldwide it was the second to be implemented, since in 2010 Banco Bilbao Viscaya sponsored and published a guide of the French Way of Santiago, during the last Holy Year.

This chapter consists of five sections. In the first section, an approach to the Augmented Reality specific technology is carried out, linking the tourism to this technology, as well as the various areas of applicability. The second section highlights the importance of the Santiago Way in cultural / religious tourism and the approach that the official entities give to it in their instruments of national and regional tourism planning. After this analysis, we describe the process leading to the creation of the Interactive Guide of the Portuguese Way of Santiago in Barcelos, as well as its different modes of use and potentialities. After explaining the methodology used in section 3, a description of the Interactive Guide is given in section 4. The chapter concludes with the main conclusions and suggestions for future research.

THE POTENTIAL OF AUGMENTED REALITY IN TOURISM FIELD

What Is Augmented Reality?

Augmented Reality is a human-computer interaction technique that shows a real-world environment, adding virtuality (Yuen, Yaoyuneyong & Johnson, 2011), and is used in a variety of fields including industries, health care, education, entertainment and mobile applications (Krevelen & Poelman, 2010; Park et al., 2014).

It allows to complement the real world through the addition of virtual objects (created by the computer) that seem to coexist in the same space of the real world (Krevelen & Poelman, 2010). In this paper, we present a set of three-dimensional virtual objects that can be created in a virtual environment (Milgram et al., 1994).

For that, Augmented Reality Technologies help us enhance our perception and can help us experience in different ways how we see, hear and feel the environment (Krevelen & Poelman, 2010).

The first Augmented Reality technology was developed in 1968 at Harvard University and at University of Utah when researcher Ivan Sutherland (called the "father of computer graphics"), along with his students, created a head-mounted display system (Oakes, 2007; Krevelen & Poelman, 2010). In the following decades, university labs, companies and national agencies created advanced Augmented Reality systems for wearables and digital displays. The US Air Force's Armstrong Laboratory, the NASA Ames Research Center, and the University of North Carolina were the most important during the 1970's and 1980's (Krevelen & Poelman, 2010).

The first commercial application of Augmented Reality appeared in 2008 (Strauss, 2008). It was developed for advertising purposes by a German advertising agency in a printed magazine advertisement of a mini car model, which, when performed in front of a computer camera, projected the same virtually on the monitor. Since the virtual model was linked to specific markers in the ad, the user was able to control the three-dimensional model of the car on the screen and move it to view the different angles simply by manipulating the piece of paper. This application was one of the first campaigns that allowed the interaction with a digital model in real time (Javornik, 2016). However, the term Augmented Reality was only used, as of 1990, by Boeing researcher and now Professor of the University of New Mexico, Thomas Caudell (University of New México, 2016). The year 2007 was considered the year of the emergence of the usage of Augmented Reality (Krevelen & Poelman, 2010). In 2011, Yuen, Yaoyuneyong & Johnson (2011) predicted that Augmented Reality, by 2014, would be widespread in US college campuses and that education will be one of the most exciting fields of application of this technology. The application of Augmented Reality can be observed in several fields. Besides design, construction and maintenance, navigation (Gervautz & Schmalstieg, 2012) design and reconnaissance are also important fields of application (Krevelen & Poelman, 2010). In advertising and marketing the Companies began to seek new ways to engage and interest potential customers. Architecture and construction, entertainment, medical, military and travel are other important fields of application (Yuen, Yaoyuneyong & Johnson, 2011).

However, the concept of Augmented Reality has only been clarified with its insertion in a wider context: that of Mixed Reality.

The Mixed Reality combines the real with the virtual (environments totally simulated by technology - Yuen, Yaoyuneyong & Johnson, 2011), covering two possibilities: Augmented Reality, whose predominant environment is the real world, and Augmented Virtuality, whose predominant environment is the virtual world (Milgram et al., 1994). The Augmented Reality can be said to be a particularization of the Mixed Reality (Figure 1).

Therefore, we can conclude that the Augmented Reality can be defined as the insertion of virtual objects in the physical environment, shown to the user, in real time, with the support of some technological device, using the real environment interface, adapted to visualize and manipulate real and virtual objects (Kirner & Kirner, 2010).

At the level of existing projection types in Augmented Reality, we can divide them into four main groups: the direct optical vision system, the direct video vision system, the monitor based video vision system and the optical vision system by projection.

The direct optical vision system works through lenses, a helmet or other mobile device, in which it is possible to directly receive an actual image, at the same time as the virtual images are projected properly adjusted with the real scenario.

The monitor-based video vision system uses the webcam to capture the real scene. Subsequently, virtual elements generated by computer and presented to the user through the computer monitor are connected to the real scenario. The user's viewing point is fixed, always depending on the position of the webcam. Examples of applications that use this kind of augmented reality are the Augmented Reality QR codes.

The system of optical vision by projection uses the surfaces of the real environment, to project the virtual images. Here the user can directly visualize all the elements (real and virtual), without needing any equipment.

Figure 1. Virtuality scale

Source: Adapted from Milgram et al., 1994, from Krevelen & Poelman, 2010 and from Yuen, Yaoyuneyong & Johnson, 2011.

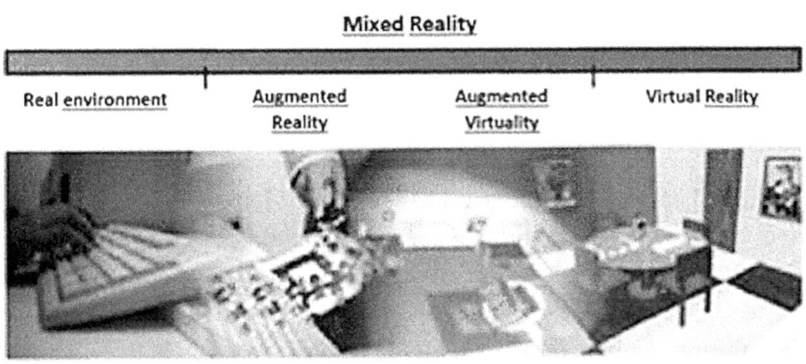

The Interactive Guide of the Portuguese Way of Santiago in Barcelos, which is presented in this chapter, uses the type of Augmented Reality called the direct video system based on a monitor. As we will see in section 4, the Guide will always need an auxiliary equipment, so that in real time we can see the mixture of the real environment with the virtual elements. Such auxiliary equipment may be a smartphone, a tablet, or Augmented Reality goggles.

The Application of Augmented Reality to Tourism Field

As mentioned in the previous item, Augmented Reality is a recent technology and its applicability to tourism is even more recent.

In fact, as ICT (Information and Communication Technologies) evolved, they have created important impacts on tourism activity. They succeeded in transforming this activity into many aspects, from the consumer (who started to use the internet to search for destination information) to the destination management (Guttentag, 2010).

As highlighted by Yuen, Yaoyuneyong & Johnson (2011) Augmented Reality can lead to newer and even more comprehensive interfaces and can show tourists (social-historical) and business (locations, services) relevant information of the surrounding in their real location. It can happen "(...) simply by checking with the user's smart-phone GPS, or when queried via a quick snapshot with the smart-phone's camera" (Yuen, Yaoyuneyong & Johnson, 2011: 126).

There are several emerging applications related to ICT applied to the World Heritage and Tourism (Fino, Martín-Gutiérrez, Fernández & Davara, 2013). This new reality that has emerged in recent years stems from the fact that people have become more familiar with new technologies as well as resulting from their quick and friendly learning.

With the increasing interest in studying and assessing the impacts of cultural tourism on cities, which are World Heritage by UNESCO, also arose the need to develop cultural activities that would make cities more attractive to tourists. The city of La Laguna (Spain) is one of the cities where an Interactive Guide has recently been applied in the field of cultural tourism (Fino, Martín-Gutiérrez, Fernández & Davara, 2013). A guide for Las Quilamas Natural Park in the field of nature tourism has also been recently developed (Martínez-Graña, Goy & Cimarra, 2013).

It is important to remember that in addition to tourists, the local population, local institutions (linked to heritage which have tours with their associates) and institutions linked to education, can also benefit from the applications in Augmented Reality and lead them to conclude their Educational and pedagogical utility (Martínez-Graña, Goy & Cimarra, 2013).

Liarokapis, Brujic-Okretic & Papakonstantinou (2006) proved the importance of Virtual and Augmented Reality interface paradigms that can provide greater location based services for urban navigation and wayfinding. Guttentag (2010) recently showed the importance of the application of the Virtual Reality in Tourism.

Also recently, the Reuben H. Fleet Science Center, in San Diego, opened the Magnet Field View Finder exhibit. Here visitors can learn more about magnetic fields using a mobile device (Gervautz & Schmalstieg, 2012).

Navigation and tourist information systems also use Augmented Reality approaches, by displaying navigation aids and information bubbles on a real-world view. A much better understanding of where to go than they would by looking on a map is what can happen with the usage of Augmented Reality applications (Gervautz & Schmalstieg, 2012).

Recently, Buhalis and Yovcheva (2015) from the University of Bournemouth developed the ten most innovative practices of Augmented Reality applicability in tourism around the world. In this chapter we highlight some of the most relevant. In terms of an enhanced booking experience, Augmented Reality is applied to tourist catalogs, brochures, leaflets and any other type of paper promotional materials. Hotels, casinos, theme parks, but also special events or virtual roller coaster trips are another kind of Augmented Reality. Indeed, Augmented Reality systems can exert a power of persuasion and provide a lucrative opportunity to market services successfully, a feature that is still very little used in the tourism industry. One of the most successful examples of this type of experience, is the application developed by the St. Petersburg Clearwater Bureau. Here, the Augmented Reality is used to provide a cutting-edge 3D experience for potential tourists (Buhalis & Yovcheva, 2015). Named "Two Treasures 3D Tour," the experience features a virtual guide that can be viewed on a desktop video camera at home. The experience features a virtual guide and provides an interactive view of world-famous beaches and museums (Buhalis & Yovcheva, 2015).

As far as Museum Interactivity is concerned, Augmented Reality provides an attractive educational environment (Buhalis & Yovcheva, 2015). In fact, education is one of the areas that have benefited greatly from the use of Augmented Reality. This technology offers a tangible interface that stimulates mental and motor activities through an intuitive interaction with an unknown content. Augmented Reality has enormous potential to actively engage tourists to foster experimentation in hitherto passive environments such as museums. More recently, interactive digital storytelling techniques have been applied to museums' programs and activity plans to increase their educational and experiential potential. For example, the Digital Binocular Station (DBS), makes the static content of a museum come alive, leading to an interactive and dynamic adventure, which increases visitor retention time and, more importantly, their return (Buhalis & Yovcheva, 2015).

AR browsers in the destination matches an Augmented Reality browser or application that suits the needs of the tourist, enriches the real world with interactive virtual information that allows visitors to recognize and identify immediately and interactively the most important and interesting points of a territory, even if they visit it for the first time. Probably the most successful example is the application of the stand-alone Yelp smartphone (Figure 2), which added an Augmented Reality view, thus providing interactive geo-information to its users. The interactive guide of the Portuguese Way of Santiago in Barcelos is part of this segment of interactive solutions offering the use of Augmented Reality (Figure 3).

There is, however, another example in Portugal linked to this good practice of Augmented Reality applicability in tourism. It is the guide of the Route of the Romanesque. It is a cultural tourism project based on built heritage (eg, churches, bridges, castles, towers and monasteries), with the Romanesque style as its common denominator. This project was born in 1998 and corresponds to the combination and integration of three pre-existing routes, namely: Vale do Sousa, Douro Valley and Vale do Tâmega. These routes are linked by road. In addition to adding a vast built heritage, this project also unites several autarchies of Portugal. This route has about 58 monuments, with 19 attached to the Route of the Sousa Valley, 25 monuments belonging to the Route of the Tâmega Valley and 14 monuments in the Douro Valley (Rota do Românico, 2014). It is a guide for smartphones, the fundamental structure of the application being executed from three sub-menus or modes of information availability (Figure 4).

Responsive Experience through Gaming is another area of application. Augmented Reality games have been instrumental in promoting physical activity, taking advantage of real-world locations and objects as part of a more immersive game. In view of the flexibility and high personalization of virtual information, different scenarios can also be applied in the field of tourism. Through these games, it's possible

Figure 2. Example of a Yelp-smartphone stand-alone app
Source: Leawo, 2016.

Figure 3. Interactive guide of the Portuguese Way of Santiago in Barcelos
Source: Own elaboration. Image Capture via iPad 2 on 2013/04/10.

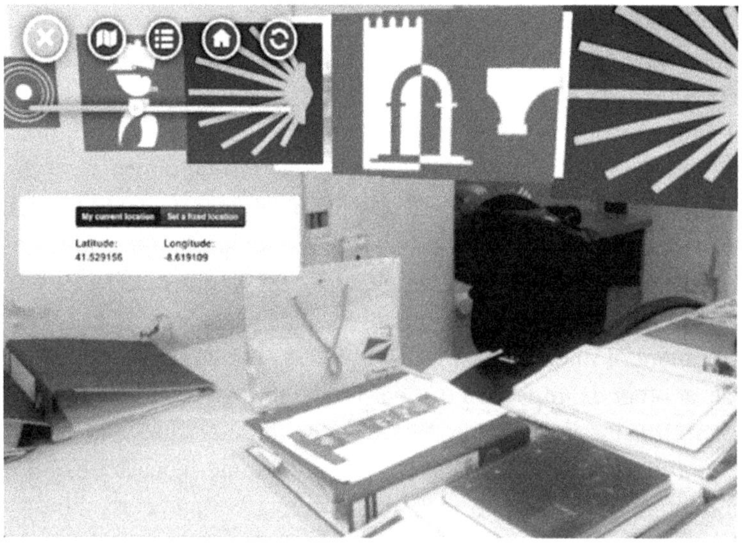

to make the interpretation of the territory something quite fun, different and interactive. An interesting example of this type of application is TimeWarp. This outdoor game of Augmented Reality, developed by researchers at the Institute of Applied Information Technology (Sankt Augustine, Germany), allows tourists to hike through the city of Cologne "jumping" through time portals and experience different historical events. Unlike the game of fiction offered by ARQuake, TimeWarp's main goal is to encourage players to interact with the city and experience its temporal changes (Buhalis 6 Yovcheva, 2015).

Figure 4. Interactive Romanic route guide
Source: Image Capture made from Iphone 5 on 1/24/2014.

Re-living Historic Life and Events, through the re-creation of ancient temples and historic buildings is a theme that naturally lends itself to Augmented Reality. The first site of the cultural heritage that benefited from an augmented virtual reconstruction of an ancient temple was Olympia in Greece, where researchers developed the ArcheoGuide AR system (Buhalis & Yovcheva, 2015).

The Augmented Reality Hotel Experience is another of the applications and it is noted that the hotel sector only now awakens to the true potential of technology. One of the few examples of good practice in this sector was developed by the Holiday Inn chain. It was also the first international hotel chain to announce the world's first Augmented Reality Hotel (Watanabe, 2012). Guests can use their smartphones to view the virtual Olympic and Paralympic athletes at the reception, lounge or in their own room.

Augmented Transportation is another area of application. Navigation and signaling were the first areas of application of Augmented Reality in tourism. This technology has the potential to reduce the mental strain necessary for both pedestrians and other means of transport.

Augmented Reality Translation is another aspect of Augmented Reality and is about interpreting unknown territory. In fact, the experience in an unknown territory can influence the tourist in his or her visit, mainly in the language level. The exploration of unfamiliar environments can be significantly influenced by the lack of clear translation of signs, instructions and other information written in a foreign language. There are Augmented Reality applications that provide translation of the elements in real time, such as: menus, train times and newspapers. These applications translate in real time the language of the country where the tourist is located to his or her native language. Word Lens and Intelligent Eye are two commercial applications of Augmented Reality that have the ability to do translations in real time, simply pointing the mobile device to the original text, overlapping it on the device display, the text already translated into the selected language (Buhalis & Yovcheva, 2015).

In the context of Participative Destination Management, it should be noted that for centuries, the planners and managers of the territory had to work with abstract and general plans in order to select a balanced mix of structures, buildings and materials. Color images, textures and shapes all play a key role in determining the aesthetic perspective of physical structures (Buhalis & Yovcheva, 2015). Augmented Reality can help planners make better decisions through on-the-spot comparisons of alternative scenarios Augmented Reality is used to overlay virtual 3D models of projects over the actual environment where this project will gain physical shape. Recently, the Netherlands Architecture Institute announced the launch of the Augmented Urban Reality application (UAR) (Buhalis & Yovcheva, 2015). Available in eight cities in the Netherlands, it allows residents and tourists to experience the urban environment of yesteryear, what could have been and was not and will be in the future. The application allows users to add comments in a database. This approach can be useful in a number of areas of tourism application, such as the construction of theme parks, resorts and other tourist structures.

THE RELEVANCE OF THE CAMINO DE SANTIAGO IN CULTURAL/RELIGIOUS TOURISM

The Camino de Santiago as a Religious and Cultural Tourism

According to the Catholic legend, after the dispersion of the Apostles throughout the world, Santiago went to preach in distant regions, spending some time in Spain, in Galicia. When he returned to Palestine in AD 44, he was arrested and beheaded by Herod Agrippa I, son of Aristobulus and grandson of Herod the Great (Cardoso & Almeida, 2005). Two of his disciples, Theodore and Athanasius, stole the master's body and boarded him (on a boat with an angelic crew), and in seven days they arrived in Galicia, more specifically, Iria Flavia, where they secretly buried him in a grove called Libredón. There is no certainty as to the date of the discovery of the apostolic sepulcher, but most Catholic sources point to dates between 813 and 820 AD (Cardoso & Almeida, 2005). Legend has it that a hermit of the forest of Libredón, named Pelagius (or Pelaio), observed for a few nights in a row a "rain of stars" on a forest hill. Prompted by the lights, the bishop of Iria Flavia, Teodomiro, ordered excavations and found a marble ark with the bones of the saint and his disciples. He then warned the King of Spain and the Pope about the discovery that was made. Alfonso II (the Casto) was the first pilgrim known to go, from Oviedo to the tomb of the Apostle, creating one of the pilgrimage routes - the Primitive Way (Cardoso & Almeida, 2005).

The Portuguese Central Way of Santiago is the most traveled route in Portugal and the second most traveled of all the Jacobean Pilgrimage Network (Oficina do Peregrino, 2016). The Portuguese Central Way of Santiago, which crosses the municipality and the city of Barcelos, is the backbone of the entire network of Jacobeans' itineraries in Portugal. It derives from other Secondary Itineraries such as the Coastal Way or the Inner Way.

In the Middle Ages, the national road network was scarce, with the fluvial network associated to the cabotage navigation as the main one. The roads of the coast, for these reasons, were rare or nonexistent, since as far as the boats arrived no roads were opened. Very different from what happened in the Modern Age, where, at the level of commercial relations, some road network at the coastal level was already perceived (Magalhães & Mattoso, 1997).

At that time the roads or paths were rare and few counties had them. In addition, it should be noted that the entire route of the Central Way, between Porto and Valença, is duly supported by technical and academic opinions of reference. There are reports, continuity in time (primordial for the definition of a Path), history and legends (e.g., the Legend of the Cock of Barcelos).

Several associations for the defense and promotion of the Central Portuguese Way of Santiago have detailed studies of the Whole Way, both on the Minho side and Galicia, with recourse, when necessary, to the support of historians, archaeologists and local researchers, in addition to the population in general (Cardoso & Almeida, 2005). In Figure 5 we can see the European Network of the Ways of Santiago.

Since 1993, a network of four Christian pilgrimage routes in the north of Spain has been inscribed in the World Heritage List. Of these routes, the French Way is the most underlined. The extension represents a network of almost 1,500 km, comprised in the territory of the Basque Country-La Rioja, Liébana and primitive routes. It includes a built heritage of historical importance created to meet the needs of pilgrims, including cathedrals, churches, hospitals, hostels and bridges. The extension covers some of the first pilgrimage routes to Santiago de Compostela, following the discovery in the 9th century of a tomb believed to be that of St. James the Greater (UNESCO, 2016).

However, in Portugal the situation is different. Although the Portuguese Way of Santiago is the second most traveled of all the European network of roads, presenting a higher rate of growth (Oficina do Peregrino, 2016), there is no effective investment by the Portuguese Government on this tourist, historical and cultural resource. Analyzing the National Strategic Plan for Tourism (NSPT) in a synthetic way, it is verified that there is no reference to this resource, throughout the document. In fact, the NSPT points out for the tourism in the north of Portugal (reference territory of the Portuguese Way of Santiago), the following resources (Ministry of Economy, 2011): touristic circuits, health tourism; short-term stays; business tourism; nature tourism; gastronomy and wines; golf; and nautical tourism.

It follows that cultural and religious tourism was not until recently a strategic tourist focus for the north of Portugal. More recently, in 2014, a new national strategic document for tourism was published - "Tourism 2020: Five Principles for an Ambition". This is a strategic and guiding document for the public and private sector, which bridges the strategic strands of national tourism and the new Commu-

Figure 5. European network of the Ways of Santiago
Source: Archicifradia del Glorioso Apóstol Santiago, 2014.

nity framework that will be in place by 2020. Also in this publication, there is no reference to cultural tourism and religious, nor particularly to the Portuguese Way of Santiago. It is lamented, therefore, that a fundamental tourism resource remains dedicated to the local strategies of each municipality. Thus, the need for the Portuguese State to assume the paternity of this resource and to work in a concerted way to preserve, promote and enhance the Portuguese Way of Santiago.

Evolution of Camino de Santiago in Portugal and at Barcelos

The Camino de Santiago has evolved significantly in recent years. In fact, we have witnessed a continuous increase in the number of pilgrims (Figure 6).

For the first time in history (since there are registrations), in 2016 the number of pilgrims may exceed the number registered in the last Holy Year (Oficina do Peregrino 2016). The Holy Years happen in the year in which the 25th of July (the day of the Apostle James) takes place on a Sunday. The last Holy Year was in 2010 and the next will occur in 2021.

Following this trend is the Portuguese Way of Santiago. As previously mentioned, the Portuguese Way of Santiago is the second most traveled route. Figure 6 reveals that the Portuguese Way of Santiago has undergone a remarkable increase of pilgrims, especially since the last Holy Year. Although the number of pilgrims is still far below the French Route (the most traveled one), its growth rate has been the highest. In 2015, there was a growth rate of 5.93% in the French Way, while the Portuguese Way of Santiago grew by 17.7%, this is the highest growth rate in all the jacobean routes (Oficina do Peregrino, 2016).

Being Barcelos, a central municipality of the Portuguese Way of Santiago, since the Middle Ages, has also denoted this effective growth of pilgrims. The land of the Legend of the Rooster has witnessed a particular dynamic of investment and return of foreign currency, coming from this pilgrims' passage to Santiago.

Figure 6. Evolution of the total number of pilgrims arriving in Santiago de Compostela between 2004 and 2015
Source: Oficina do Peregrino, 2016.

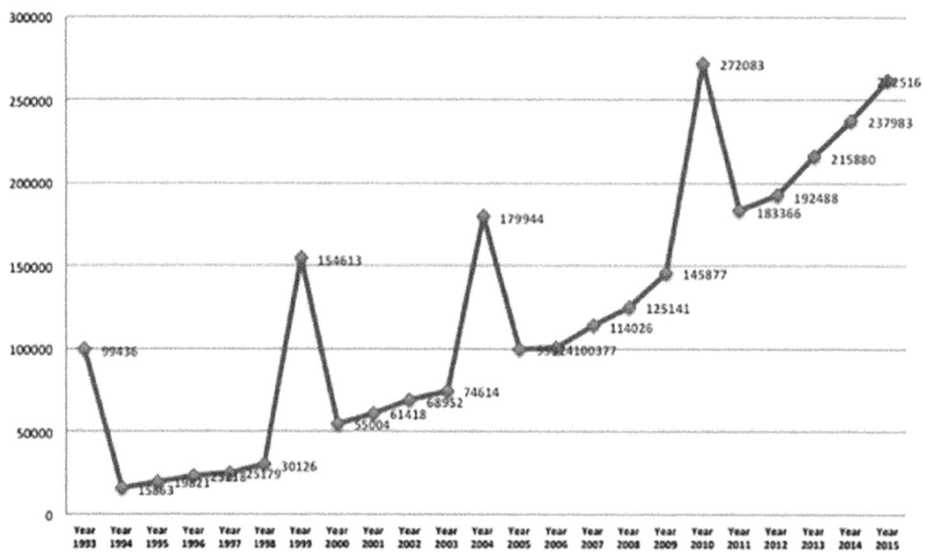

Figure 7. Evolution of total pilgrims by road between 1992 and 2015
Source: Oficina do Peregrino, 2016.

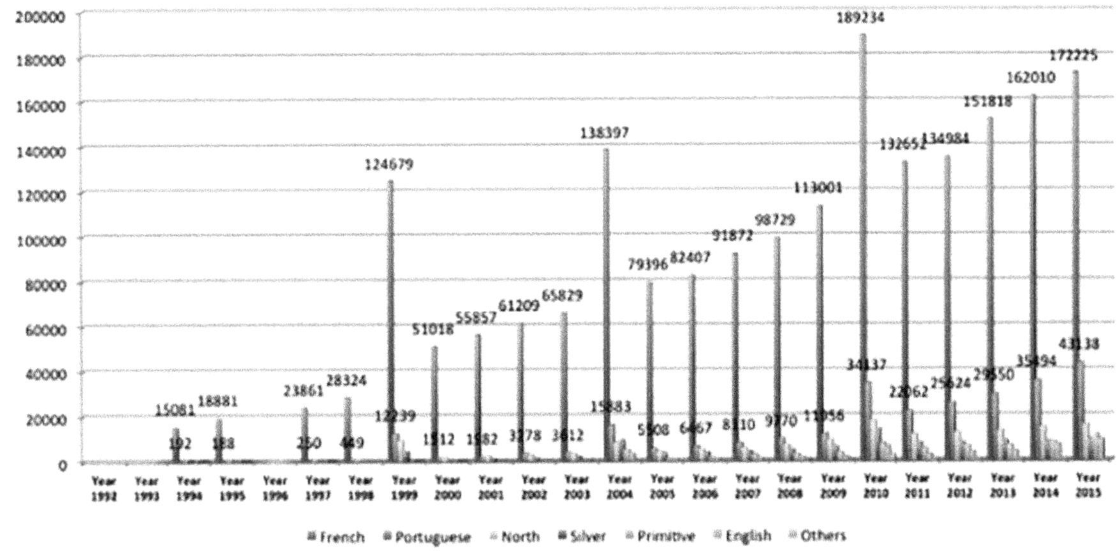

**For a more accurate representation see the electronic version.*

Although we cannot determine the dynamics of this phenomenon over time, due to the lack of data and studies, it was possible, together with the Tourism Office of the Municipality of Barcelos to quantify the dynamics and the multiplier effect generated by this route. The internal study was carried out by one of the authors of the present text, in agreement with the public and private agents directly linked to the jacobean itinerary that crosses the municipality of Barcelos. This was a team effort with the main objective of registering, for the first time, the economic impact of the Portuguese Way of Santiago in the municipality of Barcelos. The results of the study conducted in 2015 serve as a basis for the strategy to be implemented in the municipality for the upcoming years, although the study has not been published.

We can say that Barcelos receives 22,000 pilgrims annually, with 130 beds at Pilgrim's Hostel and a new Hostel dedicated to welcoming pilgrims, and attending 25% of the annual hotel occupancy rate dedicated to pilgrims. This dynamic generated around 600,000 € of direct gross revenue per year and 40 direct jobs between 2013 and 2015. It should also be noticed that 31 restaurants in Barcelos have a pilgrim menu and that there are two Help Points with 5,000 requests for support per year.

But the dynamics generated by this growing influx of pilgrims has not only translated into the economic component. Local associations and actors (public and private) have carried out a set of actions that have led to the participation of the local community. These actions are essentially aimed at strengthening the Barcelos mark in the Portuguese Way of Santiago and giving the locals an insight into the local history and the central importance that this Jacobean route has in the local and urban development of Barcelos, from its foundation to the present day. As a result of these initiatives, stands out the annual realization of ten plays with the theme of the Way, four routes of dynamization of steps of the way with an average of 55 participants per initiative, the creation of the gastronomic dish "Roasted Rooster Barcelos Style", classified as one of the 50 best dishes in Portugal and the fortifying of relations between the capital of Caminho (Pontevedra in Spain and Barcelos in Portugal).

In conclusion, the study that was conducted in 2015 revealed that for every euro invested in the Portuguese Way of Santiago in Barcelos, there is an effective return of 5.80 €. This reveals the economic power that this tourist resource has for local development, especially for small / medium sized municipalities like Barcelos. It is not surprising, therefore, that the municipality of Barcelos has been increasing its commitment to the promotion, valorization and preservation of this tourist resource.

METHODS

At the level of scientific methodology, it is important to remember that more than a discipline, it means introducing the researcher into the world of systematic and rational procedures, the basis of the formation of both the student and the professional, since both act in practice in the world of ideas (Marconi & Lakatos, 2010).

Based on the concepts inherent to the definitions described in the previous items, we can therefore affirm that the adopted methodology for the investigation was based on primary and secondary sources. As far as primary sources were concerned, fieldwork was carried out in several phases. It began in 2010 by gathering data and meetings with all stakeholders and agents in the territory. Next, a Geographic Information System was created for municipal tourism planning and management and, finally, in 2014, the interactive guide on the Portuguese Way of Santiago in Barcelos was created.

The innovation of the present investigation led to the registration of a national patent granted and published on April 12, 2012 by the National Institute of Industrial Property (NIIP), under the number 10672.

THE INTERACTIVE GUIDE PORTUGUESE CAMINO DE SANTIAGO APPLIED TO BARCELOS MUNICIPALITY

The interactive guide of the Portuguese Way of Santiago in Barcelos was officially presented at the city's festivities in May 2014, and since then it has been downloaded 685 times, being the origin of the downloads reached countries such as Australia, United Arab Emirates, South Korea, France, Germany, Spain, Italy and Norway. Currently the guide is suspended, as it is being updated and improved, and by the end of 2016 the version 2.0 is expected to be released.

The interactive guide works on any mobile device on the most relevant operating systems on the market - Apple Store and Google Play. In order for it to work, we first need to download an application adapted to Augmented Reality. While there are some on the market (e.g., Layar and Wikitude) we have chosen to use and pair the Interactive Guide to the Augmented Reality Browser Junaio. The download of this browser is free, by simply entering the name of the browser in the Apple Store or Google Play. Figure 8 shows the process for acquiring the application.

After installing the interactive guide of the Portuguese Way of Santiago in Barcelos, it is ready to be explored by the user. This exploration passes through the three existing modes of usage:

Figure 8. Process for acquiring the application
Source: Own elaboration.

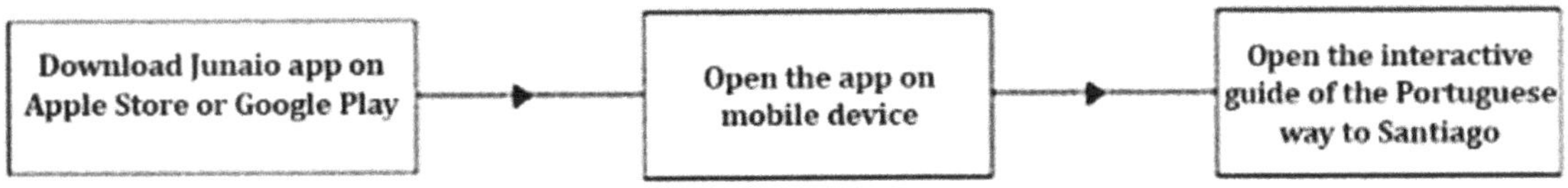

- **Augmented Reality:** Mixture of the actual image captured through the camera of the mobile device with the overlapping contextual virtual information is performed; In this mode you can set the radius of the range to view the points of interest that are around (Figure 9);
- **GPS Navigation:** The user can navigate based on conventional cartography or you can choose to navigate based on aerial photographs (Figure 10);
- **List of Points of Interest:** The user can directly search the point of interest that is within the scope range that you have set; you can also activate the associated action using the respective control button (Figure 11).

The structure of geo-data found in the interactive guide is organized by themes, symbols and actions. Actions are nothing more than ways of demonstrating and interacting geo-information with the user. This geo-information reaches the user in the following interaction modes: audio file (audio-guide), text, image, video, url link, direct telephone call and e-mail. The data structure is summarized in Figure 12.

Figure 9. Augmented reality mode
Source: Own elaboration with image capture through the iPad 2 on 10/04/2013.

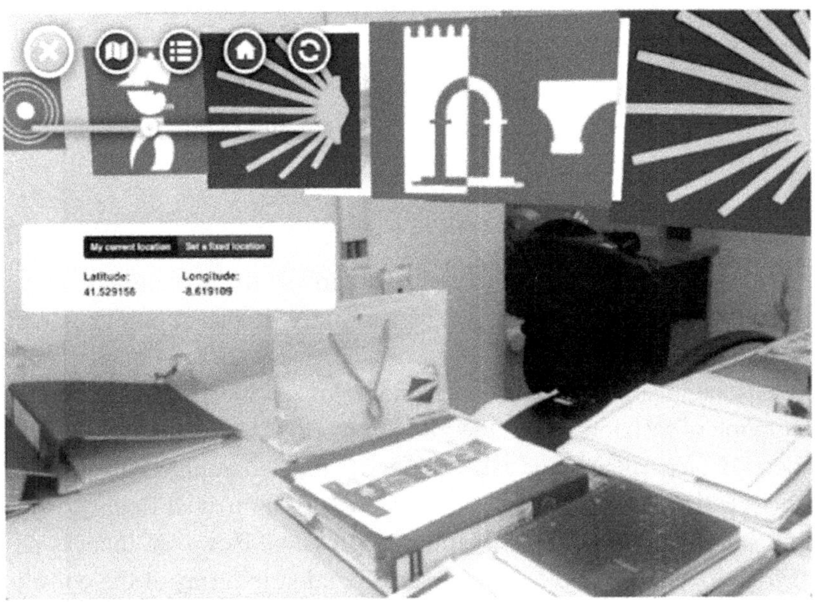

Figure 10. GPS navigation mode
Source: Own elaboration with image capture through the iPad 2 on 10/04/2013.

Figure 11. List of points of interest mode
Source: Own elaboration with image capture through the iPad 2 on 10/04/2013.

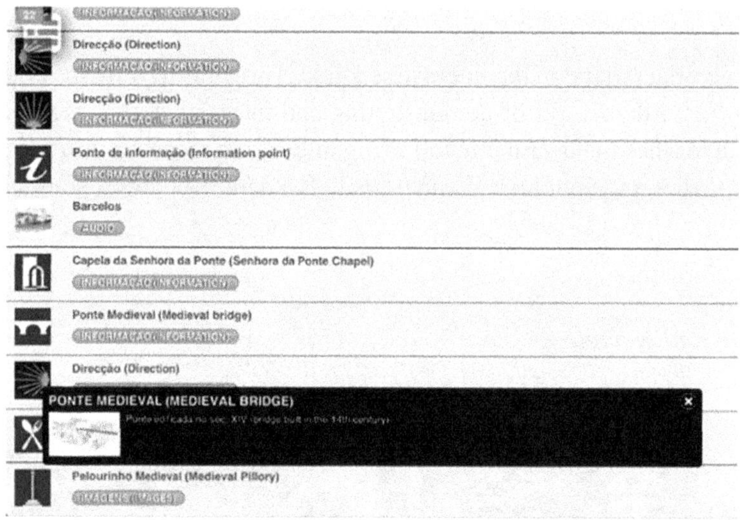

CONCLUSION

The Augmented Reality does not replace reality, but improves its contents, improving the discovery and knowledge about the patrimony existing in a certain place. It also allows to give different versions of the same object.

With regard to the relationship between new technologies and tourism, we can conclude that there is an increasing integration of technologies in the tourism world. This integration is effective and visible in its multiple aspects, from planning and management (e.g., Geographic Information Systems) to the promotion and individualization of tourist destinations (e.g., Augmented Reality). We have also noted that this integration still has considerable scope for progression. However, there is a risk of too much technological integration, which could lead to dehumanization in terms of the consumption of tourist destinations.

Figure 12. Data structure of the interactive guide of the Portuguese Way of Santiago in Barcelos
Source: Own elaboration.

TYPE	N.º	SYMBOL	TYPE OF ACTION
Direction	82		Message Box
Danger	9		Message Box
Monuments	16		Message Box/HD images/URL link/Phone call
Main monuments	12		Audio
Foutains	6		Message Box
Acommodation	5		Message Box/HD images/URL link/Phone call
Pilgrim Hostels	3		Message Box/HD images/URL link/Phone call
Transport interface	2		Message Box/Phone call/URL link/e-mail
Security forces	2		Panic button (direct phone line)
Informative video	1		Video
Others points of interest	14		Message Box/Phone call/URL link/e-

At the level of the future lines, it is our intention that the territorial scope of the application constructed extends to all the territory crossed by the Portuguese Way of Santiago. From the moment that it has been proven that the application works for the territory in question, it will make sense to add, in this platform, the entire Portuguese Way of Santiago. However, we believe that this possibility can only be realized when the basic problems in Portugal are solved, as regards to the structuring and management of the Santiago Way network.

In political terms, it is urgent that the Government considers the Portuguese Way of Santiago as a structuring product for the Country and, especially, for the North of Portugal. For this to take place, it is necessary to create a public institute with the sole responsibility of structuring and managing the network of the Santiago Pilgrims in Portugal. With this open and inclusive vision, everyone wins: public agents, private agents and pilgrims. On the other hand, when we structure the Santiago Way network we will institutionally link an effective hierarchy of the Santiago Way in Portugal. This hierarchy will be based on several elements of analysis, such as: historical, geographical, ethnographic, cultural, toponymal and quantification elements of pilgrims who have traveled in overall and who travel each jacobean itinerary in Portugal. As in Spain, the Portuguese Way of Santiago, designated as the Central Way, which starts in Lisbon, passing through Coimbra, Porto, Barcelos, Ponte de Lima and Valença, stands for the Camino de Santiago network in Portugal, as the French Way is on the Camino de Santiago network in Spain. As we have seen, this Central Path is the second most traveled of the entire network of Pathways in Europe, and it is currently the highest effective growth rate (Oficina do Peregrino, 2016). Consequently, this proposal could culminate in the effective classification of this itinerary, similar to what already exists for the French Way, as Cultural and Intangible Heritage of Humanity.

Finally, we hope that the results of this research will contribute to the rapprochement between the pilgrim, information, new technologies and the territory.

REFERENCES

Ajanki, A., Billinghurst, M., Gamper, H., Jarvenpaa, T., Kandemir, M., Kaski, S., & Tossavainen, T. et al. (2010). An augmented reality interface to contextual information. *Virtual Reality (Waltham Cross)*, *15*(2-3), 455–470.

Archicifradia Del Glorioso Apóstol Santiago. (2014). Credencial do Peregrino. Edição própria, Santiago de Compostela.

Augment Blog. (2016). *Virtual Reality vs. Augmented Reality*. Retrieved October 6th, 2015, from http://www.augment.com/blog/virtual-reality-vs-augmented-reality/

Azuma, R. (1997). A Survey of Augmented Reality. *Teleoperators and Virtual Environment*, *6*(4), 355–385. doi:10.1162/pres.1997.6.4.355

Buhalis, D., & Yovcheva, Z. (2015). *Augmented Reality in tourism: 10 unique applications explained. Digital Tourism Think Tank*. Dorset: Bournemouth University.

Butler, A. (2016). *Virtual reality and new technologies increasingly a part of the travel industry*. Melbourne: Lonely Planet.

Cardoso, A., & Almeida, L. (2005). O Caminho Português de Santiago. Editora Lucerna, 1.ª edição, Cascais.

Castells, M. (2002). *A sociedade em rede*. Lisboa: Fundação Calouste Gulbenkian.

CDN Media. (2016). *Google translate word Lens*. Retrieved April, 3rd, 2015, from http://cdn-media-2.lifehack.org/wp-content/files/2015/04/google-translate-word-lens.jpg

Charara, S. (2016). Virtual reality versus augmented reality: Which is the future?. Wearable blog, London.

CNBC. (2016). *Virtual reality devices could transform the tourism experience*. Retrieved January, 8th, 2016, from http://www.cnbc.com/2016/01/08/virtual-reality-devices-could-transform-the-tourism-experience.html

Dennis, K., & Urry, J. (2009). *After the car* (1st ed.). Cambridge, UK: Polity Press.

Digital Binocular Station. (2016). *The digital binocular station*. Retrieved January, 9th, 2016, from http://www.digitalbinocularstation.com/

Fino, E. R., Martín-Gutiérrez, J., Fernández, M. D. M., & Davara, E. A. (2013). Interactive Tourism Guide: Connecting Web 2.0, Augmented Reality and QR Codes. *Procedia Computer Science*, *25*, 338–344. doi:10.1016/j.procs.2013.11.040

Gervautz, M., & Schmalstieg, D. (2012). Anywhere interfaces using handheld Augmented Reality. *Computer*, *45*(July), 26–31. doi:10.1109/MC.2012.72

Graham, L. (2016). *Virtual reality devices could transform the tourism experience*. CNBC.

Guttentag, D. A. (2010). Virtual Reality: Applications and Implications for Tourism. *Tourism Management*, *31*(5), 637–651. doi:10.1016/j.tourman.2009.07.003

Inamo Restaurant. (2016). *Interactive Menu*. Retrieved, August, 3rd, 2016, from http://www.inamo-restaurant.com

Javornik, A. (2016). *The Mainstreaming of Augmented Reality: A Brief History*. Harvard Business Review.

Kirner, C., & Silva, K. A. C. (2010). *Vantagens educacionais no uso de jogos em Realidade Aumentada*. Renote. *Revista Novas Tecnologias na Educação*, *8*(3), 10–15.

Krevelen, D. W. F., & Poelman, R. (2010). A Survey of Augmented Reality Technologies, Applications and Limitations. *The International Journal of Virtual Reality*, *9*(2), 1–20.

Leawo. (2016). *Yelp app*. Retrieved October, 18th, 2016, from http://www.leawo.com/

Liarokapis, F., Brujic-Okretic, V., & Papakonstantinou, S. (2006). Exploring Urban Environments Using Virtual and Augmented Reality. Journal of Virtual Reality and Broadcasting, 3(5).

Lonely Planet. (2016). *Virtual reality and new technologies increasingly a part of the travel industry*. Retrieved, April, 30th, 2016, from http://www.lonelyplanet.com/news/2016/04/11/travel-tourism-virtual-reality/

Magalhães, J., & Mattoso, J. (Eds.). (1993). História de Portugal: Vol. 2. A Monarquia Feudal. Círculo de Leitores, Lisboa.

Marconi, M., & Lakatos, E. (2010). Fundamentos da metodologia científica: Técnicas de pesquisa (7th ed.). Atlas, São Paulo.

Martínez-Graña, A. M., Goy, J. L., & Cimarra, C. A. (2013). A virtual tour of geological heritage: Valourising geodiversity using Google Earth and QR code. *Computers & Geosciences*, *61*, 83–93. doi:10.1016/j.cageo.2013.07.020

Milgram, P., Takemura, H., Utsumi, A., & Kishino, F. (1994). *Augmented reality: a class of displays on the reality-virtuality continuum*. Telemanipulator and Telepresence Technologies.

Oakes, E. (2007). *Encyclopedia of World Scientist*. Infobase Publishing.

Oficina del Peregrino. (2016). *Estadísticas oficiales*. Retrieved November, 13th, 2017, from https://oficinadelperegrino.com/estadisticas/

Park, M., Lim, K., Seo, M., Jung, S., & Lee, K. (2014). Spatial augmented reality for product appearance design evaluation. *Journal of Computational Design and Engineering*, *2*(1), 38–46. doi:10.1016/j.jcde.2014.11.004

Prweb. (2016). *Digital frontiers media uses augmented reality to market St. Pete/Clearwater tourism with miles media*. Retrieved May, 1st, 2016, from http://www.prweb.com/releases/2011/03/prweb5141134.htm

Rota do Românico. (2014). *O território da Rota do Românico*. Retrieved from http://www.rotadoromanico.com/vPT/Paginas/Homepage.aspx

Rota do Românico. (2016). *Aplicativo da rota do Românico*. Retrieved May, 15th, 2016, from http://www.rotadoromanico.com/vPT/Paginas/Homepage.aspx

Strauss, P. (2008). *Mini Augmented Reality Ads Hit Newstands*. Chicago: Technabob.

Turismo de Barcelos. (2014). *Impacto económico do Caminho Português de Santiago no concelho de Barcelos. Relatório interno não publicado*. Câmara Municipal de Barcelos, Barcelos.

Turismo de Portugal. (2011). Plano Estratégico Nacional do Turismo versão 2.0. Turismo de Portugal, I.P., Lisboa.

Turismo de Portugal. (2014). Turismo 2020: cinco princípios para uma ambição. Turismo de Portugal, I.P., Lisboa.

UCL Faculty of the Built Environment. (2016). Augmented Urban Reality. The Bartlett Space Syntax Laboratory, The Bartlett School of Architecture, London.

UNESCO. (2016). *Routes of Santiago de Compostela: Camino Francés and Routes of Northern Spain*. Retrieved October,14th, 2016, from http://whc.unesco.org/en/list/669

University of New Mexico. (2016). *Thomas Caudell Biography*. Retrieved May, 15th, 2016, from http://ceet.unm.edu/about/people/thomas-caudell.html

Watanabe, A. (2012). *Inside 'world's first augmented reality hotel*. The Australian Journal.

Yuen, S., Yaoyuneyong, G., & Johnson, E. (2011). Augmented Reality: An overview and five directions for AR in Education. *Journal of Educational Technology Development and Exchange*, *4*(1), 119–140. doi:10.18785/jetde.0401.10

KEY TERMS AND DEFINITIONS

Augmented Reality: Augmented Reality (AR) defined as enhancement of the real environment by computer-generated content allows its users to see the real world together with an additional virtual world added in real time to the same field of view.

Barcelos: A city and a municipality in Braga District in the Minho Province, in the north of Portugal. The population in 2011 was 120,391. It is one of the growing municipalities in the country, and is well known by its textile and adobe industries. Originally a Roman settlement, it expanded and became the seat of the First Duke of Bragança in the 15th century. One of the most importante points of passage for pilgrims to Santiago, since Middle Age.

Mixed Reality: Mixed Reality (MR) is an area surrounding the real environment and virtual environment.

Mobile Augmented Reality: Augmented reality applications that are used on many mobile platforms. Mobile augmented reality (MAR) has emerged as the most popular and most convenient form of augmented reality, especially because of the proliferation of mobile devices.

Mobile Devices: A mobile device is a computing device small enough to hold and operate in the hand.

Pilgrim: From the Latin peregrinus "pere acres" is a traveler (literally one who has come from afar) who is on a journey to a holy place.

Santiago Way: The Camino de Santiago, also known by the English names Way of St. James, St. James's Way, St. James's Path, St. James's Trail, Route of Santiago de Compostela, and Road to Santiago, is the name of any of the pilgrimage routes, known as pilgrim ways, to the shrine of the apostle St. James the Great in the Cathedral of Santiago de Compostela in Galicia in northwestern Spain, where tradition has it that the remains of the saint are buried.

Chapter 7
Reconstructing the Past:
Providing an Enhanced Perceptual Experience

Luís G. Magalhães
Centro Algoritmi, University of Minho, Portugal

Telmo Adão
University of Trás-os-Montes e Alto Douro, Portugal & INESC TEC, Portugal

Emanuel Peres
University of Trás-os-Montes e Alto Douro, Portugal & INESC TEC, Portugal

ABSTRACT

Accurate modeling/reconstruction and visualization of real environments, particularly archaeological sites, is both a major challenge and a crucial task. This work will address the entire process of the virtual reconstruction of archaeological sites, since the construction of the virtual model until its visualization. The chapter begins with an introduction to the process of virtual reconstruction of archaeological sites, where the several stages that should take place to obtain a faithful virtual representation of an archaeological site and its artifacts are identified. Moreover, each stage is characterized and its main methods and techniques are identified, in dedicated sections. The authors' contribution for the state of the art will be highlighted in each stage. The chapter ends with the authors' vision about future trends for this field and unveils what could be their contributions to this vision.

INTRODUCTION

Accurate modeling/reconstruction and visualization of real environments, particularly archaeological sites, is simultaneously a major challenge and a crucial task. It allows the digital preservation and the visualization of not only current cultural assets, but also of those who no longer exist, resulting in a true glimpse of the past. This enables experts to study and to interact with their objects of interest, while allowing the general public to visualize such virtual environments, fostering cultural, social and scientific participation. By using mobile devices, such as smartphones or tablets, virtual models can be visualized

DOI: 10.4018/978-1-5225-2927-9.ch007

in loco, giving the experts a better understanding of how objects of interest integrate in their original environment and providing the general public an enhanced perceptual experience.

Despite sometimes being used as synonyms, in the context of this chapter "modeling" and "reconstruction" are considered as similar concepts, but with different working objects. The modeling task aims to build a model of an existent object while the reconstruction task is concerned with building models of no longer existent objects or model (reconstruct) the original shape of damaged objects, based on some information.

Highly accurate modeling/reconstruction is a very complex and time consuming task. To achieve a faithful representation of the object of interest all stages of the reconstruction and visualization processes must be carefully executed. These stages include constructing the object's virtual model, mimic the ancient original illumination conditions, to render and visualize the model, under the correct context.

This work will address the entire process of the virtual reconstruction of archaeological sites, since the construction of the virtual model until its visualization. The chapter begins with an introduction to the process of virtual reconstruction of archaeological sites, where the several stages that should take place to obtain a faithful virtual representation of an archaeological site and its artifacts are identified. Moreover, each stage is characterized and its main methods and techniques are identified, in dedicated sections. The authors' contribution for the state of the art will be highlighted in each stage. The chapter ends with the authors' vision about future trends for this field and unveils what could be their contributions to this vision.

VIRTUAL RECONSTRUCTION PROCESS

The use of computers in Archaeology dates back to the late 1950s and early 1960s, essentially for the statistical treatment of information collected during excavations (Reilly & Rahtz, 1992). At that time, the use of computers was confined to a very limited set of archaeologists. In the early 1970s, a group of enthusiasts and experts in the use of computers in Archaeology joined in and started a cycle of international conferences designated as "Computer Applications in Archaeology", which still takes place with the title "Computer Applications and Quantitative Methods in Archaeology". In the following years, the use of computers in Archaeology has evolved to the use of computer aided design (CAD) systems, database management systems (DBMS) and geographic information systems (GIS). The first, besides allowing to digitally store the topographic survey carried out during the field work also enabled, based on the acquired data, some earlier works on the 3D reconstruction of both the terrain and the archaeological site's existing structures. While both DBMS and GIS allowed storing data acquired during the excavation, GIS enabled storing, manipulating and visualizing data with a spatial nature. The term "Virtual Archaeology" as a reference to the use of Virtual Reality in Archaeology was first mentioned by Reilly (1990), but the creation of virtual reconstructions in the field of archaeology began in the 1980s.

Since then, the use of computers, particularly the virtual reconstruction as a support to research and promotion of cultural heritage, has gained an increasing interest. Presently there are several international conferences dedicated to this topic. In the last years there has been a significant increase in the number of projects involving some sort of historical reconstruction as well as its web promotion, which causes a greater impact and consequently affects more people. This increase can be related to two factors: (i) the technological development, which allows to obtain these reconstructions more easily; (ii) the increased interest of people in issues related to their cultural and architectural past. This interest in the humankind past and in the use of computers for its study has been reflected in the creation of dedicated research lines in the European framework programs, increasing the research in this area.

However one main issue in these virtual reconstructions is their validity. Many of the earlier virtual reconstructions, especially in the 1990s, were made based on the information available but without the involvement of an archaeologist to corroborate some of the assumptions made. In the beginning of the 2000s, the community awareness about the importance of scientific rigor and accurate representations of both the available knowledge and its uncertainty had raised. Various documents and initiatives included these concerns and highlighted their importance. One of those documents is the London Charter, which was conceived in 2006 and its current draft dates from 2009. The London Charter "aims to enhance the rigour with which computer-based visualisation methods and outcomes are used and evaluated in heritage contexts, thereby promoting understanding and recognition of such methods and outcomes" ('London Charter', 2009, p. 2). The Seville principles (Lopez-Menchero & Grande, 2011) proposed a set of guidelines to implement the London Charter in the case of Virtual Archeology. They define virtual reconstruction as "using a virtual model to visually recover a building or object made by humans at a given moment in the past from available physical evidence of these buildings or objects, scientifically-reasonable comparative inferences and in general all studies carried out by archaeologists and other experts in relation to archaeological and historical science" (p. 3).

The virtual reconstruction of archaeological sites is simultaneously a great challenge and a task of considerable complexity, in which all stages of the image synthesis process must be carefully executed to obtain a faithful representation of the study object. Nevertheless, most of the approaches for virtual reconstructions are more focused on how to produce a virtual model, neglecting the visualization step. Only a few works (*e.g.* Happa *et al.* (2009); Quattrini, Pierdicca, Frontoni & Barcaglioni (2016)) consider also the accurate illumination of the virtual model and how it is visualized. Figure 1 presents a complete virtual reconstruction process proposal, which considers the entire process, from the modeling until the visualization stage. The proposed virtual reconstruction process is composed by the following stages: modeling, lighting, rendering and visualization.

Figure 1. Complete virtual reconstruction process proposal

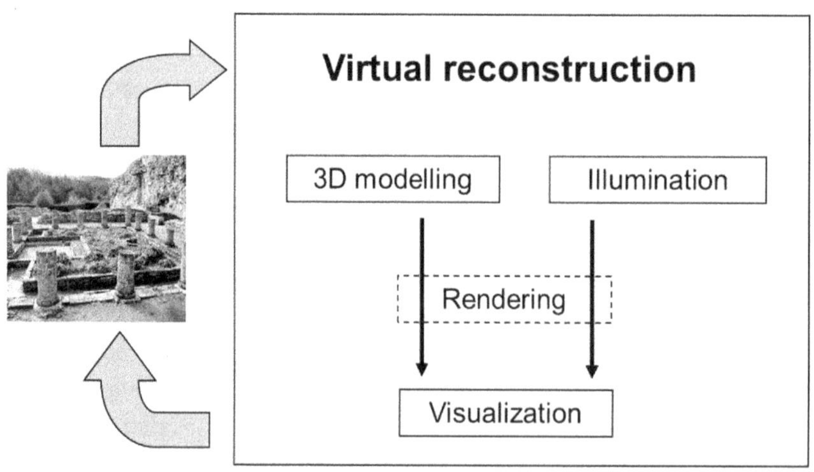

In the modeling stage, the first step is to gather information about the archaeological site, which includes surveying tasks and bibliographic studies. However, available information about archaeological sites may be sparse and incomplete. Moreover, the existing structures are often ruins for which, frequently, there is only partial information. Textual descriptions and geospatial information gathered *in situ* by archaeologists, as well as document descriptions or the comparison with similar structures of the same historical period, can be used to overcome the lack of visual information. However, the degree of uncertainty can be very high. Thus, the archaeological site's modeling task must be accompanied by Archeology experts, so that the virtual models constitute a faithful representation of the original structures. To reduce the task's completion time and/or the cost, virtual models can be created by using a modeling software or by adopting methods and techniques that automatize the process or make it more expeditious.

The way how virtual reconstructions are visualized is particularly important to have a correct historical interpretation of the represented archaeological site. Lighting is an important factor in providing the intended interpretation. To obtain a lighting configuration as similar as possible to the original, it is necessary to determine the objects' radiometric properties and to characterize the existing light sources. These radiometric properties are used to characterize how objects' surfaces react to light coming from light sources. However, it is also necessary that the virtual simulation integrates real physical data from the light sources used in the historical period under consideration.

Based on the geometric and radiometric model of the structures present in the archaeological site and on the characteristics of each light source, images are generated through a rendering process, which can be visualized in various scenarios and platforms. Virtual models' images can be visualized as part of a video or of an interactive application. This visualization may occur in the archaeological site using a variety of platforms (*e.g.* a multimedia kiosk, a screen projection, an immersive CAVE-type environment, a mobile device), near it by using a mobile device's screen as a window to the past or in another place (*e.g.* at home, via the web).

MODELING AND RECONSTRUCTION

This first stage aims to build a virtual model as detailed and faithful as possible, based on all available information about the archaeological site. This means that this stage includes a data acquisition step which is usually done before the actual modeling task, but only ends when the modeling stage finishes.

One of the most important aspects to consider in the reconstruction of real environments is the type of data to use. Data sources can include building footprints, CAD drawings, hand sketches, textual descriptions, ancient documents, 3D scans and images. The type of data to use and the corresponding data sources depend on the modeling techniques chosen. Different types of devices can be used to acquire data, such as standard cameras, LIDAR (LIght Detection and Ranging), SAR (Synthetic Aperture Radar) and laser technology. Selecting the device depends on different factors, such as the needed resolution, equipment/technology cost and even the acquisition's environmental conditions. To apply the London Charter and the Seville principles, all acquired data should be evaluated according to both its reliability and accuracy (Georgopoulos, 2014). Moreover, a consistency check between the different data sources should also be done (Pletinckx, 2008). This procedure is important to guarantee that the most faithful model is produced, based on the data and knowledge available.

Models can be created using a CAD system, which usually is a rather time-consuming task and involves intensive labor, therefore resulting in a higher cost with human resources. Due to this drawbacks, several strategies have arisen to try to automate the modeling process using techniques to automatically extract information from a particular source (*e.g.* photographs, video, data from 3D scanners, aerial and satellite images). Another approach is to use procedural modeling techniques to allow a semi-automatic modeling of structures, based on a set of rules. Hence, modeling/reconstruction techniques can be broadly classified into one of the following types:

- Non-automatic techniques;
- (Semi-) Automatic Techniques:
    - Image-based;
    - Range scanning (ex: 3D Scanner, LIDAR);
    - Procedural Modeling.

However, many of these techniques are only used to model what already exists (modeling) or to provide a model with little detail that is then necessary to complement using other techniques. Furthermore, each technique may be more suitable for some situations and incompatible with others. Therefore, in most cases, several techniques and approaches are combined to obtain a virtual model of the archaeological site, based on the available information (Beraldin, Gonzo, Whiting, Jemtrud & Valzanoe, 2005).

The following subsections briefly describe each type of modeling/reconstruction technique, present application examples and highlight the authors' works.

Non-Automatic Techniques

This is the traditional approach where a modeling software - such as a CAD type software - is used to create the virtual model. It is a time consuming and manual process, which entails a higher labor cost. The process of creating the virtual model is generally based on the data gathered from the topographic survey made on the archaeological site and excavations, in the building footprints, drawings, textual descriptions, among others. The obtained models are usually simple and lacking in detail. Sometimes, to complete them, models generated by using other techniques are used.

Regardless of its drawbacks, this approach has been successfully used over the past few years by itself or together with other techniques. It still is used in some virtual reconstruction projects. For example, non-automatic techniques were used to create a virtual model of Bracara Augusta (Portugal) (Bernardes, 2002), to model some of Conimbriga's (Portugal) buildings (Gonçalves, 2002) and to model the city of Lisbon (Portugal) before the 1755 earthquake (Câmara, Murteira & Rodrigues, 2009).

One of the authors has participated in a project which the goal was to produce a virtual model of Vila Velha, name by which the city of Vila Real, Portugal, was known in the 13th century (Lebres, 2011). The virtual model (Figure 2) was created based on data gathered during the excavations, from a topographic survey, on-site evidences, discussions with the Director of the Vila Velha's Museum and with the Archaeologist responsible for the excavations, the analysis of similar structures (such as the Castle of Trancoso) and of documents provided by the Museum and by the Archaeologist.

Based on that virtual model, a video that presents - with a fly-over perspective – Vila Velha's various aspects in the thirteenth century, was created.

Figure 2. Virtual model of Vila Velha, Vila Real, Portugal
Lebres, 2011.

(Semi-) Automatic Techniques

As a result of the previously referred traditional techniques' disadvantages, several other approaches have emerged that try to automate the virtual model's creation process or to reduce human intervention while making model's visualizations more photo-realistic. A number of these approaches can be classified according to the type of data they use as source - some use images or video and others use data acquired from a laser scanning device – and others resort to procedural modeling to generate virtual models. The following subsections briefly describe each of these three types of approaches.

Image-Based

3D reconstruction from images allows the construction of an object's model from its projections - the images obtained by an image acquisition device like a camera - what represents a transformation from a 3D model (the scene in the camera's field of view) to a 2D model (the image). This transformation process usually follows the perspective model, also known as pinhole model, which assumes that the camera performs a perspective projection (Figure 3). In this model, all projecting rays pass through a single point (C), called projection center. The image (P') of each point (P) in the scene, is formed by the intersection of the projecting ray with the projection plane, perpendicular to the Zs axis, which is at a distance f – the focal length - from the projection center. Parameters related to the camera's characteristics must still be added to the perspective model. Therefore, the relation between a point's image coordinates and its 3D coordinates is defined by the equation (Faugeras, 1993):

Figure 3. Perspective or pinhole model
Couto, Magalhães, Melo-Pinto & Gabriel, 2005.

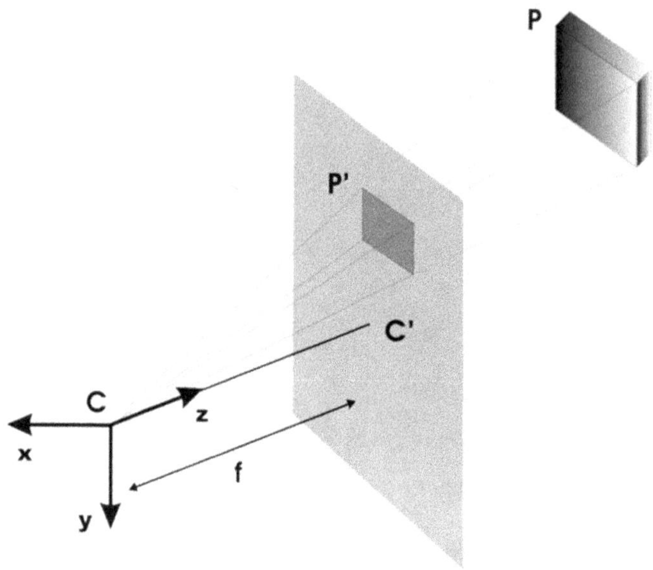

$$\tilde{p} \cong K \cdot \left(R^T - R^T \cdot t\right) \cdot \tilde{P} \tag{1}$$

in which $\tilde{p}$ and $\tilde{P}$ correspond to the homogeneous coordinates of the image point and to the 3D point coordinates, respectively. Matrix R and vector t constitute the camera's external (or extrinsic) parameters, which respectively define the camera's orientation and its position relatively to a global coordinate system. The K matrix contains the camera's internal (or intrinsic) parameters, i.e. those that depend only on the camera's characteristics.

The perspective model is only an approximation to the image's formation process. There is a set of additional effects that must be considered and that depend heavily on the camera's characteristics and of its lens. Usually a set of radial and tangential distortion parameters are added to the internal parameters.

The 3D reconstruction problem can be seen as an inverse perspective projection problem where the aim is to determine the 3D point coordinates, given its 2D coordinates and the knowledge of both the internal and external camera parameters. On this subject's vast bibliography, several techniques that try to solve the 3D reconstruction problem can be found. These techniques can be classified based on the number of images used and on the known set of camera parameters. Thus, they perform the reconstruction:

- Based on a single image;
- Based on two or more images
    - Fully calibrated (internal and external parameters known);
    - Only the internal parameters are known;
    - Uncalibrated: both the internal and external parameters of the cameras are unknown.

With a single image the problem is not determined, since there are several solutions for P. However, if geometric constraints are added in a sufficient number (for example, points have to belong to planes, points are collinear or there are known angles) then the problem becomes solvable. Etienne Grossmann and José Santos-Victor (Grossmann & Santos-Victor, 2005) proposed a method that performs 3D reconstructions from a single image or from multiple images, taking advantage of geometric constraints provided by the user. The method was applied to obtain a virtual model of the Eiffel Tower from a postcard.

If two or more images are used and the corresponding camera's positions and its internal parameters are known, the problem has a simple solution using a triangulation technique. From a geometrical perspective, it is simply the determination of the corresponding projecting rays' intersection point. Due to the presence of noise, triangulation techniques usually obtain the solution by minimizing an error. However, the internal and external camera's parameters are usually not known in advance. In most cases, a calibration process is used to determine each camera's internal parameters, before the image acquisition step. Then, the camera's external parameters - position and orientation - can be obtained based on the correlation between projections of various points in the different images. After having both the internal and external parameters estimated, a triangulation technique can be used to compute the 3D points' coordinates. Once the solution is obtained, a refinement process is usually applied to the obtained parameters and 3D points' coordinates, by using a technique called bundle adjustment (Triggs, McLauchlan, Hartley & Fitzgibbon, 1999). This technique has been used in the field of photogrammetry since the 1950s, both in the case of aerial photographs and in the case of close-range photogrammetry.

When the camera's internal parameters are known a different approach is applied which involves the inclusion of geometric constraints by imposing that points must belong to a given geometric entity (*e.g.* a parallelepiped). This is called a model-based approach. In 1996, Paul Debevec (1996) proposed an approach which became quite popular, originating an application: Facade. Moreover, it was also the inspiration for some commercial applications, such as PhotoModeler™ or ImageModeler™. These approaches require the user's intervention to define the geometric model and to associate it to image points.

When the camera's internal and external parameters are not known, the reconstruction that is obtained using only information from the image's correspondences, is projective. Therefore, it is necessary to apply a process, called self-calibration, to transform the projective reconstruction into a metric one. This transformation may be achieved by imposing some restrictions on the internal parameters, as for example, by imposing that they have to be constant for all images or that only the focal distance may vary. The final solution can also be refined by using the bundle adjustment technique. Pollefeys (1999) proposed a method to obtain a 3D reconstruction from uncalibrated images – that is, without knowing the camera's parameters – which is subject to the condition that the internal parameters remain constant with the exception of the focal length, which may vary. This method was applied in the virtual reconstruction of the archaeological site of Sagalassos, in Turkey (Pollefeys, Van Gool, Akkermans, De Becker & Demuynck, 2001), together with other techniques. More recently, a similar method using images gathered from the Web, more specifically from Flickr, obtained 3D reconstructions of some monuments (*e.g.* Colosseum of Rome) or locations (*e.g.* St. Mark's Square) in three European cities, Rome, Venice and Dubrovnic (Agarwal *et al.*, 2011).

Range Scanning

This type of technique uses a range scanning device to obtain a model of the object of study. It can be applied at various scale levels, which implies the use of different devices and with different precisions.

At larger scales, range scanners such as satellite-mounted sensors (*e.g.* RADARSAT, ERS and ASAR) or airplane-mounted sensors (*e.g.* LIDAR) can be used to obtain a digital terrain model or to obtain an approximate model of the entire archaeological site. Actually, radar data captured by satellites was used to detect and map archaeological ruins of the Maya civilization, which gave good results even in forested areas (Lira, López & Rodríguez, 2005). Using a LIDAR device it is possible to obtain data at a smaller scale and with a greater precision as it was made in some archaeological projects where LIDAR data was used to obtain a terrain's digital model with an accuracy of 1 m, thus enabling the detection of archaeological ruins (Challis, 2006). LIDAR data can also be used to create 3D buildings' models (Rodrigues, 2005).

At smaller scales, laser scanning devices are usually used. These devices can be classified into two types - TOF (Time of Flight) and Triangulation - depending on the technique that is used to make the measurements. TOF devices have a lower resolution but a higher scanning volume. Therefore, the size of the object to be scanned is what's going to determine the type of scanning device to use. However, it may be necessary to perform several acquisitions considering the size of the area to be scanned, each one at a different position. This implies the use of an alignment process for the acquired data to have a single reference, enabling to merge the data into a single object model. The alignment process is also known as registration and it can be performed by using several techniques, being most of them based on the ICP (Iterative Closest Point) approach (*e.g.* Nishino & Ikeuchi (2002). Laser scanning devices have long been used in the field of archeology for archaeological sites modeling (Allen *et al.*, 2003; Beraldin *et al.*, 2005) or to create artifacts' models (Kampel, Mara & Sablatnig, 2006).

Procedural Modeling

Procedural modeling consists in a collection of semi-automatic processes and techniques applied to generate virtual environments and structures, with a reduced demand for user interaction. These techniques have been studied, developed and applied by several researchers and professionals who recognize the potential of procedural modeling in reducing development time in projects requiring the massive production of virtual structures, such as traversable buildings or extensive urban environments. From the perspective of some business and research areas (*e.g.* architecture, archeology, video games producers) procedural modeling's major strength lies in the reduction of technological resources and skilled labor, while ensuring faster progresses towards the production of virtual content through computer-based processes. An ideal scenario would be that a few user inputs would be enough to trigger the generation of a realistic city.

The application fields are numerous and the video games industry is perhaps one of the most obvious cases, due to the use of complex road networks and rich urban environments, pretty noticeable in titles such as Grand Theft Auto (GTA by Rockstar, 1998) or Need For Speed (NFS by Electronic Arts, 1998). Actually, NFS was a case study for Watson *et al.* (2008) who had underlined the applicability and importance of procedural modeling in the production of certain game contents - such as buildings and road networks - due to its cost-effective and dynamic nature. Moreover, they suggest that designers who demand for automatic ways of generating game contents to avoid tedious and repetitive hand-made tasks, can be supported by procedural modeling tools to generate the first set of urban objects, that afterwards can be customized to make them look like what they have projected. Another application field is 3D cinema. Enterprises like Pixar (1990) or Dreamworks Animation (1998) are specialized in producing 3D movies that include human and animal characters, cities, villages and forests. Some of their productions already take advantage from procedural modeling techniques. For example, in the Monsters Inc. (Pixar) movie, the hair of Sulley character is procedurally animated (Cohen, 2001). Fracturing and debris technique is another valid example of a procedural approach that was applied in several Kung-Fu Panda movie scenes (Dreamworks) involving massive destruction of structures (Lee, Pavlov & Animation, 2008). During the last few decades, several works targeting areas that include – but are not limited to - urban planning, architecture and archeology were developed, addressing the generation of building exteriors uniquely composed by outer facades (*e.g.* Parish & Müller (2001); Wonka, Wimmer, Sillion & Ribarsky (2003); Müller, Wonka, Haegler, Ulmer & Van Gool (2006b); Carrozzino, Tecchia & Bergamasco (2009); Silva & Coelho (2011)) and traversable buildings with interior divisions (*e.g.* Hahn, Bose & Whitehead (2006); Marson & Musse (2010); Merrell, Schkufza & Koltun (2010)).

Notwithstanding procedural modeling advantages, it is important to consider that some of its applications are more suitable than others. For example, Generative Modeling Language proposed by Hohmann *et al.* (2010) enables the virtual replication of real-world buildings - including interior rooms - with a good degree of resemblance, but it also demands programming skills and several hours of user interaction. On the other hand, the L-system-based approach developed by Parish and Müller (2001) enabled the rapid propagation of procedural rules with a reduced number of inputs (such as geographic maps and population density) for automatically producing large-scale cities. For concept proof purposes, a virtual representation of Manhattan city was generated with 13000 buildings in approximately 10 minutes. Procedural modeling is particularly beneficial for experts on archeology and related areas, more specifically, for those who work towards the recovering of cultural heritage - such as ruins - inasmuch as it offers expeditious and cost-effective processes that allow to propose hypothetical virtual models based on historical evidences/facts that aim to reach to plausible digital reconstructions of severely damaged or completely destroyed monuments.

Procedural Modeling of Buildings

Research and business areas like architecture, archeology or video games demand the use of virtual building models to satisfy different requirements, committed with their own business models or researching purposes. Traditionally, the production of such models requires intense labor and large ranges of time, resulting in high costs of production. To tackle with this issue, many researchers developed semi-automatic techniques to expeditiously produce virtual building models which are presented in the next subsection, along with some projects towards the reconstruction of severely damaged or lost cultural heritage. The two following subsections - Overview of major techniques and Approaches for Cultural Heritage - are based on the literature review made in Adão, Magalhães & Peres (2016). This section ends with ERAS project (Adão, Batista, Peres, Magalhães, & Coelho, 2013), which is a solution for the digital recovery of cultural heritage sites that combines rules extraction from textual descriptions with a procedural modeling approach.

Overview of Major Techniques

This subsection focuses on some of the most important procedural modeling techniques for the generation/reconstruction of buildings, covering approaches for both exteriors (outer facades) and interiors (traversable buildings).

Regarding the procedural modeling of exteriors, one of the first reported approaches was a technique known as L-System which was originally applied to study plant development by Lindenmayer (1968) and several years later applied for city generation by Parish and Müller (2001). Essentially, this approach consists in an iterative replaceable system working with symbols that reflect a geometric transformation. In spite of being predominantly used for exteriors, Rodrigues *et al.* (2014) used L-systems for the virtual generation/reconstruction of traversable roman buildings, more specifically at the floorplan generation step. Split grammars constitute another known technique proposed by Wonka *et al.* (2003) to detail outer facades. The process starts with an initial shape that undergoes a process of consecutive splits and replacements that aim to enhance a certain element (for example, a window). It ends when a final shape is reached, which is the same to say that there are not more shapes to split or replace. Also towards feature detailing, Finkenzeller *et al.* (2005) launched a method based on floor planned modules (fpms) which can be seen as aggregations of ground marks to describe a building morphology, regarding structural elements (*e.g.* balconies). Other techniques for building reconstruction might rely on manual modeling tasks to setup building components based on picture surveys, rule-based comparison of building outlines provided by GIS with topologies, extrusions and attributions of building components to the extruded walls (Dikaiakou, Efthymiou & Chrysanthou, 2003). Random extrusions (Greuter, Parker, Stewart & Leach, 2003) showed to be pretty effective in the generation of urban environments. The process starts with an elementary set of geometries, at the building top. Then, an extrusion forms a volume and primitives are added to a subsequent level. The process is repeated until reaching the building's ground level. Computer generated architecture (CGA) proposed by Müller *et al.* (2006b), produces hollow buildings in the following steps, essentially: (1) a mass model is created considering the aggregation of volumetric shapes; (2) outer facades are generated; (3) finally doors and windows are placed. CGA became useful in some works related with cultural heritage reconstructions, as it was demonstrated by Müller *et al.* (2006a), Dylla *et al.* (2010), Besuievsky and Patow (2013) and also Tepavčević and Stojaković (2013), whose works will be analyzed in more detail the next subsection. Procedural approaches based on digital image processing of facades were also proposed by Müller *et al.* (2007) and Koutsourakis *et al.* (2009). Whilst the former (CGA) focus the decomposition of a real facade picture into architectural elements that will be integrated in a tree-based shape grammar definition, the latter combines facade image processing, parametric grammars and optimizations based on Markov Random Field formulations, to generate 3D buildings' models.

Other authors proposed techniques for procedurally producing buildings with interiors, most of them focused on floor plans. Rau-Chaplin *et al.* (1996) explored the potential of shape grammars in the design engine of LaHave House service. On the other hand, Martin (2005) proposed a technique for generating houses based on graphs and expansion algorithms. The former defines rooms' layouts and connections, while the latter is responsible to make those rooms expand and fill the building's layout, until an equilibrium state is reached. Bradley (2005) opted by constructive solid geometry algorithms to carry out the geometric transformations of traversable buildings. At the floor plan production stage, empty rectangular cells are created inside the building's layout to hold internal rooms that are distributed through a recursive approach for cells occupation. A lazy strategy for building parts' generation on real-time based on random numbers was proposed by Hahn *et al.* (2006). Voronoi diagrams were explored by Rinde (2008) to generate rooms inside a confined building region. Rooms' connections are ensured by a graph, as in Martin (2005). In Rodrigues *et al.* (2008a,b,c), the most prominent used technique relied on connecting rooms' graphs at the floor plan production stage. They are set up based on: a) user rules or b) spontaneous L-Systems. Another well-known strategy for generating interior rooms - explored in

Marson & Musse (2010) and Mirahmadi & Shami (2012) - is the squarified treemaps (Bruls, Huizing & Wijk, 1999) which consists in splitting a building's layout into rectangular areas considering a set of weights and the following key rule: in each division, it must be ensured that the aspect ratio has the closest value to 1. After that crucial step, the rest of the floor plan is achieved and, then, the 3D model. Bayesian network was a strategy used by Merrell *et al.* (2010) for rooms connectivity, i.e. for topology optimization. Geometric optimization is achieved with a greedy Metropolis algorithm. An approach inspired on architect grids was developed by Lopes *et al.* (2010). Their technique is part of the floor plan generation stage and considers some constraints to place rooms' sets inside grids and make them expand until the limits. Programming-based modeling approaches (Hohmann *et al.*, 2010; Leblanc, Houle & Poulin, 2011) can also be considered as procedural approaches. However, they are not so obvious since programming skills are demanded. As an alternative, other authors (Lewis & Séquin, 1998; Santos, Dionísio, Rodrigues & Pereira, 2011) suggest semi-automatic based processes working with manual floor plans that, in turn, are converted into digital drawings for further extrusions and completions.

Ontologies have been considered for both interior and exterior generation/reconstruction approaches. Liu *et al.* (2008) proposed a solution for recovering ancient China's outer facades with an ontology-based extensible system, capable of covering other oriental styles. Also relying on ontologies, Bellotti *et al.* (2011) proposed a solution that uses them to categorize building facades and to properly decorate them. A procedural framework covering building interiors that uses semantic information to make the selection of the proper procedural technique accordingly with the stage of generation was developed by Tutenel *et al.* (2011). Another solution using ontologies to regulate the generation of buildings guided by the specification of activities was developed by Trescak *et al.* (2010). Recently, a method combining shape grammars and multi-coordinate systems was proposed by Edelsbrunner *et al.* (2016) to endow their procedural modeling solution with tools capable of generating ancient buildings with spherical and cylindrical shaped structures.

Approaches for Cultural Heritage

Procedural reconstruction of cultural heritage sites focused in buildings' exteriors was addressed by several authors. For instance, Dikaiakou *et al.* (2003) proposed a methodology capable of digitally preserving the ancient city of Nicosia through a partially automatic method, which combines geographic data of building bases, building classification and style-concordant buildings' components, such as doors and balconies. Two distinct processes integrate the proposed method. One consists in photographing particular elements of the city to model realistic virtual buildings' components. The other is a rule-based automatic process that starts by comparing the outline of each building - obtained from GIS data - with templates, to determine the building's topology. Then, the ground edges are transformed into 3D walls. The previously modeled virtual buildings' components are applied to each wall, accordingly with the building's topology classification and with the available wall space. Finally, using a straight skeleton computation approach (Aichholzer & Aurenhammer, 1996; Felkel & Obdrzalek, 1998), each building's roof is properly produced and applied.

CGA was also applied in some works aiming virtual reconstructions (Besuievsky & Patow, 2013; Dylla *et al.*, 2010; Müller, Vereenooghe, Wonka, Paap & Van Gool, 2006a; Tepavčević & Stojaković, 2013). Müller *et al.* (2006a) used it with the purpose of reconstructing Puuc-style buildings that are similar structures to the ones found in Xkipché, México. To fulfill the architectonic requirements of

Puuc-style buildings, the authors created a grammar which defines a building accordingly with the typical design of those structures: first, the base is defined; then, middle walls are addressed, considering the building's accesses; upon these walls, a middle-layer is produced, designated by medial molding; the last rules define frieze, cornice molding and completion ornaments.

The same methodology was applied by Dylla *et al.* (2010) who produced a 3D reconstruction of ancient Rome through the combination of manually designed structures and procedurally generated buildings, in the same virtual environment. Each element's class defines what kind of approach is needed. For known positions, dimensions and design, class I elements are loaded from models created using a commercial CAD software. If some information is missing, class II elements are generated procedurally using CGA shape methodology.

Besuievsky and Patow (2013) developed their own CGA shape rules to reconstruct historic buildings and urban environments for serious games. As input, they use 2D data provided by GIS with corrective mechanisms to deal with map issues, like distortion. This allows the acquisition of relevant features, such as building outlines, for further extrusions, forming mass models. The production of building facades is made through a user-friendly tool which hides the grammar to improve the easiness of use. The application of this methodology produced some interesting results on the virtual reconstruction of Carcassone's old town, in France. The tool's flexibility was demonstrated through the virtual reconstruction of two other cities with different architectonic styles: Nantes of France and Girona of Spain.

Tepavčević and Stojaković (2013) developed a reliable mathematical model that combines fuzzy logic and probabilistic calculations to produce stochastic CGA's shape rules, which are used to generate realistic Neo-Gothic chapels. Each set of rules defining a chapel starts by specifying a building's lot and a mass model. The mass model is decomposed into three main parts: apse, nave and tower. Apse and tower mass model's parts are replaced with appropriate shapes and the subsequent steps will detail the model until the final 3D form.

An ontology-based solution was proposed by Liu *et al.* (2008). The authors embraced the challenge of recovering the cultural heritage of ancient China. To accomplish such challenge, a city generator was developed, capable of producing virtual models based on an ontology and on user input: a grammar for building definitions. Moreover, a style checker was implemented to avoid generation inconsistencies, such as buildings upon streets. Their work is also one of the few cases of an extensible ontology application that covers other architectonic styles. This system followed their previous work (Liu, Xu, Pan & Pan, 2006) in which a semantic-based modeling system was proposed. The objective was to improve users' focus on its specific implementation, while the geometric details are encapsulated by the semantic elements such as walls, doors and windows. In short, a user propagates a building's semantic information using a XML format and then a document-type definition verifies the XML conformity. Finally, in case of success, a procedural modeler produces the geometry according with a user demands.

Recent works include some additional features. Yong *et al.* (2012) reported the improvements made to the previous semantic-based solution (Liu *et al.*, 2006) that intended to overcome some noted issues regarding procedural modeling, such as the lack of annotations for digital architectural heritage, which also impacts in the identification of procedural rules for digital reconstruction of missing monuments. Such issues triggered the proposal of an approach that puts together semantics, machine intelligence, data mining and automatic annotations. Later, a granular ontology approach was suggested by Liu *et al.* (2014) to allow a collaborative ontology design based on the sub-concepts provided by users of different expertise areas.

Recently, Edelsbrunner *et al.* (2016) proposed a procedural modeling solution, based on shape grammars, that aims the production of spherical and cylindrical shaped structures through coordinate selection and manipulation of a so-called "cylindrical coordinate system". Attachments, cuts, splits and intersections are examples of supported operations towards the creation of structures such as towers, barrel vaults and crossed-vaults. According the authors, their approach can be useful for the generation of the conic parts that are often present in historical buildings.

The production of ancient buildings with interiors has not been receiving so much attention by the scientific community. Still, there are some works that are noteworthy. In that scope, Rodrigues (Rodrigues *et al.*, 2008a; Rodrigues, 2010) proposed a rule-based method capable of generating Portuguese houses (regulated by RGEU, 2008) as well as reconstructing ancient roman houses (following Vitruvius rules reinterpreted by Maciel (2006)). Several steps such as room graph definition, floor plan composition using shapes and extrusions considering doors and windows, lead to the 3D model achievement. Rodrigues *et al.* (2008c) revealed, in detail, the methods and processes carried out to generate roman houses, which include spontaneous L-systems, multilayer graphs defining containers and also room connections, among other relevant procedural operations. Later, Rodrigues *et al.* (2010) extended their work to provide virtual buildings' models in several formats (for example, X3D and VRML). The improvement foresees the integration with virtual platforms like Second Life. The aforementioned works culminated on a doctoral thesis (Rodrigues, 2010) that has some images depicting virtual reconstructions of roman houses.

Lately, Adão *et al.* (2016) implemented an ontology-based procedural modeling approach for the production of coarse virtual building models with floor-plans outlined by arbitrary shapes and divisions formed by convex polygons. Ontology-based grammar rules specifying buildings constitute the main input of the procedural modeling methodology that processes it after a proper validation step to catch typos and geometric inconsistencies at the floor-plan level. Regarding the subsequent procedural modeling process, a modified treemap approach and a fake-concave technique providing support to the subdivision of building layouts into floor-plans outlined by arbitrary shapes are proposed, along with a method that allows the adaptation of contour walls belonging to interior rooms. Markings for doors and windows, wall extrusions and completions precede the resulting virtual model. This work begun in ERAS project that aimed the reconstruction of missing cultural heritage monuments through the automatic extraction of rules from textual descriptions and its propagation to a procedural modeling module, capable of reconstructing complying ancient buildings. ERAS is presented in more detail in the following subsection.

ERAS Project

To address the digital reconstruction of severely damaged ancient structures, without the need for extensive document analysis and simultaneously ensure rapid generations and reliable virtual representations, a research project entitled "Expeditious Reconstruction of Virtual Cultural Heritage Sites" (ERAS, FCT/PTDC/EIA-EIA/114868/2009) was launched (Adão *et al.*, 2013). Two specialized modules in traversable buildings virtual reconstruction are part of the ERAS system. Each module focuses on a different thread to decrease the complexity and to properly respond to the issues raised by the referred problems. The case-study of ERAS was a subset of roman ruins situated on Conimbriga.

The information extraction module holds the process which is responsible for converting a textual description into an ontology-based data structure, in a specific roman architectural data model. Grammatical rules to parse textual descriptions of Conimbriga's missing roman buildings (Correia, 2002) were developed on Nooj (Bontcheva, Cunningham, Tablan, Maynard & Hamza, 2002), through a graphical editor in which text patterns were identified and notes were added to complement the information extracted. Over 70 reusable grammatical rules were defined for the different building's elements specified on a pre-stablished building ontology (Adão *et al.*, 2012), such as building's parts, floors, divisions, transitions, etc. To fill some gaps on the textual description about buildings' dimensions and locations (Baptista *et al.*, 2012), other sources of information such as geographic data provided by GIS were also included. Regarding the internal organization of the building's divisions resulting from these textual descriptions, they had to be mapped into a 2D matrix representing the relative position of each division on the building's floor plan, as well as their connections. After properly processing that data, the information extraction module outputs a XML file as its final result, representing specifications complying with the aforementioned building ontology, in which each *building* tag represents a new cultural heritage building's definition, with dimensions and organization, i.e., nested *buildingpart* structures. Each *buildingpart* tag specifies floors which, in turn, group the *room* structures. Transitions between rooms are also declared in the aforementioned XML file. Both rooms' arrangements and transitions are defined in concordance with the previously mentioned 2D matrix map.

The procedural modeling module receives the XML file produced in the information extraction module, and uses it to populate an ontology-based class structure. Then, an architect class starts the generation process dealing with the populated classes. The process implements several steps that can be grouped into four main stages: floor plan definition, wall extrusion, roof placement and building's detailing. The first stage is to define a restriction polygon for the building. That area is then divided into several subareas following a treemap approach to generate the floor plan. Basically, the main polygon is recursively divided into smaller polygons, according to the weights defined in the reference division tree populating the class structure, to reach a floor plan organization. After rooms' distribution upon the restriction polygon, it is time to flag windows and doors. Firstly, the architect - the class entity that manages the modeling process - checks the rooms with entry doors and windows and places them properly in the frontier between the referred rooms and the building limits. Then, it queries the rooms' graph to properly flag the doors between connecting rooms. In the second stage, the walls are extruded considering the doors and windows previously flagged. Ground and ceilings are also placed in each room. Then, the geometry of the roof is created accordingly to the type of roof defined in the building's part. Currently, the supported roof types are: flat, pyramided, hipped, mansard, holed mansard and none. The final stage focuses on the enrichment of the building's model generating the geometry for the building's base, the entrance's stairs, rooms' footers, frame portals for doors and windows and other structures, with a similar level of detail.

The whole process results in a traversable building that can be observed using the previewer included in the modeling tool. To ensure portability, the model can also be exported into a wavefront file format (.obj), which is widely accepted by most CAD software tools.

Some experiments were made to test the feasibility of ERAS in reconstructing ancient buildings, based on textual information available in Conimbriga's website (Correia, 2002), an ancient Roman City located in Portugal. Four ancient buildings with clean textual descriptions were chosen: skeleton house, fountain house, insula aqueduct and via south stores. The results are presented on Figure 4. The virtual reconstruction includes the buildings' exterior facades, the buildings' interiors, roofs and buildings' details.

Figure 4. The results of the expeditious reconstruction performed by ERAS to some ancient Conimbriga's buildings, which includes buildings' facades, buildings' interiors and special structures such as gardens and impluvium/compluviums
Adão et al., 2013.

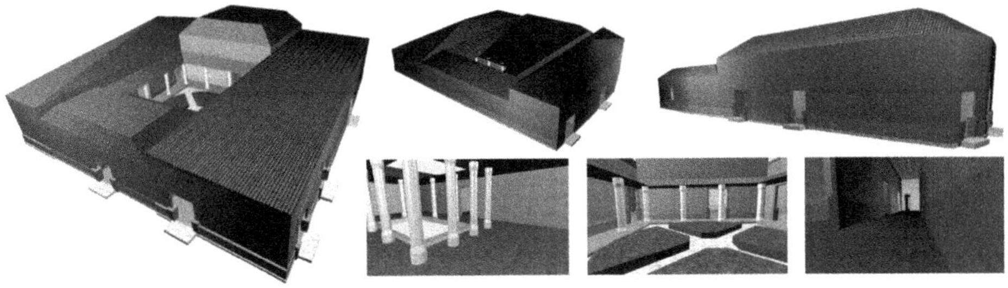

AUTHENTIC ILLUMINATION

To truly illuminate the virtual reconstruction of an archaeological site, it is necessary to replicate all the data related to it as accurately as possible. This implies to obtain objects' geometry, the photometric properties of the materials that compose the objects' surfaces and characterize all light sources.

To obtain realistic and high-quality images, the virtual models must include information about the properties of the materials that exist in the real environment. Precise simulation of light reflection and transport is of paramount importance in several areas, such as in archaeological reconstructions to investigate how a particular site or artifact may have been visualized in the past. Determining the materials' photometric properties implies understanding how light interacts with the materials surfaces. The idea is to obtain a model that allows generating an image of the object seen from any angle and under any lighting setup. Of course, getting this light source's independent model is not a simple process. There are several techniques (*e.g.* Malzbender, Gelb & Wolters (2001); Debevec (2003)) that attempt to obtain the materials' photometric properties based on objects' images.

In the visualization of archaeological sites' virtual reconstructions, the type of luminaires used plays an important role in the way how the user, visitor or specialist, perceives the site. Actually, using current lighting conditions - for example, by lighting the sites or artifacts with electric light - the archaeological sites are perceived in a significantly different manner than back when they were built or used. To obtain a virtual recreation that has scientific utility, it is necessary to recreate the light sources with precision, both from a physical and an historical perspective. This can be described as *Authentic Illumination* (Chalmers, Roussos & Ledda, 2006). Therefore, it becomes necessary to obtain physical data from the light sources commonly used in the history period under consideration or, at least, from similar ones.

Only the issue of modeling light sources to recreate the original lighting conditions as faithfully as possible will be addressed within this chapter's scope.

Until the time that electric light begun to be available, only two types of lighting were used: natural light (sun, stars or moonlight) and artificial light (fire/flame, through lamps, torches, etc.) (Forbes, 1966). This section will present methods and techniques that try to recreate natural light and flame-based artificial light. The medium through which light travels (especially the participated media) is also one of the factors to be considered. There are some approaches that try to simulate it (*e.g.* Jarosz, Donner, Zwicker & Jensen (2008); Jensen & Christensen (1998)). However, this section will not address it.

Natural Light

Several researchers have addressed the natural light simulation topic, with daytime light simulation being the one that has attracted more attention. When simulating daytime light, attention must be paid not only to the light coming from the sun but also to the atmospheric effects. Preetham *et al.* (1999) present an analytical model that provides an approximation to the daylight spectrum for different atmospheric conditions. It also includes an approximation to the atmosphere's effect - known as aerial perspective - which influences the way how distant objects are viewed, through desaturation and color shift. Most commercial or academic 3D modeling tools include rendering engines that enable - based on physical principles – the simulation of both the sunlight and the daytime skylight, when certain attributes are provided, such as the day, time and geographic location. Jensen *et al.* (2001) present a night sky's model that is based on physical principles. The model considers most of the existent natural light sources in a night sky, such as the moon and the stars. It was created considering its use for the generation of realistic night scenes' images and its applicability was demonstrated through their generation using a Monte Carlo ray tracer.

In some archaeological sites' reconstruction projects techniques have been used to simulate the effect of sunlight. One such project (Sundstedt, Chalmers & Martinez, 2004) concerned the virtual reconstruction of the Kalabsha temple, Egypt, which was literally removed from its original location due to the rise of the Nile river after the construction, in 1959, of the Aswan High dam. This virtual reconstruction's objective was to study the impact that solar illumination could have in all the architectonic and religious interpretation of the Kalabsha temple, through the simulation of its relighting by considering both its original position and the existent solar conditions at the time of its construction.

Ancient Artificial Light

It is clearly documented, mainly through archaeological finds, that candles and oil lamps were the most common sources of artificial light in the past (Forbes, 1966). The visual appearance of a scene illuminated by this type of light source depends on the flame's physical properties which, in turn, depend on the used fuel. A flame is one result of the chemical process of combustion between a fuel and the air, which defines all its attributes, such as the color, the luminance and the shape. In the case of candles, fires or torches, solid fuels such as wood, wax or animal fat are used. In the case of candles, fires or torches, solid fuels such as wood, wax or animal fat are used. In the case of oil lamps, liquid fuels such as olive oil, sesame oil, fish oil or Castor oil are used. The type of fuel used at a particular location or time depended on the available material. Sometimes, fuels have additives added, which changes their chemical composition and, consequently, the flame's attributes. Although the fuel used is one of the main factors that influence the flame's attributes, there are others that must also be considered. The physical shape and the material used in the luminaire's production also have implications on the properties of the produced light. For example, in oil lamps, the nozzle's temperature causes a preheating of the fuel, thus ensuring a more complete combustion (Egon, 2003). On the other hand, the wick can also have a significant influence on the attributes of the flame. Factors such as the material used in its construction, its height above the nozzle, its capillary capacities and its thickness must be considered.

To obtain a physically correct flame's representation, it is necessary to consider the light that it emits. Therefore, several research projects (*e.g.* Devlin & Chalmers (2001); Roussos & Chalmers (2003); Gonçalves, Magalhães, Moura & Chalmers (2008)) followed a specific procedure to characterize the light emitted by the flame-based light source, to obtain an illumination model that allows high-fidelity simulations. The procedure starts by a physical reconstruction of the luminaire (a replica of the one used in the time period under consideration). Then, the spectral distribution of the light that it emits is measured. When physically reconstructing luminaires, the materials used should be carefully chosen to create a replica as similar as possible to the original one. The same precaution should exist when selecting both the fuel and wick. Lastly, a spectroradiometer can be used to measure the flame's spectral distribution, returning readings at different wavelengths. Due to the flame's volatility and also to deal with incorrect and mismatched readings, several measurements should be made and their average value used. The data captured by the spectroradiometer can be directly used or converted to RGB, to characterize the virtual light source's photometric properties.

Once the photometric data is acquired, the next step is to model the flames. There are several approaches to do this. One of the most common is to simulate flames using particle systems: it was used in early approaches of fire simulation (*e.g.* Reeves (1983)). Moreover, while some approaches simulate only static behavior (*e.g.* Inakage (1990)), most consider the flames' dynamic behavior (*e.g.* Raczkowski (1996); Beaudoin, Paquet & Poulin (2001); Devlin & Chalmers (2001)). Some of the approaches relate to fire simulation (*e.g.* Beaudoin *et al.* (2001), some simulate flames from candles or lamps (*e.g.* Devlin & Chalmers (2001)) and others simulate flames which result from gases' combustion (*e.g.* Melek & Keyser (2002)).

There are some examples of archaeological sites' reconstruction projects (*e.g.* Devlin & Chalmers (2001); Chalmers *et al.* (2006); Gonçalves *et al.* (2008)) where the aforementioned approaches were used to simulate artificial light and to understand its influence in the visual perception of both the sites' and their existent artifacts.

VISUALIZATION

The 3D geometric model of an archaeological site, together with information about the photometric properties of the materials that make up its objects' surfaces and with its light sources' complete characterization and location in the scene, are used by the rendering engine to generate images of the archaeological site. These images can be viewed /experienced in the context of either a virtual reality or augmented reality scenario.

Virtual Reality

A virtual reality environment intends to present the user an immersive and multisensory experience of participation in a completely synthetic environment, i.e. computer generated. The immersion level as well as the number of stimulated senses depend on the technology used. Usually, only vision and hearing are stimulated, but with a greater emphasis on vision. However, in some projects such as Virtual Cocoon (Communications of the ACM, 2009), the remainder senses - smell, taste and touch - were also considered.

One of the simplest solutions to visualize archaeological sites' virtual reconstructions is to have films or interactive animations displayed on a computer's screen or on a multimedia kiosk, as was the case of Bracara Augusta project (Bernardes, 2002). There are also several projects that make use of the Web to provide ways of visualizing archaeological sites' virtual reconstructions. For example, in Conimbriga's website it is possible to access an interactive visualization of the Flavian Forum of Conimbriga (Gonçalves, 2003). Rome Reborn (Frischer, 2009) is another project where the Web was used to provide images and films of the virtual reconstruction of the city of Rome from 320 BC. Another example is to use Google Earth and/or Second Life® to visualize virtual reconstructions as, for example, a Rome Reborn project's preview (Frischer, 2009) and a visit to the city of Lisbon before the 1755's earthquake (Câmara *et al.*, 2009), respectively. However, these solutions do not allow an immersive experience to the user. By using Head Mounted Displays (HMD) or 3D glasses, the user can have a more immersive experience. Another way is by using a CAVE environment.

Augmented Reality

Augmented Reality (AR) is characterized by the addition - by overlapping - of virtual data or elements to the real world and by their visualization through some technological process in the real environment, where they seem to coexist in the same physical space. It also allows real-time interaction between virtual and real objects (Milgram & Kishino, 1994). However and unlike virtual environments, it is not intended a complete user immersion. AR has been applied in several areas, including Cultural Heritage. In the museums' context, AR can be used to complete the existing information about exposed or the unexposed collections, enabling, for example, to present or superimpose a virtual model (a reconstruction) of a partially destroyed piece.

The use of mobile devices allows the visualization of AR experiences in any location. As such, it is possible, for example, to provide to an archaeological site's visitor a richer experience by overlapping buildings' virtual models in the view that the visitor has of the current ruins. Thus, the visitor has a better perception of the object or structure in question and of its framing. The European project ArcheoGuide was one of the pioneers in the development of mobile augmented reality systems for archaeological sites (Vlahakis *et al.*, 2002). The system consisted of a mobile unit composed by an HMD with a camera and a position sensor, by a portable computer with sufficient processing capacity and a wireless connection and by a server that had all the information and contents. This system was tested in Olympia, Greece. Another reference project is LIFEPLUS (Papagiannakis *et al.*, 2002) and the works that followed it (Magnenat-Thalmann & Papagiannakis, 2010) are also worth of mention. In LIFEPLUS, besides the development of a mobile AR guide, it was also included a system to simulate virtual life which allows to add virtual characters to the AR experience. These characters then play historical narratives based on the scenes represented in the archaeological site's frescoes. LIFEPLUS was used to develop a guided tour of the streets of Pompeii in AD 79, just a few minutes before of being destroyed by a major eruption of the Vesuvius volcano.

MixAR: An Adaptative Mixed Reality System for the Virtual Reconstruction of Cultural Heritage Sites

Considering the deterioration or complete destruction of ancient buildings and monuments as being of major concern for the archeology field, the MixAR project was proposed in Magalhaes *et al.* (2014) and Narciso, Pádua, Adão, Peres & Magalhães (2015) as an adaptive Mixed Reality (MR) system that aimed to achieve the visualization of in situ ancient buildings' virtual reconstructions, properly superimposed and aligned with real-world ruins. Moreover, it provides navigability among buildings' interiors and exteriors through the soft transition feature given by a MR manager module, as long as the majority of the points-of-interest (POIs) marked for tracking remain in the scene. A POI is defined as an element for visitation (*e.g.* a ruin) which has an associated tracking configuration that, in turn, is used to trigger the augmentation of virtual models (*e.g.* monument reconstruction).

MixAR is formed by two main components, besides the network infrastructure: (1) the server that stores configurations for the MR experiences and provides a GIS module that allows to manage the geographic area where visitations will take place; and (2) the client-side Mobile Augmented Reality System (MARS) devices, responsible by managing the MR experience at the user's side. Figure 5 depicts the overall system's architecture.

MixAR's server-side is composed by a GIS and a repository that is used to store and retrieve virtual models and configurations to mobile units. The GIS module enables to georeference MR experiences areas. There is also the possibility of managing levels-of-detail (LOD) with the aim of improving performance on the user's side through the strategic exhibition or occultation of certain virtual models' parcels, depending on the distance between the viewer and the POI. Each LOD's definition is stored in a database which is consulted to build the configuration set transferred to the mobile unit, along with the models. Furthermore, the server-side implements some services that are consumed by the user's platform at runtime: (1) enable MR experiences' configurations to the mobile device, due to absence or outdated data; (2) determine the nearest POI for visitation, which is assumed to be the tracking element; and (3) retrieve a list of buildings properly identified with the right LOD, calculated considering the user's position, for computational burden management purposes. If the network infrastructure has enough quality to ensure fast communications, it should be used to balance the processing burden with the MixAR server. Otherwise, the mobile platform is able to handle the processing by itself (at least, after the first interaction with the server, that aims to retrieve MR configurations).

The client-side consists of a MARS - addressed in detailed by Pádua *et al.* (2015) - which is composed of three main components: visualization, context and processing component. To keep the mobile unit working autonomously, a power supply is also integrated. The connectivity is ensured through the network interfaces. The visualization component enables a user to see the augmented models during

Figure 5. MixAR general architecture, proposed in Magalhaes et al. (2014) and updated in Narciso et al, (2015), formed by three main components: a mobile unit carried by the user; a MR server that stores retrievable contents and handles burden processing tasks; and finally, a network infrastructure that establishes the communication among mobile units and the MR server

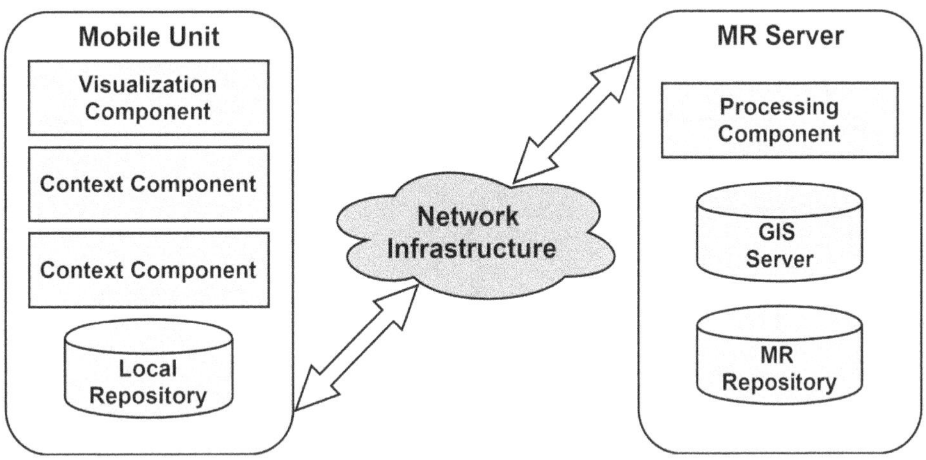

the MR experiences. Context component holds the set of sensors that permits to get aware of the surrounding environment through cameras as well as inertial and positional sensors. Data acquired from the previous component passes by the processing component which is responsible for making the required calculations and presenting the results on the visualization component.

On its very first execution, the mobile application that manages the MR experience in the MARS starts by downloading the tracking configurations - whose preparation will be explained later on - which are available on the server. Then, the CAD-based tracking configuration of the nearest POI is prepared, accordingly with the downloaded files. A virtual representation of the line model extracted from a real world target structure is loaded as a visual representation, which aims to aid the user aligning the mobile device with the POI marked for being augmented with virtual content. While the user moves within the environment where the experience is taking place, the MARS updates the tracking configurations accordingly with its location and considering the nearest building. Figure 6 presents the tracking configurations' update through a flowchart.

MixAR experiences are developed in off line tasks. After selecting the POIs, their lines, surfaces and visual aids' models must be produced to fulfill the requirements of the adopted CAD-based tracking approach. Here is a brief explanation about them (Narciso *et al.*, 2015):

- **Line Model:** Represents each structure's contours and is used to find the correct camera pose through the alignment of the virtual edges with the real-world edges, obtained from captured frames;
- **Surface Model:** It is used to determine the 3D location of projected feature points through Simultaneous Localization and Mapping (SLAM) tracking as well as to detect the visible lines of the line model, based on self-occlusion;
- **Visual Aid Model:** Aims to provide the user with visual orientation during the manual alignment of the implicit line model with the edges of the real-world structures. When a match occurs, it triggers the augmentation of the real-world structure with proper virtual content.

Figure 6. Tracking configurations' update algorithm that is carried out while the user is visiting the cultural heritage's site
Adapted from (Narciso et al., 2015).

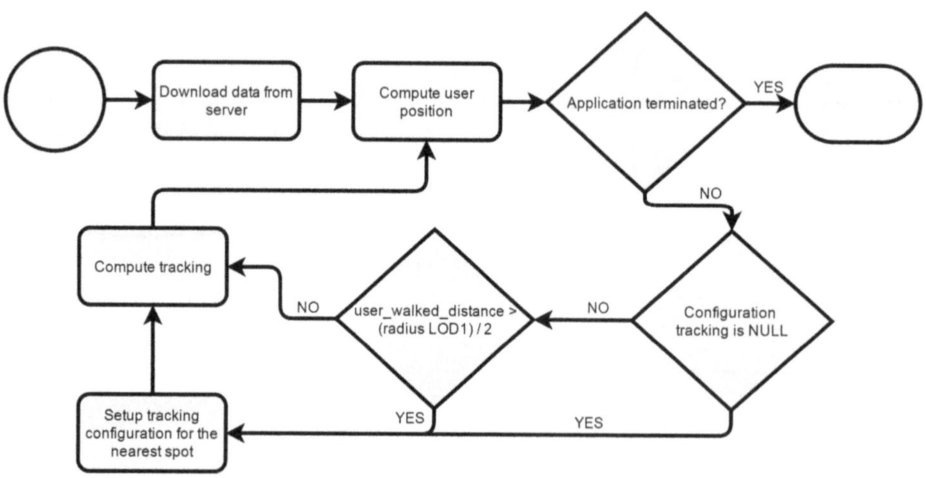

Afterwards, a procedural modeling tool (Adão *et al.*, 2016) is used to produce the virtual buildings for post-tracking augmentation. Some corrections regarding buildings' dimensions and orientations are then carried out in Blender® (Blender Foundation, 2000) upon the geographic 3D model that is retrieved by MixAR's server (it requires a previous configuration that consists in the POIs' delimitation as well as LOD definition). The desired LODs for each virtual building (i.e., different versions of the same building, with distinct details) should also be worked on in the aforementioned CAD software. Both the models and the tracking configurations are then uploaded to the server.

A set of preliminary tests was made in situ, using some of the University of Trás-os-Montes e Alto Douro (Vila Real, Portugal) structures and some POIs near the Vila Velha's Museum. Either during the tracking configurations' updates, triggered by position changes or in the post-tracking virtual models' presentation (real-scene augmentation), both a coherent and a robust behavior was noticed. Figure 7 shows some of the tests' results.

Figure 7. Preliminary tests with MixAR's mobile app running on MARS: Top row - different spots of the University of Trás-os-Montes e Alto Douro (Vila Real, Portugal) superimposed by different virtual models, assigned to check system's operable capabilities; Bottom row - CAD-based tracking approach being used in a chapel near of Vila Velha's Museum (Vila Real, Portugal), augmented after a successful tracking with exterior and interior perspectives of the virtual model
Narciso et al., 2015.

FUTURE RESEARCH DIRECTIONS

It is expected that in the future the current interest in the application of Information and Communication Technologies (ICT) to Cultural Heritage and, in particular, to the virtual reconstruction of archaeological sites, will continue. The existence of specific calls for research and development (R&D) projects for this area in the previous FP6[1] and FP7[2], as well as in the current H2020[3], shows the relevance that this area has assumed and how important ICT is in supporting the preservation and dissemination of our cultural heritage.

Despite all the R&D that has been done, there are still research directions that can be followed to improve the archaeological sites' virtual reconstruction process. Over the last years there has been a considerable research effort in automating the modeling/reconstruction stage, i.e., to define methods that automatically allow to obtain a model of the object under study. The use of reconstruction techniques from images or from range scanning data allows to automate this process somewhat, but the final result (usually a point cloud) needs always to be transformed into something with geometrical meaning. Recently, there has been an increased interest on the R&D of automatic semantic segmentation and annotation tools applied to several data sources, including point clouds. The recent Cult-Coop-9-2017 (H2020) call (European Commision, 2016) is devoted to this topic, which shows its relevance. It specifically asks for proposals that should address the "automatic contextualisation and identification of content" and the development of "innovative tools and methods to extract meaning from digital artifacts". With regard to procedural modeling, a great effort has been made to automate the process of obtaining the rules that are used in the virtual models' generation.

Inverse Procedural Modeling (IPM) is a new research field that has emerged recently. It aims to discover both the parameterized grammar rules and the parameter values that, when applied in a particular sequence, yield a pre-specified output (Musialski & Wimmer, 2013). There are two approaches to determine the referred rules. The simplest one assumes a predefined grammar and determines its derivation and parameters. It requires a rule set which has to be manually constructed and is suitable for reversing parameters on urban environments strongly characterized by patterns. The other approach focuses on the recognition of both the grammar and its parameters. Most of the IPM techniques assume that a manually designed grammar is available, which limits the reconstruction techniques to a handful of building styles for which pre-written grammars exist. Only a few approaches (*e.g.* Bokeloh, Wand & Seidel (2010)) have tackled the general IPM problem using polygonal meshes and point clouds. The authors intend to focus their attention on devising a new general IPM methodology - applicable to any structure - to extract style-specific grammars from polygonal meshes and point clouds. Another issue that also merits some attention concerns on how to deal with uncertainty regarding the generated model. In most cases, only partial information exists and it is necessary to use it to generate hypotheses. It may make sense to devise a mechanism to test various hypotheses and verify to what extent are they valid. Some of the generated hypotheses may act as constraints to other hypotheses that may arise and having a sufficient number of correlated hypotheses may enable to arrive at a solution with a smaller number of valid hypotheses. It is also necessary to reason about how these hypotheses should be shown and the mechanism to use to switch between the various hypotheses.

In the visualization stage, research is moving towards a greater realism and a greater user's immersion feeling. Using High Dynamic Range (HDR) images or videos and HDR viewing devices, highly realistic visual experiences can be provided. With regard to immersion, some researchers advocate the stimulation of all senses - not just sight and hearing - to increase the user's immersion feeling. The authors believe that based on this approach and on the aforementioned HDR technologies, it will be possible - in a near future - to provide museums' or archaeological sites' visitors with a time travel experience, that allows each visitor to fully sense a chapter of humankind history or how it would be to live in another time. Other interesting concept, which the authors hope to investigate in the coming years, is "A window to the past": a mobile device (*e.g.* a tablet) may be converted into a window for another world, which allows to have a glimpse of the past. The notion is to combine HDR images visualization with photorealistic AR, in which the environmental conditions (*e.g.* lighting, humidity, temperature) are considered so that the generated virtual models integrate perfectly with the real scene.

CONCLUSION

This chapter has presented the virtual reconstruction of archaeological sites as a process composed by a set of stages, aiming to produce a faithful and more complete virtual representation, which will allow an enhanced perceptual experience. To achieve this goal, all stages must be conducted rigorously and carefully. Moreover, the involvement of archaeological and historical experts throughout the process is crucial to guarantee the virtual reconstruction's validity. Nevertheless, it should not be forgotten that a virtual reconstruction constitutes a virtual representation of the object under study, which is based on the existent evidences and experts' interpretations. A set of methods and techniques were presented and discussed for each stage, which enables the reader to choose the ones which best suit its objectives.

The modeling stage is undoubtedly the most laborious and costly. Thus and without surprise, there has been a huge research effort on proposing and developing methods and techniques to automate it. However, there is not a "one size fits all" solution. Hence, in most cases, depending on the data available and on the goal set, there is the need to use more than one method or technique to get a complete and valid model, efficiently.

The illumination setup is often neglected in most virtual reconstructions' works, which results in visualizations that do not correspond with the original illumination conditions. Hence, the authors argue that to get an historically correct perceptual experience, the original illumination conditions should be simulated as accurately as possible. This chapter has presented some research works that propose methods which make it attainable.

The way how virtual models are both presented and experienced is important to give the user an enhanced perceptual experience. While a virtual reality scenario enables a control over all parameters and to stimulate each one of the user's senses, which provides a more immersive experience, to visualize the virtual models in situ by using AR technologies gives a more contextualized experience. Regarding the type of visualization to be used, it greatly depends on the effect that is intended to cause in the user.

One of today's hot topics is the development of both methods and tools to provide semantically annotated digital models, which will allow to create digital models' repositories that can be easily queried. This means that the semantic information contained in those repositories' models can be accessed and (re)used to help modeling other objects for which there is not enough information available. A huge research effort is being made to get an almost fully automatic reconstruction tool. The authors believe that the conjunction of forward and inverse procedural modeling techniques with the access to semantically annotated models of similar objects, will make that possible.

Current and future research on virtual and augmented reality will deliver more engaged and vivid experiences by providing multisensory and immersive environments that can be or not merged with actual ruins. The authors believe that in a near future it will be possible to provide museums' or archaeological sites' visitors with "time traveling" experiences, during which they can see and feel what it was like to live in a specific place and/or time period.

REFERENCES

Adão, T., Batista, R., Peres, E., Magalhães, L. G., & Coelho, A. (2013). Reconstructing traversable buildings for archaeology with ERAS. Proc. Virtual and Networked Organizations: Emergent Technologies and Tools - ViNOrg '13.

Adão, T., Magalhães, L. G., Bessa, M., Coelho, A., Sousa, A., Rodrigues, N., . . . Reis, L. P. (2012). ERAS - An Ontology-Based Tool for the Expeditious Reconstruction of Virtual Cultural Heritage Sites. In Actas do 20o Encontro Português de Computação Gráfica, Viana do Castelo, Portugal.

Adão, T., Magalhães, L., & Peres, E. (2016). *Ontology-based Procedural Modelling of Traversable Buildings Composed by Arbitrary Shapes*. Springer International Publishing. doi:10.1007/978-3-319-42372-2

Agarwal, S., Furukawa, Y., Snavely, N., Simon, I., Curless, B., Seitz, S. M., & Szeliski, R. (2011). Building Rome in a day. *Communications of the ACM*, *54*(10), 105–112. doi:10.1145/2001269.2001293

Allen, P. K., Troccoli, A., Smith, B., Murray, S., Stamos, I., & Leordeanu, M. (2003). New methods for digital modeling of historic sites. *IEEE Computer Graphics and Applications*, *23*(6), 32–41. doi:10.1109/MCG.2003.1242380

Baptista, R., Reis, L. P., Magalhães, L., Rodrigues, R., Coelho, A., & Sousa, A. (2012). Extração de informação de texto formal para a modelação expedita de edifícios monumentais. In Actas do 20º Encontro Português de Computação Gráfica, Viana do Castelo, Portugal.

Beaudoin, P., Paquet, S., & Poulin, P. (2001). Realistic and controllable fire simulation. Graphics Interface, 2001, 159–166.

Bellotti, F., Berta, R., Cardona, R., & De Gloria, A. (2011). An architectural approach to efficient 3D urban modeling. *Computers & Graphics*, *35*(5), 1001–1012. doi:10.1016/j.cag.2011.07.004

Beraldin, S. E.-H. J.-A., Gonzo, L., Whiting, E., Jemtrud, M., & Valzanoe, V. (2005). A hierarchical 3D reconstruction approach for documenting complex heritage sites. *The XX CIPA International Symposium*, Torino, Itália.

Bernardes, P. J. C. (2002). *Arqueologia urbana e ambientes virtuais: um sistema para Bracara Augusta*. Universidade do Minho.

Besuievsky, G., & Patow, G. (2013). Procedural modeling historical buildings for serious games. *Virtual Archaeology Review*, *4*(9), 160–166. doi:10.4995/var.2013.4268

Blender Foundation. (2000, April 4). Retrieved 29 January 2017, from https://www.blender.org/

Bokeloh, M., Wand, M., & Seidel, H.-P. (2010). A connection between partial symmetry and inverse procedural modeling. *ACM Transactions on Graphics*, *29*(4), 1. doi:10.1145/1778765.1778841

Bontcheva, K., Cunningham, H., Tablan, V., Maynard, D., & Hamza, O. (2002). Using GATE As an Environment for Teaching NLP. In *Proceedings of the ACL-02 Workshop on Effective Tools and Methodologies for Teaching Natural Language Processing and Computational Linguistics* (Vol. 1, pp. 54–62). Stroudsburg, PA: Association for Computational Linguistics. doi:10.3115/1118108.1118116

Bradley, B. (2005). *Towards the procedural generation of urban building interiors* (M. Sc. thesis). Game Programming, University of Hull.

Bruls, M., Huizing, K., & van Wijk, J. (1999). Squarified Treemaps. In *Proceedings of the Joint Eurographics and IEEE TCVG Symposium on Visualization* (pp. 33–42). Press.

Câmara, A. G., Murteira, H., & Rodrigues, P. (2009). City and spectacle: a vision of pre-earthquake Lisbon. In *Virtual Systems and Multimedia, 2009. VSMM'09. 15th International Conference on* (pp. 239–243). IEEE. doi:10.1109/VSMM.2009.43

Carrozzino, M., Tecchia, F., & Bergamasco, M. (2009). Urban procedural modeling for real-time rendering. *Proceedings of the 3rd ISPRS International Workshop 3D-ARCH.*

Challis, K. (2006). Airborne laser altimetry in alluviated landscapes. *Archaeological Prospection*, *13*(2), 103–127. doi:10.1002/arp.272

Chalmers, A., Roussos, I., & Ledda, P. (2006). Authentic illumination of archaeological site reconstructions. In *Conference on Colour in Graphics, Imaging, and Vision* (Vol. 2006, pp. 431–434). Society for Imaging Science and Technology.

Cohen, K. (2001). Monsters, Inc.: The secret behind why pixar is so good. *Animation World Magazine*, (6), 6–12.

Communications of the ACM. (2009, November 5). *Virtual Cocoon Could Simulate Five Senses*. Retrieved 28 February 2017, from http://cacm.acm.org/news/26100-virtual-cocoon-could-simulate-five-senses/fulltext

Correia, V. (2002). *Conimbriga Ruínas - Museu monográfico*. Retrieved from http://www.conimbriga.pt/portugues/ruinas0.html

Couto, P., Magalhães, L., Melo-Pinto, P., & Gabriel, R. (2005). Caracterização do Movimento Tridimensional de Corpos Articulados. In Atas do 13o Encontro Português de Computação Gráfica. Vila Real.

Debevec, P. (1996). *Modeling e Rendering Architecture from Photographs*. Berkeley, CA: University of California. doi:10.1145/237170.237191

Debevec, P. (2003). Image-based techniques for digitizing environments and artifacts. In *3-D Digital Imaging and Modeling, 2003. 3DIM 2003. Proceedings. Fourth International Conference on* (pp. 234–241). IEEE. doi:10.1109/IM.2003.1240255

Devlin, K., & Chalmers, A. (2001). Realistic visualisation of the pompeii frescoes. In *Proceedings of the 1st international conference on Computer graphics, virtual reality and visualisation* (pp. 43–48). ACM.

Dikaiakou, M., Efthymiou, A., & Chrysanthou, Y. (2003). Modelling the Walled City of Nicosia. In *Proceedings of the 4th International Conference on Virtual Reality, Archaeology and Intelligent Cultural Heritage* (pp. 61–70). Aire-la-Ville, Switzerland: Eurographics Association. https://doi.org/10.2312/VAST/VAST03/061-070

Dreamworks Animation. (1998, September 7). Retrieved 1 May 2015, from http://www.dreamworks-animation.com/

Dylla, K., Frischer, B., Müller, P., Ulmer, A., & Haegler, S. (2010). Rome Reborn 2.0: A Case Study of Virtual City Reconstruction Using Procedural Modeling Techniques. In *37th Proceedings of the CAA Conference* (pp. 62–66). EG.

Edelsbrunner, J., Havemann, S., Sourin, A., & Fellner, D. W. (2016). Procedural Modeling of Round Building Geometry. In *2016 International Conference on Cyberworlds (CW)* (pp. 81–88). https://doi.org/10.1109/CW.2016.19

Egon, F. (2003). *Wick and fuel information for Egan Bronze Oil Lamps.* Retrieved 23 January 2012, from http://www.eganbronze.com/Pages/wicksfuel.html

Electronic Arts. (1998, July 6). *Need For Speed (NFS).* Retrieved 1 May 2015, from http://www.need-forspeed.com/

European Commission. (2016). *CULT-COOP-09-2017.* Retrieved 3 January 2017, from https://ec.europa.eu/research/participants/portal/desktop/en/opportunities/h2020/topics/cult-coop-09-2017.html

Faugeras, O. (1993). *Three-dimensional computer vision: a geometric viewpoint.* MIT Press.

Finkenzeller, D., Bender, J., & Schmitt, A. (2005). *Feature-based decomposition of façades.* Proc. Virtual Concept.

Forbes, R. J. (1966). *Studies in Ancient Technology* (Vol. 6). Holanda.

Frischer, B. (2009, May 15). *Rome Reborn.* Retrieved 29 January 2017, from http://romereborn.frisch-erconsulting.com/

Georgopoulos, A. (2014). 3D virtual reconstruction of archaeological monuments. *Mediterranean Archaeology and Archaeometry, 14*(4), 155–164.

Gonçalves, A. (2003). *O Forum Flaviano de Conimbriga.* Retrieved 26 January 2012, from http://lsm.dei.uc.pt/forum/

Gonçalves, A. J. M. (2002). Reconstrução de ambientes históricos utilizando o VRML: o caso do Fórum Flaviano de Conimbriga. Tese (Mestrado em Engenharia Informática). Departamento de Engenharia Informática, Universidade de Coimbra.

Gonçalves, A., Magalhães, L., Moura, J., & Chalmers, A. (2008). Accurate modelling of roman lamps in conimbriga using high dynamic range. In *Proceedings of the 9th International conference on Virtual Reality, Archaeology and Cultural Heritage* (pp. 101–108). Eurographics Association.

Greuter, S., Parker, J., Stewart, N., & Leach, G. (2003). Real-time Procedural Generation of `Pseudo Infinite' Cities. In *Proceedings of the 1st International Conference on Computer Graphics and Interactive Techniques in Australasia and South East Asia*. New York: ACM. https://doi.org/10.1145/604471.604490

Grossmann, E., & Santos-Victor, J. (2005). Least-squares 3D reconstruction from one or more views and geometric clues. *Computer Vision and Image Understanding*, *99*(2), 151–174. doi:10.1016/j.cviu.2005.01.002

Hahn, E., Bose, P., & Whitehead, A. (2006). Lazy Generation of Building Interiors in Realtime. In *Electrical and Computer Engineering, 2006. CCECE '06. Canadian Conference on* (pp. 2441–2444). https://doi.org/10.1109/CCECE.2006.277767

Happa, J., Williams, M., Turley, G., Earl, G., Dubla, P., Beale, G., & Chalmers, A. et al. (2009). Virtual relighting of a roman statue head from herculaneum: a case study. In *Proceedings of the 6th International Conference on Computer Graphics, Virtual Reality, Visualisation and Interaction in Africa* (pp. 5–12). ACM. doi:10.1145/1503454.1503456

Hohmann, B., Havemann, S., Krispel, U., & Fellner, D. (2010). A GML shape grammar for semantically enriched 3D building models. *Computers & Graphics*, *34*(4), 322–334. doi:10.1016/j.cag.2010.05.007

Inakage, M. (1990). A simple model of flames. In *CG International'90* (pp. 71–81). Springer.

Jarosz, W., Donner, C., Zwicker, M., & Jensen, H. W. (2008). Radiance caching for participating media. *ACM Transactions on Graphics*, *27*(1), 7. doi:10.1145/1330511.1330518

Jensen, H. W., & Christensen, P. H. (1998). Efficient simulation of light transport in scenes with participating media using photon maps. In *Proceedings of the 25th annual conference on Computer graphics and interactive techniques* (pp. 311–320). ACM.

Jensen, H. W., Durand, F., Dorsey, J., Stark, M. M., Shirley, P., & Premože, S. (2001). A physically-based night sky model. In *Proceedings of the 28th annual conference on Computer graphics and interactive techniques* (pp. 399–408). ACM.

Kampel, M., Mara, H., & Sablatnig, R. (2006). Automated investigation of archaeological vessels. In *Signal Processing Conference, 2006 14th European* (pp. 1–5). IEEE.

Koutsourakis, P., Simon, L., Teboul, O., Tziritas, G., & Paragios, N. (2009). Single view reconstruction using shape grammars for urban environments. In *Computer Vision, 2009 IEEE 12th International Conference on* (pp. 1795–1802). IEEE. doi:10.1109/ICCV.2009.5459400

Leblanc, L., Houle, J., & Poulin, P. (2011). Component-based Modeling of Complete Buildings. In *Proceedings of Graphics Interface 2011* (pp. 87–94). Ontario, Canada: Canadian Human-Computer Communications Society. Retrieved from http://dl.acm.org/citation.cfm?id=1992917.1992932

Lebres, F. (2011). *Reconstrução fidedigna da vila velha no séc. XIII. Universidade de Trás-os-Montes e Alto Douro*. Vila Real.

Lee, L., Pavlov, N., & Animation, D. (2008). Procedural fracturing and debris generation for Kung-Fu Panda. In *ACM SIGGRAPH 2008 talks* (p. 59). ACM. doi:10.1145/1401032.1401108

Lewis, R., & Séquin, C. (1998). Generation of 3D building models from 2D architectural plans. *Computer Aided Design*, *30*(10), 765–779. doi:10.1016/S0010-4485(98)00031-1

Lindenmayer, A. (1968). Mathematical models for cellular interactions in development I. Filaments with one-sided inputs. *Journal of Theoretical Biology*, *18*(3), 280–299. doi:10.1016/0022-5193(68)90079-9 PMID:5659071

Lira, J., López, P., & Rodríguez, A. (2005). Detection of Mayas archaeological sites using high resolution radar images. *International Journal of Remote Sensing*, *26*(6), 1245–1260. doi:10.1080/0143116 0512331326512

Liu, Y., Xu, C., Pan, Z., & Pan, Y. (2006). Semantic modeling for ancient architecture of digital heritage. *Computers & Graphics*, *30*(5), 800–814. doi:10.1016/j.cag.2006.07.008

Liu, Y., Xu, C., Zhang, Q., & Pan, Y. (2008). The Smart Architect: Scalable Ontology-Based Modeling of Ancient Chinese Architectures. *IEEE Intelligent Systems*, *23*(1), 49–56. doi:10.1109/MIS.2008.16

Liu, Y., Zheng, X., Tang, F., & Chen, X. (2014). Ontology design with a granular approach. *Expert Systems with Applications*, *41*(10), 4867–4877. doi:10.1016/j.eswa.2014.02.019

London Charter. (2009). Retrieved 14 November 2016, from http://www.londoncharter.org/fileadmin/templates/main/docs/london_charter_2_1_en.pdf

Lopes, R., Tim, T., Smelik, R. M., Jan de Kraker, K., & Bidarra, R. (2010). A Constrained Growth Method for Procedural Floor Plan Generation. In *GAMEON'10*. Retrieved from http://graphics.tudelft.nl/~rafa/myPapers/bidarra.GAMEON10.pdf

Lopez-Menchero, V. M., & Grande, A. (2011). The principles of the Seville Charter. In *XXIIIrd International CIPA Symposium* (*Vol. 2011*, pp. 2–6). Prague, Czech Republic: Academic Press.

Maciel, M. (2006). *Vitrúvio - Tratado De Arquitetura*. Ist Press.

Magalhaes, L. G., Sousa, J. J., Bento, R., Adao, T., Pereira, F., Filipe, V., & Peres, E. (2014). Proposal of an Information System for an Adaptive Mixed Reality System for Archaeological Sites. *Procedia Technology, 16*, 499–507. https://doi.org/10.1016/j.protcy.2014.10.117

Magnenat-Thalmann, N., & Papagiannakis, G. (2010). Recreating Daily life in Pompeii. *Virtual Archaeology Review*, *1*(2), 19–23. doi:10.4995/var.2010.4679

Malzbender, T., Gelb, D., & Wolters, H. (2001). Polynomial texture maps. In *Proceedings of the 28th annual conference on Computer graphics and interactive techniques* (pp. 519–528). ACM.

Marson, F., & Musse, S. R. (2010). Automatic real-time generation of floor plans based on squarified treemaps algorithm. *Int. J. Comput. Games Technol., 2010*, 7:1–7:10. https://doi.org/10.1155/2010/624817

Martin, J. (2005). Algorithmic beauty of buildings methods for procedural building generation. *Computer Science Honors Theses*, 4.

Melek, Z., & Keyser, J. (2002). Interactive simulation of fire. In *Computer Graphics and Applications, 2002. Proceedings. 10th Pacific Conference on* (pp. 431–432). IEEE. doi:10.1109/PCCGA.2002.1167889

Merrell, P., Schkufza, E., & Koltun, V. (2010). Computer-generated residential building layouts. *ACM Trans. Graph., 29*(6), 181:1–181:12. https://doi.org/10.1145/1882261.1866203

Milgram, P., & Kishino, F. (1994). A taxonomy of mixed reality visual displays. *IEICE Transactions on Information and Systems, 77*(12), 1321–1329.

Mirahmadi, M., & Shami, A. (2012). *A Novel Algorithm for Real-time Procedural Generation of Building Floor Plans.* CoRR, abs/1211.5842

Müller, P., Vereenooghe, T., Wonka, P., Paap, I., & Van Gool, L. (2006a). Procedural 3D Reconstruction of Puuc Buildings in Xkipché. In *Eurographics Symposium on Virtual Reality, Archaeology and Cultural Heritage (VAST)* (pp. 139–146). EG.

Müller, P., Wonka, P., Haegler, S., Ulmer, A., & Van Gool, L. (2006b). Procedural modeling of buildings. *ACM Transactions on Graphics, 25*(3), 614–623. doi:10.1145/1141911.1141931

Müller, P., Zeng, G., Wonka, P., & Van Gool, L. (2007). Image-based procedural modeling of facades. *ACM Transactions on Graphics, 26*(3), 85. doi:10.1145/1276377.1276484

Musialski, P., & Wimmer, M. (2013). Inverse-procedural Methods for Urban Models. In *Proceedings of the Eurographics Workshop on Urban Data Modelling and Visualisation* (pp. 31–32). Aire-la-Ville, Switzerland: Eurographics Association. https://doi.org/10.2312/UDMV/UDMV13/031-032

Narciso, D., Pádua, L., Adão, T., Peres, E., & Magalhães, L. (2015). MixAR Mobile Prototype: Visualizing Virtually Reconstructed Ancient Structures In Situ. *Procedia Computer Science, 64*, 852–861. https://doi.org/10.1016/j.procs.2015.08.638

Nishino, K., & Ikeuchi, K. (2002). Robust Simultaneous Registration of Multiple Range Images. *5th Asian Conf. Computer Vision*, 454–461.

Pádua, L., Adão, T., Narciso, D., Cunha, A., Magalhães, L., & Peres, E. (2015). Towards Modern Cost-effective and Lightweight Augmented Reality Setups. *International Journal of Web Portals, 7*(2), 33–59. doi:10.4018/IJWP.2015040103

Papagiannakis, G., Ponder, M., Molet, T., Kshirsagar, S., Cordier, F., Magnenat-thalmann, N., & Thalmann, D. (2002). LIFEPLUS: Revival of life in ancient Pompeii. *Proceedings of the 8th International Conference on Virtual Systems and Multimedia (VSMM '02)*, 25–27.

Parish, Y. I., & Müller, P. (2001). Procedural modeling of cities. In *Proceedings of the 28th annual conference on Computer graphics and interactive techniques* (pp. 301–308). ACM.

Pixar. (1990, December 20). Retrieved 1 May 2015, from http://www.pixar.com/

Pletinckx, D. (2008). Interpretation Management: How to Make Sustainable Visualisations of the Past. *EPOCH Conference on Open Digital Cultural Heritage Systems.*

Pollefeys, M. (1999). *Self-calibration and metric 3D reconstruction from uncalibrated image sequences* (PhD thesis). ESAT-PSI, KU Leuven.

Pollefeys, M., Van Gool, L., Akkermans, I., De Becker, D., & Demuynck, K. (2001). A guided tour to virtual Sagalassos. In *Proceedings of the 2001 conference on Virtual reality, archeology, and cultural heritage* (pp. 213–218). ACM. doi:10.1145/584993.585027

Preetham, A. J., Shirley, P., & Smits, B. (1999). A practical analytic model for daylight. In *Proceedings of the 26th annual conference on Computer graphics and interactive techniques* (pp. 91–100). ACM Press/Addison-Wesley Publishing Co.

Quattrini, R., Pierdicca, R., Frontoni, E., & Barcaglioni, R. (2016). Virtual Reconstruction of Lost Architectures: from the Tls Survey to AR Visualization. *XXIII ISPRS Congress.*

Raczkowski, J. (1996). Visual simulation and animation of a laminar candle flame. *International conference on image processing and computer graphics.*

Rau-Chaplin, A., MacKay-Lyons, B., & Spierenburg, P. (1996). The LaHave House Project: Towards and Automated Architectural Design Service. In *Proceedings of the International Conference on Computer Aided Design (CADEX-96)* (pp. 62–66). IEEE.

Reeves, W. T. (1983). Particle systems—a technique for modeling a class of fuzzy objects. [TOG]. *ACM Transactions on Graphics*, *2*(2), 91–108. doi:10.1145/357318.357320

Reilly, P. (1990). Towards a virtual archaeology. In *Computer Applications in Archaeology* (pp. 133–139). Oxford, UK: British Archaeological Reports.

Reilly, P., & Rahtz, S. (1992). Introduction: archaelogy and the information age. In *Archaeology and the information age: a global perspective* (pp. 1–28). London, UK: Routledge. doi:10.4324/9780203168349_chapter_1

RGEU. (2008). *Regulamento Geral das Edificações Urbanas, Decreto n.º 38382*. RGEU.

Rinde, L. (2008). *Procedural Generation of Indoor Environments*. Charmers University of Technology.

Rockstar. (1998, November 30). *Grand Theft Auto: The Official Site*. Retrieved 1 May 2015, from http://www.rockstargames.com/grandtheftauto/

Rodrigues, N. (2010). *Rule-based Generation of virtual traversable architectural-period houses*. University of Trás-os-Montes e Alto Douro.

Rodrigues, N. C. S. (2005). *Visualização de superfícies dinâmicas*. Lisboa: N. C. S. R.

Rodrigues, N., Dionísio, M., Gonçalves, A., Magalhães, L. G., Moura, J. P., & Chalmers, A. (2008a). Incorporating Legal Rules on Procedural House Generation. In *Proceedings of the 24th Spring Conference on Computer Graphics* (pp. 59–66). New York: ACM. https://doi.org/10.1145/1921264.1921279

Rodrigues, N., Dionísio, M., Gonçalves, A., & Magalhães, L. M. G., & P, M. J. (2008b). Rule-based Generation of Houses. *Computer Graphics & Geometry*, *10*(2), 49–65.

Rodrigues, N., Magalhães, L. G., Moura, J. P., & Chalmers, A. (2008c). Automatic reconstruction of virtual heritage sites. In *Proceedings of the 9th International conference on Virtual Reality, Archaeology and Cultural Heritage* (pp. 39–46). Eurographics Association.

Rodrigues, N., Magalhães, L., Moura, J., & Chalmers, A. (2014). Reconstruction and generation of virtual heritage sites. *Digital Applications in Archaeology and Cultural Heritage, 1*(3–4), 92–102. https://doi.org/10.1016/j.daach.2014.06.003

Rodrigues, N., Magalhães, L., Moura, J., Chalmers, A., Santos, F., & Morgado, L. (2010). ArchHouse-Generator - A Framework for House Generation. *Journal of Virtual Worlds Research*, *2*(5). Retrieved from https://journals.tdl.org/jvwr/index.php/jvwr/article/view/846

Roussos, I., & Chalmers, A. (2003). High fidelity lighting of knossos. In *Proceedings of the 4th International conference on Virtual Reality, Archaeology and Intelligent Cultural Heritage* (pp. 195–202). Eurographics Association.

Santos, D. S., Dionísio, M., Rodrigues, N., & Pereira, A. (2011). Efficient Creation of 3D Models from Buildings Floor Plans. *International Journal of Interactive Worlds*, *2011*, 1–30. doi:10.5171/2011.897069

Silva, P. B., & Coelho, A. (2011). Procedural Modeling for Realistic Virtual Worlds Development. *Journal of Virtual Worlds Research*, *4*(1). Retrieved from https://journals.tdl.org/jvwr/index.php/jvwr/article/view/2109

Sundstedt, V., Chalmers, A., & Martinez, P. (2004). High fidelity reconstruction of the ancient Egyptian temple of Kalabsha. In *Proceedings of the 3rd international conference on Computer graphics, virtual reality, visualisation and interaction in Africa* (pp. 107–113). ACM. doi:10.1145/1029949.1029970

Tepavčević, B., & Stojaković, V. (2013). Procedural modeling in architecture based on statistical and fuzzy inference. *Automation in Construction*, *35*, 329–337. doi:10.1016/j.autcon.2013.05.015

Trescak, T., Esteva, M., & Rodriguez, I. (2010). A Virtual World Grammar for automatic generation of virtual worlds. *The Visual Computer*, *26*(6–8), 521–531. doi:10.1007/s00371-010-0473-7

Triggs, B., McLauchlan, P. F., Hartley, R. I., & Fitzgibbon, A. W. (1999). Bundle adjustment—a modern synthesis. In *International workshop on vision algorithms* (pp. 298–372). Springer.

Tutenel, T., Smelik, R. M., Lopes, R., de Kraker, K. J., & Bidarra, R. (2011). Generating Consistent Buildings: A Semantic Approach for Integrating Procedural Techniques. *Computational Intelligence and AI in Games, IEEE Transactions on, 3*(3), 274–288. https://doi.org/10.1109/TCIAIG.2011.2162842

Vlahakis, V., Ioannidis, M., Karigiannis, J., Tsotros, M., Gounaris, M., Stricker, D., & Almeida, L. et al. (2002). Archeoguide: An augmented reality guide for archaeological sites. *IEEE Computer Graphics and Applications*, *22*(5), 52–60. doi:10.1109/MCG.2002.1028726

Watson, B., Muller, P., Wonka, P., Sexton, C., Veryovka, O., & Fuller, A. (2008). Procedural Urban Modeling in Practice. *Computer Graphics and Applications, IEEE, 28*(3), 18–26. https://doi.org/10.1109/MCG.2008.58

Wonka, P., Wimmer, M., Sillion, F., & Ribarsky, W. (2003). Instant Architecture. In *ACM SIGGRAPH 2003 Papers* (pp. 669–677). San Diego, CA: ACM. doi:10.1145/1201775.882324

Yong, L., Mingmin, Z., Yunliang, J., & Haiying, Z. (2012). Improving procedural modeling with semantics in digital architectural heritage. *Computers & Graphics*, *36*(3), 178–184. doi:10.1016/j.cag.2012.01.003

ENDNOTES

1. Sixth European Union Framework Programme for Research and Technological Development (2002/2006).
2. Seventh European Union Framework Programme for Research and Technological Development (2007/2013).
3. Eighth European Union Framework Programme for Research and Technological Development (2014/2020).

Chapter 8
Assessing the Use of Archaeological Sites as Cultural Tourism Resources:
The Case of Segóbriga (Spain)

Nuria Huete-Alcocer
University of Castilla-La Mancha, Spain

María Pilar Martínez-Ruiz
University of Castilla-La Mancha, Spain

Víctor Raúl López-Ruiz
University of Castilla-La Mancha, Spain

ABSTRACT

This chapter offers an in-depth analysis of archaeological sites and the value they represent to the field of cultural tourism. Specifically, this chapter discusses the suitable means of studying and managing archaeological sites, which represent tangible examples of cultural tourism. Managed properly, such sites may attract a larger number of visitors and thereby contribute to the region's socioeconomic development. In order to illustrate this line of research, this analysis will focus on one archaeological site in particular, namely the Archaeological Park of Segóbriga in the province of Cuenca, Spain. More specifically, the chapter reviews survey data collected over several years by related public institutions. The findings lend support to several measures that may improve the management of such sites in the context of cultural tourism. The most important of these is the dissemination and promotion of information about the site through WOM and eWOM.

DOI: 10.4018/978-1-5225-2927-9.ch008

INTRODUCTION

As one of the main economic activities in the world, tourism has become an important source of income for many countries (Su & Lin, 2014), as well as a creator of jobs in various service industries (Yang, Lin, & Han, 2010). This is particularly true in Spain, which has become one of the world's most important tourism powers—placing third just behind France and the United States (World Tourism Organization, 2016). Spain not only possesses many attractions, but also rivals China and Italy in terms of the number of goods it produces (UNESCO, 2015). Meanwhile, Spain's position on the World Heritage list (a marketing tool used by national tourism campaigns to attract a large number of visitors; Li, Wu, & Cai, 2008) speaks to the richness of its historical and archaeological heritage (Boto, 2016). As cultural tourism has gradually become pivotal to a destination's attractiveness (McKercher, Ho, & Du Cros, 2005), Spain has outpaced many other countries in leveraging its cultural resources, becoming the second-most important country for this type of tourism (Santos & Meléndez, 2016). Case in point: In 2015, the total volume of visitors to Spain exceeded 68 million foreigners, a year-on-year increase of 4.9% (INE, 2016).

In short, culture constitutes an important part of tourism, as it increases the attractiveness and competitiveness of tourist destinations (Hennessey, Yun, & MacDonald, 2014; Pal, 2015). Indeed, several studies have shown that tourists are particularly drawn to destinations with a richer cultural or natural heritage (e.g., Bille & Schulze, 2006; Cooke & Lazzaretti, 2008; Su & Lin, 2014; Yang et al., 2010). Through cultural tourism, visitors gain insight into the history, culture and way of life of other regions of the world (Pal, 2015). As cultural tourism gains ever more importance (Chen & Chen, 2010), it is worth noting that the fastest-growing places are those that offer tourists a glimpse into both the tangible and intangible sides of cultural experience(Datta et al., 2015).

Considering the above, this work places special emphasis on a cultural destination – Segóbriga – that possesses a unique archaeological heritage. Located in the province of Cuenca, Segóbriga is one of the five archaeological parks of Castilla - La Mancha. Having ascended as a cultural destination in recent years, this area serves as a useful case study in how tourism management can leverage archaeological sites as tangible cultural resources. Through proper management, such sites may attract more visitors and thereby contribute to the socio-economic development of the areas involved. In order to illustrate this line of research, this chapter will explore how the archaeological park of Segóbriga can act as an important historical resource for cultural tourism in that area.

BACKGROUND

In order to accomplish the above goal, we need to first establish some conceptual distinctions regarding cultural tourism and, more specifically, archaeological heritage.

Cultural tourism emerged in the early 1990s, originally for the benefit of elite clientele, but was eventually generalized as an alternative to mass tourism that values the culture of the visited community (Jovicic, 2016). Silberberg (1995) offered one of the first and most enduring definitions of cultural tourism: namely, as "visits by people outside the host community motivated in their entirety or partly by interest in the historical, artistic, scientific or lifestyle offerings, heritage of a community, region, group or institution" (p. 361). Similarly, Wall and Mathieson (2006) defined cultural tourism in terms of "tourists who experience and have contact with a host population and its cultural expressions, experiencing the uniqueness of culture, Heritage and the characters of its place and people" (p. 261; see also Lynch et al., 2011). Thus, cultural tourism is effectively a synonym for heritage or ethnic tourism—a way for travelers to access the charm of local communities' traditions, folklore, spaces and values (Rodzi, Zaki, & Subli, 2013). It is, in short, a way to bring tourists to the past (Díaz-Andreu, 2014) - or more precisely, a particular vision of the past that can then influence present and future cultures (Funari, Manzato, & Alfonso, 2013).

In most countries, cultural resources comprise some of the most important attractions. These can encompass both the material (historical/archaeological resources) and the immaterial (ethnographic resources) - for instance, the remains of the life of a people or the place transmitted from one generation to another (Ezenagu & Iwuagwu, 2016). Along the same lines, Caro, Luque, and Zayas (2015) noted that the resources of cultural tourism are tangible assets (e.g. objects and archaeological sites, historical, artistic, ethnographic, technological, religious, etc), intangible cultural heritage (e.g., folklore, music, traditions, etc.) and even the landscape. Such resources are transferred from past to present generations, which creates the cultural heritage that underlies this brand of tourism (Pal, 2015). Archeology – defined as the result of surveys, excavations and other empirical studies designed to interpret and retrieve the past (Walle & Asgary, 2015) - is one such form of cultural heritage that governments frequently sponsor and promote as part of their tourism efforts.

Tourist destinations that have many heritage sites to visit, in particular, stand to gain from capitalizing on these resources, but other types of destinations can utilize their heritage, as well (Caro et al., 2015).

Archeology as a Tourism Resource in the Field of Cultural Tourism

Countries with a competitive advantage in attracting tourists typically possess good 'raw material' - that is, various types of tourist destinations, such as historical sites, natural landscapes or artistic traditions, among others (Mestanza & Revilla, 2016; Yang et al., 2010). When developing its tourism industry, a country must account for its natural and cultural resources, and assess their value as touristic assets (Yang et al., 2010). Thus, for those countries with an archaeological heritage, it is natural to center cultural tourism on these assets in order to generate wealth in the region. In other areas it has been implemented and has generated economic growth and reversed the migration process through demographic change by exploiting own heritage (Buckley, 2012).

Some studies (e.g., Li & Qian, 2016) show that many tourist destinations are beginning to leverage cultural and archaeological resources as a development option (Jovicic, 2016). In both developed and developing nations, but particularly in the latter, archaeological tourism is being used to foster economic development (Pacifico & Vogel, 2012). Indeed, several authors (e.g., Funari et al., 2013) note that monuments or archaeological ruins attract an enormous number of tourists; thus, it follows that such cultural resources, if used properly, can fundamentally affect a country's tourism sector (Alexandros & Jaffry, 2005; Ezenagu & Iwuagwu, 2016). Patrimonial resources, in particular, can help both tourists to know the past of the site they visit, its antiquity, etc., as well as to help the people who are economically with the economic benefits that this type of tourism can generate local or ethnic communities (Alazaizeh et al., 2016). However, the benefits of archeological tourism must be considered in the context of tensions that arise between different interested parties (e.g., government, property, administration, etc.; Funari et al., 2013). Thus, achieving sustainable heritage tourism requires good tourism management, which entails in such a way that one of its objectives is understanding the value of such resources to all stakeholders, including the tourists themselves (Alazaizeh et al., 2016).

When talking about cultural heritage management, to be part of the tourist offer, it must be borne in mind that it is mixing two very different sectors, such as culture and tourism. Leadership in both systems is carried out by different actors pursuing different goals: on the one hand, the private sector, whose main objective is to obtain economic benefits thanks to tourism. On the other hand, there is the cultural heritage, which is developed in the public sector and whose purpose is to obtain social benefits, guaranteeing their existence and conservation (McKercher & Du Cros 2002, González, 2009).

Usually, in the decisions that have been taken in the tourism management of the heritage, only the opinion of the professionals has been taken into account (managers, promoters or sellers of tourist services, etc.) (Timothy & Boyd, 2003), without taking into account that of the tourists themselves (Alazaizeh et al., 2016). However, there is value in allowing tourists to participate in the management of patrimonial tourism, in such a way that they help to improve the quality of the own experience of the trip (Alazaizeh et al., 2016). Therefore, in order to obtain a better view on heritage management, we need to account for the different stakeholders in the decision-making process (Bruyere, Beh, & Lelengula, 2009).

The Sources of Information and Their Contribution to the Tourist Promotion of Archaeological Resources

Although there has been extensive scientific research on archaeological sites such as Segóbriga, few studies have explored how visitors acquire and use information about these sites—both in terms of when they decide to travel and how their concept of such destinations is influenced by the information they encounter.

It is apparent, at least, that the attraction capacity of a tourism space is directly related to the dissemination of its heritage (Caro et al., 2015). Effective dissemination can not only improve tourist numbers, but also yield residual effects: For instance, some studies suggest that the diffusion of archeological heritage improves both the environment and the local community (Li & Qian, 2016). Spain has been a frontrunner in this regard, spreading knowledge about Spanish archeology through television programs, radio programs, magazines and books. Ruiz Zapatero (2013) suggests that the importance that archeology can be transmitted both through images and narrative. However, it is also apparent that the rapid proliferation of tourism options means that heritage can no longer be based on a supply-side motive and must evolve with consumers' interests (Datta et al., 2015). Any tourist destination that wants to be competitive must continuously outfit its visitors with the most useful and up-to-date information, as tourists look for and use travel information both online and offline. This can also serve as a reference for managers of any type of tourism to develop a more effective online search as marketing strategies (Ho, Lin & Chen, 2012).

However, information can be used another way—namely, to anticipate tourists' choice of destination (Camprubí & Coromina, 2016). As Datta et al. (2015) notes, tourism consumers interact "with [their] environment of choice, seek and take information from various sources, process this information, and then make a selection" (p. 19); in other words, they continuously consult the available sources of information in order to decide where to travel (Sparks & Pan, 2009). Of course, tourists do not possess the same prior knowledge about destinations, nor do they consult the same sources of information. Individuals differ greatly in the number and type of sources they consult, which produces wide discrepancies in their degree of knowledge (Camprubí & Coromina, 2016). For example, tourists who are culturally motivated require a great deal of information (Caro et al., 2015), but the different sources they use will alter their mental concept of the tourist destination (Beerli & Martín, 2004). Other studies agree that information sources constitute an important factor in tourists' perception of a destination (e.g., Alvarez & Campo, 2011; Llodrà-Riera et al., 2015).

There are several ways to classify tourism information sources. Building on previous studies (e.g., Gartner, 1994; Gunn, 1988), Beerli, Martín, and Moreno (2003) conceived five classifications that apply to most any destination: The first is the open induced, which refers to the different advertising venues (television, radio, Internet, etc.). The second is the covert induction, which refers to the publicity generated by highly prestigious and recognizable characters, who make the destination more salient and attractive in tourists' minds. The third is autonomous information, which is received through agents (e.g., news or popular culture) or media (e.g., documentaries, news, films, etc.). The fourth is organic information, which represents word-of-mouth passed through people known to the tourist (family, friends, etc.; see also Tasci & Gartner, 2007). The fifth is simply one's own experience of visiting the destination itself.

Of course, the expansion of lifestyle media (e.g., series, travel television programs, etc.) and the Internet (e.g., social media) has imbued tourists with even broader access to information (Sparks & Pan, 2009). In general, the progress of information and communication technologies (ICT), and in particular electronic commerce, offers new opportunities for tourism (Law, Buhalis & Cobanoglu, 2014). A tourist who benefits from the Web and communication 2.0 and plans his trip by searching for information on the Internet, is of great importance to online sources of information (Márquez-González & Caro, 2017). Camprubí and Coromina (2016) suggest that, apart from the information received from friends and family, online information sources are the best showcase of how tourists accumulate images of a destination. Social networks, in particular, have substantially transformed the field of tourism communication (Månsson, 2011): For instance, experiences that were previously private can now be shared publicly (Munar & Jacobsen, 2014), which allows tourists to engage with their experiences and showcase destinations in ways that may appear more authentic than country-controlled marketing. For example, Tseng et al. (2015) examined the role of blogs in China's recipient tourism and found that heritage and cultural elements were most influential when discussed by international bloggers. The breadth of this effect has spurred some researchers to claim that "social networks are changing the culture of tourism", mainly by altering how tourists search for information and make decisions, how countries promote tourism, and how companies interact with travelers (Zeng & Gerritsen, 2014, p. 32).

The advent of these new technological tools has inspired a distinction between WOM and eWOM. The latter form ostensibly encompasses online reviews and recommendations, and differs most from regular WOM in terms of its reach (i.e., number of people influenced) and speed of interaction (Cantallops & Salvi, 2014). In other words, through eWOM, consumers can obtain more information and make evaluations more quickly (Cantallops & Salvi, 2014). The main driver of eWOM, particularly with regard to tourism, is customer satisfaction—in general, greater satisfaction entails a greater possibility of positive messages (Santos & Meléndez, 2016). Therefore, the goal of eWOM is to attract new visitors by creating a positive image of a destination and simultaneously increasing people's knowledge about it (Phillips et al., 2013). However, amidst the decades' worth of research into sources of organic information, there is still a poor understanding about the consequences of WOM and eWOM recommendations on travelers' emotions, especially in cultural tourism (Santos & Meléndez, 2016). In particular, research on the relationship between archaeological tourism or cultural heritage and the eWOM source of information are also scarce. For example, the study by Márquez-González and Caro (2017) analyzed the best positioning of Heritage Cities in eWOM tools. One of its results was that Cuenca ranked thirteenth in a list of fifteen cities declared World Heritage in Spain. This is why it is necessary to improve or solve the problem, not only in Cuenca but also in the area that occupies the present study, an archaeological park located in the province of Cuenca. The incorporation of eWOW tools in many tourist destinations, as in this case, can improve and offer all its users a unique and different experience. This contributes added value and enhances the heritage resources that make up the destination (Márquez-González & Caro, 2017).

MAIN FOCUS OF THE CHAPTER

This work analyzes the case of Segóbriga, a cultural destination with an archaeological heritage. In 1980, Spain's Ministry of Culture coined the term 'archaeological park' in order to identify the country's most important and well-preserved scientific sites for the later purpose of promoting their social value (Ruiz Zapatero, 1998). Segóbriga soon emerged as an archaeological park that could promote tourism in this area and thereby boost the economy.

Segóbriga is located about 104 km from the capital of Spain, in the municipality of Saelices and the province of Cuenca. The site lies close to other heritage resources in the province, such as the towns of Uclés (about 10 km from Segóbriga) and Belmonte (about 42 km), as well as locations that do not qualify as parks but can still be visited, such as the Roman cities of Valeria (77.5 km) and Ercávica (located 69.5 km), and the soon-to-be-utilized Roman villa of Noheda (84 km) (Provincial Diputation of Cuenca, 2016).

Various archaeological excavations have gradually revealed the history of Segóbriga. This archaeological complex features the most relevant plateau and one of the westernmost cities of the Roman Empire, both largely preserved from their original state. The name Segóbriga derives from a Celtic word meaning "Victorious City" or "City of Victorious." While data on the city's origins are scarce, there are signs that it could have been founded by the Celtiberians (Abascal, Cebrián, & Almagro, 2004). Indeed, the site seems to represent a Celtiberian fort that dominated the northern part of the city until being conquered by the Romans in the second century and becoming the capital of the plateau. Following the immigration of Roman citizens, the city underwent an economic boom due to being a mineralized center of translucent crystallized gypsum (also known as *lapis specularis*), which was used for window enclosures. Because this type of plaster was in high demand in this period, the city gained great fame within the Roman Empire. The city's other economic foci were agriculture, livestock, and stone artistry (Abascal et al., 2004).

During this same period, Segóbriga became a communications junction, which was particularly important for the transhumant lifestyle of the Eastern plateau. As a result, the city's currency (made of bronze and copper) expanded to much of the southern peninsula and part of the Celtiberia. The city reached peak development in the final decades of the first century with the construction of monumental structures, including an amphitheater, a theater, a basilical classroom and baths. These expansions necessitated simultaneous improvements to the city's water supply (Abascal et al., 2004).

In the fourth century, the city's main monuments – such as the theater, the amphitheater and the circus – were abandoned. Nonetheless, the city of Ségóbriga remained important into the fifth century. Between the years 589 and 693, city officials ordered the construction of a great basilica and the surrounding necropolis, but these efforts did not curtail the reductions in urban life. That situation continued until the Islamic invasion, at which point the ruling elites went north to the Christian kingdoms. It was also at this time that an Arab wall was built on the old acropolis, which was situated at the top of the hill. In spite of this, the city gradually lost importance throughout the Islamic period, eventually being renamed *Cabeza del Griego (Greek´s head)* when it became a rural center dependent on the people of Uclés (Abascal et al., 2004).

With this history behind the site, two public institutions the Junta de Comunidades of Castilla-La Mancha and the Provincial Diputation of Cuenca (the latter as a promoter of this archaeological park since 2014), have begun utilizing this resource to boost regional tourism and, by extensión, the local economy. However, there are various factors surrounding the site that need further consideration in order to strengthen tourism in the area. However, it is worth noting the long road that this archaeological site has yet to travel with the purpose of strengthening tourism in this area.

In its current state, the archaeological park of Segóbriga is considered an inland tourist destination, located as it is in the capital of Cuenca and around other, local resources. Many weekends, holidays, thousands of citizens decide to leave the city in which they reside to move to environments that have a historical-heritage or architectural appeal, that is, places rich in heritage that can be seen in one or two days. (Vela & Tarrés, 2005). This site receives the majority (53.44%) of its visitors on weekends. Its record number of visitors on a single day was 1,064 tourists on April 3, 2014, which coincided with Good Friday (Provincial Diputation of Cuenca, 2015).

Likewise, it also has collected data on park visits since 2002. There was substantial growth between 2002 and 2003 (158%), which tapered off considerably in the following years. The negative growth between 2008 and 2013 corresponds with the global recession and its effect on Spain. More recent years have demonstrated some slight improvements: As Table 1 shows, there was a total of 49,317 visitors in 2015, which was 5.64% higher than 2014 (46,681 visits) and 22% higher compared to 2013 (38,234 visitors) (Provincial Diputation of Cuenca, 2016).

Looking now at the seasonality of visits, Table 2 shows a slight positive variation in the number of tourists during the majority of 2015 compared to 2014 (the record was lower in February, April, May, June

Table 1. Number of visitors to the archaeological park of Segóbriga by year

Year	Number of Visitors	Rate of Change
2002	28536	
2003	73825	158,71
2004	74270	0,60
2005	75258	1,33
2006	65708	-12,69
2007	78516	19,49
2008	73768	-6,05
2009	73522	-0,33
2010	61668	-16,12
2011	57378	-6,95
2012	45792	-20,19
2013	38234	-16,50
2014	46681	22,09
2015	49317	5,64

Data Source: Provincial Diputation of Cuenca, 2016.

Figure 1. Number of visitors to the archaeological park of Segóbriga by year
Source: Provincial Diputation of Cuenca, 2016.

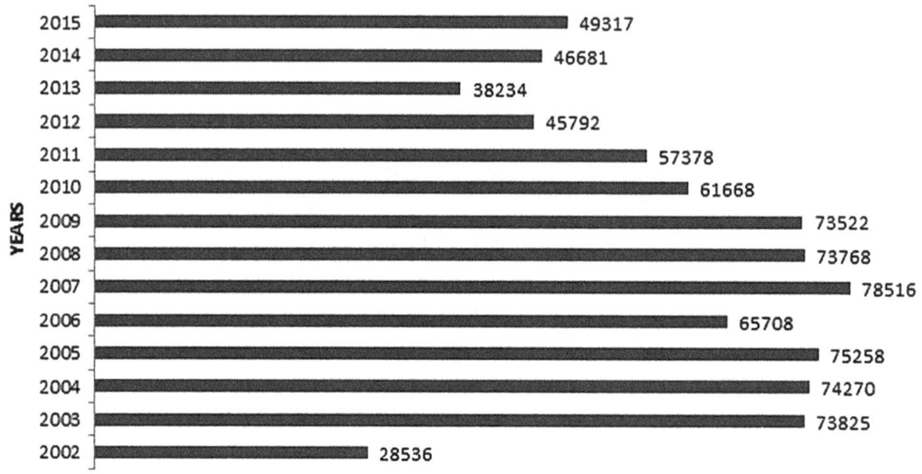

Table 2. Total visits to the archaeological park of Segóbriga per month in 2014 and 2015

Month	2014	2015	Percentage Change
January	1.307	1.727	32,13
February	2.283	2.203	-3,50
March	3.928	4.752	20,98
April	10.938	9.811	-10,30
May	7.731	7.119	-7,92
June	3.607	3.457	-4,16
July	2.079	1.182	-43,15
August	3.769	4.374	16,05
September	2.150	2.802	30,33
October	3.656	5.117	39,96
November	3.149	3.446	9,43
December	2.084	3.327	59,64
Total	**46.681**	**49.317**	5,65

Source: Provincial Diputation of Cuenca, 2016.

and July). However, in both years, the months of April and May exhibited the greater influx of visitors to the park. During 2015, 43.96% of visits happened in the spring months, 23.96% in the summer, 24.11% in the autumn, and 7.97% in the winter. In fact, it was the first year since the park's opening where the autumn season saw more visits than the summer season (Excma. Provincial Diputation of Cuenca, 2016).

During the year 2014, the Hon. Provincial council of Cuenca collected more detailed data about the park's visitors through tourist questionnaires. The data was collected from 286 respondents between March 5 and October 8, 2014. Specifically, visitors to the park were asked to complete a paper-based

Figure 2. Total visits to the archaeological park of Segóbriga per month in 2014 and 2015
Source: Provincial Diputation of Cuenca, 2016.

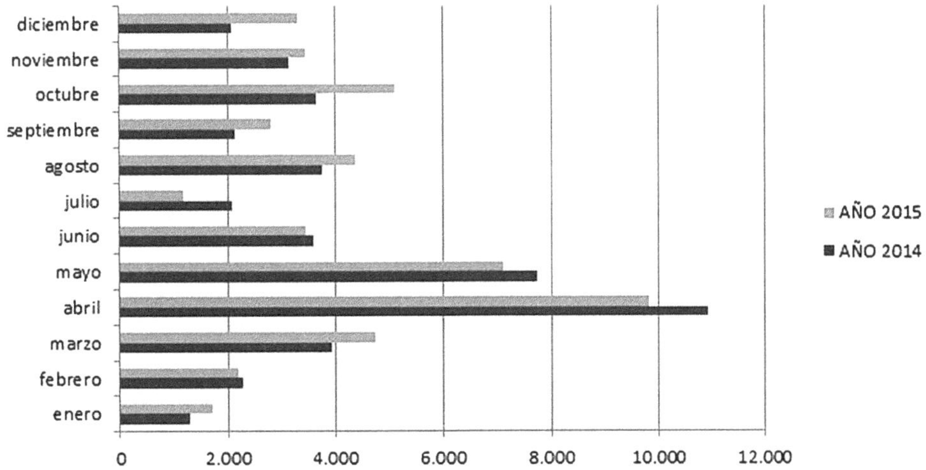

satisfaction survey as they exited the area. This questionnaire asked visitors about some personal details and their degree of satisfaction, as well as their ideas and suggestions in terms of improving the quality of the site's services (Provincial Diputation of Cuenca, 2015). The personal details included questions about visitors' age, provenance, level of studies (such as university studies, basic studies, etc.) and intended destination, as well as the sources of information they used, the duration of their stay, the reason for the visit to the province, and their knowledge of other resources near the archaeological park, among others.

The survey produced some valuable insights: For instance, in 2014, about 73% of visitors came by themselves, while the rest came in groups. Among those who visited individually, there were no gender differences, but the most prevalent age group was 41 to 60 years (followed by 26-40, 60+, 17-25 and 5-16 years). Meanwhile, students comprised most of the group visitors: The greatest number of these came from Compulsory Secondary Education (38.2%) followed by Baccalaureate (17.50%), Primary Education (8.5%), university (6.24%) and international colleges (2.78%). In terms of non-educational groups, cultural associations accounted for 11.48% of these visits while retired tourists represented 15.30%. Another 2% of visits, designated as "others", corresponded with the informative days held by the Ministry of Education. Finally, visitors to Segóbriga were particularly characterized by high levels of academic achievement: two-thirds had completed university studies, while 8% had completed graduate studies. Meanwhile, only 23% had only completed high school and 3% lacked any type of studies (Provincial Diputation of Cuenca, 2016).

Among all 2014 visitors, 78.48% came from Spain, particularly from Madrid, followed by Valencia, Cataluña, Castilla – La Mancha, and Andalucía; the rest were international visitors. In terms of the visitors' primary destination, most were traveling to the capital of Cuenca, followed by those who were traveling to other parts of the region, those who were traveling to the province itself, and those who simply wanted to visit the archaeological park of Segóbriga. Regardless of tourists' end destination, more than 50% of those surveyed had only planned a single-day trip. Those who planned to stay either two days or three-plus days accounted for a little more than 20% each. Among all surveyed visitors, more than 70% had visited the province of Cuenca more than once, while the rest were first-time visitors (Provincial Diputation of Cuenca, 2016). This is important, as some studies (e.g., Guedes & Jiménez, 2015) show that tourists consider both the cultural resources and the duration of their stay when analyzing a tourist package.

When asked about their knowledge about other heritage resources in the province of Cuenca, the greatest number of respondents noted that they were familiar with the capital of Cuenca, followed by the town of Uclés (very close to Segóbriga), the Ciudad Encantada (*Enchanted City*), and the town of Belmonte. Very few were familiar with similar sites that do not technically qualify as parks, such as the Roman cities of Valeria or Ercávica, and the Roman town of Noheda (Provincial Diputation of Cuenca, 2016). In terms of how they acquired information about the deposits, the 2014 respondents answered that word-of-mouth (organic information) was their most used, followed by the Internet (induced information). Interestingly, the third most important source for many tourists was the sign indicating the exit to the archeological park. Many of them indicated that the sign highlighting the exit to the archaeological park (located along highway A-3) was a relevant source of information. However, visitors placed little emphasis on more traditional information sources, such as printed media (brochures), travel agencies, tourist offices, news, reports, documentaries, etc. (Excma. Disputacion Provincial of Cuenca, 2016).

Regarding their level of satisfaction after visiting the park, 92.85% of respondents rated it very positively, highlighting its cleanliness and maintenance. The park's facilities were rated as 'excellent' by 64.28% of respondents and 'good' by 28.57%. Furthermore, 77.38% of respondents thought that the park's guided tour service (offered for free on weekends and public holidays) added value to their visit. In terms of inconveniences or issues, 23.52% of the total respondents and 76.31% of those over 61 years of age reported problems with physically completing the tour. Other comments highlighted the substantial distance between the interpretation center and the archaeological site, the lack of more shaded areas during the tour, and above all, the impossibility of visiting the site among disabled individuals. In terms of how to improve the reservoir, respondents proposed giving the site more publicity, expanding the summer schedule, and offering more information in other languages such as English (Provincial Diputation of Cuenca, 2016).

Figure 3. Sources of information used by visitors to the site
Source: Provincial Diputation of Cuenca, 2016.

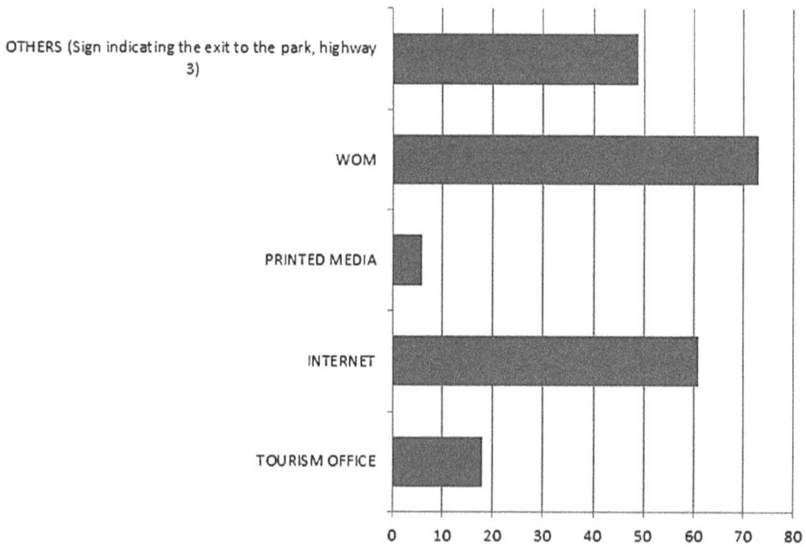

FUTURE RESEARCH DIRECTIONS

New research on cultural tourism should be carried out through applications of qualitative and quantitative methods, with the aim of further analyzing the importance of cultural resources, including archaeological resources, in attracting visitors to a destination.

In order to attract more visitors to this type of cultural destinations, it would be convenient to elaborate a management model applied to the marketing analyzing first its image. See how the image of archaeological sites is formed and see which elements influence it. That is, to identify the most common variables in this area of study, as well as those that influence the tourist to decide to visit it, taking into account both their personal aspects as the sources of information used and to see how they influence the formation of that image and its subsequent behavior. All this with the intention of contributing to the improvement of the management of the image of archaeological sites.

Another of the future investigations would be the role of the local residents in the formation of the image of the destination and its recommendation as destiny suggest a management model applied to marketing for

To study the factors that determine and motivate the tourist to choose this type of cultural destination. As well as the sources of information that are most used to recommend such a destination.

SOLUTIONS AND RECOMMENDATIONS FOR MANAGEMENT

Obviously, any analysis of potential touristic resources is beholden to the prospect of creating a tourist product that attracts a growing number of visitors and thereby contributes to the area's socio-economic development. However, properly managing archaeological resources requires that one consider a given deposit's specific characteristics, which can differ even among parks of the same typology. First and foremost, it must be understood that archaeological sites only exist due to conservation efforts; therefore, they must be carefully preserved, managed, interpreted and disseminated in parallel with those efforts in order to be most valuable. That said, dissemination should not only promote the archaeological site to experts, but to any type of hiker. In doing so, managers must account for the broad disparity in tourists' level of cultural interest—whereas some are motivated by knowledge, others are simply accompanying their relatives (Hernández, De Calle, & García, 2015).

In this regard, managers should draw on the literature regarding tourism destination image. In recent decades, the increasing competitiveness between tourist destinations at the international level has prompted an interest in offering and managing a positive image in order to gain a better positioning (Tasci & Gartner, 2007). Heritage tourism is a valuable means of creating a national image and solidifying a national identity (Li et al., 2008). However, even when the value and meaning of heritage resources are understood, they are not always included in the management process (Carter & Bramley, 2002). To overcome this problem, managers need to develop empirically sound marketing programs and study the factors that motivate tourists to choose a given destination (Tigu et al., 2014). To this end, the initial stages of transforming a destination into a touristic resource should involve learning, research, adaptation and collaborative marketing (Char-lee et al., 2014).

In addition, managers need to account for the information sources that tourists use and determine which channels are the most useful. And on the other hand, in the question of social networks, it is also necessary to observe the use made of them and their transcendence among followers, since if a social network does not show activity it reduces potential tourists, and this for the future followers can be qualified as a negative aspect (Caro et al., 2015). Similarly, some researchers (e.g., Zeng & Gerritsen, 2014) have pinpointed a lack of analysis on the effectiveness of social media with regard to destination marketing and management. In this vein, Phillips et al. (2013) proposed using the WOM of previous visitors for marketing purposes. Given that the most used sources of information for Segóbriga in 2015 were WOM and the Internet, it stands that such destinations could benefit from the use of WOM and eWOM.

The tourism destination managers consider eWOM as a very relevant medium for the promotion and dissemination of tourism products. This is why it is necessary for the Global Destinations Organizations to start developing eWOM management strategies, creating online feedback between the user and the destination, so that by analyzing these comments, visitor satisfaction is improved (Litvin, Goldsmith & Pan, 2008).

Ideally, good management of an area's cultural heritage would lead to positive consequences in both the archaeological heritage and the local population, in terms of boosting the local economy and promoting the heritage of its population (Boto, 2016). Granted, it might seem that local communities would have difficulty exploiting their archaeological resources given that other economic assets may be much more profitable (Díaz-Andreu, 2013). This is why several researchers (e.g., Poria, Reichel, & Biran, 2006) note that heritage tourism needs to account for tourists' socio-psychological needs and perceptions as part of the planning and management process. Indeed, countries that have begun pursuing heritage tourism are already making great efforts to involve their visitors with culture (Bryce et al., 2015). at the same time, There can also be a positive relationship between heritage-related behaviors and loyalty, so managers must encourage and facilitate such behaviors with the aim of increasing loyalty to a destination (Bryce et al., 2015).

In short, tourism based on archaeological resources can be an instrument of power for local communities, as it allows them to preserve their past and leave their cultural mark on the present (McKercher & Du Cros, 2002). Future scholars should aim to develop and apply a management model for this kind of destination and its marketing.

CONCLUSION

The cultural tourism literature lacks insight into the relevance of cultural resources, especially archaeological ones. To inspire more research in this direction, this work focused on the importance of cultural resources in the archaeological park of Segóbriga in terms of developing tourism in the local area. It appears that treating this deposit and its surrounding elements (e.g., Uclés, Ercávica, Valería and Noheda, among others) as cultural resources could help boost tourism and strengthen the area's competitiveness in the province of Cuenca. Of course, accomplishing this goal would require that citizens participate in and disseminate the area´s heritage, fundamental pillars for the development of a strategy of linking tourism and cultural heritage. It is therefore suggested that citizens participate in and disseminate the area's heritage, which is a fundamental pillar in the strategy to link tourism and cultural heritage.

ICT have changed the way of promoting cultural heritage, in this case the archaeological heritage, in the field of tourism (Caro et al., 2015). Tourists have been changed into tourists 2.0, many more experienced, demanding and technological. This means that destinations also do so and that is why it is necessary that those responsible for managing these tourist destinations, benefit from the opportunities offered by Web 2.0 to boost or promote them, thanks to new sources of information, such as online tools, considered eWOM (Márquez-González and Caro, 2017). The large amount of information generated by these social networks or online tools, and which in turn is shared by tourists, is increasingly influential when making a travel decision. Therefore, tourism companies, in charge of managing destinations, can take advantage of the free access they have to these information channels to understand the demands and expectations of their visitors, in such a way that serves as a guide to make future improvements of distribution and promotion (Zhang & Cole, 2016).

Therefore, the use of these social media would be a measure for managers to promote archaeological tourism, due to the constant use by tourists of these social media. For example, the social media Facebook developed search tools that allows companies to use it as a distribution channel (Law et al., 2014). Proof of this is the study by Lee, Xiong and Hu (2012), which analyzed the use of these social media in promoting events and their results showed that emotional comments on Facebook have a great impact of effectiveness of such marketing.

Based on the data we analyzed about the park and its visitors, we can suggest numerous measures that may improve that management of these touristic resources. For one, it seems especially valuable to spread information about the site's heritage via social media, and specifically through eWOM. According to the data obtained by the Provincial Diputation of Cuenca (2015), visitors' most used sources of information were WOM and the Internet; thus, it seems appropriate to disseminate information about these heritage resources through more modern sources. Through eWOM, it is possible to be in constant contact with tourists, which is a growing expectation in the domain of cultural tourism.

Our analysis also revealed that visitors lack knowledge about other archaeological resources that are similar and can be visited, but do not technically qualify as parks, such as the Roman cities of Valeria and Ercávica, or the Roman villa of Noheda. It is possible that information about these resources is not sufficiently disseminated in the media. In any case, there should be a thorough review of these resources and a determination of how to best market them. One option might be to highlight them in promotions of Segóbriga, perhaps through social networks, which could induce tourists to stay in the area for much longer. At the same time, the efficient management of resources like Segóbriga may eventually trigger economic growth in the region (in the form of inviting new businesses, creating new jobs, etc.), which might then produce residual effects for surrounding sites.

ACKNOWLEDGMENT

This work has been funded by Reference Research Project ECO2014-59688-R, "Planning and implementation of optimal management strategies of the physical, online and mobile POS, based on ICT and innovation", Ministry of Economy and Competitiveness.

REFERENCES

Abascal Palazón, J. M., Cebrián Fernández, R., & Almagro Gorbea, M. (2004). *Segóbriga. Guía del parque arqueológico*. Alicante: Miguel de Cervantes Virtual Library.

Alazaizeh, M. M., Hallo, J. C., Backman, S. J., Norman, W. C., & Vogel, M. A. (2016). Value orientations and heritage tourism management at Petra Archaeological Park, Jordan. *Tourism Management*, *57*, 149–158. doi:10.1016/j.tourman.2016.05.008

Alexandros, A., & Jaffry, S. (2005). Stated preferences for two Cretan heritage attractions. *Annals of Tourism Research*, *32*(4), 985–1005. doi:10.1016/j.annals.2005.01.004

Alvarez, M. D., & Campo, S. (2011). Controllable versus uncontrollable information sources: Effects on the image of Turkey. *International Journal of Tourism Research*, *13*(4), 310–323. doi:10.1002/jtr.838

Beerli, A., & Martín, J. D. (2004). Factors influencing destination image. *Annals of Tourism Research*, *31*(3), 657–681. doi:10.1016/j.annals.2004.01.010

Beerli, A., Martín, J. D., & Moreno, G. S. (2003). *Los agentes que conforman la imagen de los destinos turísticos. Sitio Web I Coloquio Predoctoral Europeo de Turismo y Ocio ESADE-IMHI*. Cornell-ESSEC.

Bille, T., & Schulze, G. G. (2006). Culture in urban and regional development. Handbook of the Economics of Art and Culture, 1, 1051-1099.

Boto, C. T. (2016). Archeology as development of local tourism. *International Journal of Scientific Management and Tourism*, *2*(3), 355–368.

Bruyere, B. L., Beh, A. W., & Lelengula, G. (2009). Differences in perceptions of communication, tourism benefits, and management issues in a protected area of rural Kenya. *Environmental Management*, *43*(1), 49–59. doi:10.1007/s00267-008-9190-7 PMID:18777191

Bryce, D., Curran, R., OGorman, K., & Taheri, B. (2015). Visitors engagement and authenticity: Japanese heritage consumption. *Tourism Management*, *46*, 571–581. doi:10.1016/j.tourman.2014.08.012

Buckley, R. (2012). Sustainable tourism: Research and reality. *Annals of Tourism Research*, *39*(2), 528–546. doi:10.1016/j.annals.2012.02.003

Camprubí, R., & Coromina, L. (2016). La influencia de las fuentes de información en la formación de la imagen turística. *PASOS. Revista de Turismo y Patrimonio Cultural*, *14*(4), 781–796.

Cantallops, A. S., & Salvi, F. (2014). New consumer behavior: A review of research on eWOM and hotels. *International Journal of Hospitality Management*, *36*, 41–51. doi:10.1016/j.ijhm.2013.08.007

Caro, J. L., Luque, A., & Zayas, B. (2015). Nuevas tecnologías para la interpretación y promoción de los recursos turísticos culturales. *Pasos. Revista de Turismo Y Patrimonio Cultural, 13*(4), 931-945.

Carter, R. W., & Bramley, R. (2002). Defining heritage values and significance for improved resource management: An application to Australian tourism. *International Journal of Heritage Studies*, *8*(3), 175–199. doi:10.1080/13527250220000/18895

Char-lee, J. M., Ritchie, B. W., Ruhanen, L. M., & Moyle, B. D. (2014). An institutional assessment of three local government-level tourism destinations at different stages of the transformation process. *Tourism Management*, *41*, 107–118. doi:10.1016/j.tourman.2013.09.007

Chen, C. F., & Chen, F. S. (2010). Experience quality, perceived value, satisfaction and behavioral intentions for heritage tourists. *Tourism Management*, *31*(1), 29–35. doi:10.1016/j.tourman.2009.02.008

Cooke, P. N., & Lazzeretti, L. (Eds.). (2008). *Creative cities, cultural clusters and local economic development*. Edward Elgar Publishing.

Datta, P., Bigham, G., Zou, Z., & Hill, G. (2015). A global study of heritage site ecology, proclivity and loyalty. *Journal of Hospitality and Tourism Management*, *25*, 19–29. doi:10.1016/j.jhtm.2014.12.002

De Rojas, C., & Camarero, C. (2008). Visitors experience, mood and satisfaction in a heritage context: Evidence from an interpretation center. *Tourism Management*, *29*(3), 525–537. doi:10.1016/j.tourman.2007.06.004

Díaz-Andreu, M. (2013). Ethics and archaeological tourism in Latin America. *International Journal of Historical Archaeology*, *17*(2), 225–244. doi:10.1007/s10761-013-0218-1

Díaz-Andreu, M. (2014). Turismo y arqueología. Una mirada histórica a una relación silenciada. [). Elsevier.]. *Anales de Antropologia*, *48*(2), 9–39. doi:10.1016/S0185-1225(14)70242-5

Ezenagu, N., & Iwuagwu, C. (2016). The role of cultural resources in Tourism development in Awka. *African Journal of Hospitality. Tourism and Leisure*, *5*(2), 1–12.

Funari, P. P. A., Manzato, F., & Alfonso, L. P. (2013). Tourism and archaeology in Brazil: Postmodern epistemology in two case studies. *International Journal of Historical Archaeology*, *17*(2), 261–274. doi:10.1007/s10761-013-0219-0

Gartner, W. C. (1994). Image formation process. *Journal of Travel & Tourism Marketing*, *2*(2-3), 191–216. doi:10.1300/J073v02n02_12

González, M. V. (2009). Gestión turística del patrimonio cultural: enfoques para un desarrollo sostenible del turismo cultural. *Cuadernos de turismo*, (23), 237-254.

Guedes, A. S., & Jiménez, M. I. M. (2015). Spatial patterns of cultural tourism in Portugal. *Tourism Management Perspectives*, *16*, 107–115. doi:10.1016/j.tmp.2015.07.010

Gunn, C. A. (1988). *Vacationscape: Designing tourist regions*. New York: Van Nostrand Reinhold.

Hennessey, S., Yun, D., & MacDonald, R. M. (2014). Segmenting and profiling the cultural tourism market for an Island destination. *International Journal of Management and Marketing Research*, *7*(1), 15–28.

Hernández, J. M. G., de la Calle Vaquero, M., & García, M. D. C. M. (2015). Cultura y patrimonio en las prácticas turísticas de la población madrileña. *International Journal of Scientific Management and Tourism*, *1*(4), 97–124.

Ho, C. I., Lin, M. H., & Chen, H. M. (2012). Web users behavioural patterns of tourism information search: From online to offline. *Tourism Management*, *33*(6), 1468–1482. doi:10.1016/j.tourman.2012.01.016

Hughes, H., & Allen, D. (2005). Cultural tourism in Central and Eastern Europe: The views of induced image formation agents. *Tourism Management*, *26*(2), 173–183. doi:10.1016/j.tourman.2003.08.021

Instituto Nacional de Estadística (INE). (2016). Retrieved March 2, 2016 from http://www.ine.es/

Jovicic, D. (2016). Cultural tourism in the context of relations between mass and alternative tourism. *Current Issues in Tourism*, *19*(6), 605–612. doi:10.1080/13683500.2014.932759

Law, R., Buhalis, D., & Cobanoglu, C. (2014). Progress on information and communication technologies in hospitality and tourism. *International Journal of Contemporary Hospitality Management*, *26*(5), 727–750. doi:10.1108/IJCHM-08-2013-0367

Lee, W., Xiong, L., & Hu, C. (2012). The effect of Facebook users arousal and valence on intention to go to the festival: Applying an extension of the technology acceptance model. *International Journal of Hospitality Management*, *31*(3), 819–827. doi:10.1016/j.ijhm.2011.09.018

Li, H., & Qian, Z. (2016). Archaeological heritage tourism in China: The case of the Daming Palace from the tourists' perspective. *Journal of Heritage Tourism*, 1-14.

Li, M., Wu, B., & Cai, L. (2008). Tourism development of World Heritage Sites in China: A geographic perspective. *Tourism Management*, *29*(2), 308–319. doi:10.1016/j.tourman.2007.03.013

Llodrà-Riera, I., Martínez-Ruiz, M. P., Jiménez-Zarco, A. I., & Izquierdo-Yusta, A. (2015). A multidimensional analysis of the information sources construct and its relevance for destination image formation. *Tourism Management*, *48*, 319–328. doi:10.1016/j.tourman.2014.11.012

Lynch, M. F., Duinker, P. N., Sheehan, L. R., & Chute, J. E. (2011). The demand for Mikmaw cultural tourism: Tourist perspectives. *Tourism Management*, *32*(5), 977–986. doi:10.1016/j.tourman.2010.08.009

Månsson, M. (2011). Mediatized tourism. *Annals of Tourism Research*, *38*(4), 1634–1652. doi:10.1016/j.annals.2011.02.008

Márquez-González, C., & Caro, H. (2017). World Heritage Cities of Spain: eWOM as an element of tourism development. *PASOS: Revista de Turismo y Patrimonio Cultural*, *15*(2), 437–457.

McKercher, B., Cros, H. D., & McKercher, R. B. (2002). *Cultural tourism: The partnership between tourism and cultural heritage management*. New York: Haworth Hospitality Press.

McKercher, B., Ho, P. S., & du Cros, H. (2005). Relationship between tourism and cultural heritage management: Evidence from Hong Kong. *Tourism Management*, *26*(4), 539–548. doi:10.1016/j.tourman.2004.02.018

Mestanza, J. G., & Revilla, R. G. (2016). Cultural tourism in Malaga. Museums challenge. *International Journal of Scientific Management and Tourism*, *2*(3), 121–135.

Munar, A. M., & Jacobsen, J. K. S. (2014). Motivations for sharing tourism experiences through social media. *Tourism Management*, *43*, 46–54. doi:10.1016/j.tourman.2014.01.012

Pacifico, D., & Vogel, M. (2012). Archaeological sites, modern communities, and tourism. *Annals of Tourism Research*, *39*(3), 1588–1611. doi:10.1016/j.annals.2012.04.002

Pal, B. (2015). Heritage Tourism and Bishnupur "The City of Archaeological Monuments". *Asian Journal of Multidisciplinary Studies*, *3*(10). Retrieved from http://ajms.co.in/sites/ajms2015/index.php/ajms/issue/view/31/showToc

Phillips, W. J., Wolfe, K., Hodur, N., & Leistritz, F. L. (2013). Tourist word of mouth and revisit intentions to rural tourism destinations: A case of North Dakota, USA. *International Journal of Tourism Research*, *15*(1), 93–104. doi:10.1002/jtr.879

Poria, Y., Reichel, A., & Biran, A. (2006). Heritage site management: Motivations and expectations. *Annals of Tourism Research*, *33*(1), 162–178. doi:10.1016/j.annals.2005.08.001

Provincial Diputation of Cuenca. (2015). *Memoria anual 2015 del parque arqueológico de Segóbriga.* Salelices, Cuenca. Retrieved March 2, 2016 from https://www.dipucuenca.es/noticias/-/publicador/el-parque-arqueologico-de-segobriga-cerro-2015-con-casi-50-000-visitantes-un-5-34-mas-que-en-2014

Rodzi, N. I. M., Zaki, S. A., & Subli, S. M. H. S. (2013). Between tourism and intangible cultural heritage. *Procedia: Social and Behavioral Sciences*, *85*, 411–420. doi:10.1016/j.sbspro.2013.08.370

Ruiz Zapatero, G. (1998). Fragmentos del pasado: La presentación de sitios arqueológicos y la función social de la arqueología. *Treballs d'Arqueologia*, *5*, 7–34.

Ruiz Zapatero, G. (2013). La divulgación arqueológica: Las ideologías ocultas. *Cuadernos de Prehistoria y Arqueología de la Universidad de Granada*, *19*, 11–36.

Santos, M. J. C., & Meléndez, A. P. (2016). The role of satisfaction in cultural activities word-of-mouth. A case study in the Picasso Museum of Málaga (Spain). *Tourism and Management Studies*, *12*(1), 145–152. doi:10.18089/tms.2016.12115

Silberberg, T. (1995). Cultural tourism and business opportunities for museums and heritage sites. *Tourism Management*, *16*(5), 361–365. doi:10.1016/0261-5177(95)00039-Q

Sparks, B., & Pan, G. W. (2009). Chinese outbound tourists: Understanding their attitudes, constraints and use of information sources. *Tourism Management*, *30*(4), 483–494. doi:10.1016/j.tourman.2008.10.014

Su, Y. W., & Lin, H. L. (2014). Analysis of international tourist arrivals worldwide: The role of world heritage sites. *Tourism Management*, *40*, 46–58. doi:10.1016/j.tourman.2013.04.005

Tasci, A. D., & Gartner, W. C. (2007). Destination image and its functional relationships. *Journal of Travel Research*, *45*(4), 413–425. doi:10.1177/0047287507299569

Tigu, G., Cristache, S. E., Mahika, E. C., & Totan, L. (2014). Analysis of the cultural tourism trends and perspectives in Romania. *ESSACHESS – Journal for Communication Studies, 7*(1), 191-208.

Timothy, D. J., & Boyd, S. W. (2003). *Heritage Tourism*. New York: Prentice Hall.

Tseng, C., Wu, B., Morrison, A. M., Zhang, J., & Chen, Y. C. (2015). Travel blogs on China as a destination image formation agent: A qualitative analysis using Leximancer. *Tourism Management*, *46*, 347–358. doi:10.1016/j.tourman.2014.07.012

UNESCO. (2015). Retrieved March 2, 2016, from http://www.unesco.org/

Vela, M. R., & Tarrés, C. S. (2005). El turismo rural-cultural: un modelo de gestión del marketing turístico a nivel local basado en la medida de la imagen del destino. *Cuadernos de turismo*, *16*, 197-222.

Wall, G., & Mathieson, A. (2006). *Tourism: Change, Impacts, and Opportunities*. New York: Prentice Hall.

Walle, A. H., & Asgary, N. (2015). Archaeological tourism in the Middle East: A community-based resource management model. *Middle East Journal of Management*, *2*(1), 36–52. doi:10.1504/MEJM.2015.069008

World Tourism Organization. (2016). Retrieved March 2, 2016, from http://www2.unwto.org/

Yang, C. H., Lin, H. L., & Han, C. C. (2010). Analysis of international tourist arrivals in China: The role of World Heritage Sites. *Tourism Management*, *31*(6), 827–837. doi:10.1016/j.tourman.2009.08.008

Zeng, B., & Gerritsen, R. (2014). What do we know about social media in tourism? A review. *Tourism Management Perspectives*, *10*, 27–36. doi:10.1016/j.tmp.2014.01.001

Zhang, Y., & Cole, S. T. (2016). Dimensions of lodging guest satisfaction among guests with mobility challenges: A mixed-method analysis of web-based texts. *Tourism Management*, *53*, 13–27. doi:10.1016/j.tourman.2015.09.001

KEY TERMS AND DEFINITIONS

Archaeological Parks: Archaeological Parks (AP) are classified as the most important and well-preserved scientific sites in the country whose purpose is to promoting their social value.

Archeology: Archeology (A) is defined as the result of surveys, excavations and other empirical studies designed to interpret and retrieve the past and it is one such form of cultural heritage that governments frequently sponsor and promote as part of their tourism efforts.

Cultural Heritage Management: Cultural Heritage Management (CHM) is carried out by different actors pursuing different goals: on the one hand, the private sector, whose main objective is to obtain economic benefits thanks to tourism. And on the other hand, the public sector, whose purpose is to obtain social benefits, guaranteeing their existence and conservation.

Cultural Heritage: Cultural Heritage (CH) is a way to bring tourists to the past, or more precisely, a particular vision of the past that can then influence present and future cultures.

Cultural Resources: Cultural Resources (CR) are the goods that have been valued and transformed by human activity or knowledge.

Cultural Tourism: Cultural Tourism (CT) is effectively a synonym for heritage or ethnic tourism—a way for travelers to access the charm of local communities' traditions, folklore, spaces and values.

Electronic Word of Mouth: Electronic Word of Mouth (eWOM) is informal person to person communication, mediated through the internet, about a product or service.

Worth of Mouth: Worth of Mouth (WOM) is informal person to person communication about a product or service.

Chapter 9
Accessibility Improvement Interventions at Byzantine Monuments:
Use of Technology for Facilitating Accessibility of Visitors With Sensory Disabilities

Aristotelis Naniopoulos
Aristotle University of Thessaloniki, Greece

Panagiotis Tsalis
Aristotle University of Thessaloniki, Greece

ABSTRACT

The accessibility of monuments and archaeological sites by disabled persons and persons with restricted mobility in general, constitutes a social, financial and political demand. The project "PROSPELASIS" attempted to counter this problem by focusing on creating a methodology for facing monuments' accessibility and perceptibility problems for people with disabilities and testing its application at Byzantine monuments of Thessaloniki. In six major monuments included in UNESCO's World Heritage List, significant accessibility improvements were realized. A Wi-Fi information system was installed in all of them via which an audio and visual information system was created with audio information in three languages, description of visual information, text information, information in Greek and International Sign Language. Additionally, in Rotunda and Heptapyrgion monuments three dimensional models were developed. The successful validation of the proposed methodology constitute the results of this project not only pertinent to Thessaloniki or Greece, but worthy of a wider application.

DOI: 10.4018/978-1-5225-2927-9.ch009

INTRODUCTION

A visit to an archaeological site or monument is a unique experience that also constitutes a main tourist attraction. A visit to a monument allows the composition of all stimuli into a unique experience, consisting of the following:

- **Visual Stimuli:** Shapes, colours, textures, images, sense of the real scale of the site.
- **Tactile Stimuli:** The floor's texture and the way in which it is perceived (e.g. gravel or stone) or the texture of the seats (e.g. wood, marble, metal).
- **Auditory Stimuli:** The soundscape of the surrounding area, either natural or artificial, the sound of interaction between man and the environment, walking, the swish of plants when walking through them.
- **Olfactory Stimuli:** Natural scents (depending on the season, time, weather) and artificial scents (e.g. scents of diverse materials or deliberately diffused scents and incenses).
- **Gustatory Stimuli:** Tastes referring to the site and underlining its uniqueness, such as fruits from the trees of a garden, the water of a fountain, the treat in a monastery.

In Thessaloniki, a city with rich heritage, monuments constitute isolated "islets", with the modern cityscape "drowning" them, allowing no visual connection between them, making their identification, their understanding, and physical access to them difficult for visitors in general and persons with restricted mobility in particular. This problem is exacerbated by the fact that the current city's ground level is often four to five meters above the level, where the entrance to the monuments is. Thus, any attempt to "socialize" the cultural heritage of the city has to pursue the following two objectives: a) to provide easy access to monuments for all visitors, including persons with disability and restricted mobility, and b) to help visitors through the provision of adequate information and the indication of ways of moving from one monument to another, connecting the" pieces of the puzzle" (Naniopoulos et al., 2011b.).

The present chapter describes the process of improvement of accessibility in selected Byzantine monuments of Thessaloniki using a methodology created in the frame of the "PROSPELASIS" project, financed by a grant from Iceland, Liechtenstein and Norway through the EEA Financial Mechanism 2004 – 2009 (50%) and from the public investments programme of the Hellenic Republic (50%). The project was realized by the cooperation of the Aristotle University of Thessaloniki (project leader) and the 9th Ephorate of Byzantine Antiquities. The chapter describes the background and the needs that lead to the development of the methodology, the methodology itself, its implementation and the accessibility improvement interventions carried out at selected Byzantine monuments of Thessaloniki. The authors aspire that the adoption of the proposed methodology can lead to further actions that will improve monuments' and archaeological sites' accessibility at national and international level.

BACKGROUND

Addressing, at an international level, the problems of protection, conservation, restoration and management of historical centres, archaeological sites, architectural aggregations, monuments and works of art, has been a major issue. Nowadays, we are not only interested in the monuments' past; we are also interested in their preservation, restoration and role in direct relation to their present and future environment, their integration into modern life and their connection with economic, educational, tourist and social aspects in particular.

Access to culture is a fundamental right of people with disabilities (EU Council, 1993; UN, 1993). Article 30 of the Convention for the Rights of Persons with Disabilities requires that States parties recognize the right of persons with disabilities to take part in cultural life on an equal basis with others. They are required to take all appropriate measures to ensure that persons with disabilities:

1. Enjoy access to cultural materials in accessible formats;
2. Enjoy access to television programmes, films, theatre and other cultural activities, in accessible formats; and
3. Enjoy access to places for cultural performances or services, such as theatres, museums, cinemas, libraries and tourism services, and, as far as possible, enjoy access to monuments and sites of national cultural importance. (UN, 2013)

Leisure experiences and participation provide unique and valuable opportunities that may result in a variety of positive physical, social and psychological benefits, as well as enhance one's overall quality of life. When people with disabilities participate in leisure experiences, they obtain benefits on a par with their non-disabled counterparts (Stumbo, Wang, & Pegg, 2011).

It should also be noted that making tourist attractions more accessible to people with disabilities, is considered a "golden opportunity" for businesses. In Europe it is estimated that at least 80 million people have a declared disability, a number due to increase because of demographic ageing and the correlation between disability and old age. Yet, this market appears not to be served properly (EC, 2014). Despite the existence of different legal provisions in the EU dealing with equal opportunities, there appears to be a general "inertia" among providers of tourism services in engaging in accessible tourism. (EC, 2014). This was the main reason that lead the World Tourism Day of 2016 to be dedicated to "Tourism for all – Promoting universal accessibility".

A visit to an archaeological site or monument in particular, is an original, unique experience, and constitutes a main attraction in Greece for tourists. Although there are movable findings from all historical periods of Greece in museums around the world, the main archaeological sites and monuments can be found only in their original place. A visit to an archaeological site provides direct contact with the area and the monument, an authentic experience which cannot be substituted by any representation and entails the use of one's senses allowing the composition of all stimuli in something unique.

Barriers that hinder disabled visitors form visiting archaeological sites and monuments exist at various levels, and are identified as:

- Organizational issues, such as lack of staff or lack of support for access improvements
- Physical issues, such as lack of accessible signage and information, narrow paths and entrances, loose or uneven path surfaces, steep slopes and long distances, steps, lack of seating and shelter, luck of accessible toilets and baby changing facilities
- Intellectual issues, e.g., complex or text-only information
- Social and cultural issues, e.g., publicity does not promote access, inaccessible website, lack of information shared with local community etc.
- Financial issues, such as charges for activities, like guided tours, cost of travelling to and from a site. (Ioannidis & Vozikis, 2007)

In order to grant accessibility to cultural environments, activities on two levels need to take place:

- Public awareness needs to be risen as far as cultural heritage is concerned, so that the public interest will start at younger ages and
- Necessary infrastructure needs to be provided, in order to guarantee accessibility to all population groups.

However, archaeological sites and monuments, by their nature, do not allow major interventions to their structure. There is an obvious need for balance between access rights and conservation of the archaeological sites, which demands the development of the relevant access legislation and technical standards. Any intervention to improve accessibility should be made carefully, so as not to alter the monument's character, or damage it visually or structurally (Naniopoulos & Marki, 2003; English Heritage, 2004; NDA, 2011).

The concept of accessibility, as used here, includes:

- Usability and possibility of independent physical access and movement; and
- Perceptibility, referring to the way one perceives, understands the environment (Fertier, 2003).

As far as monuments and archaeological sites in particular are concerned, some efforts have been made in order to improve physical access, focusing mostly on improving access to specific monuments. For example, in August 2004, just before the inauguration of Athens' Olympic Games, one of the most significant Monuments of the world cultural and architectural heritage, the Acropolis of Athens, became accessible to disabled persons via a lift on the north slope of the Sacred Rock. The lift, which was installed with the approval of the Greek Central Archaeological Council, can be reached by a special entrance just north of the main entrance to the archaeological site and the northwest section of the ancient promenade. The highest level of the lift concludes to a lightweight iron balcony-bridge which leads to a level space northwest of Erechtheum. From this point via specific routes, the visitor can tour the most significant Monuments of Acropolis and reach up to the old Acropolis Museum which can be accessed via a platform lift, which has been installed in its yard. (Hellenic Ministry of Culture, 2017)

Cases where monumental buildings are asked to house modern day activities are also of particular interest. This is the case of the National Archaeological Museum of Athens, which is the largest museum in Greece and one of the world's great museums. Although its original purpose was to secure all the findings from the nineteenth century excavations in and around Athens, it gradually became the central National Archaeological Museum and was enriched with finds from all over Greece. Its abundant collections, with more than 11,000 exhibits, provide a panorama of Greek civilization from the beginnings of Prehistory to Late Antiquity. The museum is housed in an imposing neoclassical building of the end of the nineteenth century, which was designed by L. Lange and remodelled by Ernst Ziller.

In order to facilitate visitors with disability and people with restricted mobility in general during the modernization of the Museum for the Olympic Games of 2004, the following interventions took place:

- A second entrance was created at the part of the building adjacent to Vasileos Irakleiou Str. which is accessible. It is connected to the street via a bridge, while access is also achieved via a 5% gradient ramp from the area in front of the Museum's main entrance. Close to the ramp's edge there are 5 allocated parking spaces for visitors with disability.

- Two lifts were built at the museum's atriums. At one of these atriums, close to the staircase that leads to the exhibition areas, a large lift was installed facilitating movement on the floor and at the service yard. Right across the exit of the floor there is a vertical lift which covers a small height difference and allows access to the room where the exhibits from Thira are located. At the other atrium, which is located at the left of the of the main entrance, a smaller lift was installed in order to serve access from the ground floor to the public toilets, the canteen and the Museum's shop. Wheelchair users can also access these areas via a stair lift which is placed at the main entrance.
- Toilets for visitors with disability and ramps which cover small height differences were constructed
- Exhibits are placed so that they can be viewed by visitors with disabilities
- Guided tours and educational seminars are held in sign language (Naniopoulos et al., 2011a).

As far as access to information for visitors of monuments and heritage sites is concerned, various efforts have been made exploiting the advantages offered by ICT applications. One of the first examples of current possibilities for increased information access through digital technology was the ARCHEOGUIDE project, first developed at the site of Olympia in Greece. This offers heritage information to the visitor through an ICT system that links augmented reality, 3D-visualisation, mobile computing, and multi-modal interaction techniques. The ARCHEOGUIDE system consists of a site information server and a set of mobile units that are carried by visitors. A wireless local network allows the mobile units to communicate with the site information server. When in use, the visitor can access information about the specific areas he or she is walking through and gain a visual impression of the original appearance of the site through augmented reality reconstructions (Vlahakis et al., 2002).

Many applications also use ICT particularly for the benefit of visitors with sensory impairments. These include, for example, Manchester Museum Touch and Discover Systems. Access was achieved to a small number of objects that cannot be handled by developing a Haptic Interactive. The interface consists of a touch-enabled computer system which allows the user to investigate and explore the topography of an artefact within a 3-dimensional digital environment through a feedback stylus. The addition of sound associated object was another important element, giving vocal instructions and an indication of the objects material qualities and character. For example a broken ceramic gives a dull sound whereas a high-fired ceramic can give a musical ring. The haptic interface does not replace the handling experience, but it can augment a visitors understanding of an object and increase their knowledge and enjoyment on a visit (AMBAVis, 2015).

The PROSPELASIS project described in the current chapter combines the above, following a holistic approach to access of disabled visitors, with interventions carried out to improve both access to information for visitors with sensory impairments and access to infrastructure for visitors with physical impairments. The objective of the current chapter is to pinpoint the methodology for accessibility improvement carried out in Byzantine monuments of Thessaloniki, depicting the process followed, the obstacles encountered and the lessons learned in order to promote the concept of accessible monumental and cultural infrastructure through a combination of information provision (focusing mainly to visitors with sensory impairments) and infrastructure improvements (focusing mainly to visitors with physical impairments).

METHODOLOGY

The research team's first step was the definition of a theoretical approach model for the improvement of accessibility in monuments, which has been further elaborated through its application to Byzantine monuments of Thessaloniki. This approach contained the following steps:

- Definition of parts of the monument that can become accessible
- Evaluation of existing accessibility level and identification of obstacles
- Definition of information provision needs
- Definition of alternative solutions at pre-study level
- Creation of final studies and implementation of accessibility improvement interventions
- Training of personnel involved

The ideal aim concerning accessibility of monuments is of course that all areas in a monument should become accessible. Thus, from the first stages of a study, the research team had to determine the parts of a monument that can be made accessible, as well as those that do not provide this possibility (English Heritage, 2005).

This process was followed by the evaluation of the existing accessibility level. Appropriate checklists were devised which cover both the monuments' physical access as well as their perceptibility and current use (it should be noted that most of the assessed monuments still host religious activities). In order to create the checklists, first the needs of visitors with disabilities at these particular surroundings had to be determined (Tsalis & Naniopoulos, 2008). This lead to the creation of a task model which was constructed through communication with people with disabilities, cooperation with associations of people with disabilities, in situ observation of the use of infrastructure, communication with experts specialised in accessibility as well as use of the results of relevant research concerning accessibility of the environment, including works by the Royal National Institute for the Blind, the Americans with Disabilities Act Accessibility Guidelines team and the British Department for Transport (RNIB, 1995; ADAAG, 1992; DfT, 2002). The checklists created in the PROSPELASIS project were structured so that the accessibility auditor would not have to be an engineer specialized in accessibility, thus ensuring the methodology's sustainability.

The implementation of the checklists lead to the construction of reports describing the existing situation for each monument, the identification of the visitors' needs and, next, to the definition of alternative solutions for the improvement of accessibility.

In the case of the Byzantine monuments examined in the frame of the project, the historic conservation was the utmost priority and, thus, any solution that did not respect this was rejected, despite the fact that it could be beneficial from the tourist image or economic development point of view. Thus the following principles were followed:

- All of the modern constructions which were necessary for improving the accessibility of monuments, and particularly large scale interventions such as ramps, corridors, lifts etc., were installed in a way which does not insult the aesthetical and archaeological values of the monument.
- These constructions were not projected on the monument and were not fixed on the monument in any permanent way. Bearing in mind that monuments of Thessaloniki are usually at a lower level than that of the street level, these constructions were fixed in the ground slopes of their sur-

roundings and stand out as extension of the equipment of a modern city, rather than as part of the monuments.

- In order to avoid confusion, these constructions do not look like old ones, and their size and shape does not exceed what is required for functionality purposes.
- The use of modern technology is restricted to a degree that does not compromise the principles of monument restoration.

All the above were necessary in order to improve physical accessibility for visitors with mobility impairments. However, they did not provide direct benefits in improving perceptibility for visitors with sensory impairments, despite the fact that contemporary management of heritage resources aims to facilitate a broad public awareness and appreciation of cultural heritage sites and that ICOMOS (International Council on Monuments and Sites) recognizes that the accessibility of these sites should be of both physical and intellectual character, providing the public with the opportunity to visit a site, and to have the benefit of detailed, up-to-date historical information about it. (Brizard, Derde, & Silberman, 2007). This appears to be common practice in Greece since, in many cases, accessibility interventions take into account only the needs of persons with physical impairments and become synonymous with the installation of lifts and ramps, following a short-sighted approach.

Technology has much to offer to enhance visitors' in situ experience and digital models are used increasingly to:

- Provide access by making easier to view details and allow items that are physically inaccessible to be documented and viewed
- Provide insights and interpretations of the previous condition or states of site or object (e.g. impression of an artefact in its former pristine state)
- Contextualize artefacts (e.g. demonstrate how a tool was used)
- Present representations of tangible heritage as part of the narrative of in-tangible heritage with digital story-telling (Kaminski, Benson, & Arnold, 2013).

PROSPELASIS followed a holistic approach and focused at the inclusion of all potential users, by providing access to monuments with "intangible" characteristics for visitors with physical and sensory impairments.

REALIZATION OF INTERVENTIONS

In total 20 Byzantine – UNESCO monuments were evaluated in Thessaloniki and solutions for accessibility improvement were completed, in pre-study level, for each of them (Naniopoulos et al., 2010a, 2010b). In six of these monuments (Acheiropoietos, church of Saint Demetrios, church of Saint Nicholas Orphanos, church of Hagia Sofia, Rotunda, Heptapyrgion Fortress), which were selected based on their historic significance and interest to the potential visitor, final studies were made and accessibility improvement interventions, which are presented for each monument at the following, were completed (Naniopoulos et al., 2011b). It should also be noted that, in order to create solutions of high aesthetic quality, two well-known artists have been involved in this process, Constantin Xenakis, who was occupied mainly with the signing of a route connecting three monuments, and Cris Giannakos who contributed to the design of ramps.

Interventions Aiming at the Improvement of Accessibility for Visitors With Sensory Disabilities

Development of a WiFi Information System

The research team's cooperation with local associations of persons with visual and hearing impairments resulted in a common belief that the creation and installation of an audio and visual guiding system is necessary for the perceptibility of monuments.

The reason disabled people and people with restricted mobility are not served adequately by the tourism industry is a combination of missing tourism product supply and inadequate information. The lack of reliable information is regarded as one of the major causes that prevent disabled people and others with access requirements from going on holiday (Buhalis et al., 2006).

Potential visitors with visual impairments identified as their main requirements and preferences in a visit to a monument the following:

- They would like to perceive the monuments via appropriate stimuli (audio, visual, olfactory, tactile)
- They consider a visit to a monument as both a recreational and educational activity
- The low level of light in most Byzantine monuments poses difficulties for visitors with reduced vision
- They would prefer something more "interactive", rather than a provision in Braille of the existing information material of monuments
- They did not consider tactile maps that useful, in those particular surroundings
- The creation of a three-dimensional model of the monuments, which visitors could touch, would allow them to perceive not only the monuments' shape and size, but also the different materials used for the monument's construction
- They considered that any accessibility improvement interventions would prove beneficial for the development of accessible tourism in Thessaloniki

The basic requirements of the realized system, according to potential users with visual impairments, were:

- To provide audio information in English, Greek and perhaps other languages depending on the origin of visitors who usually visit the monument
- To provide audio information similar to the one which will be provided in text
- To be easy to use
- To provide audio description of visual images
- To provide information about the monuments' form, size and shape to visitors with visual impairments
- To be compatible with any assistive technologies

Potential visitors with hearing impairments identified as the main problems they face in a visit to a monument the following:

- Lack of available information
- Communication problems with the monuments' staff
- Even though most of the respondents had experienced visits to monuments, archaeological sites and museums, none of them had any experience of using assisting technologies in situ

The basic requirements of the system, according to potential users with hearing impairments, were:

- To provide clear text information
- To be easy to use
- To provide descriptions in sign language

Following these, a review of possible solutions was carried out, taking into account the demands of the Ephorate of Byzantine Antiquities for any intervention not to require the installation of equipment (antennas etc.) which could cause irreversible damages, or visual intrusion to the monuments. Thus, the creation of a Wi-Fi application, focusing in particular to visitors with sensory disabilities, was considered the most suitable solution.

1. The System Developed

The development of the proposed Wi-Fi network was predominantly performed according to two critical criteria: a) the minimum architectural and electromagnetic disturbance of the monuments and b) the optimum performance of the wireless network by means of the smallest number of utilized components.

Toward these objectives, all the items of the selected equipment have very limited dimensions and weight, while they concurrently embody the most up-to-date technological innovations in the area of wireless communications.

The system was developed through a cooperation of the Transport Systems Research Group of the Aristotle University of Thessaloniki and the Electrical and Computer Engineering Department of the Faculty of Technology of the Aristotle University of Thessaloniki.

The key concept of the infrastructure lies on the use of two Power-Over-Ethernet (POE) access points (AP). The AP encourage open source development and allow their developers to customize their operation, create their own mesh-networking applications. Moreover, they combine a hi-gain antenna system, advanced radio architecture, and highly researched and developed firmware technology allowing throughput, stability, and capacity performance rivaling even the highest-end WiMax networks. It is important to stress, that the specific APs require only one cable (CAT 6 FTP type) for power-supply and data exchange. These were connected through a gigabit 5-port switch to a powerful, yet small-sized server PC, which is responsible for the establishment of the entire Wi-Fi application.

2. Web-oriented Application Development

A website was developed to provide audio and visual information about the monument. Since interaction with the user and support of modern multimedia systems is needed, a Web 2.0-compliant solution should be chosen. Additionally, in order for non-professional personnel to be quickly trained on it, ease-of-use and maintenance of the system is required. Taking into account the above requirements, the popular PHP-based Content Management System (CMS) Joomla! was the selected solution.

Users retrieve text information about the monument in Greek, English and Russian. Info is also available in audio format in the three languages mentioned above as well as in Sign Language, Greek and International, allowing Deaf visitors access to information, as can be seen in Figure 1. The software used is compatible with screen readers and information on the monument is also provided in Braille on an individual basis. A tablet pc is available in situ for those who don't have a Wi-Fi compatible mobile phone or own tablet PC.

To meet the requirements of the project, Phoca Gallery component was installed for the management of the monument's pictorial material. This component combines various visualization effects, including slideshow, with many interactive features, such as guest comments and geotagging. Images can be grouped into categories or displayed separately inside an article, thus providing various possible ways of presentation to choose from.

Various other functionalities can be considered and implemented during the website's design procedure or even later, according to the needs of the contractor and possible guests' suggestions. One final important point, concerning the maintenance and safety of the application, is the installation of Akeeba Backup, a component that can automatically back-up the application's files and store them locally on the server, on an everyday basis.

The finished application was evaluated in cooperation with the local association of deaf people before it was available to the public.

Figure 1. Deaf visitors retrieving information in sign language

Installation of Three-Dimensional Tactile Models of Monuments

Three-dimensional models in general can be used by persons with visual impairments for orientation and perception of the environment. In the case of the PROSPELASIS project, these were used in order to assist visitors with the perception of the monuments' volume, shape and materials.

Two tactile models of the Rotunda and Heptapyrgion monuments were created and installed at the monuments' yards. These give visitors the chance to get familiar with the monument, understand its dimensions and characteristics.

Through cooperation with the local Association of the Blind, the following requirements for the realized models were identified:

- An accompanying audio guide for visitors on the use of the tactile model was a definite requirement, since most of persons with vision impairments, particularly in Thessaloniki, do not have experience in the use of tactile models.
- The model should not, in any circumstances, pose any danger to the user. Thus, it should not have sharp edges and certain compromises should be made, if required, in the accuracy of the monument's representation.
- Depending on the model's placement (indoors or outdoors) a variety of materials can be used. The use of different materials, with different textures, can also be beneficial for the model's usefulness.
- The model's size should not be too large in order to allow the user to easily perceive it.
- Additional information could be written on the model in Braille. Text in Braille can be part of the model's manufacturing process or added at a later stage, if so desired.
- Maintenance is important, particularly for models that will be placed outdoors.
- Smaller scale models should be made during the model manufacturing process in order for the constructor to consult potential users with vision impairments and make any adjustments necessary.

In order to prepare the tactile model, a 3D computer model of the monuments had to be produced using laser scanning equipment, through the following process, aiming at recording the three-dimensional information:

- Scanning of the monument using a Laser Scanner
- Depiction of the monument through the use of a point cloud
- Restructuring of the three dimensional geography
- Creation of the three-dimensional model
- Creation of scale replicas, as in this case, or virtual tours in future applications

The laser scanners used are active depiction instruments that have the ability to collect a large number of three dimensional data, creating point clouds with x, y, z, i coordinates for each particular point.

For example, in the case of Rotunda, in order to achieve the required number of points, 25 scans in total were required, which were carried out from the monument's roof, the monument's yard as well as neighbouring blocks of flats. In total, 51 million points were collected. This was followed by reconstruction and registration followed in order to achieve the visualization of the final model (Tokmakidis, 2011).

The completed 3D model became the basis for the manufacturing process that followed. First of all, a small scale model was produced in a 3D printer (figure 2). This was used for the project implementation team to get some feedback from blind and partially sighted potential users. After some small corrections were made, the project team decided on the scale on which the monuments would be represented. This led to the cast printing and the completion of the moulding process.

An audible description of the tactile model was created and is available through the Wi-Fi system installed at the monuments. Through this, a brief description of the monument as well as a detailed description of the monument's representation through the tactile model is provided. As has already been mentioned, this was a definite requirement of the users, since most of the persons with vision impairments in Thessaloniki do not have experience in the use of tactile models.

Interventions on a Route Connecting Three Monuments

The "visual noise" in Greek cities is particularly high, the urban landscape is flooded by arbitrary and vulgar interventions (constructions, graffiti, posters, advertisements etc.). In such an environment, the two partners of the PROSPELASIS project chose a route connecting three important monuments of the city, Hagia Sofia, Acheiropoietos and Rotunda, in order to realize a colour-coded signage. The concept utilizes ideas from the "Freedom Trail" in Boston (Freedom Trail Foundation, 2015) as well as from the European project MAPLE (Naniopoulos & Nalmpantis, 2004).

Main objectives of the signage realized were:

- To facilitate orientation and movement of people with sensory and cognitive impairments

Figure 2. Tactile model for blind visitors at Rotunda

- To depict that accessibility improving facilitations can be beneficial for the general public

The artist Constantin Xenakis participated as a member of the PROSPELASIS team during the signage planning. Constantin Xenakis in his art work has been particularly occupied with the "code of the route" and also has made the plans for an artistic/poetic signing of a new settlement in France, the Moissy- Cramayel which though, has never been realised.

It should also be noted that, during the signage implementation, certain actions took place for the improvement of the physical accessibility of the selected route with the cooperation of the technical services of the Municipality of Thessaloniki. In particular, new ramps were created along the route, bridging height differences that hindered the movement of wheelchair users, signifying the Municipality's will to improve the route's accessibility level.

The planning and design of interventions, along the route, followed various stages. What has been realised is described in the following.

1. **Horizontal Signing:** Along the route connecting the three Monuments, certain pavement tiles were coloured with the colour assigned to each monument, while arrows indicated the movement direction to the monument. For each monument a colour code had been chosen

    a. Yellow for Hagia Sofia
    b. Blue for Acheropoietos
    c. Red for Rotunda

In certain selected areas where direction changes take place, as well as in front of each monument, different tiles were used with the adjacent monument's name written, accompanied with a direction arrow and the colour code selected in the background. The signing at the entrance of the Rotunda monument is depicted in Figure 3.

Particular effort was paid, on the one hand to have visual contact among the coloured tiles installed along the route, on the other hand not to intrude visually the urban landscape.

2. **Vertical Signing:** In front of each Monument a sign was installed, which included the following:

    a. Brief history of the Monument
    b. Monument's layout
    c. Diagram of the route connecting the three monuments
    d. Information about the interventions for the improvement of physical and sensory accessibility which took place in the monument
    e. Information concerning the context of the project, the sponsors etc.

The above mentioned information was written in three languages: Greek, English and Russian. The last language was chosen since all three monuments are very well known and attract many tourists from countries with Christian orthodox population, particularly from Russia.

On the upper side of the sign, a horizontal strip with the monument's colour code was located. The placement and type of the information signs were approved by the Greek Central Archaeological Council, following a relevant recommendation of the 9th Ephorate of Byzantine Antiquities. As seen in Figure 4,

Figure 3. Horizontal signing at Rotunda

Figure 4. Vertical signing at the Kamara area

in the area of Kamara, where direction change towards Rotunda takes place, a vertical column of triangular profile was installed, where on each side an artistic reference on each one of the three monuments was made, further assisting pedestrians.

Along the north east pavement of Egnatia Road, where the signage was applied, two bus stops of the local public transport company OASTh are located. Following permission by the Municipality of Thessaloniki, two posters-diagrams were installed on them which offered the following information:

- A diagram of the route connecting the three monuments which appear with their colour code
- Data concerning the realised interventions improving physical and sensory accessibility in each one of the three monuments
- Data concerning the project's identity

It should be noted that the accessible buses of OASTh, whose exterior has been designed by the Greek well-known fashion designer Yannis Tseklenis, bear also the colours yellow, blue, red, something that is in line with the PROSPELASIS interventions, does not create additional "visual noise" and makes a positive reference to the city's public transport system. Thus, the choice of colours and symbols by the PROSPELASIS team serves the grater scope of the unification of the visual communication code of the transport and mobility system of Thessaloniki.

3. **Facilitation of a Short Stop/Rest, Along the Route:** In order to facilitate short stop/rest along the route, special resting bars were designed around street trees and posts. The resting bars are semi-circular and have two levels, thus facilitating their use by people of varying heights. Their design is based on an idea of the disability expert David Finnegan, which had been first realised in Merseyside, UK.

On the resting bars an artistic intervention was created, with graphic elements on it similar to the ones of the same artist, Constantin Xenakis, on the mini buses of OASTh serving as a Demand Responsive Service for disabled people.

Interventions Aiming at the Improvement of Accessibility for Visitors With Physical Impairments

The following accessibility improvement interventions were carried out at each of the six selected Byzantine Monuments:

Acheiropoietos

The monument had two entrances to its yard, both of them used by the general public. Staircases bridged the height difference between the yard's entrance and the monument's entrance, thus making access to wheelchair users impossible (Naniopoulos et al., 2010b).

At the north side of the monument a non-modulated yard was located, where the 9th Ephorate's archaeologists had archaeological excavations in progress. A lift was installed there, its location ensuring that it causes minimum aesthetic intervention to the monument. The lift is fixed on a base made out of concrete as well as on an existing retaining wall.

However, the installation of the lift alone could not solve the problem of achieving access into the main monument. Thus, it was decided to widen appropriately a gate at the northwest side of the monument. In order to bridge the existing height difference between the outside of the new door and its surroundings, a metal platform was created. The height difference in the inside of the door was bridged through the creation of a platform with a metal staircase and a small platform lift.

Saint Demetrios (Hagios Dimitrios)

As the entrance to the monument and horizontal circulation in it did not pose significant problems, the interventions concerning physical accessibility focused on the improvement of access to the monument's public toilets, which are placed in the monument's yard. A new toilet was created, its dimensions and equipment ensuring that it can be used by visitors with restricted mobility. The colour contrasting surfaces used facilitate its use by visitors with restricted vision (PROSPELASIS team, 2012).

Saint Nicholas Orphanos (Hagios Nikolaos Orfanos)

Due to the monument's very small scale and particular characteristics, it was decided that the significant interventions required to improve physical access to it would be at odds with its particular character. Thus, only a portable ramp was purchased and is available upon request (PROSPELASIS team, 2012).

Rotunda

Rotunda had significant problems as far as physical accessibility was concerned. The large height difference between the present main entrance of the monument and its interior made access impossible for wheelchair users (Naniopoulos et al., 2010b).

As a solution which would not only improve access to the monument for visitors with restricted mobility but also highlight further its importance, the approach of the monument from the main "Imperial" gate, opened on the south side of the monument and not in use, was selected. In order to enable visitors to reach this gate, a bridge over the excavation of the south outbuildings of the Monument, was created. The bridge has a total length of 15.5 m and is constructed from metal truss section. As seen in Figure 5, the bridge's surface is constructed from perforated metal, while metal plates on the surface act as tactile signs for pedestrians with sight problems. In general, the interventions are designed so as to have the minimum possible visual impact. The artist Cris Giannakos has contributed to the design of the bridge.

In order to bridge the height difference between the entrance and the monument's floor a new staircase as well as a lift were installed inside the monument. The new staircase was created out of metal, and forms a small platform at its top. This construction, together with the "bridge", creates a single tread for wheelchair users. It should be noted also that alternative designs were presented in order to have a final approval of the Central Archaeological Council of the Hellenic Ministry of Culture.

It should be noted that the interventions for the improvement of physical and sensory accessibility that were completed at the "Rotunda" monument of Thessaloniki in the frame of the "PROSPELASIS" project received an honorary award in the UIA (Union Internationale des Architectes) competition "Friendly Spaces Accessible to All".

Figure 5. The bridge constructed at the Rotunda monument

Hagia Sofia

There are no particular problems concerning the monument's physical accessibility. Thus, the only intervention deemed necessary for the improvement of physical accessibility was the creation of a small ramp that would bridge a small height difference of 11cm at the monument's entrance threshold.

The monument is also part of the "Cultural route" connecting it with Acheropoietos and Rotunda.

Heptapyrgion Fortress

The monument has two entrances to its yard, only one of them being used by the general public. The staircase in front of the monument's main entrance makes access to it by wheelchair users impossible (Naniopoulos et al., 2010b).

The main entrance leads to a corridor inside the monument, where offices are located and to a second entrance with a staircase in front of it. Thus, even if the visitor negotiates the main entrance, further access to the monument is prohibited for wheelchair users and is difficult for users with restricted mobility. A secondary entrance, which was closed, appeared to be a better solution for a visitor with restricted mobility to access the monument. This led directly to the monument's main area. It should be noted, however, that this entrance had a height difference with its surroundings. In order to bridge the height difference between the entrance and the surroundings' ground the construction of a ramp was deemed necessary. The ramp was constructed from sheet metal grid with a length of 8.00m and 5% slope, to allow the unhindered movement of wheelchair users (PROSPELASIS team, 2012).

It should be noted that the participation of users during the implementation of interventions was achieved through continuous cooperation with local associations of persons with disability and restricted mobility and was deemed essential in order to pinpoint and correct any mistakes before the interventions were opened to the public (Naniopoulos et al., 2011).

ISSUES, CONTROVERSIES, PROBLEMS

The realization of the described interventions revealed procedures which were not known to the research team from the beginning of this project, mainly concerning the approval of the proposed interventions from the Central Archaeological Council of Greece (CAC).

The Central Archaeological Council is the highest advisory body on all matters pertaining to the protection of ancient monuments, archaeological sites and sites of exceptional historical or legendary importance up to 1830.

The Central Archaeological Council:

- Recommends to the Ministry of Culture on principles governing the protection of the cultural heritage and the annual programs of expropriations or direct purchases, excavations, restorations, conservation as well as other works on monuments.
- Gives advisory opinion, among others, on the protection of monuments entered on the World Heritage List, as well as other monuments and archaeological or historical sites of outstanding importance, interventions of major importance to monuments and sites, the designation and establishment of archaeological and historical sites and protection zones in accordance with the provisions of the law.

The CAC is composed of seventeen (17) members, while rapporteurs to the CAC are the respective heads of Directorates of the Ministry's Central Services depending on the issue to be discussed.

The CAC approves or rejects the proposals made or provides suggestions for further elaboration, by majority voting. Following the CAC decision, next the relevant Ministry of Culture and Tourism (MCT) Directorates undertake to elaborate it. The MCT Directorates communicate with the Ephorate and, depending on the case, they inform on:

- The approval of proposal as it is
- The rejection of the proposal
- The approval of the proposal with certain changes

In the third case, a new proposal may be asked to be presented to the CAC or the Directorates will undertake the follow up of their appropriate elaboration.

Due to the importance of the monuments where the interventions took place (UNESCO monuments), all accessibility improving constructions had to be approved by the CAC In the case of the PROSPELASIS team's proposed interventions, the head of the Directorate of Restoration Works presented the

PROSPELASIS team proposed interventions, together with the opinion and recommendation of the MCT Directorates.

Furthermore, as far as the application of the structural interventions is concerned, the following problems were identified:

- The detailed nature of the checklists for the evaluation of the existing accessibility level allowed its application from non-engineer staff members and the self-evaluation of monuments and archaeological sites. However, it resulted in a large number of data, the recording of which can prove to be time consuming. This also became obvious during the checklists' application in situ, since the research team members who were specialized on accessibility could more easily identify the checklists' more important elements, thus reducing the time required for each evaluation.
- The cooperation with staff members of the evaluated monuments pinpointed accessibility requirements that the research team itself had not identified.
- The solutions proposed at pre-study level were not evaluated nor approved by the aforementioned relative public bodies (CAC and MCT Directorates). Thus, some of the proposed solutions may not have received approval, if the project team had proceeded with their realization at final study level.

Some problems were also encountered in the design and installation of the WiFi information system. These included restrictions in the placement of the system's antennas due to aesthetic or infrastructural reasons which affected the system's effectiveness. Another problem encountered, which was not envisaged by the research team during the system's installation, was the fact that power cuts were common in some of the monuments. Since the system was not designed to restart automatically, an intervention by one of the monuments' employees was required, something that was not always realized on time. Cooperation with the local association of persons with vision impairments pinpointed some problems in the WiFi application's compatibility with screen readers. Finally, copyright issues prohibited the project team from exploiting all the information material available.

SOLUTIONS AND RECOMMENDATIONS

Recognising the difficulties the lack of knowledge of the aforementioned processes can pose to future accessibility improvement interventions carried out at monumental spaces or archaeological sites, the project implementation team created, as part of the project deliverables, a "Handbook of basic principles for the realization of accessibility improvements in monumental spaces". The handbook aspires to provide interested stakeholders a clear "step by step" approach for the implementation of accessibility improvement interventions as well as the experience the project team gained during the interventions' implementation.

In particular, the handbook's contents include the following:

- Description of disabled visitors' needs at monumental environments
- Description of basic restrictions and demands in the realization of interventions
- Identification of the authorities involved in the approval of interventions at monumental sites

- Description of the approach followed at the PROSPELASIS project
- Methodology for assessing the existing accessibility level
- Description of the realized interventions.

The project handbook is available at:

http://www.prospelasis.com/sites/default/files/pdf/handbook_edit_final.pdf

As far as the issues encountered in the application of the methodology itself, on a more practical level, the following solutions were identified:

- The creation of a "short" version of the checklist could prove beneficial, particularly in cases when the responsible auditor does not have previous relevant experience.
- The cooperation with staff members who are familiar with each monument's peculiarities should be made before the suggestion for accessibility improvement interventions even in pre-study level.
- The installation of information systems should take into account particular problems encountered in each monument, including infrastructural issues.

FUTURE RESEARCH DIRECTIONS

Europe is a key cultural tourism destination, with a large number of major monuments and archaeological sites. It is estimated that cultural tourism accounts for around 40% of all European tourism. The great variety of European cultural heritage – both material and immaterial – represents an important competitive advantage. (EC, 2014)

In order to maintain Europe's tourism leadership, a need to modernise and innovate the European tourism offer is recognised. Diversifying tourism products and capitalising on common and rich heritage (natural, cultural, historical, industrial etc.) is the first priority listed in the European Commission's Action Plan for tourism issued in 2010. It is also a stated intention of the Commission to capitalise on those initiatives and look for synergies with similar or complementary initiatives undertaken by other International and European Organisations, such as the UNESCO world heritage sites.

The interventions carried out in the "PROSPELASIS" project combine these characteristics, as the implemented large scale accessibility improvement interventions in major monuments of Thessaloniki which are included in the UNESCO World Heritage list. It should be noted that UNESCO is focusing in particular on the connection between cultural heritage and development through the Mexico City Declaration on Cultural Policies (UNESCO, 1982) and the Report of the World Commission on Culture and Development "Our Creative Diversity" (UNESCO, 1996).

Thus, the methodology and process developed constitute a precedent for further actions in other monuments of similar importance, not only in Greece but at European and international level, since it does not rely on a particular country's legislation, characteristics and authorities' structure.

However, the PROSPELASIS experience also showed that there might still be research potential and an open market for the development and application of an accessibility standard for monumental and archaeological sites. Even though accessibility guidelines have been developed in various countries, with some of them focusing on accessible heritage sites, there is no common accessibility standard applied at

European level focusing on the whole mobility chain (infrastructure, perceptibility, information, service provision). The adoption of a common "accessibility label", following the example of the various "eco-labels" developed and applied, could prove a potential critical advantage for the European tourist market.

CONCLUSION

Promotion of accessibility, usability and perceptibility of archaeological sites and monuments for people with disabilities is desirable for social, financial and political reasons.

Improving accessibility of cultural spaces provides people with disabilities with the opportunity to live the unique experience of visiting a monument or archaeological site.

The fact that a large number of archaeological sites and monuments exist in Greece is particularly important, since they are a unique feature and a powerful attraction for tourists. In Thessaloniki in particular, there are numerous monuments that could become friendlier to all visitors and not just to people with disabilities, if their accessibility and perceptibility were improved with the necessary interventions.

Actions concerning the accessibility, usability and perceptibility of a city's monuments and archaeological sites cannot be fragmentary. On the contrary, they must comply with a "systematic approach", according to which all necessary measures and actions are considered in a way that promotes the principles of Inclusive Design, accessibility and perceptibility throughout the entire "chain" related to a person's transport and reception in a site of interest.

The created methodology provides a "step by step" guide for the successful implementation of accessibility improvement interventions in monuments and archaeological sites.

The realization of these interventions, as well as the training seminars realized during the "PROSP-ELASIS" project, have provided invaluable experience for all involved actors (including authorities of antiquities, tourist guides, organizations of people with disabilities etc.). Moreover, the interventions have initiated a cooperation between involved stakeholders, with common actions concerning access to Thessaloniki's cultural heritage that have already taken place.

The evaluation of the Wi-Fi applications by users with hearing impairments showed that they were quite satisfied with the functionalities provided, particularly with the inclusion of the descriptions in sign language.

Concerning the audio guide of the tactile model for people with visual impairments, it proved to be useful and necessary, particularly if it is accompanied by additional information provided by an experienced tour guide.

The project participants aspire that this experience can lead to further actions that will improve monuments' and archaeological sites' accessibility at national as well as at international level.

REFERENCES

AMBAVis Project: Access to Museums for Blind and Visually Impaired People through 3D-Technology (2015). *The use of tactile models in museums Status quo and best practice.* Retrieved April 26, 2017, from http://www.ambavis.eu/wp-content/uploads/2016/01/150805-AMBAVis-BestPractice_Final-disclaimer.pdf

Americans with Disabilities Act Accessibility Guidelines (ADAAG). (1992). *Checklist for Buildings and Facilities*. Retrieved October 20, 2008, from http://www.access-board.gov/adaag/checklist/a16.html

Brizard, T., Derde, W., & Silberman, N. (2007). *Basic Guidelines for Cultural Heritage Professionals in the Use of Information Technologies. How can ICT support cultural heritage?. The Interactive Institute AB*.

Buhalis, D., Eichhorn, V., Michopoulou, E., & Miller, G. (2006). *Accessibility Market and Stakeholder Analysis*. Retrieved April 21, 2017, from http://www.accessibletourism.org/resources/ossate_market_analysis_public_final.pdf

Council, E. U. (2003). *Council Resolution of 6 May 2003 on accessibility of cultural infrastructure and cultural activities for people with disabilities (2003/C 134/05)*. Official Journal of the European Union.

Department for Transport. (2002). *Inclusive mobility*. London: DfT.

English Heritage. (2004). *Easy access to historic buildings*. Swindon, UK: EH.

English Heritage. (2005). *Easy access to historic landscapes*. Swindon, UK: EH.

European Commission (EC). (2014). Transnational Cultural Tourism Products and Tourism and Accessibility for all – Call for Proposals. EC.

Fertier, A. (2003). EUCREA International: Policy, objectives and programme of action. In *Access to culture and sports for people with disabilities conference proceedings*. Hellenic Ministry of Culture.

Hellenic Ministry of Culture. (2017). *Respecting the rights of the disable people: Access by lift to the top of the Acropolis*. Retrieved April 26, 2017, from http://www.yppo.gr/files/g_423.pdf

Ioannidis, Ch., & Vozikis, K. Th. (2007). *Application of a GIS for the accessibility of archaeological sites by visitors with disability and visitors with reduced mobility. XXI International CIPA Symposium*, Athens, Greece.

Kaminski, J., Benson, A. M., & Arnold, D. (2013). *Contemporary Issues in Cultural Heritage Tourism*. Routledge.

Naniopoulos, A., Antonopoulos, C., Karadedos, G., Polychroniou, I., Tsalis, P., Genitsaris, E., . . . Palantzas, G. (2011a). Handbook of basic principles for the realization of accessibility improvements in Monumental spaces. PROSPELASIS project Deliverable. Thessaloniki: AUTh.

Naniopoulos, A., Giannakos, C., Xenakis, C., Papanikolaou, E., Kalliagra, S., Kourbeti, C., Tselegidis, I., & Digbasbani, A., (2010a). *Proposal of functional alternative solutions in pre-study level for selected Monuments/spaces*. PROSPELASIS project Deliverable. Thessaloniki: AUTh.

Naniopoulos, A., Giannakos, C., Xenakis, C., Papanikolaou, E., Kalliagra, S., Sakantamis, K., … Karagiorgos, F. (2011b). *Proposal of functional solutions in final study level for selected Monuments/spaces*. PROSPELASIS project Deliverable. Thessaloniki: AUTh.

Naniopoulos, A., & Marki, E. (2003). Accessibility and Comprehensibility of Monuments and Archaeological Sites for people with Restricted Mobility. A Preliminary Investigation for the Application of a Methodology on Sites of the 9th Ephorate of Byzantine Antiquities. In *Access to culture and sports for people with disabilities conference proceedings*. Hellenic Ministry of Culture.

Naniopoulos, A., & Nalmpantis D. (2004). *An overview of: Problems, suggestions and good practices concerning the situation in Greece.* Maple project deliverable. Thessaloniki: AUTh.

Naniopoulos, A., Papanikolaou, E., Kalliagra, S., Tsalis, P., Palantzas, G., Nalmpantis, D., Genitsaris, E., Kyriakopoulos, N., & Tokmakidis, P. (2010b). *Evaluation and mapping of the existing situation in selected Monuments/spaces.* PROSPELASIS project Deliverable. Thessaloniki: AUTh.

National Disability Authority of Ireland (NDA). (2011). *Code of practice on accessible heritage sites.* Dublin: NDA.

PROSPELASIS Team. (2012). *D7: Interventions realized in selected Monuments.* PROSPELASIS project Deliverable. Thessaloniki: AUTh.

Royal National Institute for the Blind. (1995). *Building sight.* London: JMU.

Stumbo, N. J., Wang, Y., & Pegg, S. (2011). Issues of Access: What Matters to People with Disabilities as They Seek Leisure Experiences. *World Leisure Journal, 53*(2), 91–103. doi:10.1080/04419057.2011.580549

The Freedom Trail Foundation. (2015). *Explore the trail.* Retrieved August 2, 2016, from http://www.thefreedomtrail.org/freedom-trail/

Tokmakidis, K. (2011). *The process of creating haptic models.* Presentation in the frame of the 4th PROSPELASIS Seminar "Maintenance and Management of accessibility improvement interventions", Thessaloniki, Greece.

Tsalis, P., & Naniopoulos, A. (2008). *Needs of people with disabilities in tourist activities. MEDRA Project deliverable.* Toroslar Municipality.

UN Committee on the Rights of Persons with Disabilities. (2013). *General comment on Article 9: Accessibility.* Retrieved April 24, 2017, from www.ohchr.org/HRBodies/CRPD/GC/DGCArticle9.doc

UNESCO. (1982). *Mexico City declaration on cultural policies.* World Conference on Cultural Policies, Mexico City, Mexico.

UNESCO. (1996). *Our Creative Diversity, report of the World Commission on Culture and Development.* Paris: UNESCO.

United Nations. (1993). *United Nations General Assembly Rules on the Equalization of Opportunities for Persons with Disabilities Resolution 48/96.* Author.

Vlahakis, V., Ioannidis, N., Karigiannis, J., Tsotros, M., Gounaris, M., Stricker, D., & Almaida, L. et al. (2002). Archeoguide: An augmented reality guide for archaeological sites. *IEEE Computer Graphics and Applications, 22*(5), 52–59. doi:10.1109/MCG.2002.1028726

KEY TERMS AND DEFINITIONS

Accessibility: As used here, includes: usability and possibility of independent physical access and movement; and perceptibility, referring to the way one perceives, understands the environment.

Byzantine Monuments: Also referred to as the Eastern Roman Empire, was the continuation of the Roman Empire in the East during Late Antiquity and the Middle Ages c. 330 – 1453b.

Central Archaeological Council: The highest advisory body in Greece on all matters pertaining to the protection of ancient monuments, archaeological sites and sites of exceptional historical or legendary importance up to 1830.

EEA Grants: Represent the contribution of Iceland, Liechtenstein and Norway to reducing economic and social disparities and to strengthening bilateral relations with 16 EU countries in Central and Southern Europe and the Baltics.

ICT: Information and Communication Technologies.

Tactile Models: In this chapter the term is used to describe 3D models of Byzantine monuments created to assist persons with vision impairments.

UNESCO World Heritage List: List of sites of outstanding universal value that meet at least one out of ten selection criteria, as described in The Operational Guidelines for the Implementation of the World Heritage Convention.

Chapter 10

A Framework Supported by Modeling and Virtual/ Augmented Reality for the Preservation and Dynamization of Archeological-Historical Sites

Mauro Figueiredo
University of Algarve, Portugal

João Pedro Bernardes
University of Algarve, Portugal

José I. J. Rodrigues
University of Algarve, Portugal

César Gonçalves
University of Algarve, Portugal

ABSTRACT

This chapter presents an approach for the preservation and exploration of the archaeological-historical information using the most modern methods of Building Information Modelling (BIM) together with virtual and augmented reality adapted to archaeology. It was made a survey of the archaeological site using an unmanned aerial vehicle (UAV) and laser scan to obtain accurate information of existing structures which is stored in a BIM model. By using BIM methodologies, all existing information is organized in one place, shared and preserved for future memory. This 3D model is used to virtually reconstruct the Milreu archeological site, bringing this ancient Roman villa to life again, and supports the virtual reality platform and augmented reality tourism application for mobile devices, used for the promotion of the archaeological site, in an innovative way, in order to ensure a high degree of satisfaction to regular visitors and attract new public, looking for the visits to the archaeological-historical site to become a memorable experience.

DOI: 10.4018/978-1-5225-2927-9.ch010

INTRODUCTION

The ruins of Milreu are a good example of a Roman villa of great archaeological importance (Santos, 1972), that is not immediately visible to the visitor without professional or specialized knowledge to directly get a correct idea of what that place would be like at the time.

This chapter presents an approach that enhances the preservation of information in a centralized system that allows exploration and valorization of all archaeological information.

This approach is supported by Building Information Modeling (BIM) methodologies allowing the integration of different types of archaeological information into a shared database, constituting a source of 2D and 3D information that is shared and exploited by visitors and / or specialists.

An unmanned aerial vehicle (UAV) conducts a topographical survey of the ruins of Milreu and thus obtain accurate information of the existing constructions, which is the basis that will allow the recording of all the existing information about Milreu. Such records include information about the interventions, interpretations and models of the different epochs.

Virtual and augmented reality technologies are integrated in the tourism application is used to improve the interpretation and the understanding of Milreu to the visitors, using mobile devices as an artifact mediator in the discovery of this archaeological site. Virtual 3D models of some spaces where historical-archaeological information exists were built to support the virtual and augmented reality platform for mobile devices. In this way, the visitor is able to explore a three-dimensional virtual environment on the web and on a smartphone or a tablet that helps him to interpret the archaeological site.

The creation of the virtual space of Milreu allows the visitor the interactive and immersive exploration in a 2D / 3D environment presenting the history not visible directly from the archaeological site. In this way, the three-dimensional virtual reconstruction of the archaeological heritage reveals the importance of these places at the time to the general public by allowing, in an easy and interactive way, the visualization, understanding and exploration of these spaces through Internet.

On the other hand, when using augmented reality, the visitor obtains information superimposed on reality, when he is physically visiting the ruins of Milreu. Which helps him to read and interpret the different spaces, vestiges, objects and existing buildings and, in this way, to transform the visit into a memorable experience.

MILREU

The ruins of Milreu, located in Estoi, 7 Km from Faro, correspond to a Roman villa with a long period of occupation between the 1st century and 5th century, being one of the largest and best preserved Roman villa in the southwest of the Iberian Peninsula. It is classified as a national monument since 1910, after the excavations of the 19th century, carried out by archaeologist Estácio da Veiga, have revealed the archaeological importance of the site (Santos, 1972). From then, becomes a reference among the Portuguese archaeological sites, beginning a wide-ranging programme of excavations from de1971, coordinated by Theodor Hauschild. It is then that is definitely in sight the residential and richest part of the villa, the *pars urbana*, which was acquired by the State and is valued and converted into a visitable archaeological site. In this part, are to highlight the mosaics with marine motifs, the temple, the baths and the residential area organized around a peristyle and an atrium (Hauschild & Teichner, 2002; Lancha & Oliveira, 2013). The *pars rustica*, i.e. the part corresponding to the agricultural dependencies, stables and accommodation for slaves organized around a courtyard, clearly visible in the 19th-century plant raised by Estacio da Veiga (Figure 1), is nowadays occupied by agricultural land.

The site was first occupied in the first half of the 1st century AD. Then it was relatively modest rural place. From its foundation and until the middle of the 4th century the villa had 4 or 5 programs of works that reshaped successively the initial space (Bernardes, 2006, p. 141-142; Teichner, 2008, p. 165-173, fig. 73). The ruins that are nowadays visible in the archaeological site, for the most part, to the last phase of reconstruction of the villa, when the temple is built and the site reaches its maximum splendor.

With the fall of the Roman Empire, Milreu is not abandoned. Although most of the dependencies are abandoned, some structures are (re) built, (re) using the materials from the ancient Roman buildings. People continued living on the site however decadent and Christianized. With the Muslim occupation, in the first half of the 8th century, at least one family continues to occupy the place that continues to register occupation in the middle ages. In the 16th century is built on Roman ruins a farm house. Remodeled in the 18th century, takes the configuration that still have currently. This rural house remained inhabited until the 60 years of the 20th century.

The site of Milreu is a remarkable example of continuity of occupation over 2000 years. So it is not limited to the ruins of the different phases of the Roman period but also the human occupations of several times. It is understandable, therefore, that is not easy the musealisation of a place with these characteristics. Indeed, the interpretation and presentation to the public of such great complexity of structures is not easy, since they often are interspersed, interrupted or superimposed on structures of various times (Figure 2).

Figure 1. Milreu plant of the 19th century
Source: Santos, 1972.

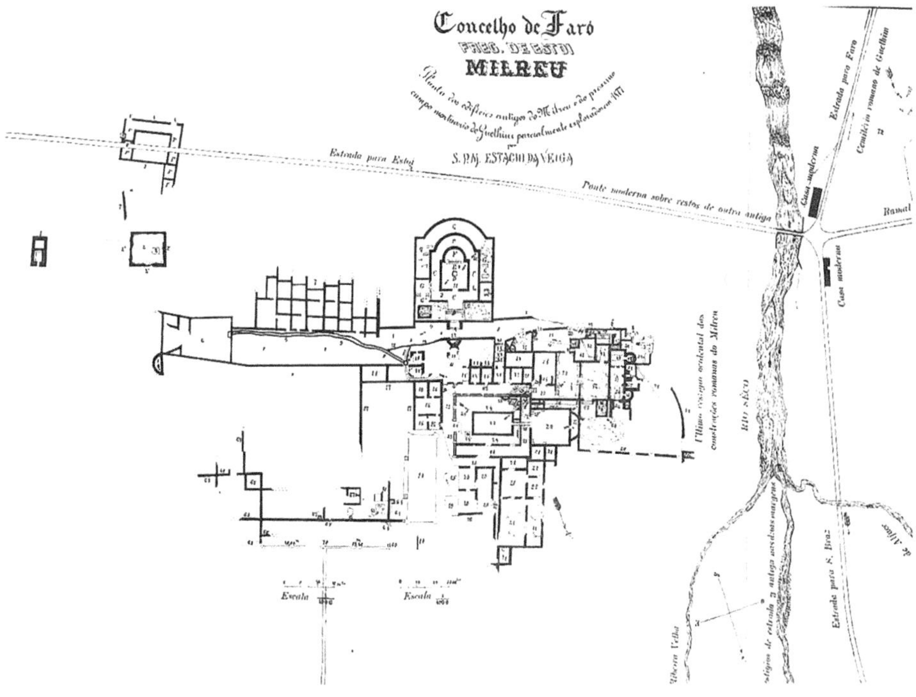

Figure 2. Mosaic pavement of Milreu (4th century)

According to the 2014 activities report of the Regional Direction of Culture of the Algarve, more than 15 000 people visited Milreu in that year, of which 79% are foreigners (Rafael, 2015, p.4-6). Despite having a circuit with explanatory panels of different parts that make up the ruins, it is very difficult to the common visitor imagine volumes and architectural proportions and understand the links between the different dependencies. Sometimes, due to the interleaving of structures from different eras or the disappearance of parts of them, it becomes impossible for a non-specialist to have a correct idea of how it was during the Roman era the appearance of buildings which belonged to those ruins. With the use of UAVs technologies, rigorous survey of structures and later reconstructions of 3D models, it is possible for visitors the cabal understanding of how were those ruins, as well as understand the evolution of the site over time. For the times and sites with archaeological-historical data available, it is possible to reconstruct buildings or built sets, revealing that the ruins of a place like Milreu correspond, in fact, not one but several constructive realities that were succeeding and that reflect our history of the last 2000 years.

This reconstituted from all the information available, in order to enable a better interpretation and reading of archaeological sites to visitors, is similar to the process of anastylosis, i.e. the re-composition of the dismembered parts of the historical monument, as defined in the Athens Charter (October 1931) for the Restoration of Historic Monuments. It is, however, a virtual anastylosis, unlike the real one, can go beyond, until to the total reconstruction of the building from not identified elements but buildings and facilities imagined, since the primary objective is to provide the visitor easy reading and closer to what the monument was. And this is possible because this is a virtual process, without ever compromising the identity and historical integrity of the object or reconstituted building.

THE RECONSTRUCTIONS AND SURVEYS OF THE MILREU RUINS IN THE PAST

After several campaigns of excavations since the late nineteenth century, in 1971 the German Archaeological Institute began, under the direction of Theodor Hauschild, systematic excavations in Milreu (Hauschild & Teichner, 2002, p. 13). Since then, its characteristics of wide and rich residential house, as well as its potential for the musealisation of the site, have been revealed, starting so the restoration of mosaics and consolidation of visible structures. Already before that architect German and archaeologist had developed a rigorous survey and study on the roman temple of the site, which still maintained much of its original volume, published in Germany in 1964 and in Portugal in 1988 (Hauschild, 1964; Hauschild, 1984-1988). This work presents, for the first time, a survey and a complete three-dimensional reconstruction of the temple, resulting in a model that is nowadays in the Centre of Interpretation of the archaeological site of Milreu. This is the only fully reconstituted building available to the general public of the entire space of the villa. It is true that other architectural reconstructions of this Roman villa were produced, but, as a rule, are for specific research purposes and do not reach the general public. A 3D virtual reconstruction of the Temple of Milreu based on previous works of T. Hauschild to a television program issued in 2015 and 2016 (*Escrito na Pedra*, 1, in RTP 2), prepared by Paulo Bernardes (from the multimedia laboratory of the Archaeology Unit of the University of Minho), allowed to disclose a digital model of the Temple of Milreu to the general public. But this model nowadays is not available to the thousands of visitors to the site, or contributes to clarify what would be those ruins from 4th century AD. The same can be said of the 3D survey, using MeshLab, applied to a thermal swimming pool covered with figured mosaics of marine motives (Bernardes et al., 2014). Félix Teichner, who continued working in Milreu after T. Hauschild, did a survey and a reconstruction of the oil mill at the site, excavated for himself, as well as a freehand reconstitution how would be all this roman place 1600 years ago (Teichner, 2011-2012).

All these reconstructions of buildings and villa of Milreu integrated studies and scientific articles. So the general public that nowadays visit Milreu does not have access and do not know these works of reconstruction, with the exception of the model of the temple according to the proposal of T. Hauschild. For the visitor, there is in place only a brochure and a guide to the ruins of Milreu (Hauschild & Teichner, 2002). It is true that the guide is very clear in the explanation of the different parts of the site, but for the common visitor the place isn't intelligible from some foundations sometimes cut or overlaid by other.

The new tools and current methodologies allow us to give back to the community and the visitors, in a simple way and perceptive, the knowledge that experts have about the past of these ruins, in the perspective of a true archaeology for the public. The dialogue between researchers, the archaeological site and the society in general, provided by virtual reconstructions, will allow everyone to gain and that archaeological sites are increasingly recognized and valued.

BUILDING INFORMATION MODELING (BIM)

Although the first contributions to the BIM development have been taken specifically with the intention of creating an information model for the construction, with developments in the extent of its applicability to the management, operation and maintenance of buildings, there are also contributions to the applicability of BIM methodologies in other areas. In particular, in the scope of archaeological heritage modeling there some developments in the literature (Murphy & Pavia, 2009; Noh *et al.*, 2009; Garagnani & Manferdini, 2013; Scianna *et al.*, 2014).

BIM is a digital representation of the physical and functional characteristics of a building or construction, providing a shared knowledge database. In BIM technology, the geometry, function, data and the respective behavior are integrated, allowing to establish relationships between them. Many authors related with AEC/FM (Architecture, Engineering, Construction and Facilities Management) (Eastman *et al.*, 2011; Gonçalves, 2014) report that BIM is a process of production/communication/collaboration supported by modeling technology, analysis and simulation of the behavior of buildings (energy, structural, acoustic, sustainability, etc.). BIM methodology gets involved in the design of all specialties in the life cycle of a project, sharing a common digital model that is used for the design and engineering processes in construction projects (Grilo & Tavares, 2008). The use of BIM in archaeology on the one hand strengthens the organization in a single shared database of all relevant information of an archaeological-historical site.

The BIM database stores the three-dimensional models, two-dimensional plans and sections, quantitative data, specifications and properties of materials and various information associated with the constructions, as well as related with interventions throughout its use at different times.

Richards-Rissetto *et al.* (2012) refers that the BIM concept, extended to Cultural Heritage, facilitates the organization, storage, query, web-based visualization, and communication of archaeological data. These authors refer that the heritage community has realized the benefits of using computers, 3D models, and advanced databased on the web to enrich their studies, and often at lower costs.

In recent years, the application of BIM has also been extended to the field of historic architecture (Pauwels *et al.,* 2008; Fai *et al.*, 2011). The literature discusses the BIM tools capability in the graphical representation of constructions, in the historical documentation storage and technical information and explores the interoperability of tools in the sharing of data through the use of web platforms.

A new 3D modeling system of historic structures is proposed by Murphy and Pavia (2009), using BIM software and data survey through a laser scanner combined with terrestrial digital cameras. To these developments, the authors denominated by *Historic building information modelling* (HBIM). The final product of HBIM technique is a 3D model that includes details behind the object's surface concerning its methods of construction and material make-up (Murphy *et al.*, 2011). This methodology aims to have a 3D model with associated data that allows automatic generation of full engineering drawings, orthogonal projections, sections, details, costs and scheduling of historical structures conservation works, adding intelligence to point cloud data. The parametric objects are constructed by HBIM methodology using the *Geometric Descriptive Language* (GDL), incorporated at the BIM software. 3D models are so georeferenced, involving 3D Geographic Information Systems (Dore & Murphy, 2012).

Garagnani and Manferdini (2013) are also of the opinion that the BIM has become a collaborative strategy in documentation and modeling of historic structures, making this information available to researchers involved in cultural heritage preservation.

Scianna *et al.* (2014) present a framework to create integrated 3D archaeological models with databases through BIM. Using the Revit Autodesk software, the authors created a 3D model of a Roman structure; decomposed into parts and elements; classified into semantic categories (architectural component, materials and phases of construction); a structured model based on families and different levels of detail. According to Scianna *et al.* (2014), this methodology allowed the photo-realistic visualization with 3D identification, through stored data related to morphology, typology and construction. Even in the Portuguese case the presentation and valuation of archaeological remains from these tools is an increasingly common reality. See, for example, the works in the Roman city of Ammaia (Marvão), where exploration and archaeological excavation supported the virtual reconstruction of the entire city, at the level of the urban network and even the volumetrics of buildings and Major arteries (Corsi & Vermuleen, 2012). However, Scianna *et al.* (2014) and Garagnani and Manferdini (2013) report that the BIM applications still have some limitations in the field of archaeology. Namely, the fact that there are libraries of materials, which are suitable to assign to modern and contemporary constructions, but do not include irregular features and constructive asymmetries in the ancient context of many historic buildings.

VIRTUAL AND AUGMENTED REALITY

The Internet and the World Wide Web continue to evolve at an unstoppable pace in these first decades of the twenty-first century. Web 2.0, cloud computing, and mobile computing devices are responsible for profound changes in the traditional activities associated with the World Wide Web and for a dramatic impact on many aspects of life in modern societies.

Virtual Worlds (MV), Augmented Reality (AR) and Web 2.0-based Games are emerging technologies and can also be explored in archaeology-historical sites.

According to Makzan (2010), a virtual world is a digital environment similar to the real world. Users can enter the virtual world and explore their three-dimensional space or just interact with each other. The established interactions can be of different types, from the establishment of a relation of collaboration or entertainment. Virtual worlds can be used in different areas, including archaeology.

For example, the Roma Virtual project (Dylla, Kimberly, Bernard Frischer et al., 2010) allows real-time navigation in a three-dimensional model of Rome in the fourth century. The use of scanners also allows archaeologists to map and reconstruct archaeological sites of great historical interest, as happened in the virtual reconstruction of Parthenon, exhibiting all its sculptural details (Tang, 2012). The animations and images of this model were used in the promotion of the Olympic Games of Athens in 2008.

Azuma (1997) presented the most popular definition for Augmented Reality, which still stands today, as the system in which 3D virtual objects are integrated into a real-time 3D environment in real time. In general, augmented reality allows to add information to the environment in order to facilitate human-computer and human interactions with the environment (Van Krevelen & Poelman, 2010; Li & Fu, 2012; Figueiredo et al., 2014, Guimarães et al., 2015).

With the emergence, increasing computing capacity and ubiquity of smartphones and tablets based on iOS and Android operating systems, a growing number of applications and augmented reality platforms have emerged that have made AR accessible to the average consumer (Roche, 2011). An augmented reality application can contain various functions, dedicated to interactions or content display. The type of AR applications are only limited by the imagination and capabilities of the mobile computing device (Ward, 2012).

Noh et al. (2009) present some concrete applications of augmented reality in the reconstruction, technical exploration and virtual presentation of archaeological sites. They also argue that with this technology, visitors to archaeological sites can immerse themselves and understand culture better, learn history by interacting in the real environment through mobile devices, share social space with the virtual world, visualize virtual models of monuments that only partially exist, view scenes from inaccessible points of view, interact with objects without running the risk of harm. Noh et al. (2009) emphasizes the importance of the digital reconstruction of archaeological heritage to preserve, protect and interpret our culture and history.

DEVELOPMENT OF A VIRTUAL AND AUGMENTED REALITY PLATFORM TO PRESENT HIDDEN STORIES OF HERITAGE

The technological developments in the domains of the Internet and the technologies of entertainment, information and communication, can nowadays support new forms of archaeological sites promotion with innovative ways of disseminating and enriching its services that can offer visitors unforgettable experiences, increasing the degree of satisfaction, and attract new audiences to the archaeological sites. This chapter presents its implementation through a tourism application that takes advantage of virtual and augmented technologies.

The first approach consists in the use of a Web platform in which the visitor explores the archaeological site in a virtual three-dimensional environment (Figure 3) created in the BIM model. This platform allows visitors to experience the various archaeological spaces that will increase interest in visiting and interacting physically with the archaeological spaces showing all the hidden structures of the archaeological site.

Recent computational development enables support to the creation of new entertainment environments based on virtual reality techniques that allow the recreation of new realities for individuals, in which the user's sense of presence in these new realities is greatly expanded. Entertainment based on virtual reality, or with a strong component of virtual reality, have characteristics that make them very popular, because it can induce the feeling of being part of a virtual world where the visitor is able, for example, to manipulate objects representations as if they were real. Objects that respond to user interactions providing an engagement that motivates visitors to explore the virtual environment.

The creation of an archaeological exploration site for a virtual visit, in which the tourist still at home can explore in an interactive and immersive 2D / 3D environment, also allows the exploration of the hidden history of the archaeological site. From the virtual reconstruction of the three-dimensional archaeological sites, it reveals the importance of these places at the time by allowing the public to easily

Figure 3. Survey carried out with an UAV that is used to support the virtual reconstruction of Milreu

and interactively view and explore these structures and buildings through the Internet and accessible world-wide. In this way, the visitor explores the archaeological site, while still at home or traveling, in an interactive, motivating and challenging way, through the use of virtual reality concepts, which will result in a greater number of visits and greater sustainability of these archaeological-historical sites.

The second approach is to use an augmented reality application for mobile devices (tablets and smartphones) and multiplatform (Android, iOS), which can be downloaded for free from the Apple or Google store. This augmented reality application will allow the activation of content in the form of texts, videos, animations, 2D / 3D models or games, that will work only when the tourist is in the archaeological site. The visitor uses the app to explore the archaeological site making the visit an exciting treasure hunt. By using this augmented reality application, visitors get information that is complementary to the information visible where they are located (Figure 4). In this way, the visitor has a better understanding of the different structures making the visit in an even more enriching experience. This information can be presented using gamification strategies, which will make interactions with the archaeological-historical site even more challenging, especially for the school-age population. This application will also integrate transmedia storytelling methodologies to automatically create the narrative of the visitor experience at the archaeological station, which can be used by the visitor for future memory or to share on social networks. This feature will have marketing multiplier effects for the archaeological-historical site.

CONCLUSION

BIM methodologies have been extensively used in the construction of models involving specialists in the life cycle of modern buildings, from design, construction, to operation and maintenance, from an Engineering and Facilities Management perspective. This chapter shows that BIM tools already provide

Figure 4. Approximate 3D virtual reconstruction of the temple using BIM methodologies for the mobile application of augmented reality

valuable contributions in the modelling of the archaeological heritage, that can be explored in sites like Milreu, allowing the preservation and valorisation of archaeological information. BIM is a collaborative strategy in the documentation and virtual reconstruction of historical structures, making information available to researchers and visitors. In addition to the use of 3D models as auxiliary tools in archaeological research and interpretation, the visualization in different perspectives, through the possibilities of rotation, translation, magnification, reduction, sectioning of 3D models, allow any visitor a better understanding of the ruins they visit. These three-dimensional models integrated in a virtual reality environment are important to help visitors to get a better understanding of the historical-archaeological sites and the reality of the past related to them. It also contributes to simplify the construction of Museological discourses. The virtual exploration of an archaeological tourism application online makes it available anywhere on the planet and to feed the user's curiosity, inviting him to physically visit the ruins. Already on the archaeological site, with the tourism application that takes advantage of augmented reality, visitors have access to additional information for a more complete and easy interpretation of the archaeological site and can compare the reality with the original virtual structures that is shown with augmented reality technology. The visitor can discover and visualize inaccessible structures from different points of view, interact with objects and share enriching experiences. Such combination of existing structures with virtual models can contribute to motivate and attract more visitors to a memorable experience in the archaeological site.

REFERENCES

Azuma, R. T. (1997). A survey of augmented reality. *Presence (Cambridge, Mass.)*, *6*(4), 55–385. doi:10.1162/pres.1997.6.4.355

Bernardes, J. P. (2006). O peristilo da villa romana de Milreu: novas Interpretações. *Promontoria, 4,* 127-160.

Bernardes, P., Magalhães, F., Ribeiro, J., Madeira, J., & Martins, M. (2014). Image-based 3D Modelling in Archaeology: Application and Evaluation. In *22nd International Conference in Central Europe on Computer Graphics, Visualization and Computer Vision*. Plzen: University of West Bohemia.

Corsi, C., & Vermeulen, F. (Eds.). (2012). *Ammaia I: The Survey. A Romano-Lusitanian Townscape Revealed. Archaeological Reports Ghent University (ARGU) 8*. Ghent: Academia Press.

Dore, C., & Murphy, M. (2012). Integration of Historic BIM (HBIM) and 3D GIS for Recording and Managing Cultural Heritage Sites. *Proceedings of the 18th International Conference on Virtual Systems and Multimedia (VSMM)*, 369–376.

Dylla, K., Frischer, B., Mueller, P., Ulmer, A., & Haegler, S. (2010). Rome Reborn 2.0: A Case Study of Virtual City Reconstruction Using Procedural Modeling Techniques. *CAA 2009. Making History Interactive*, 62-66.

Eastman, C., Teicholz, P., Sacks, R., & Liston, K. (2011). *BIM Handbook – A Guide to Building Information Modeling for Owners, Managers, Designers, Engineers, and Contractors* (2nd ed.). Hoboken, NJ: John Wiley & Sons, Inc.

Fai, S., Graham, K., Duckworth, T., Wood, N., & Attar, R. (2011). Building Information Modeling and heritage documentation. *Proceedings of the XXIII International CIPA Symposium*, 43–48.

Figueiredo, M. J. G., Gomes, J., Gomes, C., & Lopes, J. (2014). Augmented reality tools and learning practice in mobile-learning. In C. Stephanidis & M. Antona (Eds.), Lecture Notes in Computer Science: Vol. 8514. *Universal Access in Human-Computer Interaction. Universal Access to Information and Knowledge* (pp. 301–312). Springer International Publishing. doi:10.1007/978-3-319-07440-5_28

Garagnani, S., & Manferdini, A. (2013). Parametric Accuracy: Building information Modeling Process Applied to the Cultural Heritage Preservation. *International Archives of the Photogrammetry, Remote Sensing and Spatial Information Sciences.*

Gonçalves, C. (2014). *Gestão da Manutenção em Edifícios: Modelos para uma abordagem LARG (Lean, Agile, Resilient e Green).* Tese de Doutoramento em Engenharia Industrial. Universidade Nova de Lisboa, Faculdade de Ciências e Tecnologia.

Grilo, A., & Tavares, L. (2008). *Building Information Model e a Competitividade do sector da Construção.* Lisboa: OPET – Observatório de Prospectiva da Engenharia e da Tecnologia.

Guimarães, F., Figueiredo, M. J. G., & Rodrigues, J. I. (2015). Realidade Aumentada e Transmedia Storytelling em Museus e Património Cultural: Artefacto Digital I-Lugar. *Proceedings of 7th International Conference on Digital Arts*, 259-263.

Hauschild, T. (1964). *Der Kultbau neben dem römischen Ruinenkomplex bei Estoi in der Provinz Lusitania.* Berlin (TU).

Hauschild, T. (1984/88). O edifício de culto do complexo das ruínas romanas perto de Estoi, na provincia da Lusitânia. *Arqueologia e História*, 10(1-2), 123-150.

Hauschild, T., & Teichner, F. (2002). *Milreu – Ruínas.* Lisboa: IPPAR (Colecção "Roteiros da Arqueologia Portuguesa", 9).

Lancha, J., & Oliveira, C. (2013). *Corpus dos mosaicos romanos de Portugal / Corpus des mosaïques romaines du Portugal: II, Conventus pacensis: 2, Algarve Este.* Faro: Universidade do Algarve.

Li, W. H. A., & Fu, H. (2012). Augmented reflection of reality. *Proc. ACM SIGGRAPH 2012 Emerging Technologies.* doi:10.1145/2343456.2343459

Madden, L. (2011). *Professional Augmented Reality Browsers for smartphones: Programming for junaio, Layar, and Wikitude.* Chichester, UK: John Wiley & Sons, Ltd.

Makzan. (2010). *Flash Multiplayer Virtual Worlds.* Olton, UK: Packt Publishing, Ltd.

Murphy, M., McGoverna, E., & Pavia, S. (2011). Historic Building Information Modeling – Adding Intelligence to Laser and Image Based Surveys. *4th ISPRS International Workshop "3D Virtual Reconstruction and Visualization of Complex Architectures".*

Murphy, M., & Pavia, S. (2009). Historic Building information modelling (HBIM). *Structural Survey: Journal of Building Pathology and Refurbishment*, *27*(4), 311–327. doi:10.1108/02630800910985108

Noh, Z., Sunar, M., & Pan, Z. (2009). *A Review on Augmented Reality for Virtual Heritage System. Learning by Playing. In Game-based Education System Design and Development. Springer*. doi:10.1007/978-3-642-03364-3_7

Pauwels, P., Verstraeten, R., De Meyer, R., & Van Campenhout, J. (2008). Architectural Information Modeling For Virtual Heritage Application. *Proceedings of the 14th International Conference on Virtual Systems and Multimedia*, 18–23.

Rafael, L. (2015). "Monitorização de indicadores (2014)". In *Relatório de Atividades 2014*. Faro: Direção Regional de Cultura do Algarve. Retrieved October 14, 2016, from http://www.cultalg.pt/pt/drca/instrumentos-de-gestao

Richards-Risseto, H., Remondino, F., Agugiaro, G., Robertsson, J., Schwerin, J., & Girardi, G. (2012). Kinect and 3D GIS in Archaeology. *18th International Conference on Virtual Systems and Multimedia (VSMM)*. DOI: doi:10.1109/VSMM.2012.6365942

Roche, K. (2011). *Pro IOS 5 Augmented Reality*. New York: Apress. doi:10.1007/978-1-4302-3913-0

Santos, M. L. E. V. (1972). Arqueologia romana do Algarve (vol. 2). Lisboa: Associação dos Arqueólogos Portugueses.

Scianna, A., Gristina, S., & Paliaga, S. (2014). Experimental BIM Applications in Archeology: A Wok-Flow. Lecture Notes in Computer Science, 8740, 490-498. DOI: doi:10.1007/978-3-319-13695-0_48

Tang, X.-X. (Ed.). (2012). *Virtual Reality - Human Computer Interaction*. InTech.

Teichner, F. (2008). Zwischen Land und Meer – Entre tierra y mar. *Studien zur Architektur und Wirtschaftsweise ländlicher Siedlungen im Süden der römischen Provinz Lusitanien. Stvdia Lvsitana,* 3.

Teichner, F. (2011-2012). La producción de aceite y vino en la villa romana de Milreu (Estói): El éxito del modelo catoniano en la Lusitania. *AnMurcia*, *27-28*, 471–484.

Van Krevelen, D., & Poelman, R. (2010). A survey of augmented reality technologies, applications and limitations. *Int. J. of Virtual Reality*, *9*(2), 1.

Ward, T. (2012). *Augmented Reality using Appcelerator Titanium Starter*. Birmingham, UK: Packt Publishing Ltd.

KEY TERMS AND DEFINITIONS

Archaeological Site: A place in which evidence of past activity is preserved.

Augmented Reality: Real time integration between digital information, with live video and the user's environment.

Building Information Modeling: A process involving the generation and management of digital representations of physical and functional characteristics of places.

Laser Scan Survey: A surveying method that analyses a real-world object or environment to collect data on its shape and possibly its appearance. The collected data can then be used to construct digital three-dimensional models.

Milreu: Roman villa in the South of Portugal from 1st to 5th century AD.

Mobile Device: Small computing device, small enough to hold and operate in the hand and having an operating system capable of running mobile apps.

Unmanned Aerial Vehicle: Commonly known as a drone, unmanned aircraft system (UAS), or by several other names, is an aircraft without a human pilot aboard.

Virtual Reality: Three-dimensional, computer generated environment which can be explored and interacted with by a person.

Chapter 11
Architecture, Tourism, and Technological Innovation in the Jesuit Mission of São Miguel, Brazil

Pedro de Alcântara Bittencourt César
Universidade de Caxias do Sul, Brazil

Julia Luise Altmman
Universidade de Caxias do Sul, Brazil

Caroline Peccin da Silva
Universidade de Caxias do Sul, Brazil

Bruna Tronca
Universidade de Caxias do Sul, Brazil

Michele Pinheiro Trentin
Universidade de Caxias do Sul, Brazil

ABSTRACT

The contemporaneity demands a better relation between the object and the subject. In this article, it is expected to understand how has been developed this bond of Jesuit architecture and its understanding by the visitor. In this way, it is searched to explore the touristic technological means in Missões Guaraníticas. It questions the use of technology to a better extent of dissemination of local and cultural legacy - existing architecture. The methodology presents an exploratory research of technological platforms of information. It is noticed that its use increases tourism, favoring the culture and history of the region, besides promoting accessibility, reducing the social and physical barriers. The technology helps to preserve and disseminate the historical importance of the site. New information media has influenced and has increased the tourism, stimulating the local trade, and also it encourages the preservation of historical heritage. The approach of historical study of the region / country has great potential for increasing interest in historical architecture and culture.

DOI: 10.4018/978-1-5225-2927-9.ch011

INTRODUCTION

Before presenting some determinants results of the relationship between technology and tourism as a feature of the architectural tourist attraction, an overview is introduced of this current environment. In it, ideas of a society as a holder of a traditional modernity has been surpassed by diverse values that conditions to a new world context. The subjects, men and women, distinctly, have transformed technological props in support of their daily lives.

Another aspect of this activity portrays Lash and Urry (1998, p.16) when referring to mobility. These social scientists are directed to the capitalist economy in postmodernity, characterizing its currently striking aspects. In this condition, this social factor is determined as the structure of objects and subjects. This value not only configures the recognition of products that are formed by movements between project, components and ideas which overcome local and national physical barriers, from its origin to the final use (consumption); but also of subjects who are increasingly in different transits and forming global networks of flows of people.

In this issue, points are established with more interest in being accessed, which in Critical Geography can be denominated as luminous points of world capitalism (Santos, 2008). It is known that for various interests often they stand out for having their appeal associated with major world themes, reworking values, such as cultural, by structures based on information and communication. "Thus, places are redefined: as points of interest of long and short-haul, global and locals, manifested by a range of classifications that are expanding and changing" (Santos, 2008, p.18).

The present moment, called by Lash and Urry (1998) of disorganized capitalism, presupposes "a predominance of the culture, global, local and a concern for the environment, all aspects that characterize the trip and the hospitality in contemporary era" (Lash & Urry, 1998, p.348). Previously these displacements were directed to instructions of specialized guides, diverse printed matter and with little universal access. Nowadays, the traveler hopes to absorb an enormous amount of artifact and information, cultures and sense systems (Lash & Urry, 1998, p.345). In this condition, he (the traveler) uses various technologies. Corroborates in this context, the positioning of the localities, often predetermined as a place of tourist interest, not by determinism but by capitalist reproduction's logic, and in many ways are positioned, like those qualified as a World Heritage Site by Unesco, offering a landscape among other expectations to the future visitor.

It is also important to note that "the study of the relationship between the digital and the social tends to be characterized by technological determinism or by indeterminacy" (Sassen, 2010, p.192). In these conditions, the use of technology can be seen in several ways, as an independent relationship to a performance relationship. However,

The digital and the social can shape and condition each other, but each one is, and remains, specific and distinct. And this interaction can occur in short or long chains, where a social result contributes with a new technical element and so on (Sassen, 2010, p.192).

It is also observed that the digital space confronts the dominant idea previously referred to it. Not always, necessarily, but in it adds an imminent value of contradiction in the places' affirmation. This panorama can be easily observed with the reading of Augé (1994). This anthropologist and researcher highlight the necessity to determine a status of the concept of non-place by associating it with various connotations.

Thus, even without directly affirming, the areas where a strong informational presence prevails are associated, such as, for example, the environments of airport circulation. Currently, can be extended the concept portrayed by a representational logic, such as virtual gaming environments, that uses virtual realities and formulates ephemeral spaces of super modernity.

Besides, the technology collaborates for the actions of Education and Heritage Interpretation. "The transformation into a show manifests to other scales and in many ways: in the plastering of the buildings, in the cities embellished with flowers, in the restoration of the ruins, in the 'light and sounds' shows" (Augé, 2008, p.69). Thus, "it can't be denied that certain tourists also have the curiosity, the desire to observe and to learn, although, without a doubt, it is a case that happens very rarely and only between minority" (Augé, 2007, p.63).

It may be interesting to observe that the informational technology allows visual access to a particular location. In this way, currently it is possible to enter and visualize great museums around the world by accessing the world-wide computer network. In this condition, it is given a three-dimensional notion of something, being in front of the screen, an electronic object or even into virtual realities. However, with all these possibilities that may reduce physical interest, "the informatization increases mobility, including what is often considered immobile or not-mobile" (Sassen, 2010, p.193).

METHOD AND OBJECT

This chapter presents an essay involving the relations of the tourist appropriation of the historical architectural attraction with the use of digital technology tools. However, despite this free character of the format, it is expected to present an article with methodological theoretical bases, structured in defined epistemological fields, refuting and giving necessary characteristics for such undertaking. In this way, preliminary structures, involving broader issues, are portrayed. The exhibition presented here is not restricted to the existing conceptual fields or their state of the art.

Another challenge is given in the recognition of acting agents in the formation of their scientific body. This becomes an abstraction of difficult concreteness, which demands certain methodological arrangements. For that, some features are used: one determines the clipping and the other one the way of locating them. It approaches a hermeneutic understanding. Panorama that overlap, since:

Hermeneutics is something traditional in methodology, because it refers to the art of interpreting texts and especially to human communication. Part of the realization that social reality, and especially the phenomenon of human communication, has such varied, nuances and even mysterious dimensions that it is necessary to pay attention not only to what is said but also to what is not said. There is hidden meaning in communication, whose rule is to escape from the rules (Demo, 1995, p.247).

In this condition, it is worked with a superficial hermeneutics for the composition of this process. However, its recognition leads us to think of Ricoeur (1978, p.16), which reflects that:

(...) each interpretation, by definition, reduces this richness, this multivocity, and translates the symbol according to a grid of reading that is its own. The task of this criterion is to show that the form of interpretation is relative to the theoretical structure of the considered hermeneutic system.

It starts from the recognition of contemporary society, a task that seems easy after all it is one of its most current values: the use of technology. However, this apparent condition hides its complexity, which leads, with the support of Sociology (mainly) to present clues of its values and current panorama. With this support, the attractive is portrayed which is commonly presented between the urban and the architectural object. Thus, its recognition is strengthened through several areas of knowledge.

With these characteristics, there is the spatial (historically determined) clipping: the current legacy of the Jesuit-Guarani Missions which existed in South America between the XVII and XVIII centuries. From this, it is positioned and reflected its condition as attractive and tourist product. In this panorama, it is given a survey of the ways that information technology has enabled this place as a touristic product, and especially, presenting it as a facilitator of an Education and Heritage Interpretation.

THE RECOGNITION OF ARCHITECTURE AND ITS RELATION WITH THE VISITOR

In this essay, the subject is referred by his visitor's gaze, as the consumer of a contradictory space between the virtual and the vital. In this dimension, the appropriation of the urban-architectural areas of the Jesuit Missions is studied. The social representation which has this subject as a consumer of landscape among other representations, that reinforce the inexistence of a limit established between the real world and that of the computerized screens. Thus, if since the past times, the act of traveling was born of the intention of the temporary displacement and the consumption of dreams and diverse landscapes; today, its realization usually begins by actions of representational formulations with the use of the world-wide computer network. It is known that even at the time of on-site consumption, the use of these resources is not dispensed.

In this way, as defined by Zevi (1992), if Architecture deals with the recognition that surpasses a built-in box, it can be demystified by any layman with the use of suitable tools, if previously this person had a treatment for it. Thus, there is in this study the pointing to the role of this object as guide in the recognition of a memorial space's representation that is adjectival of constructions and cybernetic spaces, depending on its dimensions and visibilities. After all, are there limits to these approaches in the information society between the virtual and the real?

Understanding the architecture of a locality like São Miguel das Missões (RS-Brazil) leads to involve theories as the ones proposed by Rowen and Koetter (2006). In it, the City-collage predicts the existence of a plural society that justifies in symbolic responses the social needs (Rowen & Koetter, 2006, p.294). However, this understanding does not justify an "appreciation of the quality" (Rowen & Koetter, 2006, p.295) of its constituted urban landscape. In it, artificial physical forms seek, in a Marcusian perspective, to substitute freedom of choices by directed relation of consumption.

With these authors, whose ideas found the base of Contextualism, it is not expected to justify the values met in the urban scenario studied by such approach. It is only sought, with the use of the approximate epistemological look, to recognize and analyze its urban-architectural configuration. In the logic of spatial reproduction of the mission areas of strong memorial appeal, it is necessary to renew the understanding of this place as a locus of diverse pluralities.

The distancing between the edified and its memory, in this case, becomes present in its understanding of the historical relationship, and its many possible cuttings for diverse identities projects. It is also seen that "the symbol dominates the space. Architecture is not enough. As spatial relations are made more by symbols than by forms, architecture in this landscape becomes symbol in space before form in space" (Venturi & Brown, 2006, 343).

JESUIT MISSIONS IN AMERICA: SOME ASPECTS FOR AN UNDERSTANDING OF THE OBJECT

The Guarani missions were extended through the South American territory called Province of Paraguay (which did not exactly correspond to the area of this nation today[1]). Its extension occupied the current area of the south of Brazil, the northeast of Argentina and the south of Paraguay. From this, there are recognized the distribution of, respectively, seven, fifteen and eight settlements, totalizing 30 settlements, or reductions (Figure 1). However, this list fails to consider other sites that can be understood as an area of Jesuit expansion, because of their architectural legacies and even because of the diverse cultural aspects left behind.

Figure 1. Location of the Jesuit Missions in South America
Source: Cesar, Tronca, 2016, p.234.

It is also noted that the Guarani Jesuit Missions of San Ignacio Miní, Santa Ana, Nuestra Señora de Loreto and Santa Marí ala Mayor (Argentina), Ruins of São Miguel das Missões (Brazil) and Jesus and Trinity in Paraguay are recognized by Unesco (United National Educational, Scientific and Cultural Organization) as Heritage of Humanity. To their formation is associated the occupation by the European people and specifically by the Jesuit religious.

In Portuguese America, these religious disembarked in 1549, in a group of six, with Father Manoel de Nóbrega as the superior of the group. After they established themselves, it was necessary to increase the number of this group. Thus, from 1554, more Jesuits arrived to Spanish America and among these young people, José de Anchieta that had the mission of expanding the missionary activity along the coast and the mountain range, assisting in the delimitations established by the Treaty of Tordesilhas (Frazen, 2003). Through these last ones, the beginning of the formation of the Jesuit missions dates in 1609, initiating a project of politicization and catechization of the Guarani people in the region.

The reductions, that is, settlements for catechesis in an area far from those of European conviviality, were done for the control and defense of the natives (Tavares & Dalton, 1999). Its formation was defined by justifications of the counter-reformation and in the "Europeanization" of the South American Indian. These settlements refer to the reproduction of architectural forms and to the urban formation with unique characteristics that reinforce the degree of socioeconomic development of these settlements (César & Tronca, 2016). In a comparative between the Spanish settlements and the Portuguese, it is observed that the Jesuits maintained a common goal that was the socialization of the Indian with the European customs.

Men of the Catholic Reformation, the Jesuits wished to create an improved model in relation to that which monitors in Europe. (...) The way to achieve these goals is that it will be different because they are Jesuits of different nationalities (Portuguese, Spanish) committed to their respective crowns, similar commitments, but different due to the characteristics of each crown (Frazen, 2003, p. 37).

There was a fundamental difference between settlements (Portuguese) and the reductions (Spanish), mainly in the way of sustaining themselves. The reductions were suppliers of food and raw material; they were a source of agricultural production. Their production maintained the reduction fed and their surplus was marketed in large centers such as Buenos Aires and Asuncion. On the other hand, what was produced in the villages served only for the subsistence of the people living there and their families, they were like small farmers, producing for their livelihood (Frazen, 2003).

Thus, it can be observed that the reductions in the Spanish part have become independent and active autonomous units. The Jesuits maintained the organization of the Indians, preparing them for religious life and for the struggles, where the Indians defended the Spanish ideals. In the occupation of Portuguese America the main purpose developed was the catechization of the Indians and the teachings of organized labor, ideas of the Society of Jesus. In summary, both Spanish and Portuguese Jesuits used the Indian's strength and territory knowledge, so they ended up determining an indigenous territory, when they settled and left the status of semi nomadic. The remaining lands could be destined to the settlers (Frazen, 2003).

In addition to attempts to catechize, the Jesuits had the task of trying to save the Indians from the growing slave market. Thus, "it is clear from the relationships that the major problem for the Jesuits was to face the greed of the slave traders, who came down from Saint Vincent, and of the Indians, their intermediaries" (Frazen, 2003, p.19).

The Indians, who lived together in their reductions and settlements with the Spaniards and Portuguese, also suffered with the unknown diseases brought by the Jesuits. However, the reduction, due to their remoteness and isolation from contact with Europeans, suffered less from this (Frazen, 2003, p.41), since they were independent, had no link with a crown. In order to meet the Portuguese expansionist project, the Pioneer explores (in portuguese: "bandeirantes") began to travel through the territory of southern Brazil, and thus clashed with the Indians and Jesuits (Spanish).

The process of decay of the missionary history was carried out in the middle of the XVIII century, due to the expulsion of the Jesuits and the administrative exchanges of the colonies between Portugal and Spain, through treaties. This process culminated in Guarani wars. The Indians, with an interest in defending their lands, were defeated and forced to abandon the reductions. The destruction generated by the clashes characterized what is now known as the patrimony of humanity (César & Tronca, 2016).

In recent history, these places do not have a marked social presence of the ancient people and their dominant groups. Its uses are associated to scientific use (mainly in the areas of Architecture and Urbanism, History and Anthropology) and tourist visitation, which adds to the guided visit of educational character. Thus, since the middle of the last century the localities have been positioned for these purposes. However, there is a lack of integrated recognition of policies and actions as an integrated territory.

Unesco has sought to overcome this panorama. For more than a decade, efforts have been made jointly with the leaders of these three countries to consolidate the International Circuit of the Jesuit Missions with an appeal to visit the areas recognized as World Heritage Sites and their missionary environment. However, the transit of the visitor, especially the Brazilian, is subjected to a series of bureaucratic barriers, missing clarity about the limits of locomotion. It is observed that the bureaucratic process of mobility is not updated in its contemporary perspective.

A CONTEMPORARY PANORAMA

Three values can be listed that portrays the present moment. It is known that the understanding of these is not closed to the social understanding. The constitution of values for the understanding of the society is much more than its communicational, consumerism and spectacle constitutions. However, it is expected with these to reflect on some elements that collaborate in the context of the informational use in the locality and in the tourist attraction.

By stating that "we are more communicative and immersed in information than ever" (Netto, 2014, p.127), it can easily remember of the everyday means between communication devices (WhatsApp, Msn, Skype, mobile telephony, torpedoes, etc.) and informational (internet, channel of cable television, etc.). Today without much external stimulus, the equipment seeks to dialogue with the users, identifying where it is and was, trying to interact when proposing evaluations of objects and localities, and even reminding the user of what was done in the past. It develops, what can be termed, an oral, written and imaginary communication. The subject is challenged in his daily life to confront with usual and new meanings, re-elaborating them at all times.

In this panorama:

It is interesting that the relationship between the concreteness of urban spaces and the elusiveness of digital in our actions seemed, until recently, a contradiction - an impossible synthesis, as if the digital put in check the concrete in an electronic overcoming of the old space, making it obsolete. There was a destructive and apparently inexorable dualism (Netto, 2014, p. 162).

The vital space acquires infinity of adjectives, and even often occupies protagonist conditions. Thus it may be called by cybernetic, informational network, cybercity, space of flows, city of bits or network, among other possibilities (Netto, 2014, p.164). In this way, Iphone, mobile phone, tablets, between other features that are yet not presented for use and consumption are made possible in the cognitive dimension.

The physical environment is now represented, among other conditions, as a result of an informational space also adding this status. However, in its communicational dimension, its scope allows, for a low monetary value, to exchange data, images, to communicate with someone anywhere on the planet. In this panorama, some scientists approach this condition as an overcoming of modernity, which for some results in the idea of postmodernity, for others of hypermodernity (Netto, 2014, p.173), among other possibilities.

All this technological apparatus and its conditions can be portrayed as consumption conditions (with a rare exception). But this consumption is not the determinant, it is the dialectical condition of society, also qualifying and forming status to this social environment. Thus,

(...) the consumer society, synonymous of the expressions society of information, of knowledge, of spectacle, of disorganized capitalism and of risk, among others, refers the reader to a certain dimension, perceived as specific and therefore delimiter, for some, of contemporary societies (Barbosa, 2004, p.7).

The consumer society, as an intrinsic condition of the contemporary subject, gives the idea presented by Theodor Adorno at the Frankfurt School of Cultural Industry (Gatti, 2008). The productive means appropriates of all imaginable possibilities capital's reproduction by reaching the respective expressions and manifestations (material and immaterial) of culture.

In this context, the society is presented, between the informational and consumerist, to the spectacle. Thus, the spectacularization is reinforced, presents and enhances these values, among others, the creation and creativity in the hierarchical sense of their respective localities. Sure it is, occurs currently with values of informational devices. In this way;

The informatics conception of the work of art is, today, a cultural phenomenon as shocking as the paradoxical or absurd objects of Dadaist and Surrealist aesthetics were in their time - and this is for similar reasons. Its effect of surprise and fascination is still to confront us with the expression of the innermost, with the plastic mystery of a subjective emotion or even of a reality vision in an object in which, at the same time, we recognize the absence of all human trace (Subirats, 1989, p.26).

The show incorporates values of informational communication. In it, it becomes a social formulation that, with some sauce, can be treated as a synthesis of the society's conditions. It portrays part of a broad revolution of social mores.

ARCHITECTURE, URBANISM, AND SPACE IN AREAS OF VISITATION: DETERMINING THE RESOURCE AND THE TOURIST AND CULTURAL ATTRACTIVE

A locality, by stimulating the desire of visitation in an individual, assumes a role that has the purpose of transforming itself in what can be called tourist space, that is, a territory appropriated for the tourist visitation. The tourist dimension is commonly elaborated, in the traveler's mind, with symbols and fantasies that qualify a dualism between the mythification of the tourist space and a space of the others' social daily life. This condition can be broken when thinking the virtual space entering this logic and this recognition.

In the determination of an appropriated territory, Santos (1997) recalls that, when a place is available, it is transformed into territory by its characteristics and capacity. This space is "delimited by the quality of the relations established with it, as in objective terms, by the living testimony of the constructed, circulated, public and green spaces that are built up as a result of that" (Santos, 1997, p. 17). The tourist territory seeks for an economic element for the requalification of space, since "the artistic value of monumental heritage is hierarchically the last: status comprehensible at a time when, saved in a cultivated and enlightened environment, the concept of art remains imprecise, and in which, the notion of aesthetics has just appeared" (Choay, 2000, p. 99). In this way, it is possible to think that the "character of historicity is to transcend the value of use and material value of the artifact. For that, to presuppose the preservation of a good, in this context, it is necessary to give it symbolic social meaning" (Camargo, 2000, p.4), which is reinforce through the reflection between this place and its communication with the market within, of the process of 'touristification'.

However, the use of tourist areas should presuppose that "the metamorphosis of its use value into economic value is achieved through 'cultural engineering', a vast public and private enterprise, at the service of which a multitude of animators, communicators, development agents, engineers, cultural mediators work" (Choay, 2000, p. 185). In reflecting on the construction of the tourist space and its mythical essence, Hobsbawm and Ranger (1984) define as:

(...) invented tradition (...) a set of practices usually regulated by tacit or openly accepted rules; such practices, of a ritual or symbolic nature, seek to inculcate certain values and norms of behavior through repetition, which automatically implies: a continuity with the past (Hobsbawm & Ranger, 1984, p. 9).

The tourism can be a promoter and a requalifier of traditions, either of customs, traditional costumes, through gastronomy or folk dances (Hobsbawm & Ranger, 1984, p. 9). Regarding this issue, Yázigi (2001) states that:

Modern society is equally resurrecting or inventing traditions in the form of a spectacle, because the tourist place lives and charges much the 'typical'. (...) Several authors present long lists of traditions invented, deliberately, considered as legitimate nowadays. The organizations, linked directly or indirectly to the market, create their own in function of to the profit they represent. There the tourist gives vent to nostalgia and his kind of commitment to history (Yázigi, 2001, p. 271).

For Hobsbawm and Ranger (1984, p. 16), there is a difference between "old customs" and "invented practice". However, it is known that all manifestations are the result of an action of someone on something, that is, an act of creation or invention that can make the community of equal value to any other. Menezes (1999) states that:

(...) the universe of culture is the universe of choice, of option, and therefore of meaning, of value. But it should be noted that the values that qualify objects, practices and ideas are not immanent, do not arise from these same practical objects and ideas. For example, what we call cultural goods do not have their own identity, but the identity that social groups impose on them (Menezes, 1999, p. 93).

Therefore, a tourist destination, a monument or a work of art, present values that transpose its functionality, due to the value of tourist attractiveness. However, in every situation there are objects (material, hybrid and immaterial) to be visited, which are the attractions. In this way, it is expected to raise some questions about the object of study: the spatial transformations materialized as urban and architectural object.

In the case of the Jesuit Missions, these portray in ruins of old architectural and urban objects determined in the old configuration of previous centuries. Thus, for its recognition and positioning it becomes necessary to justify a historical-cultural appeal in its visitation. Recognizing the urban and architectural aspects of a legacy such as the Guaraní Missions involves its recognition in specific historiography and its values in these areas of knowledge.

Although it is recognized, as Waisman (2013) points out, the need to formulate a Latin American history, historical stylistics with different historical durations based on the center-periphery relationship (2013, p.xiii), this chapter will not get in this merit. With this positioning the historical-architectural and urban legacies so unknown become values that will deepen to any heritage understanding, presented by traditional means (books, etc.) or contemporary (such as digital). Its understanding enables "a double reading of the subject matter and the ideology of the historical moment in which it was studied" (Waisman, 2013, p. 4).

For the historian Fernand Braudel, it is hoped to achieve the transference of the individual to social groups and their specific daily lives of the contexts analyzed. But it is worth emphasizing that the subject (when aggregating the informational use) identified here is not positioned as subject of history as is the proposal of this historian although he noticed that the use of technology makes it possible to get in touch with unimaginable dimensions of edification. Condition that can be difficult or impossible to obtain in the real world, from direct contact with the object.

It is also important to understand the difference between general historiography and architecture. While the first exercises the look to the immersion in the past, reconstructing the historical object; the second will always have contemporaneity as point of analysis. It can be inserted in it certain technological character. The historical dimension has its value in the judgment of its understanding, but *is not complete in this* (Waisman, 2013, p. 13).

According to Waisman (2013, p. 15) an architectural work could be a monument, for the typological understanding of other works; or a document, as reference. "The works of the architects who acted in colonial times, for example, would be incomprehensible without the knowledge of the books from the writers who circulated in Latin American countries" (Waisman, 2013, p.19). The architecture elaborates codes of communication to art and its forms of vision, even if its historiography comprises a distinct field, independent of art (Waisman, 2013, p. 26).

In Latin America, by certain lack of cultural awareness, giving an aspect of periphery,

(...) the transposition of architectural ideology often becomes one of the many processes of alienation that daily suffer in the social, economic or political field. (...) However, for some time now, some international criticism has considered as one of the positive tendencies of the current architecture the regionalism as a form of constructive opposition to the various negative forms of universalism, by the way of strengthening or maintaining regional identities (Waisman, 2013, p. 92).

The urban formation differs between European cities and those of America, especially the Spanish. While the first developed their structures from several monuments, the second one settled from rigid orthogonal scheme (Waisman, 2013, p.107). This situation is observed in the Missions, although religious built objects tend to give a monumental appearance in the settlements.

In the use of tourist areas, it should be assumed that:

(...) the modern city cannot aggregate and function except at the expense, at least in part, of the old city. Since not everything can be preserved, it is necessary to establish what must be preserved at all costs. In addition, it must be taken into account that the survival condition of the remaining ancient nuclei is determined by the general urbanistic solution and by the criteria with which is disciplined, around the so-called historical nucleus, the disastrous periekon of the urban peripheries (Argan, 1995, p.77).

It is assumed that the cultural tourist territory has areas of monumental relevance, formulated as a tourist product, which have: attractiveness (either for the novelty, singularity, etc.); leisure structure; opportunity for its incorporation in economic activities, structure of hospitality, gastronomy, services and shopping, wellness, comfort and security. "The modern city becomes the space for excellence of a constant interaction between social groups, where the diversity and the resulting social conflicts intensify and gain greater visibility and dramaticity" (Frúgoli Jr., 2000, p. 20).

In order to understand the space of the missionary ruins like those of São Miguel, there is a distance in the level of the contents. Thus, a dichotomy is created, between a ruin, legacy and keeper of many stories and the local city, although this with bucolic aspects of a late modernity. In this condition, it positions the attractive and its relation with the patrimony as memorial and of studies area and the observed visitor.

It is worth remembering Bruno Zevi (1992), when he reports on "seeing the architecture" and presents a relation between interior spaces, slightly unfolding his analysis to the external space, that would be of urban analysis and not architectonic, as the architect defines it. In this condition, it is visited the urban rather than the architectural, in the non-virtual relationship (that is presential). The virtual dimension and the use of technological resources make it possible to confront the rigidity of these limits.

About heritage, it is believed that it should have a language, a way of understanding and approaching its socio-spatial context. Its interactive insertion between society and architecture / urbanism can be made possible by this understanding. In remembrance Waisman (2013) it is hoped just to reinforce that, according to the author, there is not the use of a language that is unknown. After all, what is the historiography of Latin American architecture? In this situation, a gap is created in how to understand it. It is hoped that all learn to understand reflecting with diverse ontological distortions in this presented object.

TECHNOLOGY LINKED TO TRAVEL

Amadeus Brasil (2013a), a reference company in the development of technology linked to the travel industry, has given importance in the recognition of the information and technology formation process in the tourist displacement. In this way, it is interesting to note in its research and reflections how this context have been evolved and what accessories and resources have become necessary for the traveler.

Two surveys become interesting. One refers to the main innovations that have definitely changed the way of traveling, which stand out: the invention of the aircraft, which the world press gives little prominence to Santos Dumond; the wheel case; the creation of the online reservation system for the hotel industry, among other sectors (whose complexity starts with the creation of the reserve and its incorporation of informational technology); electronic ticket processing for transportation (highlighting the air sector, although this extends for many others) and finally the GPS (Global Positioning System) (Amadeus Brasil, 2013a).

To these, it is also added the interesting technological innovations that definitely change the travels around the world (Brasil, 2014). Amadeus Brasil (2013b) still carries out surveys about the technologies used in the tourism sector. In this context, five tolls stand out: the ATM, which makes it possible to avoid the transport of securities; the creation of online translation dictionaries, in their most diverse forms, making it possible to consult words in small conversations; the smartphone, creating the possibility of storing information, telephony, as a photographic machine, that is, with expanded functions of a computer and a mobile phone; and finally, the credit card, of use without territorial limits, between the national and international use, that even allows small purchases of insurance to rent a car or for health care.

It is known that technology gives us many other possibilities. Contemporary life has in fact been sustained by technology and without a strong appeal of hospitality, viability and safety for the traveler. To these, it is possible to counterpoint tendencies as Carvão (2009), specialist linked to the UNWTO (Word Tourism Organization), says:

The increase of communities: communities of interests, of online activities and communities; the' increasing level of specialization of both demand and supply; the search for physical well-being with the development of the demand / offer of wellness products, as well as psychological, which are examples of yoga retreats; the search for complementarity in all travel options (for example, beach holidays complemented by nature activities, etc.); the increase of 'tailor-made' trips facilitated by consumer knowledge and the Internet's ability to purchase several services and compose the own package; the search for the authentic and the refusal of the artificial that lead to the development of new destinations and products in which the consumer can have access to authentic products of local culture such as gastronomy; the new luxury: the concept of luxury has been changing. Luxury more than a limo, a 5 stars hotel and a sophisticated restaurant is access to something that is unique and exclusive; the best of both worlds, which combines for example a safari in Africa with the best offer of accommodation; knowledge: as there is a growing demand for an authentic experience of the destination (s), there is also an increasing demand for experiences that represent for tourists a possibility and increase and expand their knowledge; in short, the consumer no longer seeks a product, but rather an experience in all its components (holistic view) (Coal, 2009, pp. 30-31).

Tangentially, it can be noted that much of these contemporary trends and demands pervade the use of technology, not to create an environment of ostensive wealth, but to make an ambience that although with a certain simplicity, with the personalization that the technological means provide.

TOOLS USED IN MISSIONS

The technologies provide a high flexibility for the individual who uses it, bringing him closer to the places, that virtually or physically, were previously inaccessible. The technological means in the tourism area arrived to stimulate the integration of cultures, facilitating since the planning until the accomplishment of the trip. The users can, in the comfort of their residence, use these tools to program themselves without facing waiting lines or last-minute unforeseen, for example. It also provides access to virtual worlds through auditory, visual and tactile conception, reproducing experiences that the touristic real world cannot offer.

That is the case of this research object, Missions of São Miguel. In this research were analyzed technological tools that contribute to the ease of knowing more about the Ruins of São Miguel in Santo Ângelo - RS, Brazil. To have access to real-time images of how construction was originally, are things that only technology could provide. It helps to preserve and disseminate the historical and architectural importance of the region, stimulating and also optimizing local commerce.

(...) the crucial concept of virtual scenarios is interactivity, which leads the human senses and capacities to relate to non-real situations, but having the sensation that they are (Molina, 2003, p. 74).

'Museum without Walls' is an application developed by designer Karolina Ziulkoski in her Master's thesis at the Interactive Telecommunications Program at New York University. It is a virtual 3D reconstruction on top of the existing architecture in which it is possible to contemplate the original construction, allowing an augmented reality (Ziulkoski, 2013). The tool consists of audio guides in English and Portuguese and mini audio guides made from community stories. This is an application for tablets and smartphones that uses augmented reality technology to allow on-site exploration. It can only be accessed when the user is in the Ruins of São Miguel, thus stimulating the visitation to the site. The download can be done through the Play Store tool. The application was the winner of the Inovapps award from the Ministry of Communications - Brazil.

São Miguel das Missões is a meticulous app that tells the story of the Jesuits and the Guaraní Indians. It narrates each precinct of the archaeological site, explaining in detail its history. It tells how the Indian residences, the Church, the Baptistery, the Cemetery, and other places were. It provides images so that we can better understand them visually. It also has an explanatory map, showing where each place of the Jesuit Missions is. It provides to people, who do not have easy access to the site and want to find out about the subject, audio explanatory guides in multiple languages (favoring the diversity of users worldwide). It also facilitates independent visitation to the region, for those who opt for tourism without the presence of guides. Thus, the application helps to preserve and disseminate the historical and architectural importance of the place.

While the 'Museum without Walls' application encourages on-site tourism, the Sete Povos Application brings the user closer, being in anywhere, to learn about the history and functioning of a Jesuit reduction in the 18th century in southern Brazil. It allows you to live the daily life of the Jesuits only through the cell phone. There is also the Missões Jesuíticas Project - a game developed by Atomic Rocket Entertainment (Machado, 2016), an experimental studio of game development of the Technological Graduation in Digital Games of Unisinos (Universidade do Vale do Rio dos Sinos). Through the fun that the games provide, it is possible to know the reality of the daily life of the Jesuits.

Beyond that, a video in the form of a 3D model was produced by Unisinos (Universidade do Vale dos Sinos) in São Leopoldo, RS, for didactic material on the Jesuit Missions. The model provides amplitude for the understanding of the original formation of the construction and daily life of Jesuits and Indians was like. The video makes it possible to see what the orchard, school, church was like.

Among these tools, there is the Sound and Light Show performed since 1978 in the ruins of São Miguel, had its technology recently changed recently, becoming more economical and realistic. There were changes in lighting, to have RGB projectors and reflectors with LED lights, in order to enable greater collaboration in the show, making everything more realistic and generating new tones, also reducing the expense of electricity (Viagem, ZH, 2014). Furthermore, there was the installation of four speakers behind the audience, and eight ahead, making the sound more fascinating. The show, lasting 48 minutes, does not have a human cast, but there are trees, rocks and ruins. It has presentations in Portuguese, English and Spanish.

CONCLUSION

This chapter presented a theoretical-practical essay with certain epistemological contours with a course bringing a series of values. Architecture and its understanding, by a technological dimension, are not common among the areas of academic knowledge. However, in everyday life they are present, even if little recognized.

When seeking an association between the architectural object and the dimensions present in the social and technological contemporaneity - on a subject valued in the tourist's eyes - this work is formulated. It is known that many other possibilities can be developed in this relationship by different areas. The recognition of the existence practices involving the use of technology for tourism dates from the middle of the last century.

An important caveat is made to the South American patrimony and the inexistence of an architectural historiography. In this way, this study adopts an exploratory research character, when analyzing the Jesuit Missions Guaranis. The scarcity of studies about this object hampers its recognition. In this journey between the pioneering of the Sound and Light Show until the use of technologies has a long step, but inserted in a great hiatus, which can even be observed by those who develop these tools of heritage interpretation.

As a Unesco World Heritage Site, the Jesuit Missions of São Miguel deserve greater attention because of their historical importance. With the presence of the applications and videos became easier to stimulate the trip to the place. The technological means came to favor tourism facilitating access to knowledge and valuing the local architectural culture.

REFERENCES

Argan, G. C. (1995). *História da arte como história da cidade*. São Paulo, SP: Martins Fontes.

Augé, M. (1994). *Não lugar: introdução a uma antropologia da supermodernidade*. Campinas, SP: Papirus.

Augé, M. (2007). *Por una antropologia de la movilidad*. Barcelona: Cat., Gedisa.

Augé, M. (2008). *El tiempo em ruínas*. Barcelona: Cat, Gedisa.

Barbosa, L. (2004). *Sociedade de consumo. Ciências Sociais, Passo-a-Passo, 49*. Rio de Janeiro, RJ: Jorge Zahar.

Brasil, A. (2013). *Blog 1A. "As 5 inovações que mudaram para sempre a forma como viajamos"*. Retrieved February 01, 2017, from http://amadeus1a.com.br/cms/as-5-inovacoes-que-mudaram-para-sempre-a-forma-como-viajamos/

Brasil, A. (2013). *Blog 1A. "As 5 inovações tecnológicas que transformaram a industria de turismo"*. Retrieved February 01, 2017, from http://amadeus1a.com.br/cms/5-inovacoes-tecnologicas-que-transformaram-a-industria-de-turismo/

Brasil. Ministério do Turismo. (2014). *Como a tecnologia está mudando o turismo*. Retrieved February 02, 2017, from http://www.turismo.gov.br/ultimas-noticias/415-como-a- tecnologia-esta- mudando-o-turismo.html

Camargo, H. L. (2000). *Dimensão histórica da construção e dos atrativos para o turismo no Brasil. IV Encontro nacional de turismo com base local*. Joinvile.

Carvão, S. (2009). *Tendências do turismo internacional. Revista Científica EXEDRA*. Escola Superior de Educação de Coimbra. Nº temático - Turismo e Patrimônio. pp. 17-32. Portugal. Retrieved February 01, 2017, from http://www.exedrajournal.com/docs/S-tur/02-Sandra-Carvao-32.pdf

Cesar, P. A. B., & Tronca, B. (2016). Ruins of the Jesuit - Guaranis Missions of São Miguel Arcanjo: An Overview on the UNESCO World Heritage in Brazil. In Tourism and History World Heritage: Case Studies of Ibero-American Space, Interdisciplinary. Centre of Social Sciences (CICS-NOVA).

Choay, F. (2000). *A alegoria do patrimônio*. Edições 70.

Demo, P. (1995). *Metodologia científica em ciências sociais*. São Paulo, SP: Atlas.

Frazen, B. V. (2003). *Jesuítas portugueses e espanhóis no sul do Brasil e Paraguai coloniais*. São Leopoldo, RS: EdUnisinos.

Gatti, L. F. (2008). Theodor W. Adorno: Indústria cultural e crítica da cultura. In *Curso livre de teoria crítica*. Campinas, SP: Papirus.

Hobsbawm, E., & Ranger, T. (1984). A invenção das Tradições. São Paulo, SP: Paz e terra.

Júnior, F. H. (2000). Centralidade em São Paulo: trajetória, conflitos e negociação na metrópole. São Paulo, SP: Cortes e Edusp.

Lash, S., & Urry, J. (1998). Economias de signos y espacio: sobre el capitalismo de la posorganización. Buenos Aires, CF: Amorrortu, 1998.

Machado, M. (2016). *General format*. Retrieved February 02, 2017, from www.unisinos.br/noticias/universidade/a-historia-dos-sete-povos-na-palma-da-sua-mao

Menezes, U. T. B. (1999). Os 'usos culturais' da cultura: contribuição para uma abordagem crítica das práticas e políticas culturais. In *Turismo: espaço paisagem e cultura* (pp. 88–99). São Paulo, SP: Hucitec.

Molina, S. (2003). *O pós-turismo*. São Paulo, SP: Aleph.

Netto, V. M. (2014). *Cidade e sociedade: as tramas da prática e seus espaços*. Porto Alegre, RS: Sulinas.

Ricoeur, P. (1978). *O conflito das interpretações: ensaio de hermenêutica*. Rio de Janeiro, RJ: Imago.

Rowen, C., & Koetter, F. (2006). Cidade Colagem. *Cosac Naify*, *2006*, 293–321.

Santos, M. (1997). Metamorfoses do espaço habitado (4th ed.). São Paulo, SP: Hucitec.

Santos, M. (2008). Técnica, espaço, tempo: Globalização e meio técnico-científico e informacional (5th ed.). São Paulo, SP: EdUSP.

Sassen, S. (2010). *Sociologia da globalização*. Porto Alegre: Artmed.

Subirats, E. (1989). *A cultura como espetáculo*. São Paulo, SP: Nobel.

Tavares, E., & Dalto, R. (1999). *Missões Jesuítico Guaranis*. São Leopoldo, RS: Unisinos.

Venturi, R., & Brown, D. S. (2006). Uma significação para os estacionamentos dos supermercados. A&P ou Aprendendo com Las Vegas. In *Uma nova agenda para a arquitetura: antologia teórica 1965-1995* (pp. 337–354). Cosac Naify.

Viagem, Z. H. (2014). *General format*. Retrieved February 02, 2017, from http://zh.clicrbs.com.br/rs/vida-e-estilo/viagem/noticia/2016/04/espetaculo-som-e-luz-nas-ruinas-de-sao-miguel-arcanjo-ganha-nova-roupagem-a-partir-desta-sexta-5788650.html

Waisman, M. (2013). *O interior da história*. São Paulo, SP: Perspectiva.

Yázigi, E. (2001). *A alma do lugar: turismo, planejamento e cotidiano*. São Paulo, SP: Contexto.

Zevi, A. (1992). Saber ver a arquitetura (3rd ed.). São Paulo, SP: Martins Fontes.

Ziulkoski, C. (2013). *General format*. Retrieved February 02, 2017, from http://www.karolinaziulkoski.com/Museum-Without-Walls

KEY TERMS AND DEFINITIONS

App: Abbreviated form of the word "application".

Architecture (Missionary): Characterized as architecture (missionary) in Brazil, an architecture developed mainly by the Missions of the Company of Jesus and strong baroque influence.

Cultural Tourism: An economic activity that is related to events and organized trips and directed to knowledge and leisure with cultural elements such as: monuments, architectural complexes or symbols of historical nature, as well as artistic / cultural / religious, educational, informative events or of an academic nature.

Jesuit Missions: Settlements or reductions proposed in the Counter-Reformation context for the expansion of Catholicism through indoctrination and politicization of the Guarani people (Indian) that lived in the South America region.

Technology: A term that involves the technical and scientific knowledge and the application of this knowledge through its transformation in the use of tools (Internet and mobile apps).

Unesco: United Nations Educational, Scientific and Cultural Organization.

World Heritage: It relates to a resource that must be conserved in the present and transmitted to future generations as a common good for all people around world, regardless of their geographical position.

ENDNOTE

1 The Province of Paraguay from the colonial period comprises the territory that currently constitutes: Rio Grande do Sul (Brazil), Argentine provinces of Corrientes and Misiones, beyond the southern region of Paraguay. The Jesuit actions were in part of the Spanish territory, where the Jesuit-Guarani western reductions appeared (1626-1639) and later the Seven People (1682-1750) on the eastern side.

Chapter 12
Should Festival Be Smarter?
ICT on Mass Events – The Case of the Exit Festival (Novi Sad, Serbia)

Uglješa Stankov
University of Novi Sad, Serbia

Vanja Pavluković
University of Novi Sad, Serbia

Juan Miguel Alcántara-Pilar
University of Granada, Spain

Marija Cimbaljević
University of Novi Sad, Serbia

Tanja Armenski
University of Novi Sad, Serbia

ABSTRACT

The trend of information and communication technologies (ICT) employment to enhance transactions and to deliver better experience to visitors of mass events has been growing increasingly popular over the years. The emergence of "smart tourism" agenda which highlights new, more sustainable ways of business management, experience enhancement and destination management also creates new opportunities for ICT employment in mass event. Thus, this chapter discusses existing ICT holding potential for smart approach employment on mass events. An additional case of Exit festival was used as an exploratory evidence to support the main idea of the chapter. Based on comprehensive literary review and additional information on visitors' familiarity with ICT gained from the Exit festival, recommendations for mass event managers are presented.

DOI: 10.4018/978-1-5225-2927-9.ch012

INTRODUCTION

Various mass events are becoming increasingly prolific as communities and destinations attempt to differentiate themselves from others and appeal to visitors. With increased competition for visitors, mass events are constantly striving for innovation by diversifying their programming. A wide range of information and communication technologies (ICT) can be used to enhance the event experience (Halpenny, Salenieks, Song, Van Winkle, & MacKay, 2013). Research in event tourism is fundamentally changing due to an explosive growth of ICTs (Rubinstein, 2015; Lee, Boshnakova, & Goldblatt, 2016). The event industry is also being transformed by digital proliferation and business innovations where ICT plays a crucial role enhancing tourist experiences on the mass events and prove more opportunities for their management. In this chapter, the use of ICTs on mass events is examined to help planners, managers and operators understand the current state of technology employment. Particularly, event organizers, with their constrained budgets and limited human resources capacity, must make choices about embracing these technologies smartly. The emergence of "smart tourism" agenda which highlights new, more sustainable ways of business management, experience enhancement and destination management (Cannon Hunter, Chung, Gretzel, & Koo, 2015) also creates new opportunities for ICT employment in mass event. These choices must be made with full knowledge of what each event is about, who their audience is, and what resources are required to support the implementation of ICT (Halpenny, Salenieks, Song, Van Winkle, & MacKay, 2013).

Thus, the purpose of this chapter is to review the current state of ICT implementation on the mass events and to advocate for the smart tourism approach employment. The proof-a-concept approach of this paper is based on an extensive literary review. To gain access to users' familiarity with ICT, the chapter examines the additional representative study of Exit festival, one of the leading music festivals in Europe and in the world. Based on the comprehensive literary review and results of the exploratory case, basic recommendations for smart approach employment for mass event organizers are given.

The chapter is structured as follows. Section one points to basic characteristics of smart approach in ICT design with the focus on travel industry that, among first disciplines, openly employed this concept. Section two examines some of the existing and forthcoming examples of ICT on mass events. Section three presents the exploratory case of Exit festival. The final section identifies main recommendations, contribution and limitations of presented research.

ICT ON MASS EVENTS: TOWARDS SMART TOURISM APPROACH

The review of the relevant literature showed that all ICT applications in this field can be roughly distinguished to two basic types according to its main purpose – visitors-centric applications and managerial ones (Catherwood & Van Kirk, 1992; Lee, Boshnakova, & Goldblatt, 2016). Visitor-centric applications are usually intended to serve various pre- and on-festival experiences enabling visitors' easier interaction, identification, transaction and enhancing the experience thought co-creation. For example, Tomorrowland's (Boom, Belgium) tickets come in the form of radio-frequency identification (RFID) wristbands that employ personal ticket information and facilitate a "cashless" environment. At the same time, wristbands allow wearers to connect with one another on social media sites and embedded LED lights can be remotely triggered by the festival, producing light shows from the crowd (Rubinstein, 2015). Managerial applications are usually concerned with visitors' management in the preparation phase, event organization, on-site applications and analysis phase. Again, in the driving Tomorrowland's example, RFID wristband allow real-time transaction reporting and audience insight for post-festival personalized communication. Another example is the innovative use of ultra-fast wireless access coupled with network attached storage devices at The Vieilles Charrues Festival in Carhaix, France, to support organizers, press representatives and volunteers. Likewise mass event, this three-day festival has a challenge with a wealth of data to store and to share using temporary infrastructure that has to be stable and easy-to-use (Buffalo, 2014). The study of Lexhagen, Nysveen and Hem (2005) from Storsjöyran music festival held in Östersund, Sweden, showed the importance of mobile coordination and efficient implementation of mobile services that were perceived as enjoyable and useful among both festival goers and organization staff.

However, just the use of ICT does not make festival smart. In fact, "smartness" as a new buzzword in research practice has become a very fuzzy concept. "Smart" epithet is often applied to point out some special capabilities of technology, the intelligence of its use or connectivity functionality (Gretzel, Werthner, Koo, & Lamsfus, 2015). Sometimes, the "smartness" is simplified just to the use of mobile apps, open data initiatives or even simple use of WiFi in the context of tourism and travel experiences. Although these examples can be important in the smart tourism implementation, they still do not provide the full picture (Gretzel, Sigala, Xiang, & Koo, 2015). In its broad sense, smart tourism should imply the increasing dependence of tourism destinations and travel industries on ICT as well as reliance of tourists on emerging forms of ICT and its application that allows for vast amounts of data to be produced and further transformed into value propositions (Gretzel, Sigala, Xiang, & Koo, 2015). "Smartness" is also a social phenomenon arising from the convergence of ICT with the tourism experience (Hunter, Chung, Gretzel, & Koo, 2015; Boodnah, Armoogum, Jaunky, & Armoogum 2016).

From the demand side, ICT has provided tourists with access to unique opportunities during pre-, on-, and after-travel phases that effectively reshaped the nature of tourism experience (Neuhofer, Buhalis, & Ladkin, 2014; Tussyadiah, 2013; Wang & Xiang, 2012). For the future period, for instance, Yeoman (2013) point out a mobile living as one of the most important trend on consumers side to affect events and festivals. From the supply side, tourism destination management offices or event organizers are rapidly changing due to the ubiquitous presence and influence of the internet and mobile devices. One of the facing challenges of the tourism sector to achieve smartness is putting together various business interests of numerous stockholders that simultaneously operate on the level of tourism destination (Buhalis & Amaranggana, 2015).

USE OF SMART ICT IN EVENT MENAGEMENT

ICT does not a priori create a significant value for all kinds of event types, situations and experiences. As visitors exhibit different user profiles depending on specific situations (Manes, 2001) smart approach should have various implications for the different stages of event organization. For example, the pre-event phase generally receives a large portion of interest among event organizers. Pre-event phase is largely impacted by the use of various kinds of ICTs in everyday life and represents fertile ground for employment of principles of smart approach. In many cases, event marketing contributes to overall information overload. Namely, during travel information search, users are "under attack" of different kind of travel offers, lured by discounted offers and sales promotion (Park & Jang, 2013). However, information is acknowledged to be the "lifeblood" of mass events and tourism industry because, without information, the visitors' motivation and ability to travel would be severely limited (O'Connor & Frew, 2002). In spite of having this great power of having access to travel information and control over information search, many consumers use novel services and intermediaries to filter various products offered in the market (Chaffey, Ellis-Chadwick, Mayer, & Johnston, 2006). Previously mentioned conditions, strongly imply the necessity to employ smart approach, mainly in event promotion, in order to multiply benefits of event differentiation such as the use of more intelligent search engines, smart posters, etc.

On-site phase concerns situations where information, event program and content is needed in real time and specifically provided to the user, "on demand" or most often determined by the changing context (Manes, 2001). The rise of on-destination ICT services is driven by the growth of the mobile usage, personalisation trend and peer-to-peer trend (Euromonitor, 2014). In that context, before smart services could take place, significant prerequisite should have to be done in creating smart environments, i.e. a physical settings interwoven with network connected sensors, displays and processors units, embedded in the everyday objects (Cook & Das, 2005; Weiser, Gold, & Brown, 1999). Finally, in the data driven industry, most mass event organizers will have the intention to continue to interact with visitors in order to send them notifications, advertisements or offer customer services in the post-event phase.

The employment of smart approach for mass events sits on the top of key existing and forthcoming supporting technologies ranging from items mostly used by visitors such as smartphones, wearable technologies, various audio-video display units, biometric technologies, smart environments, intelligent software agents, etc. Examples of basic smart ICT employment for an event are shown in Figure 1. The presented examples are ranged from smart online travel promotion and distribution, smart social media communications, smart event co-creation to smart operations and identification. It is also important to note that presented examples of smart approaches are neither conclusive nor exclusive for only one event phase, but rather can be applied in each phase of event management concurrently.

Smart online promotion and distribution are mostly based on the existing technologies for information editing, information enrichment and on technologies that respect users' characteristics and preferences. More and more travel search engines and recommendation systems are designed in such a way to reduce information and choice overload (Park & Jang, 2013). The context-awareness and pre-selection of interaction with users during information search were made possible with the advances in intelligent systems (Gretzel, 2011). In many cases, the main search results are enhanced with additional information that can influence decisions, such as consumer reviews, ranking, user comments, weather condition, etc (Angskun & Angskun, 2008).

As a result of significant progress in geospatial technologies, online virtual globes (e.g. Google Earth) could represent a good example of technology that could add 'smartness' to the process of information search (Peng, Chen, & Tsai, 2010). Virtual globes join information from various sources, including maps, textbooks and Internet together in one application that is designed in such a way that the users can start using the features intuitively without any effort or training (Rakshit & Ogneva-Himmelberger, 2008). Beside cartographic symbols, virtual globes are enhanced with a type of data that users can communicate more naturally, such as photos, live camera videos, or even audio. An excellent example for this is the reality street view applications enabled by some online map providers. For example, *Google Street View* allows users to watch the scenery in the streets and various places as if they are present there. Furthermore, human-computer interaction models are increasingly accepting geographic approaches (Hecht, Schöning, Erickson, & Priedhorsky, 2011). Geolocation services in the digital era represent an excellent example of using maps to facilitate location awareness. While on traditional maps user had first to locate them on the map and then to locate the point of interest, geolocation enables mobile maps to put the user in its centre. Furthermore, geotagging represents easy-to-use and an enjoyable way to identify the

Figure 1. Examples of smart ICT applications on events and key supporting technologies
Source: Authors.

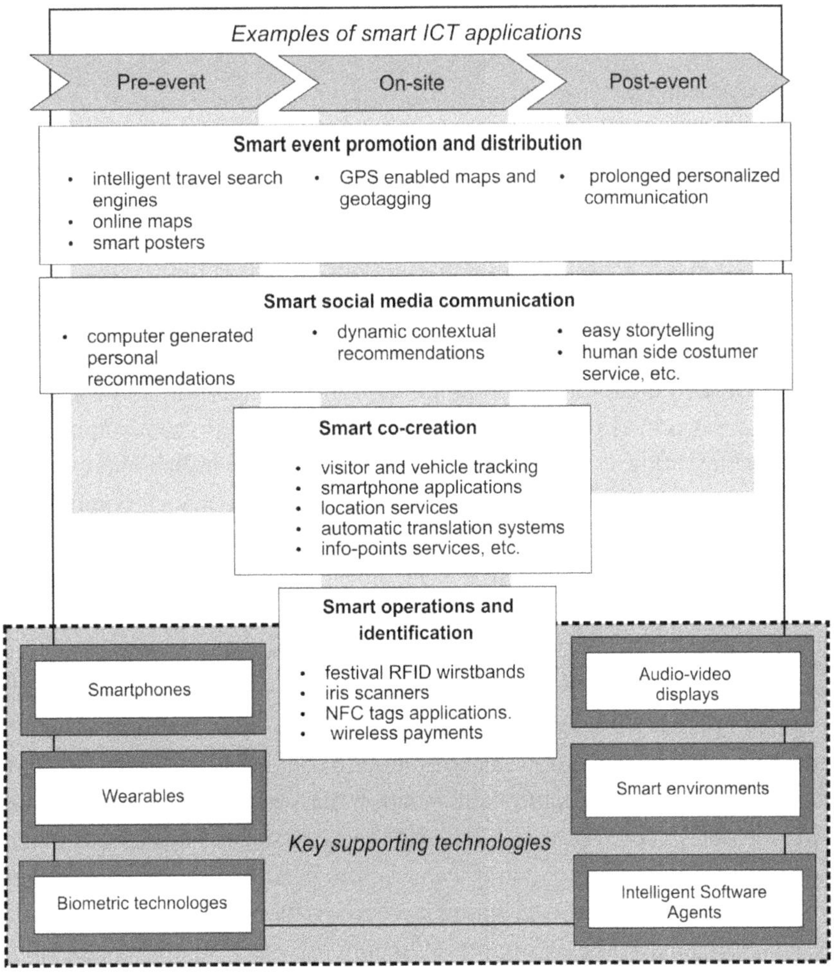

user's location in relation to other people or to add location information to the various content in order to show touristic experiences (Chung & Lee, 2016).

Mostly younger generations are accustomed to the omnipresence of social media as part of their communication patterns (Pang, 2013; Stankov, Jovanović, & Dragićević, 2014). For example, in June 30 2015, *Facebook* had reached the symbolic number of 1.49 billion monthly active users (Facebook, 2015) that is almost half of the world's estimated online population (Internet World Stats, 2015), which arguably makes it one of the biggest media organizations in the history of humankind (Rieder, 2013). Social media as a mixture of private and public spaces, information and communication (Hohl, 2009) become a way of passing desirable messages on less intrusive way than traditional media channels, as some regular user' groups become resistant to distracting effects maintain relationships with social media that keep them in control (Pang, 2013). Comparing to traditional Web searching and browsing, the Facebook event pages are capable of generating more users' emotions through interaction and sharing among users (Lee, Xiong, & Hu, 2012). Therefore, applications of social media that bring more contexts into marketing communication (Buhalis & Foerste, 2015) are a valuable tool for the smart approach. In that sense, social media automatic messages (i.e. *Facebook* users' personal news feeds) or contextual advertisement are one of the most important services of social networks as they are intended to recommend personalized contents to users based on dynamical behaviour of users and content they create (Wang, Zhu, Cui, Sun, & Yang, 2013).

Documenting travel and storytelling using social media became much easier. Visitors of mass events have always engaged in storytelling to communicate their experiences, but social media became a regular mean of telling stories supported by digital images or streaming videos (Stankov et al., 2014). Unlike websites and blogs, social media enable users to easily share information about travelling, not just in post-travel, but in all travel phases (Chung, Lee, & Han, 2015). Easy access to past and present visitors' experiences provided on social media sites and in virtual communities could represent a valuable source of information for event organizers.

Smart event experience co-creation can represent one of the most important benefits for visitors of the employment of smart approach, as they already have access to various mobile applications, services of proximity and location marketing, etc. Currently, event organizers put high hopes on mobile applications during the on-site phase. After 2005, smartphones rapidly started to change communication landscape transforming mostly single-function communication device into a computer-like device that eventually led to the "mobile movement" (Google and IPSOS, 2011). However, when mobile applications are incorporated in event experience, there is a list of possible technical factors that should be prearranged, such as network connectivity, charging stations, lighting conditions, roaming charges, etc. Furthermore, more sophisticated mobile app services require involving various separate services and product providers that open a question of application interconnectivity, costs and system stability (Chiu & Leung, 2005).

A currently operating global navigation systems, mobile triangulation, Bluetooth and RFID location systems revealed opportunities for proximity and location marketing, that is of great importance for "in situ" marketing (Yamamoto, 2009). However, besides the necessity to have access to the mobile equipment in order to participate in proximity marketing, visitors must further satisfy preconditions: such as giving permission for push notifications, accepting increased battery consumptions, mobile data transfer, roaming charges, etc. Still, based on the example of Ghent Festival, Belgium, Versichele and colleagues (2012) argue for Bluetooth employment for tracking mass event visitors as it offers significant advantages with respect to other and more prominent technologies.

Near field communication (NFC) and QR code enabled common objects to become smarter. According to Pesonen and Horster (2012), NFC could have significant application in smart approach applications. Some examples may include smart posters, paperless transaction, wireless check-in and check-out procedures, NFC payment options, visitor tracking (especially indoor tracking), virtual coupons, etc.

Although human-to-machine communication is still a major problem to overcome (Case, 2015), in the realm of designing smart technologies, human-to-human communication is the field that can significantly be improved in the future. Recent advances in audio wearable are very promising for the event industry. For example, despite many challenges (Nakamura, 2009), viable automatic speech translation technology is emerging (Cunningham, 2016). Functioning smart earpiece to translate foreign languages instantly for visitors could represent a good example of future smart technology for events and travel industry in general.

The e-info-points (audio-video displays) are traditional devices that can become smarter. Using video displays, important information can be provided to visitors in their own language, while the consistency of user interface (UI) can be provided by using one of the common mobile operating system interfaces, such as Android or Windows 10.

Smart operations and visitor identification on mass events are provided by using technological advances in wearable and biometric technology applications. According to Elwood (2010), the concept of embedding ubiquitous computing extends beyond hand-held devices. In that sense, wearable technologies, that are the different forms of body mounted technologies (Atembe, 2015) represent an emerging trend that finds purpose during travel. Wearable technologies provide various opportunities for creating tailored experiences based on users' location, past preferences or even user current moods (Dibble, 2015). As noted by Tussyadiah (2013), consumers' usage patterns of wearable technologies even suggest a potential transformation of their behaviour due to the new ways of interacting with technology and the surroundings. As stated before, more and more wearables can access some vital body parameters (Chan, Estève, Fourniols, Escriba, & Campo, 2012) and possibly sense someone's emotional status that can be used to deliver emotion-based contents services (Lee & Kwon, 2010). Geographical and emotional context brought by wearables can help transform promotional push tactic to service and informant practices that dissolve the annoyance sometimes associated with advertisements (Jebbit, 2015).

A smarter event can be induced by the use of biometric identification technology, such as fingerprint and iris scanning, facial and voice recognition, hand geometry or signature recognitions. Biometrics have been around for a number of years and recently the tourism and travel industry have started considering its use to regulate internal processes and to improve services, such as access to control systems, payment systems, time and attendance systems (Kang, Brewer, & Bai, 2007). For example, in order to prevent crime and to get better insights of visitors' patterns a fingerprint authentication system is tested in the preparation of the 2020 *Tokyo Olympic and Paralympic Games*. This system is expected to provide payment of goods and services, identification for tax exemption and substitute for presenting passports at a hotel (The Japan News, 2016). Still, biometric identification has to overcome issues such as a lack of legislation, user privacy concerns, misunderstanding of the system functioning, relatively high cost of the system, etc. (Kang et al., 2007; Neo, Rasiah, Tong, & Teo, 2014). In all such instances, Neo et al. (2014) pointed out that designers should carefully address the issue of security and privacy when managing fingerprint scanners in the realm of visitors' satisfaction.

THE CASE OF THE EXIT FESTIVAL

The Exit is a summer music festival held annually at the Petrovaradin fortress on the river Danube in the city of Novi Sad, Serbia. It started as a student protest against the past political regime of Yugoslavia and movement toward embracing the democracy in Serbia. First time held in 2000, so called "zero" Exit lasted for 100 days and attracted predominantly local population, but in short time the festival gained international recognition and became one of the most visited music festivals in Europe. Currently, the festival is held annually in the first week of July and lasts for four days. To its international recognition, Exit won numerous awards including the "Best Major European Festival Award" on European Festival Awards 2013 as well as the "Best European Festival" award at the UK Festival Awards in 2007. It was also ranked in the top 10 best major festivals at European Festival Awards 2009, 2010, 2011, 2012 and 2013, the "Best Major European Festival" at the EU Festival Awards 2014 and one of the 10 Best Overseas Festivals at UK Festival Award 2014 and Best Summer Music Festival in Europe for 2016 by travel portal "European Best Destinations" awarded in cooperation with the European Commission.

More than 2.5 million people from over 60 countries around the world have visited the festival so far (Kovačević, 2014). The festival contributes to Serbian economy with an annual income of more than 15 million euro (expenditure of festival goers during their stay in Novi Sad), with the total contribution to Serbian tourist industry of over 100 million euro so far (Milošević, 2016). As one of the leading, but jet growing award-winning summer music festival, Exit provides unparallel access to research of ICT adaption and its application in the context of mega music events.

Instrument

To examine visitors' familiarity with ICT, the research was conducted in summer 2016 during the 17th Exit festival. The questionnaire adapted the study of Wang and colleagues (2016) that indicates the important aspects that tourists take into account when evaluating smart tourist attractions and destinations. The first part of the questionnaire refers to socio-demographic characteristics of respondents (gender, age, education, occupation, monthly income) and second part measure their familiarity of ICTs which they could come in contact with during their Exit festival experience. Five point Likert scale was used for evaluating respondents' familiarity with ICTs (see Table 1). The questionnaire was translated in Serbian and English language as the research targeted both local and international festival visitors. A total of 100 questionnaires were distributed in Novi Sad among a convenience sample of tourists who have visited Exit festival in the period from 7 to 10 July 2016. Visitors were informed about the study and the participation was confidential and voluntary.

Results

The research sample consists of 63% male and 37% female respondents, most of them in the age group of 20-30 (75%). The majority of respondents have a bachelor degree (42%) followed by high school (38%) and master degree (17%) whereas 3% of respondents has PhD degree. Consequently, regarding their occupation, the highest share of respondents are students (55%).

The results on visitors' familiarity with ICTs on the Exit festival in respondents' opinion are ranged from 2.58 to 4.10 showing fair familiarity level. The highest scores are recorded to ICTs that respondents had an opportunity to personally interact with such as online information access, e-tour map, tourist attraction home pages, e-tourism recommendation system, online booking, blogs, electronic toll systems or weather forecast apps. The high score is also recorded by ICT concerning the safety of visitors at the destination, such as smart emergency response system. Queuing-time forecast gets the lowest score, although it can be very useful. Table 1 shows the mean values and standard deviation scores on the evaluated ICTs. The results are discussed in detailed in the following chapter.

Respondents had the opportunity to indicate if they were not familiar with some of the ICTs used by Exit festival. As expected, among five most familiar ICTs are technologies used in practical processes, such as travel preparation or on-site activities including free WiFi (95%), weather forecast apps (89%), online information access (87%), online booking (81%) and e-tour maps (78%). On the other side, visitors are least familiar with augmented reality (40%), smart vehicle scheduling (43%), e-complaint handling (44%), virtual tourist experiences (47%), crowd handling (48%) and real-time traffic broadcast solutions (48%). The main reason for the low level of familiarity with certain types of the ICT rests in the short time of visitation during which visitors are unable to become familiar with all technological details and offers at the destination. In addition, the majority of visitors pointed out that they were not generally

Table 1. Visitors' familiarity with various ICTs employment during Exit festival trip

List of ICTs	Number of Respondents Not Familiar With the Examined ICT	Respondents Familiar With the Examined ICT		
		N	Mean Value	Std. Deviation
Free WiFi	5	95	3.147	1.360
Online information access	13	87	3.505	1.032
Queuing-time forecast	38	62	2.580	1.300
E-ticketing system	29	71	3.169	1.298
Short messaging service and multimedia-messaging service	30	70	3.142	1.299
Smart environment	36	64	2.984	1.061
Traffic safety protection	25	75	3.426	1.002
Mobile payment	29	71	3.380	1.046
Touch screen	36	64	3.093	1.243
E-tour map	22	78	3.641	1.184
Festival activity forecast	29	71	3.422	1.283
Mobile application	31	69	3.362	.999
Tourist attraction home pages	28	72	3.500	.839
Personally itinerary design	44	56	2.910	.977
Tourist flow monitoring	48	52	2.692	1.039
Intelligent guide system	44	56	2.946	1.016
E-tourism recommendation system	32	68	3.500	1.029
Weather forecast	11	89	4.101	1.077
Crowd handling	52	48	2.625	1.178
Smart card (band)	43	57	3.193	1.216
E-entrance guard system	47	53	3.000	1.414
Quick response code	48	52	2.961	1.220
Online booking	19	81	4.049	.934
Tourist flow forecast	41	59	3.322	1.136
Guiding information service	43	57	3.315	1.002
Intelligent environment monitoring	50	50	3.020	1.203
Real-time traffic broadcast	52	48	2.916	1.107
Online coupons	43	57	3.421	1.179
Smart education	50	50	3.080	1.103
Smart emergency response system	41	59	3.576	1.053
Call service center	51	49	3.142	1.154
E-complaint handling	56	44	2.818	1.084
Smart vehicle scheduling	57	43	2.767	1.211
Electronic toll collection	43	57	3.561	1.102
Virtual tourist experience	53	47	3.127	1.244
Blogs of tourist attractions	38	62	3.854	1.005
Virtual travel community	49	51	3.411	1.416
Augmented reality	60	40	2.725	1.280

Note: Likert scale ranging: 1-poor, 2-fair, 3-good, 4-very good, 5- excellent

familiar with the terminology and application method of certain technologies; therefore it is specified as the reason for a lack of knowledge regarding implementation of particular ICTs at the Exit festival. Another important fact is that during their visit to Exit festival, certain visitors were not at all interested in using some of these ICTs, hence they did not further inform about it.

Discussion of Case Results

Exit festival visitors see websites as a good source of information when planning a trip (3.50). They have also shown confidence towards blogs that are often perceived to be more credible and trustworthy than traditional marketing communications (3.85). The festival's visitors rated e-tourism recommendation system moderately (3.50). These technologies can provide valuable information and help visitors to discover and select the points of interest that best fit their preferences. Contrariwise, the e-complaint handling system, that can identify deficiencies in the standard services through feedback and complaints of visitors, is fairly rated (2.82). Many visitors were using the internet as a medium for the search of tourist information as well as in planning their trip. Therefore, it has been also confirmed that visitors have a good familiarity with online information access (3.51) and online reservations (4.05).

Today, mobile services are perceived as enjoyable and useful in delivering festival content (Lexahagen, Nysveen & Hem, 2005). Importantly, the increased capabilities of smartphones support thousands of mobile apps which extend the functionality of mobile phones to a wide range of information services such as specialized information search, social networking, navigation, store information, etc.). For example, within the experiential phase (i.e., during the trip), smartphones provide access to location-based services (i.e. guiding-information service) that can recognize the current location of visitors and provide relevant suggestions based on tourists' inquiries including restaurants, souvenir shops, gas stations, etc. Particularly important are personally-itinerary design and e-tour maps that with the use of collaborative tour-planner systems can help visitors to design personal itineraries. Additionally, they can use GPS capabilities to collect information and to determine exact locations and directions. Festivals recognize the growing importance of QR codes on smart posters allowing people to easily copy information on their phones. Most of these technological applications proved to be, to some extent, significant for visitors of Exit Festival, such as applications for checking weather forecasts (4.10), guiding-information service (3.32), as well as e-tour maps (3.64). However, respondents think otherwise for QR codes (2.96) and personal-itinerary design (2.91), probably because these ICTs are not yet sufficiently adopted at Exit festival. Certainly, it is important to mention the fact that almost the half of respondents is not familiar with the application of these ICTs. Therefore, relatively low ratings should be attributed to this. While the results reveal that smartphones with social networks (e.g. Facebook) and mobile applications (e.g. Viber) are very popular for communication, it is surprising that the short messaging service and multimedia messaging service are also quite often used (3.14). This may be due to the large portion of local visitors in the research sample who used messaging services of their local telecommunication providers to communicate preferable to data-limited and pricey local mobile internet access. For a large number of festival visitors, who have smartphones and who seek to connect immediately it is critical that seamless WiFi infrastructure is in place to allow them to do so. With the high volume of people in a concentrated area often an open WiFi network, poorly installed and managed, can render insufficient coverage. It was one of the main reasons why WiFi is not rated highly at the site where the festival was held (3.15), even though the respondents indicated that they were mostly satisfied with the WiFi in accommodation facilities.

Another popular market that relies on mobile devices is purchasing services through mobile sites and applications (3.38). In the tourism industry the use of online coupons has become increasingly important. For festival visitors, online coupons can provide certain cost savings (3.42). Nowadays, very popular technological innovations are smart cards that can be useful for storing authentication data and for contactless transactions. Smart card received a good score at the Exit festival (3.19). However, slightly more than 40% of respondents are not familiar with its application in Novi Sad. Similarly, the electronic-ticketing systems stand out, and their main characteristic is that tickets are stored in an electronic device, such as smart cards or mobile phones. They utilize RFID and can be used for tourist sites, leisure events or even festivals. Access control and ticket sales management (reporting, accounting, etc.) can help festival organizers to browse transactions and with insight on festival goers related commodities they can adjust offerings to stimulate the spending. Their employment on the Exit festival is estimated as good.

Electronic touch screens (3.09) and intelligent-guide systems (2.95) can be pointed out as a form of smart information systems. Tourists believe that these systems can improve experience during their stay at the destination and provide them with more or different information. What visitors listed as an advantage of electronic touch screen technology is providing information 24 hours a day and they are slightly better rated than the intelligent guide system.

Access to relevant and accurate information is crucial in tourism, and intelligent tourism management system tries to bridge the gap providing relevant information about tourists at a certain time. On the other side, tourists are seeking more personalized tourism products and services, and they are expecting intelligent and proactive access to relevant high quality information at anytime and anywhere. Therefore, in the context of intelligent tourism management, it is possible to single out electronic-entrance guard system, tourist-flow monitoring, and crowd handling as well as smart education. In the context of smart destination, particularly important issues are related to determining the value of information and ensuring safety and security in rather open and ubiquitous info-structures. The real sense of smart tourism destinations is to focus on tourists' needs by combining the ICTs with a range of attraction, services and tourist innovation industry in order to promote service quality. This especially applies to the intelligent environment-monitoring, which is of a certain importance for visitors in obtaining relevant information (3.02). As an important aspect of the festival in terms of safety, visitors have stated traffic-safety protection and smart emergency response system (showing good familiarity). Using "smart materials" such as electronic sensors or security equipment it is possible to realize intelligent warning and emergency response through a wireless sensor network.

ICTs on the Exit festival regarding intelligent traffic are not highly ranked. The venue of a festival should have a vehicle-scheduling system that utilizes radio-frequency identification technology, wireless local area networks (WLAN) and other technologies. Nevertheless, more than 50% of respondents noted that they were not familiar with this technology, which among other is quite low rated (2.77). It is similar to the real-time traffic broadcast (2.92), where due to the lack of knowledge, visitors do not easily adopt these ICTs. These items represent the weaknesses of Exit festival ICT infrastructure and deserve further attention and investments. Apart from this, electronic toll collection is considered to be somewhat important, because it can improve the efficiency of the toll station (3.56).

An accurate forecast of visitor flow in the festivals can boost the business of tourism and optimize the allocation of resources. Using mobile applications, it is possible to forecast festivity information to visitors or to forecast and provide queuing time for visitors. Regarding this, festival-activity forecast (3.42) has a good implementation on the Exit festival, according to the respondents' ranking.

The last set of ICTs implies items concerning virtual tourist attraction. ICTs that provide virtual tourism experience and augmented reality can create a sort of tele-presence which allows people to experience a destination without actually visiting it. However, visitors have not emphasized their performance on the Exit festival. Also, it should be indicated that the vast majority of respondents are not familiar with this sort of ICT. In a typical GPS-based smartphone augmented reality application for outdoor use, the tourist points the device towards physical objects in the real world. Based on that, a person is able to see additional virtual information overlaid on top of the camera view through virtual annotations. However, these ICTs might be more functional and beneficial when applied to a specific tourism attraction in the destination rather than in the organization of festival itself. Certainly personalized interactive information can improve the tourist experience (Buhalis & Foerste, 2015). Those pleasurable experiences are transferred via virtual travel communities that make it easier for people to obtain information, maintain connections, develop relationships, etc. Exit Festival visitors stated that travel virtual communities represented an important source of information upon arrival in Novi Sad (3.41). In addition to the Internet, call service centers are used to provide useful and timely information for planning trips. According to the festival visitors, this type of information has received the good score of 3.14 respectively.

RECOMMENDATIONS FOR MASS EVENT ORGANIZERS

Based on the presented research, several recommendations can be made for mass event organizers:

- **ICT Hardware and Software Optimization:** Usually, one of the initial intentions of ICT implementation at the mass events was to provide tools to reduce costs. However, the high costs of ICT services are often a major barrier to ICT uptake, in particular, for mass event organized in low-income economies. Redundancy, overlapping and extensive use of ICT resources can often occur when various parties are evolved into a mass event organization. As a consequence, this sometimes requires spending organisers' limited funds on the use of extensive or even unnecessary ICT. Hence, the event organiser should strive to optimize the use of ICTs when trying to make a mass event smarter. First steps in optimization should include making a list of available ICT and the goals of particular mass event that should be accomplished with the help of ICT.
- **ICT Integration for Achieving Smartness:** The list of ICT priorities for certain mass event should be evaluated in its possibilities for integration. This is the curtail milestone in the process of leveraging smartness of a mass event. The integration of ICT in the mass event has nothing to do with a simple interconnection of ICT devices but should be understood rather as an innovative procedure based on the set of goals. It should be shifted from the traditional ICT integration transmitting towards more autonomous, active, and collaborative procedures often including visitors' active participation in ICT employment.
- **Experience Co-Creation Using ICT:** If a previous prerequisite for a smart environment is set, an experience of co-creation by using ICT can occur effectively at mass events. Most of the visitors are already equipped with necessary tools, such as smartphones, wearables, etc. This facilitates the delivery of event digital content to visitors (for example, virtual or augmented reality, smartphone on-site navigation, smart watch identifications, etc) through the users' environment they are already accustomed to.

- **New Business Models' Development:** One of the goals of „transition to smartness" could be the capabilities of mass event's organizers to offer new experiences for visitors in the form of innovative services or products. The better insight to visitors' characteristics and their consumers' patterns as well as real-time overview of the whole event activities offers a lot of new information for leveraging overall event's performance. Furthermore, as visitors seek the ways of trimming the budgets, without cutting their comforts the trend of collaborative economy have been greeted with much enthusiasm in travel industry. Besides obvious economic reasons there were several other drivers for collaborative economy development such as: technological innovation in networking and mobile movement (primary driver), visitor's motivations (e.g. empowerment, openness, altruism), environmental pressures (e.g. climate change, resource use) and newly formed digital institutions (e.g. review trust generating mechanisms) (Peeters, Dijkmans, Mitas, Strous, & Vinkensteijn, 2015). In the domain of mass events, with the help of collaborative models facilitated by ICT visitors can have the opportunity to gain insight into the knowledge of the hosts. These services link to trends in social media dealing with the travel industry, such as recommendation engines for travels, travel friend finders, special interests networks, tools to share trips and trends of creating communities around certain products (Urmann, 2012).

CONCLUSION

This chapter strives to demonstrate the use of the variety of ICTs, both by visitors and event organizers that can contribute to smarter tourism concept. The chapter makes two main contributions to the body of existing knowledge. First, it analyzes the concept of smart tourism in the context of mass events. Second, it gives insights to the visitors' familiarity with ICT at one of the major music festivals in Europe. The chapter extends the on-going discussion on the role of smart approach in the domain of mass event management, providing some insights into the strengths and weaknesses of ICT use at mass events.

It is important to define what are the right smart services and products that are important to visitors. In order to understand tourist preference of the "smart" offer, at first, it is necessary to examine the familiarity with the certain ICTs. Therefore, in the quest for "smart agenda" implementation this research could give organizers a guideline of key ICTs which may contribute to improving the organization of mass events and enhance visitors' experience. In the case of Exit festival, the most important items preferred by visitors are free WiFi, weather forecast apps, online information access, online booking and e-tour maps. Those items still need to be given priority when organizing a mass event. The findings also indicate that majority of visitors are not familiar with the certain ICT-s such as augmented reality, smart vehicle scheduling, e-complaint handling, virtual tourist experiences, crowd handling and real-time traffic broadcast solutions, as well as their application. In general, results indicate that the "level of smartness" of Exit festival is relatively low. Most importantly, it means that the intended use of some ICTs do not necessarily meet visitors' needs and interests. Going further, this could also mean that ICT hardware and software optimization and integration is not adequate, consequently leading to fewer possibilities for experience co-creation using ICT and for offering new services based on smart approach.

Finally, some important limitations of ICT employment for mass events are highlighted. This is important since the key challenge for ICT to become smarter can be found in the scope of currently existing technological limitations. Limitations are classified by the general constraints experienced by the tourism and hospitality companies in adopting new technologies as suggested by Wasan (2014).

This author summarizes those constrains into internal barriers (i.e. operational barriers, financial barriers, human resources barriers) and external barriers (i.e. market forces, law, policies and standards, customer barriers, rapidly changing technology, construction challenges). Considerable effort has been done to develop theoretical frameworks presented in Figure 1, such as proactive computing, ambient awareness, multifunctional sensors, etc. Still, as interesting as these endeavours have been they still do not match up to the desirable level of "smartness", mostly from cost-benefit point of view. In a case of the event organization, a prerequisite for smart technology implementation seems to be trivial for some events, but crucial for others. For example, enabling seamless WiFi coverage during a mass event is still a major challenge for some events. On another, certain smart technologies sometimes need an expensive infrastructure to implement and manage which could intensify the commercial pressures on the mass event organizer. The future development of certain ICTs on a mass event will depend on their capacity to get adapted to end-users needs and their alignment with the organizers' interests.

REFERENCES

Angskun, J., & Angskun, T. (2008). Online Trip Planners for the Tourism Industry. *Suranaree Journal of Social Science*, *2*(1), 33–45.

Atembe, R. (2015). The Use of Smart Technology in Tourism: Evidence From Wearable Devices. *Journal of Tourism and Hospitality Management*, *3*(6), 224–234.

Boodnah, K. D., Armoogum, V., Jaunky, V. C., & Armoogum, S. (2016). Towards Smart Tourism: An individual appreciation of Porlwi-By-Light festival. In *Emerging Technologies and Innovative Business Practices for the Transformation of Societies (EmergiTech)*. Port Louis: IEEE. doi:10.1109/EmergiTech.2016.7737360

Buhalis, D., & Amaranggana, A. (2015). Smart Tourism Destinations Enhancing Tourism Experience Through Personalisation of Services. In I. Tussyadiah & A. Inversini (Eds.), *Information and Communication Technologies in Tourism 2015* (pp. 377–389). Cham: Springer International Publishing. doi:10.1007/978-3-319-14343-9_28

Buhalis, D., & Foerste, M. (2015). SoCoMo marketing for travel and tourism: Empowering co-creation of value. *Journal of Destination Marketing & Management*, *4*(3), 151–161. doi:10.1016/j.jdmm.2015.04.001

Buhalis, D., & Law, R. (2008). Progress in information technology and tourism management: 20 years on and 10 years after the Internet – The state of eTourism research. *Tourism Management*, *29*(4), 609–623. doi:10.1016/j.tourman.2008.01.005

Cannon Hunter, W., Chung, N., Gretzel, U., & Koo, C. (2015). Constructivist Research in Smart Tourism. *Asia Pacific Journal of Information Systems*, *25*(1), 105–120. doi:10.14329/apjis.2015.25.1.105

Case, A. (2015). *Calm technology: principles and patterns for non-intrusive design*. Sebastopol, CA: O'Reilly Media, Inc.

Catherwood, D. W., & Van Kirk, R. L. (1992). *The Complete Guide to Special Event Management: Business Insights, Financial Advice, and Successful Strategies from Ernst & Young, Advisors to the Olympics, the Emmy Awards and the PGA Tour*. New York: John Wiley & Sons.

Chaffey, D., Ellis-Chadwick, F., Mayer, R., & Johnston, K. (2006). *Internet Marketing: Strategy, Implementation and Practice. Practice* (Vol. 3). Upper Saddle River, NJ: Prentice-Hall, Inc.

Chan, M., Estève, D., Fourniols, J.-Y., Escriba, C., & Campo, E. (2012). Smart wearable systems: Current status and future challenges. *Artificial Intelligence in Medicine*, *56*(3), 137–156. doi:10.1016/j.artmed.2012.09.003 PMID:23122689

Chiu, D. K. W., & Leung, H. (2005). Towards ubiquitous tourist service coordination and integration. In *Proceedings of the 7th international conference on Electronic commerce - ICEC '05*. New York: ACM Press. doi:10.1145/1089551.1089656

Chung, N., & Lee, H. (2016). Sharing economy in geotag: What are the travelers goals sharing their locations by using geotags in social network sites during the tour?. *International Journal of Tourism Cities*, *2*(2), 125–136. doi:10.1108/IJTC-08-2015-0022

Chung, N., Lee, S., & Han, H. (2015). Understanding communication types on travel information sharing in social media: A transactive memory systems perspective. *Telematics and Informatics*, *32*(4), 564–575. doi:10.1016/j.tele.2015.02.002

Cook, D., & Das, S. (2005). *Smart environments: technologies, protocols, and applications*. Hoboken, NJ: John Wiley.

Cunningham, P. (2016). *No more lost in translation – smart earpiece to translate foreign languages instantly for travellers*. Retrieved July 19, 2016, from http://www.lonelyplanet.com/news/2016/05/18/new-earpiece-instant-translation/

Dibble, T. (2015). *Technology is changging travel*. Retrieved July 18, 2015, from https://www.screenpilot.com/2015/03/wearables-wanderlust-how-technology-is-changing-travel/

Elwood, S. A. (2010). Embedding Ubiquitous Technologies. In J. Symonds (Ed.), Ubiquitous and Pervasive Computing: Concepts, Methodologies, Tools, and Applications (pp. 511–519). Hershey, PA: IGI Global. doi:10.4018/978-1-60566-960-1.ch033

Euromonitor. (2014). *Online Travel Intermediaries: A Fast Changing Competitive Landscape*. Retrieved July 29, 2016, from http://www.slovenia.info/pictures/TB_board/atachments_1/2014/Online_Travel_Intermediaries_A_Fast_Changing_Competitive_Landscape_19150.pdf

Facebook. (2015). *Company Info | Facebook Newsroom*. Retrieved October 10, 2015, from http://newsroom.fb.com/company-info/

Google and IPSOS OTX MediaCT. (2011). T*he Mobile Movement Understanding Smartphone Users*. Think Mobile with Google. Retrieved October 20, 2015, from https://ssl.gstatic.com/think/docs/the-mobile-movement_research-studies.pdf

Gretzel, U. (2011). Intelligent systems in tourism. *Annals of Tourism Research*, *38*(3), 757–779. doi:10.1016/j.annals.2011.04.014

Gretzel, U., Sigala, M., Xiang, Z., & Koo, C. (2015). Smart tourism: Foundations and developments. *Electronic Markets*, *25*(3), 179–188. doi:10.1007/s12525-015-0196-8

Gretzel, U., Werthner, H., Koo, C., & Lamsfus, C. (2015). Conceptual foundations for understanding smart tourism ecosystems. *Computers in Human Behavior*, *50*, 558–563. doi:10.1016/j.chb.2015.03.043

Halpenny, E. A., Salenieks, T., Song, L. D., Van Winkle, C., & MacKay, K. (2013). Albertan festivals' Adoption of Social Media and Mobile Digital Technology. In *TTRA Canada Annual Conference 2013 Academic papers*. Ottawa: TTRA Canada Chapter.

Hecht, B., Schöning, J., Erickson, T., & Priedhorsky, R. (2011). Geographic Human-Computer Interaction. In *CHI '11 Extended Abstracts on Human Factors in Computing Systems*. Vancouver: AMC Press. doi:10.1145/1979742.1979532

Hohl, M. (2009). Calm Technologies 2.0: Visualising Social Data as an Experience in Physical Space. *Parsons Journal for Information Mapping*, *1*(3), 1–7.

Hunter, W. C., Chung, N., Gretzel, U., & Koo, C. (2015). Constructivist research in smart tourism. *Asia Pacific Journal of Information Systems*, *25*(1), 105–120. doi:10.14329/apjis.2015.25.1.105

Internet World Stats. (2015). *Internet Usage Statistics. The Internet Big Picture*. Retrieved October 10, 2015, from http://www.internetworldstats.com/stats.htm

Jebbit. (2015). *3 Ways that Wearables are Transforming Marketing Interactions*. Retrieved May 29, 2016, from https://www.jebbit.com/blog/3-ways-wearables-transforming-marketing-interactions/

Kang, B., Brewer, K. P., & Bai, B. (2007). Biometrics for Hospitality and Tourism: A New Wave of Information Technology. *Hospitality Review*, *25*(1), 1–9.

Kovačević, D. (2014). *Record edition of the best major European Festival*. Retrieved May 29, 2016, from http://vojvodinahouse.eu/uploads/images/bilteni/Vojvodina%20World%204.pdf

Lee, H., & Kwon, J. (2010). Combining Context-Awareness with Wearable Computing for Emotion-based Contents Service. *International Journal of Advanced Science & Technology*, *22*, 13–24.

Lee, S. S., Boshnakova, D., & Goldblatt, J. (2016). *The 21st Century Meeting and Event Technologies Powerful Tools for Better Planning, Marketing, and Evaluation*. Waretown: Apple Academic Press.

Lee, W., Xiong, L., & Hu, C. (2012). The effect of Facebook users arousal and valence on intention to go to the festival: Applying an extension of the technology acceptance model. *International Journal of Hospitality Management*, *31*(3), 819–827. doi:10.1016/j.ijhm.2011.09.018

Lexhagen, M., Nysveen, H., & Hem, L. E. (2005). Festival coordination: An exploratory study on intention to use mobile devices for coordination of a festival. *Event Management*, *9*(3), 133–146. doi:10.3727/152599505774791167

Manes, G. (2001). The Tetherless Tourist: Ambient Intelligence in Travel & Tourism. *Information Technology & Tourism*, *5*(4), 211–220. doi:10.3727/109830503108751144

Milošević, Ž. (2016). *Dušan Kovačević: Promoting CoMuntry's Image and Economic Contribution*. Retrieved October 29, 2016, from http://www.diplomacyandcommerce.rs/dusan-kovacevic-promoting-countrys-image-and-economic-contribution/

Nakamura, S. (2009). Overcoming the Language Barrier with Speech Translation Technology. *NISTEP Quarterly Review*, *31*, 35–49.

Neo, H.-F., Rasiah, D., Tong, D. Y. K., & Teo, C.-C. (2014). Biometric technology and privacy: A perspective from tourist satisfaction. *Information Technology & Tourism*, *14*(3), 219–237. doi:10.1007/s40558-014-0014-8

Neuhofer, B., Buhalis, D., & Ladkin, A. (2014). A Typology of Technology-Enhanced Tourism Experiences. *International Journal of Tourism Research*, *16*(4), 340–350. doi:10.1002/jtr.1958

OConnor, P., & Frew, A. J. (2002). The future of hotel electronic distribution: Expert and industry perspectives. *The Cornell Hotel and Restaurant Administration Quarterly*, *43*(3), 33–45. doi:10.1016/S0010-8804(02)80016-7

Pang, A. S.-K. (2013). *The distraction addiction: getting the information you need and the communication you want without enraging your family, annoying your colleagues, and destroying your soul*. New York: Little Brown and Company.

Park, J.-Y., & Jang, S. (2013). Confused by too many choices? Choice overload in tourism. *Tourism Management*, *35*, 1–12. doi:10.1016/j.tourman.2012.05.004

Peeters, P., Dijkmans, C., Mitas, O., Strous, B., & Vinkensteijn, J. (2015). *Research for Tran Committee: Tourism and the sharing economy: challenges and opportunities for the EU*. Brussels: European Parliament. Retrieved from http://www.europarl.europa.eu/RegData/etudes/STUD/2015/563411/IPOL_STU(2015)563411_EN.pdf

Peng, C., Chen, B.-Y., & Tsai, C.-H. (2010). Integrated Google Maps and smooth street view videos for route planning. In *2010 International Computer Symposium (ICS2010)*. Tainan: IEEE. doi:10.1109/COMPSYM.2010.5685494

Pesonen, J., & Horster, E. (2012). Near field communication technology in tourism. *Tourism Management Perspectives*, *4*, 11–18. doi:10.1016/j.tmp.2012.04.001

Rakshit, R., & Ogneva-Himmelberger, Y. (2008). Application of Virtual Globes in Education. *Geography Compass*, *2*(6), 1995–2010. doi:10.1111/j.1749-8198.2008.00165.x

Rieder, B. (2013). *Studying Facebook via data extraction*. In *Proceedings of the 5th Annual ACM Web Science Conference on - WebSci '13* (pp. 346–355). New York: ACM Press. doi:10.1145/2464464.2464475

Rubinstein, P. (2015). *The Use of Technology to Enhance Music Festivals*. Retrieved May 29, 2016, from http://www.youredm.com/2015/03/07/the-use-of-technology-to-enhance-music-festivals

Stankov, U., Jovanović, T., & Dragićević, V. (2014). Facebook Travel Related Usage Patterns of Tourism Students. In *SINTEZA 2014 Impact of Internet on Business activities in Serbia and Worldwide*. Belgrade: Singidunum Univeristy. doi:10.15308/sinteza-2014-743-749

The Japan News. (2016). Fingerprints to be tested as "currency". *The Japan News*. Retrieved from http://the-japan-news.com

Tussyadiah, I. (2013). Expectation of Travel Experiences with Wearable Computing Devices. In *Information and Communication Technologies in Tourism 2014* (pp. 539–552). Cham: Springer International Publishing. doi:10.1007/978-3-319-03973-2_39

Urmann, D. (2012). *7 Ways Social Travel Sites are Engaging Users*. Retrieved April 16, 2017, from https://www.socialfresh.com/travel-social-media-tools/

Versichele, M., Neutens, T., Delafontaine, M., & Van de Weghe, N. (2012). The use of Bluetooth for analysing spatiotemporal dynamics of human movement at mass events: A case study of the Ghent Festivities. *Applied Geography (Sevenoaks, England)*, *32*(2), 208–220. doi:10.1016/j.apgeog.2011.05.011

Wang, D., & Xiang, Z. (2012). The New Landscape of Travel: A Comprehensive Analysis of Smartphone Apps. In M. Fuchs, F. Ricci, & L. Cantoni (Eds.), *Information and Communication Technologies in Tourism 2012* (pp. 308–319). Vienna: Springer Vienna. doi:10.1007/978-3-7091-1142-0_27

Wang, X., Li, X. R., Zhen, F., & Zhang, J. (2016). How smart is your tourist attraction?: Measuring tourist preferences of smart tourism attractions via a FCEM-AHP and IPA approach. *Tourism Management*, *54*, 309–320. doi:10.1016/j.tourman.2015.12.003

Wang, Z., Zhu, W., Cui, P., Sun, L., & Yang, S. (2013). Social Media Recommendation. In N. Ramzan, R. van Zwol, J.-S. Lee, K. Clüver, & X.-S. Hua (Eds.), *Social Media Retrieval* (pp. 23–42). London: Springer - Verlang. doi:10.1007/978-1-4471-4555-4_2

Wasan, P. (2014). Sustainable Technology in Hospitality Industry. In V. Jauhari (Ed.), Managing Sustainability in the Hospitality and Tourism Industry Paradigms and Directions for the Future (pp. 101–135). Boca Raton, FL: CRC Press.

Weiser, M., Gold, R., & Brown, J. S. (1999). The origins of ubiquitous computing research at PARC in the late 1980s. *IBM Systems Journal*, *38*(4), 693–696. doi:10.1147/sj.384.0693

Yamamoto, G. T. (2009). *Mobilized Marketing and the Consumer: Technological Developments and Challenges*. Hershey, PA: Business Science Reference.

Yeoman, I. (2013). A futurists thoughts on consumer trends shaping future festivals and events. *International Journal of Event and Festival Management*, *4*(3), 249–260. doi:10.1108/IJEFM-06-2013-0017

KEY TERMS AND DEFINITIONS

Biometric Identification Technologies: The process of identification is related to human characteristics. Typically includes fingerprint and iris scanning, facial, voice, hand geometry or signature recognition.

Co-Creation: An approach to bring together parties (e.g. event organizer and visitor) in a business process in order to jointly create a mutually desirable outcomes.

Event Management: Project management of the event itself. It involves creating and managing different activities of an event before actually launching the event.

Mass Events: A planned gatherings of a larger body of people at a specific location and for a specific purpose. It requires sophisticated coordination of all related operations.

Mobile Movement: The extensive use of smart phones creates more opportunities for smarter business models. Smart phones are always with consumers and they are always on serving not just for communication, but for information search, socializing, entertainment, shopping, etc.

RFID: It stands for radio-frequency identification and refers to the use of radio waves to access information stored on tags attached to different objects.

Smart Destination: A new step in the evolution of ICT that enables destinations to build their competitiveness based on the interoperability of systems and co-creation of tourism products.

Chapter 13
New Cultural Mediators, Cocreation, and the Cultural Consumption of Creative Tourism Experiences

Rui Miguel Ferreira Carvalho
University of Aveiro, Portugal

Carlos Manuel Martins da Costa
University of Aveiro, Portugal

Ana Maria Alves Pedro Ferreira
University of Évora, Portugal

ABSTRACT

Creative tourism has been a proficuous ground for the implementation of ICT's (Information and Communications Technology) strategies and the so-called creative industries. New cultural mediators are changing tourism consumption. Postmodern consumers have brought new perceptions to cocreation processes through user-generated content, eWOM (Electronic Word of Mouth), peer-to-peer exchange, collaborative economy, SoLoMo (social-local-mobile) tourists, among others. Booktubers and music fans/consumers in Chile constitute examples of diverse consumption through virtual and physical mediation, as capital construction enables social practices. In this exploratory study, the authors discuss how creative experiences are being consumed through cultural mediation made possible by technological developments. The creative tourism network website is analysed in the light of postmodern cultural mediation and capital construction.

DOI: 10.4018/978-1-5225-2927-9.ch013

INTRODUCTION

Creative tourism can be understood as a postmodern type of tourism (Molina, 2016) where tourists engage with locals directly and are given the chance to develop their cultural capital (Bourdieu, 1984, 1986, 2010). ICT's and new technologies play an important role where new consumers act as cultural mediators influencing cultural and tourism consumption. New cultural mediators (Arriagada & Cruz, 2014; Jeffman, 2014), present themselves as being part of a specialized group of consumers which proactively influence consumption choices in several fields. In this exploratory study, two examples are analyzed in order to connect new approaches to cultural mediation in the sociology of culture and tourism. Booktubers and music consumer fans represent two important examples where cultural mediation exceeds virtual purposes. New ways of cultural capital creation are present as the establishment of new virtual and physical networks crucial for tourism and culture fruition, boosts social phenomena. The aim of this chapter is to discuss how creative tourism experiences are being consumed by a new cultural mediation made possible by technological developments. The creative tourism network website is analyzed (http://www.creativetourismnetwork.org) using content analysis (Carvalho, Costa, & Ferreira, 2015; Ratz, 2016). This exploratory research seeks to perceive how cultural mediation occurs in relation to this special niche tourism (Richards, 2016), how the website allows for social engagement and how creative destinations are been promoted in terms of cultural mediation processes. The chapter is organized in several sections. The Background is divided in three theoretical areas in which the paper is based. In the next section the main focus of the chapter treats in detail the creative tourism network website, followed by future research directions and conclusions sections.

BACKGROUND

Specialised Cultural Consumption in Postmodern Tourism

I am someone who can adapt to any cultural way-of-life, any fashion style, or any cultural good as I flexibly accumulate a broad range of diverse experiences. (Thompson, 2000, p. 130)

The statement above made by Thompson (2000), illustrates the versatile character of postmodern consumers where cultural fruition, mediation and symbolic capital are present. Postmodernism consists of the dissolution of borders, not only between high and low culture, but also between different cultural forms, such as tourism, art, education, photography, television, music, sports, shopping and architecture (Urry, 2002). "Architecture, the representational arts, and all branches of the humanities and the social fields have been energized (…) by the turn to things postmodern" (Thompson, 2000, p. 118). In short, the mass communication era has transformed the tourist gaze and many of the features of "postmodernity" have already prefigured in part on existing tourism practices (Urry, 2002). This also influences tourism outcomes as the new tourist is motivated by higher-level motivations, driven by post-materialistic values and consciously seeks the experiences important for him (McLeod, 2006).

The concept and its meaning has been discussed in different ways, for example for Giddens, (2002) the word "post-modernity" is often used as a synonym for "postmodernism" or post-industrial society". For the author, postmodernism is appropriated to refer to styles or movements in literature, painting and architecture. It has to do with the aesthetic reflexion about the nature of modernity (Giddens, 2002). Despite its "cultural disorder", postmodernity has been seldom identify has a post-industrial society (e.g. Bell, 1976); in economic thought by Baudrillard, (1998); in philosophy put forward by Lyotard, (1989); addressed in sociology as "Reflexive Modernity" by Giddens, (2002) or "Liquid Modernity" by Bauman, (2001), just to name a few.

Others debate whether it is a "natural consequence of modernity" (e.g. Thompson, 2000) or a "reflexive" or "radical modernity" (e.g. Giddens, 2002). "Many commentators on the postmodern condition" in its many variegated forms espouse a "periodizing view", which portrays modernism and post-modernism as distinct historical/cultural societal eras (…) [with its] common reference point in the 1960s" (Thompson, 2000, p. 120). Charles (2011), when introducing the postmodern thought of Lipovestky, (2007), Lipovetsky and Charles, (2011) mentions postmodernity not as a unidimensional phenomenon but as a double one. "Basically, we need to understand post modernity in the form of a paradox and that its two logics coexist closely, one that favors autonomy, the other which increases dependency. (...) On the one hand, more accountability and, secondly, most deregulation" (Charles, 2011, p. 23).

Although this is important to the discussion around postmodernity, it is widely accepted that consumption is crucial for the postmodern consumer, as it is considered to be influenced by several postmodern characteristics. "The consumer, that figure born as an imposed figure after the fall of the Berlin wall, globalised, which has appropriated all classical modern categories and even premodern ones: spectators, creations, artists, operas, patrons were all substituted by the figure of the tout court consumer, the main actor of everything which is part of the global markets chain" (Ribeiro, 2015, pp. 55-56).

Everyday life (…) [is] penetrated and transformed by mass media and marketing; time space compression is hyper intensified by advances in information technologies and the digital revolution; no "real" distinctions about the real and fiction, facts, images, simulations among others where everything is ephemeral (Baudrillard, 1981; Thompson, 2000; Giddens, 2002). In tourism literature, postmodernity is represented as an important paradigm through which is used to analyse tourism consumption. It has given rise to different approaches to themes such has authenticity, symbolic consumption, the *Mcadonalisation* of tourism commodities and destinations, liminal phases of touristic events, globalised consumption and staged touristic experiences (MacCannell, 1999; Wang, 1999; Urry, 2002; Reisinger, 2009; Goffmann 1959 as cited in Heitmann, 2011).

In the present work, the authors agree with the argument posited in favour of postmodernity as a "continuity", despite having its own set of "conditions and characteristics", it is still connected to modernity as a whole. As Walsh (1992) suggests: (…)" [Post]-modernity is a condition - one which is not an experience of radical rupture, nor so different from modernity that the two share no characteristics at all, but rather one that is an intensification of those experiences and processes which emerged during the eighteenth and nineteenth centuries especially" (Walsh, 1992, p. 53, as cited in Macleod, 2006, p. 180). Consumption has developed itself as an epithet for self-actualisation, self-development, specialized consumption and personal meaning (Scitovksky, 1992; Thompson, 2000; Lipovetsky 2007).

Consumption is done for each one's sake. "A postmodernist no longer seeks unity and synthesis but instead reveals heterogeneity, polysemy and difference" (Thompson, 2000, p. 123). The ultimate goal of postmodern consumption is to avoid being typed, classified, predicted and controlled. (…) They are self-conscious producers who use the marketplace for endless acts of self-recreation (…) they are motivated by a multiplicity of goals and desires, some of them more modernist or hyper modernist (due to a reflexive self-awareness) than those taken for granted by modern consumers (Thompson, 2000).

"They express discernible historical currents that have given rise to a reflexive and ironic stance toward modernist conventions" (Thompson, 2000, p. 126) and this has been so for quite some time, especially in the array of mass production goods, typical of the industrial revolution. "Baudelaire called attention to the fragmented dehistoricized, aestheticized experiences of the nineteenth century urban flaneaur and the visual spectacle of the city. Benjamin developed these baudeleairain themes in relation to his own notions of "aestheticized, consumer dream worlds" and he discussed the rupture between objects, meaning and tradition created by mechanical reproductions (i.e. simulations) and capitalism's intertwining of aesthetics and the marketplace" (Thompson, 2000, p. 122). However, Benjamin, (1936) also mentions the loss of the special aura present during the production of the unique/original cultural good, where the *"hic et nunc"* (here and now) significance disappears and the act of alienation occurs, separating producer and the object massively produced (Assoun, 1989).

Not only the act of production and reproduction of art goods loses its value, but also cultural fruition on the part of the consumer results in a forced action. "The reproducible artwork loses its value as a "cultural good" in favour of its "showable" reality (…) as the social meaning of art diminishes, a crescent divorce is witnessed between critical opinion and pleasure conduct" (Assoun, 1989, p. 108). It may look like that consumption is done to fulfil temporary quirks, typical as the ones portrayed in postmodern literature (hedonism, ephemeral consumption, and so forth), but never as the consumer been so alert and demanding as before taking part and influencing the outcome of the majority of consumption acts. It makes part of both supply and demand sides when these two sides become indistinct through the process of cocreation and the ICT's. These consumers also use social networks to "tell their version" of the experience, evaluate, share and create new knowledge, influencing others.

In this context, the authors argue that the term of specialized consumption by Scitovsky, (1992) is applicable to the present discussion of tourism consumption. In his work, the author proposes to find out why acts of consumption would be more pleasant and fulfilling for ones and not to others. In addition, in what concerns to leisure activities as these enter the tourism atmosphere, a special amount of time and skills are needed. "Consumption of leisure activities, especially those devoted to intellectual pursuits, requires time, in fact often a lot of time, as is obvious if one thinks of the investment in skills that these activities ask" (Bianchi, 2003, p. 4).

What is important about the work of Scitovsky is that he informs us that creative activities do take some amount of time, as people need skills to choose and enjoy activities in order to develop their cultural capital. This is consistent with Bourdieu's cultural capital theory, as family and school makes its inculcation possible, through a long period (Bourdieu, 1986). "What makes creative activities so pleasurable – is that these activities, because of the skills they require, their complexity and variety, and their separateness from mere need, can be a constant source of novelty and change" (Bianchi, 2003, p. 8). Skilled consumption or specialized consumption can make the difference in choosing a creative tourism activity. This is why postmodern tourists are important, as they not only know exactly what they are consuming, they are difficult to categorise (Thompson, 2000).

The actual role of the consumer encompasses several new ones filled with symbolism (Thompson, 2000; Silva, 2004). New functions as user generated content, online reputation, ICT's presence in all phases of the trip, the sharing of pictures, videos and testimonies among others (Barros, 2015), makes possible for the exchange of cultural capital influencing and generating tourism consumption behaviors (Arriagada & Cruz, 2014).

This makes sense if we think of recent tourism literature where individualized forms of tourism try to answer alternatively to massive forms of tourism consumption (Poon, 1993). Since de conference in Manila in 1980, organized by the WTO that "new" tendencies and approaches to tourism analyses are well known. A general assembly organized by the WTO in Sofia in 1985, pointed out new approaches to tourism praxis: where economic aspects are no longer definitely important to the tourism sector but also factors such as politics, society, economy, culture, education, environment protection and quality of live deserve more attention. In addition, immaterial resources enhance its importance, attention is based now on value, predominant active tourism forms and differentiated products, emancipated tourists and the integration of local communities in the tourism business are new areas of intervention (WTO, 1980, 1985; Poon, 1993; Neves, Magalhães, & Lourenço, 2007).

These changes had repercussions on both production and organization levels in tourism. Furthermore, the prominence of special interest tourism niches (Ratz, 2016), the growing importance of cocreation in tourism (Binkhorst and den Dekker, 2009), the role that technology plays in tourism consumption (Neuhofer, Buhalis, & Ladkin 2012, 2013), as new forms of tourism such has creative tourism (Raymond and Richards, 2000), are *a fortiori* developed. Moreover, disintermediation made possible by technology and new service offers such as Airbnb, Uber among others, help to reshape the consumption of tourism. In short, postmodernity centralizes the individualised consumer as a central figure, which plays an important role in the specialised cultural consumption of tourism. Personal and practical knowledge act as symbolically forms of cultural capital, in the process of cocreation, where new types of mediation emerge in creative tourism.

ICT's, Cocreation, and New Cultural Mediators in Tourism Experiences

As we have seen in the section above, the consumption of culture and tourism experiences have been a place where technology as developed an essential role in the postmodern paradigm. Tourism is the area where the power of information and communication technologies is being increasingly implemented (…) as their effects are evident (Mihajlović, 2014). Some of these effects have to do with the availability of information via Internet, growing opportunities for tourists in the organization of independent travels (…) effects on tourist's behaviour, as virtual experiences may stimulate travel acquisitions (Mihajlović, 2014). This has profound implications on the design of tourism experiences.

Briefly, the discourses of experiential marketing have been mainly based on predicting tourists behaviour, sensorial marketing, among others. This follows the widely accepted and seminal work of Pine and Gilmore's, (1999) the experience economy, where the staging of experiences is crucial to the ever more engaging customer. However, costumers want a more active role in the cocreation of their own experiences. As referred by Neuhofer, et al., (2013), the idea of cocreation has been fostered by Prahalad and Ramaswamy, (2004) who argue that instead of consuming staged experiences, consumers now seek after more authenticity and expect a balance between the experience stager and their role as co-creators of experiences and value (Binkhorst, 2006; Ramaswamy & Gouillart, 2008)" (Neuhofer et al., 2013, p. 546).

Cocreation paradigm has been developed under new approaches between companies and consumers portrayed as B2B, B2C and C2C connections. However, the term itself needs revaluation. In the evaluation done by Rihova, (2013) she identified three discourses in marketing literature "Features and Benefits", "Value in "and "Inter subjectivity value" discourses (Rihova, 2013). The authors focus on the third one. "This perspective emphasises socially constructed, co-created value (…) processes of valuing rather than as realised in subjective value perceptions" (Rihova, 2013, p. 57). The authors of this chapter try to call the attention to the symbolic aspects of the experience, even technological mediated ones.

"Two major paradigm shifts are drastically changing the nature of experiences. (…) Experiences are a) transforming consumers to play an active part in cocreating their own experience and b) technology is increasingly mediating experiences" (Neuhofer et al., 2012, p. 36). Not only it is important to acknowledge that technology alone plays a crucial role in cultural and tourism fruition but also to take into account, who new (inter) mediators are and also how they are present online and how they are rapidly shaping tourism experiences virtually and physically.

The power of ICT's increasingly tests the power of intermediaries (Mihajlović, 2014). Virtual networks of specialized consumers and their presence online allows for the use of cultural capital (Bourdieu, 1986), seen as digital capital by Arriagada, (2014) as knowledge used to influence cultural consumption and arguably shaping cultural and tourism experiences (Richards, 2013, 2016). "Knowledge is created, shared, and accessible to users with minimal costs" (Mihajlović, 2014, p. 44). Creative tourism is seen as a type of tourism, which confers special attention to cultural capital possession and development, where innovation, ICC's and technology are present (Richards, 2016) and new ways of mediation are developed.

Cultural intermediaries have been a productive device for examining the producers of symbolic value in various industries, commodity chains and urban spaces, highlighting such issues as the blurring of work and leisure (Maguire & Matthews, 2012). Research on cultural intermediaries has generally followed two different (although not incompatible) directions: cultural intermediaries as exemplars of the new middle class involved in the mediation of production and consumption (Bourdieu, 1984, 2010) and cultural intermediaries as market actors involved in the qualification of goods, mediating between economy and culture (Maguire & Matthews, 2012). In the context of cultural economy, cultural intermediaries are distinguished as knowledgeable agents that shape the necessities and desires of consumers (Maguire & Mathews, 2010).

In cultural capital theory developed by Bourdieu, (1986, 2010) social agents which possess great amounts of cultural capital (knowledge in their several forms: embodied, objectified and institutionalized) are the ones better prepared to understand the arts and in general cultural fields. Such agents use their knowledge to move between fields always in their own interest. Building on Bourdieu the authors refer to a vision of social conflict, crucial to the French sociologist to refer to these social individuals that "frame particular cultural products as legitimate (…) and valuable" (Smith & Mathews, 2010 as cited in Arriagada & Cruz, 2014, p. 152). It is the struggle for power over who gets to define cultural and symbolic value (Arriagada & Cruz, 2014). Cultural intermediaries (Bourdieu, 1984 as cited in Arriagada & Cruz, 2014) are examples of the petit-bourgeoisie, which are involved in the mediation between cultural

Table 1. Cultural intermediaries and mediators

Cultural Intermediaries According to Bourdieu	Mediators According to Latour
"Cultural intermediaries" have a significant role in the reproduction of consumer economies, particularly because they stand between the production and consumption of goods, acting as "shapers of taste and the inculcators of new consumerist dispositions (Nixon & Du Gray, 2002, p. 497).	"Actors and "actants" (human and non-human, respectively) transform, translate, distort, and modify the meaning or the elements they are supposed to carry" (Latour, 2007, p. 39).

Source: Own elaboration based on (Nixon & Du Gray, 2002, p. 497) and (Latour, 2007, p. 39) both cited in (Arriagada & Cruz, 2014).

production and consumption. Cultural mediators becomes an important concept because they are in a way holders of cultural capital that influence behaviour and the life style of others.

Despite this, Arriagada and Cruz, (2014) refer that in the context of the Chile's music scene mediation, "This processes (…) do not map neatly the practices of contemporary music scenes, thoroughly postmodern (that is, rejecting "high" and "low" culture; Jameson, 1992) and suffused with digital technology as they are" (Arriagada & Cruz, 2014, p. 153). In short, the authors mention that the notion of Latour better serves their purposes. "Individuals as cultural mediators make explicit efforts to shape the music scene in ways that are attractive to specific ("niche") audiences as well as increasingly important market agents, often making use of new media. (…) This assemblage of actors and actants (the internet), as a set of technologies to facilitate the production, reproduction, distribution and consumption of information about a [musical] scene, and a group of active mediators who both document the scene and make it attractive to market agents, thus acquires and important role in the growth and dynamism of contemporary cultural participation" (Arriagada & Cruz, 2014, p. 53).

In the necessity of actualisation of the term of Bourdieu, the authors resolve the problem around postmodern consumption patterns, the new media, the internet and new technology not yet available at this time. In addition, the concept of cultural capital is updated in the same context (Carvalho, Costa, & Ferreira, 2016). According to Bourdieu, (1984, 1986, 2010) cultural capital is mainly formed by the social agent's family and school attendance. Several authors have developed different forms of cultural capital formation (Setton, 2005; Prieur, Roselund, & Skjott-Larsen, 2008; Prieur & Savage, 2011, 2013; Prieur, 2013). Others conceptualise various forms of cultural capital such as "relational capital" as local knowledge, skills exchanged between locals (switchers) and tourists (Richards, 2013). "Digital capital" in relation to cultural production as "practical fluency with the assemblage of technologies necessary to produce and maintain not only a website but also a social network linking an array of actors with a diversity of interests. "Digital capital" becomes as important as social, cultural and economic capital (…) becoming integral to all three" (Arriagada, 2014, 2015; Arriagada & Cruz, 2014). Finally, "intercultural capital" as monuments, international agreements or declarations with inherent intercultural dimensions, intercultural universities, among others as put forward by Pöllmann (2013, 2016).

The creation and transfer of these types of symbolic capital is done through virtual networks and technological enhanced situations. The authors use two examples to show the interconnection of the ICT's, internet and social networking in the cultural Chile music scene and cultural consumption of indie music (Arriagada, 2014, 2015; Arriagada & Cruz, 2014) and the case of you tubers and vloggers who use YouTube to promote their tastes in books (Jeffman, 2014). What is common in both cases is that the cultural capital of the users no only refers to the use of social media (ex. how to work with ICT's) but also the knowledge used to legitimate forms of culture (ex. Defining what is culturally valid).

In the Chile case, the authors refer to the presence of "digital capital". This knowledge cannot be understood as a linear system of inputs and outputs, causes and effects but as a junction of different capital mediations and associations between actors, practices, discourses and objects (Arriagada, 2014). Websites are perceived as "practices with digital technologies in the creation and maintenance of music websites [which] are the result of different types of knowledge, objects, emotions, and activities that are stabilized and assembled on websites and social networking profiles" (Schatzki 2001; 2002 as cited in Arriagada, 2015, p. 5). Using the musical event case "Corona clash" organized by a publicity enterprise in the Chile context, the authors argue that the event is seen as the result of a set of different interactions of technological mediation, between different entities – musicians, consumers, producers, label companies, brands and publicity agencies. "The fluidity of the Santiago scene is due in large part to the

Internet, and websites are the key means of making and connecting this diversity of activity to a range of locales and, perhaps more importantly, to market agents" (Arriagada & Cruz, 2014, p. 155).

Therefore, through the appropriation and use of digital technologies, consumers have become an integrating part of production and value circulation *vis a vis* cultural fluxes, becoming mediators (Arriagada, 2014; Arriagada & Cruz, 2014). This situation seems to favour the consumer's role in the context of postmodern cultural consumption. Influence factors and possession of cultural capital as knowledge of several cultural fields, are determinants to the new consumer play role acting as cultural mediator while he co-creates value. Through the internet, websites and social networks, mechanisms in the sense of Latour, are used to emphasize "cultural critic" and the opinion of the subjective habitus.

Nonetheless, the nature and users intentions exceeds the objectives of digital platforms, websites or social networks (Jeffman, 2014). A social network can be seen as a set of two elements: actors (people, institutions and groups) and their connections (interactions or social bonds). Jeffman (2013) distinguishes between several typologies of social networks. General social networks (e.g. Facebook, Twitter); segmented (RSS) (e.g. Skoob, Flickr) (Cadé, 2009); niche social networks (Malavolta, 2010) or theme based social networks (Montardo, 2008 as cited in Jeffman, 2013, p. 7). In short, segmented social networks are directed to specific audiences. According to Dourado (2010) vertical social medias are social networks that evolve around a specific theme and because of that are capable of engaging users that share the same consumption and leisure habitus (as cited in Jeffman, 2013, p. 7).

Another good example of new cultural mediators are booktubeers. By using a general social network (Youtube) of media content, a group of attentive consumers developed a set of videos specialized on the books they read, surpassing the design and purpose of YouTube itself (Jeffman, 2014). "Therefore, it is necessary to go beyond the pre-defined definitions of the site, so that the researcher can understand the peculiarities of their uses and their users" (Jeffman, 2014, p. 3). Booktubers talk about books they like to read, explain why they did so, answer to questions about a set of literary genres and suggest new readings. This way the cocreation of value is highlighted through the videos objectives that "invites a reaction, a criticism, an answer. They generate discussions about specific subjects" (Jeffman, 2014, p. 6). Other users can ask questions while exchanging new information about books. This will influence their own reading and buying of books.

These two cases demonstrate that cultural consumption has been extended by technologies and the multiple role of consumers. They hold the necessary cultural capital to dominate the ICT's but also the necessary legitimization while "specialized consumers" in their cultural fields. With the presence of internet, ICT's and other forms of technology, cultural and tourism mediation changes also, as it seems to be the case mentioned by (Richards, 2013). In terms of authenticity, a negotiation is done between locals and tourists. "The interesting new dimension of this authenticating system is that it happens directly, without intermediaries (although bloggers try hard). Whereas the travel industry used to be the major entry point, now locals themselves can facilitate access by putting their flat on couchsurfing.com or acting as Greeter (Richards, 2013, p. 4). Online user generated content has replaced professional reviewers (Viglia, Minazzi & Buhalis, 2016).

This has repercussions in the promotion of destinations and tourism experiences (Neuhofer, et al., 2012, 2013). "We used to take our (physical) stuff with us, our food, our newspapers, our pubs and just replicate them physically in the destination. Now that we have been freed from stuff by the Internet, and globalisation has also made our physical stuff ubiquitous, we are effectively also free to engage in the local" (Richards, 2013, p. 5). User generated content is replacing guidebooks and other officials sources of information as the authenticating agent for the local (Richards, 2013). "This new source of information on the one hand offers a richer and more varied set of reviews with a significantly wider coverage of products" (Viglia et al., 2016, p. 2035).

No doubt that technology as changed the ways we communicate, share information virtually and create value in the tourism industry.

By embracing ICTs, tourism organizations are able to create enhanced tourism experiences with tourist throughout their journey from early inspiration to the on-site travel experience and post travel recollection in the online world (...) the pre-travel and post-travel stages, as socially intense phases (Gretzel & Jamal, 2009), are predestine for the integration of ICT's to foster interaction and co-creation among tourism providers, tourists and other tourism consumers alike. (Neuhofer et al., 2013, p. 549)

Arguably, creative tourism consists of a type of tourism where these changes are present. Creative tourism literature characterizes creative tourism as a more authentic way of experiencing other cultures and pragmatically developing one's cultural capital near local communities. Both participant actors (supply and demand agents) create value through the process of cocreation and negotiate cultural mediation. "In the process of the development of creative tourism, the experts on tourism, planning and other matters, are mediators" (Molina, 2016, p. 211). In this sense, the concept of cultural capital also has to be updated in the light of the present discussion. Carvalho et al. (2016) argue that several factors influence the current formation of cultural capital such as the Internet, social networks and the new technologies. They conceptualise cultural capital as "specialized knowledge, mediated and recreated by new technologies in the appropriation and cultural usage phases, although influenced by family, school and cultural baggage through a lasting period of time. It is present in a global and experiential network, is shared and revaluated virtually thus remaining updated" (Carvalho et al., 2016).

Because of the generative nature of creative tourism, it presents itself as a coherent paradigm to analyse the role of new cultural mediators and new behaviours on the fruition of cultural and creative experiences, in the light of new technologies. "The future of etourism will be focused on technologies that will help to detect new trends in the consumer behaviour" (Mihajlović, 2014, p. 49). Creative tourism and creative experiences are characterized in the following section.

The Pertinence of Creative Tourism

The participation of the Creative tourism network in the International Congress on World Civilizations and Creative Tourism organized by the UNTWO and the Ministry of Tourism of Bulgaria in November of 2016, resulted in the meeting of ministers of tourism from all over the world "eager to introduce the creative tourism in their strategic development" (Creative Tourism Network, 2014). "Creativity, culture, heritage, economy and society". These several terms are used to characterize creative tourism. The development of this special interest tourism niche is bound to every one of them. "Creative tourism expands the very concept of tourism as a whole, driving a shift from conventional models of heritage-based cultural tourism to new models of creative tourism centred on contemporary creativity, innovation and intangible content" (OECD, 2014, p. 7).

Creative Tourism can be defined as tourism, which offers visitors the opportunity to develop their creative potential through active participation in learning experiences, which are characteristic of the holiday destination where they are undertaken (Richards & Raymond, 2000). This type of tourism is not just based on cultural heritage, but also on the knowledge generated by contemporary creativity by both producers and consumers (OECD, 2014). Creative industries and other creative strategies have been used to help differentiate cities from other touristic destinations due to the massive consumption of tourism in these areas. The creative industries can be defined as "knowledge-based creative activities that link producers, consumers and places by utilising technology, talent or skill to generate meaningful intangible cultural products, creative content and experiences" (OECD, 2014, p. 7).

As culture develops a more central role in society (Urry, 2002), it has grown beyond its original socialization role to become the oil of the new economy and a vital reservoir of symbolic resources (Richards, 2014). In the same way, that cultural tourism has overthrown the sea, sun and sand tourism paradigm, so creative tourism seems to offer something more than cultural tourism, to the postmodern tourist as it thrives to cope with processes of individualization, self-development, and reflexivity and to differentiate consumption choices by using its cultural capital. According to Richards and Wilson (2006) "the rise of skilled consumption, the importance of identity formation and the acquisition of cultural capital in (post) modern society point towards the use of creativity as an alternative to conventional cultural tourism" (Richards & Wilson, 2006, p. 1209).

"Tourism has always involved the consumption of culture" (Richards, 2014, p. 1). This new type of tourism, coined by Richards and Raymond (2000), arguably represents a departure from traditional models of cultural and heritage tourism, moving away from tangible heritage as the key asset towards creative and symbolic capital. (…) Faced with this massification of cultural consumption, many tourists have sought refuge in less tangible forms of cultural consumption that require even higher levels of cultural capital and competence to master (Richards, 2014), when compared with massive cultural tourism forms.

The development of creative tourism had the goal to offer the opportunity for more engaging and authentic experiences to tourists, developed near local communities. This would permit to differentiate this type of consumption from massified forms of tourism such as cultural tourism: based on a "cultural system of museums and monuments [which] where the backbone of tourist consumption as people gathered the symbols of the countries they visited" (Richards, 2014, p. 2). The use of creativity in tourism is not new (Richards & Wilson, 2006, 2007; Richards, 2011, 2012, 2013) as it has been used to develop tourism products and experiences, revitalize cultural and creative assets, provide economic spinoffs for creative development, enhance tourism experiences and to create buzz and atmosphere. The social dimension of creativity is strengthen by the fact that value, in terms of creativity is socially determined within networks (Richards, 2012).

Being "creative tourism a process of postmodernity" (Molina, 2016, p. 210), it offers new ways for local communities to engage in the tourism business. It is based on bottom up approaches established in a system of cocreation between producers and consumers (Richards, 2016), puts local communities in charge of tourism issues (Molina 2016), alerting to the protection of the environment of the destinations helping to improve undeveloped countries. Nonetheless, creative tourism is also important because it uses creativity and renewable immaterial resources to develop destinations and impacts on material resources diminishes, among others (Richards, 2011).

In short, creative tourism is based in an important shift from traditional forms of tourism while suggesting a creative role for both producers (who have to be creative in using resources to develop active participation) and tourists (who need to engage creatively with the destination), (Richards, 2014). Both need to develop their own cultural capital through the process of cocreation (Prahalad & Ramaswamy, 2003, 2004; Binkhorst & den Dekker, 2009). "The study of creative tourism is very recent (Richards, 2011) and research has been developed mainly on the supply side and not enough on the demand side

(Tan et al, 2013)" (as cited in Carvalho, et al, 2015, p. 4). The authors offer us a description of the main characteristics of this niche tourism.

Creative tourism literature is proficuous in indicating several business models. Richards and Wilson's triad (Creative spaces, creative events and creative tourism activities) (2006, 2007); the use of creativity as an activity or as a backdrop, Richards (2011) or the overall creative tourism development portrayed in the OECD (2014) report on Tourism and the creative economy (private sector led initiatives, public sector led initiatives and public and private partnerships). According to Molina (2016), "creative tourism is not based in a unique model which can be reproducible in different environments. If creativity confers power to a place, creative tourism that works successfully in a place can fail in another with similar characteristics if simple transpositions of models occurs. Creative tourism seeks the possibility for each place to structure one unique and not reproducible model" (p. 213). In addition, Richards (2016), points out to vehicles for cocreation in tourism as Courses, Creative spaces, Networks and Events.

As it has been mentioned earlier, the influence of the experience economy and cocreation has been important in the tourism industry as in the case of creative tourism. Because several creative strategies have been developed to help shape cultural and tourism consumption, so the modes of consumption have evolved and mediation has changed. Cocreation gives the consumer more importance in the consumption of experiences as their role as "opinion makers" helps to influence others. Today's social media reviews and user generated content can make the difference in the decision making process of tourism services (Carvalho et al., 2015).

Cocreation enhances the role of the tourist as the co-author of his effective experience. Binkhorst and den Dekker (2009) state that tourism should be considered a global network of cocreation. "Theoretically this would mean: no separation between supply and demand, company and customer, tourist and host, tourism spaces and "other" spaces, but viewing tourism as a holistic network of stakeholders all connected in experience environments in which everyone operates from different time spatial contexts" (Binkhorst & den Dekker, 2009, p. 318). Although (Prahalad & Ramaswamy, 2004; Binkhorst & den Dekker, 2009) conceptualize and mention a greater participation and influence of the demand in the outcome of the experience, the supply side is still very important. In the majority of cases ICT's, the internet and new technologies are used to push forward this type of tourism and develop memorable experiences.

Richards, (2016) sums up two types of experiences. Pine and Gilmore's (1999) "first generation experiences are criticized for being too staged, commercial and artificial and therefore not suitable to today's customers" (Boswijk et al., 2005; Nils & Peter, 2002 as cited in Richards, 2016, p. 2). "The "second generation" of experiences that emerged around the turn of the Millennium were therefore based on cocreation between company and client, enabling customer-driven product development, and, in the context of tourism, more meaningful encounters between tourists and their hosts (e.g. Binkhorst, 2007)"

Table 2. Main characteristics of creative tourism

• Resources used for the development of creative tourism are both tangible and intangible implying a broader use of culture;
• Creative spectacles, creative spaces and creative tourism constitute strategies for the development of this type of tourism in cities;
• Creativity can be used as an activity (e.g. Workshops) and function as a backdrop (e.g. Processions);
• Creative tourism offers the possibility for tourists to develop their creative capital instead of just consuming, as both sides of supply and demand need to develop their creative capital;
• Brings sustainable and profitable development to small communities, where the supply side offers crafts, arts, culinary and other creative activities, thus creating a close link between the tourists, the local population and its cultural heritage.

Source: (Carvalho et al., 2015, pp. 4-5).

(Richards, 2016, p. 3). Mediation in creative tourism seems to be different than it was in cultural tourism. The shift to cultural tourism was marked by the migration of art historians to tourism in order to translate cultural capital into economic capital; we are now seeing the emergence of the ex-pat as a new cultural intermediary (Richards, 2013). The author refers to long stay visitors or expats, "paralocals" which have fixated in some destinations as Dutch expats case of bike hire firms in Barcelona (Richards, 2013). New forms of tourism services that go beyond traditional tours, city buses, and sightseen circuits, among others, have been developed recently (Richards, 2013; Rátz, 2016). In addition, the sharing economy has been an important "place" for the development of new firms and service providers in the tourism sector (Uber, Blablacar, Couchsurfing, and Airbnb, among others).

This makes clear that things have changed since people began using their cultural capital to earn more money from cultural tourism in the 1980s. People are now using relational and locational capital to earn a living. The fact that you are in a particular place that attracts tourists and you can communicate effectively with them is enough. So in theory, any "local" with good communication skills should be able to become a postmodern tourism "switcher." (Richards, 2013, p. 6)

Not only have more directed forms of tourism services providers have been present in creative tourism but also authenticity, cultural capital development and proximity to local communities become tacit.

In this sense, the design of cocreation experiences in tourism implies a number of key elements or qualities: mutual interest, interaction, learning, creativity, and factors, which have largely to do with the way in which people are able to use their own skills in the tourism experience (Richards, 2016). The same author points out such factors as "spaces for dialogue and creativity; narratives linking to the experience world of the tourist; integration of landscape and culture; experiences based on the senses; networks evolving several actors from and outside of the destination while putting local communities in charge (adapted from Richards, 2016).

Despite the fact that, in recent forms of tourism such as creative tourism "the scene of the tourist-host encounter displaces itself from the package hotel, themed attraction of the beach into new settings, such as the home of the local resident, local communities spaces, artist's workshops (…) the roles of "tourist" and "host" disappear, to be replaced by the creative interaction of equals" (Richards, 2016, p. 2). Therefore, new technologies can be put forward to change and improve co-creation interaction, experience design and fruition. Interaction with the consumer is usually generated through blogs and other forms of long-distance interaction (Richards, 2016). This is true if we think about Trip advisor's reviews that, even though gives the opportunity for tourists to engage in the sharing of opinions about accommodation, transport, and restaurants providing services, it doesn't brings a real interaction in the sense defended by the author. Nor the rating star system of Booking.com allows a complete interactive, creative and co-created experience not to mention for example Trivago.com, an accommodation price-comparing website.

"ICT's have drastically changed the nature of the tourism experience by empowering co-creation and extending the space in which experiences can be co-created" (Neuhofer et al., 2012, p. 42). Building on the work of the authors an holistic conceptualisation of Technology Enhanced Destination experiences bases itself in recognizing a co-creation space encompassing (pre, during and post travel phases), physical and virtual co-creation levels and multiple levels of engagement (tourist consumers on destination, tourism suppliers, social networks and co-consumers (Neuhofer et al., 2012). A Fully Technology-Enhanced tourism experience is conceptualised "in reflecting the social, interactive dimension of cocreation and the integration of technology, this experience is realised when a tourist is highly involved, actively participating and co-creating by using various ICT's to empower this very process" (Neuhofer et al., 2013).

In the next section, the authors analyse the www.creativetourismnetwork.org website concerning the theoretical principles portrayed in the previous sections. Co creation processes (C2C), cultural capital presence, and transformation, creative experiences design and mediation are considered using content analyses (Carvalho et al., 2015).

MAIN FOCUS OF THE CHAPTER

Case Study of the Tourism Creative Network

Websites are the result of different types of knowledge, objects, emotions, and activities that are stabilized and assembled on websites and social networking profile (Schatzki 2001; 2002 as cited in Arriagada, 2015). www.creativetourismnetwork.org is the official website of the *Creative Tourism Network,* an international organization created with the aim of fostering Creative Tourism around the world. According to the website, the network was created in Barcelona in 2010, by the Fundação Sociedade e Cultura (FUSIC) which also boosted the pioneering platform Barcelona Turismo Criativo in 2005.

Among the services provided by the organization, the authors point out: "consultancy for the creation and management of destination's creative tourism programs, tailored communication and press services, promotion in fairs and other events, partnerships with tourism and transports companies, cultural associations, recognition as "Creative Friendly Destinations", identification of creative tourists and their motivations, academic and professional training and the development of a Charter for best practices of creative tourism".

Tourism destinations can apply for membership where social media and internet are mentioned as services provided (website, social networks and newsletters development), are important for international connections. In addition, private entities managing projects related to creative tourism can apply. Whether you are individual students, Universities, (future) entrepreneurs, tourist boards, private companies or public bodies, interested in the creative tourism, management-training courses, workshops, masterclasses among others, are offered by the creative tourism network team in the destination to be developed. Among partner cities present in the network we point out Porto Alegre, Brazil; Biot and the region of Louvre-Lens in France; the Province of Namur in Belgium, Barcelona, Ibiza and Lucena in Spain, Saint-Jean-Port-Joli (Quebec) in Canada, Tuscany in Italy, Bangkok in Thailand and Loulé in Portugal. Also direct links to creative platforms are displayed.

The website seems to provide a wide scope of services to whoever seeks to develop their cultural capital on creative and responsible tourism matters. The development of international conferences and expert meetings ensures mediation between physical and virtual networks. The presence of creative platforms helps tourists, tourism enterprises get in touch directly to tourism service providers in the destination undergoing creative tourism development.

Important conferences, lectures, trainings and presentations about creative tourism are listed on the website. News, press articles and press releases shows us the much active creative platform in promotion and events organizations in the partner destinations. Probably one of the most important distinctions developed by this platform is the "Creative Tourism Awards", distinction given to "companies, projects and destinations worldwide" which have distinguished in the development of creative tourism programs in innovative and sustainable tourism.

Table 3. Creative platforms

Cerdeira Village Art&Craft – Portugal www.cerdeiravillage.com	This platform offers artistic residencies and creative retreats services in the natural Portuguese ambience. Also, Master workshops and creative programs (glass decoration, ceramic chalk techniques, Nuno-felting techniques, tile painting and woodcarving).
StudiainItalia www.studiainitaly.com	This Italian agency is specialized in language travel education. It offers language courses, cultural courses, study programs and crafts, fashion, design, jewellery, gastronomy creative activities among others.
Guatemala www.llatzer.com.gt/pages/studytour	Anchored in communitarian tourism principles the Guatemalan platform proposes the study tour Ruta Textil Maya.
Put a face to tourism- Spain www.ponlecaraalturismo.com	The PCAT enterprise suggests activities in the theme of industrial tourism and local initiatives to travel agencies, tour operators and tourists.
EasyFrascati www.easyfrascati.com	This Italian group the tourist courses and creative activities like wine tasting experiences, cookery, drawing and painting courses, barista and photography courses.
Airserve www.airserve.jp/activities-tours/	Creative activities are available in Japan such as home cooking classes, traditional arts, nail technique, organic tea in Kyoto among others.
Creative Tourism Austria http://www.kreativreisen.at/en	The platform divulges crafts workshops, seminars and creative courses, wine and gourmet workshops, cooking courses and others.
Madagascarexplorer www.madagascar-explorer.net	This inbound tour operator offers creative experiences such as woodcarving, silk scarf and the Antemoro paper experience.

Source: (Creative Tourism Network, 2014).

FUTURE RESEARCH DIRECTIONS

Creative tourism research has been done mainly on the supply side, as more research is needed. The ICT's and new technologies have relevant impacts in tourism research, as new cultural mediation seems to offer new ways for tourist to co-create and design creative experiences. New research can be developed in the line of the ones mentioned by the others as new technologies change the nature of tourism experiences and cultural capital creation. Experience design research is one of the most important areas that can help tourism providers and tourist to enhance their experiences in order to develop tourism. Future research perspectives should focus on the analysis of social impact experiences where locals act as cultural mediators and deliver creative experiences while virtually connecting with tourists and leaving their mark on the community (ex. Airbnb social impact experiences). More attention should be paid to specialized consumers in the context of the sharing economy. More research should be developed about how user-generated content and cocreation are being used to exceed websites design and consumer goals.

CONCLUSION

The creative tourism network website offers crucial information about creative tourism and the means to develop creative programs for friendly creative tourism member destinations. Not only develops the means to do so but also puts tourism providers, tourism organizations and other private identities in contact in order to co-create creative experiences. This approach available to everyone is done mainly in a B2C perspective where creative enterprises seek forms to developed and divulge their programs near potential markets. It's a fact that co-creation processes are present in this direct connection, essentially between tourism providers in the search for more authentic and local experiences (Richards, 2016).

The website overcomes distance obstacles by providing not only important information about creative tourism characteristics, tourism destinations and creative platforms but also provides tourism services based in responsible tourism approaches corresponding to creative tourism literature and assuring cultural capital presence. The main goal projected by the online website is accomplished by the realization of numerous events, workshops, training courses, seminars among others, resulting in cultural capital transmission and transformation between social agents. By empowering local providers and tourism firms with important creative capital (reckoning main cultural and creative resources of destinations), the website makes possible the dissemination of best practices. By recognizing best practices and best examples in the creative tourism context, the website acts as a tourism mediator in bringing both sides closer.

Using several ICT's and virtual tools, the creative tourism network establishes important contacts among key partners in the pursuit of tourism design experiences (Richards, 2016). It enhances success rates for creative tourism business by promoting events and workshops where creative and innovate ideas are exchanged. The major influence of the website is indeed a *vis a vis* situation between firms, local tourism providers and creative tourists. Virtual and physical opportunities are given to tourists, enterprises and destinations to develop their creative potential while improving information about who creative tourists are and their motivations (demand) and the right tools to develop creative experiences (supply).

Arguably, creative tourism, a postmodern type of tourism (Molina, 2016) offers new ways for tourism providers, local communities and tourists to co-create authentic experiences (Wang, 1999). ICTs and the internet are crucial in tourism (Neuhofer et al., 2012, 2013) and for the new consumer (Thompson, 2000), where a wider understanding of culture acts as a magnet for destinations to differentiate themselves (Richards & Wilson, 2006, 2007; Richards, 2011). The Creative Tourism Network represents a good example of cultural mediation where experts in creative tourism can design better and sharper experiences near social agents.

Despite allowing the presence, transfer and development of digital capital in the sense of Arriagada and Cruz (2014) this approach is mainly based in B2B and B2C interconnections in the website context. Nonetheless, this capital transfer happens widely in onsite locations and events organization provided by the organization. The website seems to lack a direct link between costumers (C2C) (Rihova, 2013) as the case portrayed by Jeffman (2013, 2014). Here costumers have the opportunity to influence cultural consumption with their opinions and their cultural baggage (Page & Connel, 2009 as cited in Shirt, 2011). While undergoing a culinary creative experience in Loulé in the Algarve, Portugal, the authors of this exploratory research where asked to give their opinion about the overall experience on the Portuguese website. Still this is not yet available in the main creative tourism network website.

Space should be available for creative tourists to share and discuss their creative experiences with other creative costumers by using on sight videos, short testimonies after experience consumption or photo sharing. The website functions as a cultural mediator while bringing together key partners in the creative tourism business and allowing the development of cultural capital among several social agents. Despite the fact that the website fulfils its function, new ways should be made available for creative tourists to share their opinions after the consumption of creative experiences, enhancing even further its purpose. Experience categories can be used to classify or review cultural capital development, creativity usage and creative tourist's experience with new ICT's present on site destinations.

REFERENCES

Arriagada, A. (2014). *Cultural mediators and the everyday making of 'digital capital' in contemporary Chile* (Doctoral Dissertation). Available from LSE Theses Online. Retrieved July 16, 2016, from http://etheses.lse.ac.uk/id/eprint/913

Arriagada, A. (2015). Unpacking the "digital habitus" of music fans in Santiago's indie music scene. In The production and Consumption of Music in the Digital Age. London: Routledge.

Arriagada, A., & Cruz, V. (2014). Music Fans as Mediators in the Age of Digital reproduction. In L. Duits, K. Zwaan, & S. Reijnders (Eds.), *The Ashgate Research campanion to fan cultures* (pp. 149–162). Ashgate Publishing.

Assoun, P. L. (1989). *A Escola de Frankfurt*. Lisboa, Portugal: Editora Dom Quixote.

Barros, V. G. (2015). *Turismo em Portugal*. Lisboa, Portugal: Fundação Francisco Manuel dos Santos.

Baudrillard, J. (1981). *Simulacros e Simulação*. Lisboa, Portugal: Editora Relógio D'Água.

Baudrillard, J. (1998). *The Consumer Society Myths and Structures*. London: Sage Publications. doi:10.4135/9781526401502

Bauman, Z. (2001). *Modernidade Liquida*. Rio de Janeiro, Brasil: Zahar Editor.

Bianchi, M. (2003, June). A Questioning Economist: Tibor Scitovskys Attempt to Bring Joy into Economics. *Journal of Economic Psychology*, *24*(3), 391–407. doi:10.1016/S0167-4870(03)00019-9

Binkhorst, E., & den Dekker, T. (2009). Agenda for Co-creation tourism experience research. *Journal of Hospitality Marketing and Management*, *18*(2-3), 311–327. doi:10.1080/19368620802594193

Bourdieu, P. (1984). *Distinction: A Social Critique of the Judgment of Taste*. London: Routledge.

Bourdieu, P. (1986). The forms of capital. In J. G. Richardson (Ed.), *Handbook for Theory and Research for the Sociology of Education* (pp. 241–258). Academic Press.

Bourdieu, P. (2010). *A Distinção. Uma Crítica Social da Faculdade do Juízo*. Lisboa, Portugal: Edições 70.

Carvalho, R. (2014). A literature review of the role of cultural capital in creative tourism. In *Contemporary Issues in Tourism & Management Studies TMS Conference Series 2014* (pp. 17-28). University of the Algarve, School of Management, Hospitality and Tourism.

Carvalho, R., Costa, C., & Ferreira, A. M. (2015). *Community based tourism festivals in the Médio Tejo Region, Portugal – A potential for the specialized cultural consumption of Creative Tourism*. Paper presented at IV International Congress on tourism – Tourism in the 21st Century, Management School of Polytechnic Institute of Cávado e Ave, Guimarães.

Carvalho, R., Costa, C., & Ferreira, A. M. (2016). *Turismo Criativo – Uma leitura contemporânea de capital cultural*. Communication presented at the PDT Meeting, University of Aveiro.

Charles, S. (2011). O individualismo paradoxal – Introdução ao pensamento de Gilles Lipovetsky. In Os Tempos Hipermodernos. Lisboa, Portugal: Edições 70.

Creative Tourism Network. (2014). Retrieved from http://www.creativetourismnetwork.org/

Giddens, A. (2002). *As consequências da modernidade*. Lisboa, Portugal: Celta Editora.

Heitmann, S. (2011). Authenticity in Tourism. In *Research themes for Tourism* (pp. 45–58). CAB International.

Jeffman, T.M.W. (2013). Redes socias segmentadas: Socialidade, consumo e segmentação na era digital. *Artigo submetido ao NT 1 Sociabilidade, novas tecnologias e práticas internacionais do SIMSOCIAL 2013*. Performances Interacionais e Mediações Sociotécnicas Salvador - 10 e 11 de outubro de 2013.

Jeffman, T.M.W. (2014). Literatura que cabe na tela: Uma análise da cultura participativa, consumo e conexões nos booktubers. *VII Encontro Nacional de Estudos do Consumo, III Encontro Luso-Brasileiro de Estudos do Consumo, I Encontro Latino-Americano de Estudos do Consumo. Mercados Contestados – As novas fronteiras da moral, da ética, da religião e da lei. 24, 25 e 26 de setembro de 2014*, Pontifícia Universidade Católica do Rio de Janeiro (Puc-Rio).

Karlsson, S. (2005). The Social and the Cultural Capital of a Place and their Influence on the Production of Tourism – A Theoretical Reflection based on an Illustrative Case Study. *Scandinavian Journal of Hospitality and Tourism*, *5*(2), 102–115. doi:10.1080/15022250510014408

Lester, J., & Scarles, C. (2013). *Mediating the Tourist Experience. From Brochures to Virtual Encounters*. Routledge Taylor and Francis Group.

Lipovestky. (2007). *A era do vazio: ensaios sobre o individualismo contemporâneo*. Lisboa, Portugal: Relógio d'Agua.

Lipovetsky, G., & Charles, S. (2011). *Os Tempos Hipermodernos*. Lisboa, Portugal: Edições 70.

Lyotard, J. F. (1989). *A condição pós-moderna*. Lisboa, Portugal: Editora Gradiva.

MacLeod, N. (2006). Cultural Tourism: Aspects of Authenticity and Commodification. In M. Smith & K. Robinson (Eds.), *Cultural Tourism in a Changing World. Politics, participation and (re)presentation*. Cleveland, OH: Channel View Publications.

Maguire, J. S., & Mathews, J. (2010). Cultural intermediaries and the media. *Social Compass*, *4*(7), 405–416. doi:10.1111/j.1751-9020.2010.00285.x

Maguire, J. S., & Mathews, J. (2012). Are we all cultural intermediaries now? An introduction to cultural intermediaries in context. *European Journal of Cultural Studies*, *15*(5), 551–562. doi:10.1177/1367549412445762

Mihajlović, I. (2014). ICT and New Trends in Consumer Behaviour – New Experiential knowledge, Opportunities or Challenges for Intermediaries. *Journal of Marketing Management*, *2*(1), 43–64.

Molina, S. (2003). *O Pós-Turismo*. São Paulo, Brasil: Aleph.

Molina, S. (2016). Turismo creativo. *Turismo: Estudos & Práticas*, *5*(1), 205-223.

Neuhofer, B., Buhalis, D., & Ladkin, A. (2012). Conceptualizing Technology enhanced destination experiences. *Journal of Destination Marketing & Management*, *1*(1-2), 36–46. doi:10.1016/j.jdmm.2012.08.001

Neuhofer, B., Buhalis, D., & Ladkin, A. (2013). Experiences, Cocreation and Technology: A conceptual Approach to Enhance Tourism. Tourism and Global Change: On the Edge of something big. *CAUTHE 2013 Conference Proceedings.*

Neves, A., Magalhães, A., & Lourenço, F. (2007). *Oferta educativa e formativa em Turismo: Articulação com o mercado de emprego*. Lisboa, Portugal: Gráfica Europan, Lda.

OECD. (2014). *Tourism and the Creative Economy, OECD Studies on Tourism*. OECD Publishing. 10.1787/9789264207875-en

Pine, J., & Gilmore, J. (1999). Welcome to the Experience Economy. *Harvard Business Review*, 97–105. PMID:10181589

Pölmann, A. (2013). Intercultural Capital: Toward the Conceptualization, Operationalization, and Empirical Investigation of a Rising Marker of Sociocultural Distinction. *SAGE Open*, 3. Retrieved July 7, 2016, from http://sgo.sagepub.com/content/3/2/2158244013486117.full

Pölmann, A. (2016). Habitus, reflexivity, and the realization of intercultural capital: The (unfulfilled) potential of intercultural education. *Cogent Social Sciences*, *2*, 1–12.

Poon, A. (1993). *Tourism, technology and competitive strategies*. Wallingford: CABI.

Prahalad, C. K., & Ramaswamy, V. (2003). The new frontier of experience innovation. *MIT. Sloan Management Review*, *44*(4), 12–18.

Prahalad, C. K., & Ramaswamy, V. (2004). Co- creation experiences: The next practice in value creation. *Journal of Interactive Marketing*, *18*(3), 5–14. doi:10.1002/dir.20015

Prieur, A., Rosenlund, L., & Skjott-Larsen, J. (2008). Cultural Capital Today: A Case Study from Denmark. *Poetics*, *36*(1), 45–71. doi:10.1016/j.poetic.2008.02.008

Prieur, A., & Savage, M. (2011). Updating cultural capital theory: A discussion based on studies in Denmark and in Britain. *Poetics*, *39*(6), 566–580. doi:10.1016/j.poetic.2011.09.002

Prieur, A., & Savage, M. (2013). Emerging Forms of Cultural Capital. *European Societies, 15*(2), 246-267. DOI: 566_58010.1080/14616696.2012.748930

Priuer, A. (2013). Contemporary Cultural Capital: Two New Tendencies; Emerging Cultural Capital and New Forms of Distinction. *Workshop, LSE.*

Rátz, T. (2016, May 29). 'Be global, go local' – Innovation and creativity in the development of alternative guiding services in Budapest. *Journal of Tourism and Cultural Change*, 1-14.

Reisinger, Y. (2009). *International Tourism Cultures and Behavior*. Elsevier Inc.

Ribeiro, A. P. (2015). *Paradoxos da "oferta cultural". In Políticas culturais para o desenvolvimento.* Conferência ARTEMREDE.

Richards, G. (2011). Creativity and Tourism - The state of the Art. *Annals of Tourism Research*, *38*(4), 1225–1252. doi:10.1016/j.annals.2011.07.008

Richards, G. (2012). *Tourism, Creativity and Creative industries*. Paper presented at the Conference Creativity and Creative Industries in Challenging Times, NHTV Breda.

Richards, G. (2013). *Creating relational tourism trough exchange*. Paper present at the ATLAS Annual Conference, Malta.

Richards, G. (2014). *The challenge of creative tourism*. Working draft. February 2014.

Richards, G. (2016). Co-designing experiences with consumers: the case of creative tourism. Input for a workshop on experience design, Tromsø.

Richards, G., & Raymond, C. (2000). Creative Tourism. *Atlas News*, *23*, 16–20.

Richards, G., & Wilson, J. (2006). Developing creativity in tourist experiences: A solution to the serial reproduction of culture? *Tourism Management*, *27*(6), 1209–1233. doi:10.1016/j.tourman.2005.06.002

Richards, G., & Wilson, J. (2007). Tourism development trajectories: from culture to creativity? In G. Richards & J. Wilson (Eds.), *Tourism, creativity e development* (pp. 1–33). Routledge.

Rihova, I. (2013). *Customer-to-customer co-creation of value in the context of festivals* (Doctoral Dissertation). Available from Eprints Bournemouth University. Retrieved December 2, 2016, from http://eprints.bournemouth.ac.uk/21072/

Schatzki, T. (2001). Introduction: Practice Theory. In The Practice Turn in Contemporary Theory (pp. 10-23). London: Routledge.

Schatzki, T. (2002). *The site of the social: a philosophical account of the constitution of social and change*. University Park, PA: The Pennsylvania State University Press.

Scitovsky, T. (1992). *The Joyless Economy: The Psychology of Human Satisfaction* (revised edition). Oxford, UK: Oxford University Press.

Setton, M. G. C. (2005, January/April). Um novo capital cultural: Pré disposições e disposições à cultura informal nos segmentos com baixa escolaridade. *Educ. Soc. Campinas*, *26*(90), 77–105. doi:10.1590/S0101-73302005000100004

Shirt, G. (2011). Cultural Tourism and Accessibility. In P. Robinson, S. Heitmann, & S. Dieke (Eds.), *Research Themes for Tourism* (pp. 160–175). Cabi International.

Silva, F. (2004). *A Quadratura do Circulo. Desenvolvimento, Sustentabilidade, Criação de valor, Emancipação*. Lisboa, Portugal: Editora Caminho.

Smith, M. K., & Robinson, M. (2006). *Cultural tourism in a changing world. Politics, participation and (re)presentation*. Cleveland, OH: Channel View Publications.

Thompson, C. J. (2000). Postmodern Consumer Goals Made Easy. In *The Why of Consumption: Contemporary Perspectives on Consumer Motives, Goals, and Desires* (pp. 118-137). New York: Routledge. Retrieved January 6, 2016, from https://www.researchgate.net/publication/292726261_Postmodern_consumer_goals_made_easy

Urry, J. (2002). *The Tourist Gaze* (2nd ed.). London, UK: Sage.

Viglia, G., Minazzi, R., & Buhalis, D. (2016). The influence of e-word-of-mouth on hotel occupancy rate. *International Journal of Contemporary Hospitality Management*, *28*(9), 2035–2051. doi:10.1108/IJCHM-05-2015-0238

Wang, N. (1999). Rethinking authenticity in tourism experience. *Annals of Tourism Research*, *26*(2), 349–370. doi:10.1016/S0160-7383(98)00103-0

WTO. (1980). Manila Declaration on World Tourism. *World Tourism Conference.*

WTO. (1985). *Tourism bill of rights and tourist code.* General Assembly of the World Tourism Organization, Sofia, Bulgaria.

KEY TERMS AND DEFINITIONS

Co-Creation: Process through which the customer participates in the production and consumption of products, services or experiences.

Creative Experiences: New ways for tourists to engage in cultural experiences based in activities characteristic of the touristic destination where they are undertaken.

Creative Tourism: Special interest tourism alternative to massive forms of cultural consumption of tourism, where the tourists have the possibility to develop their creative capital through engaging with locals.

Creativity: Problem-solving strategy or innovation process used to design more engaging and memorable tourism experiences.

New Cultural Mediators: These new cultural agents endowed with digital capital are present in virtual networks with physical manifestations that influence and change cultural/creative tourism consumption by overcoming traditional cultural production systems.

Specialized Consumption: Reflexive consumption made by conscious consumers who often know more about the experience/service than who is providing them.

Technological Mediated Experiences: Consumer experiences negotiated and enhanced by virtual platforms, websites and the internet where intervenients make use of technology to improve tourism phenomenon.

Chapter 14
"España Verde": Tourism Destination Image among German Facebook Users

Till Maximilian Schuh
University of Algarve, Portugal

Dora Agapito
University of Algarve, Portugal

Patrícia Pinto
University of Algarve, Portugal

ABSTRACT

This study aims at measuring the image of the tourism brand "España Verde" by using the social media platform Facebook. The ever-increasing competition within the tourism industry makes it vital for destinations to address their target group by tailored marketing measures. Furthermore social media channels are changing the interaction between Destination Management Organizations (DMOs) and customers. With the aim of exploring España Verde's image, a three components approach—cognitive, affective and conative was applied. Related to the measurement of the cognitive component, the study also focuses on España Verde's touristic potential ranging from a rich and diverse culture as well as a unique natural heritage to a suitable infrastructure for touristic purposes. Although the supply side seems to fit the target group's desires when choosing a vacation destination, the exploratory results reveal that there is currently only little awareness for España Verde on the German market.

INTRODUCTION

The tourism brand España Verde was founded in 1989 and unites four Spanish autonomous communities - Galicia, Asturias, Cantabria and the Basque Country. The area ranges from the French border, along the northern Spanish coast until the western end of the Iberian Peninsula. The destination is characterized by a broad touristic supply and represents an alternative to the typical "sun and beach" vacations. The brand was founded in order to establish a strong brand image which clearly represents the characteristics

DOI: 10.4018/978-1-5225-2927-9.ch014

of the participating communities (Cano Fuentes, 2006). These autonomous communities consider tourism as an industry that supports mutually the economic development as well as the natural and cultural heritage of the region (Ivars Baidal, 2004).

Tourism destinations like España Verde are competing in an environment where it is vital to be differentiated from competition and to focus on unique selling points (Echtner & Ritchie, 1991). It is of increasing importance to attract the tourist's attention in order to be considered as a possible holiday location (Gartner, 1993). Hence, the destination image held by target markets is essential in order to build and manage a strong tourism brand (Bigné, Sánchez & Blas, 2009; Martín & Bosque, 2008). Additionally, new Information and Communication Technologies (ICTs) are deeply affecting the tourism industry and changing the interaction between destinations and tourists (Buhalis & Law, 2008). New ICTs, as for instance Social Media, provide a broad range of possibilities for destinations such as countries, regions and cities to address customers and to influence their decision - making - process by tailored marketing measures (Stepaniuk, 2015).

In the annual journal "España Hoy" (Spain Today) – published by the Ministry of Presidency – the Spanish State Secretariat for Communication gives a current overview of Spain including descriptions of the measures and decisions undertaken by the government such as the new policy for promoting tourism abroad as committed by the Spanish General Secretariat of Tourism TURESPAÑA. In Spain Today's version of 2015, the first measure of this policy aims to apply new ICTs as well as Social Media, due to the technological advances, which are also affecting the tourism industry. The policy regarding mature markets, as for instance Germany, is to increase the tourist's loyalty and to attract new demand segments demanding products towards art and culture, urban tourism, local gastronomy and nature (Ministry of the Presidency, 2015).

According to the ranking of international tourist arrivals by country of residence, as presented by the National Institute of Statistics (Instituto Nacional de Estadística, 2016), the incoming tourism from Germany to entire Spain amounts to 10,293,964 arrivals or about 15% of the total inbound tourism in 2015. Considering those numbers, Germany is ranked on the third position. Hence, the German market can be considered as a mature market. In view of the tourism supply of España Verde, as outlined at a later stage of this chapter, it becomes evident that its supply side is suitable for the attraction of new demand segments and the diversification of the array of products. Statistics, achieved from the tourism promotion board of Cantabria (CanTur – Sociedad Regional Cántabra de Promoción Turística) show that Germany was ranked on the fourth position regarding the number of tourists who visited España Verde in 2015 between January and September (IET Instituto de Estudios Turísticos, 2015)[1], and can, therefore, be considered as a strategic market for this Spanish destination.

This study aims at analyzing the destination image of the tourism brand España Verde amongst the German market by using a Social Media channel. The results provide the groundwork for the development and application of suitable marketing measures for connecting the destination with its target audience.

This chapter follows the following structure: a) in the background section, a literature review on the destination image construct and related concepts is provided, as well as on the relationship between destination image and social media, which is followed by a summarized presentation of the tourism supply of España Verde; b) the section related to the methodology, presents the objectives and the research questions, followed by the design of the questionnaire, the process for data collection, and the summary of instruments for data analysis; c) in the section data analysis, the results for each of the research questions are depicted ; d) in the discussion and conclusion section, the findings are discussed and the main contributions of this scientific work are presented.

BACKGROUND

Brand Image vs. Brand Identity

The concept of image has already been studied in various scientific fields, including social and environmental psychology, consumer behavior and marketing (Stepchenkova & Morrison, 2008). An object of marketing management is to examine and improve the brand image continuously because the perceived image of a product or a brand is strongly connected to the consumer's buying decision (Ferreira Lopes, 2011). Hence, the management of a proper brand image is a major factor for a company's success (Aaker, 1991). The brand image relates to the perception the customers have of a brand, whereas the brand identity is how the brand aims to be perceived by the customers (Aaker, 1996). Aaker defines brand identity as: "...a unique set of brand associations that the brand strategist aspires to create or maintain. These associations represent what the brand stands for and imply a promise to customers from the organization members. Brand identity should help establish a relationship between the brand and the customer by generating a value proposition involving functional, emotional, or self-expressive benefits." (Aaker, 1996, p. 68)

It is crucial to mention that the image which a customer perceives can vary from the image a marketing campaign wants to implement. There can be considerable differences between a consumer's perception of a brand and its actual performance. Hence, it is vital to analyze the perceived image (Gartner, 1993; Martín & Bosque, 2008). The final perception of an image, even of a holiday destination's image, arises from the interaction of three different components, the cognitive, the affective and the conative behavioral dimension (Agapito, Mendes & Valle, 2010; Ferreira Lopes, 2011; Gartner, 1993; Pike & Ryan, 2004; Stepchenkova & Morrison, 2008).

The Construct of Destination Image

Since the early seventies, this complex and subjective concept of image has also been studied in the field of tourism (Stepchenkova & Morrison, 2008). Basic work was done by Echtner and Ritchie (1991) and Gartner (1993). Echtner and Ritchie introduced the three-dimensional continuum approach, including a functional–psychological, an attribute–holistic as well as a common–unique continuum. Gartner (1993) proposed an approach that contains a cognitive, an affective and a conative component.

The definitions of destination image used in different studies vary a lot. Gallarza, Saura and García (2002, p. 59) claim that "there are almost as many definitions of image as scholars devoted to its conceptualization". Crompton (1979, p. 18) defines destination image as "the sum of beliefs, ideas and impressions that a person has of a destination." Lawson and Baud Bovy (1977, p. 10) believe that it is "...the expression of all objective knowledge, impressions, prejudice, imaginations, and emotional thoughts an individual or group might have of a particular place." According to Bigné, Sanchez and Sanchez (2001), it is the subjective interpretation of reality made by a tourist.

Image Formation and Impact on Travel Decision

The literature proposes several models for understanding the formation process of a destination image, its impact on the travel decision and the related factors of influence. Baloglu and McCleary (1999) argue that the image a person holds of a destination is mainly influenced by personal factors and stimulus factors.

Personal factors split up to psychological factors such as values, motivations and personality and social factors as for instance age, education, marital status and others. Stimulus factors can be distinguished in information sources, previous experience and distribution (Figure 1).

Gunn's model (1988) of seven phases of travel experience deals with the various information sources and their influence on the image formation in the different phases of the model:

1. Accumulation of mental images about vacations experiences
2. Modification of those images by further information
3. Decision to take a vacation trip
4. Travel to the destination
5. Participation at the destination
6. Return home
7. Modification of images based on the vacation experience

Image formation takes place at the phases 1, 2 and 7. During the first phase of the model the potential tourist develops an organic image by gathering non-touristic, non-commercial information such as general media, education or word-of-mouth of family and friends. In the second phase, the organic image is transformed into an induced image under the influence of commercial sources of information as for instance travel brochures, travel agents and travel guidebooks. The last modification of the image takes place in the seventh phase of travel experience. After returning home, the travel experience changes the induced image and adjusts it to reality.

Gartner (1993) identified eight image formation agents which determine the process of image formation. Those agents are the different sources, channels or persons which spread information about a destination towards a potential tourist. The author argues the right mix of formation agents should be individually selected for each destination and depends on the available budget, characteristics of the target market, demographic characteristics, the right timing as well as the projected type of image. The researcher also claims that a destination should attract the awareness of the decision taker to be considered as a possible alternative and should implement a favorable image in the customer's mind in order to pass the competitive evaluation process.

Figure 1. Framework of destination image formation
Baloglu & McCleary, 1999.

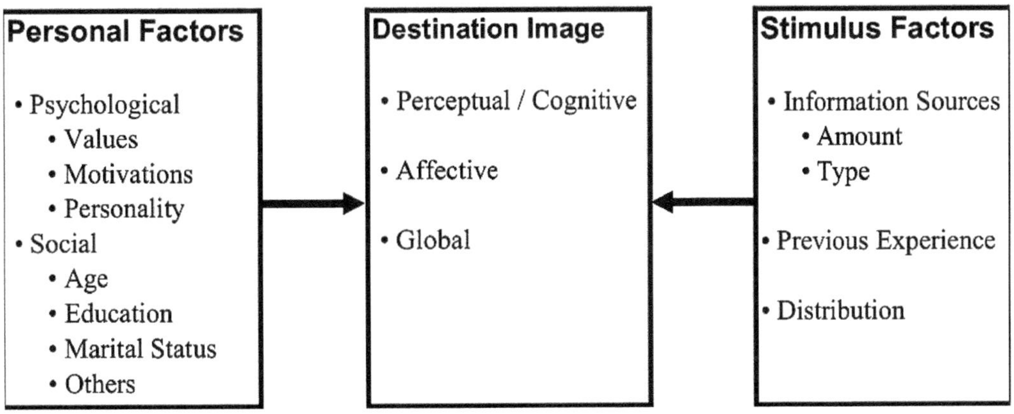

Those remarks underline that there is a substantial coherence between the image of a touristic destination and the consumption decision of a potential customer (Ferreira Lopes, 2011; Hunt, 1975; Pearce, 1982). Therefore, it is crucial for destinations to determine their unique selling points (Echtner & Ritchie, 1991) and to develop a strong brand image for taking influence in the decision-making process of a tourist (Gartner, 1993). Thus, destinations can assert themselves in a more and more competitive market (Echtner & Ritchie, 1991; Martín & Bosque, 2008).

Destination Image and Social Media

The Spanish General Secretariat of Tourism TURESPAÑA has committed a new policy for promoting tourism abroad (Ministry of the Presidency, 2015). The first measure of this policy aims to apply new ICTs as well as Social Media, due to the technological advances, which are also affecting the tourism industry. Buhalis and Law (2008, p. 610) underline that "Not only do ICTs empower consumers to identify, customize and purchase tourism products but they also support the globalization of the industry by providing effective tools for suppliers to develop, manage and distribute their offerings worldwide." Estêvão, Carneiro and Teixeira identified four dimensions where eTourism – the application of new ICTs within the tourism sector – facilitates the interaction between Destination Management Organizations (DMOs) and customers, namely information, communication, relationship and transaction (2014). Especially for information and communication, Social Media platforms such as Facebook provide convenient features to link with the target group and promote user-generated content as for instance videos, photos, blogs or comments (Mariani, Di Felice & Mura, 2016). According to Kim and Johnson (2016), website stimuli and brand related user-generated content influence the consumer's emotions and cognitions and thus the willingness to pass-along information. Functions such as clicking "like" or "share" and the possibility to post contents on a friend's Facebook will facilitate word-of-mouth recommendation. Thereby Social Media platforms enable DMOs to address information to the customer's cognitive and affective perception and thus to influence their behavioral intensions (Stepaniuk, 2015) with higher efficiency but lower costs than with traditional media (Kaplan & Haenlein, 2010; Királ'ová & Pavlíčeka, 2015). For those reasons, Social Media's role in destination marketing is of increasing importance and DMOs must adjust their marketing measures to the potentials arising from the use of Social Media platforms as destination marketing tools (Mariani et al., 2016; Pike & Page, 2014). This justifies the investigation of a destination's image among Social Media users, as this group can be reached and positively influenced in their perception of a specific destination.

The Three Components Approach

The image of a destination is a composition of multiple components and influences (Baloglu & McCleary, 1999; Echtner & Ritchie, 1991; Gartner, 1993) and can be viewed from different perspectives. As brought up in a previous section, basic work towards the conceptualization and measurement of destination image was done by Echtner and Ritchie (1991) as well as Gartner (1993). Both studies consider a destination's image as a construct, composed by the cognitive evaluation of attributes as well as a customer's general feeling towards a certain destination. As this study applies Gartner's approach, the following comments refer to the three components of destination image - the cognitive component, the affective component as well as the conative component.

- **The Cognitive Component:** The cognitive component refers to the beliefs or the knowledge a potential tourist holds towards the characteristic attributes of a destination (Agapito et al., 2010; Baloglu & McCleary, 1999; Chen & Phou, 2013; Ferreira Lopes, 2011; Gartner, 1993). The characteristic attributes of the cognitive component are directly observable, descriptive and measurable (Chen & Phou, 2013; Walmsley & Young, 1998).
- **The Affective Component:** The affective component stresses the feelings and emotional responses towards the features of a destination (Agapito et al., 2010; Baloglu & McCleary, 1999; Chen & Phou, 2013; Ferreira Lopes, 2011). The influence of the cognitive component on the affective component has been approved by Agapito et al. (2013).
- **The Conative Component:** The conative component refers to the behavioral manifestation from the tourist side (Chen & Phou 2013, Gartner, 1993; Pike & Ryan, 2004) and determines if a tourist plans to revisit the destination or to suggest it to friends or family (Agapito et al., 2010; Pike & Ryan, 2004). According to Agapito et al. (2013), the conative component is influenced by the cognitive as well as the affective perception a tourist has of a destination.

The Measurement of Destination Image

Two basic methodologies can be applied in order to measure a destination's image; structured methods or unstructured methods. Most of the previous destination image studies focused on structured methods, but there is a common agreement among tourism destination image researchers, that structured and unstructured methodologies should be combined, in order to capture the image of a destination. (Baloglu & McCleary, 1999; Echtner & Ritchie, 1993; Jenkins, 1999).

Structured Methodologies

Structured methods measure the destination image based on attributes which are evaluated on scales. The attributes which were used in previous studies by tourism destination image researchers for measuring the cognition differ a lot, due to the idiosyncrasies of the destinations as well as the different methods applied for the selection process. A problem in designing a list is the validity of the selected attributes. Approaches towards the development of such a list can be either the use of secondary sources such as literature reviews and opinions of experts or a qualitative research with consumers (Echtner & Ritchie, 1991).

The affective as well as the conative component can also be measured on scales. According to Russel, Ward and Pratt (1981) two independent bipolar scales ranging from unpleasant to pleasant and sleepy to arousing are appropriate for the measurement of an individual's affective perception of a specific place (Agapito et al., 2010; Beerli & Martín, 2004a). The conative component can be analyzed by asking the participants of a survey to state their revisit intention as well as their willingness to recommend the destination to friends and family on a scale (Agapito et al., 2010, Pike & Ryan, 2004).

Unstructured Methodologies

As mentioned before, unstructured methods should be conducted as well for the measurement of a destination's image. By using open-ended questions, the participants of a survey are allowed to think freely about a destination and to submit their impressions or beliefs without the constraint of a scale. Echtner and Ritchie (1993) formulated three open-ended questions which can be used in destination image studies:

- What images or characteristics come to your mind when you think of XXX as a vacation destination?
- How would you describe the atmosphere or mood you would expect to experience while visiting XXX?
- Please list any distinctive or unique tourist attractions you can think of in XXX.

The Tourism Supply of España Verde

The following comments refer to the supply of the tourism brand España Verde. In order to explore the supply of this destination, an analysis of the official websites of the tourism promotion boards of the four autonomous communities was conducted due to the fact that a common website still does not exist. The examined websites are: turismo.gal, turismoasturias.es, turismodecantabria.com and turismo.euskadi.eus. Furthermore, the tourism boards were contacted in order to collect information regarding the supply and characteristics of the area. In this context, the tourism promotion board of Cantabria provided an unpublished brochure "Green Spain – The spirit of the North Press Kit"[2]. Furthermore, sources such as official publications were considered as well. It must be mentioned that it is beyond the scope of this study to give a comprehensive overview of all components which constitute the supply of España Verde. This section merely aims to give an impression of the supply side of the research area.

The area is topographically dominated by the Basque Mountains and the Cantabrian Range (Ministry of the Presidency, 2014). The Cantabrian Mountains proceed 460 km along the coast, and their altitude varies from 2,128 m (Peña Trevinca) in the Trevinca Massif to 1,548 m (Aizkorri) in the Basque Mountains. The highest peak, Torre Cerrado, has a height of 2,648 m and rises in the Picos de Europa, an area located about 20 km away from the coast with many peaks above 2,000 m (Rodríguez-Rodríguez, Jiménez-Sánchez, Domínguez-Cuesta & Aranburu, 2015).

The Basque Country, Asturias, Cantabria and Galicia are located in the Bay of Biscay. The western seaside of Galicia looks to the Atlantic Ocean. The entire length of España Verde's coastline amounts to 1,966 km (CanTur, 2015), representing about 40% of the Spanish coastline, compared with the entire length of 5,755 km (Ministry of the Presidency, 2014). The coastline contains 1.042 beaches. The total area amounts to 52,608 km^2. There are 424 protected areas located within this region, which constitute about 30% of the entire area (CanTur, 2015).

The area of España Verde contains 14 biosphere reserves, 25 nature parks as well as three national parks (CanTur, 2015). The "Parque Nacional Picos de Europa" which was founded in 1918 and reclassified in 1995 ranges over a territory of 671,27 km2. It was the first national park founded in Spain (Organismo Autonomo Parques Nacionales, 2014).

España Verde's climate is Atlantic or oceanic, due to the proximity to the Atlantic Ocean (Ministry of the Presidency, 2014). The vegetation of the green Spain is dominated by rich grasslands and groves of broadleaves species. It also has a very rich fauna, including species such as wolves, chamois, roe deer and capercaillies. There is a great number of marine bird species living along the coast and even eagles, vultures and goshawks can be found on the territory (CanTur, 2015). Endangered species as the Cantabrian Brown Bear find protection in the natural parks (Ministry of the Presidency, 2014).

Six international airports are located in the area of España Verde. These airports provide connections to 35 European cities. There are direct flights from the German Cities Frankfurt, Düsseldorf and Munich to España Verde. The connection by car is provided by the A8 motorway, which leads along the coast from Galicia until the Basque Country (CanTur, 2015). The Spanish National Railway Network (renfe) provides connections from Madrid to all capitals of the autonomous communities. Besides, the sightseeing train "Transcantabrico" connects San Sebastian with Santiago de Compostela (TURESPAÑA, 2016).

The tourism destination España Verde offers a wide range of hotels and accommodation facilities. There are about 1,976 Hotels with 122,104 places, 243 campsites with 103,450 places, 667 tourist apartments with 19,999 places, 2,068 boarding houses with 38,395 places, 3,452 rural lodging facilities with 41,291 places, 32 Spas, 11 Thalassotherapy centres and 19 National state-run luxury hotels. There are 46 restaurants with overall 56 Michelin Starts. The Basque Country is, together with Catalonia, the region with the highest amount of Michelin Stars of entire Spain. Besides, España Verde is an outstanding location for wine tourism. There is a new route for visiting palaces and wine cellars all across the four autonomous communities (CanTur, 2015).

The cultural supply of España Verde is determined by the strong regional identities of the autonomous communities. This diversity finds expression, for instance in three different languages which are spoken within the territory. Besides, Castellano, the regular Spanish language as it is generally spoken in Spain, there are considerable parts of the population speaking Galician language and Basque language. The Galician language is a romance language. It is spoken by about 4.5 million people and has, besides Castellano, an official status in Galicia (Gonzáles Gonzáles, Rodríguez Banga, Campillo Díaz, Méndez Pazó, Rodríguez Liñares & Iglesias Iglesias, 2008). The Basque language is named Euskara and it is considered as an isolated language. Euskara is not an Indo – European language and its origin is still unexplored (Mercador, 2008). Although there are just about 800,000 Basque speakers, it has an official status in the Basque Country (Echeverria, 2010).

España Verde offers a wide range of cultural sites as for instance the city Donostia-San Sebastian which is designated as the European Capital of Culture 2016 by the European Union (EU). There are 18 caves with Palaeolithic paintings located on España Verde's territory which are declared as World Heritage Sites by the UNESCO. Furthermore, Green Spain offers cultural and historic sites such as the "Guggenheim Museum" in Bilbao, the "Painted Forest" created by the Basque painter and sculptor Augustin Ibarrola or the Cathedral of Santiago de Compostela. The City is the final destination of the "Way of St. James" and is also declared as a World Heritage Site. The northern route of the St. James Way proceeds along the coast across entire España Verde (CanTur, 2015).

The north of Spain offers numerous outdoor sports facilities, due to its location upon the Cantabrian Sea as well as to the topography of the landscape. There are outstanding conditions for sports such as hiking, mountaineering, climbing, canyoning, canoeing and mountain biking. Furthermore, the region is equipped with 53 golf courses (CanTur, 2015). The Basque Country is a famous surf area with surf spots such as San Sebastian, Getxo, Zarautz, Sopelana, Bakio and Mundaka.

International Festivals take place in España Verde. Particularly mentionable are the Santander International Festival (FIS) and the San Sebastian International Film Festival (Zinemaldia). The Santander International Festival deals with culture and performing arts and tries to keep a balance between tradition and innovative trends. The Zinemaldia Festival is one of the most relevant film festivals in Europe (CanTur, 2015).

METHODOLOGY

This study aims to analyze the image of the tourism brand España Verde among German Facebook users following the three components approach as introduced by Gartner (1993). In order to reach the aforementioned research objective, the following main questions were formulated:

- Which attributes should be addressed for the measurement of the cognitive component of España Verde?
- To what extent is the German market aware of the destination España Verde?
- What is important for the target group when choosing a holiday destination and what does this group associate with España Verde?
- Are there significant differences regarding the perception of España Verde between people who already visited the destination and people who did not?

Unstructured as well as structured methods (Jenkins, 1999) were applied for the measurement of España Verde's image. A three-step process became passed through in order to develop a questionnaire that captures the cognitive component, the affective component as well as the conative component of destination image. First of all, a literature review of the essential destination image literature was conducted. According to this literature review, the three components approach of Gartner (1993) was found appropriate for measuring España Verde's image. A first list of attributes was identified in order to find out the cognitive component. Furthermore, questions for capturing the affective and conative component were included according to the literature and a first draft of the questionnaire was developed. In a second step, the tourism supply of the research area was determined in order to adjust the list of attributes to the territory of España Verde. In a third step, the list that arose from this process was sent to a tourist promotion board of the research area for verification. After this procedure, the questionnaire was distributed via the Social Media platform Facebook. The results were analyzed by using the programs Excel, SPSS, NVivo as well as the word-cloud generator Tagxedo.

Development of the Questionnaire

Measuring the Cognitive Component

Gallarza et al.'s list of attributes (2002) was chosen as a starting point for the development of a suitable list of attributes that fits the characteristics of the research area. In a first step, those attributes were selected, which were used in at least 50% of the studies, namely: landscape/surroundings, cultural attractions, nightlife/entertainment, shopping facilities, sports facilities, accommodation, gastronomy, price/value/cost and resident's receptiveness.

The second step dealt with the adjustment of the list to the research area as the attributes must cover the characteristics of the setting. Therefore, the tourism supply of España Verde was identified as described in the regarding section. Relevant contents concerning the supply were categorized. The initial categories were determined according to the attributes selected from Gallarza et al.'s (2002) collocation. Thereby, attributes which fit the research area but were excluded from the list due to the 50% restriction could be added, and attributes which do not fit the area could be adjusted or excluded. Furthermore, the breakdown of the supply made it possible to identify attributes which were not included in Gallarza et al.'s initial list due to their specific relation to España Verde.

The outcome was a list containing 18 attributes covering the universal features of the cognitive component of a destination's image as well as the specific characteristics of España Verde. In order to ensure the completeness and the validity, the list was sent to the tourism promotion board of Galicia, since in 2016 the "Agencia Turismo de Galicia" is the coordinator among the autonomous communities which are involved in España Verde. The list was supplemented and approved by tourism experts of the research area. Therefore it can be considered as appropriate for measuring the cognitive component of España Verde's image.

The participants of the study were asked to evaluate the performance of the destination related to each attribute, either according to their knowledge, for instance from personal experience, or according to their imagination of España Verde as a vacation destination on five-point Likert scales, as applied by Agapito et al. (2010), Baloglu and McCleary (1999), Bigné et al. (2009) and Stepchenkova and Morrison (2008). The scales range from 1 (very low level) to 5 (very high level). Afterwards, the mean of each attribute was calculated.

Measuring the Affective Component

Two seven-point semantic scales were used for the measurement of the affective component as applied by Agapito et al. (2010) and Beerli and Martín (2004b). As suggested by Russel et al. (1981), two independent bipolar dimensions were considered as sufficient and therefore appropriate to capture the affective perception an individual holds of a specific place such as a travel destination. According to Russel et al. (1981), the scales should range from unpleasant to pleasant and from sleepy to arousing. Indeed, the participants in this study were asked to evaluate their feelings towards a stay at the vacation destination España Verde on scales which range from unpleasant to pleasant as well as from sleepy to exciting.

The variation of the adjective "arousing" is due to the different linguistic usage in Germany. As the questionnaire had to be translated into German in order to ensure its comprehensibility, it was important to translate the adjectives according to their actual meaning.

Measuring the Conative Component

Measuring the conative component aims at investigating the behavioral intentions a person has in terms of willingness to repeat a trip and in terms of willingness to give recommendations to other people (Boulding, Karla, Staelin & Zeithaml, 1993). In this context, two statements were added to the questionnaire: (1) I can imagine spending my holidays again in España Verde within the next two years. (2) I would recommend España Verde to my friends and family as a vacation destination. Following Bigné et al. (2009), Pike and Ryan (2004) as well as Agapito et al. (2010), the participants were asked to state their level of agreement on two five-point Likert scales which range from "strongly disagree" to "strongly agree".

Open Ended Questions

Additional to the aforementioned methods for capturing the three components of the destination image, two open-ended questions were added to the questionnaire. The first open-ended question (What is important for you when choosing a holiday destination?) aimed to find out terms and expressions of specific importance for the participants in their decision-making process when choosing a holiday destination. The second question (Which characteristics come to mind when you think of España Verde as a vacation destination?) was added in order to give the participants the possibility to think freely about the location and to submit their impressions or thoughts of España Verde without the boundaries of a scale. The latter one follows the first one of the open-ended questions as suggested by Echtner and Ritchie (1993). For reasons of clarity and comprehensibility, the participants were asked to answer both questions with three terms or expressions.

Previous Experience

When comparing the statistics of German tourist arrivals to España Verde with the arrivals to entire Spain, one can assume that the research area is not very well known on the German market. Therefore it is of distinct relevance for this study to find out whether the participants had visited the research area already before, respectively, the reasons they had for not visiting España Verde.

Therefore, the participants were asked to state if they already had visited the destination and afterwards, in case of a negative answer, they were asked to select from three possible reasons for not visiting, namely: (1) I have never heard anything about this travel destination, (2) This travel destination is not interesting for me and (3) Other reason.

Data Collection

The Social media platform Facebook was chosen for the distribution of the questionnaire for two reasons. First of all, because of the aforementioned outstanding features, Facebook offers for interacting with customers; secondly, because of Facebook's reach among Social Media users in Germany. The public relations consulting agency for enterprise and sales communication "Faktenkontor GmbH" publishes an annual report about the Social Media usage in Germany in collaboration with the IMWF institute for management and economic research and the panel provider Toluna. The base of the study is a representative online panel survey among 3,500 internet users. Some of the results for 2015 are published on the website of the Faktenkontor GmbH. According to the study, 87% of German Social Media users were also using Facebook. Only the video platform YouTube attained a higher result of 88% (Faktenkontor GmbH, 2016). Therefore Facebook was selected as its features are more suitable for destination marketing measures.

The questionnaire was created with the tool Google Forms. A pre-test among 10 persons was conducted in order to eliminate obscurities regarding the questions and problems with the functionality of Google Forms. Afterwards, the questionnaire was sent to 30 persons. It was tried to implement a pyramid scheme (snowball technique), so those people were asked to respond and then to pass along the questionnaire to other people and so on. Additionally, the questionnaire was posted into four public Facebook groups for surveys.

Instruments for Data Analysis

In the aftermath of the distribution of the questionnaire and the collection of replies, the data were transformed from Google Forms into Excel-sheets. Afterwards, the data were analyzed with the program IBM SPSS Statistics 22. Methods of descriptive statistics were used in order to provide an initial characterization of the sample.

The frequency of socioeconomic variables as well as variables concerning the previous experience the participants had with España Verde were measured and the results were visualized in tables and charts.

Furthermore, the means of the attributes were calculated and provided in a table containing an overall column, a column with replies from people who had already visited the destination as well as a column of people without previous experience with the research area. The Mann-Whitney test was applied, and the p-values were analyzed in order to assess if the means show significant differences between the groups of visitors and non-visitors[3].

In order to interpret the results of the open-ended questions, the terms and expressions mentioned by the participants were grouped into categories with a common meaning. For instance, the terms "sun", "nice weather" and "climate" were summarized under the term "good weather". The software NVIVO was used in order to count the frequency of specific words and to determine their weighted percentage in relation to the overall amount of terms mentioned.

In order to visualize the results, the words mentioned more than five times were presented in word-clouds. The clouds were made with the online word-cloud generator Tagxedo.

DATA ANALYSIS

Sociodemographic Characteristics

The sociodemographic characteristics of the survey participants are presented below. As this study aims to analyze the destination image of the tourism brand España Verde on the German target market, the sample was collected among German Facebook users. By using a filter, replies of people with another than German nationality could be removed from the sample afterwards. The entire amount of collected replies amounts to 206 (Table 1).

The distribution regarding gender shows that an almost balanced sample could be achieved. In numbers, 101 replies out of the total amount were achieved from men compared to 105 replies from women (Figure 2). This distribution exactly corresponds the gender-ratio of German citizens in 2015 (Destatis, 2016) and therefore benefits the study, since all members of a strategic market, independently of their gender, can be considered as potential customers. Within the group of visitors, 40.7% (11) are males,

Table 1. Socio-demographic characteristics of the sample

Variables	Distribution of Answers
Nationality	German: 100 %
Gender	Female: 51 %; Male: 49 %
Age	18-24: 19.5 %; 25-34: 55.1 %; 35-44: 11.2 % 45-54: 8.8 %; 55+: 5.4 %; mean: 31.7; Std. 10.122
Educational Level	Hauptschule: 1.5 %; Realschule: 13.1 % Gymnasium: 30.1 %; University: 55.3 %

Figure 2. Distribution of visitors compared to non-visitors within the groups of gender

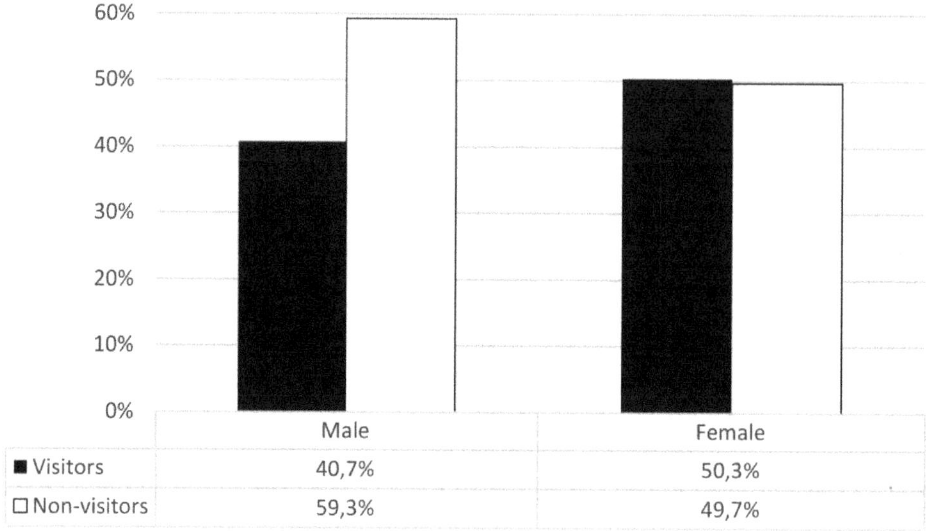

whereas 59.3% (16) are females. Among the non-visitors, 50.3% (90) are men compared to 49.7% (89) of respondents that are women.

Regarding age, people between 18 - 24 as well as 25 - 34 represent the largest groups. In numbers, the group 18 - 24 contains 40 persons, the group 25 - 34 comprises 114 persons, the group 35 - 44 contains 23 persons, the group 45 - 54 comprises 18 persons, and the group 55+ contains 11 persons. The mean regarding age is 32 years old, and the standard deviation is 10.122. Replies of people younger than 18 years were not collected.The figure below shows the age distribution among the visitors and the non-visitors. In numbers, the group 18 - 24 contains four persons, the group 25 - 34 comprises 15 persons, the group 35 - 44 contains five persons, the group 45 - 54 comprises one person and three people among the visitors are older than 55. The non-visitors group of 18 - 24 comprises 36 persons, the group 25 - 34 contains 100 persons, the group 35 - 44 comprises 18 persons, the group 45 - 54 contains 17 persons and 8 persons among the non-visitors are over 55 years old (Figure 3).

For visualizing the different educational levels of the survey participants, the groups were arranged according to the main steps of education in Germany. The first three groups namely "Hauptschule", "Realschule" and "Gymnasium" constitute the school education in Germany[4]. Those terms were not translated, due to the lack of corresponding expressions in English. The fourth group represents people holding an academic degree. The sample contains 55.3% academics compared to 44.7% non-academics. In numbers, the sample comprises 3 graduates of the Hauptschule, 27 graduates of the Realschule, 62 graduates of the Gymnasium as well as 114 university graduates. A graphic of the educational level of the groups of visitors, non-visitors and people who never have heard of España Verde is presented below. It becomes evident that the percentage of people holding an academic degree is higher among the visitors than among the groups of non-visitors and people who have never heard of the destination (Figure 4).

Figure 3. Distribution of age within the groups of visitors and non-visitors

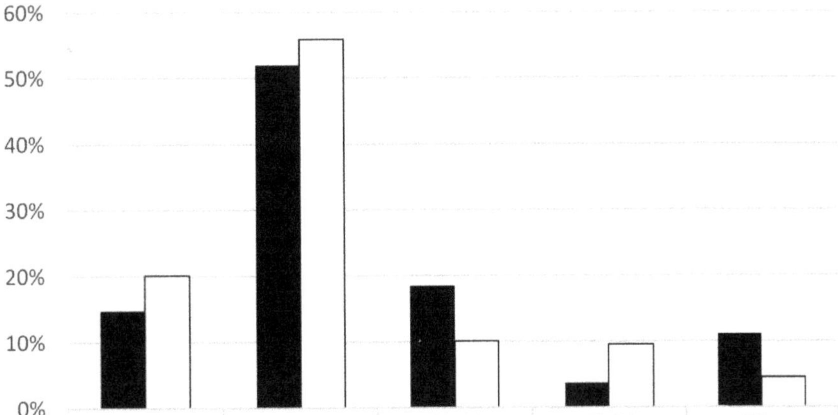

	18-24	25-34	35-44	45-54	55+
■ Visitors	14,8%	51,9%	18,5%	3,7%	11,1%
□ Non-visitors	20,1%	55,9%	10,1%	9,5%	4,5%

Figure 4. Educational level of the different groups

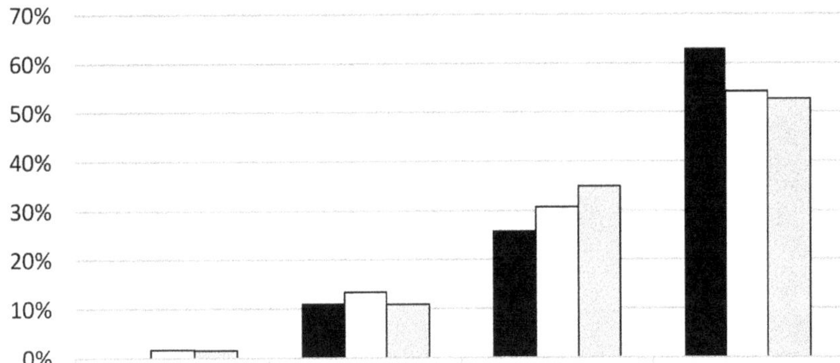

	Hauptschule	Realschule	Abitur	University
■ Visitors	0,0%	11,1%	25,9%	63,0%
□ Non-visitors	1,7%	13,4%	30,7%	54,2%
□ Never heard of "España Verde"	1,6%	10,9%	34,9%	52,7%

Previous Experience in "España Verde"

This section aims to explore to what extent the participants of the survey have experience with the research area as it can explain differences in the evaluation of the destination's performance. Furthermore, important information regarding the revisit intention and the willingness to give recommendation can be achieved by identifying the people who already travelled to España Verde and thus the conative component of destination image can be analyzed. Therefore, the participants were asked to state if they had already visited one of the four autonomous communities: Galicia, Asturias, Cantabria and the Basque Country. The results show a strong ascendance of non-visitors, since 86.9% (179 persons) did not visit España Verde compared to 13.1% (27 persons) who already visited the research area (Figure 5).

When asking the non-visitors for their reasons, 72.5% stated that they had never heard of España Verde, 23% stated that they are not interested in this destination and 4.5% had other reasons for not visiting the research area. In numbers, 130 persons had not heard of it, 41 persons are not interested, and 8 respondents stated other reasons (Figure 6).

Figure 5. Previous experience in "España Verde"

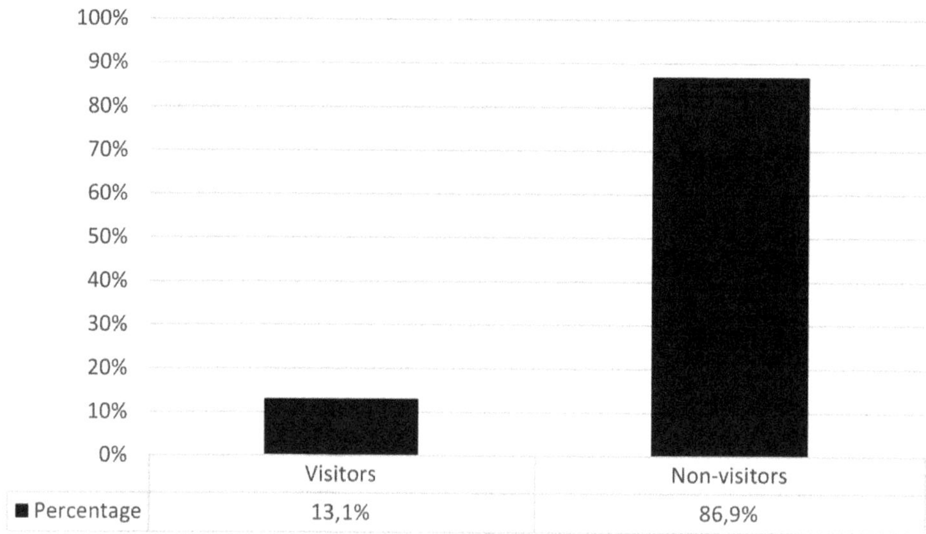

Figure 6. Reasons for not visiting the destination

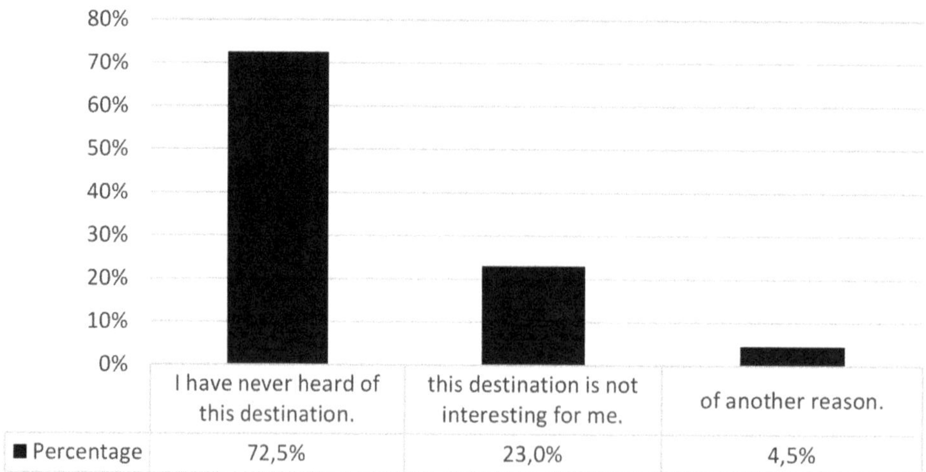

Open-Ended Questions

This section refers to terms and expressions which are important factors for the participants when choosing a holiday destination (What is important for you when choosing a holiday destination?). Overall, 596 terms were stated. In Table 2 as well as in the word-cloud shown in Figure 7, the terms respectively expressions which were mentioned more than five times by the survey participants are presented. Those ones mentioned more often are presented in the word-cloud in larger letters. For instance, the term "good weather" represents 14.6% of the overall amount of terms and is therefore written in bigger letters than "culture", which just represent 7.9% of the overall amount. The terms most important for the participants (terms which represent more than 5% of the overall amount of terms) are: good weather, culture, beach, costs, landscape and sea.

The results of the first open-ended question explain which criteria are important for the survey participants in their decision-making process. In spite of the subjective nature of the evaluation of a destination's performance regarding a specific attribute, it becomes evident that there are many similarities between the preferences of the German target group and the tourism supply of the destination España Verde. This can be seen by comparing the chapter "Tourism supply" with the above-noted results. Furthermore, it becomes apparent that España Verde's supply side fits TURESPAÑA's objectives regarding mature markets, as presented in the publication "Spain today 2015". Table 3 illustrates those coherences.

Table 2. Important criteria in the decision-making process

Word	Weighted Percentage (%)	Word	Weighted Percentage (%)
Good weather	14.6	Safety	2.3
Culture	7.9	Quiet	1.8
Beach	5.7	Sport facilities	1.7
Costs	5.4	Surroundings	1.7
Landscape	5.4	Location	1.5
Sea	5.0	Child-friendly	1.3
No mass tourism	4.2	Experience	1.3
Sights	4.0	Value for money	1.3
Leisure activities	3.5	Excursions	1,2
Nature	3.4	Diversity	1.0
Recreation	2.8	Cleanliness	0.8
People	2.8	Infrastructure	0.8
Gastronomy	2.7	Language	0.8
Accessibility	2.3		

Figure 7. Word-cloud of important criteria in the decision-making process

Table 3. Comparison of TURESPAÑA's objectives, España Verde's supply side and important criteria for the target group

Policy for Promoting Tourism Abroad - Spain Today 2015	Tourism Supply of España Verde	Important Criteria when Coosing a Vacation Destination
	- World heritage sites	- Culture
"...and attracting new demand	- 1.042 Beaches	- Beach
segments that consume	- Ca. 40% of Spanish coastline	- Landscape
products other than traditional	- Cantabrian mountains	- Sea
tourism products (art and	- Wildlife	- Sights
culture, urban tourism, Spanish	- Surfing, Hiking, Golf, etc…	- Leisure activities
gastronomy, nature and	- Wine, Cidra, Pintxos	- Nature
conference tourism)."	- 56 Michelin Stars	- Gastronomy
(Ministry of the Presidency,	- Six international airports	- Accessibility
2015)	- Hotels, rural losging, etc…	- Sports facilities
	- (see chapter tourism supply)	- Infrastructure

The second open-ended question (Which images or characteristics come to mind when you think of España Verde as a vacation destination?) enabled the participants to think freely about the destination and to state terms or expressions they associate with España Verde. Those expressions can originate from knowledge, beliefs or imagination. The total amount of terms stated sums up to 458. Table 4, as well as the word-cloud in Figure 8, show the terms and expressions which were mentioned more than five times. The terms, the participants associate the most with España Verde (terms which represent more than 5% of the overall amount of terms) are: good weather, sea, landscape, green, mountains, nature, beach.

The word-cloud of the second open-ended question illustrates the people's associations with España Verde. When comparing the results with the frequently mentioned terms and expressions of the first open-ended question one can observe a number of coherences. The survey participants associate 10 terms with the destination, which are also important in their decision-making process, namely: good

Table 4. Associations with "España Verde"

Word	Weighted Percentage (%)	Word	Weighted Percentage (%)
Good weather	13.1	Forest	2.0
Sea	8.7	People	1.7
Landscape	7.9	Wine	1.5
Green	7.0	Green Spain	1.3
Mountains	6.3	Coast	1.3
Nature	6.1	Quiet	1.3
Beach	5.2	No mass tourism	1.1
Gastronomy	3.5	Rural	1.1
Recreation	3.1	Tapas	1.1
Spain	2.6		

Figure 8. Word-cloud of associations

weather, sea, landscape, nature, beach, gastronomy, recreation, people, quiet, no mass tourism. In spite of the threat of people making connections between both open-ended questions, the results indicate that the participants assume España Verde to be suitable to plenty of their desires.

Measuring the Cognitive Component

This section aims to analyze the cognitive component of destination image. All participants, visitors as well as non-visitors, were asked to evaluate the destination's performance regarding each attribute on Likert-scales ranging from 1 (low-level rating) until 5 (high-level rating).

The results were separated according to the different groups, the values were added up and the means were calculated. For analyzing if there are significant differences between the ratings of people who already visited the destination and people who did not, the Mann-Whitney test was applied. This test was chosen due to the small sample size of the group of non-visitors. Twelve of these differences are statistically significant at a 10% significance level ($p < 0.10$). The final results are presented in Table 5.

When looking at the overall results, it becomes obvious that 16 out of 20 attributes are rated higher than the neutral value of three. A rating of four or close to four was just achieved in two cases, namely Landscape/Surroundings and Natural parks/Nature. Attributes which achieved a lower overall rating than three are highlighted with a frame.

When comparing the results of non-visitors and visitors, one can observe that 15 out of 20 attributes are higher rated by the participants who already visited España Verde. Ratings higher than 4 (on a Likert scale ranging from 1 until 5 with 5 as the highest value) by visitors were achieved in three cases namely:

Table 5. Evaluation of the attributes as well as averages and results from the Mann-Whitney Test (p-value)

Attributes	Overall	Visitors	Non-Visitors	Mann-Whitney Test (p-value)
Landscape / Surroundings	4.1	4.1	4.1	0.713
Natural parks / Nature	3.9	3.6	4.0	0.138
Rural villages	3.7	4.1	3.6	0.021
Outdoor sports facilities	3.6	3,7	3.6	0.579
Rural accomodation	3.6	3.6	3.6	0.657
Value for money	3.5	3.8	3.4	0.017
Mountains	3.5	3.6	3.5	0.418
Gastronomy	3.5	4	3.5	0.002
Cultural sites (Cultural heritage / In general)	3.4	3.7	3.4	0.069
Marine villages	3.4	3.6	3.4	0.187
Animal watching / Wildlife activities	3.3	2.9	3.4	0.023
Beaches	3.3	3.5	3.3	0.241
Receptiveness of the locals	3.3	3.7	3.3	0.032
Hotels	3.2	3.4	3.2	0.044
Religious sites	3.1	3.6	3	0.003
Health and wellness	3.1	3.1	3.1	0.946
Cities	2.9	3.7	2.8	0
Fairs / Exhibitions / Festivals	2.9	3.6	2.9	0
Shopping facilities	2.9	3.3	2.8	0.002
Nightlife / Entertainment	2.8	3.5	2.7	0

landscape/surroundings (4.1), rural villages (4.1) and gastronomy (4.0). Just the attribute "animal watching / wildlife activities" was rated lower than the neutral value of three by the visitors (2.9).

Ratings close to the neutral value by non-visitors can be explained by the 72.5% of people who never have heard of the destination. It can be assumed that those persons just have little or no knowledge of España Verde and therefore tend to neutral ratings. Neutral ratings of visitors might be partly explained by a lack of knowledge due to the diversity of España Verde's supply side.

By looking at the results of the Mann-Whitney test, significant differences can be found in 12 cases between the ratings of visitors and non-visitors (considering a 10% significant level). There are 11 attributes which achieved a significant higher-rating by people who have already visited España Verde than by people who have not been there.

Measuring the Affective Component

For the measurement of the affective component the participants were asked to rate their feelings towards España Verde on two seven-point semantic scales ranging from 1 (unpleasant) to 7 (pleasant) respectively 1 (sleepy) to 7 (exciting). In order to analyze if there are significant differences in the perception between visitors and non-visitors, the Mann-Whitney test was applied. The results indicate that both groups, visitors and non-visitors, consider a stay at the destination as pleasant, as their ratings exceed the neutral value of 3.5. Visitors though gave higher ratings than non-visitors did.

When looking at the results of the second question, it becomes evident that visitors consider a stay at España Verde as more exciting than non-visitors would expect it to be. The results of the Mann-Whitney test show a significant difference (Table 6).

Measuring the Conative Component

In order to analyze the revisit intention and the willingness to recommend España Verde to friends and family, the visitors were asked to state their opinion on five-point Likert-scales ranging from 1 (strongly disagree) to 5 (strongly agree). The results were added up, and the means were calculated. For both questions, the visitors gave a high rating almost approaching 4, what indicates a high willingness to revisit and recommend the destination (Table 7).

Table 6. Comparison of the affective perception of visitors and non-visitors (Mann-Whitney test – p-value)

Measuring the Affective Component of D.I.	Overall	Visitors	Non-Visitors	Mann-Whitney Test (p-value)
How do you consider a stay at España Verde on Scale ranging from 1 (unpleasant) until 7 (pleasant)?	4,6	5,0	4,6	0,185
How do you consider a stay at España Verde on Scale ranging from 1 (sleepy) until 7 (exciting)?	3,9	4,5	3,8	0,023

Table 7. Revisit intention and willingness to recommend

Revisit Intention and Willingness to Recommend	Visitors
I can imagine to spend my holidays again in España Verde within the next two years.	3,9
I would recommend España Verde as a holiday destination to my friends and family	3,9

CONCLUSION

This study was conducted in order to fill the gap of research and knowledge regarding the image of the destination brand España Verde on the German market. Since the Spanish General Secretariat of Tourism TURESPAÑA aims to attract new demand segments on mature markets that consume other products than the traditional sun and beach tourism, it becomes vital to identify suitable destinations and to analyze their image on target markets. This study highlights the destination's supply side and reveals the perception of España Verde on the German market. Thus, this study supports the understanding of problems and facilitates the development of marketing measures to strengthen the brand's image and to increase the awareness of the target group. The study was carried out via the Social Media platform Facebook, due to the growing importance of Social Media in tourism marketing as well as TURESPAÑA's objective of increasing the usage of Social Media for promoting tourism abroad. The explanatory results reveal that there is currently low awareness for the destination España Verde on the German market as only 13.6% of the survey participants have already visited the destination. When focusing on non-visitors' reasons for not visiting the destination, it becomes evident that 72.5% of the respondents do not have specific information regarding the destination.

The analysis of España Verde's supply side that had to be conducted for the development of the list of attributes used for measuring the cognitive component shows the suitability of the destination to TURESPAÑA's objectives regarding mature markets. The touristic supply of España Verde seems to be suitable to the desires of the survey participants as can be observed when looking at the results of the first open-ended question (What is important for you when choosing a holiday destination?). Many of the terms and expressions mentioned more than five times as important criteria in the participant's decision-making process can also be associated with España Verde. By looking at the results of the second open-ended question (Which images or characteristics come to mind when you think of España Verde as a vacation destination?), it becomes apparent that, despite the lack of knowledge of the destination, ten terms or expressions associated with the research area, which were stated more than five times, can even be found among the aforementioned important criteria.

These findings are in line with the OECD report regarding tourism trends and policies in 2016 which stresses the change in consumer trends towards more unique and personalized experiences in alternative destinations (OECD, 2016). Supporting arguments can be found in an article in the German newspaper "Die Welt". The executive director of enterprise communications of the "TUI Deutschland GmbH" states that he considers trips across the green north of Spain to hold big potentials and TUI contemplates to broaden its product line (Die Welt, 2016).

The results of the measurement of the cognitive component show a number of significant differences in the cognitive perception of visitors and non-visitors. The visitors rated 15 attributes higher than the non-visitors did, with significant differences in 12 cases. Just two attributes achieved a higher rating by non-visitors and only in one case, namely "animal watching / wildlife activities", the difference can be considered as significant. That indicates that people who have already visited España Verde usually appreciate the destination more than non-visitors would expect it to appreciate. However, both groups, visitors and non-visitors, rated many attributes closer to the neutral value of three than to the highest value of five. In the case of the non-visitors, that might be explained by a lack of knowledge considering the 72.5% who have never heard of the destination. Even the visitor's rating behavior could be explained by a lack of knowledge of the diversity of the destination's broad supply side. Many attributes would have been expected to achieve higher ratings by visitors, when taken into account the potentials identified by the analysis of España Verde's tourism supply, as for instance the attributes "natural parks/nature" and "animal watching/wildlife activities".

The results of the measurement of the affective component seem to reflect the cognitive results which are not surprising regarding the interrelation of the components. Visitors consider a stay at España Verde as more pleasant than non-visitors would expect it to be. The destination is considered as significantly more exciting by visitors than by non-visitors, what can be explained by the previous experience and the associated advance in knowledge of the destination. The measurement of the conative component makes evident that people who have already visited the destination can imagine to revisit España Verde as well as to recommend the destination to friends and family.

The findings of this study raise two questions:

- Which marketing measures can be applied by España Verde's DMOs in order to attract the attention of the German target group?
- Why are there not more and higher significant differences between the ratings of non-visitors compared to visitors and how can the destination achieve a higher appreciation regarding its performance among the group of visitors?

Altogether, the findings of this study indicate that the communication policy of the destination brand España Verde regarding the German target market should be improved. The low awareness of the brand on the German market raises the question of adequate measures in order to attract the attention of this target group. Even if it is far beyond the scope of this research to develop a comprehensive marketing strategy, some suggestions can be made on how the Social Media performance of the brand could be improved. The following suggestions focus on the Social Media appearance of the brand as the study was carried out via Facebook and the participants can be reached via this platform.

Even if the tourism boards of the four autonomous communities, Galicia, Cantabria, Asturias and the Basque Country, run their own Facebook pages, their common brand España Verde indeed is still not represented on Facebook. That might be due to a lack of willingness to "share" the potentials of the target markets. Even if it is understandable to promote the autonomous communities as different destinations on the domestic market, it seems to make sense to use the synergies between them and to push into the German marked supported by a strong overall brand image. Therefore, a Facebook page in the German language should be created for extending the range of marketing measures and thus increasing the awareness of the German target market.

As already mentioned before, the features Facebook offers, provide outstanding possibilities to reach the people's cognitive and affective perception and to facilitate positive word-of-mouth. Destination marketing via Facebook should accelerate user generated content and user engagement by measures such as opinion polls, games, quizzes and contests involving visual content as claimed by Mariani et al. in their study "Facebook as a destination marketing tool: Evidence from Italian regional Destination Management Organizations" (2016). According to their study, the above-mentioned strategies would also benefit other DMOs even in different geographical contexts.

There are limitless possibilities for engaging potential customers and creating a buzz in Social Media. The following comments refer to campaigns and measures which give an idea of how up to date Social Media marketing for España Verde could look like. A very basic strategy to achieve awareness of a specific customer group is to work with key social influencers for this segment. The broad touristic supply of España Verde allows collaborating with influencers from a wide range of areas including food and wine, outdoor sports or art and culture. By inviting social influencers relevant to the target market who share their experiences via Facebook, one can reach their respective followers and teach them about the destination's touristic supply.

The results of this study reveal that there is only a little knowledge about the destination among the German target group. Therefore, it seems appropriate to create a platform that tells about the destination by using a unique resource: The local people. Local artists, producers or sportsmen tell their stories and talk about their home base, their passions, and experiences. In order to avoid the platform being a one-way road, measures should be applied that motivate visitors to share their own impressions and experiences and thus creating a community which emotionally engages like-minded travelers.

For example, in the course of a campaign named "#Night At", successfully launched by Airbnb, the company created outstanding hotel rooms at unusual places where guests could win an overnight stay, for instance in a cable car in the French Alps, in an airplane or even a night in a floating house on the river Thames. The idea to use "pop-up hotels" for generating content to share via Social Media and thus originating buzz among the users seems appropriate for España Verde as well, due to the outstanding landscape and the diverse touristic supply which provides various opportunities for creating such rooms.

Those are only a few examples of how the creation of stimulating content could engage Facebook users and thus increase the awareness for the destination. Of course, it seems recommendable to develop new concepts tailored to the destination rather than copying already existing campaigns but looking at ideas such as "Sheep View", a highly successful campaign launched by the DMO of the Faroe Islands, helps to understand what it is all about. For this campaign, some sheep were equipped with 360-degree cameras. The sheep walked around the islands and uploaded images. The campaign reached high awareness among media all around the world and boosted tourism. Key is to develop unique and creative ideas which are appropriate to link with the target group and to use Social Media platforms such as Facebook to reach a large audience and to make it a viral success.

The second question goes hand in hand with a limitation of this study, namely the small sample of people who have already visited España Verde. As mentioned before, it is possible that even people who visited the destination were not able to achieve a comprehensive overview about the touristic potentials, due to the diversity of the tourism supply. This matter would again concern the communication policy. Nevertheless, future research should analyze if a higher sample of visitors would change the results among them and the DMOs should compare the brand's performance with the visitors' perception in order to choose the right marketing measures for increasing the customers' awareness, knowledge, and appreciation of the tourism destination España Verde.

ACKNOWLEDGMENT

This work was supported by FCT- Portuguese Foundation for Science and Technology [grant number UID/SOC/04020/2013].

REFERENCES

Aaker, D. A. (1991). *Managing brand equity: capitalizing on the value of a brand name*. The Free Press.

Aaker, D. A. (1996). *Building strong brands*. Simon & Schuster UK Ltd.

Agapito, D., Mendes, J., & Valle, P. (2010). Destination Image – Perspectives of Tourists versus Residents. *European Journal of Tourism. Hospitality and Recreation*, *1*, 90–109.

Agapito, D., Valle, P., & Mendes, J. (2013). The cognitive-affective-conative model of destination image: A confirmatory analysis. *Journal of Travel & Tourism Marketing*, *30*(5), 471–481. doi:10.1080/10548408.2013.803393

Baloglu, S., & McCleary, K. W. (1999). A Model of Destination Image Formation. *Annals of Tourism Research*, *26*(4), 868–867. doi:10.1016/S0160-7383(99)00030-4

Beerli, A., & Martín, J. D. (2004a). Tourists characteristics and the perceived image of tourist destinations: A quantitative analysis-a case study of Lanzarote, Spain. *Tourism Management*, *25*(5), 623–636. doi:10.1016/j.tourman.2003.06.004

Beerli, A., & Martín, J. D. (2004b). Factors influencing destination image. *Annals of Tourism Research*, *31*(3), 657–681. doi:10.1016/j.annals.2004.01.010

Bigne, J. E., Sanchez, M. I., & Sanchez, J. (2001). Tourism image, evaluation variables and after purchase behaviour: Interrelationship. *Tourism Management*, *22*(6), 607–616. doi:10.1016/S0261-5177(01)00035-8

Bigné Alcañiz, E., Sánchez García, I., & Sanz Blas, S. (2009). The functional-psuchological continuum in the cognitive image of a destination: A confirmatory analysis. *Tourism Management*, *30*(5), 715–723. doi:10.1016/j.tourman.2008.10.020

Boulding, W., Karla, A., Staelin, A., & Zeithaml, V. (1993). A Dynamic Process Model of Service Quality: From Expectations to Behavioral Intensions. *JMR, Journal of Marketing Research*, *30*(1), 7–27. doi:10.2307/3172510

Buhalis, D., & Law, R. (2008). Progress in information technology and tourism management: 20 years on and 10 years after the Internet - The state of eTourism research. *Tourism Management*, *29*(4), 609–623. doi:10.1016/j.tourman.2008.01.005

Cano Fuentes, M. (2006). Las estrategias de promoción exteriror del turismo deportivo y naturaleza español por parte del instituto de turismo de España. *Estudios Turísticos*, *169-170*, 39–49.

CanTur - Sociedad Regional Cántabra de Promoción Turística (2015). *Green Spain – The Spirit of the North Press Kit*. Author.

Chen, C.-F., & Phou, S. (2013). A closer look at destination: Image, personality, relationship and loyalty. *Tourism Management*, *36*, 269–278. doi:10.1016/j.tourman.2012.11.015

Crompton, J. L. (1979). An assessment of the image of Mexico as a vacation destination and the influence of geographical location upon that image. *Journal of Travel Research*, *17*(1), 18–23. doi:10.1177/004728757901700404

Die Welt. (2016). *„Wir haben kein einziges Bett mehr frei"*. Retrieved May 21, 2016, from http://www.welt.de/153592079

DSTATIS Statistisches Bundesamt. (2016). *Bevölkerung nach Geschlecht und Staatsangehörigkeit*. Retrieved May 21, 2016 from https://www.destatis.de/DE/ZahlenFakten/GesellschaftStaat/Bevoelkerung/Bevoelkerungsstand/Tabellen/Zensus_Geschlecht_Staatsangehoerigkeit.html

Echeverria, B. (2010). For whom does language death toll? Cautionary notes from the Basque case. *Linguistics and Education*, *21*(3), 197–209. doi:10.1016/j.linged.2009.10.001

Echtner, C. M., & Ritchie, J. R. B. (1991). The Meaning and Measurement of Destination Image. *The Journal of Tourism Studies*, *14*(1), 37–48.

Echtner, C. M., & Ritchie, J. R. B. (1993). The Measurement of Destination Image: An Emperical Assessment. *Journal of Travel Research*, *31*(4), 3–13. doi:10.1177/004728759303100402

Estêvão, J. V., Carneiro, M. J., & Teixeira, L. (2014). The Evolving Value of eTourism for Suppliers and Visitors. In J. Gamon (Ed.), *Handbook of Research on Enterprise 2.0: Technological, Social and Organizational Dimensions* (pp. 486–510). Hershey, PA: Business Science Reference. doi:10.4018/978-1-4666-4373-4.ch026

Faktenkontor Gmb, H. (2016). *Social Media-Atlas 2015/2016*. Retrieved March, 21, from http://social-media-atlas.faktenkontor.de/2015/nutzung-einzelner-kanaele.php

Ferreira Lopes, S. D. (2011). Destination image: Origins, Developments and Implications. *PASOS. Revista de Tourismo y Patrimonio Cultural*, *9*(2), 305–315.

Gallarza, M. G., Saura, I. G., & Garcia, H. C. (2002). Destination image: Towards a conceptual framework. *Annals of Tourism Research*, *29*(1), 56–78. doi:10.1016/S0160-7383(01)00031-7

Gartner, W. C. (1993). Image formation process. *Journal of Travel & Tourism Marketing*, *2*(2/3), 191–215.

Gonzáles Gonzáles, M., Rodríguez Banga, E., Campillo Díaz, F., Méndez Pazó, F., Rodríguez Liñares, L., & Iglesias Iglesias, G. (2008). Specific features of the Galician language and implications for speech technology development. *Speech Communication*, *50*(11-12), 874–887. doi:10.1016/j.specom.2008.02.004

Gunn, C. (1988). *Vacationcapes: Design tourist regions*. New York: Van Nostrand Reinhold.

Hunt, J. D. (1975). Image as a factor in tourism development. *Journal of Travel Research*, *13*(3), 1–7. doi:10.1177/004728757501300301

IET Instituto de Estudios Turísticos. (2015). *Turistas extranjeros: ¿DE DÓNDE VIENEN?*. Sociedad Regional Cántabra de Promoción Turística.

Instituto Nacional de Estadística. (2016). *Statistics of Tourist Movements at Borders (FRONTUR) Total year 2015. International tourist arrivals by country of residence.* Author.

Ivars Baidal, J. A. (2004). Tourism Planning in Spain – Evolution and Perspectives. *Annals of Tourism Research, 31*(2), 313–333. doi:10.1016/j.annals.2003.12.001

Jenkins, O. H. (1999). Understanding and Measuring Tourist Destination Images. *International Journal of Tourism Research, 1*(1), 1–15. doi:10.1002/(SICI)1522-1970(199901/02)1:1<1::AID-JTR143>3.0.CO;2-L

Kaplan, A., & Haenlein, M. (2010). Users of the world, unite! The challenges and opportunities of Social Media. *Business Horizons, 53*(1), 59–68. doi:10.1016/j.bushor.2009.09.003

Kim, A., & Johnson, K. (2016). Power of consumers using Social Media: Examining the influences of brand-related user-generated content on Facebook. *Computers in Human Behavior, 58*, 98–108. doi:10.1016/j.chb.2015.12.047

Királová, A., & Pavlíčeka, A. (2015). Development of Social Media Strategies in Tourism Destination. *Procedia: Social and Behavioral Sciences, 175*, 358–366. doi:10.1016/j.sbspro.2015.01.1211

Lawson, F., & Baud Bovy, M. (1977). *Tourism and recreational management.* London: CBI Pub. Co.

Mariani, M., Di Felice, M., & Mura, M. (2016). Facebook as a destination marketing tool: Evidence from Italian regional Destination Management Organizations. *Tourism Management, 54*, 321–343. doi:10.1016/j.tourman.2015.12.008

Martín, H. S., & Bosque, I. A. R. (2008). Exploring the cognitive-affective nature of destination image and the role of psychological factos in its formation. *Tourism Management, 29*(2), 263–277. doi:10.1016/j.tourman.2007.03.012

Mercator European Research Centre on Multilingualism and Language Learning. (2008). *Basque: The Basque language in education in Spain* (2nd ed.). Author.

Ministry of the Presidency (2014). *Spain Today 2014.* NIPO (official publication identification number): 002-14-032-0.

Ministry of the Presidency. (2015). *Spain Today 2015.* Retrieved March 19, 2016, from http://www.lamoncloa.gob.es/lang/en/espana/spaintoday2015/Paginas/index.aspx

OECD. (2016). *OECD Tourism Trends and Policies 2016*. OECD Publishing. 10.1787/tour-2016-en

Organismo Autonomo Parques Nacionales. (2014). *Amplicacion del Parque Nacional Picos de Europa en 2.467,59 ha.* Author.

Pearce, P. L. (1982). Perceived changes in holiday destinations. *Annals of Tourism Research, 9*(2), 145–164. doi:10.1016/0160-7383(82)90044-5

Pike, S., & Page, S. (2014). Destination Marketing Organizations and destination marketing: A narrative analysis of the literature. *Tourism Management, 41*, 202–227. doi:10.1016/j.tourman.2013.09.009

Pike, S., & Ryan, C. (2004). Destination Positioning Analysis through a Comparsion of Cognitive, Affective and Conative Perceptions. *Journal of Travel Research*, *42*(4), 333–342. doi:10.1177/0047287504263029

Rodríguez-Rodríguez, L., Jiménez-Sánchez, M., Domínguez-Cuesta, M. J., & Aranburu, A. (2015). Research history on glacial geomorphology and geochronology of the Cantabrian Mountains, north Iberia (4342°N/42°W). *Quaternary International*, *364*, 6–21. doi:10.1016/j.quaint.2014.06.007

Russel, J., Ward, L., & Pratt, G. (1981). Affective quality attributed to environments: A factor analytic study. *Environment and Behavior*, *13*, 259–288.

Smith, S. L. J. (1994). The Tourism Product. *Annals of Tourism Research*, *21*(3), 582–594.

Stepaniuk, K. (2015). The relation between destination image and Social Media user engagement – theoretical approach. *Procedia: Social and Behavioral Sciences*, *213*, 616–621. doi:10.1016/j.sbspro.2015.11.459

Stepchenkova, S., & Morrison, A. M. (2008). Russia's destination image among American pleasure travelers: Revisiting Echtner and Ritchie. *Tourism Management*, *29*(3), 548–560. doi:10.1016/j.tourman.2007.06.003

TURESPAÑA. (2016). *Travelling in Spain.* Retrieved February 26, 2016, from http://www.spain.info/en/informacionpractica/transportes/reportajes/viajar_por_espana_1.html

Walmsley, D. Y., & Young, M. (1998). Evaluative images and tourism: The use of personal constructs to describe the structure of destination images. *Journal of Travel Research*, *36*(3), 65–69. doi:10.1177/004728759803600307

KEY TERMS AND DEFINITIONS

Cultural Heritage: The cultural heritage are the cultural resources of an area such as language and customs of the residents but also resources and activities as for instance: fine arts, literature, history, music, dancing, shopping and sports facilities.

Destination Image: The subjective perception a person has of a particular destination either according to knowledge or imagination.

España Verde: A tourism brand consisting of the four Spanish autonomous communities Galicia, Cantabria, Asturias and the Basque Country.

Natural Heritage: The natural heritage of a region contains essential components of the tourism supply like air and climate, physiography, landforms, terrain, flora, fauna, bodies of water, beaches or natural beauty.

Social Media: Social Media are digital channels which provide the possibility for the interactive exchange of information.

Spain Today: The annual journal "España Hoy" (Spain Today) gives a current overview of Spain including descriptions of the measures and decisions undertaken by the government.

Tourism Supply: The tourism supply of a destination is formed by the natural and cultural heritage as well as the touristic infrastructure of a destination.

ENDNOTES

1 Statistics of the "IET Instituto de Estudios Turísticos" achieved on demand via e-mail from the tourism promotion board of Cantabria (Sociedad Regional Cántabra de Promoción Turística).

2 The unpublished brochure "Green Spain – The spirit of the North Press Kit", was provided by the tourism promotion board of Cantabria "CanTur – Sociedad Regional Cántabra de Promoción Turística". This brochure is cited in the text as: "CanTur, 2015" and in the bibliographical references as: "CanTur - Sociedad Regional Cántabra de Promoción Turística (2015). Green Spain – The spirit of the North Press Kit."

3 Although the sample is not a random sample, these statistical tests were applied with academic purposes to enrich the analysis, and aiming to enlarge the researcher's skills. Accordingly, the tests' results should be interpreted with care.

4 Hauptschule covers the school years 5 until 9 and is the lowest degree. Realschule covers the school years 5 until 10 and is the middle educational achievement. The Gymnasium covers the school years 5 until 12 and is the highest possible degree in Germany.

Chapter 15
Gastronomy in Cultural Tourism:
Use of Mobile Instant Messaging to Look for Gastronomic Recommendations

Maria Romero-Charneco
Universidad de Málaga, Spain

Ana-María Casado-Molina
Universidad de Málaga, Spain

Pilar Alarcón-Urbistondo
Universidad de Málaga, Spain

ABSTRACT

Cultural tourism consumers seek advice and recommendations from others before making buying decisions. The mobile instant messaging (MIM) boom could create a channel not only for social communication but also for information about cultural tourism and specifically the choice of restaurant. In this research we study which channels are most used by consumers when asking for gastronomic recommendations and, in particular, the factors behind the use of MIM as the preferred channels when obtaining tourist information. For this, an online survey was carried out with a sample of 393 individuals in Spain and descriptive statistical techniques were applied to the processing and analysis of the data. The results obtained show that: (1) its use is determined by its instantaneousness and permanent availability; and (2) people use it due to a lack of knowledge about the area.

INTRODUCTION

Tourism is undergoing major changes. One of these changes is that tourists are seeking destinations that allow them to enjoy different experiences (De la Rosa, 2003; Cracolici & Nijkamp, 2008). At the same time, cultural tourism has been transformed, adapting to the new demands of travellers (Guzmán-López & Jesús, 2011). This has resulted in it undergoing an evolution influenced by the conceptual changes

DOI: 10.4018/978-1-5225-2927-9.ch015

that have taken place in the area of cultural heritage, social changes and consequently by changes in demand, looking for new forms of cultural consumption (Ibarra, 2001).

Cultural tourism can still be defined as that which includes all aspects of the trip, allowing the tourist to learn about the history, heritage or current ways of living and thinking (Richards, 2001). However, the way this is experienced has changed. Cultural tourism had always prioritised the visual sense over the rest of the senses, turning the tourist into a mere observer of reality, a passive tourist. However, tourists have evolved, changing from a mere collector of photos to wanting to seek out experiences. This search by the tourist for trips offering new experiences entails the greater involvement of the other senses in order to understand the customs of the place (McCabe, 2014; Ricky & Scott, 2017).

Thus, today's traveller wants to have a full sensory experience and this includes taste. Through food, the cultural tourist obtains a greater understanding of the place they are visiting, beyond the simple observation mentioned previously (Cohen & Avieli 2004; Kivela & Crotts, 2006; Molz, 2007; Mak et al., 2012; Oliveira, 2007). In addition, it should be noted that gastronomy forms part of the cultural, social, environmental and economic history of places and their inhabitants, reflecting a particular lifestyle and being deeply rooted in the culture and tradition (Mitchell & Hall, 2006). In fact, one of the elements of cultural tourism is gastronomy, with strong cultural links between gastronomy and tourism (Ritzer, 1995; Richards, 2002; Roden, 2003; Dos Santos & Antonini, 2004; López-Guzmán & Sánchez-Cañizares, 2008; Sánchez-Cañizares & López-Guzmán, 2011). In addition, it is a factor that has traditionally been used by destinations to improve their image and create a differentiated positioning (Hjalager, 2010).

It is in this context that wine tourism, culinary tourism and olive oil tourism are becoming more important, with the gastronomic factor being either the main motivation or a key part of the cultural trip, rather than simply a necessary activity at the destination (Flavián & Fandos, 2011).

Therefore, gastronomy and culture are closely related. When tourists travel they do not just go to restaurants to satisfy their need for food. Fields (2002) identifies four types of gastronomic motivation: physical, cultural, interpersonal, and status and prestige. In this study we focus on cultural motivations. In these, the importance of food in the culture of a country is taken into account. According to Vinha (2004), food has always been a key element of the culture of each society and tourists increasingly perceive gastronomy as an important factor in better understanding the culture of a place. In this sense, gastronomic tourism is understood not only as the act of going to a restaurant and tasting the typical dishes, but also being aware of the rituals and habits associated with the local gastronomy and of the option to visit museums and other attractions on this topic.

In cultural tourism, and specifically in gastronomic tourism, the Internet plays a very important role (O'Connor 2011). In the Web 2.0 environment, users become the main channels for the dissemination of online information, generated in turn by them and allowing for electronic word of mouth dissemination, or e-word of mouth as it is known *(e-WOM)*. This type of information is called User-Generated Content (UGC) (Burgess et al., 2009).

In addition, the buying decisions of tourists are influenced by the ratings and comments made by other gastronomic tourism consumers. Several authors (Borja et al., 2002; Borja & Gomis, 2009; O'Connor, 2011) argue that this type of tourist in particular is influenced during the pre-purchase stage, purchase stage and post-purchase stage, not only by offline recommendations from friends/family and traditional channels but also by the online environment: *word of mouth* of the blogs, websites such as *TripAdvisor* or social networks like *Facebook*. So when it comes to making a decision, the recommendations taken from the social media become a key element influencing the evaluation of the information on the tourist products and services by the user who wishes to consume them (Cho & Fesenmaier, 2001; Buhalis, 2003; Buhalis & Law, 2008; Xiang & Gretzel, 2010; Hays et al., 2012; Albacete, 2012; Burguess & Kerr, 2012; Roque & Raposo, 2013; García, 2016;).

In this way, the Internet has enabled users to become experts or social influencers on a particular subject or product in a very short time (Xiang & Gretzel, 2010). Likewise, it is argued that *e-word of mouth* is becoming increasingly important in the decision making process for tourist consumption. The success of this form of communication is due to the fact that the information generated is not for commercial purposes and is therefore seen as having greater credibility by potential gastronomic tourists seeking objective information to evaluate their alternatives.

Today's gastronomic tourist consumer is a consumer and generator of recommendations through the social media that allow these users to leave comments, exchange experiences, collaborate and help others in their decision making (Borja et al., 2002; Xifra & Chias, 2008; Rosen, 2009). These media, based on online participation and recommendations, turn consumers into prosumers at the same time, since they offer direct participation mechanisms.

In addition, in view of this situation, it can be seen that gastronomic tourist consumption is being influenced by how these consumers are using mobile technology not only to speed up the search for alternatives and make purchases, but mainly to obtain recommendations that increase the confidence of tourist consumers in those products and services researched. When looking for information on the gastronomic destination and its tourist services, the following aspects stand out: search for accommodation, restaurants or activities near the traveller's location, alerts on possible flight delays, receiving personalised offers or discounts on services linked to the trip, among others (Gasdia & Rheem, 2012; Salgado *et al.,* 2013; García, 2016).

In addition, the use in recent years of mobile instant messaging (MIM) services, such as WhatsApp, *WeChat, and LINE*, is changing the way in which we communicate and maintain relationships with others, turning MIM into the main channel for social communication. In fact, it is argued that it will become a platform for entertainment, business and work (Wu & Lu, 2013). Its rapid growth and high acquisition rate make MIM an ideal medium for the dissemination of information on tourist products and services.

The intention with this research is to gain a better understanding of which information channels are most used by tourist consumers using *WhatsApp* when obtaining recommendations in the gastronomic tourism sector and what factors are the most important for these tourist consumers affecting their decision to do so through *WhatsApp*.

This paper contains the following sections: first, a review of the literature on: (1) the gastronomy within cultural tourism and the consumer types;(2) the search for tourist information in Web 2.0 channels; (3) Instant messaging as a tourist information channel, dealing *chatbots*; and (4) the factors that influence the use of Web 2.0 channels and MIM in the search for tourist information. Once this review has been completed, the objectives and methodology of this paper are defined. Third, we present the results that allow us to identify the information channels used and the most relevant factors for *WhatsApp* users when obtaining recommendations on tourist products and services. Finally, we conclude with the main contributions of this scientific work.

This study provides the foundation for identifying the trends in the use by tourists of MIM with *chatbots* when seeking and receiving gastronomic recommendations or any other type of tourist information.

BACKGROUND

Gastronomy Within Cultural Tourism: Consumer Types

Tourism is increasingly characterised as an activity that provides the traveller with an opportunity for personal and cultural enrichment (Ávila & Barrado, 2005). Tourist mobility has developed from being a simple physical displacement to being identified as an introspective experience. Thus, all of those elements of the tourist offer of a destination that allow the traveller to experience this personal growth during their trip begin to play an important role. If we limit ourselves to cultural tourism, local traditions, understanding lifestyles and the typical gastronomy stand out as the main factors of the destination. Thus, gastronomy is positioning itself as an important diversification element and as a tool for defining the brand and image of an area, country or culture (Hjalager, 2010). Food is becoming an element of the local culture and expression of the history, customs and traditions of a community or a certain geographical area (Lee & Crompton, 1992; Kivela & Crotts, 2006).

So much so that gastronomy is starting to contain different categories of travellers (Fox, 2007; Acevin, 2012). The word 'foodies' is used to identify those tourists who are sensitive to the food heritage of the destinations they visit and understand gastronomy as a complex and cultural experience. Thus, the typical product or traditional dish of the local gastronomic culture has a cultural communication function and is not only seen as a way to satisfy the need for food (Mogollón et al., 2015). Within foodies there are degrees ranging from those who consider gastronomy as an important and differentiating element of the destination to the so-called gastronomic tourist who travels with the discovery of a different gastronomy as their main motivation, who seeks to learn more about it to enrich them culturally (Fields, 2002; Cambourne *et al.,* 2003; Torres 2003; Vinha, 2004;).

According some authors (Fields, 2002; Torres 2003; Vinha, 2004;), the type of tourist who values gastronomy when travelling actively searches for information about where to eat and selects channels that guarantee the authentic experience and not the classic tourist offering. So they look to specialists Internet channels and other information sources which they consider to be equally genuine, such as e-word of mouth, as a way of gaining knowledge. In contrast, the general tourist accepts lower quality food (Oliveira, 2007).

Gastronomic consumption by the cultural tourist can be fitted into any of the decision-making prototypes of the Assael model (1987). Inspired by his model, 4 types of gastronomic tourist are proposed (see Figure 1). These depend on whether the gastronomic consumer knows the different gastronomic alternatives that the destination offers them and the degree to which gastronomy is the focus of the trip:

- The expert gastronomic tourist has complex buyer behaviour. The process of making a decision about the gastronomy of the destination to experience closely resembles how the decision is made about the destination of the trip itself. It is a rational decision and searching for information prior to the visit is very common (Herbert, 2001), as is the importance of analysing the information channels used and the intensity of the search using them (Fodness & Murray, 1997).
- The pure gastronomic tourist goes to the destination as a result of their desire to discover the gastronomy of the place, but is not knowledgeable about the destination and does not differentiate between one gastronomic offering and another. This tourist decides which gastronomic offering they want to try through the process of dissonance reduction (they are not guided by brands or

Figure 1. Henry Assael buyer behaviours 1987
Assael, 1987.

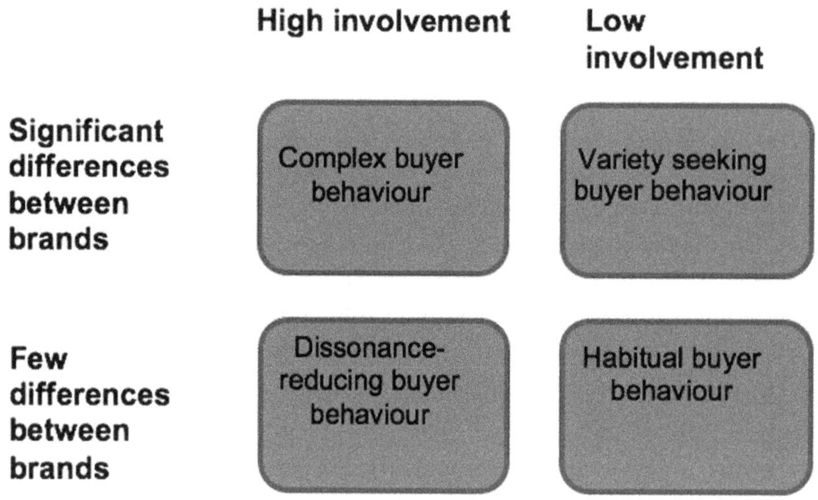

recognition, but make a comparison depending on the needs that they want to satisfy) and looking at information beforehand or once at the destination.

- The classic cultural tourist with gastronomic sensitivity. For this tourist the gastronomic decisions are usually made at the destination, or from home but very close to the departure date of the trip. This is a tourist sensitive to brands, a tourist that differentiates between brands, but is not as involved as the first type of tourist previously mentioned. This type of tourist is attracted by trying different alternative so they look at information once at the destination and base decisions on social recommendations about the various gastronomic offerings.
- The cultural tourist with little gastronomic sensitivity. This type does not look for recommendations on gastronomic offerings, their priority is the destination and not the gastronomy.

Although each of these decisions has a certain profile, mixed profiles may appear in certain cultural tourism decisions depending on the circumstances and context in which they arise.

As previously mentioned, the search process is different for each type of consumer; the number of channels consulted, type of query, moment of the query, etc. In any case, the Internet and mobile instant messaging have changed the information search habits of these consumers.

The Search for Tourist Information in Web 2.0 Channels

Before making a purchase, consumers evaluate the products they want to buy. Products can be classified into two broad groups: search products and experience products (Nelson, 1970; Korgaonkar et al., 2006). The first can be evaluated in more detail before the purchase because they are characterised by having specific functional attributes that facilitate their analysis prior to use. However, experience products, such as restaurants, are subject to intangible attributes that are not known until their purchase is made and evaluations about them can only be verified by experiencing or consuming the product (Barrios, 2012).

Tourist consumers rely on the opinions of those who are "the same as me" as the main evaluation criterion to validate the credibility of the information and source consulted (Zhang & Watts, 2008). For this validation they use online social media where they can see the opinions of other people who provide ratings. This includes *TripAdvisor, Booking, and Foursquare*, among others.

In this respect, the ratings and evaluations of other consumers are vitally important in the decision making process of the consumers since social information is what they trust most (Cheung et al. 2009; Yoo et al., 2009). This is why when travelling to an unknown place a tourist uses the opinions of others as a way to reduce their situational uncertainty or other types of risk (Gretzel & Yoo, 2007; Ayeh et al., 2013b).

In the decision-making process for tourist consumers, the Internet has today become the main source of information when planning a trip (Cai et al., 2004; Fernandes et al., 2010; O'Connor, 2011; Ayeh et al., 2013a), becoming an information tool to help and give tangibility to the images of the tourist services, improving communication and the interactivity of tourism services (Parra-López et al., 2011). However, consumers continue to heed the advice of friends, family members and other groups of individuals in the decision-making process for tourist products (Litvin et al., 2008).

Looking in more detail at the Internet, a number of *Web 2.0* information channels are those most frequently used to help users with their consumption decisions. Table 1 shows these tourist information channels used by consumers.

As shown in Table 1, some tourist information channels 2.0 are consulted in the inspiration phase, during the trip and after it, such as *TripAdvisor, Virtual Tourist, Yelp, and Minube Foursquare.* All of these are easy to use: (1) prior to the trip to evaluate alternatives based on the opinions of other tourists; (2) a posteriori, once at the destination you can go back and do a more detailed search of the tourist

Table 1. Web 2.0 tourist information channels used by consumers

Web 2.0 Information Channels	Classification	Trip Phase (García, 2016).	Access	Authors
TripAdvisor VirtualTourist Yelp Minube Foursquare	Community of travellers based on UGC.	Inspiration. During. After.	Website. App.	(Cruz et al., 2011). (Chung & Buhalis, 2008). (Mendes-Filho & Santos, 2014) (Hsu & Lin, 2008) (Wang & Fesenmaier, 2004) (Bigné et al., 2010). (Melián et al., 2010). (García, 2016). (Ariyasriwatana, 2014). (Ariyasriwatana, & Quiroga, 2016). (Hudson et al., 2016)
Youtube Facebook Twitter	Social Networks	Inspiration. After.	Website. Mobile Application.	(Cruz et al., 2011). (Parra et al., 2011). (Alonso et al, 2008). (Fotis et al., 2012).
Booking Hotel Tonight Airbnb	Comparison website	Inspiration. Purchase.	Website. Mobile Application.	(Mendes-Filho & Santos, 2014). (Melián et al., 2010).
Trivago Kayak Expedia	Metasearch engine	Inspiration.	Website. Mobile Application.	(García, 2016).

Data Source: Own research.

services by location; and (3) once back from the trip tourists can report their experience in these virtual communities and this serves as an aid in the decision-making of other tourists. It should be noted that the most frequently used information channels within the community of travellers category are those that have the functionality to search for restaurants (*TripAdvisor, Yelp, Foursquare and Minube)*. In contrast, metasearch engines and comparators are mainly used in the buying phase for comparing and booking accommodation and transportation at the destination. The social networks are used by tourists in the pre and post trip stages.

The accessibility of these *Web 2.0* channels through any device, and particularly through mobile telephones, allows for a direct and instant search, eliminating geographical and time barriers at the moment of need. However, there is no immediate response to consumer questions about tourist products and services. Currently an immediate response, rather than an immediate search, and direct communication are only possible through mobile instant messaging. In fact, there are tourism companies that are currently adopting this form of communication to relate to their customers and deal with their queries. According to the Asociación para la Investigación de Medios de Comunicación (2016), more than 57.5% of users use mobile instant messaging applications on a daily basis, among which what stands out are *WhatsApp* with a 91.6% market share followed by *Telegram* with 16.8%. These studies show that MIM is a potential channel for receiving and sending tourist information.

Instant Messaging as a Tourist Information Channel

The enormous penetration of smartphones and access to mobile broadband has made it possible for mobile instant messaging (MIM) to become a significant communication alternative to the traditional short message system (Ha et al., 2015). This, coupled with the boom in smartphones, has favoured the development of mobile instant messaging in such a way that *WhatsApp, WeChat and LINE* are changing how we communicate and maintain relationships with others, becoming the main channels for social communication (Bere, 2016). The popularity of MIM has meant that it has rapidly evolved and has achieved a large mass of users. The advantages include sending and receiving messages, images, videos and audio for free. Authors like Wu and Lu (2013) argue that mobile instant messaging will become a platform for entertainment, commerce and work.

The uses of MIM are becoming closer to those of the social networks in terms of participation and the distribution of information. However, it has the advantage of being able to establish a dialogue in the same way as a conversation between two or more people takes place in the offline environment. In the case of MIM, it is not only plain text that is sent and received, but also multimedia content such as videos or images, which enrich the conversation.

Moreover, a study on mobile instant messaging for companies carried out by Segittur (2016), a Spanish state company dedicated to the management of innovation and tourist technologies, in collaboration with various entities, has identified different real cases of tourist companies and destinations using MIM to communicate with their customers. The following initiatives stand out among these: Nextel Travel - XiXi Travel, Istanbul Tourist Pass, Hotel Barceló Illetas Albatros, Casual Hoteles (see Table 2).

Table 2. Tourist brands with coverage in mobile instant messaging

Brand	MIM	Function	Area	Stage (Garcia 2016)	Chat-bot	Coverage	Language
Nextel Travel-XiXi Travel.	WeCh[1]	Promotion of product	Destination	Inspiration	No	Global	Eng.[2]
Istanbul Tourist Pass.	WA[3]	Tourist Information	Destination	During	No	Local	Eng.
Hotel Barceló Illetas Albatros.	WA	Customer service	Hotel	During	No	National	Sp.[4]
Casual Hoteles.	Line WA	Sales. Customer service	Hotel	During	No	National	Sp.
British Airways	FBM[5]	Customer service Sales	Flights	Inspiration Purchase	Yes	Global	Eng.
Expedia	Skype FBM	Search Comparison Sales	Flights	Inspiration Purchase During	Yes	Global	Eng.
Austrian Airlines	FBM	Search Sales Customer service	Flights	Inspiration	Yes	Global	Eng.
Skyscanner	Skype FBM	Search Sales	Flights	Inspiration Purchase	Yes	Global	Eng.
Kayak	FBM Slack	Search Sales	Flights Hotel	Inspiration Purchase	Yes	Global	Eng.
Foursquare	Slack Skype	Search	Destination Food	During	Yes	Global	Eng.
Ask Vicente	WA FBM	Search	Destination Food	Inspiration During After	Yes	National	Sp. Eng.

Data source: Own research.

Chatbots in Mobile Instant Messaging for Searching for Information About Tourist Products and Services

Mobile instant messaging (MIM) channels such as *WhatsApp* and *Facebook Messenger* allow for the sending of messages one by one through a chat as if you were having a face-to-face conversation. This advantage of maintaining a real-time dialogue with another person creates a new communication scenario through which brands can interact with their consumers. The interface of these channels through dialogue allows for private, personalised and direct interaction with each customer, through either man-machine (Hill et al., 2015) or peer-to-peer communication. The first form of communication consists of implementing a *chatbot*, that is, software based on artificial intelligence that allows for communication with humans, providing an automated response to consumer requests (Shah et al., 2016). In contrast, peer-to-peer communication is that where there are no automated processes to respond to the needs of the consumer/customer (AbuShawar & Atwell, 2016).

The pioneering brands starting to implement services for their consumers through existing mobile instant messaging applications, or even developing conversational mobile instant applications, come from the tourist sector where the goal is to better serve the customers.

The fact that there are brands that provide coverage through third-party mobile instant messaging applications instead of creating their own mobile applications is mainly due to the high friction that exists about downloading a new application and the large amount of time that consumers spend using MIM applications (Oghuma et al., 2016). Therefore, it is easier to create a new consumer-brand communication channel in the existing instant messaging applications that consumers already use on a daily basis than in their own which consumers would only use occasionally.

Table 2 shows the main tourist product and service brands that provide coverage through mobile instant messaging channels, using either a *chatbot* or a person. This is difficult to estimate since the advances in technology allow the dialogue process to be personalised through natural language processing, which makes it difficult to identify this difference at a glance. However, some brands identify their type of communication and whether or not the intervention is through a human.

The presence of the brands in MIM channels that do not use *chatbots*, as can be seen from Table 2, is mainly to provide customer service, providing specific services and adapted to the exclusive needs of the customers during the trip. These are responded to by a human through open dialogue. In contrast, the brands that have implemented *chatbots* in the mobile instant messaging channels have a predefined and automated dialogue structure. They mostly address the inspiration stage and the phase of purchasing the trip, so they are companies that deal with the search for the destination and accommodation. Moreover, it should be noted that the *Web 2.0* information channels *Kayak, Foursquare and Expedia* have started to use MIM as another alternative channel to provide the service.

However, we have not found a generic *chatbot* that covers everything from the inspiration stage of the trip to the planning of the trip with transport and accommodation decisions, all the way through to the recommendations made in the destination or post-consumption.

Factors That Influence the Use of Web 2.0 Channels and MIM in the Search for Tourist Information

This section discusses the factors that influence the use of *Web 2.0* channels based on User-Generated Content (UGC) in social media to search for and evaluate tourist products and services, comparing them with the factors that determine the use of a gastronomic recommendations channel through the mobile instant messaging (MIM) service *WhatsApp.*

This table shows that the factors influencing the use of *Web 2.0* information channels to evaluate tourist products and services relate to: (1) learning, that is, how difficult or easy it is to use; (2) value for money; and (3) trust of the community in the contents generated.

Analysing the literature, it has not been possible to identify any authors looking at factors that influence the use of MIM in the search for tourist information or recommendations. However, it is interesting to see whether the factors found for the *Web 2.0* channels are applicable to specific MIM channels with *chatbots* in the gastronomic tourism field.

OBJECTIVES AND METHODOLOGY OF THE RESEARCH

The general objective of this research is to gain a better understanding of which information channels are most used by tourist consumers using WhatsApp when obtaining recommendations in the gastronomic

Table 3. Factors in the use of Web 2.0 sources in the search for tourist information

Factors	Authors
Attitude	(Casaló et al., 2010).
Confidence	(Bressler & Grantham, 2000; Chung & Buhalis, 2008; Filieri and Mcleay, 2013).
Collaborative environment	(Bressler & Grantham, 2000; Wang & Fesenmaier, 2004; Chung & Buhalis, 2008).
Reduced cost	(Binney et al., 2003;Taño et.al., 2013).
Ease of use	(Meroño, 2005; Taño et.al., 2013; Silva & Mendes, 2014).
Time optimisation	(Binney et al., 2003).
Time-independence	(Taño et al., 2013).
Intention to use	(Wang et al., 2002; Wang & Fesenmaier, 2004; Hsu & Lin, 2008; Parra et al., 2011; Hsu & Huang 2012).
Perceived usefulness	(Huh et al., 2009; Ryu et al., 2009).

Data base: Own research.

tourism sector and which factors are the most important for these tourist consumers affecting their decision to do so through WhatsApp.

In order to achieve this general objective, the following specific objectives have been established:

1. To identify the situations in which these consumers use the gastronomic recommendations service through *WhatsApp.*
2. To understand the perception of these consumers about gastronomic recommendations extracted from this MIM channel, *WhatsApp*.
3. To define the factors that these consumers value most about gastronomic recommendations through the *WhatsApp* channel.
4. To identify additional information channels offering gastronomic recommendations of restaurants used by the types of consumers studied.

Table 2 shows that only the MIM channel using *chatbot* called *Ask Vicente* offers coverage in Spain in English and Spanish, while the rest are only available in English with international coverage. It is important to study this channel for three reasons: (1) the penetration of *WhatsApp* in the Spanish market in recent years (according to data from PwC's Strategy& consultancy company, in 2015 Spain was the fourth ranked country in the world in the use of *WhatsApp* with a penetration rate of 70% among mobile telephone users); (2) the importance of gastronomic tourism in Spain; and finally (3) because it is the only MIM channel with *chatbot* that uses *WhatsApp* to deal with user queries in the three phases of the purchase of the tourism product and service (inspiration, during and after). For these reasons we will focus on *Ask Vicente* and analyse the factors that influence its use by *WhatsApp* consumers. Focusing on a brand using a *chatbot* means that there should be a series of variables that are easy to measure. In contrast, the brands providing the service through humans have measurement difficulties because it is a dialogue without parameterisation. In addition, those MIMs that have *chatbots* consider the usefulness for generic tourist consumption, independently of the services of the brand itself or its customers, as previously considered.

The methodology applied is then delimitated according to the research phase covered in this work. The phases are:

- **Preliminary Phase:** Proposal of the study objective through the collection of information from secondary sources to establish the state of the debate, theoretical framework, research objectives and study variables. This involves the reading of the bibliography and an analysis of the real/professional context of the sources of tourist information in the *Web 2.0* and mobile instant messaging in Spain and internationally.
- **Phase 2:** Establishment of the design of the research: population, sample, scope of the research, period, type of research and research technique to apply. These research was carried out on a population of tourist consumers who use mobile instant messaging channels as possible sources to obtain information on such gastronomic tourism services.

For convenience, the selected sample was 393 users who use *WhatsApp* as a channel for gastronomic recommendations in Spain. The company, called Ask Vicente (the only company to deal with user queries in the three phases of the purchase of the tourism product and service), contacted with these users. This company distributed the online survey (see annex 1) between all its active users through WhatsApp.

In this research, this questionnaire included 15 questions, of which 5 of them were selected to address the objectives of this study. The characteristics of these five questions are: 1 open question with multiple answers (alternative channels to *WhatsApp* to obtain gastronomic recommendations), 2 open-closed questions (use of gastronomic *chatbot* through *WhatsApp* and the perception of its use) and another 2 closed multiple answer questions (factors most valued in the information on the recommendations through *WhatsApp* and other relevant factors for users about the information that should be provided in this channel through *WhatsApp*), which address the issues in relation to the general and specific objectives of this study.

The scope of the research is Spain and the field work was carried out from 15 August to 15 October 2016. The type of research carried out is quantitative.

- **Phase 3:** Processing and analysis of the information with the application of descriptive statistical techniques.
- **Phase 4:** Description of results.

In Table 4, the sheet used in the field work for this investigation is shown.

As can be seen in Table 4, the sample is 393 respondents. The profile of the respondents is as follows: 52.4% are women and 47.1% are men. The age range of the sample is from 18 to 56 years and older, distributed as follows: 27.9% of the respondents are aged between 18 and 25, 30.9% between 26 and 35, 18.7% between 36 and 45, 15.1% are aged between 46 and 55 and the remaining 7.4% are aged 56 upwards. Of the total sample, only 13.04% of those who use *WhatsApp* do not use services to obtain gastronomic recommendations.

Table 4. Technical sheet

Study population	*WhatsApp* users
Geographical scope	Spain.
Research technique	Online survey.
Processing and analysis	Descriptive Statistics.
Type of research	Quantitative.
Confidence Margin	95%.
Sample size	393 respondents.
Period of research	15 of August to 15 of October 2016.

Data source: Own research.

RESULTS OF THE RESEARCH

The situations in which users use the MIM *WhatsApp* to obtain tourist service recommendations, as shown in Figure 1, are mainly as follows: first, to look for gastronomic recommendations when in an unknown area; second, to look for recommendations for gastronomic places for celebrations; and finally, to include such gastronomic recommendations in weekend activities or to request a specific recommendation related to a typical dish. Of little importance are the cases related to work circumstances or company meals. These are very closely linked, the first being during the working day and the second because of work commitments but not necessarily during the working day.

Therefore, the situations in which these users rely most on the *chatbot* service for gastronomic recommendations through *WhatsApp* are consultations about the area they are in and to plan celebrations, obtaining the information necessary to reduce their uncertainty (see Figure 2).

Figure 2. Use of the gastronomic chatbot through the MIM service WhatsApp
Data base: Own research.

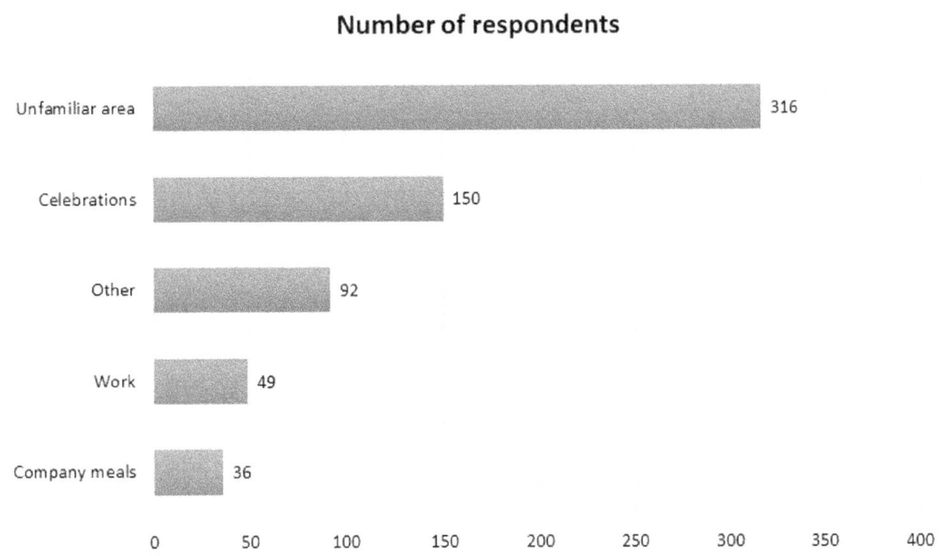

The main perceptions of these consumers about the gastronomic recommendations received from the recommendations channel generated through the *WhatsApp* mobile instant messaging service are (see Figure 3): (1) This channel allows a meal to be planned at an any time and in any place; (2) Channel of recommendations always available when needed; (3) Fast channel in supplying the response. These first three perceptions are related to functional rather than emotional attributes. Regarding the other three perceptions with a lower rating (fun, enjoyable and entertaining), these are related to the empathy of the interactions with the gastronomic recommendation channel through *WhatsApp*. Likewise, it was observed that the responses given by the users in "others" were synonymous with one of the three emotional perceptions mentioned above, so they were recoded.

As can be seen from Figure 4, the factors that these consumers value most when receiving gastronomic recommendations through *WhatsApp* are:

1. The adaptation of the recommendation to their preferences (42%); and
2. Proximity to the location of the users at the time of requesting the gastronomic recommendation (33%). In a lower percentage they value factors related to extra information about the recommended gastronomic place in terms of: accessibility of the recommended place (9%), whether there is a terrace or not (7%) and whether it has parking (6%). This indicates that the factor most valued by users when requesting information from the *chatbot* recommendation service is the proximity of the gastronomic establishment.

Among the alternative tourist information channels for gastronomic restaurant recommendations consulted by the types of consumer studied, Figure 5 shows, in order from most to least, that what stands out are the communities of travellers (*TripAdvisor, El Tenedor, Yelp and Foursquare)* with a figure of 30.27%, among which *TripAdvisor* (21.71%) stands out, followed by the *Google* search engine (16.45%).

Figure 3. Perception of the user of the gastronomic recommendations chatbot through WhatsApp
Data base: Own research.

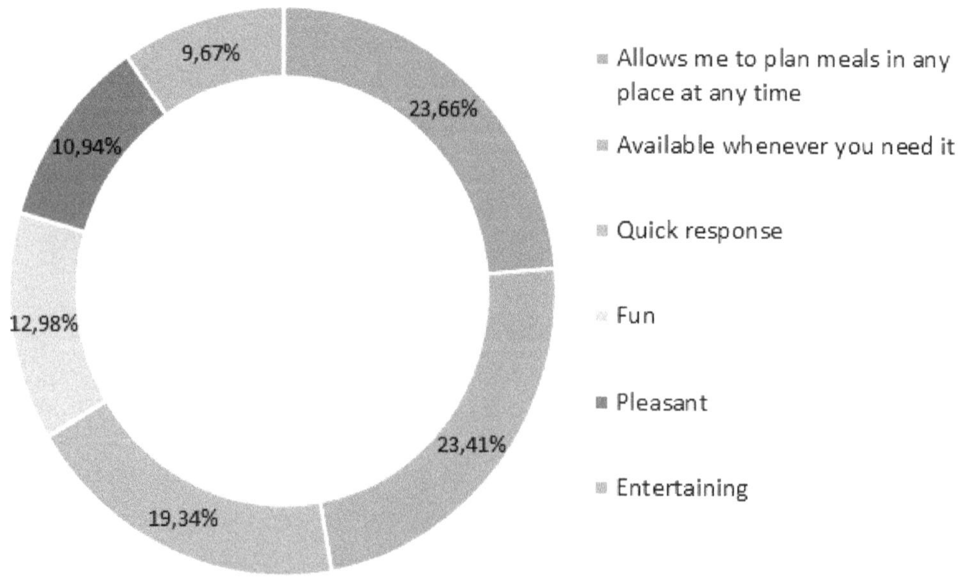

**For a more accurate representation see the electronic version.*

Figure 4. Factors most valued about the gastronomic recommendations through WhatsApp
Data source: Own research.

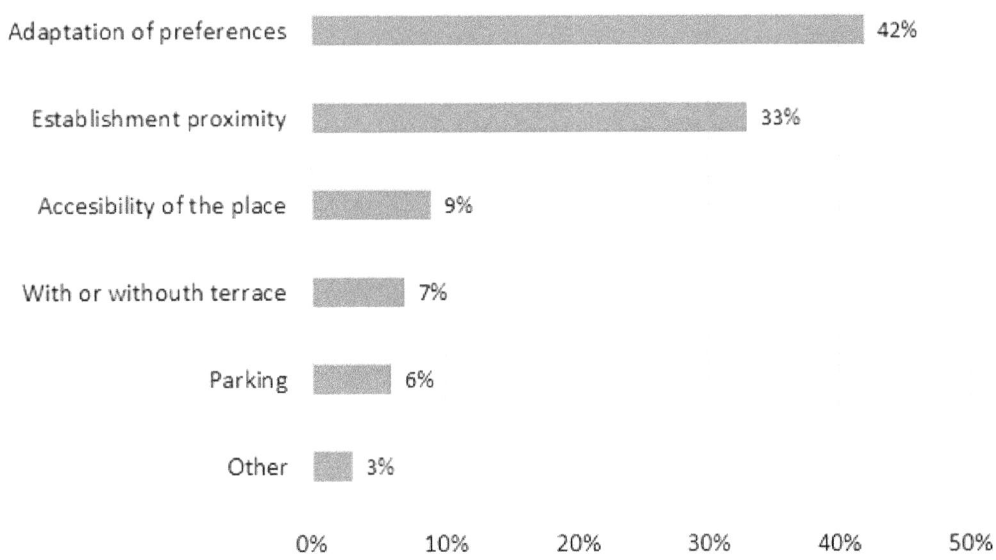

Figure 5. Alternative channels for finding a place to eat
Data source: Own research.

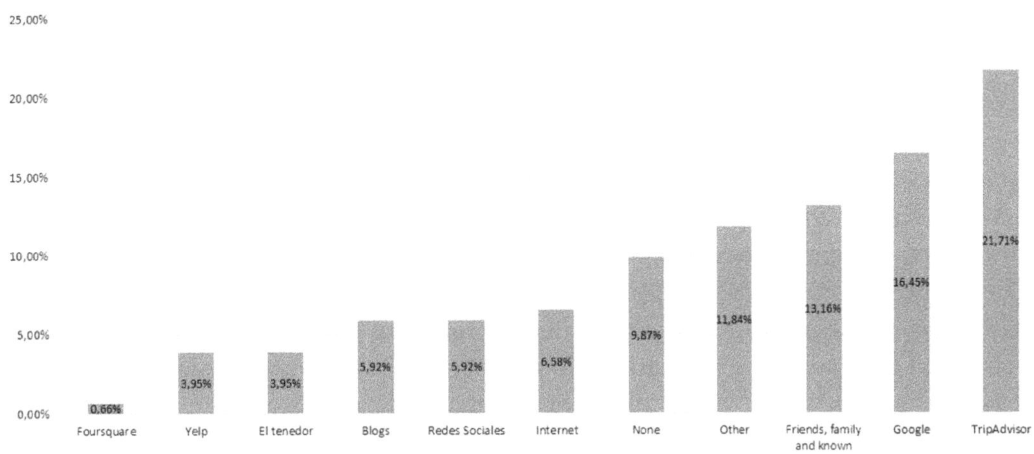

In third place is *offline* advice from friends, acquaintances and family (13.16%), followed by an Internet search in general, (unspecified websites - 6.58%) and social networks and blogs (5.92%).

In terms of the other sorts of tourist product and service recommendations that are relevant for the consumers studied and to be consulted through the MIM channel *WhatsApp,* the following stand out in a range between 20% and 17%: recommendations on offers for shows, of tourist routes in the area, transport and travel recommendations (see Figure 6).

Figure 6. Other types of information on tourist recommendations of interest to the user to be consulted through the MIM channel WhatsApp
Data source: Own research.

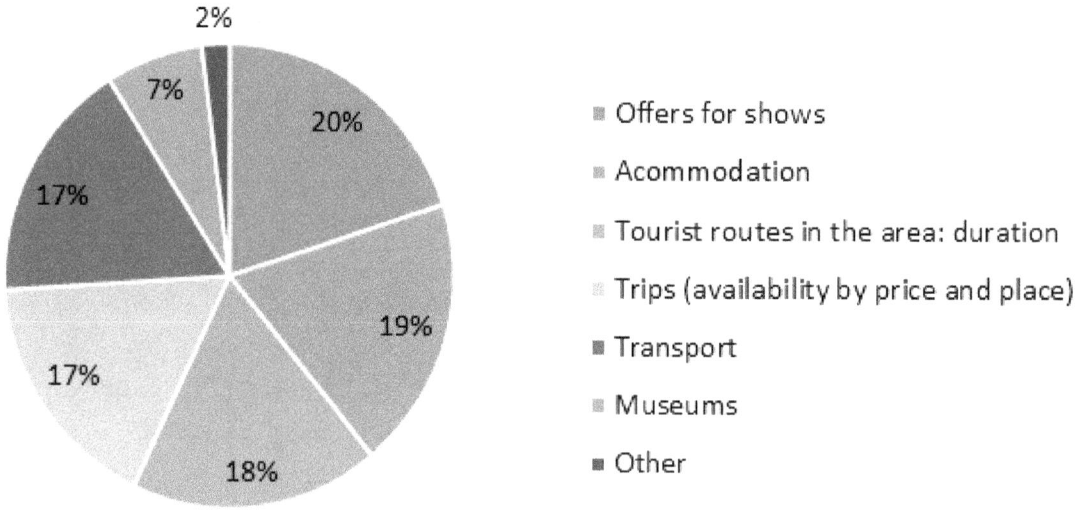

CONCLUSION

This research is based on the contrasted idea that cultural tourism and gastronomy are not two separate areas. Both of them are realities that converge in the daily life of the consumer of cultural tourism. In addition, as it has been the common note in recent years both spheres are under the influence of the Internet. In this last aspect, the Internet incursion into tourism and / or gastronomy has evolved as the online scenario itself. So it goes from the static and official tourist web to forums and social networks. However, it is not easy to imagine that evolution is going to continue. In this sense it is aimed at the entry force of virtual reality or new forms of dialogues more related to Smart-phone such as chatbots.

In this context, the study shows that there is a tendency to use increasingly the mobile instant messaging channels for the search of recommendations, and in particular the new forms of communication within this channel, the chatbots, for the both different profiles of gastronomic tourist (the pure gastronomic tourist and the classic cultural tourist with gastronomic sensitivity) in order to know and enjoy different cultures as if they are profiles of people who live in the places of destination and who make gastronomic cultural consumption

From this research, it can be inferred that the system of dialogue in gastronomic recommendations in particular, but also in tourism in general, plays a decisive factor in all of the stages of the cycle of a trip. So much so that *Web 2.0* channels such as *Kayak, Foursquare* and *Expedia* have also made the move into MIM with the implementation of automated chats to provide coverage and meet the demands of their customers. As seen in this article, the tourist services that have adopted mobile instant messaging applications as an alternative source of information are mainly those related to the search, consultation and booking of flights and accommodation in English and to a lesser extent the information channels recommending gastronomic establishments, where there is only *Ask Vicente*, whose coverage is national. However, there are indications in this research that illustrate the future performance of this *chatbot* to offer a complete process of gastronomic recommendations for consumers. With only two years old, Ask Vicente is used by 9.87% as the main information channel for making gastronomic consumption decisions in Spain.

The typology of chatbots with the characteristics of Ask Vicente, as shown in this study, provides companies in the gastronomic sector with a new technological perspective in the gastronomic recommendation services offered to customers that allow the option of: dialogue and immediacy generated by word of mouth through WhatsApp; permanent availability; and time-independent nature when consulting it to plan a meal. With this type of chatbot of recommendations allows a more satisfactory experience with the tourist consumer, specifically this type of chatbot allows an interpersonal and conversational communication. This protocol of conversation gives humanity to the gastronomic recommendation. The consumer talks to the "peer-to-peer" advocate, causing him greater confidence and trust in the recommendations generated by this gastronomic chatbot.

From this research, it can be seen that the situations in which consumers use a *chatbot* for recommendations through the mobile instant messaging service *WhatsApp* when looking for a gastronomic establishment are determined by circumstantial factors. As a result, since they often are used in moments of leisure such as celebrations, what is appreciated most is the functional characteristics of this channel along with the characteristics of experience in using it.

Therefore, this type of gastronomic cultural tourism consumer positively values its permanent availability and time-independent nature when consulting it to plan a meal. These factors in the use of this MIM channel coincide with some of the factors in the use of web 2.0 channels for tourism queries. In addition, this type of consumer perceives that it operates in a way, which is pleasant, fun and entertaining. These characteristics should be highlighted because these traits are found in almost none of the Web 2.0 channels analysed; they are more related to experience of use than functionality. This reflects the fact that the type of consumer who uses this sort of query channel is not only the pure gastronomic tourist but also the classic tourist with gastronomic sensitivity, that is to say, the one who goes out to eat for leisure and whose use of this channel is based on situational circumstances.

The study reveals the role played for this user by their immediate environment, specifically friends, family and acquaintances, when it comes to obtaining information and recommendations in this area. The results show that the gastronomic tourist consumer is still using recommendations based on *word of mouth*, through either *offline* channels or *Web 2.0* channels. We therefore find that the option of dialogue and immediacy generated by *word of mouth* through *WhatsApp* is a differential advantage, meaning that in the coming years the Mobile Instant Messaging (MIM) channels, here specifically referring to *chatbots*, will be the preferred option in the consultation of gastronomic tourism.

The three aspects most highly rated when looking for gastronomic recommendations through the *WhatsApp* channel are: adaptation to the preferences of the user, proximity to the location and accessibility. The user demands recommendations based on their geolocation and for a specific moment when they want their need to be addressed. Again, it is confirmed that a *chatbot* of gastronomic recommendations through MIM offers the option of not only helping when planning to go to a restaurant but also meeting immediate and instant needs through a conversation, without having to carefully evaluate the information generated by other users, as is the case with *Web 2.0* tourist information channels. In addition, these users affirm that *WhatsApp* would be a good channel for searching for, requesting and consulting information related to other tourist products and services, beyond gastronomy, such as exhibitions, accommodation and cultural routes.

From this research it can be seen that the factors that determine the use of a *chatbot* for tourist recommendations through *WhatsApp* when searching for a restaurant during a cultural trip are related to the factors that influence the use of the *Web 2.0* tourist information channels based on user-generated content. Among these factors, what stands out is it being time-independent, that is, the option of consulting these channels with no time or geographic limitations, and the way they adapt to the preferences of the consumer to offer recommendations according to indications and needs.

However, this study reveals that there is a key factor in the use by consumers of gastronomic recommendations through WhatsApp that does not apply to some *Web 2.0* information channels, namely the immediacy of response. This advantage also means that the future of these MIM channels with the implementation of a *chatbot* is one of the best options for finding an immediate response that provides the gastronomic recommendation of interest requested by the pure and classic gastronomic tourist.

Because of all this, it has been demonstrated that cultural tourism and gastronomy are not two separate spheres, but realities that converge in the daily life of the cultural tourism consumer and under the influence of the Internet. This study shows that, for both the different types of gastronomic tourist (the pure and classic with gastronomic sensitivity) who travel from their places of origin to the chosen destinations in order to experience and enjoy different cultures and for the types of people who live in the places of destination and enjoy gastronomic cultural consumption, there is an increasing tendency to use mobile instant messaging channels in the search for recommendations, and in particular the new forms of communication within this channel, *chatbots*.

This investigation uses descriptive methodologies. Although this methodology could be considered a weakness of this study, however, given the novelty of the topic, this research helps the readers to get a first idea on the subject. Moreover, due to the limitation of time and resources, this research has been developed in the country of Spain. In this geographical scope of the study, there is a small number of platforms that currently offer this service of gastronomic *chatbots* and an incipient knowledge on the part of the Spanish society of these gastronomic services versus other countries. Given these limitations, we have considered the study sample only customers of this type of gastronomic *chatbots* and specifically those customers of a single platform of *chatbots* that is operative in Spain, Ask Vicente.

Faced with these limitations, we consider that in future research lines should extend the geographic scope of study and contemplate other platforms to define the variables determining the use of *chatbots* specialised in gastronomic tourism through mobile instant messaging to contribute to improving the experience of the tourist in the search of information.

ACKNOWLEDGMENT

This research has been possible thanks to the funding of the Universidad de Málaga, Andalucía-Tech.

This research has been possible thanks to the collaboration of the company levelbots for the *Ask Vicente* field study.

REFERENCES

AbuShawar, B., & Atwell, E. (2016). Usefulness, localizability, humanness, and language-benefit: Additional evaluation criteria for natural language dialogue systems. *International Journal of Speech Technology*, *19*(2), 373–383. doi:10.1007/s10772-015-9330-4

Acevin. (2012). *Informe de visitantes a bodegas asociadas a las Rutas del Vino de España. Año 2011.* Ministerio de Industria Energía y Turismo e Instituto de Turismo de España.

Albacete, C. A. S. (2012). *Las tecnologías de la información y comunicación en el sector turístico: una aproximación al uso de las redes sociales*. Madrid: Universitaria Ramón Areces.

Alonso, A., Figueroa, C., Rodríguez, J., & Talón, P. (2008). *El impacto de la tecnología social en las decisiones de consumo turístico.* TURITEC 2008, VII Congreso de Turismo y Tecnologías de la Información y de las Comunicaciones, Málaga.

Ariyasriwatana, W., Buente, W., Oshiro, M., & Streveler, D. (2014). Categorizing health-related cues to action: Using Yelp reviews of restaurants in Hawaii. *New Review of Hypermedia and Multimedia*, *20*(4), 317–340. doi:10.1080/13614568.2014.987326

Ariyasriwatana, W., & Quiroga, L. M. (2016). A thousand ways to sayDelicious!' Categorizing expressions of deliciousness from restaurant reviews on the social network site Yelp. *Appetite*, *104*, 18–32. doi:10.1016/j.appet.2016.01.002 PMID:26774047

Ávila, R., & Barrado, D. A. (2005). Nuevas tendencia en el desarrollo de destinos turísticos: Marcos conceptuales y operativos para su planificación y gestión. *Cuadernos de Turismo*, *15*, 27–43.

Ayeh, J. K., Au, N., & Law, R. (2013a). Predicting the intention to use consumer-generated media for travel planning. *Tourism Management*, *35*, 132–143. doi:10.1016/j.tourman.2012.06.010

Ayeh, J. K., Au, N., & Law, R. (2013b). Do we believe in TripAdvisor? Examining credibility perceptions and online travelers attitude toward using user-generated content. *Journal of Travel Research*, *52*(4), 437–452. doi:10.1177/0047287512475217

Barrios, M. (2012). Marketing de la Experiencia: Principales conceptos y características. *Palermo Business Review*, *7*(1), 67–83.

Bere, A., & Rambe, P. (2016). An Empirical Analysis of the Determinants of Mobile Instant Messaging Appropriation in University Learning. *Journal of Computing in Higher Education*, *28*(2), 172–198. doi:10.1007/s12528-016-9112-2

Bigné, E., Hernández, B., Ruiz, C., & Andreu, L. (2010). How motivation, opportunity and ability can drive online airline ticket purchases. *Journal of Air Transport Management*, *16*(6), 346–349. doi:10.1016/j.jairtraman.2010.05.004

Borja, L., Andreu, J. C., & Bosch, R. C. (2002). *El Consumidor Turístico*. Madrid: ESIC Editorial.

Borja, S. L., & Gomis, J. M. (2009). *El nuevo paradigma de la intermediación turística*. Madrid: Ediciones Pirámide.

Bressler, S. E., & Grantham, C. (2000). *Communities of commerce: Building internet business communities to accelerate growth, minimize risk, and increase customer loyalty*. McGraw-Hill Professional.

Buhalis, D. (2003). *E-Tourism: Information technology for strategic tourism Management.* Pearson Education.

Buhalis, D., & Law, R. (2008). Progress in Information Technology and Tourism Management: 20 years on and 10 years after the internet in The state of eTourism Research. *Tourism Management, 29*(4), 609–623. doi:10.1016/j.tourman.2008.01.005

Burgess, S., Sellitto, C., Cox, C., & Buultjens, J. (2009, June). User-generated content (UGC) in tourism: Benefits and concerns of online consumers. ECIS, 417-429.

Burguess, L., & Kerr, G. (2012, June). Australian Traveller's Use of the Internet: Understanding Australian Online Planning and Booking Behaviour. *8th Annual International Conference on Tourism*, 11-14.

Cai, L. A., Feng, R., & Breiter, D. (2004). Tourist purchase decision involvement and information preferences. *Journal of Vacation Marketing, 10*(2), 138-148.

Cambourne, B., Mitchell, R., Hall, C. M., Sharples, L., & Macionis, N. (2003). *Food tourism around the world: Development, management and markets*. Amsterdam: Elsevier Ltd.

Cheung, M. Y., Luo, C., Sia, C. L., & Chen, H. (2009). Credibility of electronic word-of-mouth: Informational and normative determinants of on-line consumer recommendations. *International Journal of Electronic Commerce, 13*(4), 9–38. doi:10.2753/JEC1086-4415130402

Cho, Y., & Fesenmaier, D. R. (2001). A new paradigm for tourism and electronic commerce: Experience marketing using the virtual tour. *Tourism Distribution Channels: Practices, Issues and Transformation*, 351-370.

Chung, J. Y., & Buhalis, D. (2008). A study of online travel community and Web 2.0: Factors affecting participation and attitude. *Proceedings Enter, 2008*, 267–278.

Cohen, E., & Avieli, N. (2004). Food in tourism: Attraction and impediment. *Annals of Tourism Research, 31*(4), 755–778. doi:10.1016/j.annals.2004.02.003

Cracolici, M. F., & Nijkamp, P. (2009). The attractiveness and competitiveness of tourist destinations: A study of Southern Italian regions. *Tourism Management, 30*(3), 336–344. doi:10.1016/j.tourman.2008.07.006

Da Cruz, G., Velozo, T., & Elvas Falcão Soares, A. (2011). Twitter, Youtube e innovación en la promoción turística online: Análisis de las estrategias del Ministerio de Turismo de Brasil. *Estudios y perspectivas en turismo, 20*(3), 627-642.

De La Rosa, B. M. (2003). Nuevos turistas en busca de un nuevo producto: El patrimonio cultural. *Pasos. Revista de Turismo y Cultura, 1*(2), 157–159.

Dos Santos, R. J., & Antoninni, B. O. (2004). La gastronomía típica de la Isla de Santa Catarina (Brasil). *Estudios y Perspectivas en Turismo, 13*, 89–110.

Ejemplo de Mealhada–Portugal, U. (2007). La importancia de la gastronomía en el Turismo. *Estudios y Perspectivas en Turismo, 16*, 261–282.

Fernandes Galhanone, R., Marques, J. A., Toledo, G. L., & Mazzon, J. A. (2010). Turismo de lujo e internet: Oportunidades para las agencias de viajes. *Estudios y perspectivas en turismo, 19*(6), 888-908.

Fields, K. (2002). Demand for the gastronomy tourism product: motivational factors. In Tourism and gastronomy (pp. 36-50). London: Routledge.

Filieri, R., & Mcleay, F. (2013). E-WOM and Accommodation: An Analysis of the Factors That Influence Travelers Adoption of Information from Online Reviews. *Journal of Travel Research, 53*(1), 44–57. doi:10.1177/0047287513481274

Flavián, C., & Fandos, C. (Eds.). (2011). Turismo gastronómico: estrategias de marketing y experiencias de éxito. Zaragoza: Prensas Universitarias de Zaragoza.

Fodness, D., & Murray, B. (1997). Tourist information search. *Annals of Tourism Research, 24*(3), 503–523. doi:10.1016/S0160-7383(97)00009-1

Fotis, J., Buhalis, D., & Rossides, N. (2012). *Social media use and impact during the holiday travel planning process* (pp. 13–24). Springer-Verlag. doi:10.1007/978-3-7091-1142-0_2

Fox, R. (2007). Reinventing the gastronomic identity of Croatian tourist destinations. *International Journal of Hospitality Management, 3*(3), 546–559. doi:10.1016/j.ijhm.2006.03.001

García, J. J. (2016). Estrategias de las empresas turísticas a través de dispositivos móviles. AECA. *Revista de la Asociación Española de Contabilidad y Administración de Empresas, 113*, 16–20.

Gasdia, M. & Rheem, C. (2012). *Mobile Hits the Mainstream: Leisure and Business Traveler Trends.* PhoCusWright.

Gómez, M. M., & Rubio, F. R. (1999). Turismo cultural: el caso de Sevilla. *Cuadernos de turismo, 4*, 33-50.

González, M. V. (2009). Gestión turística del patrimonio cultural: enfoques para un desarrollo sostenible del turismo cultural. *Cuadernos de turismo, 23*, 237-254.

Gretzel, U., Yoo, K. H., & Purifoy, M. (2007). *Online travel review study: Role and impact of online travel reviews.* Laboratory for Inteligent Systems in Tourism, Texas A&M University.

Guzmán-López, T., & Jesus, M. M. (2011). Turismo, cultura y gastronomía. Una aproximación a las rutas culinarias. *Encontros Científicos-Tourism & Management Studies*, (1), 915-922.

Ha, Y. W., Kim, J., Libaque-Saenz, C. F., Chang, Y., & Park, M. C. (2015). Use and gratifications of mobile SNSs: Facebook and KakaoTalk in Korea. *Telematics and Informatics, 32*(3), 425–438. doi:10.1016/j.tele.2014.10.006

Hays, S., Page, S. J., & Buhalis, D. (2013). Social media as a destination marketing tool: Its use by national tourism organisations. *Current Issues in Tourism, 16*(3), 211–239. doi:10.1080/13683500.2012.662215

Henry, A. (1987). *Consumer behavior and marketing action.* Boston: Academic Press.

Herbert, D. (2001). Literary places, tourism and the heritage experience. *Annals of Tourism Research, 28*(2), 312–333. doi:10.1016/S0160-7383(00)00048-7

Hill, J., Ford, W. R., & Farreras, I. G. (2015). Real conversations with artificial intelligence: A comparison between human–human online conversations and human–chatbot conversations. *Computers in Human Behavior, 49*, 245–250. doi:10.1016/j.chb.2015.02.026

Hjalager, A. M. (2010). A review of innovation research in tourism. *Tourism Management, 31*(1), 1–12. doi:10.1016/j.tourman.2009.08.012

Hsu, C. H. C., & Huang, S. (2012). An extension of the theory of planned behavior model for tourists. *Journal of Hospitality & Tourism Research (Washington, D.C.), 36*(3), 390–417. doi:10.1177/1096348010390817

Hsu, C. L., & Lin, J. C. (2008). Acceptance of blog usage: The roles of technology acceptance, social influence and knowledge sharing motivation. *Information & Management, 45*(1), 65–74. doi:10.1016/j.im.2007.11.001

Hudson, S., Huang, L., Roth, M. S., & Madden, T. J. (2016). The influence of social media interactions on consumer–brand relationships: A three-country study of brand perceptions and marketing behaviors. *International Journal of Research in Marketing, 33*(1), 27–41. doi:10.1016/j.ijresmar.2015.06.004

Huh, H. J., Kim, T., & Law, R. (2009). A comparasion of competing theoretical models for understanding acceptance behavior of information systems in upscale hotels. *International Journal of Hospitality Management, 28*(1), 717–724. doi:10.1016/j.ijhm.2008.06.004

Ibarra, J. G. (2001). Análisis de la oferta de turismo cultural en España. *Estudios turísticos*, 15-40.

Kivela, J. Y., & Crotts, J. (2006). Tourism and gastronomy: Gastronomys influence on how tourists experience a destination. *Journal of Hospitality & Tourism Research (Washington, D.C.), 3*(3), 354–377. doi:10.1177/1096348006286797

Korgaonkar, P., Silverblatt, R., & Girard, T. (2006). Online retailing, product classifications, and consumer preferences. *Internet Research, 16*(3), 267–288. doi:10.1108/10662240610673691

Lee, T. Y., & Crompton, J. (1992). Measuring novelty seeking in tourism. *Annals of Tourism Research, 4*(4), 732–737. doi:10.1016/0160-7383(92)90064-V

Litvin, S. W., Goldsmith, R. E., & Pan, B. (2008). Electronic word-of-mouth in hospitality and tourism management. *Tourism Management, 29*(3), 458–468. doi:10.1016/j.tourman.2007.05.011

López-Guzmán, T., & Sánchez Cañizares, S. M. (2012). La gastronomía como motivación para viajar. Un estudio sobre el turismo culinario en Córdoba. *Guía de Estilo para Autores, 10*, 575.

López-Guzmán, T. J., & Sánchez-Cañizares, S. M. (2008). La creación de productos turísticos utilizando rutas enológicas. *Pasos. Revista de Turismo y Patrimonio Cultural, 2*, 159–171.

Mak, A. H. N., Lumbers, M., Eves, A., & Chang, R. C. Y. (2012a). Factors influencing tourist food consumption. *International Journal of Hospitality Management, 3*(3), 928–936. doi:10.1016/j.ijhm.2011.10.012

Marrero Rodríguez, J. R., & Abdul-Jalbar, B. (2012). Turismo cultural y planificación del viaje: un estudio de caso. *Tourism & Management Studies*, (8), 41-47.

McCabe, S. (2014). Towards a better theory of tourism experience? A response to Gnoth and Matteucci. *International Journal of Culture. Tourism and Hospitality Research*, *8*(2). doi:10.1108/IJCTHR-04-2014-0026

McCabe, S. (2014). Towards a better theory of tourism experience? A response to Gnoth and Matteucci. *International Journal of Culture. Tourism and Hospitality Research*, *8*(2). doi:10.1108/IJCTHR-04-2014-0026

Melián González, S., Bulchand Gidumal, J., & González López-Valcárcel, B. (2010). La participación de los clientes en sitios web de valoración de servicios turísticos. El caso de Tripadvisor. *Revista de Análisis Turístico*, *10*, 17–22.

Mendes-Filho, L., & Santos Dantas De Carvalho, M. (2014). Factores que influyen en el uso del contenido generado por el usuario en Internet: Un Estudio Preliminar Con Viajeros Brasileños. *Estudios Y Perspectivas en Turismo*, *23*(3), 607-625.

Millán, M. G., & Agudo, E. M. (2010). El turismo gastronómico y las Denominaciones de Origen en el sur de España: Oleoturismo. Un estudio de caso. *Pasos. Revista de Turismo y Patrimonio Cultural*, *1*, 91–112.

Mogollón, J. M. H., Di Clemente, E., & Guzmán, T. J. L. G. (2015). El turismo gastronómico como experiencia cultural. El caso práctico de la ciudad de Cáceres (España). *Boletín de la Asociación de Geógrafos Españoles*, (68), 407-428.

Molz, J. G. (2007). Eating difference: The cosmopolitan mobilities of culinary tourism. *Space and Culture*, *10*(1), 77–93. doi:10.1177/1206331206296383

Nelson, P. (1970). Information and consumer behavior. *Journal of Political Economy*, *78*(2), 311–329. doi:10.1086/259630

O'Connor, P. (2011). *An Analysis of the use of Facebook by International Hotel Chains (Comunicação apresentada no International Council on Hotel, Restaurant and Institucional Education – CHRIE)*. Denver, CO: Conference.

Oghuma, A. P., Libaque-Saenz, C. F., Wong, S. F., & Chang, Y. (2016). An Expectation-Confirmation Model Of Continuance Intention To Use Mobile Instant Messaging. *Telematics and Informatics*, *33*(1), 34–47. doi:10.1016/j.tele.2015.05.006

Oliveira, S. (2007). La importancia de la Gastronomia en el turismo. *Estudios y Perspectivas en Turismo*, *16*, 261–282.

Parra-López, E., Bulchand-Gidumal, J., Gutiérrez-Taño, D., & Díaz-Armas, R. (2011). Intentions to use social media in organizing and taking vacation trips. *Computers in Human Behavior*, *27*(2), 640–654. doi:10.1016/j.chb.2010.05.022

Richards, G. (2001). El desarrollo del turismo cultural en Europa. *Estudios turísticos*, 3-14.

Richards, G. (2002). Gastronomy: An essential ingredient in tourism production and consumption. *Tourism and Gastronomy*, *11*, 2-20.

Rickly, J. M., & McCabe, S. (2017). Authenticidad para Turismo Diseño y experiencia. In Design Science in Tourism (pp. 55-68). Springer International Publishing.

Ricolfe, J. S. C., Merino, B. R., Marzo, S. V., Ferrandis, M. T. R., & Rodríguez, C. M. (2008). Actitud hacia la gastronomía local de los turistas: Dimensiones y segmentación de mercado. *PASOS. Revista de Turismo y Patrimonio Cultural*, *6*(2es), 189–198.

Ritzer, G. (1995). *The McDonaldization of society*. London: Sage.

Roden, C. (2003). *Local food and culture in Local Food & Tourism International Conference: Larnaka, Cyprus 9-11 November 2000* (OMT, Coord.). Madrid: World Tourism Organization.

Roque, V., & Raposo, R. (2013). *Os Media Sociais como uma Ferramenta de Comunicação e Marketing no Turismo: uma análise das atividades online dos principais atores portugueses*. Academic Press.

Rosen, E. (2008). *Buzz Marketing de Boca em Boca*. Cascais: Gestãoplus.

Ryu, M. H., Kim, S., & Lee, E. (2009). Understanding the factors affecting online elderly users participation in video UCC services. *Computers in Human Behavior*, *25*(3), 619–632. doi:10.1016/j.chb.2008.08.013

Salgado Criado, J., Bujarski, L., & Merten, R. (2013). *European Online Travel Overview* (9th ed.). Phocuswright.

Sánchez-Cañizares, S., & López-Guzmán, T. (2011). Gastronomy as a tourism resource: Profile of the culinary tourist. *Current Issues in Tourism*, *3*, 229–245.

Schlüter, R. G. (2003). *Gastronomia e turismo*. São Paulo: Editora Aleph.

Segittur. (2016). *Ministerio de Energia,Turismo y Agenda Digital*. Segitur Turismo e Innovación. Retrieved from http://www.segittur.es/es/inicio/index.html

Shah, H., Warwick, K., Vallverdú, J., & Wu, D. (2016). Can Machines Talk? Comparison Of Eliza With Modern Dialogue Systems. *Computers in Human Behavior*, *58*, 278–295. doi:10.1016/j.chb.2016.01.004

Silva, M. M., & Mendes Filho, L. (2014). Intenção de Uso de Comentários de Viagem Online na Escolha de um Meio de Hospedagem: Fatores Influenciadores. *Revista Brasileira De Pesquisa em Turismo*, *8*(3), 419–434. doi:10.7784/rbtur.v8i3.805

Silva, M. M., & Mendes Filho, L. (2014). Intenção de uso de Comentários de Viagem Online na Escolha de um Meio de Hospedagem: Fatores Influenciadores. *Revista Brasileira De Pesquisa Em Turismo*, *8*(3), 419–434. doi:10.7784/rbtur.v8i3.805

Taño, D. G., Gidumal, J. B., Armas, R. J. D., & López, E. P. (2013). Antecedentes del Uso de los Medios Sociales por el Turista: Motivación, Oportunidad Y Capacidad. *Cuadernos De Turismo*, (31), 153-173.

Torres Bernier, E. (2003). Del turista que se alimenta al turista que busca comida. In *Gastronomía y Turismo. Cultura al Plato* (pp. 305–316). Buenos Aires: CIET.

Toselli, C. (2006). Algunas reflexiones sobre el turismo cultural. *Pasos. Revista de turismo y patrimonio cultural, 4*(2), 175-182.

Vinha, I. (2004). *Gastronomia. Atracção turística primária (Estudo de caso os "domingos gastronómicos")*. Tesis de Licenciatura, Universidade de Aveiro.

Wang, Y., & Fesenmaier, D. R. (2004). Towards Understanding Members› General Participation In An Active Contribution To An Online Travel Community. *Tourism Management*, *25*(6), 709–722. doi:10.1016/j.tourman.2003.09.011

Wichels, S. (2014). *Nuevos desafíos en Relaciones Públicas 2.0: La creciente influencia de las plataformas de online review en Turismo*. Academic Press.

Wu, J., & Lu, X. (2013). Effects of extrinsic and intrinsic motivators on using utilitarian, hedonic, and dual-purposed information systems: A meta-analysis. *Journal of the Association for Information Systems*, *14*(3), 153.

Xiang, Z., & Gretzel, U. (2010). Role of social media in online travel information search. *Tourism Management*, *31*(2), 179–188. doi:10.1016/j.tourman.2009.02.016

Xifra, J., & Chias, J. (2008). *Las Relaciones Públicas y el Marketing*. Barcelona: UOC.

Yoo, K. H., Lee, Y., Gretzel, U., & Fesenmaier, D. R. (2009). Trust in travel-related consumer generated media. *Information and communication technologies in tourism 2009*, 49-59.

Zhang, W., & Watts, S. A. (2008). Capitalizing on content: Information adoption in two online communities. *Journal of the Association for Information Systems*, *9*(2), 73.

KEY TERMS AND DEFINITIONS

Ask Vicente: *Chatbot* of gastronomic recommendations through mobile instant messaging.

Chatbots: Software based on artificial intelligence that allows communication with humans in text conversations through interfaces. Provides automated responses to user requests.

Foodie: In this context this refers to a tourist consumer whose main motivation for travelling is the gastronomy at the destination. These are "food lovers" who enjoy going out to eat and trying new dishes rather than just satisfying their need for food.

Peer to Peer (MIM): Person to person communication and is the way of communicating without automated processes to respond to the needs of the user through mobile instant messaging channels.

UGC - User Generated Content: This is information created by the users in the Web 2.0 channels.

Web 2.0 (Web Social): Set of online channels (social networks, websites, blogs, wikis, etc.) that facilitate the sharing of information within a community where the user has control of publishing content and sharing it with the rest.

Wine Tourism: A type of tourism focused on wine production areas. It has a close relationship with gastronomic tourism and can also have a relationship with cultural tourism depending on the historical or artistic nature of the wine industry in the area, taken as industrial heritage.

ENDNOTES

1 WeCh: *WeChat*
2 Eng: English
3 WA: *WhatsApp*
4 Sp: Spanish
5 FBM: *Facebook Messenger*

APPENDIX

The questionnaire questions that addressed the objectives of this research are the following:

1. I use Ask Vicente for the following reason:
    a. Work
    b. Company meals
    c. Celebrations
    d. Unfamiliar areas
    e. Others:____________________
2. The use of Ask Vicente for you is:
    a. Fun
    b. Pleasant
    c. Entertaining
    d. Available when ever you need it
    e. Quick response
    f. Allows me to plan meals in any place at any time
    g. Others:_________________
3. Aspects that you value about the recommendations of Ask Vicente:
    a. Establishment proximity
    b. Accessibility of the place
    c. Parking
    d. With or without terrace
    e. Adaptive of preferences
    f. Others:____________________
4. Other channels consulted in addition to Ask Vicente to find a place to eat:
    a. Tripadvisor
    b. Yelp
    c. Foursquare
    d. El Tenedor
    e. Google
    f. Blogs
    g. Internet
    h. Friends, family and known (WoW)
    i. Social Networks
    j. Others
    k. None
5. Other type of recommendations from Ask Vicente that you are interested in knowing:
    a. Museums
    b. Offers for Shows
    c. Transports
    d. Trips (Availability by price and place)
    e. Tourist Routes in the area: Duration
    f. Accommodations

Chapter 16
Information Mycological Systems and Traditional Ecological Knowledge:
The Case of Mycological Tourism in Central Mexico

Humberto Thomé-Ortiz
Universidad Autónoma del Estado de México, Mexico

ABSTRACT

Wild edible fungi are non-timber forest products that have great relevance for forest communities in central Mexico. Texcaltitlán is a rural community known for its traditional ecological knowledge on the use and identification of wild edible mushrooms. The aim of this work is to link Geographic Information Systems and Traditional Ecological Knowledge, in order to generate Mycological Information Systems. This is a qualitative, quantitative and exploratory research, which seeks to determine the usefulness of Geographic Information Systems (GIS) to systematize and locate mycological resources for use as a tourist attraction. The results show the existence of a wide variety of edible mushrooms in the region, along with a wide mycological traditional knowledge. Both aspects reflect the existence of unique natural and cultural features that can be the basis to build a unique tourism product in central Mexico. It is concluded that GIS are useful tools to build a multifunctional vision of mushrooms.

INTRODUCTION

This chapter is part of a basic scientific research entitled "Evaluation of the recreational dimension of wild edible mushrooms, their socioeconomic interest and their perspectives of rural development", supported by the National Council of Science and Technology of Mexico. This project contains three central components: (i) a participatory approach integrating local stakeholders as promoters of mycological tourism; (ii) generating mycological information systems based on traditional ecological knowledge

DOI: 10.4018/978-1-5225-2927-9.ch016

and scientific knowledge; and (iii) proposing a strategy for the tourism management of mycological resources in the central Mexican plateau.

Mycological tourism consists of experimenting with the natural and cultural dimensions of wild edible mushrooms, through an articulated offer of goods and services that allow a recreational experience to be lived. Its main activities are the identification, harvesting and tasting of the mushrooms in close contact with the nature and mushroom picking communities. This tourist modality is part of the new trends in rural tourism that are characterized by their high specialization, focused on a product anchored to the territory.

Mycological tourism is an example of the valorization of forests as a tourist resource in contemporary societies. The growing importance of forest spaces as tourist scenarios is associated with the specific characteristics of these ecosystems. This value can be increased by modifying forest management practices; For example, by maintaining the abundance of certain local resources of special interest (Bostedt & Mattsson, 1995). However, tourism exploitation of forests also generates environmental, social and cultural risks (Kuvan, 2005). Aspect by which planning is a central theme.

In the case of Geographic Information Systems, the interconnections between tourism and new technologies not only reveal the location of tourist attractions in a specific territory. Rather, they allow the mobilization of local resources, converted into cultural goods, as a distinctive sign of contemporary tourist leisure (Hannam, Butler & Morris, 2014).

The objective of this chapter is to analyze the relationship between mycological tourism and Geographic Information Systems as a tool for tourism planning in rural areas. All this from a participatory approach in which traditional ecological knowledge serves as a source of information and a point of reference to guide policies for economic restructuring of rural areas.

For this the text is divided into six parts. After this introductory section the relationship between Geographic Information Systems and Mycological Tourism is presented. Later, the use of GIS in the planning of mycological tourism is explored as a tool for generating data that can be analyzed from an integral and participatory perspective for the determination of the tourist potential of the territory and its adequate spatial projection. Later, the case study in a forest community in central Mexico is presented, where the characteristics of the observation unit and the methodological design of the research are discussed. Next, the application of the Mycological Information System is presented, through the evaluation of local mycological resources and a proposal of paths for mycological tourism. Finally, the conclusions and some considerations for the future of the research are presented.

BACKGROUND

Geographic Information Systems Applied to Tourism

The use of local resources for tourism can produce the opportunity to generate processes of socio-economic transformation that help to improve the quality of life of rural inhabitants. However, the introduction of new non-agricultural rural activities such as tourism requires the development of systematized information platforms for the success of development strategies.

In the case of nature-based tourism, many of the resources in which the activity is focused can be documented through spatial information sources that indicate the quantity and characteristics of tourism resources, as well as the socio-economic impacts that can derive from their use as tourist capital.

Traditionally, the application of Geographic Information Systems (GIS) has focused on environmental issues and resource management (Robinson, 1992). Equally important are the works on rural space planning developed by Haines-Young, Bunce and Parr (1994). Both cases are important background on the use of GIS in the planning and management of tourism in rural areas.

The use of GIS can be a useful tool for tourism planning and management in rural areas where there is a clear lack of systematic information on local resources and where it is essential to avoid the negative impacts of tourism. This is of particular relevance in contexts where natural and cultural resources are vulnerable to anthropic, economic and political pressures related to tourism.

Having quality information is a key aspect of tourism spatial planning, to detect the multifunctional use of the territory, and to avoid the emergence of new social tensions among local actors linked to key resources. From a vision of the data that integrates socioeconomic and environmental variables, a set of negative effects and potential risks that tourism can generate in natural resources can be prevented. GIS can be an important tool to analyse the scenarios of the productive transformation of rural space.

According to the above, it is intended to detect the conflicts generated by tourism, to prevent negative impacts and to have elements for making decisions (Bahaire & Elliot-White, 1999), which is why GIS can play an important role in the planning, development and evaluation of the tourist activity.

There are several uses of GIS related to tourism, among which are: database design, map production, spatial analysis, spatial modelling and support for making decisions. In this way, it is possible to create multiple tourist applications such as resource inventories, tourism feasibility assessment, impact measurement, route design and the development of prospective tourism scenarios (Bahaire & Elliot-White, 1999).

There are pioneering works where GIS has been used as a tool for the analysis of resources related to tourism (Gunn, 1994). Through the overlapping of maps the tourism potential of the territory is identified through the selection of active and interpretive tourism zones, depending on the characteristics of the natural resources. In the same direction, Boyd and Butler (1996) use GIS to identify suitable spaces for the development of ecotourism through the association between natural resources and the specific characteristics of the landscape.

Some papers have explored the relationship between GIS and tourism planning in North America. In this regard, it is essential that local actors have key information about the location and availability of tourism resources, assessing the points of conflict and complementarity between tourism and other activities, and predicting the fragility of local resources (Williams, Paul & Hainsworth 1996).

GIS, Mycological Resources and Mycological Tourism

Spain is the pioneer in the management and use of mycological resources, through the use of GIS as a tool to generate data about wild edible mushrooms. With this objective, MICODATA was created, which is a system for the collection and management of data on wild edible mushrooms with socioeconomic importance in the province of Castilla y León. This system is based on soil and climate variables to generate useful information for the collectors and to provide advice for the management of mycological resources.

The objectives of MICODATA can be summarized as follows: (i) generate a mycological information system; (ii) have objective criteria for assessing the sustainable management and socio-economic impact of mycological resources; (iii) provide general information on the productivity, regulation and conditions of mushroom harvesting, through a web platform; and iv) contribute to the regulation and management of mycological resources (Martínez-Peña, et al., 2009).

From the MICODATA model, the need for a Mycological Information System with a participatory approach in central Mexico is proposed, for this it is necessary to integrate Geographic Information Systems, applied forest mycology, ethno-mycology and an approach from the tourist studies (Thomé-Ortiz, 2015).

The participatory approach proposed in this work is a tool for tourism planning based on the involvement of local mushroom pickers in the decision making process and the benefits of tourism. It seeks to integrate the vision of local pickers respect to tourism and the incorporation of other local actors such as traders, service providers and producers. The process includes a basic social consensus and the formation of new tourism-oriented capabilities (Dallen, 1999).

This is due to the fact that, in the case of Mexico, mycological resources are part of a common good from which apparently all people can enjoy except that knowledge about wild edible mushrooms is an access barrier that only allows the use of these resources by small groups where mycological knowledge is transmitted from generation to generation.

In this sense it is important to evaluate the recreational potential that wild edible mushrooms have as tourist attraction. This implies processes of productive innovation in rural areas, based on their territorial capacity to offer cultural services, aimed at urban societies in the context of globalization. The objective is also to promote multifunctional and sustainable management of forests that enhances and integrates the ecological, social and economic functions of wild edible mushrooms.

Mycological tourism can be defined as a recreational activity focused on the conservation and protection of mycological resources to promote economic development and improve the living conditions of the population, which implies local mycological knowledge and may constitute a sustainable strategy for rural development (De Castro, 2009).

Although mycological tourism is practically unknown in Mexico, European experiences clearly show that it is a lucrative activity. According to data from the Micosylva + project, the average annual value generated by mycology in the province of Castilla y León is estimated at 65 million euros. Of this amount, 20 per cent is derived from the income generated by mushrooms collectors, 40 per cent is obtained from the added value generated by the collection and processing companies, and the remaining 40 per cent is generated by mycological tourism (Europa Press, 2014).

Mycological tourism is an activity that requires professional knowledge so it is necessary to have mycological information systems that promote correct practices of harvesting and management of mushrooms, in order to avoid any kind of risk derived from the consumption of toxic mushrooms, degradation of the environment and fragmentation of the social structure in the harvesting communities.

The development of Mycological Information Systems can also benefit tourists, since these systems can provide an interpretive framework for mycological resources. This requires that the information gathered is presented as mushroom picking guides and digital applications with information on seasonality, availability and location of fungi.

MAIN FOCUS OF THE CHAPTER

Geographic Information Systems as a Planning Tool for Mycological Tourism

The application of GIS in mycological tourism planning represents an important tool for the development of various tasks that are fundamental for the proper development of tourism activity, among which can be highlighted: the generation of data, inventory of tourism resources, analysis of the data, zoning and a participatory approach.

The generation of data about mycological resources is a central aspect for their use for recreational purposes. Traditionally, forest management has focused on timber resources with the consequent oversight of the importance of non-timber forest resources for the ecological balance of forests and the economic well being of communities.

Certainly, wild edible mushrooms are resources of great socioeconomic importance for communities living in the forest. In Mexico, its use has been restricted to harvesting for their own consumption, exchange and sale, being a marginal activity that often does not reflect a fair return for the work and time invested.

This is why it is essential to explore some options, such as mycological tourism, that allow adding value to the use of mushrooms and retaining the income generated within the harvesting communities (De Frutos, Martínez & Esteban, 2012; Lázaro, 2008).

The recreational use of wild edible fungi requires accurate information systems to determine which are the most appropriate mechanisms for the management of these resources as tourist attractions. To do this it is necessary to develop the two dimensions of GIS. The first refers to a spatial perspective, focused on locating data at a specific point on Earth. While the second is related to the attributes of the data, qualitatively and quantitatively, they reflect the characteristics of a geo-referenced entity (Grimshaw, 1993). In this sense, it is possible to think of its usefulness both for the location of the mushrooms and for their detailed characterization.

From the point of view of the location it is important to detect in what type of forest fructify certain species of mushrooms. With this it is possible to establish the relationship between mycological resources and a certain type of vegetation, can also be associated with soil types and humidity. All of these are useful aspects for the location of mushrooms within pre-established mycological paths.

On the other hand, the attributes of the data usually provide more detailed information on the characteristics of the mushrooms. Among these characteristics are its shape and color, fruiting periods, availability, cultural importance and economic value. All of these data may be important elements for the planning of mycological tourism activities as will be discussed below.

In addition to the aspects related to wild edible mushrooms, the development of a mycological tourism project must have an inventory of tourism resources that can evaluate the existence of a set of goods and services that support the tourism experience. To obtain these data, a quantitative and qualitative approach is necessary to establish the levels of attraction, accessibility, presence of infrastructure and levels of degradation of resources (Priskin, 2001).

In the case of mycological tourism, the levels of attraction are directly related to the natural and cultural resources associated with mushrooms. This refers fundamentally to the specific characteristics of forests, their landscapes, ethno-mycological knowledge and mycogastronomy.

The conformation of interrelated data systems allows a comprehensive view of the management of wild edible mushrooms as a multifunctional resource. This provides an appropriate perspective on the possible complementarity or conflict between mycological tourism and other economic activities such as harvesting for self-consumption or harvesting for commercial purposes. In the same way it can help to understand the social tensions originated by the use of the common spaces for diverse purposes or the disputes between local and external actors for the use of the endogenous resources.

A complementarity should be sought between new activities (tourism) and traditional activities (mushroom harvesting). In accordance with the above, the following criteria should be observed for the sustainable management of mycological tourism (Garau, 2015):

1. Protection of natural and cultural resources:
    a. Environmental sustainability (preservation of ecosystems, use of environmental management systems, protection of the productive vocation of the territory).
    b. Economic sustainability (development of landscape quality, development of nearby markets for products and services, innovation in environmental management).
    c. Social sustainability (generate a social awareness about the importance of mushrooms, develop participatory approaches and improve the network of relationships between stakeholders).
2. Development of sustainable mycological tourism:
    a. Local economic development (creation of local businesses, generation of employment, alliances between public and private sectors)
    b. Sustainable environmental development (small-scale tourism, protection of natural and cultural heritage, certification of tourist practices).
    c. Social development (integration between different productive sectors, development of a place-based perspective, detection of the opportunities of the exclusive resources of the territory).

The data obtained through GIS technology are an important reference for zoning in mycological tourism. The generation of mycological paths is more efficient through the use of accurate and georeferenced data to establish the fruiting areas of mushrooms and those places where the integrity of local resources is not compromised.

In the case of the Spanish province of Castilla y León, the existence of mycological information systems has allowed the development of 100 mycological paths, whose journey lasts between four and five hours. These paths contain elements to recognize the beginning and end of the trail, information on the natural environment in which they are located, instructions for the safe mushroom harvesting and criteria for identifying the species collected (De Frutos, Martínez & Esteban, 2012). In the same direction, it is important to determine the commercial areas, spaces for the development of sports activities and the spaces where housing and food infrastructures can be located.

One of the advantages of using GIS in mycological tourism planning is that it encourages community participation in tourism planning and decision-making (Hughes & Shirmer, 1994). In the case of wild edible mushrooms, the information generated comes from local informants and includes aspects such as location, identification, temporality and use of mushrooms, which is part of the traditional ecological knowledge about these resources (Jímenez, Thomé -Ortiz & Burrola, 2016).

On the other hand, the information generated through GIS has to be validated through processes of feedback and permanent consultation to the community. This implies a high level of involvement of the social actors and the collective appropriation of the tourism strategy. According to Harris, Weiner, Warner and Levin (1996), a participatory GIS allows the integration of local knowledge with the technical expertise of external actors, taking advantage of spatial representation of local knowledge.

Case Study of a Mushroom-Harvesting Community in Central Mexico

Study Area

The village called Ejido Venta Morales (La Laguna) is located in the municipality of Texcaltitlán, State of Mexico at an altitude of 2860 meters (figure 1). It is within the Natural Protection Area of Nevado de Toluca Volcano, in the GPS coordinates Length (dec) -99.895000 and Latitude (dec) 18.983333.

The community has electricity, potable water, radio signal and television signal, but only a small percentage has telephone service and no home has Internet signal. The average schooling of the population is 6.88 years. It has approximately 373 inhabitants, distributed in 110 houses, of which 179 are men and 194 are women, with a fertility rate of 2.95 children per couple.

Its predominant climate is temperate humid with rains in summer and has an average annual temperature of 19 C. Its territory is divided into communal and ejido lands and sits on pinus spp and abies religiosa forests, among which there are streams and waterfalls from the melting of the Nevado de Toluca volcano. Its population is mestizo and was evangelized by catholic missionaries, who founded the village church in the eighteenth century (INEGI, 2017).

This village is renowned in the region for its vocation as mushroom pickers, whose products are sold at the roadside or in the nearby markets. The mushrooms harvesting is an activity that brings important benefits to the economy of rural families since it generates additional income and contributes a food of self-consumption during the rainy season.

The learning process on the identification and harvesting of fungi starts from childhood. The first times children go out alone and collect everything they find, when they get home their mother teaches them which mushrooms are edible. The operation is repeated until the children show a satisfactory ability to identify good mushrooms to eat. Each picker family knows specific places where, according to altitude and vegetative dominance, certain species of mushrooms fructify. Harvesting should begin at an early hour to prevent others from finding edible mushrooms in accessible places (Mariaca, Silva & Castaños, 2001).

Mushrooms harvesting has a positive impact on the family economy. Through this practice families ensure mushrooms consumption between one and three times a week during the rainy season and can purchase basic food for at least three months. They usually exchange mushrooms in local markets for products such as oil, sugar, coffee, tomatoes, onions, salt, soap, candles and other necessities (Mariaca, Silva & Castaños, 2001).

Despite the socioeconomic importance of the mushrooms, it can be seen that the work of pickers does not have a fair payment as it only reaches the average of 5 dollars per day. In this regard, some studies indicate that mycological tourism has the capacity to produce between 7 and 9 times the income that the exclusive harvesting and sale of mushrooms generates (Lázaro, 2008).

Information Mycological System Based on Ethno-Knowledge

During the rainy season of 2015, a case study was carried out in Ejido Venta Morales village. The case study approach was relevant because from this it is possible to make theoretical constructs on emerging phenomena, based on predominantly qualitative analysis (Yin, 2009), but at the same time allows the flexibility to use mixed methods (Stake, 1994).

Figure 1. Map: Location of Texcaltitlán, Estado de México
Source: INEGI, 2012.

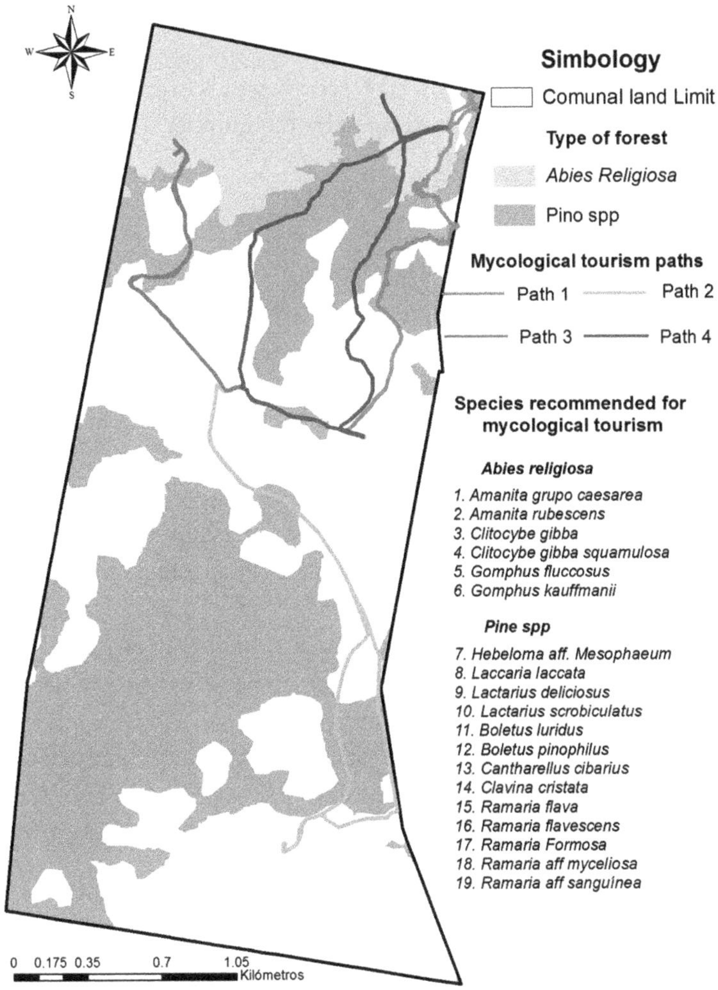

The fieldwork was developed during the mushroom season, which, according to the villagers, occurs between June and December. Two harvests were carried out per month. This led to an inventory of the main mushrooms with socioeconomic relevance in the study area.

In order to determine the species of edible mushrooms existing in the region, fourteen harvests were carried out, which were guided by local pickers who, from their traditional ecological knowledge, provided relevant data on the relation of fungi to certain tree species, soil type and weather. To collect field data a GPS (Global Positioning System), Garmin brand, model Map 64S with an accuracy of +/- 10 meters was used. The routes were made using the automatic route plotting function of the GPS equipment and in addition, the points were marked where the mycological species of interest were found. At each point the species, the scientific name, the availability and the approximate location were referenced.

Subsequently, a group of collectors was selected, who helped determine the index of cultural importance of each species and the index of economic importance. The selection of informants was based on the following criteria: (i) that they were locally recognized actors because of their knowledge about mushrooms; (ii) that among its daily productive activities there will be the mushrooms harvesting; and (iii) that they had received their knowledge about mushrooms in an intergenerational manner. The sample included eleven informants and was determined using the non-probabilistic snowball sampling technique (Goodman, 1960).

The index of cultural importance (Signorini, 2009) corresponds to the percentage value of the number of times the specific uses of the taxon are mentioned by the number of informants and was calculated by the following formula:

$$CI_S = \sum_{u=u1}^{U_{NC}} \sum_{1=1_1}^{1_N} UR_{U1} / N$$

where u is the use category, NC is the total number of different use categories (of each "i" species), UR is the total number of uses reported by each of the species (corresponding in the study to the " Citations ") and N is the total number of informants in the study.

To calculate the NC, it was defined as the total number of uses-category (for each species the different number of secondary uses as NC was considered, taking into account that is more detailed and uses numerous than-category). Once obtained the index of each species were grouped under the criteria: high, medium and low.

To calculate the economic value (Reyes-Garcia, Huanca, Vadez, Leonard & Wilkie, 2006) of mushrooms was used as reference the local price of species, from its sales value in the markets, roadside and into the community.

For those species of mushrooms that did not present a market value, analogies has to be made about their exchange value for other products and investigating the relationship between the time invested in their harvest and the value of time reflected in income from other paid activities. The following formula was used:

$$EV_e = Me_e * Pe_e$$

where EV_e is the economic value of species e. Me_e is the number of species mentioned and Pe_e is the price of species e. After obtaining the economic value of each species were grouped under the criteria high, medium and low.

The points and routes obtained in the field were related to the availability of mycological resources, their index of importance and economic value. These data were exported from the file in GPX format (GPS format) to ArcGis 10.2.2 software. Subsequently, the information obtained in the field was overlapped with the vegetation type layers of the V series, in .shp format, at scale 1: 250,000 of INEGI (National Institute of Statistics and Geography, for its acronym in Spanish). With this overlap, it was possible to identify the type of forest and the mycological species of the study region suitable for mycological tourism.

Evaluation of the Wild Edible Mushrooms of Texcaltitlán

36 species of wild edible mushrooms were detected (Table 1). Most of these species are distributed in different parts of the forest, associated with forests of pinus spp and abies religiosa. A small percentage

Table 1. Wild edible fungi of Texcaltitlán, State of Mexico

Local Name	Scientific Name	Location	Availability	Cultural Significance	Economic Value
1. Chicale	*Amanita grupo caesarea*	Abies Religiosa Forest	Medium	Low	Low
2. Mosco	*Amanita rubescens*	Abies Religiosa Forest	High	Low	Low
3. Zorrita	*Hebeloma aff. Mesophaeum*	Pinus Spp. Forest	High	Low	Low
4. Jocoyol	*Laccaria laccata*	Pinus Spp. Forest	High	Low	Low
5. Tejamanilero	*Clitocybe gibba*	Abies Religiosa Forest	High	Medium	Low
6. Tejaminilero	*Clitocybe squamulosa*	Abies Religiosa Forest	High	Medium	Low
7. Clavito o Jarero	*Lyophyllum aff. Connatum*	Pinus Montezumae Forest	High	High	Low
8. Blanco	*Russula brevipes*	Abies Religiosa Forest	High	Medium	Low
9. Enchilado azul	*Lactarius deliciosus*	Pinus Spp. Forest	High	Low	Low
10. Enchilado blanco	*Lactarius scrobiculatus*	Pinus Spp. Forest	Low	Low	Low
11. Cema	*Boletus appendiculatus*	Pinus Montezumae and Abies Religiosa Forest	Low	High	Low
12. Pancita	*Boletus barrousii*	Quercus Ilex Forest	Low	Medium	Low
13. Pancita	*Boletus edulis*	Quercus Ilex Forest	Low	Medium	Low
14. Pancita	*Boletus edulis var. Clavipes*	Quercus Ilex Forest	Low	Medium	Low
15. Galambo	*Boletus luridus*	Pinus Spp. Forest	Low	Low	Low
16. Cema	*Boletus pinophilus*	Pinus Spp. Forest	Low	Medium	Low
17. Naranjo	*Cantharellus cibarius*	Pinus Spp. Forest	Low	Low	Low
18. Corneta roja	*Gomphus fluccosus*	Abies Religiosa Forest	High	Low	Low
19. Corneta blanca	*Gomphus kauffmanii*	Abies Religiosa Forest	Low	Low	Low
20. Pata de pajaro	*Clavulina cristata*	Pinus Spp. Forest	Low	Low	Low
21. Pata de pájaro	*Ramaria flava*	Pinus Spp. Forest	Low	Low	Low
22. Pata de pájaro	*Ramaria flavescens*	Pinus Spp. Forest	Low	Low	Low
23. Escobeta	*Ramaria Formosa*	Pinus Spp. Forest	Low	Low	Low
24. Escobeta	*Ramaria aff myceliosa*	Pinus Spp. Forest	Low	Low	Low
25. Escobeta	*Ramaria aff sanguinea*	Pinus Spp. Forest	Low	Low	Low
26. Gachupín	*Helvella crispa*	Abies Religiosa Forest	Low	Medium	Medium
27. Gachupín	*Helvella fusca*	Abies Religiosa Forest	Low	Medium	Medium
28. Gachupín	*Helvella lacuosa*	Abies Religiosa Forest	Low	Medium	Medium
29. Gachupín	*Champiñon pithiophyla*	Abies Religiosa Forest	Low	Medium	Medium
30. Olote	*Morchella elata*	Quercus Ilex Forest	Low	High	High
31. Olote	*Morchella esculenta*	Quercus Ilex Forest	Low	High	High
32. Olote	*Morchella conica*	Quercus Ilex Forest	Low	High	High
33. Matas	Unidentified scientific name	All kinds of forest	Low	High	Medium
34. Coyote	Unidentified scientific name	All kinds of forest	Low	Low	Low
35. Juanito (Champiñón)	Unidentified scientific name	Plains	Low	Low	Low
36. Hongo de ocote	*Trocholoma magnivelare*	Pinus Montezumae Forest	Low	High	High

Source: Own elaboration based on fieldwork, 2015.

of the mushrooms are located in quercus ilex and pinus montezumae forests and in a lesser amount in the plains. According to data provided by the informants it is observed that in a good amount of species, it is increasingly difficult to determine their exact location, an aspect that is related to variables such as forest fragmentation, anthropic pressure and climate change.

Of the identified mushrooms, only 9 species with high availability and 27 with low availability were geo-referenced. Mushroom pickers describe that finding mushrooms has become more difficult, that the places where they habitually found them have changed drastically and that there is disappearance of some species.

18 species of low cultural importance were detected, 11 with medium cultural importance and 7 with high cultural importance. This aspect is related to those species with greater gastronomic value and those whose collection involves a high degree of difficulty. Species of high cultural importance often have a high economic value, and even some locally highly valued species are not sold and are exclusive to local consumption.

Regarding economic value, there are 27 low value species, 5 medium value species and 4 high value species. This is associated with the loss of value experienced by mushroom pickers, related to the intermediaries who sell the mushrooms to the final consumers. This justifies the development of strategies that help to retain and add value within the mushroom picking territories.

Design of Mycological Tourism Paths

Of the 36 species identified, it is only proposed to use 19 for mycological tourism (Table 2). Which are intended to respect the criteria of ecological, cultural and economic sustainability. Those species with very low availability, which are culturally significant for the population and those with high market price, are excluded from the recreational harvesting. With this, it is sought that mycological tourism does not generate new social tensions around mycological resources.

All species with tourism potential are found in the abies religiosa and pinus spp forest ecotones, which cover most of the study area and have been divided into four mycological paths with different degrees of difficulty and different scenic attractions (Figure 2). This allows articulating different recreational experiences that are halfway between nature and culture. For this purpose, it was important to take into account three fundamental considerations: (i) that the type of land tenure in which the proposal would be developed is communal, so it is important to respect the collective management of resources; (ii) harvesting areas accessible to a wide range of tourists; and (iii) that the interests of the local population would not be affected.

According to the results it was determined to select those paths that have better conditions for the development of mycological tourism. It was determined that the mycological paths were composed, 70%, by those rural roads used by the villagers to carry out other productive activities. This has the objective of not generating new paths that produce impacts such as noise pollution, soil compaction and ecosystem fragmentation. On the contrary it is intended to generate a strategy based on the multifunctional use of existing rural infrastructure.

This prevents tourists from entering the forest and only visiting specific areas that have a high concentration of mushrooms. On the other hand, due to the seasonality of the activity, there are no apparent conflicts due to the land use of forest and tourist use. It is important to emphasize that the use of communal roads, for tourism purposes, encourages the collective appropriation of tourism strategy and limits the participation of external actors.

Table 2. Recommended mushroom species for mycological tourism

Species	Fruiting Time	Keys for Localization
1. *Amanita grupo caesarea*	July – September	In sandy soils under large trees
2. *Amanita rubescens*	July – September	Within the forests, associated with the roots of the trees
3. *Hebeloma aff. Mesophaeum*	June – July	It is widely distributed in coniferous forests
4. *Laccaria laccata*	June – September	In wet soils under trees
5. *Clitocybe gibba*	October – December	Under shady trees in coniferous forests
6. *Clitocybe squamulosa*	October – Diciembre	Under shady trees in coniferous forests
7. *Lactarius deliciosus*	July – October	Under the pines
8. *Lactarius scrobiculatus*	June – September	Under the pines
9. *Boletus luridus*	September – October	In mossy areas
10. *Boletus pinophilus*	May – June	In pinus spp forests in areas rich in moss
11. *Cantharellus cibarius*	June – October	In coniferous forests, in areas rich in moss
12. *Gomphus fluccosus*	August	In abies religiosa forests in areas rich in moss
13. *Gomphus kauffmanii*	August	In coniferous forests in soils rich in organic material
14. *Clavulina cristata*	July – August	In coniferous forests, in moist areas, near rotten wood
15. *Ramaria flava*	July – December	Inside the forest in humid and dark areas
16. *Ramaria flavescens*	July – August	In litter in mixed forest areas
17. *Ramaria Formosa*	July – August	Grow under the trees
18. *Ramaria aff myceliosa*	July – August	It grows on land and rarely in moist logs
19. *Ramaria aff sanguinea*	July – August	Woody substrate, under the ground, in coniferous forests

Source: Own elaboration based on fieldwork (2015).

Figure 2. Map: mycological tourism paths in Texcaltitlán, State of Mexico
Source: Own elaboration based on field work, 2015.

FUTURE RESEARCH DIRECTIONS

The use of GIS as a planning, management and evaluation tool has been widely used in tourism studies. However, there are few examples of the use of these systems applied to rural tourism focused on local resources such as mycological tourism.

In this direction, the use of GIS as a tool for planning and management of mycological tourism should be conceived in the context of an integrated strategy for sustainable forest management. This is important because traditional ecological knowledge, linked to the use of mushrooms, should not only be a source of information, but must provide a perspective and a way of seeing the world that influences development policies and strategies for the rural space. This gives an ethical dimension to the application of GIS that has a positive impact on the actors affected by the way information is presented.

Accordingly, GIS is an important tool for tourism planning since in the rural space it is essential to generate information on endogenous resources that will help local actors to face the challenge of diversifying their productive activities towards tourism. This requires precise data on the set of goods and services that is useful to determine the tourist potential of the territory.

Nevertheless, some aspects to investigate are still pending, such as the perspective of the tourist demand, the carrying capacity and the mechanisms of regulation of this new activity in the territory.

CONCLUSION

One of the main advantages of the analysis conducted through GIS is that it allows a comprehensive perspective on the interrelations between the data collected, which allows an adequate spatial projection of the sustainable tourism strategy in the social, economic and environmental dimensions. For this, it is necessary that the data feeding and its subsequent interpretation be based on a participatory approach.

The results show that there are an important variety of wild edible mushrooms in the study area, whose use through commercialization and self-consumption provides marginal benefits for the mushroom pickers. In this regard it can be concluded that mycological tourism can diversify the traditional activities of the mushroom pickers and generate more lucrative benefits that positively impact on their quality of life.

Mycological tourism is not the panacea to solve the economic problems of the mushroom pickers but it is a complementary strategy that must strictly follow criteria to protect the species of threatened mushrooms and must work for the benefit of those who have been dedicated to the mushroom harvesting as an economic activity.

Mycological tourism in Texcaltitlán should be a small-scale activity, in accordance with the available accommodation infrastructure, which should be restricted to the use of the 19 species with tourist vocation and only four paths must be operated, which agree with the communal roads where the population develops other forestry activities.

This chapter is part of a basic science research aimed at exploring the tourist potential of wild edible mushrooms in the high mountain area of central Mexico. The data obtained in this research can be useful to generate mechanisms of control, management and territorial ordering around the mycological resources.

ACKNOWLEDGMENT

This work was funded by the National Council for Science and Technology of Mexico (CONACYT) through the SEP – Basic Science Joint Fund 2014; and by the Autonomous University of the State of Mexico through the Fund for Innovation and Development 2014.

REFERENCES

Bahaire, T., & Elliot-White, M. (1999). The Application of Geographical Information Systems (GIS) in Sustainable Tourism Planning: A Review. *Journal of Sustainable Tourism*, *7*(2), 159–174. doi:10.1080/09669589908667333

Bostedt, G., & Mattsson, L. (1995). The value of forest for tourism in Sweden. *Annals of Tourism Research*, *22*(3), 671–680. doi:10.1016/0160-7383(95)00007-S

Boyd, S., & Butler, R. (1996). Seeing the forest through the trees: Using GIS to identify potential ecotourism sites in Northern Ontario. In L. C. Harrison & W. Husbands (Eds.), *Practicing Responsible Tourism: International Case Studies in Tourism Planning, Policy & Development* (pp. 380–403). New York, NY: J. Wiley & Sons.

Dallen, T. (1999). Participatory planning: A view of tourism in Indonesia. *Annals of Tourism Research*, *26*(2), 371–391. doi:10.1016/S0160-7383(98)00104-2

De Castro, S. (2009). *Micoturismo: Enquadramento Estratégico em Áreas Protegidas* (Unpublished Master Dissertation). Universidad Técnica de Lisboa, Portugal.

De Frutos, P., Martínez, F., & Esteban, S. (2012). Edible wild mushroom tourism as a source of income and employment in rural areas. The case of Castilla y León. *Forest Systems*, *21*(1), 81–98. doi:10.5424/fs/2112211-02545

Europe Press. (2013 May 24). El proyecto 'Micosylva+' estima en 65 millones de euros el valor medio generado por la micología en CyL. EP Castilla y León. *Europa Press.* Retrieved from: http://www.europapress.es/castilla-y-leon/noticia-proyecto-micosylva-estima-65-millones-euros-valor-medio-generado-micologia-cyl-20130524173020.html

Garau, C. (2015). Perspectives on Cultural and Sustainable Rural Tourism in a Smart Region: The Case Study of Marmilla in Sardinia (Italy). *Sustainability*, *7*(6), 6412–6434. doi:10.3390/su7066412

Goodman, L. (1961). Snowball Sampling. *Annals of Mathematical Statistics*, *32*(1), 148–170. doi:10.1214/aoms/1177705148

Grimshaw, D. (1993). *Bringing GIS into Bussines Geoinformation.* London: Longman.

Gunn, C. (1994). The emergence of effective tourism planning and development. In A. Seaton, L. Jenkins, R. Woods, P. Dieke, M. Bennett, L. MacLellan, & R. Smith (Eds.), *Tourism The State of the Art* (pp. 10–19). Chichester, UK: John Wiley & Sons.

Haines-Young, R., Bunce, R., & Parr, T. (1994). Countryside Information System: An information system for environmental policy development and appraisal. *Geographical Systems*, *1*(4), 329–345.

Hannam, K., Butler, G., & Morris, C. (2014). Developments and key issues in tourism mobilities. *Annals of Tourism Research*, *44*, 171–185. doi:10.1016/j.annals.2013.09.010

Harris, T., Weiner, D., Warner, T., & Levin, R. (1996). Pursuing social goals through participatory GIS: Redressing South Africa's historical political ecology. In J. Pickles (Ed.), *Ground Truth: The Social Implications of GIS* (pp. 196–222). Guildford: Guildford Press.

Hughes, G., & Schirmer, D. (1994). Interactive multimedia, public participation and environmental assessment. *The Town Planning Review*, *65*(4), 399–414. doi:10.3828/tpr.65.4.n7220465t3813122

INEGI. (2017). Retrieved from: www.inegi.con.mx

Jímenez, A., Thomé-Ortiz, H., & Burrola, C. (2016). Biocultural heritage, mycological tourism and ethnoknowledge. *El periplo sustentable*, *30*, 180-205.

Kuvan, Y. (2005). The use of forests for the purpose of tourism: The case of Belek Tourism Center in Turkey. *Journal of Environmental Management*, *75*(3), 263–274. doi:10.1016/j.jenvman.2005.01.003 PMID:15829368

Lázaro, A. (2008). El aprovechamiento micológico como vía de desarrollo rural en España: Las facetas comercial y recreativa. *Anales de Geografía*, *28*, 111–136.

Mariaca, R., Silva, L., & Castaños, C. (2001). Proceso de recolección y comercialización de hongos comestibles silvestres en el Valle de Toluca, México. *Ciencia Ergo Sum*, *8*(1), 30–40.

Martínez-Peña, F., Gómez, R., Ortega, P., Cabezón, A., Francés, D., Sevillano, J., & Aldea, J. (2009). *MICODATA: Sistema de Información Geográfica sobre la producción, aprovechamiento y ordenación del recurso micológico en Castilla y León.* Paper presented at 5to. Congreso Forestal Español. Montes y Sociedad: Saber qué hacer, Ávila, Spain.

Priskin, J. (2001). Assessment of natural resources for nature based tourism: The case of Central Coast Region of Western Australia. *Tourism Management*, *22*(6), 637–648. doi:10.1016/S0261-5177(01)00039-5

Reyes-García, V., Huanca, T., Vadez, V., Leonard, W., & Wilkie, D. (2006). Cultural, Practical, and Economic Value of Wild Plants: A Quantitative Study in the Bolivian Amazon. *Economic Botany*, *60*(1).

Robinson, G. (1992). Geographical Information Systems (GIS) and planning in Scotland: The RLUIS project and andvances in GIS. *Scottish Geographical Magazine*, *108*(1), 22–28. doi:10.1080/00369229218736838

Signorini, M. (2009). Plants and traditional knowledge: An ethnobotanical investigation on Monte Ortobene (Nuoro, Sardinia). *Journal of Ethnobiology and Ethnomedicine*, *5*(6), 1–14. PMID:19208227

Stake, R. (1994). Case Studies. In N. Denzin & Y. Lincoln (Eds.), *Handbook of Qualitative Research* (pp. 236–247). Thousand Oaks, CA: Sage Publications.

Thomé-Ortiz, H. (2015). Turismo micológico, una nueva mirada al bosque. *Ciencia y Desarrollo*, *41*, 14–19.

Williams, P., Paul, J., & Hainsworth, D. (1996). Keeping track of what really counts: Tourism resource inventory systems in British Columbia, Canada. In L. Harrison & W. Husbands (Eds.), *Practicing Responsible Tourism: International Case Studies in Tourism Planning, Policy & Development* (pp. 404–421). New York, NY: J. Wiley & Sons.

Yin, R. (2009). *Case Study Research: Design and Methods*. Thousand Oaks, CA: Sage Publications.

KEY TERMS AND DEFINITIONS

Altiplano: An elevated intermontane plateau, which is generally found between two or more mountain ranges.

Central Mexico: The central region of Mexico concentrates most of the economic, political and cultural activity of the country. It is made up of Mexico City and the states of Guanajuato, Hidalgo, Mexico, Morelos, Puebla, Querétaro and Tlaxcala. Its approximate extension is of 130,000 km2.

Communal Lands: Mode of land tenure that is jointly exploited by a social group and owned by the community.

Geographic Information Systems: An organized integration of hardware, software and geographic data to capture, store, manipulate, analyze and deploy geographically referenced information in order to solve complex planning and management problems.

Mycological Tourism: Tourism and leisure activity that combines cultural, nature and sports activities. It consists of the search and collection of wild edible mushrooms with the purpose of consuming them as a gastronomic product of high quality.

Participatory Approach: A set of methodologies and approaches based on the participation of the local population and used for the diagnosis, execution, monitoring and evaluation of development projects.

Rural Tourism: All forms of tourist activity carried out in rural areas are usually small-scale and developed within the family economy. It is based on the natural and cultural resources of the rural environment.

Territorial Specialization: The new economy of rural areas is based on the productive specialization of the countryside, linked to the particular characteristics of its natural and cultural capital.

Traditional Ecological Knowledge: A qualitative, intuitive, holistic, moral and spiritual knowledge, based on empirical observation and accumulation of facts through the daily use of natural resources.

Chapter 17
Isle of the Dead:
A Study of Trunyan Cemetery (Bali)

Bintang Handayani
President University, Indonesia

Maximiliano Emanuel Korstanje
University of Palermo, Argentina

ABSTRACT

This essay aims to explain the phenomenon and effect on tourism of the Balinese cemetery in the village of Trunyan, where the dead are not buried. It is a narrative enquiry combined with critical theory largely grounded in the scholarship of dark tourism and communication theory, coupled with content analysis of the online community's reviews from the TripAdvisor website. The study indicates that (1) connectedness to death suggests the existence of spirituality needed by people, at the same time indicating understanding of mortality; (2) social connections developed as a result of visiting Trunyan cemetery not only bring self-awareness and awareness of others, revolving around intrapersonal communication about spirituality and interpersonal communication among members of the online community, but also illustrate the development of dark tourism and conceptualise the role of tourists in building authentic experience as the essence of a death site's brand image.

INTRODUCTION

The expression "Lonely in a crowd" indicates how the quality of relationships matters, and signifies a much deeper existence from postmodern perspectives where people seek for feelings shared by others. This aspect represents the roots of reciprocity as it was studied by ethnographers in non-western cultures (Malinowski, 1926). In this context, feeling of this calibre are driven by the so called dark tourism sites (Biran, Poria, & Oren, 2011; Stone & Sharpley, 2008). Although gaining in popularity, dark sites wake up a profound ethical discussion in public opinion (Tzanelli 2016). While a family of theories understand that dark sites express an emotional arousal which links community with pastime, addressing some of the existential questions of human existence (Lennon & Foley 2000; Raine 2013, Biran & Hyde, 2013; Cohen 2011; Podoshen 2013; Stone 2011); others claim beyond the quest for death, underlies a

DOI: 10.4018/978-1-5225-2927-9.ch017

sentiment of morbid voyeurism which is politically manipulated to perpetuate the legitimacy of elite, even in contexts of disasters and trauma (Bowman & Pezzullo, 2009; Hartmann 2014; Tzanelli 2016; Korstanje 2016). Likely, the Trunyan cemetery in Bali offers a fertile ground to overcome the limitations dark tourism literature shows. Despite this cemetery attracts both types of segments, overseas and domestic tourists, it is difficult to frame this space into the model of Seaton and Lennon (2004). As P. Stone (2006) puts it, dark tourism takes a wider spectrum which oscillates from battlefronts memorials which draws much attention from media, to cemeteries, where any intrusion is seen as a clear violation to private life. In this respect, B. Heidelberg (2015) dissects the case of Amityville US to understand many factors are involved at time of adopting dark tourism as the first option. Many communities, even, are far from the needs of reminding the event, and opted to silence it in the dust of oblivion. Korstanje has gathered substantial evidence during his fieldwork in Cromañón, Buenos Aires (Argentina) to confirm some communities see in tourism as an activity that very well may corrupt their memory of deads (Korstanje 2015), while in other cases, dark sites include the colloquially named perilous places, houses of horror, fields of fatality, tours of torment, and themed Thanatos, are theoretically on the dark tourism spectrum (Sharpley & Stone, 2009; Stone, 2006; Bowman & Pezzullo, 2009). Death tourism, which is defined as activities visiting unique and macabre sites such as cemeteries, appears not only to encourage human contemplation on death of the self (Stone, 2012; Korstanje and George, 2015), but also to revolve around how the death sites (those visited by tourists) serve as a distraction from one's own mortality (Korstanje & George, 2015). Coupled with the conversation on social media (Sigala, Christou & Gretzel, 2012; Nikiforova, 2013) from a postmodern perspective, i.e. the phenomenon of an online community generating e-comments and e-word of mouth (e-WOM) (e.g. see Gretzel & Yoo, 2008; Yoo & Gretzel, 2008, 2010, 2011; Xiang and Gretzel, 2010),this phenomenon of death sites in particular and the surprisingly popular dark tourism in general, leads to question whether it is tourist-demand or attraction-driven (Stone, 2006; Wilkinson, 2010).

As this backdrop, the online comments into death sites in the online community not only indicate how the role of tourists in building shared values may (or may *not*) shape the brand image of death sites, but also signifies the intertwined relationships of spirituality and specific tourist typology from the postmodern perspective. This strengthens the conceptualisation of "secular tourists" that Korstanje and George (2015) coined in their study on philosophical issues in dark tourism. The secular tourist is considered as one who may seek for authentic life experience of social connectedness and the need for otherness, which in other domains of study is identified as human needs of spirituality (e.g. Krentzman, 2013). It also indicates the magnitude of good relationships which revolve around human interactions with death and lead to contemplation of self-awareness (i.e. to intrapersonal communication) and how the conversation about death in the online community (i.e. interpersonal communication) validate the sense of spirituality and its philosophical perspectives. For example, Krentzman (2013) examines the intertwined relationship of spirituality and religion, leading to how attributes such as belief, comfort, reflection, ethics, and awe fuel the content of the shared values under discussion. Arguably, it keeps people alive and gives validation to their lives, as well as serving self-awareness (e.g. Krentzman, 2013; Holt-Lunstad, Smith & Layton, 2010).

The structure of this essay is as follows. First, the literature of dark tourism, from the tourist's and postmodern perspectives, and the purpose of life revolving around spirituality and religion are reviewed. Next, the research gap, the research methodology and an overview of the study context are outlined. The findings of the content analysis revolve around the presentation of death and its communication patterns; and how the presentation of death and religiosity emerge as commodification and affect tourists' lifeworld. Connectedness between death and tourist discourses is discussed, aiming to map how the fabrication of this attraction enriches the dark tourism spectrum. Finally, the study's limitations and directions for future work are outlined.

DARK SITES, TOURISTS, AND POSTMODERN PERSPECTIVES

Undoubtedly, the patterns of holiday-making are experiencing substantial changes. If our grand-parents enjoyed from beaches, or paradisiacal destinations in their vacations, now the apollonian concept of beautiness sets the pace to death as the primary commodity. Modern emergent segments prefer to visit spaces of mass-death, mourning or suffering not only to understand what has happened, but their place in this life. For that, Stone (2006) defined dark tourism, including dark sites, as the act of travel to sites associated with death, suffering and the seemingly macabre. Further, Stone indicates that dark sites seem to be gaining in popularity as people's fascination with death revolves around a combination of respect and reverence, and morbid curiosity or superstition. This attraction may not only indicate tourist demand but also, more importantly, be attraction-driven (Stone, 2006; Wilkinson, 2010), coupled with the phenomenon of the online community which mediates the interaction of people across different settings with common interests, such as visiting dark sites. With this in mind, the phenomenon of visiting dark sites not only involves how these sites change the tourist's lifeworld but also fuels the discourse of death as an attraction from the postmodern perspective.

The interconnection among dark sites, tourists and postmodernism occurs in the online community context, generating e-comments and e-WOM (Gretzel, Fesenmaier, Lee & Tussyadiah, 2010). The online community mediates interaction and communication between people who have similar interests and shared values (Boley, Magnini & Tuten, 2013). Further, Xiang & Gretzel (2010) suggest that online reviews on travel experience in social media context revolve around the facts of the attractions and destination, details of how to get there, and the uniqueness of the experience. In this sense, the online community is not only profoundly useful for members of the public who volunteer to share their thoughts and information (e.g. shared values and/or ideology) but it also indicates the usefulness for business, in which the service provider maps the needs, wants and desires of their target market. Yoo & Gretzel (2008) suggest that e-comments and e-WOM derived from visitors' experience are largley motivated by helping the travel service provider, concern for consumers, and the need for enjoyment or positive self-enhancement. More so, Gretzel points out that TripAdvisor site which provides review aimed is not to vent or take revenge on a business but rather to help other travellers. In this sense, review writers have other travellers in mind and try to provide helpful information (Kugel, 2011). Further, Yoo & Gretzel's (2008) findings indicate that venting negative feelings through posting is not considered an important motive. It may only be seen as expressive projected feelings derived from the experience of the visit. The later usefulness indicates the supply side of the tourism business, which involves tourism marketing.

The tourism marketing spectrum involves branding as a technique for managing the needs, wants and desires of the potential target market, communicating the brand distinctiveness of market offerings, e.g. the dark site attributes. Dark site attributes in this case are central to managing positioning (i.e. according to Maggard, 1976, involving segmentation and differentiation) and developing the e-comments (both positive and negative) of the online community into attributes of personification. Overall, the essence of e-comments is authenticity, moving towards the brand image of the dark site. E-comments derived from the online community, used wisely, are valuable. This is in line with the idea of "word power" in general and the bizzare tourism campaign which suggests maximising "negative word play" (Handayani, 2016) or "word play" (Khan, 2014) as a technique to seize public attention and arguably win the heart of the potential target market. To a certain extent, the end result of negative "word play" and "word play" also indicates the magnitude of brand loyalty, and previous studies suggest brand as the new form of religiosity (Gil Soldevilla, Palao Errando, & Marzal Felici, 2014).

Brand as the new form of religiosity relies on the power of image(s) in communicating brand identity (i.e derived from aspiration of vision and mission) and brand differentiation and/or distinctiveness which is derived from elements of authenticity or attributes of shared values (Olins, 2014). Authenticity in tourism in general can be analysed based on three approaches: objectivism, constructivism and postmodernism (Wang, 1999). Considering this study context is a dark site, Trunyan cemetery, coupled with tourists' online reviews, the postmodernist approach is applied. In this regard, it aims to investigate authenticity in the dark tourism experience and is considered more appropriate than the other approaches.

Further, studies indicate that negative experience is most likely to be used as a predetermined condition for the relationships between attribution dimensions, reliance on e-WOM and satisfaction expressed in online reviews (e.g. Jiang, Gretzel & Law, 2010). Jiang et al. (2010) suggest that negative experiences are more likely to be attributed to internal factors, and are perceived as unstable and specific. However, would these negative experiences, which lead to venting negative feelings in the online community sphere, position the philosophical dark attributes on dark sites? For this reason, the theorem that indicates dissatisfaction and negative feelings in tourists' online reviews would be in line with the proposition of tourists' perception on feelings of authenticity during and/or after visiting dark sites in general and Trunyan cemetery in particular. Past studies suggest the importance of emotional experiences in the consumption of dark tourism, and suggests adopting a hot interpretation approach (Ballantyne & Uzzell, 1993; Uzzell & Ballantyne, 1998), which denotes the importance of authenticity in dark tourism settings (Miles, 2002; Shackley, 2001; Sharpley & Stone, 2009a). However, there seems to be scant research to support this proposition. To bridge this knowledge gap, the study of Kang, Scott, Lee, and Ballantyne (2012), which highlights the importance of a hot interpretation approach to enhancing visitors' emotional experiences and the benefits gained, is appropriate for this study context. Attractions appear to be authentic because of point of view, belief, perspective, or power (Wang, 1999). With this in mind, the existential authenticity that Wang proposes can be adapted; in this study context existential authenticity is attributed to elements of the dark site, which emerge as the new form of religiosity simply through online discussions about visiting a death site. Brand as a new form of religiosity in this case is interpreted as the diffusion process derived from discourses about dark site attributes which gradually becomes the brand image of a dark site's profile.

PURPOSE OF LIFE: SPIRITUALITY AND RELIGION

A whole portion of studies focuses on dark tourism as finely-ingrained in the world of heritage consumption. For these scholars, dark tourism exhibits an historic fascination for others' death, which can be found to ancient world. Through "thanaptosis", dark sites ignite a spiritual travel to be in contact with others' pain. This cements the rise of a new heritage where experience plays a vital role mediating between past and future. Since all visitors understand they will die some later day, through dark site consuming they emulate their own end (Stone 2005; Cohen 2011; Poria 2007; Raine 2013; Johnston, 2013; White & Frew 2013).

Contrariwise, Korstanje and George (2015) pose a philosophical question about the possibility of dark tourism and pilgrimage being profoundly intertwined. While pilgrimage is considered as one of the oldest and most basic forms of population mobility in human society, and most likely associated with religion (Collins-Kreiner, 2010), dark sites are largely attributed to spirituality. The spiritual dimension of tourism, according to Willson, McIntosh & Zahra, (2013) is people seeking to understand for themselves the meaning of life and its purpose; their quest for meaning and experiences of transcendence and connectedness are objectively lived through their travel. This issue leads to a discourse on the relationships between the state of religion and spirituality, which Krentzman (2013) believes are intertwined through attributes such as belief, comfort, reflection, ethics, and feelings of awe; according to Korstanje and George (2015) this may be an indication of how humans as modern tourists understand death through the lens of other, validating feelings to anticipate and/or avoid their own death. Other studies recognise aspects of spirituality in the context of pilgrimage, and visits to dark sites are mainly for the authenticity and sense of place. While religion offers peace and a purpose to life through guidance to reach happiness, spirituality offers the essence of connectedness through experiencing dark site phenomena (Korstanje & George, 2015; Krentzman, 2013). This feeling of connectedness is derived from interaction with the dark site attributes (i.e. the dead body, the surroundings and the environmental socio-cultural topography, shared values and the characteristics of local people), helping tourists in facing their own death.

The relationship between spirituality and religion thus lies the purpose of life, which indicates human needs of otherness and connectedness. Krentzman (2013) suggests that spirituality and religion are not the same entity, although spirituality may incorporate elements of religion. Therefore, it can be inferred that the intersection of these two entities is based on attributes such as belief, comfort, reflection, ethics and feelings of awe, generated from both of spirituality and religion. This reminds that one of the main significant problems of dark tourism studies rests on the fact, fieldworkers do not distinguish the credibility of gathered information. The administration of open or closed-ended questionaries' sometimes gets biased information, simply because people sometimes lie, or in other case are incognizant of their behaviour. In other cases, interviewees are happy to meet the expectances of researchers, changing their answers in order to be in consonance to what should be uttered. This is the reason why not only fieldworkers claim for new methodologies to be applied in dark tourism issues, but also to new horizons that overcome current conceptual limitations (Korstanje & George 2015; Korstanje 2016). To fulfil this gap, we offer an alternative methodology which will be discussed in next section.

RESEARCH GAPS, RESEARCH PROBLEM, AND JUSTIFICATION OF THE STUDY CONTEXT

There are many studies into Balinese cultural heritage, particularly dark tourism (e.g. Keesing, 1974; Kunst, 1994; Picard, 1990, 1997, 2008). However, unlike "ngaben" cremation which has received much attention other specific traditional Balinese rituals, as found in the Trunyan cemetery, have received little attention despite the popularity with both overseas and domestic tourists. Accessibility and the surrounds seem to suffer from lack of maintenance. Further, study that examines online travel community in relation with destination brand image formation seems to be limited. To date, specific study that employ TripAdvisor as study context suggests that destination experts who are active throughout the TripAdvisor platform is important and influential pillars of the community (Hochmeister, Gretzel & Werthner, 2013). To bridge these knowledge gaps and lack of death sites' maintenance, this study aims to explain the phenomenon of Trunyan cemetery, where the dead are not buried; and also the impact of online travel community on tourist's lifeworld in particular and dark tourism in general. Further study will not only enrich the body of knowledge on dark tourism but may also be used as recommendations for improving the surrounds of the cemetery. The research problem is therefore: (1) how does visiting Trunyan cemetery affect the tourist's lifeworld; and (2) what are the factors which make death sites such as Trunyan cemetery attractive to tourists?

METHODOLOGY AND DISCUSSIONS

Methodologically speaking, one of the main limitations of applied-research in the fields of dark tourism seems to be associated to two salient points. On one hand, the application of obtrusive methods as open or closed-ended questionnaires taints the obtained answers or condition what really interviewees think. In this respect, there is a dissociation between what people feel and how really they behave, which ignited a hotly debate in epistemological circles (Korstanje & George 2017). On another, as Stone (2012) claimed, dark tourism is still in its infancy in which case the abundance of abstract insights or theoretical approaches flourished. This represents serious problems to carve out a consolidated discipline that offers all-encompassing and explanatory models to understand dark tourism. In a recent book, Senior lecturers Glenn Hooper & John Lennon (2016) call the attention on the needs of mingling theory with practical study cases in dark tourism research. While media and journalism echoed from the interests of public opinion respecting to dark tourism sites, this represents a big problem for professional researchers who experienced a fragmentation of produced-knowledge as well as the dispersion of what dark tourism really means. This is the chief reason why some innovative and novel approaches should be discussed and introduced in the study of dark sites. This chapter offers a fertile ground since it utilises the benefits of narrative enquiry (or content analysis) which is combined with critical theory grounded in the scholarship on dark tourism and communication theory. R. Tzanelli gives insight on the availability of digital instruments or alternative sources of information to explore dark topics. She argues convincingly that not only websites or travelogue sites provide with a fresh answer to the limitations and stagnations of current research simply because people express freely in a way otherwise they would never done, but also she considers the content analysis of films or movies still remains as a valid platform to confront with the already-established paradigms (Tzanelli, 2016). By this way, Jennifer Germann Molz (2015) laments the resistance of scholarship to adopt ICT or digital technology as efficient instrument of dataset collection –substituting the classic field-working. In an ever-changing world, not only the nature of tourism is being radically altered starting from the premise, we are passing from psychical travels to virtual experiences, but also the used methodologies to grasp the rise of these new tourist practices.

Hence we incline to apply OGC (Online-generated content) as the main technique, which contributes for mapping the venting feelings of tourists (in these case death-seekers. Our review of existent literature suggests that venting negative feelings crystalize in negative reputation but in some extent, it does not replicate in dark sites. The classic sense of pleasure-maximization seems not to apply in sites of dark tourism. In this vein, our attempts are inscribed in the direction of Pantano & DiPietro (2013) who explore how bad or negative experiences can be sublimated in positive reputation for the involving tourist destination. In so doing, online consumer behaviour still reveals the power of media as analytic platform for future investigations.

As the previous argument given, this present chapter centres on the content analysis of online community with basis on Trip-Advisor website, which is today not only one of the well-famous tourism advisor websites but also consulted by hundred thousands of clients worldwide. In this respect, let's explain readers that *TripAdvisor* functions as a website founded by Stephen Kaufer & Langley Steinert to easily give reviews of experiences, travel-related content as well as the experience of travellers who interact with others through virtual forums. Today this site contains more than 315 million members who had cemented almost 465 million reviews. As one of the largest travel website of the world this platform encompasses the viewpoints, experiences and information of customers who had visited or will visit tourist destinations. Although dark tourism sites are not highly-consulted destinations, TripAdvisor concentrates a whole portion of reviews of people who have achieved a "dark experience". Hence we posit that the popularity of death sites not only indicates the existence of the "secular tourist" who is fascinated by the unique rituals of others' experience of death, developing into online discussions of death and immortality, but it also shapes the tourist's view of the world and attaches a brand image to death sites.

Communication theory is the lens through which the tourist's lifeworld and post-visit experience are unveiled. The critical theory is used to scrutinise the meaning of visiting death sites and how this affects tourists. Communication theory conceptualises both the secular tourist in the dark tourism spectrum and otherness through spirituality and religion, involving other people's death and cultural aspects of the death. On the other hand, online comments on the TripAdvisor website are subjected to content analysis, which aims to uncover post-visit feelings about the death sites; why Trunyan cemetery in particular is distinguished; how tourists perceive the death rituals and their shared values; and how these affect their beliefs. Fifty e-comments on Trunyan cemetery on the TripAdvisor website were reviewed on 27 December 2015 posted from 2012 to 27 December 2015. The reasons of this selection rest on two important issues. At a first glance, content analysis as a method is not based on the number of the study-cases or the range of periods but also in the deepness how information is deciphered. In this vein, we opted to draw a small sample of dataset and reviews, which was framed from 2012 to 2015 to gain further readability and prioritizing the informational tabulation. Secondly, 50 e-comments from 80 were a sufficient sample that leads towards reliable outcomes. Here it is important to understand that as a sample, drawn following non-representative methods, the findings should not be extrapolated to others universes or contexts. The sample was formed following the researchers' criteria according to The Trunyan cemetery as a tourist attraction, adjoined to other factors as the languages in which the review is written, and the dark attributes featured to Trunyan Cemetery. The novel of this approach consists in bringing reflection on the convergence of tourist experience, which is ontologically constituted in the subject's biography with the external traits which are proper of the cemetery as dark site. This investigation exhibits an exploratory study adopting a combination of techniques which would be helpful to continue in future layouts.

In terms of data handling and data analysis, Richards (2015) points out ways of seeing data and testing synthesis and patterns: (1) via coding and category handling; (2) via modelling; (3) via writing; (4) via case study; (5) via typologies; (6) via matrices. Of these six ways, handling data via coding and category was selected, although checking the frequency of occurrences and the specific cases that occur (which denotes the matrix way of seeing data) is inevitably important and is used in this study. The 50 e-comments were transcribed and analysed using content analysis. A list of themes was developed including expressions of negative feelings, positive feelings, and mixed feelings. The themes were grouped into several relevant constructs to use in the post-visit evaluation and identify how the perceived brand distinctiveness of Trunyan cemetery's attributes is formed, as a variable that delineates the dark attributes as dimensions of venting feelings in the online community.

OVERVIEW OF THE STUDY CONTEXT: VISITING TRUNYAN CEMETERY

Historically, Trunyan village was the only area of Bali not conquered by the Majapahit emperors, which means that the empire's traditions, culture and belief structures did not influence the village. This may be an indication of why rituals of shared values in Trunyan cemetery are different from other classical types of Balinese cremation. Located on the edge of Lake Batur in northern Bali, the cemetery is where people from the nearby village of Kuban bring their dead to rest on top of the ground. The only dead allowed here are those who passed away because of old age or sickness brought on by old age, not those who died through accident or any other tragic cause e.g. being murdered. The site can only be reached by boat, a small fleet of which awaits visitors at the end of a wooden jetty overlooked by the stunning Mount Batur. Crossing the lake to Trunyan takes between 20 and 30 minutes and upon arrival a small huddle of men awaits the boats. The cemetery is small and seems to be poorly maintained, but what indicates the importance of this final resting place is the great number of human skulls lined up on stone shelves (Gower, 2010; Morton, 2014).

The uniqueness of this ritual lies in not burying the body, but merely placing it under the tree named Teruyan (Teru Menyan). This tree has a strong scent, and the people of Trunyan village believe that it diminishes the smell from the dead body. In the cemetery, under the teruyan trees, the bodies of the deceased are just covered in cloth and rudimentary bamboo cages. These cages are flimsy and practically leave the body open to the elements. The bodies left out in the open will of course decompose, and the potential for unwelcome odours and even health concerns is real. The presence of a banyan tree, described as a holy tree, seems to stand guard protecting the cemetery. Its leaves carpet the ground and presumably this is part of the way in which the tree keeps the area free from unwelcome odours. In addition, once the bodies of the deceased are decomposed, old bones will be moved stone shelves, to make way for new ones. This sacred ritual profoundly indicates the shared values which distinguish the people of Trunyan from other Balinese and their cultural rituals for dealing with the death of family members. The Trunyan ritual denotes the mixed aspects of spirituality and religion with the cultural heritage.

FINDINGS AND ANALYSIS OF THE CONTENT ANALYSIS

As discussed in the methodology, the analysis and findings are as follows. Firstly, those derived from the content analysis are presented. Next, details of how the critical theory used to scrutinise the meaning of visiting Trunyan cemetery and how it affects tourists is outlined. The analysis involves discussion on the presentation of death and communication patterns and on the presentation of death and religiosity formation.

The online comments from TripAdvisor on visiting the cemetery are judged by several criteria: overall rating of the attractions (Table 1), title of the review, the review's content, types of companion (i.e. couple, family with young children, family and teens, friends, business, and solo). Additional information includes the attraction's phone number, website, recommended length of visit (1 hour, 1-2 hours, 2-3 hours, and more than 3 hours), followed by questions: (a) to what extent is the attraction free

Table 1. Rating of Trunyan Cemetery as attraction

Your Overall Rating of This Attraction	Terrible	Poor	Average	Very Good	Excellent
	1	2	3	4	5
Recommended Length of Visit	<1 hour	1-2 hours	2-3 hours	More than 3 hours	
Attraction's Profile	**Rating**				
Is this attraction free to the public?	Yes		No	Not sure	
Would this be a good rainy day activity?	Yes		No	Not sure	
Is there food available at this attraction?	Yes		No	Not sure	
Is a car required to access this attraction?	Yes		No	Not sure	
Is this attraction accessible using public transport?	Yes		No	Not sure	

to the public? (b) is a gratuity suggested at this attraction? (c) would this be a good rainy day activity? (d) is food available at this attraction? (e) is a car required to access this attraction? (f) is this attraction accessible using public transport? An optional question regarding willingness to share photos about the trip is also asked. Six questions concern the overall rating of the Trunyan cemetery as an attraction, and recommendation to visit (as depicted in Table 1) rated on the scale "yes", "no", and "not sure" (TripAdvisor, 2015). In short, these criteria can be grouped into categories: (1) overall rating derived from the visit itself, e.g. type of companion; (2) recommended length of visit and its attractions profile; (3) and the optional question on willingness to share the information about the attraction's phone number or website and willingness to share photos of the visit.

As depicted in Table 2, the languages used in the online community are English (31 respondents), Dutch (2), French (1), Bahasa Indonesian (9), Norwegian (1), Japanese (3), Russian (2), German (1). The range of visits is from 2012 to 27 December 2015. Out of 50 top listed reviews and comments, total respondents for 2015 was 23; for 2014 15; for 2013 6; for 2012 5; and no date stated 1.

Most responses are positive, and all respondents answered all the questions, leading to discussing the value of money, basic and expensive prices for accessibility, some dissatisfaction with the local people's attitude (Table 3). In addition, discussion on the distinctiveness of the Trunyan cemetery was expressed by 13 respondents indicating negative feelings, 3 comments denoting both negative and positive feelings, and a few comments about historical facts. Among the more interesting comments are the story of Gunung Batur, an ancient Taru Menyan tree, Dewi Danu, classification of resting the dead body according to criteria of children, unmarried or married, the story of Bali Aga as a marginalised tribe and its label as the poorest one are. Further, both negative and positive feelings are expressed about the Trunyan cemetery as a dark site, denoting artificial dissatisfaction not only with the graveyard and the unfriendly environment but also about the local people's attitudes; these imply Trunyan authenticity and its dark attributes are fundamentally distinct from other dark sites, signifying strong positioning. In fact, those comments that contains harsh word play coupled with negative feelings, which appear discouraging, suggests the attributes being commented on may emerge as central to authenticity and shared values, giving a brand image to the Trunyan cemetery as a premium dark sites attraction.

The word play in the online community confirms what the literature indicated. Some of the word play most used denotes sarcasm, e.g. "Ancient culture in the middle of the Island of the Gods"; "Sad that this is a tourist attraction"; "Horrible experience"; "Bad experience"; Worst attraction I've ever done";

Table 2. Language used, date of visit, and summary of venting feelings on TripAdvisor

Language Used in Online Community	Respondent Number (RN)	Date of Visit	Venting Feelings e-Comments		
			(+)	(-)	Mixed (+) and (-)
English	RN 1	December 2015	√		
	RN 2	December 2015			√
	RN 3	October 2015	√		
	RN 4	February 2015	√		
	RN 5	September 2015	√		
	RN 6	September 2015	√		
	RN 7	October 2014			√
	RN 8	August 2015	√		
	RN 9	August 2015		√	
	RN 10	July 2015		√	
	RN 11	June 2015		√	
	RN 12	May 2015	√		
	RN 13	June 2015		√	
	RN 14	March 2014	√		
	RN 15	January 2015	√		
	RN 16	December 2014		√	
	RN 17	August 2014	√		
	RN 18	November 2014	√		
	RN 19	September 2014		√	
	RN 20	-	√		
	RN 21	October 2014		√	
	RN 22	April 2014		√	
	RN 23	April 2014	√		
	RN 24	November 2012		√	
	RN 25	September 2013	√		
	RN 26	September 2013	√		
	RN 27	November 2012	√		
	RN 28	April 2013	√		
	RN 29	December 2012	√		
	RN 30	August 2012	√		
	RN 31	June 2012		√	
Dutch	RN 32	December 2015			
	RN 41	March 2015	√		
French	RN 35	August 2015	√		

continued on following page

Table 2. Continued

Language Used in Online Community	Respondent Number (RN)	Date of Visit	Venting Feelings e-Comments		
			(+)	(-)	Mixed (+) and (-)
Bahasa Indonesian	RN 33	October 2015	√		
	RN 34	October 2014	√		
	RN 36	August 2015	√		
	RN 37	August 2015	√		
	RN 39	September 2014	√		
	RN 40	January 2015	√		
	RN 46	September 2014	√		
	RN 47	July 2014		√	
	RN 49	April 2013		√	
Norwegian	RN 38	August 2014	√		
Japanese	RN 42	February 2015	√		
	RN 43	January 2014	√		
	RN 50	January 2012			
Russian	RN 44	January 2014	√		
	RN 45	September 2014			√
German	RN 48	April 2013		√	
	Total: 50 respondents	Total 2015 (23 respondents); Total 2014 (15 respondents); Total 2013 (6 respondents); Total 2012 (5 respondents); Not stated (1 respondent).			

Source: TripAdvisor online community, 27 December 2015.

"Shocking!"; "Merkelig opplevelse" ("Strange experience"); "その土地の風習、文化" ("customs of the land, culture"). Negative feelings expressed include "Nice and new experience, just shame it became too touristy"; "Terrible locals"; "Don't bother....!!!"; "Just don't go there. It is not worth it."; "Cemetery okay, but Aga Village is a disgrace!"; "We wanted to learn about Trunyan beliefs and culture, but didn't"; "Lebih Baik Bawa Guide Lokal" ("It is better to hire Balinese as tourist guide"), denoting dissatisfaction towards encountering dark site attributes; also, the overpricing, the local people's characteristics, and lack of ready accessibility. Bearing this in mind, this study's findings can be useful as a meta-theme of dark sites' attributes in general, here attributed to Trunyan cemetery's brand distinctiveness, which signifies its existential authenticity. In sum, this study's findings which denote dissatisfaction expressed in the form of negative feelings expressed online indeed delineate this true philosophical dark site's attributes.

DISCUSSION: CONNECTEDNESS BETWEEN DEATH AND TOURISTS

As outlined in the overview of this study, the ritual of just leaving the bodies of the deceased on the ground, covered by cloth and rudimentary bamboo cages, leads to the question of shared values of this ritual. Perspectives of religion and spirituality interconnect with how this fascinates tourists and how it affects their lifeworld; and what are the explanations for this phenomenon. As the literature indicates, contemporary dark tourism in general and death sites as attractions in particular lead to contemplation and consideration of human feelings about death.

The feelings of connectedness coupled with the attributes of spirituality as perceived by the people of Trunyan reflect their perceived values in finding more meaning in not burying the dead body. They denote spiritual values and a socio-cultural topography that fuel their way of life. The essence of spirituality, according to Krentzman (2013) and Willson et al. (2013), revolves around such questions as (1) where do we find meaning? (2) how do we feel connected? and (3) how should we live?

Understanding the role of teruyan trees within the cemetery, and using bamboo cages and cloths (Gower, 2010) to protect the body also signify their true belief and shared values that connect them with the universe and indicate the way to treat dead bodies. On the other hand, the tourists world determines their beliefs and values as they visit death sites, awakening their visualisation of life after death and fuelling the need for validation of modern tourists who assume they can avoid death, seen through the lens of other people's death cultural settings and shared values.

In terms of the second question, the meta-theme examined is as follows. A five-point Likert scale was used to score the answers to: (1) how did the visit to Trunyan cemetery change the tourist's lifeworld? (2) What indications can be taken as core attributes for expressing feelings in the online community? (5 indicated strong effect on the tourist's lifeworld and 1 no effect). As it depicted in Table 3, the meta-theme findings indicate that distinct dark-site attributes can be grouped into (1) value of money, (2) accessibility, (3) surrounding views at this attraction, (4) local people's characteristics and attitude, and (5) shared values and cultural rituals. These five attributes are derived from TripAdvisor, which in this sense plays a role as facilitator that mediates communication and interaction among members of the online community, and from the commitment of members of the online community in providing the information for sharing their feelings. Of the 50 respondents who shared their experience of visiting Trunyan cemetery, 34 had positive feelings, 13 negative feelings, and 3 expressed both.

Table 3. Meta-Theme of findings on dark attributes associated with Trunyan Cemetery

Posting e-Reviews and/or e-Comments					
Distinctiveness of the dark-site attributes	Value for money/ pricing	Accessibility	Surrounding views at this attraction	Local people's characteristics and attitude	Shared values and cultural rituals
	√	√	√	√	√
Total number of respondents	Positive feelings		Mixed feelings	Negative feelings	
50	34		3	13	
Overall rating of the dark site	5	4	3	2	1
	Extreme effect on tourists' lifeworld	Some effect on tourist's lifeworld	Average effect on tourist's lifeworld	Little effect on tourist's lifeworld	No effect on tourist's lifeworld
Indicator:	extreme experience visiting dark site that changed tourist's lifeworld (5) – experience visiting dark site has no effect on tourist's lifeworld (1)				

Source: TripAdvisor online community, January 2015 to 27 December 2015.

As already established from the literature review, e-comments and e-WOM about visitors' experience are largely motivated by helping a travel service provider, concerns for consumers, the need for enjoyment or positive self-enhancement, and expressing negative feelings about the site (Yoo and Gretzel, 2008); hence it is appropriate to analyse the findings further, using content analysis as explained above. Discussion of the study findings and analysis follows.

Presentation of Death and Communication Patterns

Presentation of death in this study context is arguably the reason why tourists feel akin to the local people and their shared values. Based on the e-comments on TripAdvisor, Trunyan cemetery influenced the tourists who visited it along a spectrum according to presentation of the dead body. The e-comments largely denoted sadness, projected not only by the fact that the dead body is not buried (the "first in first out" procedure broke some visitors' hearts), but also, more interestingly, by the fact that the surrounding environment, the attitude of local people, and even the entrance fee gave rise to conflicting feelings of the "secular" tourists (Korstanje and George, 2015) who were merely interested in visiting the dark site for the purpose of understanding other people's death rituals, as a distraction from their own mortality. Likewise, Krentzman's (2013) explanation of the relationships between religion and spirituality is strengthened by the tourists' e-comments, expressing conflicting feelings towards the dead bodies, the environment in particular and the other attributes identified; these are seen through the lens of their own shared values, indicating how their own values dominate this human interaction and communication. In other words, local and shared values seem to be marginalised, while at the same time producing the inevitable strange feelings and self-awareness of how humans are powerless by the time the soul and the body come to be separated. For example:

Inside of feeling creepy, we felt enriched by the experience of reaching this place by boat from the village of Trunyan. Pictures of the deceased hung on the bamboo frame over the corpse and yes, the corpse remains above ground. No stink, dry as a bone, which you also find in a pile near the pile of skulls. Remember these were once people like you and me paying bills, earning a living, eating lunch. Don't miss an opportunity to see inside Indonesian culture" (Respondent number 3).

To an extreme degree, the presentation of the Trunyan dark site indicates its authenticity, as discussed in the overview of the study and supported by the content analysis of the TripAdvisor e-comments: how dark attributes, i.e. the presentation of death, the surrounding environment, the attitude of local people and their shared values, denote not only allegory of the dark tourism attraction but also unveil the meaning of life after death, and the philosophical spectrum of the domination of spirituality on the tourist's lifeworld. In terms of the communication patterns, which lie on the spectrum of interaction between death and the tourist, mortality has never been so influential as when seen by the tourists' own eyes and discussed online. One can consider this dark site as both distracting the tourist from thoughts of his/her own death, but also as an experience of the agony of ending the human journey, all influenced by the shared values of culture and heritage, and the socio-economic topography of one tribe which has specific beliefs.

Presentation of Death and the Formation of Religiosity

Visiting dark sites to gain an understanding of other people's death or one's own mortality leads to discussion of how dark sites might result in religiosity formation. As death is something that every person has to face, the fear of having the kind of death projected in the dark attraction may strengthen the fact that the secular tourist is more concerned with spirituality and religiosity as primary needs. The formation of religiosity fulfils the cognitive and affective beliefs of tourists, projected not through specific dark-site attributes but, more importantly, through the latent meaning of e-comments in the online community. There is nothing more tragic than twisted belief structures associated with religiosity perspectives, where people cannot see or be able to differentiate between religion and spirituality. Religion arguably focuses on what practices and rituals someone should follow; what is right and wrong, true and false; leading to the sense of how civilisation emerges not only as a new form of decent culture (i.e. shared values) but also validating the superior perspectives of how certain groups of people are more civilised and decent. While others may justify this phenomenon as colonisation of people's lifeworld, marginalisation seems to be only a flicker which serves as justification of civilisation's correct way of disposing of dead bodies; for the general good, this is frequently by burying the body, although not in the case of the Trunyan cemetery rituals. This leads to philosophical questions, searching for meaning, about the purpose of life.

Spirituality, as discussed in the literature review, asks questions such as where does a person find meaning?; how does a person feel connected?; and how should one live one's life? All of these questions from the perspectives of both religion and spirituality may (or may *not*) be answered by dark sites. To sum up, the religiosity of a dark site stimulates inflicted feelings of agony about human interaction with other groups of people who do not share similar values. This is perhaps because of the feelings of awe derived from the dark site and from the shared values attributed to belief, feelings of comfort, reflection and applied ethics.

CONCLUDING REMARKS: MAJOR WOW! ANCIENT CULTURE IN THE MIDDLE OF THE ISLAND OF THE GODS

Dark sites can thus be perceived from four main viewpoints, in line with past studies of conceptualisation (e.g. Korstanje & George, 2015). First, the death of other people emerges as a main attraction of dark tourism in general and dark sites in particular. As past studies suggest, visiting dark sites is a distraction from one's own mortality for secular tourists.

Second, as the findings and analysis from the content analysis of the e-comments about the Trunyan cemetery show, dark tourism in general may be useful as a driving force for revitalising the tourist site, i.e. the dark site. In this respect, improving accessibility and the development of local people's attitude may have two sides, reflecting both advantages and disadvantages of the dark site: they may (or may not) improve the dark site's attributes attached to its profile or may diminish authenticity attributes that genuinely indicate its unique profile and shared values, making it stand out from the crowd and be true, in line with the present socio-demographical situation and condition. In this vein, the reasons why dark sites in general and Trunyan cemetery in particular fascinate tourists perhaps chiefly lie in its authentic shared values that work along with socio-cultural economic considerations and topography; these not only serve as magnetic attractions revealing the tourist's lifeworld, but also, more importantly affect the modern (secular) tourist's perception of the distinctive way of treating the dead body, which is different from his/her framework of experience. These explains one tourist's e-comments on his/her experience of the Trunyan cemetery, as "Major Wow!, ancient culture in the middle of the Island of the Gods". In short, expressing opinions through posting online not only shows how visits to Trunyan cemetery affect the tourist's lifeworld, but also denotes the usefulness of venting negative feelings and encouraging the philosophical perspective of visiting dark sites in general, and how the fear of death reveals the characteristics of the modern, secular tourist. Trunyan cemetery, like any other dark site, exhibits its authenticity and shared values which not only scare tourists but also strengthen its position as a distinctive tourist attraction that only can be enjoyed by a certain type of people as a branded attraction generating the "major wow"; but this is not for everybody.

Third, authenticity and shared values, constantly discussed throughout this study, indicate the existential authenticity which Wang (1999) believes revolves around personal or intersubjective feelings, activated by the "liminal process" of tourist activities. Wang denotes a liminal experience as what the tourist feels when they encounter the attraction, i.e authentic touristic market offerings, more freely self-expressed than in everyday life, simply because of engaging in non-ordinary activities. Visiting Trunyan cemetery, an "authentically good time" (Brown, 1996) may paradoxically indicate expressing positive feelings about the death site's attributes. Conversely, expressing negative feelings about these attributes (e.g. the difficulties in accessing the cemetery, the expensive entry fee, the characteristics of the local people and their shared values) to the online community perhaps indicates the true philosophical meaning of "dark site" and its dark attributes. With this in mind, "authentically good time" may refer to existential authenticity; in the case of Trunyan cemetery it presumably implies the dissatisfaction that shapes the conversation about death with the online community. Nevertheless, this may be useful as the essence of brand distinctiveness, as vital attribute for brand image formation. Fourth, as Stone & Sharpley (2008) observed, dark tourism rests on numerous disparate factors involving contemplation of death, addressing issues of personal meaningfulness and having more to do with life and living. With this in mind, how Trunyan cemetery changes the tourist's lifeworld post-visit lies in the intensity of meanings for various individuals within different social networks, the awareness of mortality and the anticipation of death amongst various social and cultural groups. In this study context, these issues are talked about in the online community.

THEORETICAL AND PRACTICAL IMPLICATIONS

This study confirms the usefulness of the hot interpretation approach in terms of dark tourism attractions and dark sites (e.g. Kang, Scott, Lee, & Ballantyne, 2012; Moscardo & Ballantyne, 2008; Stone & Sharpley, 2008; Uzzell & Ballantyne, 1998; Uzzell, 1989), in order to enhance dark tourism experiences. In conclusion, the findings have relevance to management and the development of dark tourism attractions and products, providing evidence that dark tourism experiences can be beneficial for destinations as well as for tourists and visitors. The findings may help management in turn to create more effective sites and tourism services, by a better understanding of the benefits gained by visitors to a site.

In terms of practical implications, this study indicates the existence of critical marketing in the tourism marketing domain. Bauman (2001) suggests that exploration of new forms of consumption move from the functionality of needs to the diffuse plasticity and volatility of desire. He argues that the principle of instability has become functional yet seems to conjure stability out of an entire lack of solidity. Critical tourism marketing revolves around the fact that some of the negative e-comments may be profoundly useful for commodification of socio-demographic attributes that shape a dark site's profile, which arguably may serve as the core in communicating brand-distinctiveness. It encourages the process of giving brand image to the dark site's personification. As a result, contemporary branding techniques would move from active development by the supply side of the business, i.e. the service providers, into the new form of sounding the shared values and authenticity attributes shaped in the publics' e-comments in the online community, as discussed in the review of literature and supported by the findings of this study's content analysis. In this sense, the online community may not only serve as a medium for people to communicate and interact but it also indicates the power of technology in bringing the audience (which used to be passive with no equal control over the information, i.e. the shared values and/or ideology) from across different settings and content i.e. the information that is being discussed online.

As depicted in Table 2, e-reviews and/or e-comments involve discussion of value for money/pricing, accessibility, surrounding views, local people's characteristics and attitude, shared values and the rituals of the attractions; thus the extreme postings of e-reviews and/or e-comments in the online community could be classified as extending the experience of visits to Trunyan cemetery and their effects on the tourist's lifeworld. This examination (as depicted in Table 3) delineates the shared values of not burying the dead body, the ritual of placing it under the Teru Menyan tree which stands in the middle of the graveyard, the myth of the lake Goddess Dewi Danu who was lured from heaven by earth sent from the Teru Menyan tree; this is represented by the opinion of respondent number 25 in particular, and the majority of respondents in general. The TripAdvisor participants were fascinated by the fact that the villagers of Trunyan leave their dead bodies under a thin blanket and a few bamboos sticks to keep animals away, and amazed that there is no smell as the tree seems to absorb it from the decomposing bodies. What is more, the eccentric characteristics of the local people and their attitude during their encounters with tourists indicate the existential state of being that Wang (1999) analytically terms existential authenticity, as a distinctive source of authentic experiences in tourism. This Trunyan cemetery phenomenon is a verification of past studies which coined dark tourism (Stone, 2006) as attractions and exhibits associated with death and the macabre. Further, dark tourism in general and death sites/dark sites are also argued by past studies as either tourist-demand or attraction-driven (Stone, 2006; Wilkinson, 2010), which leads to a discussion of the secular tourist in the dark tourism typology. Therefore, it can be inferred that this study is in agreement with the previous studies. Table 3 summarises the meta-themes of Trunyan cemetery.

THE STUDY'S LIMITATIONS AND DIRECTIONS FOR FUTURE WORK

Every study has its limitations, and this study is no exception. Here they lie in the critical evaluation of the usefulness of critical theory in tourism marketing. For instance, informants' comments come from only one online community, and the findings would be more robust if future study examined another form of community and/or other forms of e-comments in different online communities. Other than that, the study context can be re-tested with other methodologies, e.g. ethnography or phenomenology, to explain tourists' lifeworld and the lives of local people. As for generalisation, the quantitative approach can be taken to reveal the effect of this study on the lifeworld's of both domestic and overseas tourists. Gender, nationality and religion of tourists who participate in online communities can be proposed as moderating variables for future study.

REFERENCES

Ballantyne, R., & Uzzell, D. (1993). Environmental mediation and hot interpretation e a case study of District Six, Cape Town. *The Journal of Environmental Education*, *24*(3), 4–7. doi:10.1080/00958964.1993.9943496

Bauman, Z. (2001). Consuming life. *Journal of Consumer Culture*, *1*(1), 9–29. doi:10.1177/146954050100100102

Biran, A., & Hyde, K. F. (2013). New perspectives on dark tourism.*International Journal of Culture. Tourism and Hospitality Research*, *7*(3), 191–198.

Biran, A., Poria, Y., & Oren, G. (2011). Sought experiences at (dark) heritage sites. *Annals of Tourism Research*, *38*(3), 820–841. doi:10.1016/j.annals.2010.12.001

Boley, B. B., Magnini, V. P., & Tuten, T. L. (2013). Social media picture posting and souvenir purchasing behaviour: Some initial findings. *Tourism Management*, *37*, 27–30. doi:10.1016/j.tourman.2012.11.020

Bowman, M. S., & Pezzullo, P. C. (2009). Whats so darkabout dark tourism?: Death, tours, and performance. *Tourist Studies*, *9*(3), 187–202. doi:10.1177/1468797610382699

Brown, D. (1996). Genuine fakes. In T. Selwyn (Ed.), *The Tourist Image: myths and myth making in tourism*. Chichester, UK: Wiley.

Cohen, E. H. (2011). Educational dark tourism at an in populo site: The Holocaust Museum in Jerusalem. *Annals of Tourism Research*, *38*(1), 193–209. doi:10.1016/j.annals.2010.08.003

Collins-Kreiner, N. (2010). Researching pilgrimage: Continuity and transformations. *Annals of Tourism Research*, *37*(2), 440–456. doi:10.1016/j.annals.2009.10.016

Germann Molz, J. (2012). *Travel connections: Tourism, technology, and togetherness in a mobile world*. Abingdon, UK: Routledge.

Gil Soldevilla, S., Palao Errando, J. A., & Marzal Felici, J. J. (2014). Brands as New Forms of Religiosity: The Case of the World of Red Bull. *Trípodos,* (35), 57-74

Gower, S. M. (2010). Trunyan: Where the dead lie. *Jakarta Post*. Retrieved April 22, 2010, from http://www.thejakartapost.com/news/2010/04/22/trunyan-where-dead-lie.html

Gretzel, U., Fesenmaier, D. R., Lee, Y. J. & Tussyadiah, I. (2010). 11 Narrating travel experiences: the role of new media. *Tourist experience: Contemporary perspectives*, 171.

Gretzel, U. & Yoo, K. H. (2008). Use and impact of online travel reviews. *Information and communication technologies in tourism 2008*, 35-46.

Handayani, B. (2016). The Paradox of Authenticity and its Implications for Contemporary and 'Bizarre'. *Tourism Campaigns.*

Hartmann, R. (2014). Dark tourism, thanatourism, and dissonance in heritage tourism management: New directions in contemporary tourism research. *Journal of Heritage Tourism*, *9*(2), 166–182. doi:10.1080/1743873X.2013.807266

Heidelberg, B. A. W. (2015). Managing ghosts: Exploring local government involvement in dark tourism. *Journal of Heritage Tourism*, *10*(1), 74–90. doi:10.1080/1743873X.2014.953538

Hochmeister, M., Gretzel, U., & Werthner, H. (2013). *Destination expertise in online travel communities*. Springer Berlin Heidelberg.

Holt-Lunstad, J., Smith, T. B., & Layton, J. B. (2010). Social relationships and mortality risk: A meta-analytic review. *PLoS Medicine*, *7*(7), 859. doi:10.1371/journal.pmed.1000316 PMID:20668659

Hooper, G., & Lennon, J. (2016). *Dark Tourism: practice and interpretation*. Abingdon, UK: Routledge.

Jiang, J., Gretzel, U., & Law, R. (2010). Do negative experiences always lead to dissatisfaction? Testing attribution theory in the context of online travel reviews. *Information and communication technologies in tourism 2010*, 297-308.

Johnston, T. (2013). Mark Twain and The Innocents Abroad: Illuminating the tourist gaze on death. *International Journal of Culture and Hospitality Research.*, *7*(3), 199–213. doi:10.1108/IJCTHR-05-2012-0036

Kang, E. J., Scott, N., Lee, T. J., & Ballantyne, R. (2012). Benefits of visiting a 'dark tourismsite: The case of the Jeju April 3rd Peace Park, Korea. *Tourism Management*, *33*(2), 257–265. doi:10.1016/j.tourman.2011.03.004

Keesing, R. M. (1974). Theories of culture. *Annual Review of Anthropology*, *3*(1), 73–97. doi:10.1146/annurev.an.03.100174.000445

Khan, S. (2014). Word play in destination marketing: An analysis of country tourism slogans. *TEAM Journal of Hospitality and Tourism*, *11*(1), 27–39.

Korstanje, M. E. (2016). *The Rise of Thana Capitalism and Tourism*. Abingdon, UK: Routledge.

Korstanje, M. E., & George, B. (2015). Dark Tourism: Revisiting Some Philosophical Issues. *E-review of Tourism Research*, *12*(12), 127–136.

Korstanje, M. E., & George, B. (Eds.). (2017). *Virtual Traumaescape and exploring the roots of dark tourism*. Hershey, PA: IGI Global.

Korstanje, M. E., & Skoll, G. (2015). From Disasters to Religiosity: Republica de Cromañon, Buenos Aires, Argentina. In Religious tourism and pilgrimage management: An international perspective. CABI. doi:10.1079/9781780645230.0267

Krentzman, A. R. (2013). *What Is Spirituality?*. Retrieved July 10, 2013, from http://www.takingcharge.csh.umn.edu/enhance-yourwellbeing/purpose/spirituality/what-spirituality

Kugel, S. (2011). Travel Lessons From the World of Academia *The New York Times*. Retrieved December 6, 2011, from http://frugaltraveler.blogs.nytimes.com/2011/12/06/travel-lessons-from-the-world-of-academia/?login=facebook

Kunst, J. (1994). *Indonesian music and dance: traditional music and its interaction with the West*. Royal Tropical Institute.

Lennon, J. J., & Foley, M. (2000). *Dark tourism*. London: Cengage Learning EMEA.

Malinowski, B. (1926). *Myth in primitive psychology*. London: Norton.

Miles, W. F. S. (2002). Auschwitz: Museum interpretation and darker tourism. *Annals of Tourism Research, 29*(4), 1175–1178. doi:10.1016/S0160-7383(02)00054-3

Morton, E. (2014). Leave me be beneath a tree: trunyan cemetery in Bali. *Slate*. Retrieved October 23, 2014, from http://www.slate.com/blogs/atlas_obscura/2014/10/23/trunyan_cemetery_with_the_taru_menyan_tree_in_bali_indonesia.html

Moscardo, G. M., & Ballantyne, R. (2008). Interpreation and attractions. In A. Fyall, B. Garrod, A. Leask, & S. Wanhill (Eds.), *Managing visitor attractions: New directions (pp. 237-252)*. Oxford, UK: Butterworth-Heinemann. doi:10.1016/B978-0-7506-8545-0.50022-8

Nikiforova, B. (2013). Social media in travel, tourism and hospitality: Theory, practice and cases. *Journal of Tourism History*, *5*(1), 99–101. doi:10.1080/1755182X.2012.758973

Olins, W. (2014). *Brand new: The shape of brands to come*. Thames & Hudson.

Picard, M. (1990). Cultural Tourism in Bali: Cultural Performances as Tourist Attraction. *Indonesia*, *49*, 37–74. doi:10.2307/3351053

Picard, M. (1997). Cultural tourism, nation-building, and regional culture: The making of a Balinese identity. *Tourism, ethnicity, and the state in Asian and Pacific societies*, 181-214.

Picard, M. (2008). Balinese identity as tourist attraction from cultural tourism(pariwisata budaya) toBali erect(ajeg Bali). *Tourist Studies*, *8*(2), 155–173. doi:10.1177/1468797608099246

Podoshen, J. S. (2013). Dark tourism motivations: Simulation, emotional contagion and topographic comparison. *Tourism Management*, *35*, 263–271. doi:10.1016/j.tourman.2012.08.002

Poria, Y. (2007). Establishing cooperation between Israel and Poland to save Auschwitz Concentration Camp: Globalising the responsibility for the Massacre. *International Journal of Tourism Policy*, *1*(1), 45–57. doi:10.1504/IJTP.2007.013897

Raine, R. (2013). A dark tourist spectrum. *International Journal of Culture, Tourism and hospitality Research, 7*(3), 242-256.

Richards, L. (2015). *Handling qualitative data: A practical guide*. London: Sage.

Seaton, A. (2009). Purposeful otherness: Approaches to the management of thanatourism. *The darker side of travel: The theory and practice of dark tourism*, 75-108.

Seaton, A. V. & Lennon, J. J. (2004). Thanatourism in the early 21st century: Moral panics, ulterior motives and alterior desires. *New horizons in tourism: Strange experiences and stranger practices*, 63-82.

Shackley, M. (2001). Potential futures for Robben Island: Shrine, museum or theme park? *International Journal of Heritage Studies*, *7*(4), 355–363. doi:10.1080/13581650120105552

Sharpley, R., & Stone, P. R. (Eds.). (2009). The darker side of travel: The theory and practice of dark tourism. Channel View Publications.

Sharpley, R., & Stone, P. R. (2009). Life, death and dark tourism: future research directions and concluding comments. *The darker side of travel: The theory and practice of dark tourism*, 247-251.

Sharpley, R., & Stone, P. R. (2009a). (Re)presenting the macabre: interpretation, kitschification and authenticity. In R. Sharpley & P. R. Stone (Eds.), *The darker side of travel (pp. 110-128)*. Bristol, UK: Channel View.

Sigala, M., Christou, E., & Gretzel, U. (Eds.). (2012). *Social media in travel, tourism and hospitality: Theory, practice and cases*. Ashgate Publishing, Ltd.

Stone, P. (2006). A dark tourism spectrum: Towards a typology of death and macabre related tourist sites, attractions and exhibitions. Tourism: An Interdisciplinary. *International Journal (Toronto, Ont.)*, *54*(2), 145–160.

Stone, P. (2011). Dark tourism: Towards a new post-disciplinary research agenda. *International Journal of Tourism Anthropology*, *1*(3-4), 318–332. doi:10.1504/IJTA.2011.043713

Stone, P. (2012). *Dark tourism as 'mortality capital': The case of Ground Zero and the significant other dead*. Academic Press.

Stone, P., & Sharpley, R. (2008). Consuming dark tourism: A thanatological perspective. *Annals of Tourism Research*, *35*(2), 574–595. doi:10.1016/j.annals.2008.02.003

Stone, P. R. (2012a). Dark tourism as 'mortality capital': The case of Ground Zero and the significant other dead. In R. Sharpley & P. R. Stone (Eds.), *The contemporary tourist experience: Concepts and consequences* (pp. 30–45). Abingdon, UK: Routledge.

Stone, P. R. (2012b). Dark tourism and significant other death: Towards a model of mortality mediation. *Annals of Tourism Research*, *39*(3), 1565–1587. doi:10.1016/j.annals.2012.04.007

TripAdvisor. (2015). Retrieved from https://www.tripadvisor.com.my/Attraction_Review-g294225-d2628462-Reviews-Trunyan_Cemetery-Indonesia.html

Tzanelli, R. (2016). *Thanatourism and Cinematic Representations of Risk: Screening the End of Tourism*. Abingdon, UK: Routledge.

Uzzell, D. L. (1989). The hot interpretation of war and conflict. In D. L. Uzzell (Ed.), *Heritage interpretation (pp. 33-47)*. Bristol, UK: Belhaven Press.

Uzzell, D. L., & Ballantyne, R. (1998). Heritage that hurts: interpretation in a postmodern world. In D. L. Uzzell & R. Ballantyne (Eds.), *Contemporary issues in heritage & environmental interpretation (pp. 152-171)*. London: The Stationary Office.

Walter, T. (2009). Dark tourism: mediating between the dead and the living. In *The Darker Side of Travel: The Theory and Practice of Dark Tourism. Aspects of Tourism* (pp. 39–55). Bristol, UK: Channel View Publications.

Wang, N. (1999). Rethinking authenticity in tourism experience. *Annals of Tourism Research*, *26*(2), 349–370. doi:10.1016/S0160-7383(98)00103-0

White, L., & Frew, E. (2013). *Dark Tourism: Place and identity: managing and interpreting dark places.* London: Routledge.

Wilkinson, P. F. (2010). Review of "The darker side of travel: The theory and practice of dark tourism", by Sharpley & Stone. *e-Review of Tourism Research, 8*(1).

Willson, G. B., McIntosh, A. J., & Zahra, A. L. (2013). Tourism and spirituality: A phenomenological analysis. *Annals of Tourism Research, 42*, 150–168. doi:10.1016/j.annals.2013.01.016

Xiang, Z., & Gretzel, U. (2010). Role of social media in online travel information search. *Tourism Management, 31*(2), 179–188. doi:10.1016/j.tourman.2009.02.016

Yoo, K. H., & Gretzel, U. (2008). What motivates consumers to write online travel reviews? *Information Technology and Tourism, 10*(4), 283–295. doi:10.3727/109830508788403114

Yoo, K. H., & Gretzel, U. (2010). Antecedents and impacts of trust in travel-related consumer-generated media. *Information Technology and Tourism, 12*(2), 139–152. doi:10.3727/109830510X12887971002701

Yoo, K. H., & Gretzel, U. (2011). Creating more credible and persuasive recommender systems: The influence of source characteristics on recommender system evaluations. In Recommender systems handbook (pp. 455-477). Springer US.

ADDITIONAL READING

Amujo, O. C., & Otubanjo, O. (2012). Leveraging rebranding of 'unattractivenation brands to stimulate post-disaster tourism. *Tourist Studies, 12*(1), 87–105. doi:10.1177/1468797612444196

Biran, A., Poria, Y., & Oren, G. (2011). Sought experiences at (dark) heritage sites. *Annals of Tourism Research, 38*(3), 820–841. doi:10.1016/j.annals.2010.12.001

Cohen, E. H. (2011). Educational dark tourism at an in populo site: The Holocaust Museum in Jerusalem. *Annals of Tourism Research, 38*(1), 193–209. doi:10.1016/j.annals.2010.08.003

Collins-Kreiner, N. (2010). Researching pilgrimage: Continuity and transformations. *Annals of Tourism Research, 37*(2), 440–456. doi:10.1016/j.annals.2009.10.016

Dann, G. M., & Potter, R. B. (2001). Supplanting the planters: Hawking heritage in Barbados. *International Journal of Hospitality & Tourism Administration, 2*(3-4), 51–84. doi:10.1300/J149v02n03_03

Foley, M., & Lennon, J. J. (1996). JFK and dark tourism: A fascination with assassination. *International Journal of Heritage Studies, 2*(4), 198–211. doi:10.1080/13527259608722175

Gelbman, A., & Maoz, D. (2012). Island of peace or island of war: Tourist guiding. *Annals of Tourism Research, 39*(1), 108–133. doi:10.1016/j.annals.2011.05.008

González-Tennant, E. (2013). New heritage and dark tourism: A mixed methods approach to social justice in Rosewood, Florida. *Heritage & Society, 6*(1), 62–88. doi:10.1179/2159032X13Z.0000000007

Goulding, C., & Shankar, A. (2011). Club culture, neotribalism and ritualised behaviour. *Annals of Tourism Research*, *38*(4), 1435–1453. doi:10.1016/j.annals.2011.03.013

Isaac, R. K. (2009). Alternative tourism: Can the segregation wall in Bethlehem be a tourist attraction? *Tourism and Hospitality Planning & Development*, *6*(3), 247–254. doi:10.1080/14790530903363381

Kang, E. J., Scott, N., Lee, T. J., & Ballantyne, R. (2012). Benefits of visiting a 'dark tourismsite: The case of the Jeju April 3rd Peace Park, Korea. *Tourism Management*, *33*(2), 257–265. doi:10.1016/j.tourman.2011.03.004

Korstanje, M. (2016). Inglaterra y el Turismo Oscuro: Los orígenes de la thanaptosis. *RITUR-Revista Iberoamericana de Turismo*, *6*(2), 183–194.

Korstanje, M. E. (2011). Detaching the elementary forms of dark-tourism. *Anatolia*, *22*(3), 424–427. doi:10.1080/13032917.2011.620800

Korstanje, M. E. (2015). Turismo negro y crimen. *Estudios y perspectivas en turismo, 24*(3), 776-779.

Korstanje, M. E., & Clayton, A. (2012). Tourism and terrorism: Conflicts and commonalities. *Worldwide Hospitality and Tourism Themes*, *4*(1), 8–25. doi:10.1108/17554211211198552

Korstanje, M. E., & Olsen, D. H. (2011). The discourse of risk in horror movies post 9/11: Hospitality and hostility in perspective. *International Journal of Tourism Anthropology*, *1*(3-4), 304–317. doi:10.1504/IJTA.2011.043712

Lemelin, H., Dawson, J., Stewart, E. J., Maher, P., & Lueck, M. (2010). Last-chance tourism: The boom, doom, and gloom of visiting vanishing destinations. *Current Issues in Tourism*, *13*(5), 477–493. doi:10.1080/13683500903406367

Minić, N. (2012). Development of" dark" tourism in the contemporary society. *Journal of the Geographical Institute Jovan Cvijic, SASA*, *62*(3), 81–103. doi:10.2298/IJGI1203081M

Pantano, E., & Di Pietro, L. (2013). From e-tourism to f-tourism: Emerging issues from negative tourists online reviews. *Journal of Hospitality and Tourism Technology*, *4*(3), 211–227. doi:10.1108/JHTT-02-2013-0005

Simone-Charteris, M. T., & Boyd, S. W. (2011). The potential for Northern Ireland to promote politico-religious tourism: An industry perspective. *Journal of Hospitality Marketing & Management*, *20*(3-4), 457–483. doi:10.1080/19368623.2011.562438

Urry, J. (1992). The tourist gaze revisited. *The American Behavioral Scientist*, *36*(2), 172–186. doi:10.1177/0002764292036002005

Walklate, S., Mythen, G., & McGarry, R. (2011). Witnessing Wootton Bassett: An exploration in cultural victimology. *Crime, Media, Culture*, *7*(2), 149–165. doi:10.1177/1741659011407110

Wight, A. C. (2006). Philosophical and methodological praxes in dark tourism: Controversy, contention and the evolving paradigm. *Journal of Vacation Marketing*, *12*(2), 119–129. doi:10.1177/1356766706062151

KEY TERMS AND DEFINITIONS

Dark Tourism: Signals to a new trend in touring and travels that select sites of mass disaster or death as chief tourist destination.

Death Consumption: Consists in a postmodern tendency to consume spaces where disasters or catastrophes have happened. The main orientation of death consumption rests on the needs of grasping or figuring the own life through the others' death.

Holocaust Tourism: A widely used term which alludes to the curiosity of some visitors for spaces of genocide, slaughters, or mass-assassination perpetrated against a vulnerable and disarmed population.

Smart Tourism: An innovative development to forge smart destinations. This helps consumers to time-maximization process in the quest and interpretation of global information. Smart tourism is vital for consumers to reach rational choices or optimizing results in the decision making process.

TripAdvisor: A global platform where clients and travellers left their experiences and hopes respecting to countless destinations and nations. It offers not only a valid guide for tourists before travelling abroad but also situates as a forum of dialogue that transcends the borders of cultures.

Trunyan Cemetery: Geographically in the zone of Terunyan, which is a Balinese village situated on the eastern of Lake Batur.

Chapter 18
Perspectives of the Adoption of Cloud Computing in the Tourism Sector

Pedro R. Palos-Sanchez
University of Extremadura, Spain

Marisol B. Correia
ESGHT, University of Algarve, Portugal & CEG-IST, Universidade de Lisboa, Portugal

ABSTRACT

This chapter aims to expose the current situation of the adoption of cloud computing in companies in general and in enterprises of the tourism sector in particular. For this, a review of the literature has been carried out to establish the conceptual framework of technology and of the new economic model that underlies its adoption. Cloud computing is one of the technologies less known to many organizations and especially users, as it is a new technology based on the Internet, through which information is stored on servers, is provided as a service and on clients' demand. Therefore, the main theories of adoption that have been used to explain the different adoption models are presented, as well as, the different solutions that are being used in the tourist industry.

INTRODUCTION

Information and Communication Technologies, also known as Information Technology (IT) have been widely adopted by the society, but especially by the enterprises. These technologies have been widely adopted under the concept of solutions that are provided through IT services. This solution provides effective low-cost communication tools for customers (Tan & Teo, 1998). This is something to be considered for the small and medium-sized enterprise (SME), which adopts IT in a gradual and precise way, not having the need to make large investments, distributing the effort for years.

The adoption of Internet-based IT has made it possible to develop the paradigm of everything as a service, where the user pays only for the use made of the service. These services can range from software applications (Application Service Provider or ASP and Software as a Services or SaaS) to systems

DOI: 10.4018/978-1-5225-2927-9.ch018

infrastructure (Infrastructure as a Service or IaaS). This formula is intuited as a good solution for small and medium enterprises SME, in the line of jumping the barriers that prevented them to take advantage of IT. In the following section, as well as throughout the whole chapter, this concept will be expanded.

Heart and Pliskin (2002) defined this concept as "eRent" of Information Systems (IS), made through the Internet and thanks to an ASP. They say that for SMEs, the IS through "eRental" could be an attractive solution to the expensive and complex acquisitions and implementations of traditional IT.

Johansson (2004) also states that the main reason for SMEs to adopt IT by contracting an ASP is that they allow full control cost and a lower cost when adopting and maintaining them. In spite of this, it assures that if this decision is examined in detail, it is observed that the customers do not emphasize these reasons, and it induces to think that the perspective of the cost is secondary for the SME.

In this way it identifies the three main reasons why ASP clients hire their services. The main reason is that the company is looking to outsource everything that is not basic competencies of its business, which most usually meet the IS. The other two reasons are the lack of qualified personnel and the overall strategy of the organization.

The adoption of IT in the tourism sector is evolving with changes of habits of the travelers, driven by the adaptation of IT as the Internet of Things (IoT), which consists of an automated connection through the Internet of the information generated by the devices and systems. IoT can be defined as a set of interconnected things over the Internet, which have the ability to measure, communicate and act all over the world. The key idea of the IoT is to obtain information about the environment to understand and control and act on it (Díaz, Martín, & Rubio, 2016). According to these authors, the cloud computing and IoT integration, known as Cloud of Things, solves such problems as IoT's limitations, data access, computing, data analysis, and can create new opportunities.

Another adoption of IT in the tourism sector is SoLoMo (Social, Local and Mobile), which reflects consumers' preferences for sharing content and habits through the social web (social purchase, recommendations, etc.), only to say some examples (Junta de Andalucía, 2012).

Thus, travelers or tourists increasingly use different devices connected to the internet to find information, locate offers, book all services related to travel or make purchases at destination, which has resulted in the explosion of travel agencies (Online Travel Agencies), internet portals that intermediate in the booking of tourism products at worldwide level, the sale of second-hand travel through Internet, offering huge discounts through online outlet portals, or the emergence of new typologies of solutions to optimize the management of these channels and the presence based on solutions such as the Central Reservation System, Channel Managers (Channel Manager System) or online communication systems (Online Reputation, Social Networks, etc.).

The aim of this chapter is to present the different models of adoption of cloud computing by companies and organizations and, in particular, by enterprises of the tourism sector. The description and features of cloud computing, the benefits and obstacles for the companies, the added value for adopting the cloud, as well as, some examples of open source solutions are presented. Finally, the characteristics of the solutions adopted by the enterprises of the tourism sector are explained and discussed.

This chapter is structured as follows. After this introduction, a brief review of the state of the art of the literature of cloud computing is developed in Section Theoretical Background. Then, in Section Cloud and Enterprise, the basic principles of adoption of cloud computing by enterprises in general are presented, while in Section Smart Tourism Destinations and Cloud Computing in the Tourism Sector, the adoption of cloud computing by the different subsectors of activity of the tourism sector is explained.

Finally, the last section discusses the conclusions and presents some guidelines that can be addressed in future work.

THEORETICAL BACKGROUND

Theoretical Fundamentals of Cloud Computing

Cloud computing is born of the terms: cloud and computing (Torres, 2011). Cloud is the name that is generally used to represent the Internet. A concept of abstraction is established (physical systems that are not specified, storage of data in unknown locations, ubiquitous access of users and subcontracted administrations).

Computing brings together the concepts of computer science, logic of coordination and storage. Also cloud computing consists of moving the computing from the simple personal computer or conventional data center to the Internet. It is a real paradigm shift in the way the systems are used, forming a new model of supply of resources to design applications and for access of users from independent of platforms to services.

This technology as a concept can be explained in two ways. In one, the cloud and the Internet are confused in the same concept. In such a way that to refer to services of the cloud, is to do it to any service offered through Internet. It could also be understood from the most widespread concept, where cloud computing can be understood as a set of technologies that provide a number of advantages for both the customer and the service provider and make it possible through "economies of scale" in the delivery of services over the Internet, reducing costs and increasing scalability.

You cannot define the cloud without its services. For this, it is necessary to conceptualize what are the ASP. Cloud seems an evolution from the same concept, seen from the perspective of service. ASP are hosts of proprietary software, usually from a third company, to which the customer pays a monthly amount to access. In this way, applications run on the ASP, customer can access it through a web browser or may require an additional installation. In this model, an instance is executed by each customer of the ASP, i.e., it cannot serve multiple customers of different companies with the same service or software, which, as will be seen later, is a feature that cloud computing technology incorporates.

For the National Institute of Standards and Technology of the United States of America (NIST, 2011), "cloud computing is a model for enabling ubiquitous, convenient, on-demand network access to a shared pool of configurable computing resources (e.g., networks, servers, storage, applications, and services) that can be rapidly provisioned and released with minimal management effort or service provider interaction".

It is a technological proposal that allows to offer computer services over the Internet in which resources and software are offered on demand. Technology, services and applications are taken and become self-service utilities. Systems and storage can be supplied according to needs by assessing costs based on counters, allowing an agile scalability of resources, virtualizing systems, pooling and sharing resources. This model offers great possibilities for organizations, both in terms of investment and economies of scale, offshoring, access to information from any place, etc.

Cloud computing is a flexible means of proportionally expanding physical hardware according to demands and has become immediately popular in academic and industrial domains in contrast to grid computing, which can be seen as a collection of computer resources from multiple locations to reach a common goal, that has been proposed and applied mostly within academic fields (Zhou, Xu, & Kimmons, 2015).

Cloud computing is often referred to as "the fifth generation," after the mainframe, the PC, the client-server system, and the World Wide Web. It presents itself as a "democratization" of IT, making available to a great majority of people and to SME the access to new applications, platforms and infrastructure at any time and from anywhere.

History

Cloud computing is an emerging concept that has attracted much attention in both the commercial and the academic field. Strictly speaking, cloud computing is not a new concept, it can be traced back to 1997, when the term was first mentioned, but only recently has become a fashionable term (Chou & Chou, 2007; Xin & Levina, 2008; Lijun, Chan, & Tse, 2008). The use of the term "cloud" is metaphorical and usually points to a large set of available resources, hardware and software, which are easily accessible through the Internet (Vaquero et al., 2009). These characteristics of cloud computing are themselves divided into subsections, such as network computing, grid computing, utility computing, ubiquitous computing, and processing services (Voas & Zhang, 2009).

Among its most notable features are the market-oriented architecture, which, unlike a resource management architecture centered on the traditional system, is regulated by the supply and demand of cloud resources, thus in the market equilibrium and also in its flexibility (Buyya et al., 2009).

A common concept in Information System (IS) and in general in IT is scalability, that applied to IS is the desirable property of a system, based on its ability to react without losing quality, to manage fluently the continuous growth of work or to be prepared to become bigger without losing quality in the offered services (Bondi, 2000).

Applied to the subject matter of this research, it can be said that a service can be easily scaled, that scaled for its resources for optimal use, and for its ability to charge the consumer a certain amount or fee for the use of eligible resources. Services are usually provided on the basis of Service Level Agreements (SLA), based on certain customer needs and expectations, which may meet different levels of quality or service criteria. The background of cloud computing can be seen in the next pyramid presented at Figure 1 that is ordered from the 1950s to nowadays.

Cloud computing is a return to the classic computing model in which the Internet network and all its services make up a cloud of resources that can be compared to a large mainframe (Torres, 2011). Companies are therefore faced with the transition from a model where each company owned their applications or data, to a model where the data and applications of companies co-exist on shared platforms offered by cloud service providers.

Internet has many of the characteristics of what is now called cloud, offering abstraction, running using the same set of protocols and standards, with the same applications and operating systems. That is why there is a confusion between the Internet and cloud computing and, although they are strongly linked, there are differences.

Currently there are several theoretical models proposed by different authors who consider the adoption and adaptation to new technologies as the key factors that determine the success or failure of an IS. One of these processes of adoption of technology that can be seen at Figure 2 is based on the Diffusion Theory of Innovation by Rogers (1995).

Figure 1. Cloud background
Source: Authors elaboration based on Torres (2011)

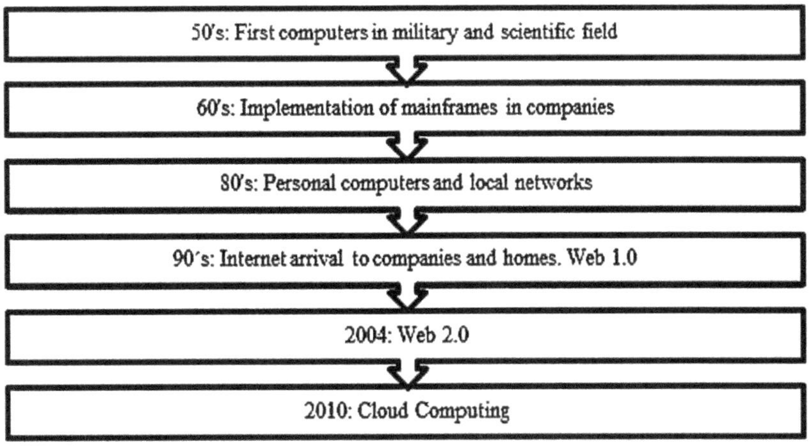

Figure 2. Process of adoption of technology: Diffusion Theory of Innovation
Source: Authors elaboration based on Rogers (1995).

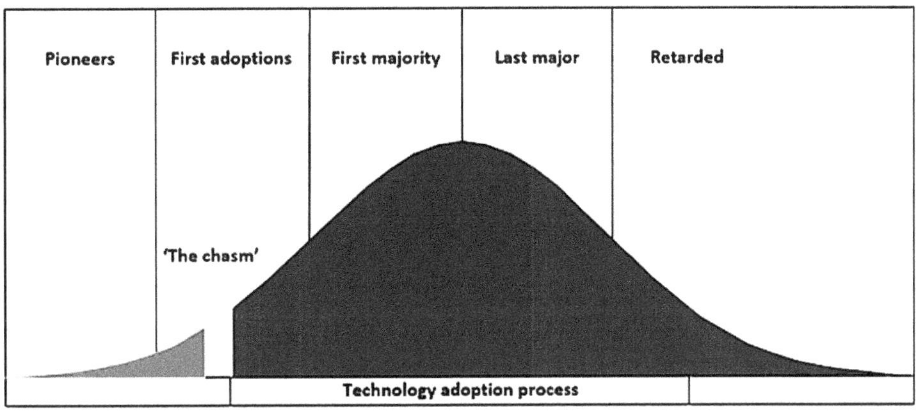

In the case of the cloud, the computer is no longer the PC, the laptop, the smartphone or the tablet, it is now the Internet cloud. The network is the computer.

Based on Rogers (1995) it is possible to affirm that at this moment companies and organizations are in a phase of "early adopters" or of first adoptions of adoptive population of this new approach (Fundación de la Innovación, 2011).

Rogers (1995) discusses the acceptance of technology based on its interrelation with the social and psychological dimensions of the user, and presents a theoretical analysis, where diffusion is the process by which an innovation is communicated in time and diffused by certain channels, among the members of a social system where such innovation is diffused. The theory on diffusion of innovations proposes elements that make up the innovation process, where it is defined as the idea, practice or perceived object as new by an individual or another unit of adoption.

Description and Characteristics

Cloud computing is structured of five essential characteristics, which can also be conceptualized as benefits (NIST, 2011):

- **On Demand Self-Service:** A consumer can unilaterally provision computing capabilities, such as server time and network storage, as needed automatically without requiring human interaction with each service provider.
- **Broad Network Access:** Capabilities are available over the network and accessed through standard mechanisms that promote use by heterogeneous thin or thick client platforms (e.g., mobile phones, tablets, laptops, and workstations).
- **Resource Pooling:** The provider's computing resources are pooled to serve multiple consumers using a multi-tenant model, with different physical and virtual resources dynamically assigned and reassigned according to consumer demand. There is a sense of location independence in that the consumer generally has no control or knowledge over the exact location of the provided resources but may be able to specify location at a higher level of abstraction (e.g., country, state, or data center). Examples of resources include storage, processing, memory, and network bandwidth.
- **Rapid Elasticity:** Capabilities can be elastically provisioned and released, in some cases automatically, to scale rapidly outward and inward commensurate with demand. To the consumer, the capabilities available for provisioning often appear to be unlimited and can be appropriated in any quantity at any time.
- **Measured Service:** Cloud systems automatically control and optimize resource use by leveraging a metering capability at some level of abstraction appropriate to the type of service (e.g., storage, processing, bandwidth, and active user accounts). Resource usage can be monitored, controlled, and reported, providing transparency for both the provider and consumer of the utilized service."

Complementary Characteristics

To these five characteristics defined by the NIST, there are the following ones (Sosinski, 2011):

- **Lower Costs:** Since cloud services operate with higher efficiency and therefore with greater use, originates a significant reduction in costs due to the law of supply and demand.
- **Ease of Use:** No software or hardware licenses are required to implement the service.
- **Quality of Service:** Quality of Service (QoS) will be something set in the contract with the supplier (service-level agreement or SLA).
- **Reliability:** The ability to provide load balancing and failover makes the system very reliable.
- **Outsourced IT Management:** Management of external IT services, while the company is focused on managing their businesses.
- **Simplified Maintenance and Updating:** Centralized systems are updated more easily. It provides an easy access to the most recent versions.
- **Low Entry Barriers:** A concept linked to the capital outlay aligned with growth and defined as variable cost.

Added Value of Cloud Computing: Drivers

Regarding the added value of cloud computing, the following is a list of the drivers of cloud computing technology (Frost & Sullivan, 2008):

- **Outsourcing Services:** The need to outsource certain services that do not need to be carried out within the organization, undoubtedly drive the cloud, given that concrete applications are normally done by an external company of services and specialized in cloud.
- **More Efficient and Less Time-Consuming Practices:** The cloud computing services industry is accustomed to carrying out software and services projects more efficiently and in less time. This is reflected both in terms of storage capacity, in computing capacity or in terms of time availability.
- **The Ubiquitous Nature:** This driver shows a capacity known as ubiquity, reflected in being there, available from any access point of the network and at any point in time. This driver gives organizations the ability to work from anywhere in the world connected to the Internet and also a multiplatform character, i.e. from a tablet, a smartphone or a personal computer.
- **Cost Savings:** It promotes this technology for the sake of assuming a cost reduction through the use of shared resources.
- **Virtualization:** This is one of the drivers that has undoubtedly managed cloud technology to reach the level of efficiency with which it is perceived and used by countless organizations around the world. Virtualization technologies or software is the major player in achieving the objectives of resource allocation among customers who share the same cloud service provider. Virtualization allows this same assignment to be simultaneously dynamic, elastic and extremely effective, without too many latencies.

According to Hwang (2008) "cloud computing has provided new opportunities to build and deploy computational infrastructure and complex services thanks to virtualization." For Ohlman, Eriksson and Rembarz (2009), another advantage of the cloud technology is that it can be accessed on demand and used from anywhere, at any time and hiding the complexities of the infrastructure to final consumers.

Barriers

However, not all are drivers, there are also real barriers to this technology. Some of the identified barriers that undoubtedly pose a challenge to the adoption of cloud computing (Frost & Sullivan, 2008) are described below:

- **Security:** It is one of the most important barriers in the expansion of cloud computing. In this sense, it is possible to say that it is not getting to know the important characteristics that cloud contributes to housing or to have servers in the own facilities of the organization, concept that has many followers.
- **Privacy:** This barrier is related with perception. For many customers and users, there is a huge distrust in this regard. This distrust exists mainly due to the lack of knowledge that the data in many cases are encrypted or because the organization itself uses the cloud as a storage support without using any privacy policy.

- **Legislation:** Hiring cloud services means that your data may be physically in one or several parts of the world. This decentralization is also subject to legislation of the country where the hardware resources or the physical center or data center are located. The perception of the user about the legislation of other countries depends a lot on the name of the country or its prestige, but the lack of knowledge of the function of replicating the data in several data centers, to obtain better yields, makes that user perceives negatively this fact from the point of view of the rights that can assist you as an intellectual property, privacy of the personal data or security of the same.
- **Restrictions:** Referred to data traffic in the network itself, since information is delayed by passing through each node, sometimes existing information highways, but in other crossings and jams very damaging to the expansion of cloud technology.
- **Control of Information:** It is indisputable that this barrier exists. Every user sacrifices that control over data for the benefit of other advantages that have already be seen. However, such a waiver for the benefit of the cloud provider does not have to mean that data is not secure and controlled. In fact, not seeing or being able to access the servers does not have to mean lack of control, although it seems obvious that responsibility always lies with the provider.

If any type of problem exists companies and organizations would be seriously affected in such essential aspects as the loss or integrity of data. There are authors who systematically detract from such arguments, explaining that the user or client will renounce a freedom that makes them truly dependent on the service provider (Weber, 2008). For this type of situation, the best recommendation seems to be to establish agreements or contracts based on SLA that detail how much the user loses control.

The SLA is a private contract between a provider of the IT sector and a customer, which has the particularity of establishing the agreed level for the quality of the service. It is increasingly used by Public Administrations and Governments. The SLA is an effective instrument that helps both parties to reach a consensus in terms such as response time to an incident, level quality of service, available documentation, staff level and human resources assigned to the service, etc.

CLOUD AND ENTERPRISE: BASIC PRINCIPLES OF ADOPTION

The cloud technology is a step forward, but its adoption must be done in a modular scheme and offer great facilities of reconfiguration, in which it is possible to flexibly accumulate resources or services that meet changing market demands.

Cloud computing is a current trend that reveals how the architecture of applications will be in the next generation of technology (Hutchinson & Castilon, 2009). While cloud services such as Webmail, Flickr or YouTube have been widely used by individuals for some time, it is not until recently, less than two decades, when organizations have begun to use the services of cloud as a tool for fulfillment of their IT needs.

For cloud computing to grow, it is important to understand the factors that can influence their rate of adoption by organizations, especially enterprises. Of note is the study by (Lin & Chen, 2012), that aims to investigate how cloud computing is perceived by IT professionals and the concerns that IT professionals have with regard to the adoption of cloud services. This study was conducted in Taiwan in 2009 when cloud computing was still a new phenomenon for most people and has provided an excellent opportunity to study how an innovation is perceived and what factors can encourage and prevent its early implementation.

The study sought the opinions of IT professionals as they are more likely to experiment, adopt or to promote the use of cloud computing. Demonstrating that the diffusion theory of innovation is the theoretical basis used to support the identification of the factors that encourage and predict its adoption (Rogers, 1995).

Models for the Delivery of Services in the Cloud

Existing models can be classified, firstly, based on the way services are delivered. This criterion divides them into three types:

- Software-as-a-service (SaaS),
- Platform-as-a-Service (PaaS),
- Infrastructure-as-a-service (IaaS).

Each type of service has different objectives and is addressed to different clients. However, they share a common business model that leases the use of computing resources, including services, applications, infrastructures and platforms for customers.

This model is similar to the ASP model in which a service provider provides the software, infrastructure, people, and maintenance which are all custom-tailored for the customer (Wang et al., 2013). Thus, both SaaS and all other service models can be understood as a variation of ASP, where customers pay, rent, or subscribe to applications or services from cloud providers, such as storage, database access or any other service, always using the Internet (Leavitt, 2009).

Both SaaS and other service models are intended to provide trouble-free performance to end users and allow corporate customers freedom from having to manage their IT resources (Pearlson & Saunders, 2009). Therefore, it can be said that Software-as-a-Service (SaaS) has emerged as an innovative way of presenting and offering the user software applications based on cloud computing (Chou & Chou, 2007). In this model, providers of SaaS deploy software applications on cloud servers which users can request depending on their needs and pay for services according to their usage (Armbrust et al., 2010).

In addition, SaaS improves the quality of software services by updating the applications and providing automatic data backup (Xin & Levina, 2008). Software as a Service (SaaS) is defined as a software distribution model, but it is also considered as a service that is accessed using the Internet with a web browser at the user's request (ONTSI, 2012).

Cloud computing has gone beyond the basic SaaS and service provision and provides IaaS and PaaS. PaaS provides a full or partial application development environment that allows developers to access resources for application development and collaborate with others online (Mathur & Nishchal, 2010). The Amazon Simple Storage Solution (S3) and Microsoft Azure Services Platform are the most well-known PaaS solutions.

IaaS offers customers an extensive set of computing resources, for example, virtual machines to provide a computing infrastructure to customers over the Internet. IaaS is aimed at IT companies and software developers to enable them to increase or decrease the number of virtual machines in operation depending on their workload, in order to promote efficiency of the use of IT resources; with the most commonly mentioned examples being Elastic Compute from Amazon Cloud (EC2) and Mosso Hosting Cloud.

Having said that, it is clear that cloud computing challenges the current understanding of IT resources. IT resources are no longer considered as mere products, but are understood as a service that can be rented and subscribed to under contract with suppliers, and with the common denominator that is always accessed through the Internet. It is, therefore, a proven argument that cloud computing represents a paradigm shift in computing and management of IT services, both for IT resource virtualization and management (Armbrust et al., 2010; Buyya et al., 2009).

Benefits and Obstacles for the Company

The potential benefits of adopting cloud computing can be evaluated both in terms of financial savings and improvements in the management of computing resources. An obvious financial benefit of cloud computing, especially for small and medium-sized businesses, is the savings made from not having to buy and maintain their own hardware and software infrastructures (Miller, 2008).

The significant capital reduction in investment in hardware and software infrastructures, in favor of contracting services in the cloud, offers companies the opportunity to acquire technological capabilities that they may not have been able to offer in the past (Grossman, 2009). Universal access to software services (SaaS) can also bring financial benefits by not having to pay for the software in terms of license fees (Palos & Correia, 2016a).

The elasticity of services in the cloud also means more flexible management of resources, which can also lead to cost savings. That is to say, companies that decide to provide their services using the cloud can expand and scale the capacity of demand, paying only for actual use. PaaS provides an agile development environment that makes it easier for IT professionals to rapidly develop applications and have them adopted instantly, since it eliminates the wait for the deployment of the right hardware and software for the applications (Greer, 2009).

In short, cloud computing enables enterprises, particularly SMEs and consumers, to access resources that could be colloquially defined as "chosen on demand", benefiting from greater flexibility and lower computer resources management costs. But not all are benefits for the company, because despite the promise of technological advancement of cloud services, there are also obstacles to its growth and adoption. The lack of constantly high-speed Internet connections is a major hurdle for cloud computing, because it relies on the Internet to offer its services (Miller, 2008).

The lack of standardization of program application interfaces and technological platforms means that platform interoperability is poor and companies will not be able to easily transfer data from one cloud provider to another. Companies are therefore faced with data lock-in with providers. This perception of lack of control may discourage enterprises from initiating the adoption of cloud computing (Armbrust et al., 2010).

Companies may also be concerned that their activities and processes, on a daily basis, are controlled, not by their own staff, but by outsourced technicians operating outside their headquarters with the data in the cloud provider, and that they may not be able to make the necessary changes to the application with ease and when needed (Leavitt, 2009, Miller, 2008). The concern for security combines privacy and data confidentiality, which is one of the most cited objections in favor of cloud computing (Armbrust et al., 2010; Zhang, Cheng, & Boutaba, 2010). It is argued that most security and privacy issues in cloud computing are due to lack of control over the physical infrastructure.

In other words, companies do not trust those who control and monitor the data center in the cloud. These obstacles result in a series of risks derived from the use of cloud computing, which can be grouped into four categories (Khajeh-Hosseini et al., 2012):

- **Political and Organizational Risks:** For example, distrust of cloud providers due to the possibility of data blockage or loss of governance.
- **Technical Risks:** Such as leakage or data loss.
- **Legal Risks:** Including data protection and software licenses.
- **Risks Not Directly of the Cloud:** But of the infrastructure on which it is dependent, such as network problems or electricity supply.

The uncertainty of service availability and reliability, especially worrying being system downtime from an unexpected outage, could deter companies from adopting cloud computing as this could increase project costs and business risks. For example, Salesforce.com customers (example of a Customer Relationship Management or CRM offered using the ASP business model) lost service for six hours because of a system upgrade, and Amazon's EC2 experienced an outage in one of the high-availability service areas on the east coast of the United States due to power outages at a data center in Northern Virginia. This caused incalculable losses, in addition to significant damage to the reputation of these two important companies' brand names.

Also, the use of IT in the IT sector is an important factor to take into account and, as a consequence, permanent training is an important challenge (Khajeh-Hosseini et al., 2012; Hutchinson et al., 2009). Therefore, if companies have or not the relevant IT professionals to manage the processes and services for cloud computing is an issue that is of major concern.

A study developed by (Gupta, Seetharaman, & Raj, 2013) presents the five factors influencing the cloud usage by micro and small businesses. These authors found that ease of use and convenience is the biggest favorable factor followed by security and privacy and then comes the cost reduction. The factor reliability is ignored as micro and small businesses do not consider cloud as reliable and these businesses do not want to use cloud for sharing and collaboration as they prefer their old conventional methods for sharing and collaborating with their stakeholders.

Cloud Computing and IT Professionals

Cloud computing raises opportunities and challenges for both businesses and IT professionals. Some of these challenges are of a technical nature that can be resolved with time, while others are related to the uncertainties arising from the commitment to a recent innovation.

The purpose of this section is to identify some of the uncertainties that IT professionals may have and that may discourage the adoption of cloud computing systems.

An innovation is an idea, practice or object that is perceived as new by an individual or other unit of adoption (Rogers, 1995). Although the novelty of cloud computing is certainly debatable, there is no doubt that its integration challenges the conventional understanding of the location and management of IT infrastructures, the nature of products and services, business processes and the use of their services (from both points of view, that of IT professionals and that of consumers).

There is a significant contrast between users who can actively use cloud computing services on the Internet (Horrigan, 2014), and others, for whom cloud computing remains a concept not yet fully understood, even for IT professionals and companies. Factors that potentially affect the intention of IT professionals to use cloud computing to deliver products and services to their customers are mainly from the diffusion of innovation theory (Rogers, 1995).

The theory identifies five variables that have a profound influence on the speed of an innovation adoption including: types of innovation, type of innovation decision, communication channels, nature of the social system, and the change in effort to promote agents. Rogers (1995) argues that the perceived attributes of innovation are important predictors of intention to adopt innovations.

Classification Criteria

Among the classification criteria when choosing vendors and virtualization software, it is possible to highlight (Mahjoub et al., 2011):

- **Main Purpose:** Cloud providers should carefully choose the platform that best fits their goals.
- **Architecture:** The architecture of a platform determines how it works and how it was built.
- **Location of Virtual Machines:** The location of the virtual machine is important, to ensure an intelligent and optimal use of resources.
- **Storage:** Networked, in line with the data, data is stored in virtualized groups to be chosen according to needs.
- **Network:** Cloud platforms must pay attention to virtual networks to help ensure performance.
- **Access Interface:** This refers to the fact that cloud clients will have access to their resources in an economic model of leasing or hosting within a particular hardware infrastructure.
- **Security:** The evolution of cloud computing technology is making it increasingly popular, especially in recent years, but as it can be seen later, data security is one of the barriers to expansion.
- **Fault Tolerance:** This is the property that allows a system to continue to function properly in case of failure or temporary or definitive failure of any of its components.
- **Load Balancing:** A method of working in computer networks, which essentially contributes to the distribution of the workload amongst several machines in order to achieve optimum utilization of resources.

The increase in the development and use of open source code or free software has been seen steadily and increasingly in recent years, particularly in the fields of programming, operating systems and software applications. However, the operating system is not yet being used intensively for the structuring and management of cloud computing platforms (Wind, 2011).

This is all the more remarkable in this particular field, where it would be easier to structure cloud management platforms efficiently and cost-effectively using the systems available today. These free software systems are available as alternatives to commercial vendors and allow private cloud solutions for the community as well as hybrids.

However, many companies, private and public institutions like government administrations and other institutions do not take advantage of this fact, partly because of the uncertainty and lack of information about such possibilities. Companies, in particular, can achieve potential savings of between 30% and 40% of costs in IT with the optimized use of their computing resources.

These cost-saving data can be even more improved by using open source software resources making more profitable platforms, independent, innovative and flexible solutions that can usually be implemented very easily (Bughin, Chui, & Manyika, 2014). For this reason, it is worth looking closely at the use of open source in terms of science, but also for the practical aspects of cloud computing.

According with the definition of NIST, which understands the cloud as a set of efficient computing management platforms (NIST, 2011), companies and organizations must be constantly calculating access needs "as needed" to Internet as a configurable set of computer resources (for example, networks, servers, storage, applications and services), which can be quickly used and released with minimum effort of management or interaction by the service provider (Grance & Mell, 2008). This cloud model promotes the concept of total availability and consists of five essential characteristics, three service models and four implementation models (see Figure 3).

Cloud computing solutions can be distinguished by four essentially different characteristics (Grance & Mell, 2008). In general, cloud computing management platforms are used to build and manage cloud architectures, regardless of the type of cloud involved. The use of these commercial platforms can establish their own cloud architectures (community, private or hybrid clouds), as well as building the infrastructure. The market for this type of platform has experienced strong growth in recent years, in addition to other proprietary solutions being developed by public cloud providers.

Presently, a large number of standard management platforms are available, which can also be used to build and manage cloud architectures. Open source cloud technology provides an overview of the entire ecosystem of the cloud management platform (see Figure 4).

SMART TOURISM DESTINATIONS AND CLOUD COMPUTING IN THE TOURISM SECTOR

This technology is being consolidated as a new scenario of IT platforms, representing a significant change in how tourism companies and public institutions can manage their IT areas. All of this proposes the generation of companies that offer services to SMEs that cannot afford to have a technology department, so that in a way they will contribute to the reduction of the technological gap existing between large and small companies (Cerezo-Medina & Guevara-Plaza, 2015).

Figure 3. Implementation models
Source: Author.

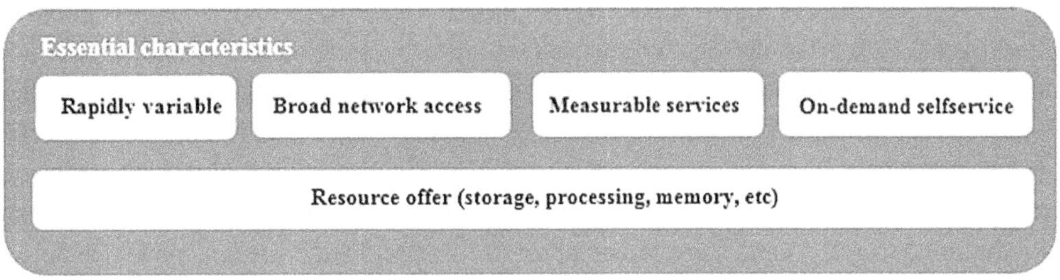

Figure 4. The cloud platform management ecosystem
Source: Author.

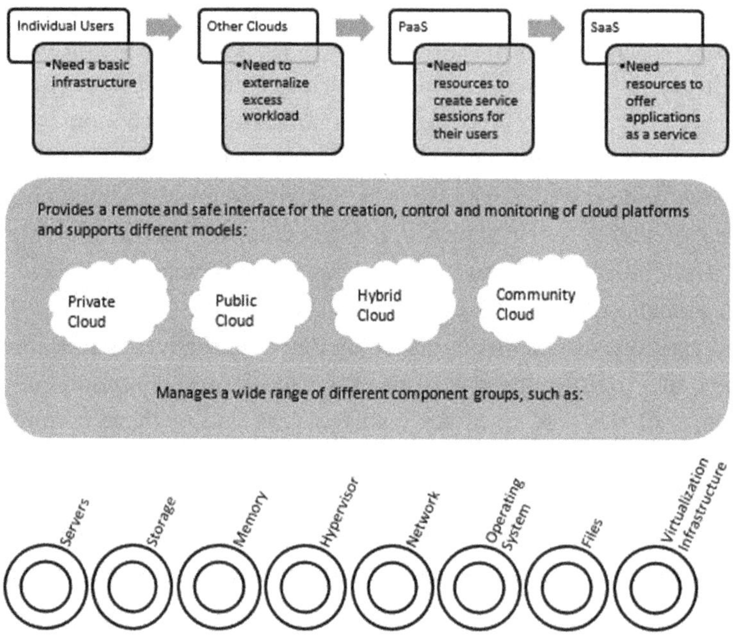

In the tourism sector, the ubiquitous access to data from tourists, from anywhere and at any time, provides significant service improvements that contribute to the loyalty of customers of international hotel chains (Guasch-Portas & Soler-Fuensanta, 2014).

The application of cloud computing is closely related to technological levers and new management systems and cloud-based solutions can boost the adoption of advanced systems by SMEs, reducing the cost (Etro, 2009) and the technological infrastructures necessary for their use (Palos & Aguayo-Camacho, 2016), while also managing the needs of users in a ubiquitous and in real time. This cost saving is estimated between 30% and 40% over traditional solutions. In short, the cloud has to help the sector to think more about the tourist business and less on technology, seeing it as a tool that facilitates the work (SEGITTUR, 2012).

Any tourist company that uses cloud computing will obtain large amounts of data to know its customer, since the real business opportunity is to understand the motivations, needs and profile of the clients, so it is essential to adapt the services to client interests (Hosteltur, 2017).

Among the specific disadvantages caused by the adoption of cloud computing among tourism companies, there are the lack of knowledge about what this new business model is and offers, the distrust of the unknown that results in a lack of security and the dependence on a third party (Gonzales, 2012). The difficulty of recovering the data or accessing them at a specific time, as well as the possibility of moving information between cloud providers (SEGITTUR, 2012) are other of the challenges that tourism companies are currently facing when choosing the cloud model. Tourism companies that considered the cloud computing trend, should have information in the cloud such as: tour packages, promotions, images, reservations, etc. and also information about the company itself, which will show the company's legitimacy and the customers' confidence in acquiring its services (Gonzales, 2012).

Smart Tourism Destinations cored in massive tourism resource data centre, supported by IoT and cloud computing, focused on enhancing tourists experience through intelligent identification and monitoring. The cloud computing services are designed to provide convenient way to access solid web platform and data storage through certain network (Gretzel et al., 2015). The relationship between these technologies and Smart Tourism Destinations is one of the keys to develop a massive tourist resources data centre, supported especially in cloud computing, focused on improving the experience of tourists, through a correct identification of data and intelligent monitoring (Buhalis & Amaranggana, 2013). However, the true meaning of Smart Tourism Destinations is to focus on the needs of tourists by combining IT with informal culture and the tourism innovation industry in order to promote service quality and to improve tourism management (Huang, Yuan, & Shi, 2012).

It is important to focus that augmented reality (AR) has been used in recent years as a tool to improve collaboration between the real world and virtual environments. Its main support is the cloud computing technology and has been used is the tourism sector. Thus, the benefits of using AR in the tourism-oriented mobile applications show that the use of AR improves the tourist experience in an innovative way and that the use of AR could also be applied as a method to improve the quality of service (Aguirre-Brito, 2015).

To understand the adoption of cloud computing in the tourism sector, the application of cloud computing solutions to the different subsectors of the tourism industry are presented (Lohmann & Netto, 2017), (Middleton et al., 2009).

Accommodation/Hospitality

Cloud computing has application in most of the solutions used in the accommodation management, being especially relevant its application in the Property Management Systems (PMS) as central nucleus of the management of the establishment.

Likewise, there are applications in cloud computing that allow to analyze and optimize the room rates, as well as others oriented to analyze the reputation of the brand in the online channels and to interact with the customers. The use of cloud solutions in turn allows to solve the current lack of technical solutions, investment capacity and personnel trained in the IT field by a large number of establishments, especially SMEs. Cloud computing solutions in the Accommodation/Hospitality area can be grouped under the following categories: Property Management System (PMS), Yield & Revenue Management, Central Reservation System (CRS), Online Communication and Backoffice (Enterprise Resource Planning).

Property Management System (PMS)

These systems address the management of the main processes and basic activities for the provision of accommodation services. A PMS does not actually manage a property in the commercial real estate sense; it helps manage virtually every aspect of a guest's visit to a property.

PMS represents the back-bone of hotel operations and interfaces with a variety of other key systems from channel management and bookings to hardware such as telephony and key rooms. PMS covers the entire guest experience, including the booking process to capturing guest data for future interaction (Grant Thornton, 2016).

Globally, cloud solutions for property management have the features of allow real-time management of aspects related to the main services of establishments such as availability, customer check-in and check-out, or invoicing. As it is the central system of hotel management, it often has integrations with

CRS or Global Distribution Systems used by intermediaries (GDS). Finally, in some cases it has back office functions (ERP). Some of the most important players are: Oracle Hospitality, Protel and Infor (Grant Thornton, 2016).

Yield and Revenue Management

It is a management technique that, making use of technological solutions, seeks to maximize the benefit through control over the price and inventory of rooms. The main typologies of these systems, in close relation with CRS and PMS are Revenue Management that allows to establish strategies of price to maximize the profit allowing particularizing the income by availability and Channel Management, which encompass the centralized management of several online channels (Internet Distribution System – (IDS), GDS, web portal, etc.) and, the prices of the competitive set in different channels. Some of the most important players are: Oracle Hospitality and Infor (Grant Thornton, 2016).

Central Reservation System (CRS)

These systems allow automatic management of the availability of accommodation spaces (rooms, apartments, etc.) and their prices, as well as the performance of booking, modification and cancellation activities in a personalized way for each distribution channel. These solutions are generally included as additional functionality in PMS or Channel Management Systems.

Online Communication

Online communication systems allow establishments to build and maintain reputation online, and must monitor the opinions expressed by users at any time and channel (online brokerage agencies, social networks, forums, blogs, etc.). Nowadays, the management of the tourism business brand is a process of great complexity, due to the high number of social platforms that allow to upload images and videos of the hotels, to rate them or to make comments on a certain establishment or brand.

Backoffice (Enterprise Resource Planning: ERP)

ERP systems are solutions that allow the integral management of the back-office activities of the lodgings, such as financial management (accounting), human resources, administration, maintenance, purchasing and logistic, etc. Generally, these systems are offered from commercial packages, not specific to the tourism sector, which have functionalities to manage these business processes, although there are also companies that offer hotel management software based on ERP packages or there are integrated as added functionality in the PMS. ERP offers numerous advantages in terms of seamless use of technology, more automation, greater visibility into hotel operations, optimised use of manpower, reduced revenue leakages and higher resultant profits.

Food & Beverage (F&B)

This activity is mainly associated with the supply of food and beverages for consumption in an establishment and generally needs systems that allow to manage the establishment occupation and the availability and supply of the resources. The cloud computing solutions for this subsector are mainly focused on the management of the processes related to the clients, such as reservations or promotions, and the organization of the activities of business, such as invoicing and warehouse. These solutions are usually classified into two subtypes: Front-end (Point of Sales - POS) and Business Management.

Front-End (Point of Sales: POS)

The cloud solutions correspond to technological solutions that focus on the POS and allow to manage the functionality of each of the attached devices, such as: barcode readers, magnetic and electronic card readers, etc. These solutions usually support a wide range of peripherals such as card readers, printers, cash, beverage dispensers, mobile terminals, coffee machines, card loading devices, and configure, manage and control all POS operations, such as controlling sales, changing prices or inserting new items while they are in operation. Finally, these solutions allow to control the statistics associated with the cash functions and have features of back-office management such as warehouse management and product availability.

Business Management

Business management is addressed through modular solutions that allow the control of different aspects of the business, such as CRM (reservations, campaigns, customer databases, etc.) or Business Intelligence, through control and analysis of business metrics (management control, reports, dashboards, Key Performance Indicators or KPI, etc.).

These solutions usually provide functionalities to manage the occupation of the establishment, through the organization of reservations and available tables, optimize the resources, mainly the activity of the waiters (shifts, tables, charges by tables, etc.), have tools to control aspects such as the customer database, the calendar and the holiday calendar, to define promotions and offers, to send emails with promotions and offers to customers and to provide a channel to manage promotions through discount coupon providers.

The business intelligence solutions in the field of F&B provide tools for capturing, processing and analyzing key business data, to provide on-demand consultation of information related to business performance at the general level, departmental, or follow-up level of strategic measures or projects and with real-time reporting capabilities.

Intermediation

Intermediation involves the activities carried out by a wide variety of agents, reception agencies (responsible for the reception of the customer at the destination and the provision of contracted services), online travel agencies, tour operators, wholesalers, etc. To manage these activities there are solutions in the cloud that support the integral management of the business processes. In addition, the appearance of online intermediaries, such as Online Travel Agencies or OTA, which allow booking and purchase of tourist products, have led to a large increase in online tourist product reserves, articulating on portals developed under cloud computing architectures. These solutions are usually classified into two subtypes: Management of intermediation agencies and OTAs.

Management of Intermediaries' Agencies

These solutions allow the integral management of the business of intermediaries such as tour operators, wholesalers or receptive agencies, providing all the information (contracts, rates, availability, etc.) of the products offered such as flights, hotels, transport, excursions, etc.

The cloud solutions generally allow the management of information on all tourism products and services offered by the intermediaries such as rates, occupancy, offers, etc., provide tools to formalize purchase and sale contracts and have integrations to make the booking and sale of different types of tourist services.

Online Travel Agencies (OTA)

Online travel agencies are services accessible from the internet that allow suppliers of tourism products to position and market their offer, creating their own space on the web in which they provide information on the characteristics and rates or prices of their products. OTA have search engines that allow to select the product according to availability, typology, location, or according to the users' score and in some cases, allow the reservation engine to be integrated into the client's website or even into their social profile, functioning as a CRS. Some examples are Expedia, Orbitz, Priceline, etc.

Transport

Within this subsector of activity are those companies whose activity is centered on the services of ground transportation, maritime and air travelers. The application of cloud computing to this subsector has special relevance in the simultaneous and comparative search of the products, as the flight search engines, that allows users to search the flight rates offered for a specific trip on the websites of different flight companies, offering a comparison that allows users to optimize their decision. Also in the application of mobile services sensitive to the context, such as tourist guides.

The cloud solutions for flights search usually have a smart search engine that enables the simultaneous search of flights, according to a set of parameters, in different travel agencies and airlines and allow to include a great variety of optional parameters to define the preferences of the trip, price range, number of stops, etc. Also, provide comparative fare information for a particular combination of flights and dates, as well as basic information about the trip, such as the duration or the stopovers to be made. Finally, enable the possibility of identifying existing offers to multiple destinations. For example: Trabber.com.-

Promotion

In this area within the tourism sector are encompassed the processes that aim to show and to market the different products and services of the sector, as well as tourist resources, in order to reach the maximum number of consumers possible. The cloud solutions generally used allow the addition of a large amount of information on tourist products and services that make up the tourist offer associated with a destination.

The smart solutions for destination promotion allow the grouping of resources to carry out a joint promotion of the destination, promoting the improvement of their joint marketing and the cross-selling of products and services (Kotler, Bowen, & Makens, 2014). These solutions generally have functionalities for the management of contents and the information of the products, allow access to the reservation and sale of these products and services, promoting cross-selling and provide information on the destination, such as weather, festivals, and so on.

CONCLUSION

Cloud computing technology is rapidly being deployed and its growth is remarkable. The advantages that have been described in this chapter are improving the services and competitiveness of organizations. Especially, this technology is being adapted to the tourism sector, where its adoption is getting important transformations that result from the deployment of cloud technology. However, there are aspects such as security, privacy and trust that is being an important brake on its implementation. On the other hand, the Internet is the support behind the cloud and its internationalization is making that legislation about data processing is being considered a source of legal uncertainty for many business organizations, among which are those operating in the tourism sector.

The main advantages that companies perceive with the use of cloud computing lies in the improvement of productivity, the best flexibility and scalability of IT resources and the reduction of costs in hardware. These conclusions are in line with previous studies (Armbrust et al., 2010). In addition, companies with fewer workers benefit more from these advantages than companies with more workers (Palos & Correia, 2016a). This fact is also confirmed in companies that are less senior and therefore are in a more entrepreneurial phase, which can indicate that there is a relationship between the degree of entrepreneurship, entrepreneurial capacity and cloud adoption (Ratten, 2013).

Apart from these factors, which condition their development, other conditions affect the adoption of cloud technology and have not been addressed in this chapter, such as the time of adoption and deployment, business cooperation to deploy private clouds and especially the standardization of interfaces and technological platforms, where the European Commission is working to create a secure legal environment with adequate standards and contracting conditions (Palos & Correia, 2016b). It should be borne in mind that cloud computing is still a recent innovation, with a not very high number of adopting organizations and users and with an industry with poor standardization. This lack of standardization affects the interface of software and technological platforms, which means that interoperability between platforms is still poor. Therefore, companies are not able to easily transfer data from one cloud provider to another and are faced with data-lock-in providers. It would therefore be a question of assessing whether this perception of lack of control can discourage companies from starting the adoption of cloud computing, as suggested by Armbrust et al. (2010).

As was explained, cloud computing is one of the alternatives used to improve the competitiveness of companies, not only at IT level, but also as a new economic model of resource sharing, of data and application usage or as service providers. There is a lack of studies about the adoption of cloud computing in the tourism sector and authors intend to study the adoption of cloud computing in the tourism sector, in particular, the tourism sector of Spain and Portugal.

Finally, it should be noted that for the tourism sector one of the sources of risk is in a wrong choice of cloud provider or a contractual relationship not adequate to the needs of the company. These facts can be real problems in the migration to future platforms of other suppliers or an inadequate support service and attention to the client that can be materialized in interruptions of service, the breach of agreements, the efficiency of the security devices and the loss or misuse of data.

The lack of standards in this technology and the influence of cloud computing in the tourism sector have been a major constraint. However, this research delves into the problem of trust and security of data in the cloud and points to future problems that privacy will represent in the management of personal data of tourists in the generation of smart destinations supported by cloud technology.

REFERENCES

Aguirre-Brito, C. N. A. (2015). Augmented reality applied in tourism mobile applications. *2015 Second International Conference On Edemocracy & Egovernment (ICEDEG)*, 120-125. doi:10.1109/ICEDEG.2015.7114484

Armbrust, M., Fox, A., Griffith, R., Joseph, A., Katz, R., & Konwinski, A. (2010). A view of cloud computing. *Communications of the ACM*, *53*(4), 50–58. doi:10.1145/1721654.1721672

Bondi, A. B. (2000). Characteristics of scalability and their impact on performance. *Proceedings of the Second International Workshop on Software and Performance*. doi:10.1145/350391.350432

Bughin, J., Chui, M., & Manyika, J. (2014). *Clouds, big data, and smart assets: Ten tech-enabled business trends to watch*. Retrieved, December 2016 from http://www.itglobal-services.de/files/100810_McK_Clouds_big_data_and%20smart%20assets.pdf

Buhalis, D., & Amaranggana, A. (2013). Smart tourism destinations. In *Information and communication technologies in tourism 2014* (pp. 553–564). Springer International Publishing. doi:10.1007/978-3-319-03973-2_40

Buyya, R., Yeo, C., Venugopa, S., Broberg, J., & Brandic, I. (2009). Cloud computing and emerging it platforms: Vision, hype, and reality for delivering computing as the 5th utility. *Future Generation Computer Systems*, *25*(6), 599–616. doi:10.1016/j.future.2008.12.001

Cerezo-Medina, A., & Guevara-Plaza, A. (2015). Necesidades formativas tecnológicas en turismo. Estudio de caso de Andalucía. *PASOS. Revista de Turismo y Patrimonio Cultural*, *13*(4), 913–929.

Chou, D., & Chou, A. (2007). Analysis of a new information systems outsourcing practice: Software-as-a-service business model. *International Journal Information Systems Change Management*, 2(4), 392–405. doi:10.1504/IJISCM.2007.017385

Díaz, M., Martín, C., & Rubio, B. (2016). State-of-the-art, challenges, and open issues in the integration of Internet of things and cloud computing. *Journal of Network and Computer Applications*, *67*, 99–117. doi:10.1016/j.jnca.2016.01.010

Etro, F. (2009). The economic impact of cloud computing on business creation, employment and output in Europe. *Review Business and Economics*, *54*(2), 179–208.

Frost & Sullivan. (2008). *Market demands for hosted UC services*. Frost & Sullivan.

Fundación de la Innovación. (2011). *Cloud computing. La tercera ola de las tecnologías de la información*. Bankinter.

Gonzales, M. L. (2012). Cloud Computing y su aplicación fuera del campo de la Informática. *Revista de Información, Tecnología y Sociedad*, 66.

Grance, T., & Mell, P. (2008). *Perspectives on cloud computing and standards*. NIST, Information Technology.

Thornton, G. (2016). *Emerging clouds in hotel technology - Spotlight on cloud-based PMS*. Retrieved January, 2017, from Grant Thornton - An instinct for growth: http://www.grantthornton.co.uk/globalassets/1.-member-firms/united-kingdom/pdf/publication/2016/emerging-clouds-in-hotel-technology.pdf

Greer, M. (2009). *Software as a service inflection point: Using cloud computing to achieve business agility*. New York: Global Authors Publishers.

Gretzel, U., Sigala, M., Xiang, Z., & Koo, C. (2015). Smart tourism: Foundations and developments. *Electronic Markets*, *25*(3), 179–188. doi:10.1007/s12525-015-0196-8

Grossman, R. (2009). The case for cloud computing. *IT Professional*, *11*(2), 23–27. doi:10.1109/MITP.2009.40

Guasch-Portas, V., & Soler-Fuensanta, J. R. (2014). Cloud Computing, turismo y protección de datos. *Revista de Análisis Turístico*, *17*, 61–68.

Gupta, P., Seetharaman, A., & Raj, J. R. (2013). The usage and adoption of cloud computing by small and medium businesses. *International Journal of Information Management*, *33*(5), 861–874. doi:10.1016/j.ijinfomgt.2013.07.001

Heart, T., & Pliskin, N. (2002). Renting restaurant applications from application service providers. *International Journal of Hospitality Information Technology*, *2*(2), 45–61. doi:10.3727/153373402803617764

Horrigan, J. B. (2014). *Use of cloud computing applications and services*. Retrieved December, 2016, from Pew Internet 2016: http://www.pewinternet.org/Reports/2008/Use-of-Cloud-Computing-Applications-and-Services/Data-Memo.aspx

Hosteltur. (2017). *Transformación digital: Cloud Computing*. Retrieved from https://www.hosteltur.com/comunidad/nota/018691_transformacion-digital-cloud-computing.html

Huang, X. K., Yuan, J. Z., & Shi, M. Y. (2012). Condition and key issues analysis on the smarter tourism construction in China. In *Multimedia and signal processing* (pp. 444–450). Springer Berlin Heidelberg.

Hutchinson, C. W., & Castilon, K. (2009). Navigating the next-generation application architecture. *IT Professional*, *1*(2), 18–22.

Hwang, K. (2008). Massively distributed systems: From grids and P2P to clouds. *International Conference on Grid and Pervasive Computing*, 5036, 1.

Johansson, B. (2004). *Exploring application service provision*. Springer.

Junta de Andalucia. (2012). *Cloud computing aplicado a los sectores de la agroindustria, eficiencia energética, industrias culturales y turismo*. Edita Consejería de Economía Junta de Andalucía.

Khajeh-Hosseini, A., Greenwood, D., Smith, J., & Sommerville, I. (2012). The cloud adoption toolkit: Supporting cloud adoption decisions in the enterprise. *Software, Practice & Experience*, *42*(4), 447–465. doi:10.1002/spe.1072

Kotler, P., Bowen, J., & Makens, J. (2014). *Marketing for hospitality and tourism* (6th ed.). Pearson Education Limited.

Leavitt, N. (2009). Is cloud computing really ready for prime time? *IEEE Computer Society Issue*, *42*(1), 15–20. doi:10.1109/MC.2009.20

Lijun, M., Chan, W., & Tse, T. (2008). A tale of clouds: Paradigm comparisons and some thoughts on research issues. *IEEE Asia-Pacific Services Computing Conference*, 468.

Lin, A., & Chen, N. (2012). Cloud computing as an innovation: Perception, attitude, and adoption. *International Journal of Information Management*, *32*(6), 533–540. doi:10.1016/j.ijinfomgt.2012.04.001

Lohmann, G., & Netto, A. P. (2017). *Tourism theory - Concepts, models and systems*. London, UK: CABI. doi:10.1079/9781780647159.0000

Mahjoub, M., Mdhaffar, A., Halima, R., & Jmaiel, M. A. (2011). Comparative study of the current cloud computing technologies and offers. *2011 First International Symposium on Network Cloud Computing and Applications (NCCA)*, 131-134. doi:10.1109/NCCA.2011.28

Mathur, P., & Nishchal, N. (2010). Cloud computing: New challenge to the entire computer industry. *2010 1st International Conference on Parallel Distributed and Grid Computing PDGC*, 223-228.

Middleton, V. T., Fyall, A., Morgan, M., & Ranchhod, A. (2009). *Marketing in travel and tourism*. Routledge.

Miller, M. (2008). *Cloud computing: Web-based applications that change the way you work and collaborate online*. QUE Publishing.

NIST. (2011). *The NIST Definition of Cloud Computing*. Retrieved November, 2016, from NIST - National Institute of Standards and Technology: http://nvlpubs.nist.gov/nistpubs/Legacy/SP/nistspecialpublication800-145.pdf

Ohlman, B., Eriksson, A., & Rembarz, R. (2009). What networking of information can do for cloud computing. 18th IEEE International Workshops on Enabling Technologies: Infrastructures for Collaborative Enterprises WETICE '09, 78-83. doi:10.1109/WETICE.2009.27

ONTSI. (2012). *El estudio cloud computing. Retos y oportunidades*. Madrid: Ministerio de Industria.

Palos, P. R., & Aguayo-Camacho, M. (2016). Los cambios organizacionales y la nube en el entorno turístico: Estudio de caso. *International Journal of World of Tourism*, *3*(5), 33–42.

Palos, P.R., & Correia, M.B. (2016a). La actitud de los recursos humanos de las organizaciones ante la complejidad de las aplicaciones SaaS. *Dos Algarves: A Multidisciplinary e-Journal*, 87-103. doi:10.18089/DAMeJ.2016.28.6

Palos, P. R., & Correia, M. B. (2016b). The paradigm of the cloud and web accessibility and its consequences in Europe. In *7th International Conference on Software Development and Technologies for Enhancing Accessibility and Fighting Info-exclusion DSAI 2016*. Vila Real, Portugal: ACM. doi:10.1145/3019943.3019995

Pearlson, K., & Saunders, C. (2009). *Strategic management of information systems* (4th ed.). Hoboken, NJ: Wiley.

Ratten, V. (2013). Cloud computing: A social cognitive perspective of ethics, entrepreneurship, technology marketing, computer self-efficacy and outcome expectancy on behavioural intentions. *Australasian Marketing Journal*, *21*(3), 137–146. doi:10.1016/j.ausmj.2013.02.008

Rogers, E. (1995). *Diffusion of innovations* (4th ed.). New York: Free Press.

SEGITTUR. (2012). *Informe y conclusiones think-tank de turismo del transporte*. Retrieved from https://es.slideshare.net/Turismoas/informe-conclusiones-think-tank-del-transporte

Sosinski, B. (2011). *Cloud computing bible*. Hoboken, NJ: Wiley & Sons.

Tan, M., & Teo, T. (1998). Factors influencing the adoption of the internet. *International Journal of Electronic Commerce*, *2*(3), 5–18. doi:10.1080/10864415.1998.11518312

Torres, J. (2011). *Empresas en la nube. Ventajas y retos del cloud computing*. Barcelona: Libros de Cabecera.

Vaquero, L. M., Rodero-Merino, L., Cáceres, J., & Lindner, M. (2009). A break in the clouds: Towards a cloud definition. *Computer Communication Review*, *39*(1), 50–55. doi:10.1145/1496091.1496100

Voas, J., & Zhang, J. (2009). Cloud computing: New wine or just a new bottle? *IT Professional*, *11*(2), 15–17. doi:10.1109/MITP.2009.23

Wang, C., Chow, S., Wang, Q., Ren, K., & Lou, W. (2013). Privacy-preserving public auditing for secure cloud storage. *IEEE Transactions on Computers*, *62*(2), 362–375. doi:10.1109/TC.2011.245

Weber, J. (2008). Cloud Computing. *Times Online*. Retrieved October 21, 2016, from http://www.fba.unlp.edu.ar/tic/archivos/Q09.pdf

Wind, S. (2011). Open source cloud computing management platforms: Introduction, comparison, and recommendations for implementation. *IEEE Conference on Open Systems ICOS*, 175-179. doi:10.1109/ICOS.2011.6079245

Xin, M., & Levina, N. (2008). Software-as-a service model: Elaborating client-side adoption factors. *International Conference on Information Systems ICIS*. doi:10.2139/ssrn.1319488

Zhang, Q., Cheng, L., & Boutaba, R. (2010). Cloud computing: State-of-the-art and research challenges. *Journal of Internet Service Application*, *1*(1), 7–18. doi:10.1007/s13174-010-0007-6

Zhou, X., Xu, C., & Kimmons, B. (2015). Detecting tourism destinations using scalable geospatial analysis based on cloud computing platform. *Computers, Environment and Urban Systems*, *54*, 144–153. doi:10.1016/j.compenvurbsys.2015.07.006

KEY TERMS AND DEFINITIONS

Cloud Computing: Model for enabling ubiquitous, convenient, on-demand and scalable networks access to a pool of configurable computing resources that can be rapidly provisioned and released with minimal management effort or service provider interaction.

IaaS: Offers to customers a comprehensive set of IT resources, as for example virtual machines to provide a computing infrastructure to customers via the Internet. IaaS is aimed at IT companies and software developers to allow them to increase or decrease the number of virtual machines in operation, depending on their workload to promote efficiency in the use of IT resources.

PaaS: Provides a full or partial application development environment that allows developers to access resources for application development and collaborate online with others.

SaaS: Model of software distribution, also considered as a service that is accessed, via the Internet, through a web browser, under the user's own demand.

Smart Tourism: Describe the increasing reliance of tourism destinations, their industries and their tourists on emerging forms of IT that allow for massive amounts of data to be transformed into value propositions.

Chapter 19
Semantic Transformation and Use of Cultural Data:
Record Once and Publish Many

Feliz Ribeiro Gouveia
Universidade Fernando Pessoa, Portugal

Sérgio Lira
Green Lines Institute for Sustainable Development, Portugal

ABSTRACT

Cultural content and cultural assets are increasingly seen as invaluable drivers for education, entertainment, tourism, knowledge, and shared memory initiatives. As such, cultural information, as stored in cultural institutions such as museums, archives, and specialized libraries is increasingly demanded by several actors, from public policy, tourism, app developers and software companies, schools and the citizen at large. To satisfy the needs of such a large spectrum of consumers and end users, the information must be format independent, multi-lingual, multi-purpose, and make use of standards, norms and national and international recommendations. In this is paper we describe our past and current efforts to develop cultural information systems that can satisfy those requirements and those of the specialized public, such as scientists and curators. We describe an inventory and content management system and the conceptual and architectural choices that were made to allow its evolution, standards' compliance and multi-purpose use.

INTRODUCTION

Cultural content and cultural assets are increasingly seen as invaluable drivers for education, entertainment, tourism, knowledge, and shared memory initiatives. As such, cultural information, as stored in cultural institutions such as museums, archives, and specialized libraries is increasingly demanded by several actors, from public policy, tourism, mobile app developers and software companies, schools and the citizen at large. To satisfy the needs of such a large spectrum of consumers and end users, the information must, as much as possible, be format independent, multi-lingual, multi-purpose, and make

DOI: 10.4018/978-1-5225-2927-9.ch019

use of standards, norms and national and international recommendations. As Libraries, Archives and Museums are arguably the oldest examples of knowledge based organization (Hedstrom & King, 2003) it is natural that they are at the forefront of the web evolution. Cultural institutions have been using several inventory management systems, and investing in cleaning, formatting and adapting data to be shown on public portals and mobile applications. Some institutions have been exporting their data, encoded in some metadata format, to aggregators with national or international dimension such as Europeana.

After data is published on the web there is a growing need for linking it from different places, themes, languages, and culture so that it can be part of the linked open data world, and be used to its full extent. It becomes virtually impossible for an institution to cope with so many requests for information, in different formats, encoding standards, languages and level of detail. Requests can come under the form of sharing in social networking sites, supplying data to content aggregators, providing programming interfaces to app developers and other end users, participating in joint portals, and virtual exhibits, for example. Additionally, published data should be correctly found by search engines, and made accessible to the general public. The use of right metadata, together with search engine optimization techniques can help disseminate a cultural institution's content. The web is an interlinked collection of resources, identified by what is called a URI (Uniform Resource Identifier). A kind of URI is what people generally type in a web browser to access a given site. To be able to make available their data so that it is found, either by searching or by looking from other data, institutions need to take a systematic approach to web publishing by providing as much context information as possible.

The so called semantic web is a web with context information, organized in a way to make search and navigation easy and accurate by providing only relevant information. The semantic web is designed to make search and discovery more efficient, and to navigate from one resource to the other as one would normally do in a web page. For example, when searching for the painter Picasso there would be irrelevant results, like those related to a car model with that same name, software packages or generic pages mentioning Picasso. Discovery is also an important behavior, as people would normally move from one page to the other by following links. The semantic web should keep and encourage that same behavior, mainly if computer programs are browsing the data as this is the only way they can move from one page to another.

The linked data movement proposed the Resource Description Framework (RDF) syntax to represent information to be exchanged (Bizer, Heath & Berners-Lee, 2009; W3C, 2014). There were several RDF vocabularies available then, and their number and availability continues to increase. Anyone can define and publish a RDF vocabulary, making it available such that other people can reuse it (see for example http://lov.okfn.org/dataset/lov/ for a database of more than 600 available RDF vocabularies).

Tim Berners-Lee (2006) summarized and defined the following characteristics for the semantic web, a web of linked data:

- Use URIs as names for things.
- Use HTTP URIs so that people can look up those names.
- When someone looks up a URI, provide useful information, using the standards (RDF, SPARQL).
- Include links to other URIs so that they can discover more things.

In 2010, Berners-Lee updated the semantic web document and defined a 5 star system to rate linked open data (LOD) projects on the web. Linked data is defined as above, and open means open license (Berners-Lee, 2006; http://5stardata.info/en/); item numbering is the number of stars:

1. Available on the web (whatever format) but with an open license, to be Open Data.
2. Available as machine-readable structured data (e.g. excel instead of image scan of a table).
3. As (2) plus non-proprietary format (e.g. CSV instead of excel).
4. All the above plus, use open standards from W3C (RDF and SPARQL) to identify things, so that people can point at your stuff.
5. All the above, plus: link your data to other people's data to provide context.

A five-star system means that the content is free to use, it can be machine processed with open, possibly free, software, and it is easily structured, and has pointers to allow navigation to and from other data. There are of course some cautions to be taken, as institutions must clearly identify the implications of an open license, for example, and the costs of converting their data to the open formats if they were in different ones. Institutions starting to make available their collections on the web start already by adopting the five-star system, and institutions having already invested on web publishing their collections can make a step by step evolution.

Institutions are primarily concerned with compliance with national and international standards, e.g. Spectrum in the UK (Spectrum, 2011), and then with providing and publishing data following the linked open data principles. Being open data, the first step would be to agree on an open license, for example the Creative Commons 'No Rights Reserved' (CC0) license. If an open license is not possible, institutions should nevertheless try to provide a flexible as possible license.

Hyvönen, Tuominen, Alonen and Mäkelä (2014) proposed two more stars:

6. Provide your data with a schema and documentation so that people can understand and re-use your data easily.
7. Validate your data and denote its provenance so that people can trust the quality of your data.

According to the authors those two additional stars would come with little effort, as most of the needed information would be provided automatically by the underlying system and not by manual coding. They would nevertheless increase the reliability and usefulness of the published linked open data.

The technology stack is still complex, and most of the cultural management systems are oriented towards inventory and management, and not towards publication and sharing of cultural data as open linked data. Recognizing the growing importance of the semantic web, the ICOM/CIDOC CRM Special Interest Group issued a recommendation on LOD for Museums (The International Council of Museums, 2011). Recently, large museums have been providing a LOD interface, thus allowing their data to be browsed, shared and reused in multiple ways (Hyvönen, 2012, 2014; de Boer *et al.*, 2013; Skevakis, 2013; Szekely, 2013; Skevakis, Makris, Arapi & Christodoulakis, 2013; Dijkshoorn, 2016; Pantoja *et al.*, 2016). By doing so, those institutions are encouraging reuse and new and innovative applications using the data they provide — there has been an increase worldwide in the number of cultural hackathons, that is, exploratory application creation marathons around museums or painters (*eg* Coding Dürer, an international and interdisciplinary Hackathon for Art History and Information Science, and Coding da Vinci, the first German open cultural data hackathon that took place in 2014).

This process can be understood as real revolutionary in the realm of cultural institutions, such as museums or even archives and libraries. Inventory, for the first two, used to be an internal tool, not to be seen or accessed by the public and rarely by experts, academics or scholars. Museum's directors and high level staff tended to keep inventory for internal work only – mainly for security reasons and because the "old times" inventory was of scarce importance to researchers. Information contained in those "primitive" forms of inventory was normally stored in strict chronological order, registered in books with numbered and signed pages – any attempt of removing items from the inventory would raise significant documental issues and that was considered one of the methods to prevent robbery. In archives and libraries, on the other hand, the inventory itself was of tremendous importance: in libraries the readers absolutely needed access to the list of available books, ordered by author, title or thematic.

In fact, libraries used to make available the inventory under these three possible organization: didascalic, onomastic and Universal Decimal Classification (UDC); in some cases, the real record files physically browsed by the readers' fingers were in fact the only complete inventory of a library... with all the inherent risk. In archives the situation is more ambiguous since a list of existing/available documents is the minimum readers and researchers need in order to use the archive, but a descriptive record of each document (or set of documents) is obviously much more helpful and avoids unnecessary access to originals.

Presently inventories for these three types of cultural institutions can fulfil multiple purposes as they are flexible (in the sense that once data is stored it can be filtered, sorted and made available in many different ways and levels). The most complete, dense, complex and information-rich inventory can easily be transformed in a simple list of items for public access, or in a research-focused catalogue, or even in an "available for barter" list of items. Inventories ceased to be tools reserved for internal-use-only and became much more complex tools; they kept their security and safety purposes but they embraced a significant number of other tasks that concern the various types of public of these institutions. As such, the quality of information stored in inventory systems is crucial and it influences the over-all quality of the service provided by museums, archives and libraries.

METADATA FORMATS

Machine readable information needs some agreement on how the data is structured, what it contains, and how it should be interpreted, for example. Metadata (or data about data) fulfils that need, by specifying for example most used attributes for a given application domain such as title, description, and owner or creation date. The values of those attributes can follow standards, for example the "creation date" attribute can use the ISO 8601 standard to represent dates as "2011-10-02". Using agreed upon standards makes it easy to store, search, discover and interchange information. Although metadata was defined and used before the internet and the web, it gained growing importance as a way of harmonizing disparate forms of representation of cultural resources and facilitating automated processing of those resources.

Metadata is used to record several types of information about a cultural resource: descriptive metadata describes the resource itself and provides access points to find the resource; rights metadata stores information concerning access, use and reproduction rights; preservation metadata stores information about actions taken or to be taken in order to preserve a resource over time. There are more specific types of metadata, for example for images and visual representations of resources. Metadata is used both at the item and at the collection, group of itens, level.

Metadata formats are most of the time represented in an incomprehensible way for non computer professionals, and most of the existing systems offer only a couple of them, and not a complete range of metadata formats. Nevertheless the use of metadata helps overcome the lack of universal standards and the lack of uniformity of cultural content, allowing institutions to use the data formats they want and to manage whatever cultural content they need to; when needed, institutions convert their data to specific metadata formats, loosing in the process eventually some of the information contents if the metadata does not have a concept for that information. Some of the most common metadata formats used for cultural resources are briefly described below.

Dublin Core (Consortium for Interchange of Museum Information, 2001) is one of the simplest and most widely used metadata formats. It has a small number of attributes, fifteen, and as such it is unable to represent many of the characteristics of complex cultural objects. Improvements to the original format were proposed, resulting in Qualified Dublin Core that aimed at meeting the needs of an increasing and diverse range of application domains. A simple Dublin Core example is taken from the documentation:

```
<dc:creator>Rose Bush</dc:creator>
              <dc:title>A Guide to Growing Roses</dc:title>
              <dc:description>Describes process for planting and nurturing
different kinds of rose bushes.
</dc:description>
              <dc:date>2001-01-20</dc:date>
```

EDM (Europeana Data Model) is the metadata format developed by the Europeana project. The Europeana portal ingests metadata encoded in EDM, intended to replace the older ESE schema (European Standard Elements). EDM metadata can use Dublin Core for the individual elements. EDM was developed embedding concepts from OAI-ORE (Open Archives Initiative Object Reuse and Exchange), DC Terms and SKOS (Simple Knowledge Organization System)(Open Archives Initiative, 2014; W3C, 2009). Europeana embraced and encouraged partner institutions to adopt open linked data principles (Isaac, Clayphan & Haslhofer, 2012). EDM is a complex and rich format, as required by the different types of cultural assets, from books to pictures to newspapers to film and music recordings, currently made available through Europeana.

LIDO (Lightweight Information Describing Objects) is also a XML schema intended to be general enough to express most of the information museum and heritage institutions need to publish and exchange (Coburn, E., Light, McKenna, Stein & Vitzthum, 2010). LIDO produces extensive information about a resource making it very rich and suitable for all kind of cultural objects. LIDO is maintained by the International Council of Museums (ICOM) and it is widely used in inventory systems.

CDWA (Categories for the Description of Works of Art) is a set of guidelines for description of art, architecture, and other cultural works. CDWA includes around 540 categories and subcategories of information. CDWA provides crosswalks to other richer formats, such as the CIDOC CRM that will be presented in the next section (CWDA, 2014).

MODS (Metadata Object Description Schema) is also a metadata encoding schema, oriented towards bibliographic data (Library of Congress, 2017). MODS is maintained by the Network Development and MARC Standards Office of the Library of Congress. MADS is a schema for encoding of authority data, and can be used with MODS. MODS has been selected for the Digital Repository of Ireland (Bustillo, 2016), overcoming the limitations of Dublin Core.

Some formats convey richer semantics and thus can be considered more powerful then simple metadata. Some of them, relevant to the cultural domain, are briefly presented next.

FRBR (Functional Requirements for Bibliographic Records) is an IFLA initiative to represent bibliographic information, at the light of the limitations of the MARC family of standards for semantic and linked information interchange (FRBR, 2015). FRBR defines the concepts work, expression, manifestation, item and relationship. The same work can have multiple expressions (for example, multiple translations), and each expression can have multiple manifestations (for example, the physical printed book, the e-book edition).

SKOS (Simple Knowledge Organization System) can be used to represent thesauri and to aid in linking data from disparate sources. SKOS can represent concepts and terms as specified in the ISO 25964 "The international standard for thesauri and interoperability with other vocabularies" (Will, 2012), using the linked open data principles. SKOS has gained wide acceptance as more and more cultural open data projects publish their vocabularies and thesauri as SKOS.

OWL (The W3C Web Ontology Language) can be used in representing ontologies, that is, knowledge about given concepts and entities, and the relationships between them. OWL ontologies are generally represented in RDF. OWL is a computational logic-based language such that knowledge expressed in OWL can be exploited by computer programs. As such, it is possible to reason over published data, and to find new information from the published data (W3C, 2013).

SPARQL is a query language for RDF triples on the web having capabilities for querying required and optional graph patterns (SPARQL Working Group, 2008). Several implementations of SPARQL endpoints exist. Mäkelä and Hyvönen (2014) proposed a configurable SPARQL browser as a service, SPARQL SAHA, which can be adapted to any underlying model.

To aid in data exchange, crosswalks exist for most common metadata standards, although the transformation process involves generally manual intervention. It would be nice to record information once, as museums normally do in their inventory systems, and then to publish everywhere, as needed, without concern for the metadata format to be used. Museum professionals should be able to see and manipulate information as they are used to, leaving to their systems, or other experts, the task to comply with the technical standards. Haslhofer and Klas (2010) identified several techniques for metadata interoperability, proposing that agreement at the meta-model level makes that task easier. In the cultural heritage domain they cite the CIDOC CRM, briefly introduced in the following section, as such an approach.

SEMANTIC REPRESENTATIONS

The ICOM/CIDOC has been producing recommendations and guidelines concerning the management of information in Museums and heritage institutions, mainly in the realm of documentation. In fact, the CIDOC Information Categories were first published in 1995 (ICOM, 1995), and they were later followed by a relational model (Reed, 1995). Other attempts were undertaken, such as the International Federation of Library Associations and Institutions proposal of a conceptual model to deal with bibliographic information (FRBR, 2015) but the fist basis for a standard conceptual reference model was published in 1998 by the Documentation Standards Group of the ICOM/CIDOC (Crofts *et al*, 1998). It became an ISO standard in 2006 — ISO, 21127:2006 (ISO, 2014).

The Conceptual Reference Model (CRM) (ICOM, 2005; Le Bœuf *et al.*, 2005) is an object-oriented information model, based on the notion of Ontologies. An ontological approach has several benefits: it is a high-level description of a domain, independent of implementation details; Ontologies can be translated to different implementation systems and formats; several institutions can share and agree upon an ontology, regardless of the specifics of their implementations; besides being shared, ontologies can be reused; once a *Time* or *Units of Measure* ontology has been created, several institutions can reuse it without them having to define themselves the ontology. As such, the CIDOC CRM is generic reference ontology for representing cultural heritage objects and documentation.

The Erlangen CRM/OWL is an OWL-DL 1.0 (a subset of OWL) implementation[1] of the CIDOC CRM (Görz, Schiemann & Oischinger, 2008). As it is defined in OWL, it is ready to be used in a web context.

Although the CIDOC CRM was introduced over a decade ago, there are few library, archive and museum systems using its concepts. The authors have been involved in the design and development of an inventory system based on the CIDOC CRM, described next.

The *Index Rerum* system is based on the CIDOC CRM, defining a meta-model that can be adapted to different representation formats and domains. *Index Rerum* is the heritage inventory and collection management system from FCo – full service company in multimedia[2]. *Index Rerum* allows for virtually any type of records to be defined, and to link those record types between them and with other information, in any way intended. It provides crosswalks with different formats by working at the meta-model level. The structure of a record is flexible, and can thus include fields designed for different purposes, for example, translations in different languages, descriptions for specific target audiences, and inventory management.

Some of the features of *Index Rerum* are:

- It can manage multiple sites in the same system, so that institutions with multiple sites can use the same *Index Rerum*, keeping an institutional design, separate records and user logins for each site. Those sites can be different physical sites, departments or even different services, for example archives and libraries.
- Fields in the records can be translated. This means a record can have a description field with entries in several languages. As not all fields are candidates for translation, the institution can select, and translate, only a small set of fields relevant to the public.
- Records can be exported in Dublin Core, Europeana ESE, Europeana EDM, Resource Description Framework, Unimarc, Excel/CSV, and PDF. *Index Rerum* has an OAI-PMH 2.0-compliant interface which allows participation in cultural repositories and aggregators (as, for example, the Europeana repository).
- Records can be made public (no authentication is required for accessing them) or private (authentication is required). Fields can also be made public or private; for example, a public record may not show details about the conservation status or costs.
- Records have a permanent URL, and it is easy to generate barcodes and QR-codes from any field for each record.
- Users can have different permissions based on their role, for example, some users are not allowed to delete records, and some users are allowed to edit any record. This makes a flexible framework where institutions can authorize different types of users to perform different actions on records.
- User actions are tracked and recorded, so that auditing can take place; users cannot change information in the logs, automatic dates in the records, or the creator of a record. A complete edit log for each user is always available for auditing purposes.

Although *Index Rerum* can be used as a front-end for a portal, providing search facilities, and inventory management, it can be used to feed specialized portals, through OAI or web services, leaving the specialized user interface issues to the client applications.

An example of a multi-language, multi-site installation, with three institutions is shown on the web at http://www.museuchapelaria.cm-sjm.pt/(FCo, 2016)

This *Index Rerum* installation manages hundreds of record types, mainly related to the shoe and hat industry, and to contemporary art. There are more than 100000 records in the system, allowing joint search in the three museums, tag cloud generation, selective export of records, and inter-record linking. This installation is an example of the *Index Rerum* being used both for inventory (authorized users can log in) and for public search and browsing. Figure 1 shows partially a record for a hat.

The next example shows the record of an ancient coin represented with the CIDOC CRM as produced by *Index Rerum*:

```
<rdf:RDF xmlns:xsd=http://www.w3.org/2001/XMLSchema#
         xmlns:dc=http://purl.org/dc/elements/1.1/
         xmlns:skos=http://www.w3.org/2004/02/skos/core#
         xmlns:owl=http://www.w3.org/2002/07/owl#
         xmlns:rdf=http://www.w3.org/1999/02/22-rdf-syntax-ns#
         xmlns:dc-term="http://purl.org/dc/terms/">
   <E22_Man-Made_Object xmlns=http://erlangen-crm.org/current/
                              rdf:about="http://indexrerum.com/id/object/13">
<P2_has_type rdf:resource="http://indexrerum.com/id/thesauri/w34"/>
<P45_consists_of rdf:resource="http://indexrerum.com/id/thesauri/w31"/>
<P51_has_former_or_current_owner
           rdf:resource="http://indexrerum.com/id/actor/1"/>
<P50_has_current_keeper
           rdf:resource="http://indexrerum.com/id/actor/1"/>
```

Figure 1. A partial view of a record for a hat

```
<P1_is_identified_by rdf:resource="http://indexrerum.com/id/object/13"/>
<P48_has_preferred_identifier
          rdf:resource="http://indexrerum.com/id/object/13"/>
<P102_has_title rdf:resource="Dracma"/>
<E54_Dimension rdf:resource="http://indexrerum.com/id/object/13/weight"/>
<P3_has_note rdf:resource="Helenic"/>
<P108i_was_produced_by
          rdf:resource="http://indexrerum.com/id/object/13/production"/>
<P138i_has_representation
          rdf:resource="http://indexrerum.com/content?16bf57b543.png"/>
   </E22_Man-Made_Object>
</rdf:RDF>
```

As records are easily customizable, the system has been evolving and adapting to new record types and collections, which is of paramount importance in a domain such as industrial heritage where there is a great diversity of objects and not all of them are known or identifiable beforehand. Being of great touristic and cultural interest, industrial heritage can greatly benefit from the linked data approach, as the number of applications and uses for the data are diverse and always changing. Another application of *Index Rerum* is described in (Gouveia & Lira, 2008).

Next we will review some of the applications of cultural linked data in semantic portals, highlighting the potential of systems based on meta-models, such as *Index Rerum*.

SEMANTIC PORTALS

CultureSampo was one the first large-scale projects of a publication and semantic portal for cultural information (Hyvönen, 2007; Hyvönen *et al.*, 2009). CultureSampo aggregated several cultural collections offering to the end-user a semantically rich interface allowing complex search and browsing operations. CultureSampo integrated also narratives, events, and semantic recommendations. Mäkelä, Hyvönen and Ruotsalo (2011) described the real world issues of integrating heterogeneous data in CultureSampo, and the lessons learned.

The Europeana portal is one of the major heterogeneous aggregators, including different languages, different levels of description of the items, different standards, and a diverse set of international contributor institutions. Europeana had to go through a complex and manual process of metadata extraction, analysis, translation to adequate formats, and curation. In 2012 Europeana introduced the Europeana Data Model (EDM) as the first move to the web of linked data, transforming on the way more than 20 million metadata, text, video and image objects (Isaac, Clayphan & Haslhofer, 2012). The hard task of the EDM was to be able to represent data from the Archives, Museums, Libraries, and Audio-Visual domains.

As we mentioned before, most of the world's largest museums are moving to the linked data approach, making their collections available to automatic manipulation; e.g. the Rijksmuseum makes available a LOD collection of more than 350000 objects in a process detailed by Dijkshoorn *et al.* (2016). The Prado Museum developed a knowledge graph containing 300000 entities (Pantoja *et al.*, 2016). This process is however complex, and time consuming. Nisheva-Pavlova, Spyratos and Stanchev (2014) review some of the issues relating to museums and their move to the semantic web.

SEMANTIC APPLICATIONS

Cultural content everywhere is used in feeding general purpose portals, tourism applications, gaming and entertainment portals, and educational portals, for example. Mobile applications use cultural content to drive games, personalized postcards, quizzes, and rough guides. Hackathons are regularly organized to develop new applications and find new ways of using the data; more and more, user generated content must be integrated with the existing content, providing annotations, comments, tagging, and additional information. Given the intrinsic educational value of cultural content, one of the most important application fields is education and learning.

Recognizing that fact, the Europeana Taskforce for Education, following the policy recommendations set forth by the European Foundation (Europeana Foundation, 2015) recently identified seven keys to unlock the potential for re-use of digital heritage in education (Europeana Task Force for Education, 2016):

1. Relevance of digital heritage for educational purposes. Collections should be used to enable specific learning outcomes.
2. Discoverability of digital heritage. For digital heritage to be easily found, ensure metadata includes search terms that educators and students use.
3. There is sufficient context information about the source, for instance, essential information such as maker, author, date, translation.
4. The source is of sufficient quality (e.g. texts are readable, essential details visible).
5. Copyright allows for re-use. It must be legally possible to use the digital heritage in open educational research that can be shared.
6. Easy and reliable access: the sources can be used beyond where they are found, for example through direct links or embed functions, and links don't change.
7. Interoperability: use via different learning platforms is possible, e.g. the standards used in the digital collections are interoperable.

Keys 2, 6 and 7 are directly linked to the technical aspects of the data, such as the quality of the metadata, as previously discussed. The other keys relate to the contents itself, and to the capability of the institutions of providing clear, focused, content at least for the cultural data intended to be made public. Another important issue is the language, and the need to provide contents in some major languages if an international public is intended. This is mainly an issue for content originally described in less spoken languages that suddenly finds an international audience, as was the case when some of this content was exported to portals like Europeana.

Another important application area is access and discovery of cultural information. Given the wealth of information already available, semantic browsers and search engines can be a useful, and much needed, tool to navigate cultural content. Next we will describe some approaches to these problems.

Wang *et al.* (2008, 2009) used semantically enriched information at the Rijksmuseum to feed a recommender system and to deal with the complexity and limitations of heterogeneous information, and lack of user ratings, for example. Mulholland, Wolff, Kilfeather and McCarthy (2014) propose a simple interface for authoring stories that can be semantically enriched with Freebase triples.

Dijkshoorn, van Ossenbruggen, Aroyo, and Schreiber (2014) proposed a search engine where search results can be enriched by expert user annotations. The authors used a small subset of the Rijksmuseum collections and demoed annotation sessions. Moving from expert users to the public at large would bring trust issues. Kovalenko, Mrabet, Schouten and Sejdovic (2015), used linked data at the British Museum to provide personalized museum tours using mobile devices. They use a mix of RDF, CIDOC CRM, and external vocabularies such as DBPedia[3].

A SPECIFIC APPLICATION

This section describes a specific application of *Index Rerum* inventorying and making available a peculiar "collection": medieval and modern seals that are stored in many different national and private archives.

Despite the fact seals are indeed material objects they are also cultural objects with significant "associated information" that must be considered when developing an inventory and collections management system. Developing the system for SIGILLVM it was taken under consideration that standard information models, such as the Relational Model, suffer from some limitations due to the fact that they deal with tabular data and that it is problematic to represent complex relationships and hierarchies between data items.

For a long time now the ICOM/CIDOC has been producing recommendations and guidelines concerning the management of information in Museums and heritage institutions, mainly in the realm of documentation. FCo made available the SIGILLVM version of *Index Rerum* for free during the first period of the project, acting as a sponsor of the SIGILLVM project. The following paragraphs present some major aspects of an application of *Index Rerum* in a very particular situation: a collection that includes only one type of object – but a demanding one – and the need to interact with other systems and inventory applications since seals are object of study in several different countries and under different approaches. A set of rules was defined to present information to the user by taking advantage of the object-oriented model: browsing, navigating and searching information follows the structure of the model. Similar approaches have been proposed by (Paton et al, 1994).

The SIGILLVM project (Gaspar, 2014) needed a modern, flexible and fully-customizable inventory system that could be at the same time a scientific tool for inventory and a public-access web-system for experts, curious and the general public. Furthermore, the SIGILLVM project needed its inventory system to be able to communicate with other systems: it must follow standards mainly on what metadata is concerned and allow some particularities such as formatted text fields for Latin expressions. On the other hand it must be easy to use, with a simple but effective interface, because SIGILLVM welcomes the participation of experts and researchers that are very specialized in seals... but not always in web-systems and similar technologies. Finally, SIGILLVM needed a system that could be used no matter where (in archives, libraries, museums, public or private institutions, at office and at home). As such, the inventory system should not be installed in one machine but available in any machine (public or personal computer, laptop, tablet, smart-phone) despite the size of the screen, hardware specs or operating system. *Index Rerum* responds to all these requirements, being a web-based system that can also run in stand-alone, disconnected devices. The solution is a web-based system that runs in a server-client basis, reachable in any device connected to the internet. Because the interface is responsive it can be used in any device, from a 4 or 5 inch smart-phone to an office computer with a huge-comfortable screen. In cases internet is not available, *Index Rerum* allows to register data in a *.xls standardized file format (generated by *Index Rerum* itself) that can be later on uploaded into the system. Using a spreadsheet format it is also a convenient way to do bulk uploads for example from data exported from other applications and easily edited in such a format.

Normally clients connect to the system using a standard browser via a network. Browsers must be JavaScript enabled and support HTML 4 or 5. For some applications, a secure connection is established using the Secure Sockets Layer protocol. The interface presented to the users introduces a minimum overhead, by reducing image and graphic elements, and by not using frames as this can bring some problems with some browsers. This allows the use of "obsolete" hardware: any PC with an old Pentium (or equivalent) CPU and 1 or 2 Gb of RAM that is connected to the internet with an updated browser will be enough to work with *Index Rerum*. This might seem like a not so important aspect but in some institutions it has proved to be quite significant.

The software architecture of the system uses a relational-object layer to present to the user an object-oriented view of the data, and to store it in a table format in a relational database. This is a common approach when the expressive power and the flexibility of the object model is the objective, and the convenience (even in cost terms) of working with a relational database. Classes with instances are mapped to tables, which contain all attributes, including inherited ones. Relationships are mapped to tables with just two object identifiers. Although this is not the most efficient strategy (e.g. see Agarwal et al. 1995), it allows for most of database accesses to be made with only one join operation. Future improvements could distinguish between different types of relationships and decide different strategies for their efficient storage in the relational database. If the size of the database grows to the point performance issues arise – which has not been the case so far – NoSQL databases (Cattell, 2011) or object-oriented databases could be used in the future (Kim, 1990).

There are several levels of access corresponding to the different profiles in the system. The first level of access only permits people to see information, and to see only some kind of information. For that reason, no username or password is necessary. Restricted data are not available to those who use the system as "normal public" – for example insurance details of the items are not available. For this visitor, the SIGILLVM inventory system appears more like a virtual tour that enhances significant or interesting issues about the seals. The second group of users (researchers) needs to retrieve other kind of information; for that purpose, the coordinator of the project is able to create temporary users, with username and password. This kind of username allows researchers to see almost all data in the system and gives permission to use special functionalities like "personal folders", where items of the collection can be virtually gathered and organized. However, researchers are not allowed to input data, neither are they allowed to edit or change record files. Staff from project has personal usernames, and those allow creating record files and inputting data into the system. Each username and password allows its user to edit and change its own work. However, no one is allowed to edit or change other users' record files, preventing accidental destruction of information. More profiles can be defined if needed, as the system manages the user's authorization to perform certain actions by checking profiles. A profile is thus a set of authorizations to perform actions.

All actions of a logged-in username are stored and so it is possible to know exactly what was done, when and by whom. This logged information is never erased, creating a permanently updated full-history of the inventory activity and providing a tool for auditing. The system administrator is the only user allowed to edit other users' work; this kind of action is also registered, and the altered record file would present the previous version(s) of the contents and the date/authorship of the change(s). The administrator is also the only user allowed to create other users, of any kind (even another administrator). No user may be deleted from the system, but the administrator is able to deny access to any user.

For the general public the only functionality available is the "search" functionality. Visitors may search the inventory by entering a keyword or a combination of keywords in the record fields. *Index Rerum* searches for it in some specific data fields. Searches may also be done in a more precise way, choosing some data fields, like "date" or "location". All other users may search the system using complete search criteria. It is possible to decide which data fields are to be searched and shown on the result; specific values for those data fields can be used as search criteria; it is also possible to decide that a specific value in a data field must be "equal", "higher" or "lower" than a specific given value. There is also a full text search functionality which allows indexing all fields and to search by relevance, by partial matches and using generic placeholders.

Researchers will have access to other functionalities, such as: personal profile, personal folders and information about the number and type of items registered in the system. The personal profile registers the user's name and surname, the username and the password.

Museum's staff accesses all researchers' functionalities and also the "create" functionality. This enables inputting data into the system. A list of blank record files is available on the screen and the user only has to choose what kind of data he/she is willing to register. Some of the fields are automatic (date, name of user, number of record file) others are to be filled. Generically, there are five main types of data fields: alphanumeric (with different lengths); values; list of choice; dates and thesaurus (either simple-choice or multiple-choice). Upload fields are also available and are used to upload files to the system, for example images or *.pdf files. Retrieving information is possible in all levels of detail. After a query is defined, users may print it, export it to an excel file or save it, for future use. Any query saved can be edited and, eventually, executed later for up-to-date results.

Administrators have all the functionalities available. They can see all information registered in the system and they are allowed to edit and change all record files. They can also create new users or disable login of existing users. Specific information is available after login in as an administrator, especially on what concerns statistics (number of record files, who created them and when, for example) and information on users sessions on-line and past sessions. It is always possible for the administrator to know who is working at each moment; statistics on each user's activity is also accessible. Another tool only available to the administrator is the import of data from standard sources (like *.xls files, for example). It is also possible to import new models (in XML format). The administrator may also export data in various formats: *.xls, *.xml and *.pdf. The system generates labels with barcodes/QR-codes, equivalent to the inventory number of each item or with any information in the system.

For the sake of exemplification, the following images show two of the main interaction screens: creating a file and retrieving information using the complete "search" mode – these are examples of the professional interface, not the public interface.

The complete search function (Figure 2) is normally used by professionals or researchers who know exactly what they are searching for and have a significant knowledge about the theme, the collection and/or the system. Search function allows to include/exclude each field and to determine if its contents should be searched for specific values. Search criteria such as "has contents", "is null", "equals", "not equals", "greater than", "less than" can be also used for each field. Finally a "and" or a "or" condition can be applied to the search criteria. Knowing the collection to be searched or having specific information on particular item this allows a very oriented and accurate search.

In order to create a record, users select a type of record and are shown a number of sections organized by types of information that should be provided. This accordion-like organization helps users go through the fields they want to fill in without having to browse a long list of fields. Some of the fields

Figure 2. Complete search interface

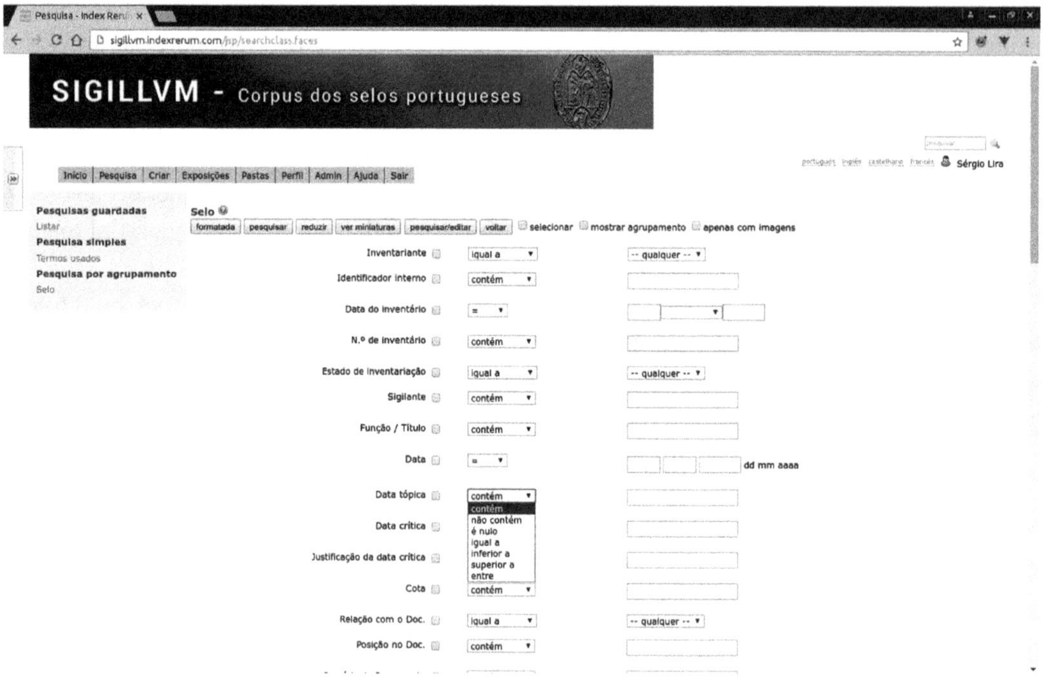

are required, others are not; some of them may have default values already filled in (Figure 3). Additional information such as help texts, thesauri, and lists of values can be attached to any input field helping users to input data and contributing to data consistency by using recommended and harmonized terms.

The SIGILLVM *Index Rerum* is in use for circa four years now and it has fulfilling its task perfectly, allowing professional work, public access and information interchange with other similar research projects. New fields have been added, removed or modified when needed, allowing for a soft evolution of the system. In such a specific domain as this, new needs for representing information can arise and the system should be prepared to adopt them without making users tied up to the initial design and choices of the records.

CONCLUSION

Cultural information is a major driver for several initiatives in several domains, and this chapter described the major issues around the cultural semantic web. Cultural institutions understand how important it is to make available the data they stored and curated for years, so that others can find new applications otherwise not possible. From games to learning materials, education, entertainment at large, or tourism, cultural data is being used everywhere. We briefly overviewed the issues institutions are facing and the range of choices they have to make data available on the web. Institutions having large inventories have a large legacy and want to be able to reuse all the work they had already done. Metadata crosswalks help institutions to translate between metadata formats with minimal effort, helping them also to support other formats in the future.

Figure 3. A form to create records

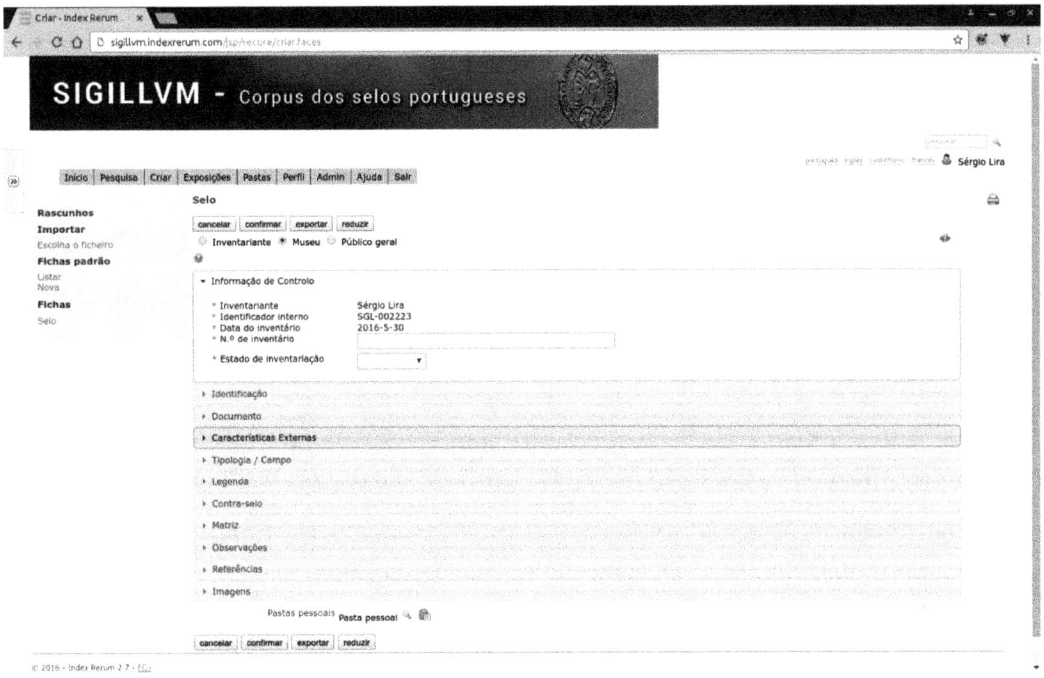

Institutions want to minimize the information burden they'll have to maintain several versions of the same museum item, and a single point of creation and edition will simplify their tasks. Being able to use crosswalks between formats is thus of paramount importance, allowing institutions to deliver their data according to the format the consumers of data want or prefer. There are, of course, other important issues we have not dealt with: copyright issues, ownership issues, just to name a few and that have been at the forefront of concerns. As institutions go global, language issues will have also an impact as institutions will be publishing their data to several target audiences, which can speak different languages; automatic large scale translation is still not a reality, and manual translation is time consuming and expensive. Those issues will have to be resolved, for LOD to become a reality in the cultural domain.

The chapter also introduced *Index Rerum*, an inventory system based on an object-oriented model using a conceptual reference model, the CIDOC CRM, as an example of managing collections and publishing data using the LOD principles. By using a conceptual model systems are able to manage information at a high-level, allowing them to switch between formats and to easily provide several representations of the same data. It also allows to represent the most disparate types of cultural assets and to interlink them in several ways. In the cultural web the capability of publishing data in several metadata formats ensures interoperability with other systems, applications and data consumers in general such as aggregator portals.

REFERENCES

Berners-Lee, T. (2006). *Linked Data. Design Issues*. Retrieved January 10, 2017, from https://www.w3.org/ DesignIssues/LinkedData.html

Bizer, C., Heath, T., & Berners-Lee, T. (2009). Linked Data - The Story So Far. *International Journal on Semantic Web and Information Systems*, *5*(3), 1–22. doi:10.4018/jswis.2009081901

Bustillo, M., Grant, R., Kenny, S., Martínez-García, A., McGoohan, C., Ní Cholla, R., . . . Webb, S. (2016). MODS and the Digital Repository of Ireland. Royal Irish Academy. DOI: doi:10.3318/DRI.2016.1

Categories for the Description of Works of Art (CDWA) (Getty Research Institute). (2014, March 25). Retrieved from http://www.getty.edu/research/publications/electronic_publications/cdwa/

Cattell, R. (2011). Scalable SQL and NoSQL data stores. *SIGMOD Record*, *39*(4), 12–27. doi:10.1145/1978915.1978919

CIMI. (2001). *Guide to best practice: Dublin Core version 1.1*. Consortium for the Computer Interchange of Museum Information, CIMI Consortium.

Coburn, E., Light, R., McKenna, G., Stein, R., & Vitzthum, A. (2010). *LIDO – Lightweight Information Describing Objects, version 1.0*. ICOM/CIDOC for the Data Harvesting Working Group.

Crofts, N., Dionissiadou, I., Doerr, M., & Reed, P. (Eds.). (1998). *CIDOC Conceptual Reference Model - Information groups*. ICOM/CIDOC Documentation Standards Group.

de Boer, V., Wielemaker, J., van Gent, J., Oosterbroek, M., Hildebrand, M., Isaac, A., & Schreiber, G. et al. (2013). Amsterdam Museum Linked Open Data. *Semantic Web – Interoperability, Usability, Applicability*, *4*(3), 237–243.

Dijkshoorn, C., Jongma, L., van Ossenbruggen, J., Schreiber, G., ter Weele, W., & Wielemaker, J. (2016). *The Rijksmuseum Collection as Linked Data. Semantic Web – Interoperability, Usability, Applicability*.

Dijkshoorn, C., van Ossenbruggen, J., Aroyo, L., & Schreiber, G. (2014), INVENiT: Exploring cultural heritage collections while adding annotations. *Proceedings of the 3rd International Conference on Intelligent Exploration of Semantic Data (IESD'14)*, 1279.

EF. (2015). *Europeana for Education and Learning*. Den Haag: Policy Recommendations. Europeana Foundation.

ETE. (2016). *Keys to unlocking digital heritage for use in education*. Europeana Taskforce for Education.

FCo. (2016). *Gestão de Coleções*. Retrieved from http://www.museuchapelaria.cm-sjm.pt/

FRBR. (2015). *FRBR object-oriented definition and mapping from FRBRER, FRAD and FRSAD (version 2.1)*. International Working Group on FRBR and CIDOC CRM Harmonization.

Gaspar, B. (2014). *Sigillvm portvgaliae*. Retrieved from http://portugal-sigillvm.net/

Görz, G., Schiemann, B., & Oischinger, M. (2008). An implementation of the CIDOC Conceptual Reference Model (4.2.4) in OWL-DL. CIDOC 2008, Athens, Greece.

Gouveia, F., & Lira, S. (2008). An Information Model for Virtual Museums. The case of an Ecomuseum. In K. Robering (Ed.), *Information Technology for the Virtual Museum. Museology and the Semantic Web* (pp. 103–111). London: LIT-Verlag Münster.

Haslhofer, B., & Klas, W. (2010). A Survey of Techniques for Achieving Metadata Interoperability. *ACM Computing Surveys*, *42*(2), 1–37. doi:10.1145/1667062.1667064

Hedstrom, M., & King, J. L. (2003). *On the LAM: Library, archive, and museum collections in the creation and maintenance of knowledge communities*. Organization for Economic Cooperation and Development. Retrieved January 10, 2017, from http://www.oecd.org/edu/innovation-education/32126054.pdf

Hyvönen, E. (2007). Semantic Portals for Cultural Heritage. In Handbook on Ontologies. Springer Verlag.

Hyvönen, E. (2012). Publishing and Using Cultural Heritage Linked Data on the Semantic Web. In J. Hendler & Y. Ding (Eds.), *Synthesis Lectures on Semantic Web: Theory and Technology*. Palo Alto, CA: Morgan & Claypool. doi:10.2200/S00452ED1V01Y201210WBE003

Hyvönen, E., Mäkelä, E., Kauppinen, T., Alm, O., Kurki, J., Ruotsalo, T.,..., Nyberg, K. (2009). CultureSampo — Finnish Culture on the Semantic Web 2.0: Thematic Perspectives for the End-user. *Proceedings of Museums and the Web 2009.*

Hyvönen, E., Tuominen, J., Alonen, M., & Mäkelä, E. (2014). *Linked Data Finland: A 7-star model and platform for publishing and re-using linked datasets. The Semantic Web: ESWC 2014 Satellite Events, Revised Selected Papers*. Springer Verlag.

ICOM. (1995). *Graphic Data Mode*. ICOM/CIDOC Data Model Working Group.

ICOM. (2005). *Definition of the CIDOC Conceptual Reference Model, Version 4.2* (N. Crofts, M. Doerr, T. Gill, S. Stead, & M. Stiff, Eds.). ICOM/CIDOC CRM Special Interest Group.

ICOM. (2011). *ICOM recommendation on Linked Open Data for museums* (N. Crofts, M. Doerr, & M. Nyman, Eds.). ICOM/CIDOC CRM Special Interest Group.

Isaac, A., Clayphan, R., & Haslhofer, R. (2012). EUROPEANA: moving to linked open data. Information Standards Quarterly, 24(2-3).

ISO. (2014). *Information and documentation — A reference ontology for the interchange of cultural heritage information. ISO 21127:2014*. Geneva, Switzerland: International Organization for Standardization.

Kovalenko, O., Mrabet, Y., Schouten, K., & Sejdovic, S. (2015). Linked Data in Action: Personalized Museum Tours on Mobile Devices. *Proceedings of the ESWC2015 Developers Workshop*.

Le Bœuf, P., Sinclair, P., Martinez, K., Lewis, P., Aitken, G., & Lahanier, C. (2005). Using an ontology for interoperability and browsing of museum, library and archive information. *International Council of Museums 14th Triennial Meeting*. The Hague: ICOM Committee for Conservation.

Library of Congress. (2017, May 18). *Metadata object Description Schema*. Retrieved from http://www.loc.gov/standards/mods/

Mäkelä, E., & Hyvönen, E. (2014). SPARQL SAHA, a Configurable Linked Data Editor and Browser as a Service. In Lecture Notes in Computer Science: Vol. 8798. The Semantic Web: ESWC 2014 Satellite Events (pp. 434-438). Springer Verlag.

Mäkelä, E., Hyvönen, E. & Ruotsalo, T. (2011). How to deal with massively heterogeneous cultural heritage data – lessons learned in CultureSampo. *Semantic Web – Interoperability, Usability, Applicability*.

Mulholland, P., Wolff, A., Kilfeather, E., & McCarthy, E. (2014). *Using event spaces, setting and theme to assist the interpretation and development of museum stories. Proceedings of Knowledge Engineering and Knowledge Management, EKAW 2014, Linköping, Sweden* (pp. 320–332). Springer.

Nisheva-Pavlova, M., Spyratos, S., & Stanchev, P. (2014), *Museum Collections and the Semantic Web. Fourth International Conference on Digital Presentation and Preservation of Cultural and Scientific Heritage*, Veliko Tarnovo, Bulgaria.

Open Archives Initiative. (2014, August 14). *ORE Specifications and User Guides - Table of Contents.* Retrieved from http://www.openarchives.org/ore/1.0/toc

Pantoja, J., Docampo, J., Martín, A., Maturana, R., & Navalón, C. (2016). *The new Prado Museum website: A (semantic) challenge.* MW2016 Museums and the Web 2016. Retrieved January 10, 2017, from http://mw2016.museumsandtheweb.com/paper/the-new-prado-museum-website-a-semantic-challenge/

Paton, N. W., Al-Qaimari, G., & Doan, K. (1994). On interface objects in Object-Oriented Databases. *12th British National Conference on Databases.* Springer-Verlag.

Reed, P. A. (1995). *CIDOC Relational Data Model. A Guide.* ICOM/CIDOC.

Skevakis, G., Konstantinos Makris, K., Arapi, P., & Christodoulakis, S. (2013), Elevating Natural History Museums' Cultural Collections to the Linked Data Cloud. *Proceedings of the 3rd International Workshop on Semantic Digital Archives (SDA 2013).*

Skevakis, G., Makris, K., Arapi, P., & Christodoulakis, S. (2013). Elevating Natural History Museums' Cultural Collections to the Linked Data Cloud. *Proceedings of the 3rd International Workshop on Semantic Digital Archives (SDA 2013).*

SPARQL Working Group. (2008, January 15). *SPARQL Query Language for RDF.* Retrieved from https://www.w3.org/TR/rdf-sparql-query/

Spectrum. (2011). InDawson, A., & Hillhouse, S. (Eds.), *SPECTRUM 4.0. The UK Museum Collections Management Standard.* The Collections Trust.

Szekely, P., Knoblock, C., Yang, F., Zhu, X., Fink, E., Allen, R., & Goodlander, G. (2013). Connecting the Smithsonian American Art Museum to the Linked Data Cloud. In *Lecture Notes in Computer Science: Vol. 7882. The Semantic Web: Semantics and Big Data: 10th International Conference, ESWC 2013.* Springer Verlag. doi:10.1007/978-3-642-38288-8_40

W3C. (2009, August 18). *SKOS Simple Knowledge Organization System Primer.* Retrieved from https://www.w3.org/TR/skos-primer/

W3C. (2013, December 11). *OWL.* Retrieved from https://www.w3.org/OWL/

W3C. (2014, June 24). *RDF 1.1 Primer.* Retrieved from https://www.w3.org/TR/rdf11-primer/

Wang, Y., Stash, N., Aroyo, L., Gorgels, P., Rutledge, L., & Schreiber, G. (2008). Recommendations based on semantically enriched museum collections. *Web Semantics: Science, Services, and Agents on the World Wide Web*, *6*(6), 283–290. doi:10.1016/j.websem.2008.09.002

Wang, Y., Stash, N., Hollink, L., & Schreiber, G. (2009). Using Semantic Relations for Content-based Recommender Systems in Cultural Heritage. *Proceedings of the 2009 International Conference on Ontology and Semantic Web Patterns (WOP'09)*, 516.

Will, L. (2012). The ISO 25964 Data Model for the Structure of an Information Retrieval Thesaurus. *Bulletin of the American Society for Information Science and Technology*, *38*(4), 48–51. doi:10.1002/bult.2012.1720380413

KEY TERMS AND DEFINITIONS

CIDOC CRM: The conceptual reference model proposed by the CIDOC for the cultural heritage domain.

Conceptual Model: An information model providing definitions and the structure for representing information in a given domain.

Crosswalk: Process using rules allowing transformation of data from one given metadata format to another.

Cultural Open Data: Data pertaining to the cultural domain that is published in the web according to the Open Data principles.

Linked Data: Data that is published on the web according to the principles set by T. Berners-Lee.

Metadata: Data about data, in practice the set of properties characterizing data in a given domain.

Semantic Portal: A web portal allowing navigation by following semantic relationships between data.

Chapter 20
A Platform for the Promotion of Energy Efficiency and Monitoring in Hotel Units

Sergey Nogin
University of Algarve, Portugal

Jânio Monteiro
University of Algarve, Portugal & INESC-ID, Portugal

Sergio Gómez Melgar
University of Huelva, Spain & LAR Arquitectura, Spain

José Peyroteo
University of Algarve, Portugal

António Mortal
University of Algarve, Portugal

Carlos Miguel A. Santos
University of Algarve, Portugal

José Livramento
University of Algarve, Portugal

Pedro J. S. Cardoso
University of Algarve, Portugal

Jorge Semião
University of Algarve, Portugal

ABSTRACT

Tourists today are more likely to be concerned with the environment and greener lifestyle choices. In this context, a green flagship of some hotels can be an important selection criteria at the time of selecting one. In the near future, buildings should become nearly zero energy, consuming as low as possible

DOI: 10.4018/978-1-5225-2927-9.ch020

and producing almost all the energy they need, using renewable energy sources. To achieve this goal, hotel buildings need to pass through a transformation process that will make them more efficient. In this process, a decision support platform would be important to help hoteliers monitor their energy consumption, identify which points are consuming more than expected, decide which investments are more cost effective and manage their equipment in an optimum way. This chapter describes the challenges involved in developing such a platform, covering several research and development fields, including Internet of Things networks, ICT, Smart Grids, Renewable Energy, Energy efficiency, as well as algorithms for machine learning and optimization.

INTRODUCTION

There has been a gradual shift in the expectations and demands of tourists, regarding hotels. Today's typical hotel guests are more likely to be concerned about environmental issues comprising greener lifestyle choices, such as recycling, fuel-efficient vehicles or organic food. While the location of hotels is still one of the most important features to select them, it is also common to find many hotels in the same region or area. In these cases, the green flagship of some of these hotels can be an important differentiating factor that make them more attractive to some tourists.

To achieve that green flagship, a better energy efficiency of hotels is required. In this field, the Directive 2010/31 of the European Union (European Parliament, council on the energy performance of buildings, 2010) makes mandatory for all new public buildings after January 2020 and all other new buildings from January 2021 onward to become nearly zero energy. This means that, they will have to consume as low as possible and at the same time will have to produce almost all the energy they need, in their own building or in their vicinity.

As tourism is one of the priorities for the economic activities of several European regions, the implications of the European Directive 2010/31 are of high importance for touristic companies and in particular for hotel units, affecting their competitiveness and image. Monitoring energy consumption to achieve the zero energy goal also helps to accomplish the sustainability of the region where the hotel is. By conveying the achievements obtained with these measures in future eTourism Applications, the image of the region as a whole can be improved.

In order for them to achieve the goals of zero energy building, a complete set of decision support tools is required that, besides monitoring consumption, could support the development of innovative methods to improve energy efficiency. Their aim is to give hoteliers and technicians a set of tools that include recommendations on building insulation, amount of renewable energy needed, automated detection and identification of excessive consumption levels, and management of consuming devices.

In some cases, as for instance in the detection and automatic identification of abnormal consumption levels, machine learning algorithms are required to compare the current level of consumption with the expected one, obtained from the consumption history of the building and weighted by several factors such as occupancy levels and environmental variables. Machine learning algorithms are thus used to perform a real time and continuous analysis, selecting the relevant information between huge amounts of data generated, e.g., by a network of IoT (Internet of Things) sensors and SCADA (Supervisory Control and Data Acquisition) devices.

Regarding the energy generation from renewable sources, the understanding of which set of solutions allows the building to reach the goal of nearly zero consumption is of crucial importance. As nearly zero means that the amount of energy generated locally should equal what is consumed in a certain time period (usually one year) the understanding of the consumption profile of the building is of crucial importance to define what should be the most appropriate installation levels.

This should also be combined with an effective reduction in energy costs, taking into consideration the tariff rates of energy suppliers. In order to accomplish it, hotel managers need to know which of the tariff rates, of the energy retailers, is the best solution for them, and also, need to adjust consumption levels accordingly. Thus not only the selection of the tariff rates should depend on the consumption profile, but also the consumption profile should change according with the contracted tariff rates. When these decisions are also based on generation from renewable energy sources, the complexity of the whole system increases significantly, as it requires maximizing the use of the locally generated energy, avoiding selling it at a lower price. Thus a set of actions should be defined that could increase the correlation between production and consumption through rescheduling of loads and the commensurate design of generation systems.

Given these considerations, the objective of this book chapter is to describe the state of the art solutions in consumption and IoT monitoring, energy efficiency and machine learning, that can be used to build a decision support tool for hoteliers. Based in a testbed implemented in one hotel building we describe the involved research and technological developments in several related fields, including sensor networks or Internet of Things, Information and communications technology (ICT), smart grids, renewable energy sources, energy efficiency, machine learning and optimization algorithms, that support the creation of innovative solutions that can be applied at a worldwide scale in touristic regions.

The structure of the chapter is the following. In the Background section, we start by describing the current state-of-the-art in terms of developments and research that is capable of improving the energy efficiency in buildings. This section includes an analysis of: (1) Decision Support Systems in Energy; (2) Passive measures capable of achieving the near zero energy consumption goal; (3) Real time Monitoring and Sensing Architectures and Solutions; and (4) Decision Support Algorithms for Energy Management.

In the subsequent section of the chapter, we present a platform capable of promoting energy efficiency in hotels. In this section we start by: (1) describing the General Architecture of a Sensor Platform; (2) continue by describing the implementation of the electronic sensor devices; (3) the structure of the monitoring platform and associated applications; (4) the solutions for anomaly detection using machine learning algorithms; (5) the decision support solutions for passive measures; and (6) discuss how these measures can be combined to build the Decision Support Platform for hoteliers.

In last two sections, we present the conclusions of the chapter and present the future research directions of the ongoing research for the improvement of Energy Efficiency in Hotel Buildings.

BACKGROUND

Globally, buildings account for nearly 40% of energy consumption and 36% of CO_2 emissions in the EU. In order to reach the 2050 goals of reducing greenhouse gas emissions by 80-95% when compared to 1990 levels, a combination of actions is needed towards the nearly Zero Energy (nZE). The European Directive on the Energy Performance of Buildings (European Parliament, council on the energy performance of buildings, 2010) imposes that after the end of 2020 all new buildings should be nearly

Zero Energy Buildings (nZEB), while for new public buildings the aforementioned requirement applies in the 1st of January 2020. Regarding all the other buildings, European Member States are required to define specific policies and measures to stimulate their transformation into nZEB.

In order to reach the nZEB goal, a very high energy performance of such buildings is required, imposing a reduction of consumption with a very significant generation of energy, using renewable sources.

In terms of renewable energy sources, the environmental conditions that Mediterranean countries enjoy, including solar and wind intensity, support a high level of energy autonomy of buildings, businesses and of the associated regions as a whole. In some of these regions, like the Algarve region in Portugal, several studies (AREAL & INETI, 2006; European Commission, Institute for Energy and Transport, 2006) show that the energy generated per square meter of solar panel reaches maximum values, comparable only with equipment installed in the Sahara Desert. Enjoying a similar condition, the region of Andalusia leads the ranking of Spanish autonomous communities, in terms of production from solar thermal installations (Agência Andaluza de Energia, 2011).

Also in these southern regions, tourism represents an important source of wealth, thus standing as a priority for their economic activities, reflected in their regional strategies, as for instance happens in the Portuguese regions of Lisbon and the Algarve (CCDR Algarve, 2015).

In the tourism sector, accommodation represents nearly 21% of CO_2 emissions (UNWTO and UNEP, 2008), mainly as a result of air-conditioning and heating systems, but not only. Hotel buildings contain equipment that consume considerable amounts of energy, in air conditioning systems, electric motors, water pumping systems for swimming pools or irrigation, water heating systems, laundries, among many other loads. Altogether these devices are characterized by having high consumption levels, much higher than lightning for example, and still allow the adjustment of its consumption over time, in accordance with the preferences of those that manage them.

As the legislation of several countries is changing to allow the so called self-consumption, i.e. to allow consumers to generate electricity for their own consumption while still being connected with the utility (Decreto-Lei n.º 153/2014, 2014), load adjustment/scheduling supports the so called demand response concept where the working hours of equipment or their consumption levels are changed in real time, to reflect the actual generation level and/or the tariff rates. Instead of producing what is consumed, we now need to consume what is being generated, when it is generated.

In this context of distributed generation (Olivares et al., 2014), a more proactive role is thus imposed to consumers, which become the so called prosumers. In this path to become prosumers, users start by asking themselves how much renewable energy they need to install, which depends on the consumption curve of the building. But, that is not all, they also need to adjust the loads of the building in response to the generation levels and the contracted tariff rate.

Overall a rethinking of a great number of existing Small and Medium (SME) Hotels, which represent 90% of the EU hospitality industry, is required. Among the several solutions that can be implemented, decision support tools for hoteliers are considered critical, not only to demonstrate the advantages of investments in nZEB, but also to help technical staff to identify and track unusual consumption levels and to help users participate in the global challenge of energy efficiency and reduction of CO_2 emissions.

Decision Support Systems in Energy

Within the 28 countries of the European Community, energy costs, on average, reach up to 30% of total business expenditure (Monteiro, Cardoso, Serra & Fernandes, 2014), with an average increment rate of approximately 9% each year (Eurostat, 2013). Although most managers worry about this problem, only a minority of them actively implement measures to increase the energy efficiency of their businesses (Duke University, 2005).

This may be due to the number of factors involved. In fact, when investing in energy efficiency solutions, these managers have to consider many options (Tournaki et al., 2016) categorized in: (1) energy management measures (including monitoring, introduction of building energy management system, energy audits, feedback systems to guests, etc); (2) measures to reduce heating and cooling demands (changing windows, insulation, installation of sun shading devices, etc); (3) energy efficiency of equipment (replace light bulbs and electrical appliances with higher energy efficiency rating, consider efficient solutions for active space cooling, use high efficiency boilers, etc) and systems (key card systems, balancing of heating, cooling and air-conditioning systems, etc); and (4) introduction of renewable energy sources (biomass boiler, solar thermal, photovoltaics, etc).

In order to alleviate such burden, Intelligent Decision Support Systems can be used to help in making such decisions. As stated by Neves-Silva (2012), Intelligent Decision Support Systems are software platforms that help people make decisions in complex environments with several sources of uncertainty, by making use of computational intelligence methods to enhance the decision making capabilities of the human being.

Some projects have addressed the development of Decision Support Systems in energy as for instance (Emprove, 2013; LifeSaver, 2013). In (Emprove, 2013) a prototype of a platform was developed to support a potential investor in making decisions on building retrofitting with energy efficiency in mind. The focus was on the return of the investment. In (LifeSaver, 2013) a platform was implemented to support decision making in industry, to find energy efficiency opportunities in operations and in the CO_2 emissions market. However, none of these platforms have combined real time monitoring of consumption, renewable energy introduction, optimization and decision support.

Given these considerations, in the following we describe some important energy efficiency measures that should be integrated in a decision support system to motivate hoteliers change their buildings according with the nearly zero energy goals. These measures include: passive measures to improve the building insolation, real time monitoring of consumption levels; detection of abnormal consumption levels; and recommendations and sizing of Renewable Energy Sources according with the consumption levels. We will now analyse the work done in each of these fields.

The Passive Contribution to the Near Zero Energy Consumption

The set of systems and equipment installed in a hotel are intended to provide the building with the services necessary for the development of its activity. Of all these systems, the air conditioning is the one that generates more demand of energy. Its function is related to the building's ability to self-regulate its internal temperature and humidity, regardless of external weather conditions.

Since the major development of Heating, Ventilation and Air Conditioning (HVAC) systems in the 1950s, 1960s and 1970s, architects and engineers usually face the problem of air conditioning of buildings using active systems dependent on a significant energy consumption necessary to make them operate. This growing technological dependence on machines and forced systems, although it facilitated a technification of the construction industry, caused the progressive renunciation of traditional construction techniques inherent to vernacular and patrimonial architecture (Chandel, Sharma, & Marwah, 2016; Gokarakonda & Kumar, 2016; Philokyprou, Michael, Malaktou, & Savvides, 2017).

The energy crisis of the 1980s, with the rising cost of fossil fuels, and the subsequent environmental crisis of the 1990s, with evidence of the contribution of GHGs (greenhouse gases) to global warming, has provided an opportunity to recover the value of these traditional techniques as a contribution to reduce the energy consumption of buildings without reducing the comfort of their users. Contemporary passive architecture is incorporating many of these traditional techniques, updating them with contributions such as new materials (phase change materials, thermo-reflexive insulation, thermo-acoustic glasses, etc) (Lee, Lim, & Salleh, 2016; Oliver, Neila, & García, 2011; Schiavoni, D'Alessandro, Bianchi, & Asdrubali, 2016), new construction techniques (ventilated facades, external thermal insulation facades, etc.) (Ciampi, Leccese, & Tuoni, 2003; Gagliano, Nocera, & Aneli, 2016), and new design tools (solar optimization, energy simulators, BIM design, etc.) (Attia, Gratia, De Herde, & Hensen, 2012; Nadarajan & Kirubakaran, 2016).

Hotel buildings, located in the Algarve region and western Andalusia are subject to a subtropical climate, with warm and dry summers, mild winters and temperate intermediate periods. The highest level of occupancy and intensity of use in hotel establishments in this area occurs during the summer, associated with sun and beach tourism, although the cultural and golf offer tries to break the seasonality in recent years. The biggest problem is therefore the warm weather and how to reduce the energy consumption of the hotel establishment under those conditions. During the summer, the level of solar radiation and the number of daily hours increase significantly, which increases considerably the potential of the photovoltaic energy to attend the whole consumptions of the building.

Having in mind the environmental maxim of reducing, reusing and recycling, the passive actions in the thermal envelope of the buildings would be framed in the first of these strategies: reduce the building's energy demand as much as possible.

The materialization of nearly zero energy hotel (nZEH) depends on their dialogue and their ability to incorporate the most efficient facilities (mainly air conditioning, but also lighting and water heating), on site renewable energy generation (solar thermal, solar photovoltaic, microeolic, geothermal and co-generation), and data analysis (analysis of consumption, temperature and humidity, power generation, coupling of generation and consumption, user feedback, etc.).

Real Time Monitoring and Sensing

Nearly all decisions that are made in the field of energy efficiency result from measurements. Although in some cases those measurements are made regularly, usually they are made only once or twice (for instance before and after an intervention). In first last case, there is a great advantage if those measurements are transmitted to an online platform that stores them and allows their real-time monitoring. In this field, there are currently several Internet based online platforms that support these functions. For instance, emoncms (2017) and thingspeak (2017) define a Web based API (Application Programming Interface) that allows any IoT device to send its data over the Internet to their servers. These Web APIs are used for machine-to-machine (M2M) communications. They use URLs and HTTP request and response messages, exchanging data that is usually structured in JSON or XML format. Similar to Web based client-server communications created for humans, the communication between hardware devices thus also relies in the Internet Protocol (IP) suit. Therefore, the same way users monitor the data stored in databases, using several types of representations or charts, hardware devices retrieve data in JSON or XML formats.

In terms of electrical power and energy, SCADA devices are typically used to obtain the associated measurements. Their interconnection with IP based solutions is typically done using gateways. SCADA relies in a master slave architecture and uses protocols like Modbus (Modbus, 2006, 2012), Building Automation Control Network (BACnet, 2001), Lonworks (Lonworks, 2009), Digital Addressable Lighting Interface - DALI (DALI Activity Group, 2001), EnOcean (EnOcean GmbH, 2016), and KNX (KNX, 2017). In order to retrieve data from non-IP SCADA devices, IP clients act as SCADA masters, periodically requesting measured values from SCADA slaves, through gateways. SCADA slaves store measurements in specific memory registers. The IP based device after retrieving them, store these data locally, or remotely, in Internet based servers, allowing subsequent processing and user access.

Besides SCADA, many other wireless and wired sensor solutions are currently used to gather data about environmental variables. Some of these are also non-IP and rely in gateways to interconnect them to IP based networks. For instance, gateways are commonly used to allow data transmission/retrieval from ZigBee (IEEE.802.15.4) and Bluetooth (IEEE.802.15) devices.

The IPv6 over Low power Wireless Personal Area Networks (6LoWPAN) is one of the protocol stacks that has gained some importance in wireless sensor networks, that supports the implementation of an IP communication over IEEE.802.15.4. 6LoWPAN and the associated set of protocols support the communication of low-power devices with limited processing capabilities with any Internet device, though a border router. Thus instead of requiring a gateway, a border router is used.

At higher layers, two protocols are gaining importance: MQTT (OASIS, 2014) and CoAP (IETF, 2014). MQTT (MQ Telemetry Transport) is an open protocol designed for lightweight M2M communications that implements a publish/subscribe messaging mechanism. A node called broker, stores and relays information between the clients. However, MQTT runs over TCP.

CoAP is similar to the HTTP protocol, but runs over UDP, instead of TCP. It follows a client server model and uses the GET, PUT, POST, and DELETE methods. While this solution requires a lower level of complexity, the communication with Internet terminals is not made directly, requiring proxies.

Besides these solutions, a growing number of sensor devices run an HTTP/TCP/IP stack of protocols. They only need to connect to the home or building networks. However, while CoAP and MQTT are bandwidth efficient, HTTP is not and requires a power usage that may affect negatively batteries of constrained devices.

Whatever the protocol architecture is, each and all of these solutions form what is called IoT ecosystem, supporting the transmission of a large number of variables to a large number of monitoring devices.

In the field of energy, these devices work as a basic mechanism that allows a greater awareness about excessive consumption. But is it enough?

Decision Support Algorithms for Energy Management

The importance of decision support tools in energy management is reflected in several studies and developed platforms. For instance, Kebir & Maaroufi (2016) present a decision-support model to evaluate the possible inclusion of a battery energy storage system into an electrical feeder. In (Spiliotis, Marinakis, Doukas & Psarras, 2016) the authors define an action plan to optimally schedule the operation of heating and electricity systems, by integrating a decision support system with smart grid infrastructures and ICT solutions. Also in (Dadda & Ouhbi, 2014) the authors present a decision support system for renewable energy plant projects using a multi-criteria decision making method. Several algorithms are used to implement such decision support tools for energy efficiency.

Traditionally, energy efficiency of hotel units is achieved through periodic analysis from technicians that use their knowledge and expertise to execute judgements and notification of consumption levels that get above the expected ones.

In order to assess the building's consumptions, machine learning algorithms can be used to perform those evaluations systematically and automatically (Costa, Cabrita, Monteiro & Semião, 2015), supporting the analysis of a large number of hotel units and considering data from a wide range of sensors and sources. The anomaly detection procedure requires the use of prediction methods based on algorithms that learn from the building's historical levels of consumption. In order to improve the accuracy of the prediction, those algorithms can also consider several variables, like the values obtained from sensors that translate occupation levels or environmental data (e.g., inside/outdoor temperature and photovoltaic radiation). These statistical methods correlate the levels of energy consumption with their determining factors, perceiving when the measured values become distant from the expected ones. In order to accomplish the abnormal consumption detection several methods exist, including regression models (Lei, F. & Hu, P., 2009) or artificial intelligence models, which comprise Neural Networks (Magoulès, Zhao & Elizondo, 2013; Ekici & Aksoy, 2009), Support Vector Machines (Dong, Cao, & Lee, 2005), Bayesian Networks (Costa, Cabrita, Monteiro & Semião, 2015; Dong, Cao & Lee, 2005; Vlachopoulou, Chin, Fuller & Lu, 2014), among others.

In the following we describe some of these models and give some examples where they were used for energy management.

Machine Learning Algorithms

Machine Learning (ML) refers to an automated learning concept that uses different methods and models to learn from past experience through the analysis of historical data (Hackeling, 2014; Witten, Frank, Hall, & Pal, 2016; Marsland, 2015). They are usually classified in Supervised Learning versus Unsupervised Learning. Supervised learning algorithms are used when the machine training is supported on sets of pairs of inputs and corresponding targets pairs. As for unsupervised learning, the training of the machine is supported only in inputs, and tries to find patterns between data. Table 1 summarizes some of the main algorithms used in each type of learning method class.

Other classification of ML tasks arises when one considers the desired output of a machine-learned system. Classification methods, typically used in a supervised way, divide inputs into classes and the learner should produce a model to assigns new inputs to one or more of those classes. Regression methods are

Table 1. A classification of machine learning algorithms

Supervised Learning		Unsupervised Learning	
Classification	**Regression**	**Clustering**	**Dimensionality Reduction**
• Support Vector Classifier (SVC) • Linear SVC • Naive Bayes • K-Nearest Neighbours • Ensemble methods	• Stochastic Gradient Descent (SGD) Regressor • Ridge Regression • Least Absolute Shrinkage and Selection Operator (LASSO) • Elastic Net • SVR (support vector regression)	• Mean Shift • K-Means • Mini Batch K-Means • Spectral clustering • Gaussian mixture models	• Principal component analysis • Isomap • Spectral Embedding • Locally Linear Embedding

also supervised, being many times their outputs continuous, rather than discrete. Clustering methods also divide inputs into groups but, unlike in classification methods, the groups are not established beforehand. In dimensionality reduction inputs are simplified by transforming them into lower-dimensional spaces.

Among these solutions, regression based supervised learning solutions have been extensively used to support energy management, including renewable energy forecast (Zhang & Wang, 2015), financial impact of energy investments, load scheduling of electric vehicles (Sarikprueck, Lee, Kulvanitchaiyanunt, Chen & Rosenberger, 2014), and feedback systems for users (Stuart & Fleming, 2014).

The k-Nearest Neighbour (k-NN) algorithm was used to group similar training sequences (Zhang & Wang, 2015) in the forecast of solar power production, supported on several parameters including temperature, atmospheric pressure, solar radiation index, and precipitation.

In order to analyse wind power generation, some investigations were carried out in the context of wind force prediction and the consequent energy production. In one of them, Alaiz, Barbero & Dorronsoro (2012) compared the performances of the Lasso, Ridge Regression and Elastic-Net algorithms. The performance analysis was obtained by calculating the MAE (mean absolute error) and the RMAE (relative mean absolute error). The Elastic-Net algorithm showed better results, when compared with the other two algorithms. Abo-Khalil & Lee (2007) presented a support vector regression algorithm to tackle the same problem, showing also good results with a prediction error margin of 3.3%.

In the economic field of energy, Barnes & Balda (2013) made a study based on the Ridge Regression algorithm. The study was carried out to calculate the ideal level of capacity and scheduling of charge/discharge of batteries, as a function of the variation of energy prices throughout the day. The algorithm proved to be robust, with a prediction error of 10%.

Sarikprueck, Lee, Kulvanitchaiyanunt, Chen & Rosenberger (2014) used a hybrid technique for scheduling loads at electric vehicle charging stations. This method consists of the integration of SVC (support vector classification) for detection of peak occurrences and SVR (support vector regression) to estimate energy prices.

Some of these ML algorithms can be used to identify abnormal consumption levels. They can also be used in Human Machine Interfacing, building the so called feedback systems that encourage energy behaviour change. While this is an important issue, very little literature exists on the design of these systems for non-domestic buildings. As verified in (Black, Davidson & Retra, 2009) users are usually non-aware of energy consumption levels and the main importance of consumption feedback stands in its ability to make energy "more visible and more amenable to control" (Whittle & Jones, 2013). In this field, Stuart & Fleming (2014) developed a method to improve human machine communication of energy consumption levels. They use a linear regression algorithm that continuously compares the actual consumption data with the forecast obtained from a linear regression model. The discrepancy between them is classified in several levels and communicated to the users using smiles/faces with different levels of satisfaction.

Integration of Renewable Sources and Demand Response Mechanisms

In terms of generation from renewable energy sources, it is of crucial importance to hotel managers to understand which set of solutions allow reaching the goal of nearly zero energy consumption (European Parliament, 2010).

While solar thermal systems have been used for many years in water heating, a more recent legislation is being introduced all across Europe that allows the so called self-consumption. This means that users are allowed to produce electricity from renewable energy sources, while using it, selling the remainder to the grid, or consuming from the difference from the utility, when necessary.

In this case, by knowing the building's consumption profile, the goal is thus to define a set of actions that increase the correlation between production and consumption through measures that include rescheduling of loads (Monteiro, Eduardo, Cardoso & Semião, 2014) and a proper sizing of production systems.

The ability to manage energy consumption according to the production is a critical feature of what is known as Smart Grids, and a base for innovation, new products and services. In order to support this capability, the communication between different devices such as meters, appliances, electric vehicles, energy management systems and distributed energy resources (including renewable energy and storage) must occur using secure, standard and open procedures. In this context, several protocols have been or are being defined that extend beyond those of real time sensing, as they were specifically developed for energy management.

In this field, one important feature is the reception of price rates information. One of the communication protocols for Smart Grids that enables that price reception from the utility is the Open Automated Demand Response - OpenADR - version 2.0 (OpenADR Alliance, 2014) protocol. The OpenADR 2.0 is an evolution and extension of the first version, developed by the Demand Response Research Center at Lawrence Berkeley National Laboratory. It relies on standard-based transport mechanisms over IP communications, such as HTTP and XML Messaging and Presence Protocol (XMPP). It is supported by the OpenADR industrial alliance, having been developed as part of the standard OASIS Energy Interoperation 1.0 (OASIS, 2012).

Another protocol, more focused in Micro Grids is the Smart Energy Profile - SEP (IEEE, 2013), which results from the collaboration between the low-power ZigBee, Wi-Fi and HomePlug power-line technologies, building a power management architecture, supported on IP networks. SEP is built around several function-sets, each one representing a minimum set of behaviours to deliver a particular functionality. For instance, a metering function set allows devices to obtain consumption information from the smart-meter or any other device that has metering capability while the pricing function set allows a utility to send pricing signals to electrical devices such as smart-appliances and programmable thermostats.

Besides these, in March 2011, the Institute of Electrical and Electronics Engineers (IEEE) announced the approval and publication of the Standard for Ubiquitous Green Community Control Network Protocol (IEEE 1888 TM) (IEEE, 2011) within the Ubiquitous Green Community Control Network Protocol (UGCCNet). Originating in China, the IEEE 1888 standard defines itself as a global standard within the IoT, which aims at energy efficiency through the management of renewable energy, through communication using Internet protocols and Information, and communication technologies.

These protocols and architectures can already be used to obtain information about tariff rates from a Distribution System Operator (DSO) and to communicate with loads. They can also be used to obtain the consumption and generation curves of respectively one appliance or inverter. However, in this architecture there is one element missing. That element is the optimizer. In fact, in order to maintain the equilibrium of the grid while reducing costs and assuring human requirements, these set of protocols need to be complemented with the development of an optimization algorithm that gives the required intelligence to the system, defining when loads should start working.

There is a wide variety of optimization techniques referenced within the scope of Smart Grids, which can be used separately or combined, forming hybrid optimization solutions. Metaheuristics such as the

Genetic Algorithms (GA), are widely used to solve a large range of problems. GAs are deeply relevant for industrial applications, because they are capable of handling problems with non-linear constraints, multiple objectives, and dynamic components properties, that frequently appear in real problems (Roeva, Fidanova & Paprzycki, 2013). Other methods are also of great value in this field of research such as Neural Network, Particle Swarm Optimization, or Ant Colony Optimization (Momoh, 2012; Rahim, Khan, Javaid, Shaheen, Iqbal & Rehman, 2015; Vachirasricirikul & Ngamroo, 2014).

Platform for Promoting Energy Efficiency and Monitoring in Hotels

In the following we describe a platform that is being implemented for energy efficiency of hotel units in Portugal. The primary goal of the platform is to constitute a decision support tool for hoteliers that help them monitor, invest and manage their buildings with the aim of improving the associated energy efficiency and achieve the objectives of the nearly zero energy. The platform relies in a network of IoT and SCADA devices that monitors environmental data and electrical consumption levels. The retrieved information can be used to implement a decision support tool that: (1) helps hoteliers make investments in renewable energy sources; (2) decide the optimum mixed combination of load scheduling and tariff rates options according with the consumption profile of the building; (3) recommend passive measures for the improvement of energy efficiency; (4) actively detect abnormal levels of consumption; and (5) communicate with users in an easy and intuitive manner to make them participate in energy management.

General Architecture of the Sensor Platform

A general architecture of the monitoring system is illustrated in Figure 1., which comprises four enthalpy measurement points and three electrical energy meters. It also comprises environmental measurement units using IoT devices.

As depicted, each enthalpy measuring module simultaneously monitors 2 points of the water heating system. At each of these points two temperatures are measured through two thermistors and one water flow through a flow meter. The enthalpy meters connect to a switch over an Ethernet cable. The purpose of the enthalpy meters is to measure the heat of a system. In this case the heat of each point is determined using two temperature sensors and one water flow rate meter. The metering device implements an HTTP server and measured data is provided in the form of a JSON object.

The switch supports not only data transfer, but also powers all modules through Power-over-Ethernet (PoE). Thus the primary objective of the Ethernet switch is to interconnect, and power, several components of the system. All PoE devices use the IEEE 802.3af standard. The central computational unit uses a PoE splitter to separate data and power connections. In the enthalpy meter a module that supports PoE (Arduino Leonardo Ethernet with PoE) was also used.

The switch (a TP-Link TL-SG108PE) has 8 Ethernet ports, with 4 of them supporting PoE. The switch is in turn connected to the hotel's router, which gives access to the Internet and, through a DHCP server, assigns the IP addresses to all connected devices.

The electrical energy meters are self-powered from the power line. In terms of electrical grid, three energy meters were installed, represented in the right bottom side of Figure 1: a) exterior south pool and indoor pool; b) pumping systems of the north Outdoor pools (in the main distribution board); c) Total consumption of the hotel (in the main distribution board). The indoor and outdoor pools are considered two major energy consumers and therefore it was considered relevant to monitor them.

Figure 1. General architecture of the monitoring devices and communication technologies

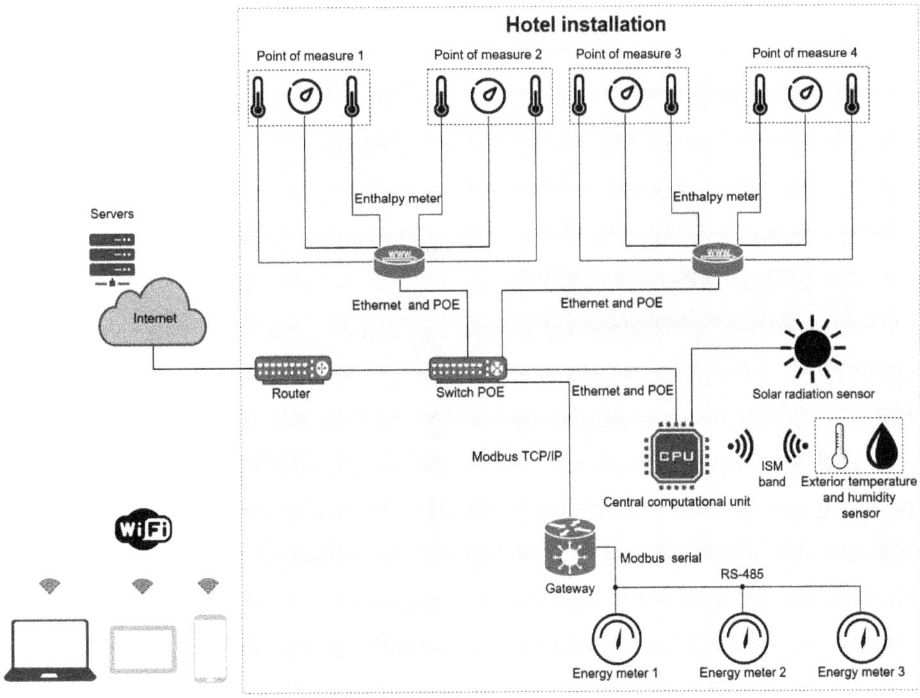

In order to monitor the three electric energy measurement points, energy meters (Schneider Electric, 2012) were used to communicate, using a Modbus protocol via a gateway (Schneider Electric, 2013), with the central processing unit. The gateway is connected to this unit through the Ethernet switch.

Each energy meter provides several parameters including voltage, current, frequency, power factor as well as active, reactive and apparent power. It also computes the total amount of active and reactive energy. All these parameters can be acquired through the Modbus serial over RS-485 network. Thus the energy meter is a Modbus Serial line Server end device. The gateway is used to interconnect Modbus serial line sub-network and TCP/IP. It is a master device on RS-485 network and consequently energy meters are slave devices. Each meter is identified explicitly by its unit identifier.

The central processing unit communicates with the gateway using the TCP/IP Modbus protocol, periodically acquiring the data from the electrical consumption and enthalpy readings. A microcomputer was used as the central unit, shown in the right image of Figure 2, which is also powered by PoE, through a PoE splitter. Collected data is sent to a cloud server on the Internet. The cloud server with a frond-end, implements an on-line platform which represents the data in different formats to different type of devices, including laptops, tablets or even smartphones.

The process of implementation of the project went through several phases. In the first phase the modules were developed and individual tests were carried out, including the calibration of the enthalpy meters. Afterwards several tests were made to verify if the whole system was working as expected.

In a second phase the developed modules were placed into operation at the hotel. Figure 2, in the left side, shows the gateway and one of the energy counters installed inside the electrical panel of the indoor and outdoor south pool.

Figure 2. Modules installed during the project: Enthalpy meter (upper left image); Electrical Energy meter (bottom left image); Central processing unit module (right image, bottom left side), POE splitter (right image, right side) and switch (right image, upper left side)

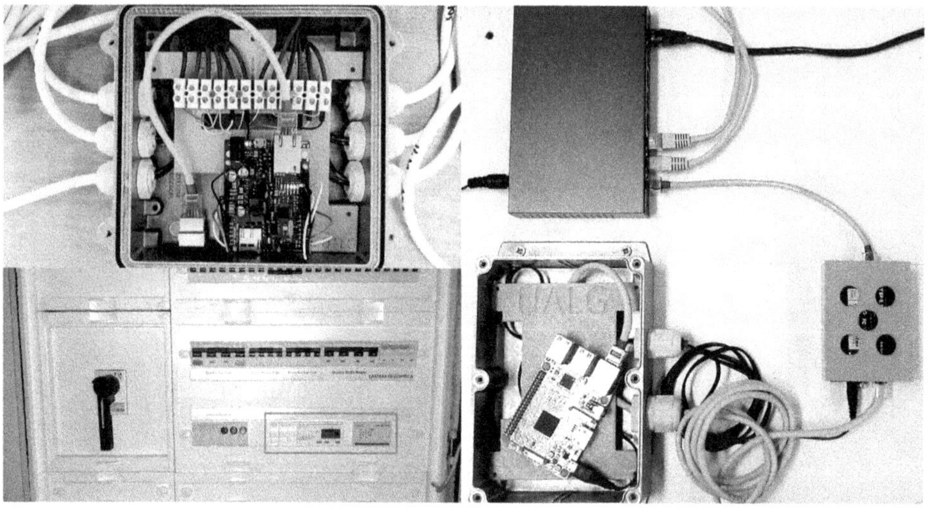

All these devices are currently integrated into the existing network infrastructure of the hotel. The switch is connected to the hotel's routers that assign static IP address for each device through its DHCP server.

Implementation of the Electronic Sensor Devices

The central computational unit features the Broadcom BCM2837 system-on-chip (SoC) and the Microchip's LAN9514. The latter is used to provide USB and 10/100 Mbps Ethernet connectivity. The device uses a Linux distribution as an operating system.

The enthalpy meter was constructed using a Atmega 32u4 microcontroller, a Power over Ethernet (PoE) module and a Wiznet W5500 embedded Ethernet controller. The Atmega 32u4 is a low-power 8-bit AVR RISC-based microcontroller. It features 32 kbyte self-programming flash program memory, 2.5 kbyte SRAM, 1 kbyte EEPROM, USB 2.0 full-speed/low speed device, 12-channel 10-bit A/D-converter, and a JTAG interface for on-chip-debug. The W5500 chip is a Hardwired TCP/IP embedded Ethernet controller that enables easier Internet connection for embedded systems using SPI (Serial Peripheral Interface).

In the enthalpy meters the heat of the system is measured through the following equation:

$$Q = 4.18 M \Delta T \quad (1)$$

where Q represents the heat, in kilowatts, M the water flow rate, in liters/second, and ΔT the temperature difference between two points, in °C.

As it has been described above there are two temperature monitoring points per channel: one for hot water in the supply line and second for cold water in the return line. The measurement is noninvasive

– thermally isolated sensors measure the surface temperature of the pipe. A Negative Temperature Coefficient (NTC) thermistor was used as a temperature sensor. The thermistor is a variable resistor, such that the resistance decreases, in a non-linear way, as temperature rises.

In these situations, a Steinhart–Hart or β parameter equation is typically used to obtain an approximation of the temperature from the resistance. In this case different mathematical models were tested to try to obtain a minimal error in the curve fitting process. In the performed tests, the best results were obtained using Weibull model:

$$t = a - be^{-cr^{d}} \tag{2}$$

where t represents the temperature, in °C, e the Euler's number, r the thermistor resistance, in Ω, and $a, b, c,$ and d are constants obtained through calibration tests. Using this model, the obtained curve was compared with the original *r-t* points.

The temperature sensors are connected to analog inputs of Atmega 32u4 using a voltage divider that places the signal around a continuous component. Thus the meters read tension values instead of resistance and then convert them to temperature values.

The flow rate is measured using a water meter, with a pulse output. The pulse output is used by the Atmega 32u4 to counts the impulses, multiplying them by the ratio between liters per pulse of the associated meter.

The central computational unit periodically gets new readings and registers the update time instance. The water flow rate is obtained by dividing the difference between two consecutive readings by the time elapsed between these readings. Then the actual heat can be calculated using the formula described above.

Monitoring Platform and Applications

The measurements made by the elements described in the previous section are sent to an online platform, based on the open platform Emoncms (Hudson, Reed, & Lea, 2017). The data received in this platform is stored in a database and can be viewed in real time. Historical data can also be downloaded.

In order to visualize the data, several dashboards were created, some were adapted to the screens of mobile terminals, and others were more oriented to the size and definitions supported by computer terminals. In addition, a mobile application was developed for mobile terminals.

For visualization from computers, several dashboards were created that allow the visualization in some detail of the various consumption parameters. An example of one of these dashboards is shown on the left side of Figure 3.

Each of the charts depicted in the Figure 3 allows the adjustment of the horizontal axis scale to display one day (D), one week (W), one month (M), or one year (Y). It is also possible to increase the horizontal definition (with the "+" button), decrease it (with the "-" button) and move it further to the left or right (with the "<" and ">" buttons).

For each of the electric and enthalpy energy meters, a specific dashboard was created, which graphically displays the various parameters monitored. In the case of the electric energy meter the parameters stored and displayed graphically are: (1) active power, (2) reactive power, (3) apparent power, (4) current and voltage in each phase, (5) power factor, and (6) frequency of the electrical network.

Figure 3. Example of a dashboard developed for computer terminals (left side) and Android application developed for hoteliers and technicians, with the main window (on the right top) and an example of a dashboard (on the right bottom)

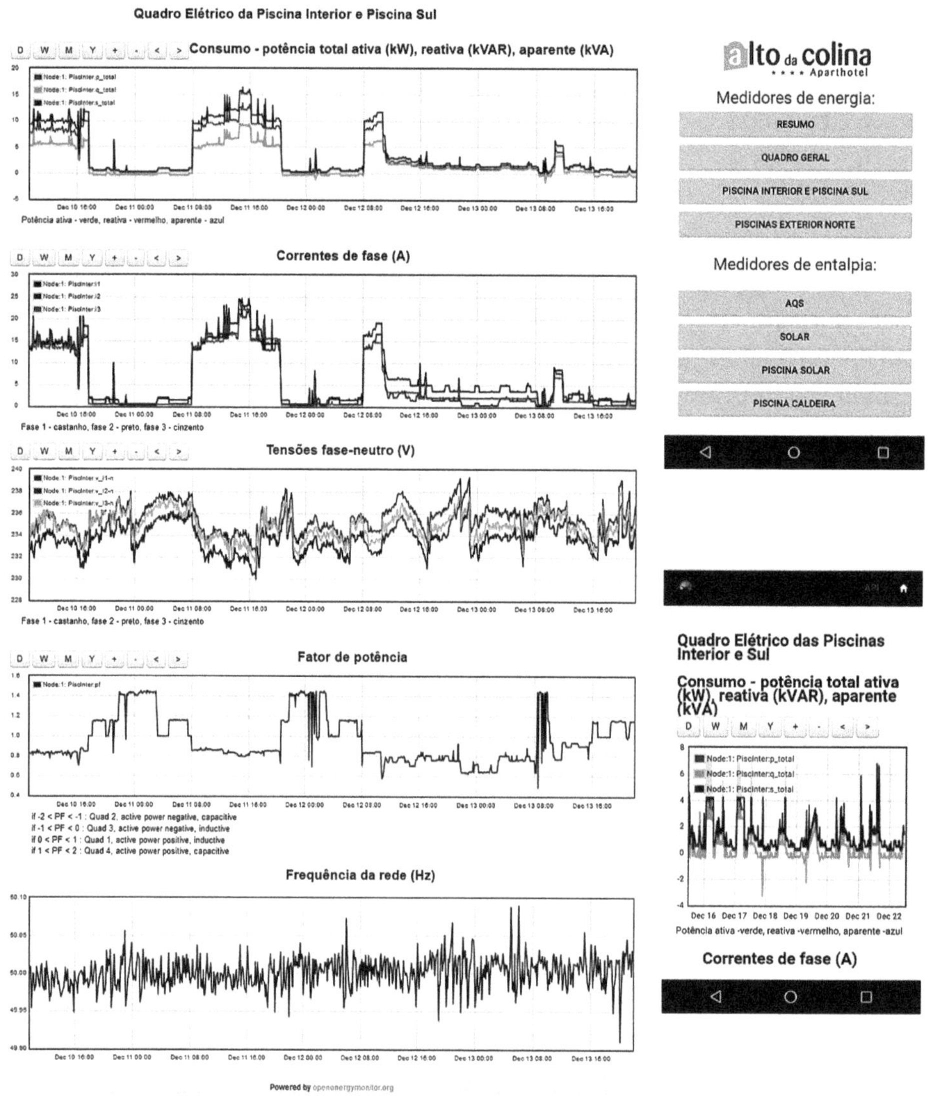

A dashboard with the summary of the active powers of the three electrical energy measurements and the daily consumption of active and reactive power by each point was also constructed.

In the case of enthalpy meters, the following parameters are represented in the associated dashboards: (1) the temperatures of water at the entrance and exit of the monitored point, (2) the flow rate, and (3) the heat.

In order to access the data from a mobile phone, an Android application (App) was developed. The main window of the application is shown in Figure 3, right side, top, with several menu options pointing to the measurement points of the hotel.

The main menu is divided in two categories: energy meters and enthalpy meters. Each menu item comprises a button that when selected opens an "Web View" container showing a dashboard adapted for the application of the intended measurement point. An example is shown in Figure 3, right side, bottom. The contents shown in the dashboard depends on the measured point.

Anomaly Detection Using Machine Learning

The data gathered during several days/weeks/months supports an important feature of the platform, that is the detection of abnormal consumption levels. Anomalies can be detected by comparing the expected value with the actual measured consumption level. The expected value is obtained by learning the building's behaviour, using historical data. Thus, if the difference between expected and measured values gets above or below a certain limit, an action will be triggered. For instance, an e-mail will be sent. However, the accuracy of detecting anomalies, is proportional to the accuracy of prediction normal consumption values. Thus before detecting anomalies the model should be able to predict the majority of the consumption values with a low level of error.

After implementing a forecast algorithm, in the tuning phase, the first steps are to test and improve its accuracy, by reducing the mean error between forecasted values and the measured ones. To translate these errors, two equations are largely used: the Mean Absolute Error (MAE) translates the mean of the absolute differences between the estimated value $\hat{y}$ and actual value y, using equation

$$MAE = \frac{1}{n}\sum_{i=1}^{n}\left|\hat{y} - y\right| \tag{3}$$

and the Mean Absolute Percentage Error (MAPE), which "normalises" the errors by dividing them by y,

$$MAPE = \frac{1}{n}\sum_{i=1}^{n}\left|\frac{\hat{y} - y}{y}\right| \tag{4}$$

Given the importance of linear regression methods in prediction models, in the following a brief description of them are presented. We will also describe some classification methods.

Linear Regression Methods

Linear regression (Hastie, Tibshirani, & Friedman, 2009) is a technique to describe, through models, the behaviour of a given system. Simple linear regression uses only one feature while the multiple linear regression incorporates several features that describe its behaviour. The behavior function can be stated as

$$h_\theta\left(x_1, x_2, \ldots, x_n\right) = \theta_0 + \theta_1 x_1 + \ldots + \theta_n x_n \tag{5}$$

where $\theta_i\left(i=0,1,\ldots,n\right)$ are the regression constant for each one of the *n* presented features. Given the behaviour function, the objective of the, Ordinary Least Squares, regression method is to minimize the quadratic mean error of the model, given by

$$J\left(\theta_0,\theta_1\ldots\theta_n\right)=\frac{1}{2m}\sum_{i=1}^{m}\left(h_\theta\left(x^{(i)}\right)-y^{(i)}\right)^2 \tag{6}$$

for a set of *m* samples of the form $\left(x^{(i)},y^{(i)}\right)$. The cost function is thus the sum of the quadratic differences between the estimated value, obtained from equation (5), with the real value $\left(y\right)$. For this equation to describe the behavior of the system, the weights of each coefficient need to be calculated, so that the cost is the minimum. Several methods can be used to accomplish this goal. The normal equation method computes the regression constants, θ, using formula

$$\theta=\left(X^TX\right)^{-1}X^ty \tag{7}$$

where X is the design matrix. One disadvantage of this method is that it imposes the computation of an inverse matrix whose complexity may imply a prohibitive computational cost if the number of features is large.

The gradient descent method is usually more appropriate to be used in systems with a large number of variables. This method is described by the following iterative expression:

$$\theta_j:=\theta_j-\alpha\frac{d}{d\theta_j}J\left(\theta_0,\theta_1\ldots\theta_n\right),\left(j=0,1,2,\ldots,n\right) \tag{8}$$

where α is the learning coefficient that is used to obtain the global minimum. If the parameter α is too small, many iterations can be necessary to obtain the global minimum, however if the parameter is too large the global minimum may not be found.

Particular methods address some of the problems of Ordinary Least Squares, like the Ridge Regression (by imposing a penalty on the size of coefficients, by minimizing them through the quadratic residual sum), the Lasso regression (estimates coefficients in a penalizing way in order to minimize or even discard some of the coefficients according to the defined penalty parameter, used to estimate sparse coefficients), or the Elastic Net regression (trained with norms L1 and L2 prior as regularizer). Combinations of the cost functions with different types of optimizers also are used to address particular cases, like the use of a stochastic gradient descent learning routine that supports various loss and penalty functions to construct a linear regression model. This method works well for a large number of samples and can be used with several error functions (e.g., quadratic error function, Huber error function or epsilon error function).

Classification Methods

Classification methods are those that establish a qualitative prediction, that is, group the data into classes. Some of the most common procedures are *k*-NN (*k*-Nearest Neighbors) and the Bayesian classifier methods.

The concept of the *k*-NN method (Murty & Devi, 2011) is to find the *k* training samples that are at a Euclidean distance closer to the point of estimation and predicting in which group it makes sense to insert that point. ON the other hand, the concept of the Bayesian method is a probabilistic classification based on the Bayes' theorem where it is possible to determine the probability of a certain point belonging to one of the classes through conditioning probabilities. In this case, a relation is made between the point and the probability of belonging to a certain class, as for the *k*-NN method the relation is made between all the points through the distances. Usually the number of classes is much lower than the number of samples, so the Bayesian method is faster since computation only affects the probabilities of the classes.

The use of this and other ML methods will be further addressed in a following section which focus on the building of the decision support platform.

Decision Support on Passive Measures

Besides active measures like the ones described previously, a platform for decision support also needs to include methods to increase the building efficiency, in terms of passive measures.

The contributions of the passive techniques in the reduction of the energy consumption in hotels are multiple. First, they approximate the interior temperature to the comfort temperature without the need for active systems, which drastically reduces the energy demand of the building. Secondly, they equate the temperature of the air with that of the walls, floor and ceiling, which results in a considerable increase of the comfort for users. The passive techniques applied to the construction of hotels, unlike those based only on the operation of air conditioning systems, improve the daily thermal stability of the environment inside the rooms. This avoids the feeling of suffocating heat when we access a room that has been unoccupied for several hours. Thanks to this thermal stability, it is unnecessary to activate the air conditioning at most hours of the day, which not only reduces energy consumption but also improves acoustic comfort compared to air-based systems. Finally, the particular conditions of the Algarve warm climate and the maximum solar radiation that occurs at noon, favours the coupling of the photovoltaic energy generation curve and the consumption curve, when it comes to the energy supply for the air conditioning systems.

The main passive strategies for improving energy efficiency in hotels are summarized below.

Reduction of the Thermal Transmittance of the External Envelope

The improvement of the thermal insulation of the enclosure results in the improvement of its capacity to reduce the flow of heat from the outside to the interior of the building in hot weather conditions. It is the best way to reduce the thermal load by conduction through the enclosure. It is important to emphasize that it is essential to eliminate thermal bridges in the enclosure, for which it is necessary to adequately plan the construction section of the enclosure, paying special attention to the singular points (columns and slabs coverings, corners, frames, blinds, etc.).

The two techniques most indicated for the improvement of the thermal insulation of the enclosure in hotels are the system of thermal insulation by the exterior (ETICS) and the ventilated facade. In the first case a certain thickness (between 5 and 25 cm) of insulation material such as plastic foams (EPS, XPS and PUR) or mineral wools (GW and RW), should be added, mechanically anchored to the outer sheet of the original enclosure. The resultant set is coated with continuous material (lime mortar, cement or similar) which provides an aesthetic improvement to the solution. In the case of the ventilated facade, the insulation material is also fixed mechanically to the original enclosure, but the finish material (consisting of large format plates of stone, ceramic, metallic or phenolic) is arranged in a different plane fixed with metal lightweight profiles (galvanized steel or aluminium), producing a continuous air chamber in between. In both cases, the advantage of applying the treatment by the exterior is that it facilitates the elimination of thermal bridges and avoids the reduction of indoor space.

For the specific case of the roof, a good solution is to improve the existing insulation by installing floating extruded polystyrene (XPS) sheets. If the cover is non-passable, it can be covered with a 10 cm thick layer of clean white gravel to keep the XPS on the site when subject to strong winds.

Improvement of Exterior Frames

As we improve the opaque part of the envelope, we will have to do the same with the exterior carpentries, installing high-performance glass-frame assemblies. Sliding joinery systems are not acceptable due to their low level of sealing, although this is an issue that we will analyse below. The most suitable frames are multi-chamber PVC and wood frames, although high performance aluminium with double thermal bridge break can be equivalent. The glasses, single chamber or double chamber filled with argon gas and with low emissive film for the reduction of the solar factor.

Solar Protection of Hollows

In hot weather it is important to protect the gaps from the direct incidence of the sun's rays, as they produce significant gains in heat from radiation. This hollow protection will be different depending on the exact latitude and orientation of the gap to be protected. In the case of hollows facing south, the most appropriate protection consists of the installation of horizontal overhangs with variable depth depending on the height of the hole. Another possible option is to install slats and lattices that fill the amount of light that enters through the well while protecting it from direct radiation. Holes with east and west orientation are more difficult to protect with fixed systems since the angle of inclination of the solar rays is much reduced at sunrise and sunset. In all cases, the solar protections must be installed on the exterior of the glass, since those arranged by the interior do not reduce the consequent greenhouse effect.

Increase of the Enclosure Albedo

The energy performance of an insulating coating on the exterior of the facade improves if we also maximize its albedo by choosing light-coloured finishes. It is the technique inherited from the white Mediterranean villages. Reflecting the greater amount of incident sunlight, we are able to minimize solar gain by radiation. This strategy is especially interesting in the south and west oriented facades since in this area of the northern hemisphere they are the ones that receive the most amount of solar radiation.

Airtightness of the Enclosure

Another factor of important incidence in the energy consumption of the hotels is related to the lack of tightness of its envelope. When uncontrolled infiltrations of outdoor air occur in hot weather, it is necessary to compensate for all those thermal gains with active systems that consume a lot of energy. Instead, the best possible strategy in warm weather is to keep the outer envelope as leak tight as possible during the day, making it permeable through cross ventilation by opening windows and doors at night to encourage the dissipation of the internal heat load accumulated during the day. Getting the conditions for this cross ventilation is not easy in a typical hotel room. Usually, two of its four limits are borders with other rooms and the third one separates it from the access corridor. In order to compensate it, the dimensions of the exterior windows must be increased, maximizing its practicable surface.

In order to achieve the objective of maximum air tightness, it will be necessary to install casement windows with very low permeability, taking care of the detail of its installation, especially in the encounter with the brick wall. In the construction tradition of massive type of the Algarve and the west of Andalusia, the opaque part of the enclosure will have to be covered in its interior of cement mortar or plaster in continuity in its entire surface. Installation ducts, including corrugated tubes for house electrical conductors, should be conveniently sealed, especially when communicating the inside (register box) and the outside (terrace light, outside plugs, etc.). A blower door test (BDT) with a result of not exceeding 0.6 rev / hr at 50 Pa will be performed to check compliance with the desired sealing objective.

Form Factor

The value of the form factor, or quotient between the outer thermal envelope surface and the internal air volume of the hotel, also has a significant impact on the final energy consumption. More compact values reduce internal heat gains and reduce the need for air conditioning. It is therefore fundamental that the architectural design of the hotel building achieves the maximum reduction of the building form factor.

Dual Flow Ventilation With Heat Recovery

The double flow ventilation with heat recovery allows the necessary airtightness of the enclosure, without impairing the quality of the indoor air of the room. Providing the system with a high efficiency heat exchanger (> 85%) allows us to take full advantage of the inverted energy to compensate for overheating without generating a load added by ventilation.

Natural Night Ventilation

On most summer nights, the outdoor temperature drops below the indoor comfort level, so it is very important to disconnect the active systems and to favour the dissipation of the thermal load accumulated during the day using the night sky as an energy sump. The effectiveness of this solution is maximized when there is cross ventilation or the possibility of generating chimney effect, objectives both difficult to achieve in a standard hotel room. It is necessary in any case, to take due care to re-close the windows before the outside temperature begins to rise from dawn.

Refreshing Radiant Ceiling System Supplied by Photovoltaic Energy

The passive solutions adopted will in any case lead us to drastically reduce the energy demand of the hotel, and yet under certain adverse weather conditions (summer noon and early afternoon) we will need a cooling system that reduces the temperature inside. The use of a system based on radiant surfaces installed in the ceiling represent a double advantage. In the first place, it is a system based on a large emission surface and a lower thermal gradient than the conventional air-based one, which greatly improves user comfort (and favours the negative temperature gradient from head to feet). Secondly, it acts as an accumulator of the energy of the photovoltaic installation in cold water tanks for the primary circuit, coupling the generation and demand curves to the maximum, since the hours of greater solar radiation coincide with those of greater need of refrigeration.

Vegetation and Landscaping

It is well known the beneficial effect that the implantation of vegetation has on the adjoining building, because it generates a microclimate that softens the impact of the high temperatures. Of special incidence is the beneficial effect that the shading of the facade and the hollows of the enclosure with trees causes in the reduction of the superheating of the building. Outdoor recreational areas and gardens are often an important aspect in the provision of services of a hotel establishment, so handled carefully by the maintenance service, can become an important resource for reducing the consumption of the building.

Building the Decision Support Platform

The decision support platform for hoteliers and technical staff should comprise several modules. In the following, we summarize them and discuss the main involved features and benefits.

Analysis of the Electricity Contract

Costs are the main driving force that is capable of motivating hoteliers to refurbish and update their installations. The most basic source of information about consumption costs are invoices. Invoices from the electricity supplier specify the amount of money that the hotel pays for each component of the spent energy. This also extends to other sources of energy.

The information in electricity invoices can give us relevant information. For instance, it can help verify if the power factor is too low and thus if the installation requires a capacitor bank. It can also help verify if the costs payed in time of use tariff periods are balanced, leading to recommendations about shifting the working periods of electrical equipment. The cost per kWh of each tariff rate is another important information that can be obtained from it. As we will discuss later these costs are required to scale and analyse the payback period of investments made in renewable energy sources.

In order to gather the information from invoices, the platform should have an online form, were hotel managers can insert the most important data found in these invoices. The platform can then identify some of the identified weaknesses and draw some basic recommendations.

Recommendations Resulting From a Real-Time Monitoring System

At a second stage, the data obtained by a real-time monitoring system enables the identification of the circuits/equipment that are consuming more energy, or that are consuming out of the normal range. The consumption profile of some electrical circuits can be used to define what electrical equipment should be rescheduled to work in the periods where tariff rates are lower, complementing the information about the costs obtained from the invoice.

In hotels, the average consumption per gest or per room is also an important metric that enables the assessment of its energy efficiency and the implementation of a comparative rating for hotels. This however requires data about the occupancy, which needs to be obtained from the hotel staff or using information obtained from other sources, like for instance the number of active Wi-Fi users.

In order to motivate the load scheduling of electrical equipment, the platform should clearly represent the cost per kWh during the day and the total instantaneous cost that is being spent. Also, a list of recommendations should be made to technical staff. For instance, the swimming pool pumps should work less in peak tariff rates periods.

Finally, the real time monitoring system also supports the comparison between different time of use tariff rates, either in the same utility company or between such companies.

Anomaly Detection

The monitoring platform, when combined with anomaly detection algorithms, can trigger alarms that inform hotel managers and technicians when the consumption of some parts, or of the global installation, gets out of its normal range. To accomplish it, these algorithms need to accurately define what are the expected consumption levels, considering the data obtained from several sensors like temperature and radiation (Costa, Cabrita, Monteiro & Semião, 2015). Occupancy is another important variable that can be used to improve the accuracy of the model.

Besides consumption, anomaly detection algorithms can also evaluate nearly all of the monitored variables. For instance the system can automatically detect if the tensions and currents in three-phase electric circuits are balanced, or if the water temperature in some points of the heating system is within their normal range.

The aim of such alarm systems is to prevent users from continuously monitor charts and values. Finally, the same algorithms can also be used to improve the awareness of clients, technical staff and hoteliers about the normal versus expected levels of consumption. The use of emoticons, like the one used in (Stuart & Fleming, 2014), is one of such tools.

Recommendations Concerning the Introduction of Passive Measures

The integration of passive measures in a decision support platform has the advantage of supporting recommendations that derive from long time measurements. Thus instead of making general recommendations, that apply to nearly all buildings, an IoT based decision support tool should be able to make recommendations that reflect the actual problems of the building, monitored by the sensor devices. For instance, by monitoring the outside and inside temperature in several hotel rooms and halls, recommendations can be made in terms of improvement of the thermal insulation of the enclosure, shading, natural night ventilation. Thus, this requires the implementation of an IoT network to gather the relevant information of the building.

Recommendations Concerning Introduction of Renewable Energy Sources

In terms of renewable energy sources two types of recommendations can be made. If the objective is to reduce the payback period of the investment, the production curve of the renewable energy sources should be maintained under the consumption curve for most of the time instants. This guaranties a reduction of the costs payed to the utility company. When the generation curve gets above the consumption level the difference between these power levels will be fed into the utility grid. When this happens the benefits are lower as the fed energy is usually payed at a lower rate. As the consumption and production levels vary significantly during week days and months of the year a long term analysis is recommended.

If in turn, the objective is to achieve the nearly zero building target, a higher payback period will likely be obtained, as more energy needs to be generated, increasing the probability of feeding energy into the utility grid.

These recommendations will result from optimization algorithms that require data from solar radiation sensors, time of use energy cost and consumption energy levels.

CONCLUSION

In order to improve the energy efficiency of hotels and even comply with the requirements of a nearly zero energy building, a significant effort must be made by hotel managers in several fields. While these measures can be categorized in passive versus active actions, a platform that helps change the building efficiency requires combining them all, integrating sensor devices, monitoring, intelligence and knowledge.

The resulting decision support platform should enable several levels of recommendations, including those that comprise or derive from: (1) the analysis of the electricity contract, (2) a real-time monitoring system, (3) anomaly detection algorithms, (4) passive measures, and (5) the introduction of renewable energy sources.

In terms of real time monitoring of consumption, the representation of data using charts or values is usually non-friendly and require continuous human verification. Thus automated methods play an important role in alleviating user intervention. These methods use the consumption profile of the building to recommending the best practices that should be taken. As different buildings have different consumption patterns and characteristics, the recommendations can differ significantly.

Knowledge about passive energy efficiency measures also plays an important role. The platform has the potential of conveying information about good construction practices, while evaluating the building behaviour with sensors. Thus, demand reduction needs to be confirmed later, with the monitoring systems.

FUTURE RESEARCH DIRECTIONS

There is still a considerable number of functions to include in the decision support platform. The IoT and SCADA networks are currently working. Using the hotel testbed, a study was also made that comprised the analysis of the electricity contract and the sizing of renewable energy sources. This study led to several recommendations.

In the next steps, we will focus in the implementation of the anomaly detection algorithms in the online platform and in the recommendations comprising passive measures.

REFERENCES

Abo-Khalil, A. G., & Lee, D. (2007). SVR-based Wind Speed Estimation for Power Control of Wind Energy Generation System. *2007 Power Conversion Conference*, Nagoya. doi:10.1109/PCCON.2007.373152

Agência Andaluza de Energia. (2011). *Andalucía Renovable. Junta de Andalucía*. Retrieved January 17, 2017, from http://goo.gl/NSvbNY

Alaiz, C. M., Barbero, A., & Dorronsoro, J. R. (2012). Sparse methods for wind energy prediction. *The 2012 International Joint Conference on Neural Networks (IJCNN)*. doi:10.1109/IJCNN.2012.6252843

AREAL & INETI. (2006). *Avaliação do Recurso Solar da Região do Algarve*. Retrieved January 17, 2017, from http://goo.gl/yj1mzQ

ASHRAE. (2003). *BACnet - A Data Communication Protocol for Building Automation and Control Networks*. Retrieved January 18, 2017, from http://www.bacnet.org/Addenda/Add-2001-135d.pdf

Attia, S., Gratia, E., De Herde, A., & Hensen, J. L. M. (2012). Simulation-based decision support tool for early stages of zero-energy building design. *Energy and Building*, *49*, 2–15. doi:10.1016/j.enbuild.2012.01.028

Barnes, A. K., & Balda, J. C. (2013). Sizing and economic assessment of energy Storage with real-time pricing and ancillary services. *2013 4th IEEE International Symposium on Power Electronics for Distributed Generation Systems (PEDG)*. doi:10.1109/pedg.2013.6785651

Black, R., Davidson, P., & Retra, K. (2009). *Facilitating energy saving behaviours among university student residents*. Institute for Land Water and Society, Report No. 53. Retrieved January 17, 2017, from https://goo.gl/Nt0ySw

Castellani, A. P., Ministeri, G., Rotoloni, M., Vangelista, L., & Zorzi, M. (2012). Interoperable and globally interconnected smart grid using ipv6 and 6lowpan. *2012 IEEE International Conference on Communications (ICC)*, 6473–6478.

Algarve, C. C. D. R. (2015). Estratégia Regional de Investigação e Inovação para a Especialização Inteligente. RIS3 - ALGARVE 2014-2020. Faro.

Chandel, S. S., Sharma, V., & Marwah, B. M. (2016). Review of energy efficient features in vernacular architecture for improving indoor thermal comfort conditions. *Renewable & Sustainable Energy Reviews*, *65*, 459–477. doi:10.1016/j.rser.2016.07.038

Chen, D., Brown, J., & Khan, J. Y. (2014). Performance analysis of a distributed 6lowpan network for the smart grid applications. *Intelligent Sensors, Sensor Networks and Information Processing (ISSNIP), 2014 IEEE Ninth International Conference on*, 1–6.

Choi, S., Lee, W., Youn, J. H., Moore, D., & Schuette, M. (2015). An energy-efficient neighbor discovery protocol for 6lowpan smart grid applications. Wireless Communications and Networking Conference Workshops (WCNCW), 2015 IEEE, 52–57.

Ciampi, M., Leccese, F., & Tuoni, G. (2003). Ventilated facades energy performance in summer cooling of buildings. *Solar Energy*, *75*(6), 491–502. doi:10.1016/j.solener.2003.09.010

Costa, H., Cabrita, C., Monteiro, J., & Semião, J. (2015). *Mecanismo de Deteção de Consumos Anómalos em Redes Energéticas Inteligentes. CRC2015*, 19–20.

Dadda, A., & Ouhbi, I. (2014). A decision support system for renewable energy plant projects. *2014 International Conference on Next Generation Networks and Services (NGNS)*, 356-362. doi:10.1109/NGNS.2014.6990278

DALI Activity Group. (2001). *Digital Addressable Lighting Interface Manual*. Retrieved January 18, 2017 from goo.gl/vVJzup

Dong, B., Cao, C., & Lee, S. E. (2005). Applying support vector machines to predict building energy consumption in tropical region. *Energy and Building*, *37*(5), 545–553. doi:10.1016/j.enbuild.2004.09.009

Echelon. (2009). *Introduction to the LonWorks® Platform, revision 2, Echelon*. Retrieved January 18, 2017, from goo.gl/iYnoHl

Ekici, B. B., & Aksoy, U. T. (2009). Prediction of building energy consumption by using artificial neural networks. *Advances in Engineering Software*, *40*(5), 356–362. doi:10.1016/j.advengsoft.2008.05.003

Emoncms. (2017). *Emoncms Platform*. Retrieved January 17, 2017, from emoncms.org

EnOcean GmbH. (2016). *EnOcean Standard ESP3 Specification V1.30*. Retrieved January 18, 2017 from https://goo.gl/JLTxou

EnPROVE. (2013). *Energy Consumption Prediction with Building Usage Measurements for Software Based Decision Support*. Retrieved January 17, 2017, from www.enprove.eu

European Commission, Institute for Energy and Transport. (2006). *Solar radiation and PV maps – Europe*. Retrieved January 17, 2017, from http://goo.gl/wIiPed

European Parliament, Council on the Energy Performance of Buildings. (2010). Directive 2010/31/EU of the European Parliament, (OJ L153 18.6.2010), 19 May 2010.

Gagliano, A., Nocera, F., & Aneli, S. (2016). Thermodynamic analysis of ventilated façades under different wind conditions in summer period. *Energy and Building*, *122*, 131–139. doi:10.1016/j.enbuild.2016.04.035

Gokarakonda, S., & Kumar, A. (2016). Passive Architectural Design Index applied to vernacular and passive buildings. *The International Journal of Environmental Studies*, *73*(4), 563–572. doi:10.1080/00207233.2016.1178982

Hastie, T., Tibshirani, R., & Friedman, J. H. (2009). The elements of statistical learning: data mining, inference, and prediction: with 200 full-color illustrations. In Linear Methods for Regression (pp. 43-94). New York: Springer.

Hackeling, G. (2014). *Mastering machine learning with scikit-learn: apply effective learning algorithms to real-world problems using scikit-learn*. Birmingham, UK: Packt Publishing Ltd.

Hglund, J., Ilic, D., Karnouskos, S., Sauter, R., & da Silva, P. G. (2012). Using a 6lowpan smart meter mesh network for event-driven monitoring of power quality. *Smart Grid Communications (SmartGrid-Comm), 2012 IEEE Third International Conference on*, 448–453.

Hudson, G., Reed, P., & Lea, T. (2017). *Emoncms: GitHub repository*. Retrieved January 17, 2017, from http://github.com/emoncms

IEEE. (2011). *IEEE standard for ubiquitous green community control network protocol*. IEEE-SA board of governors, IEEE Std, 2011, 10, 016–5997.

IEEE. (2013). IEEE Adoption of Smart Energy Profile 2.0 Application Protocol Standard. *IEEE Std, 2030*, 1–348.

IETF. (2014). *The Constrained Application Protocol (CoAP)*. IETF RFC 7252. Retrieved January 18, 2017 from https://tools.ietf.org/html/rfc7252

Kebir, N., & Maaroufi, M. (2016). Decision-support model for battery energy storage system inclusion in grid-connected PV systems for medium voltage applications. *2016 IEEE International Conference on Renewable Energy Research and Applications (ICRERA)*, 897-902. doi:10.1109/ICRERA.2016.7884465

KNX. (2017). *KNX Specifications*. Retrieved January 18, 2017 from https://goo.gl/ENqlWB

Lee, S. W., Lim, C. H., & Salleh, E. I. B. (2016). Reflective thermal insulation systems in building: A review on radiant barrier and reflective insulation. *Renewable & Sustainable Energy Reviews, 65*, 643–661. doi:10.1016/j.rser.2016.07.002

Lei, F., & Hu, P. (2009). A baseline model for office building energy consumption in hot summer and cold winter region. *International Conference on Management and Service Science (MASS'09)*, Beijing, China. doi:10.1109/ICMSS.2009.5301031

LifeSaver. (2013). *Context Sensitive Monitoring of Energy Consumption to Support Energy Savings and Emissions Trading in Industry*. Retrieved January 17, 2017, from www.lifesaver-fp7.eu

Lu, C.-W., Li, S.-C., & Wu, Q. (2011). Interconnecting zigbee and 6lowpan wireless sensor networks for smart grid applications. *Sensing Technology (ICST), 2011 Fifth International Conference on*, 267–272.

Magoulès, F., Zhao, H., & Elizondo, D. (2013). Development of an RDP neural network for building energy consumption fault detection and diagnosis. *Energy and Building, 62*, 133–138. doi:10.1016/j.enbuild.2013.02.050

Marsland, S. (2015). *Machine learning: An algorithmic perspective*. CRC Press.

Modbus. (2006). *MODBUS over Serial Line Specification and Implementation Guide V1.02, December 20*. Retrieved January 18, 2017, from http://www.modbus.org/docs/Modbus_over_serial_line_V1_02.pdf

Modbus. (2012). *MODBUS Application Protocol Specification V1.1b3, April 26*. Retrieved January 18, 2017, from http://www.modbus.org/docs/Modbus_Application_Protocol_V1_1b3.pdf

Momoh, J. (2012). *Smart grid: Fundamentals of design and analysis* (Vol. 63). John Wiley & Sons. doi:10.1002/9781118156117

Monteiro, J., Cardoso, P. J. S., Serra, R., & Fernandes, L. (2014). Evaluation of the Human Factor in the Scheduling of Smart Appliances in Smart Grids. *16th International Conference on Human-Computer Interaction*. doi:10.1007/978-3-319-07446-7_52

Monteiro, J., Eduardo, J., Cardoso, P. J. S., & Semião, J. (2014). A Distributed Load Scheduling Mechanism for Micro Grids. *IEEE International Conference on Smart Grid Communications (IEEESmartGridComm)*. doi:10.1109/SmartGridComm.2014.7007659

Murty, M. N., & Devi, V. S. (2011). *Nearest Neighbour Based Classifiers. Pattern recognition: an algorithmic approach*. London: Springer.

Nadarajan, M., & Kirubakaran, V. (2016). Simulation tools for residential buildings-A review on concepts and technologies. *Journal of Engineering and Applied Sciences (Asian Research Publishing Network)*, *11*(5), 2998–3007.

Neves-Silva, R. (2012). *Decision Support Systems for Energy Efficiency*. "Portugal — Caminhos da Excelência em Ciência e Tecnologia", Fundação Calouste Gulbenkian. Retrieved January 17, 2017, from http://ciencia2012.fct.pt/files/ciencia2012_RuiNevesSilva.pdf

OASIS. (2012). *Energy Interoperation Version 1.0*. Retrieved January 18, 2017 from https://goo.gl/4To3QZ

OASIS. (2014). *MQTT Version 3.1.1. OASIS Standard*. Retrieved January 18, 2017 from https://goo.gl/VCBTTT

Olivares, D.E., et al. (2014). Trends in Microgrid Control. *IEEE Transactions on Smart Grid, 5*(4), 1905-1919.

Oliver, A., Neila, F. J., & García, A. (2011). PCM inclusion in gypsum boards for thermal energy storage through latent heat: Thermal characterization with DSC. *Informes de la Construccion, 63*(522), 61–70. doi:10.3989/ic.09.039

OpenADR Alliance. (2014). *OpenADR 2.0 profile specification, a profile*. Retrieved January 18, 2017 from www.openadr.org/specification

Philokyprou, M., Michael, A., Malaktou, E., & Savvides, A. (2017). Environmentally responsive design in Eastern Mediterranean. The case of vernacular architecture in the coastal, lowland and mountainous regions of Cyprus. *Building and Environment, 111*, 91–109. doi:10.1016/j.buildenv.2016.10.010

Rahim, S., Khan, S. A., Javaid, N., Shaheen, N., Iqbal, Z., & Rehman, G. (2015). Towards multiple knapsack problem approach for home energy management in smart grid. In *Network-Based Information Systems (NBiS), 2015 18th International Conference on* (pp. 48-52). IEEE. doi:10.1109/NBiS.2015.11

Roeva, O., Fidanova, S., & Paprzycki, M. (2013). Influence of the population size on the genetic algorithm performance in case of cultivation process modelling. In *Proc. Federated Conf. on Computer Science and Information Systems (FedCSIS)*. IEEE.

Sarikprueck, P., Lee, W., Kulvanitchaiyanunt, A., Chen, V. C., & Rosenberger, J. (2014). Novel hybrid market price forecasting method with data clustering techniques for EV charging station application. *2014 IEEE Industry Application Society Annual Meeting*. doi:10.1109/IAS.2014.6978374

Schiavoni, S., DAlessandro, F., Bianchi, F., & Asdrubali, F. (2016). Insulation materials for the building sector: A review and comparative analysis. *Renewable & Sustainable Energy Reviews*, *62*, 988–1011. doi:10.1016/j.rser.2016.05.045

Electric, S. (2012). *iEM3100 series / iEM3200 series Energy Meters, User Manual*. Retrieved January 18, 2017 from https://goo.gl/PcdE2E

Electric, S. (2013). *PowerLogic communication devices EGX100 Ethernet gateway Technical data sheet, EGX300 Integrated gateway-server*. Retrieved January 18, 2017 from https://goo.gl/JDNrGx

Stuart, G., & Fleming, P. D. (2014). *Smart energy performance indicators for live historical and normative feedback systems*. Frankfurt: Improving Energy Efficiency in Commercial Buildings (IEECB).

Spiliotis, E., Marinakis, V., Doukas, H., & Psarras, J. (2016). Integrating a decision support system with smart grid infrastructures and ICT solutions towards energy cost reduction: An action plan to optimally schedule the operation of heating and electricity systems. *2016 7th International Conference on Information, Intelligence, Systems & Applications (IISA)*, 1-6.

Thingspeak. (2017). *Thingspeak platform*. Retrieved January 17, 2017, from thingspeak.com

Tournaki, S., Frangou, M., Tsoutsos, T., Morell, R., Guerrero, I., Urosevic, Z., & Claridge, N. et al. (2016). *Towards Nearly Zero Energy Hotels Technical Analysis and Recommendations. 5th International Conference on Renewable Energy Sources and Energy Efficiency*, Nicosia, Cyprus.

UNWTO & UNEP. (2008). *Climate Change and Tourism, Responding to Global Challenges*. Madrid: World Tourism Organization and United Nations Environment Programme.

Vachirasricirikul, S., & Ngamroo, I. (2014). Robust LFC in a smart grid with wind power penetration by coordinated V2G control and frequency controller. *IEEE Transactions on Smart Grid*, *5*(1), 371–380. doi:10.1109/TSG.2013.2264921

Vlachopoulou, M., Chin, G., Fuller, J., & Lu, S. (2014). Aggregated residential load modeling using dynamic Bayesian networks. *Smart Grid Communications (SmartGridComm), IEEE International Conference on*, 818-823. doi:10.1109/SmartGridComm.2014.7007749

Whittle, C. G., & Jones, C. R. (2013). User perceptions of energy consumption in university buildings: A University of Sheffield case study. *Journal of Sustainability Education, 5*. Retrieved January 17, 2017, from https://goo.gl/5HGN1K

Winkler, G., Meisenbach, C., Hable, M., & Meier, P. (2001). Intelligent energy management of electrical power systems with distributed feeding on the basis of forecasts of demand and generation. In *16th International Conference and Exhibition on Electricity Distribution. Part 1: Contributions*. CIRED. doi:10.1049/cp:20010857

Witten, I. H., Frank, E., Hall, M. A., & Pal, C. J. (2016). *Data Mining: Practical machine learning tools and techniques*. Morgan Kaufmann.

Zhang, Y., & Wang, J. (2015). Probabilistic solar power forecasting based on k-nearest neighbor and kernel density estimator. 2015 IEEE Power & Energy Society General Meeting, 1-5.

KEY TERMS AND DEFINITIONS

Decision Support Platform (DSP): A software capable of helping people to make decisions in complex environments with several sources of uncertainty, by making use of Computational Intelligence methods.

Internet of Things (IoT): A networks of hardware devices capable of sensing environmental and consumption data and communicate it to Internet Protocol based servers.

Machine Learning (ML): Automated learning concept that uses different methods and models to learn from past experience through the analysis of historical data.

Nearly Zero Energy Building (nZEB): A building having a very high energy performance that results from reduced consumption and a significant production of energy, using renewable energy sources, either produced in the building, or in its vicinity.

Supervisory Control and Data Acquisition (SCADA): An architecture of electronic devices and protocols capable of gathering, monitor and control industrial facilities and buildings.

Compilation of References

Aaker, D. A. (1991). *Managing brand equity: capitalizing on the value of a brand name*. The Free Press.

Aaker, D. A. (1996). *Building strong brands*. Simon & Schuster UK Ltd.

Ab Aziz, K., & Siang, T. G. (2014). Virtual reality and augmented reality combination as a holistic application for heritage preservation in the UNESCO World Heritage Site of Melaka. *International Journal of Social Science and Humanity*, *4*(5), 333–338. doi:10.7763/IJSSH.2014.V4.374

Abascal Palazón, J. M., Cebrián Fernández, R., & Almagro Gorbea, M. (2004). *Segóbriga. Guía del parque arqueológico*. Alicante: Miguel de Cervantes Virtual Library.

Abo-Khalil, A. G., & Lee, D. (2007). SVR-based Wind Speed Estimation for Power Control of Wind Energy Generation System. *2007 Power Conversion Conference*, Nagoya. doi:10.1109/PCCON.2007.373152

AbuShawar, B., & Atwell, E. (2016). Usefulness, localizability, humanness, and language-benefit: Additional evaluation criteria for natural language dialogue systems. *International Journal of Speech Technology*, *19*(2), 373–383. doi:10.1007/s10772-015-9330-4

Acevin. (2012). *Informe de visitantes a bodegas asociadas a las Rutas del Vino de España. Año 2011*. Ministerio de Industria Energía y Turismo e Instituto de Turismo de España.

Adams, E. (2016). *Most Virtual Reality Is Not Virtual Reality. Here's Why* [online article]. Retrieved December 5, 2016, from http://gearpatrol.com/2016/07/18/virtual-reality-vs-360-video/

Adão, T., Batista, R., Peres, E., Magalhães, L. G., & Coelho, A. (2013). Reconstructing traversable buildings for archaeology with ERAS. Proc. Virtual and Networked Organizations: Emergent Technologies and Tools - ViNOrg '13.

Adão, T., Magalhães, L. G., Bessa, M., Coelho, A., Sousa, A., Rodrigues, N., . . . Reis, L. P. (2012). ERAS - An Ontology-Based Tool for the Expeditious Reconstruction of Virtual Cultural Heritage Sites. In Actas do 20o Encontro Português de Computação Gráfica, Viana do Castelo, Portugal.

Adão, T., Magalhães, L., & Peres, E. (2016). *Ontology-based Procedural Modelling of Traversable Buildings Composed by Arbitrary Shapes*. Springer International Publishing. doi:10.1007/978-3-319-42372-2

Adobe. (2016). *XD Essentials: Card-based user interfaces*. Retrieved: Nov. 16, 2016 from https://goo.gl/gg8qUM

Adomavicius, G., & Tuzhilin, A. (2011). Context-aware recommender systems. In Recommender systems handbook (pp. 217-253). Springer US. doi:10.1007/978-0-387-85820-3_7

Adukaite, A. (2015). Technology Enhanced Learning in Tourism. Teachers' and Students' Perspectives in South Africa. In M. Fuchs, W. Hopken, Z. Xiang, & A. Mariussen (Eds.), *Enter 2015 PhD Workshop, Research Proposals*, (pp. 41-47). Academic Press.

Agapito, D., Mendes, J., & Valle, P. (2010). Destination Image – Perspectives of Tourists versus Residents. *European Journal of Tourism. Hospitality and Recreation*, *1*, 90–109.

Agapito, D., Valle, P., & Mendes, J. (2013). The cognitive-affective-conative model of destination image: A confirmatory analysis. *Journal of Travel & Tourism Marketing*, *30*(5), 471–481. doi:10.1080/10548408.2013.803393

Agarwal, S., Furukawa, Y., Snavely, N., Simon, I., Curless, B., Seitz, S. M., & Szeliski, R. (2011). Building Rome in a day. *Communications of the ACM*, *54*(10), 105–112. doi:10.1145/2001269.2001293

Agência Andaluza de Energia. (2011). *Andalucía Renovable. Junta de Andalucía.* Retrieved January 17, 2017, from http://goo.gl/NSvbNY

Aguirre-Brito, C. N. A. (2015). Augmented reality applied in tourism mobile applications. *2015 Second International Conference On Edemocracy & Egovernment (ICEDEG)*, 120-125. doi:10.1109/ICEDEG.2015.7114484

Ahmedi, L., Rrmoku, K., Sylejmani, K., & Shabani, D. (2017). A bimodal social network analysis to recommend points of interest to tourists. *Social Network Analysis and Mining*, *7*(1), 14. doi:10.1007/s13278-017-0431-8

Ajanki, A., Billinghurst, M., Gamper, H., Jarvenpaa, T., Kandemir, M., Kaski, S., & Tossavainen, T. et al. (2010). An augmented reality interface to contextual information. *Virtual Reality (Waltham Cross)*, *15*(2-3), 455–470.

Akiki, P. A., Bandara, A. K., & Yu, Y. (2014). Adaptive model-driven user interface development systems. *ACM Computing Surveys*, *47*(1), 9. doi:10.1145/2597999

Al Subhi, N., Bell, D., & Lashmar, P. (2015). Location based modelling for Heritage Mobile Applications. *UKAIS Conference 2015.*

Alahi, A., Ortiz, R., & Vandergheynst, P. (2012). *Freak: Fast retina keypoint.* In *IEEE Conference on Computer Vision and Pattern Recognition*, 212 (pp. 510-517). IEEE.

Alaiz, C. M., Barbero, A., & Dorronsoro, J. R. (2012). Sparse methods for wind energy prediction. *The 2012 International Joint Conference on Neural Networks (IJCNN).* doi:10.1109/IJCNN.2012.6252843

Alazaizeh, M. M., Hallo, J. C., Backman, S. J., Norman, W. C., & Vogel, M. A. (2016). Value orientations and heritage tourism management at Petra Archaeological Park, Jordan. *Tourism Management*, *57*, 149–158. doi:10.1016/j.tourman.2016.05.008

Albacete, C. A. S. (2012). *Las tecnologías de la información y comunicación en el sector turístico: una aproximación al uso de las redes sociales.* Madrid: Universitaria Ramón Areces.

Alexandros, A., & Jaffry, S. (2005). Stated preferences for two Cretan heritage attractions. *Annals of Tourism Research*, *32*(4), 985–1005. doi:10.1016/j.annals.2005.01.004

Alexopoulou, A., Liaros, N., Panagopoulou, A., & Kaminari, A. (2010). *False Colour Infrared Imaging as a Tool for the Study of Pigments Used in Ceramics from Areas Within the Mediterranean Basin.* Paper presented at the IIC Congress 2010: "Conservation and the Eastern Mediterranean", Istanbul, Turkey.

Algarve, C. C. D. R. (2015). Estratégia Regional de Investigação e Inovação para a Especialização Inteligente. RIS3 - ALGARVE 2014-2020. Faro.

Alkhamisi, A. O., & Monowar, M. M. (2013). Rise of augmented reality: Current and future application areas. *International Journal of Internet and Distributed Systems*, *1*(04), 25–34. doi:10.4236/ijids.2013.14005

Allen, P. K., Troccoli, A., Smith, B., Murray, S., Stamos, I., & Leordeanu, M. (2003). New methods for digital modeling of historic sites. *IEEE Computer Graphics and Applications*, *23*(6), 32–41. doi:10.1109/MCG.2003.1242380

Alonso, A., Figueroa, C., Rodríguez, J., & Talón, P. (2008). *El impacto de la tecnología social en las decisiones de consumo turístico.* TURITEC 2008, VII Congreso de Turismo y Tecnologías de la Información y de las Comunicaciones, Málaga.

Alvarez-Cortes, V., Zayas, B. E., Uresti, J. A. R., & Zarate, V. H. (2009). *Current Challenges and Applications for Adaptive User Interfaces*. INTECH Open Access Publisher. doi:10.5772/7745

Alvarez, M. D., & Campo, S. (2011). Controllable versus uncontrollable information sources: Effects on the image of Turkey. *International Journal of Tourism Research*, *13*(4), 310–323. doi:10.1002/jtr.838

AMBAVis Project: Access to Museums for Blind and Visually Impaired People through 3D-Technology (2015). *The use of tactile models in museums Status quo and best practice.* Retrieved April 26, 2017, from http://www.ambavis.eu/wp-content/uploads/2016/01/150805-AMBAVis-BestPractice_Final-disclaimer.pdf

Americans with Disabilities Act Accessibility Guidelines (ADAAG). (1992). *Checklist for Buildings and Facilities.* Retrieved October 20, 2008, from http://www.access-board.gov/adaag/checklist/a16.html

Anacleto, R., Figueiredo, L., Almeida, A., & Novais, P. (2014). Mobile application to provide personalized sightseeing tours. *Journal of Network and Computer Applications*, *41*, 56–64. doi:10.1016/j.jnca.2013.10.005

Anderson, E. F., McLoughlin, L., Liarokapis, F., Peters, C., Petridis, P., & De Freitas, S. (2010). Developing serious games for cultural heritage: A state-of-the-art review. *Virtual Reality (Waltham Cross)*, *14*(4), 255–275. doi:10.1007/s10055-010-0177-3

Andrew, S. R., & Eastop, D. (1994). Using ultra-violet and infra-red techniques in the examination and documentation of historic textiles. *The Conservator*, *18*(1), 50–56. doi:10.1080/01410096.1994.9995084

Angskun, J., & Angskun, T. (2008). Online Trip Planners for the Tourism Industry. *Suranaree Journal of Social Science*, *2*(1), 33–45.

APP Ammergau – Travel Alps. (2017). *Ammergau Alps - Travel.* Retrieved: January 12, 2017, from https://play.google.com/store/apps/details?id=de.ammergau.en

APP Easy Go. (2017). *Easy Go.* Retrieved: January 12, 2017, from https://play.google.com/store/apps/details?id=com.cnc.easygo&hl=pt_PT

APP Smart Tourism Taiwan. (2017). *Smart Tourism Taiwan.* Retrieved: January 12, 2017, from https://play.google.com/store/apps/details?id=tw.org.iii.ari.smarttourism

APP TripIt. (2017). *TripIt: Travel Organizer.* Retrieved: January 12, 2017, from https://play.google.com/store/apps/details?id=com.tripit

APP Visit Dubai. (2017). *Visit Dubai.* Retrieved: January 12, 2017, from http://www.visitdubai.com/en/travel-planning/travel-tools/get-the-app

April, Q. (2016). *Virtual Absence and Presence in the Museum of Stolen Art* [online article]. Retrieved December 5, 2016, from http://www.artpractical.com/column/locating-technology-the-museum-of-stolen-art/

Archicifradia Del Glorioso Apóstol Santiago. (2014). Credencial do Peregrino. Edição própria, Santiago de Compostela.

Ardissono, L., Felfernig, A., Friedrich, G., Jannach, D., Schäfer, R., & Zanker, M. (2001). Intelligent interfaces for distributed web-based product and service configuration. In Web Intelligence: Research and Development (pp. 184-188). Springer Berlin Heidelberg. doi:10.1007/3-540-45490-X_21

AREAL & INETI. (2006). *Avaliação do Recurso Solar da Região do Algarve*. Retrieved January 17, 2017, from http://goo.gl/yj1mzQ

Argan, G. C. (1995). *História da arte como história da cidade.* São Paulo, SP: Martins Fontes.

Ariyasriwatana, W., Buente, W., Oshiro, M., & Streveler, D. (2014). Categorizing health-related cues to action: Using Yelp reviews of restaurants in Hawaii. *New Review of Hypermedia and Multimedia, 20*(4), 317–340. doi:10.1080/13614568.2014.987326

Ariyasriwatana, W., & Quiroga, L. M. (2016). A thousand ways to sayDelicious!' Categorizing expressions of deliciousness from restaurant reviews on the social network site Yelp. *Appetite, 104,* 18–32. doi:10.1016/j.appet.2016.01.002 PMID:26774047

Armbrust, M., Fox, A., Griffith, R., Joseph, A., Katz, R., & Konwinski, A. (2010). A view of cloud computing. *Communications of the ACM, 53*(4), 50–58. doi:10.1145/1721654.1721672

Arriagada, A. (2014). *Cultural mediators and the everyday making of 'digital capital' in contemporary Chile* (Doctoral Dissertation). Available from LSE Theses Online. Retrieved July 16, 2016, from http://etheses.lse.ac.uk/id/eprint/913

Arriagada, A. (2015). Unpacking the "digital habitus" of music fans in Santiago's indie music scene. In The production and Consumption of Music in the Digital Age. London: Routledge.

Arriagada, A., & Cruz, V. (2014). Music Fans as Mediators in the Age of Digital reproduction. In L. Duits, K. Zwaan, & S. Reijnders (Eds.), *The Ashgate Research campanion to fan cultures* (pp. 149–162). Ashgate Publishing.

Arrizabalaga, I., Gómez-Laserna, O., Aramendia, J., Arana, G., & Madariaga, J. M. (2014). Applicability of a Diffuse Reflectance Infrared Fourier Transform handheld spectrometer to perform in situ analyses on Cultural Heritage materials. *Spectrochimica Acta, Part A*(129), 259–267.

Art, U. K. (2016). *Welcome to Art Detective* [website]. Retrieved December 21, 2016, from http://www.artuk.org/artdetective/

Artoolkit. (2016). *ARtoolKit, The world's most widely used tracking library for augmented reality.* Retrieved: Nov. 16, 2016 from http://artoolkit.org/

ASHRAE. (2003). *BACnet - A Data Communication Protocol for Building Automation and Control Networks.* Retrieved January 18, 2017, from http://www.bacnet.org/Addenda/Add-2001-135d.pdf

Association of Art Museum Directors. (2015). *Next Practices in Digital and Technology* [online book]. Retrieved December 4, 2016, from https://aamd.org/sites/default/files/document/Next Practices in Digital and Tech.pdf

Assoun, P. L. (1989). *A Escola de Frankfurt.* Lisboa, Portugal: Editora Dom Quixote.

Atembe, R. (2015). The Use of Smart Technology in Tourism: Evidence From Wearable Devices. *Journal of Tourism and Hospitality Management, 3*(6), 224–234.

Attia, S., Gratia, E., De Herde, A., & Hensen, J. L. M. (2012). Simulation-based decision support tool for early stages of zero-energy building design. *Energy and Building, 49,* 2–15. doi:10.1016/j.enbuild.2012.01.028

Attila, K., & Edit, B. (2012). Beyond reality: The possibilities of augmented reality in cultural and heritage tourism. *2nd International Tourism and Sport Management Conference,* 1-6.

Augé, M. (1994). *Não lugar: introdução a uma antropologia da supermodernidade.* Campinas, SP: Papirus.

Augé, M. (2007). *Por una antropologia de la movilidad.* Barcelona: Cat., Gedisa.

Augé, M. (2008). *El tiempo em ruínas.* Barcelona: Cat, Gedisa.

Augment Blog. (2016). *Virtual Reality vs. Augmented Reality.* Retrieved October 6th, 2015, from http://www.augment.com/blog/virtual-reality-vs-augmented-reality/

Ávila, R., & Barrado, D. A. (2005). Nuevas tendencia en el desarrollo de destinos turísticos: Marcos conceptuales y operativos para su planificación y gestión. *Cuadernos de Turismo*, *15*, 27–43.

Axon, V. R. (2016). *AxonVR*. Retrieved: Dec. 6, 2016 from http://axonvr.com

Ayeh, J. K., Au, N., & Law, R. (2013a). Predicting the intention to use consumer-generated media for travel planning. *Tourism Management*, *35*, 132–143. doi:10.1016/j.tourman.2012.06.010

Ayeh, J. K., Au, N., & Law, R. (2013b). Do we believe in TripAdvisor? Examining credibility perceptions and online travelers attitude toward using user-generated content. *Journal of Travel Research*, *52*(4), 437–452. doi:10.1177/0047287512475217

Azuma, R. T. (1997). A Survey of Augmented Reality. *Presence (Cambridge, Mass.)*, *6*(4), 355–385. doi:10.1162/pres.1997.6.4.355

Azuma, R., Baillot, Y., Behringer, R., Feiner, S., Julier, S., & MacIntyre, B. (2001). Recent advances in augmented reality. *IEEE Computer Graphics and Applications*, *21*(6), 34–47. doi:10.1109/38.963459

Babich, N. (2016). *Designing Card-Based User Interfaces, Smashing Magazine*. Retrieved: Nov. 16, 2016 from https://goo.gl/AM46gT

Bahaire, T., & Elliot-White, M. (1999). The Application of Geographical Information Systems (GIS) in Sustainable Tourism Planning: A Review. *Journal of Sustainable Tourism*, *7*(2), 159–174. doi:10.1080/09669589908667333

Balance. (2016). *The balance: Fine Art Museum Apps for Smart Phones*. Retrieved: Nov. 16, 2016 from https://goo.gl/WEsQRN

Ballantyne, R., & Uzzell, D. (1993). Environmental mediation and hot interpretation e a case study of District Six, Cape Town. *The Journal of Environmental Education*, *24*(3), 4–7. doi:10.1080/00958964.1993.9943496

Baloglu, S., & McCleary, K. W. (1999). A Model of Destination Image Formation. *Annals of Tourism Research*, *26*(4), 868–867. doi:10.1016/S0160-7383(99)00030-4

Banou, P., Kaminari, A., Moutsatsou, A., Alexopoulou, A., & Singer, B. (2010). *Investigating the Conservation Problems of Oil Paintings on Paper Supports*. Paper presented at the International Symposium "Works of Art and Conservation Science Today", Thessaloniki, Greece.

Baptista, R., Reis, L. P., Magalhães, L., Rodrigues, R., Coelho, A., & Sousa, A. (2012). Extração de informação de texto formal para a modelação expedita de edifícios monumentais. In Actas do 20º Encontro Português de Computação Gráfica, Viana do Castelo, Portugal.

Barbosa, L. (2004). *Sociedade de consumo. Ciências Sociais, Passo-a-Passo, 49*. Rio de Janeiro, RJ: Jorge Zahar.

Barnes, A. K., & Balda, J. C. (2013). Sizing and economic assessment of energy Storage with real-time pricing and ancillary services. *2013 4th IEEE International Symposium on Power Electronics for Distributed Generation Systems (PEDG)*. doi:10.1109/pedg.2013.6785651

Barrios, M. (2012). Marketing de la Experiencia: Principales conceptos y características. *Palermo Business Review*, *7*(1), 67–83.

Barros, V. G. (2015). *Turismo em Portugal*. Lisboa, Portugal: Fundação Francisco Manuel dos Santos.

Bastanlar, Y., Grammalidis, N., Zabulis, X., Yilmaz, E., Yardimci, Y., & Triantafyllidis, G. (2008). *3D Reconstruction for a Cultural Heritage virtual tour system*. Paper presented at the The International Archives of the Photogrammetry, Remote Sensing and Spatial Information Sciences, Beijing, China.

Baudrillard, J. (1981). *Simulacros e Simulação*. Lisboa, Portugal: Editora Relógio D'Água.

Baudrillard, J. (1998). *The Consumer Society Myths and Structures*. London: Sage Publications. doi:10.4135/9781526401502

Bauman, Z. (2001). *Modernidade Liquida*. Rio de Janeiro, Brasil: Zahar Editor.

Bauman, Z. (2001). Consuming life. *Journal of Consumer Culture*, *1*(1), 9–29. doi:10.1177/146954050100100102

Bearman, G., & Spiro, I. (1996). Archaeological application of advanced imaging techniques. *Biblical Archaeologist*, *59*(1), 56–66. doi:10.2307/3210537

Beaudoin, P., Paquet, S., & Poulin, P. (2001). Realistic and controllable fire simulation. Graphics Interface, 2001, 159–166.

Beerli, A., & Martín, J. D. (2004). Factors influencing destination image. *Annals of Tourism Research*, *31*(3), 657–681. doi:10.1016/j.annals.2004.01.010

Beerli, A., & Martín, J. D. (2004a). Tourists characteristics and the perceived image of tourist destinations: A quantitative analysis-a case study of Lanzarote, Spain. *Tourism Management*, *25*(5), 623–636. doi:10.1016/j.tourman.2003.06.004

Beerli, A., Martín, J. D., & Moreno, G. S. (2003). *Los agentes que conforman la imagen de los destinos turísticos. Sitio Web I Coloquio Predoctoral Europeo de Turismo y Ocio ESADE-IMHI*. Cornell-ESSEC.

Begault, D. R. (2000). *3-D sound for Virtual reality and Multimedia*. NASA Center for AeroSpace Information. NASA/ TM – 2000-209606.

Bellotti, F., Berta, R., Cardona, R., & De Gloria, A. (2011). An architectural approach to efficient 3D urban modeling. *Computers & Graphics*, *35*(5), 1001–1012. doi:10.1016/j.cag.2011.07.004

Beraldin, S. E.-H. J.-A., Gonzo, L., Whiting, E., Jemtrud, M., & Valzanoe, V. (2005). A hierarchical 3D reconstruction approach for documenting complex heritage sites. *The XX CIPA International Symposium*, Torino, Itália.

Berardi, U., Iannace, G., & Maffei, L. (2016). Virtual reconstruction of the historical acoustics of the Odeon of Pompeii. *Journal of Cultural Heritage*, *19*, 555–566. doi:10.1016/j.culher.2015.12.004

Bere, A., & Rambe, P. (2016). An Empirical Analysis of the Determinants of Mobile Instant Messaging Appropriation in University Learning. *Journal of Computing in Higher Education*, *28*(2), 172–198. doi:10.1007/s12528-016-9112-2

Bergamasco, M., Frisoli, A., & Barbagli, F. (2002). *Haptics technologies and cultural heritage applications*. Paper presented at the Computer Animation. doi:10.1109/CA.2002.1017503

Bernardes, J. P. (2006). O peristilo da villa romana de Milreu: novas Interpretações. Promontoria, 4, 127-160.

Bernardes, P., Magalhães, F., Ribeiro, J., Madeira, J., & Martins, M. (2014). Image-based 3D Modelling in Archaeology: Application and Evaluation. In *22nd International Conference in Central Europe on Computer Graphics, Visualization and Computer Vision*. Plzen: University of West Bohemia.

Bernardes, P. J. C. (2002). *Arqueologia urbana e ambientes virtuais: um sistema para Bracara Augusta*. Universidade do Minho.

Bernardo, Á. (2016). *Museums that are Accessible Thanks to Technology* [online article]. Retrieved December 19, 2016, from https://www.bbvaopenmind.com/en/museums-that-are-accessible-thanks-to-technology/

Berners-Lee, T. (2006). *Linked Data. Design Issues*. Retrieved January 10, 2017, from https://www.w3.org/ DesignIssues/LinkedData.html

Bernstein, F. (2013). Technology That Serves to Enhance, Not Distract. *The New York Times*. Retrieved from http://www.nytimes.com/2013/03/21/arts/artsspecial/at-cleveland-museum-of-art-the-ipad-enhances.html?hpw&_r=0

Bernstein, S. (2015). *Measuring Success* [online article]. Retrieved November 30, 2016, from https://www.brooklynmuseum.org/community/blogosphere/2015/08/19/measuring-success/

Bernstein, S. (2015). *The Realities of Installing iBeacon to Scale* [online article]. Retrieved November 29, 2016, from https://www.brooklynmuseum.org/community/blogosphere/2015/02/04/the-realities-of-installing-ibeacon-to-scale/

Besuievsky, G., & Patow, G. (2013). Procedural modeling historical buildings for serious games. *Virtual Archaeology Review*, *4*(9), 160–166. doi:10.4995/var.2013.4268

Bianchi, M. (2003, June). A Questioning Economist: Tibor Scitovskys Attempt to Bring Joy into Economics. *Journal of Economic Psychology*, *24*(3), 391–407. doi:10.1016/S0167-4870(03)00019-9

Biggs, K. (2014). *Mummies, mobiles and 3D printing* [online article]. Retrieved December 4, 2016, from https://blog.britishmuseum.org/2014/05/30/mummies-mobiles-and-3D-printing/

Bigné Alcañiz, E., Sánchez García, I., & Sanz Blas, S. (2009). The functional-psuchological continuum in the cognitive image of a destination: A confirmatory analysis. *Tourism Management*, *30*(5), 715–723. doi:10.1016/j.tourman.2008.10.020

Bigné, E., Hernández, B., Ruiz, C., & Andreu, L. (2010). How motivation, opportunity and ability can drive online airline ticket purchases. *Journal of Air Transport Management*, *16*(6), 346–349. doi:10.1016/j.jairtraman.2010.05.004

Bigne, J. E., Sanchez, M. I., & Sanchez, J. (2001). Tourism image, evaluation variables and after purchase behaviour: Interrelationship. *Tourism Management*, *22*(6), 607–616. doi:10.1016/S0261-5177(01)00035-8

Bille, T., & Schulze, G. G. (2006). Culture in urban and regional development. Handbook of the Economics of Art and Culture, 1, 1051-1099.

Binkhorst, E., & den Dekker, T. (2009). Agenda for Co-creation tourism experience research. *Journal of Hospitality Marketing and Management*, *18*(2-3), 311–327. doi:10.1080/19368620802594193

Biran, A., & Hyde, K. F. (2013). New perspectives on dark tourism.*International Journal of Culture. Tourism and Hospitality Research*, *7*(3), 191–198.

Biran, A., Poria, Y., & Oren, G. (2011). Sought experiences at (dark) heritage sites. *Annals of Tourism Research*, *38*(3), 820–841. doi:10.1016/j.annals.2010.12.001

Bizer, C., Heath, T., & Berners-Lee, T. (2009). Linked Data - The Story So Far. *International Journal on Semantic Web and Information Systems*, *5*(3), 1–22. doi:10.4018/jswis.2009081901

Black, R., Davidson, P., & Retra, K. (2009). *Facilitating energy saving behaviours among university student residents*. Institute for Land Water and Society, Report No. 53. Retrieved January 17, 2017, from https://goo.gl/Nt0ySw

Blackwell, R. D., Miniard, P. W., & Engel, J. F. (2001). *Consumer behavior* (9th ed.). Fort Worth, TX: Harcourt College Publishers.

Blais, F., & Beraldin, J. A. (2006). Recent Developments in 3D Multi-modal Laser Imaging Applied to Cultural Heritage. *Machine Vision and Applications*, *17*(6), 395–409. doi:10.1007/s00138-006-0025-3

Blake, J. (2013). *Natural user interface in. Net*. Greenwich, CT: Manning.

Blender Foundation. (2000, April 4). Retrieved 29 January 2017, from https://www.blender.org/

Blohm, I., & Leimeister, J. M. (2013). Gamification. *Business & Information Systems Engineering*, *5*(4), 275–278. doi:10.1007/s12599-013-0273-5

Bodnar, J. L., Candoré, J. C., Nicolas, J. L., Szatanik, G., Detalle, V., & Vallet, J. M. (2012). Stimulated infrared thermography applied to help restoring mural paintings. *NDT & E International*, *49*(0), 40–46. doi:10.1016/j.ndteint.2012.03.007

Boehner, K., DePaula, R., Dourish, P., & Sengers, P. (2007). How emotion is made and measured. *International Journal of Human-Computer Studies*, *65*(4), 275–291. doi:10.1016/j.ijhcs.2006.11.016

Boes, K., Buhalis, D., & Inversini, A. (2016). Smart tourism destinations: Ecosystems for tourism destination competitiveness. *International Journal of Tourism Cities*, *2*(2), 108–124. doi:10.1108/IJTC-12-2015-0032

Bokeloh, M., Wand, M., & Seidel, H.-P. (2010). A connection between partial symmetry and inverse procedural modeling. *ACM Transactions on Graphics*, *29*(4), 1. doi:10.1145/1778765.1778841

Boley, B. B., Magnini, V. P., & Tuten, T. L. (2013). Social media picture posting and souvenir purchasing behaviour: Some initial findings. *Tourism Management*, *37*, 27–30. doi:10.1016/j.tourman.2012.11.020

Bondi, A. B. (2000). Characteristics of scalability and their impact on performance. *Proceedings of the Second International Workshop on Software and Performance*. doi:10.1145/350391.350432

Bontcheva, K., Cunningham, H., Tablan, V., Maynard, D., & Hamza, O. (2002). Using GATE As an Environment for Teaching NLP. In *Proceedings of the ACL-02 Workshop on Effective Tools and Methodologies for Teaching Natural Language Processing and Computational Linguistics* (Vol. 1, pp. 54–62). Stroudsburg, PA: Association for Computational Linguistics. doi:10.3115/1118108.1118116

Boodnah, K. D., Armoogum, V., Jaunky, V. C., & Armoogum, S. (2016). Towards Smart Tourism: An individual appreciation of Porlwi-By-Light festival. In *Emerging Technologies and Innovative Business Practices for the Transformation of Societies (EmergiTech)*. Port Louis: IEEE. doi:10.1109/EmergiTech.2016.7737360

Borja, L., Andreu, J. C., & Bosch, R. C. (2002). *El Consumidor Turístico*. Madrid: ESIC Editorial.

Borja, S. L., & Gomis, J. M. (2009). *El nuevo paradigma de la intermediación turística*. Madrid: Ediciones Pirámide.

Bosangit, B., Hibbert, S., & McCabe, S. (2015). If I was going to die I should at least be having fun: Travel blogs, meaning and tourist experience. *Annals of Tourism Research*, *55*, 1–14. doi:10.1016/j.annals.2015.08.001

Bostedt, G., & Mattsson, L. (1995). The value of forest for tourism in Sweden. *Annals of Tourism Research*, *22*(3), 671–680. doi:10.1016/0160-7383(95)00007-S

Boto, C. T. (2016). Archeology as development of local tourism. *International Journal of Scientific Management and Tourism*, *2*(3), 355–368.

Boulding, W., Karla, A., Staelin, A., & Zeithaml, V. (1993). A Dynamic Process Model of Service Quality: From Expectations to Behavioral Intensions. *JMR, Journal of Marketing Research*, *30*(1), 7–27. doi:10.2307/3172510

Bourdieu, P. (2010). *A Distinção. Uma Crítica Social da Faculdade do Juízo*. Lisboa, Portugal: Edições 70.

Bourdieu, P. (1984). *Distinction: A Social Critique of the Judgment of Taste*. London: Routledge.

Bourdieu, P. (1986). The forms of capital. In J. G. Richardson (Ed.), *Handbook for Theory and Research for the Sociology of Education* (pp. 241–258). Academic Press.

Bower, M., Howe, C., McCredie, N., Robinson, A., & Grover, D. (2014). Augmented Reality in education–cases, places and potentials. *Educational Media International*, *51*(1), 1–15. doi:10.1080/09523987.2014.889400

Bowman, M. S., & Pezzullo, P. C. (2009). Whats so darkabout dark tourism?: Death, tours, and performance. *Tourist Studies*, *9*(3), 187–202. doi:10.1177/1468797610382699

Boyd, S., & Butler, R. (1996). Seeing the forest through the trees: Using GIS to identify potential ecotourism sites in Northern Ontario. In L. C. Harrison & W. Husbands (Eds.), *Practicing Responsible Tourism: International Case Studies in Tourism Planning, Policy & Development* (pp. 380–403). New York, NY: J. Wiley & Sons.

Bradley, B. (2005). *Towards the procedural generation of urban building interiors* (M. Sc. thesis). Game Programming, University of Hull.

Brasil, A. (2013). *Blog 1A. "As 5 inovações que mudaram para sempre a forma como viajamos"*. Retrieved February 01, 2017, from http://amadeus1a.com.br/cms/as-5-inovacoes-que-mudaram-para-sempre-a-forma-como-viajamos/

Brasil, A. (2013). *Blog 1A. "As 5 inovações tecnológicas que transformaram a industria de turismo"*. Retrieved February 01, 2017, from http://amadeus1a.com.br/cms/5-inovacoes-tecnologicas-que-transformaram-a-industria-de-turismo/

Brasil. Ministério do Turismo. (2014). *Como a tecnologia está mudando o turismo*. Retrieved February 02, 2017, from http://www.turismo.gov.br/ultimas-noticias/415-como-a- tecnologia-esta- mudando-o-turismo.html

Bressler, S. E., & Grantham, C. (2000). *Communities of commerce: Building internet business communities to accelerate growth, minimize risk, and increase customer loyalty*. McGraw-Hill Professional.

Brewster, S., Chohan, F., & Brown, L. (2007). Tactile feedback for mobile interactions. In *Proceedings of the SIGCHI conference on Human factors in computing systems* (pp. 159-162). San Jose, CA: ACM. doi:10.1145/1240624.1240649

Bringhurst, R. (1997). *The Elements of Typographic Style*. Hartley & Marks.

Brizard, T., Derde, W., & Silberman, N. (2007). *Basic Guidelines for Cultural Heritage Professionals in the Use of Information Technologies. How can ICT support cultural heritage?. The Interactive Institute AB.*

Brown, D. (1996). Genuine fakes. In T. Selwyn (Ed.), *The Tourist Image: myths and myth making in tourism*. Chichester, UK: Wiley.

Browne, J. (2014). *Simply ASK* [online article]. Retrieved November 30, 2016, from https://www.brooklynmuseum.org/community/blogosphere/2014/10/06/simply-ask/

Bruls, M., Huizing, K., & van Wijk, J. (1999). Squarified Treemaps. In *Proceedings of the Joint Eurographics and IEEE TCVG Symposium on Visualization* (pp. 33–42). Press.

Bruno, F., Bruno, S., De Sensi, G., Luchi, M.-L., Mancuso, S., & Muzzupappa, M. (2010). From 3D reconstruction to virtual reality: A complete methodology for digital archaeological exhibition. *Journal of Cultural Heritage*, *11*(1), 42–49. doi:10.1016/j.culher.2009.02.006

Bruyere, B. L., Beh, A. W., & Lelengula, G. (2009). Differences in perceptions of communication, tourism benefits, and management issues in a protected area of rural Kenya. *Environmental Management*, *43*(1), 49–59. doi:10.1007/s00267-008-9190-7 PMID:18777191

Bryce, D., Curran, R., OGorman, K., & Taheri, B. (2015). Visitors engagement and authenticity: Japanese heritage consumption. *Tourism Management*, *46*, 571–581. doi:10.1016/j.tourman.2014.08.012

Büchner, A. G., & Mulvenna, M. D. (1998). Discovering internet marketing intelligence through online analytical web usage mining. *SIGMOD Record*, *27*(4), 54–61. doi:10.1145/306101.306124

Buckley, R. (2012). Sustainable tourism: Research and reality. *Annals of Tourism Research*, *39*(2), 528–546. doi:10.1016/j.annals.2012.02.003

Bughin, J., Chui, M., & Manyika, J. (2014). *Clouds, big data, and smart assets: Ten tech-enabled business trends to watch.* Retrieved, December 2016 from http://www.itglobal-services.de/files/100810_McK_Clouds_big_data_and%20 smart%20assets.pdf

Buhalis, D. & Yovcheva, Z. (2014). *Augmented reality in tourism: 10 best practices.* Academic Press.

Buhalis, D. (2003). *E-Tourism: Information technology for strategic tourism Management.* Pearson Education.

Buhalis, D. (2003). *eTourism: Information technology for strategic tourism management.* Pearson.

Buhalis, D., Eichhorn, V., Michopoulou, E., & Miller, G. (2006). *Accessibility Market and Stakeholder Analysis.* Retrieved April 21, 2017, from http://www.accessibletourism.org/resources/ossate_market_analysis_public_final.pdf

Buhalis, D., & Amaranggana, A. (2013). *Smart tourism destinations. In Information and Communication Technologies in Tourism* (pp. 553–564). Cham: Springer.

Buhalis, D., & Amaranggana, A. (2013). Smart tourism destinations. In Z. Xiang & L. Tussyadiah (Eds.), *Information and Communication Technologies in Tourism 2014* (pp. 553–564). Springer International Publishing. doi:10.1007/978-3-319-03973-2_40

Buhalis, D., & Amaranggana, A. (2015). Smart Tourism Destinations Enhancing Tourism Experience Through Personalisation of Services. In I. Tussyadiah & A. Inversini (Eds.), *Information and Communication Technologies in Tourism 2015* (pp. 377–389). Cham: Springer International Publishing. doi:10.1007/978-3-319-14343-9_28

Buhalis, D., & Foerste, M. (2015). SoCoMo marketing for travel and tourism: Empowering co-creation of value. *Journal of Destination Marketing & Management, 4*(3), 151–161. doi:10.1016/j.jdmm.2015.04.001

Buhalis, D., & Law, R. (2008). Progress in information technology and tourism management: 20 years on and 10 years after the Internet – The state of eTourism research. *Tourism Management, 29*(4), 609–623. doi:10.1016/j.tourman.2008.01.005

Buhalis, D., & Wagner, R. (2013). *E-destinations: Global best practice in tourism technologies and applications. In Information and Communication Technologies in Tourism* (pp. 119–130). Berlin: Springer.

Buhalis, D., & Yovcheva, Z. (2015). *Augmented Reality in tourism: 10 unique applications explained. Digital Tourism Think Tank.* Dorset: Bournemouth University.

Buján, D., Martín, D., Torices, O., López-de-Ipiña, D., Lamsfus, C., Abaitua, J., & Alzua-Sorzabal, A. (2013). Context management platform for tourism applications. *Sensors (Basel, Switzerland), 13*(7), 8060–8078. doi:10.3390/s130708060 PMID:23797739

Buoso, M. C., Ceccato, D., & Zafiropoulos, D. (2009). False-Color Infra Red Photography in the Identification of Pigments Used for a Late 13th Century Illuminated Manuscript. *Laboratori Nazionali di Legnaro (LNL) Annual Report, Applied and Interdisciplinary Physics Instrumentation,* 153-154.

Burgess, S., Sellitto, C., Cox, C., & Buultjens, J. (2009, June). User-generated content (UGC) in tourism: Benefits and concerns of online consumers. ECIS, 417-429.

Burguess, L., & Kerr, G. (2012, June). Australian Traveller's Use of the Internet: Understanding Australian Online Planning and Booking Behaviour. *8th Annual International Conference on Tourism*, 11-14.

Burke, M., & Hiltbrand, T. (2011). How gamification will change business intelligence. *Business Intelligence Journal, 16*(2), 8–16.

Burke, R. (1999). Integrating knowledge-based and collaborative-filtering recommender systems. *Proceedings of the Workshop on AI and Electronic Commerce*, 69-72.

Bustillo, M., Grant, R., Kenny, S., Martínez-García, A., McGoohan, C., Ní Cholla, R., . . . Webb, S. (2016). MODS and the Digital Repository of Ireland. Royal Irish Academy. Doi:10.3318/DRI.2016.1

Butler, A. (2016). *Virtual reality and new technologies increasingly a part of the travel industry*. Melbourne: Lonely Planet.

Buyya, R., Yeo, C., Venugopa, S., Broberg, J., & Brandic, I. (2009). Cloud computing and emerging it platforms: Vision, hype, and reality for delivering computing as the 5th utility. *Future Generation Computer Systems*, *25*(6), 599–616. doi:10.1016/j.future.2008.12.001

Cabrelles, M., Seguí, A. E., Navarro, S., Galcerá, S., Portalés, C., & Lerma, J. L. (2010). *3D Photorealistic modelling of stone monuments by dense image matching*. Paper presented at the International Archives of Photogrammetry, Remote Sensing and Spatial Information Sciences. Commission V Symposium, Newcastle upon Tyne, UK.

Cai, L. A., Feng, R., & Breiter, D. (2004). Tourist purchase decision involvement and information preferences. *Journal of Vacation Marketing, 10*(2), 138-148.

Câmara, A. G., Murteira, H., & Rodrigues, P. (2009). City and spectacle: a vision of pre-earthquake Lisbon. In *Virtual Systems and Multimedia, 2009. VSMM'09. 15th International Conference on* (pp. 239–243). IEEE. doi:10.1109/VSMM.2009.43

Camargo, H. L. (2000). *Dimensão histórica da construção e dos atrativos para o turismo no Brasil. IV Encontro nacional de turismo com base local*. Joinvile.

Cambourne, B., Mitchell, R., Hall, C. M., Sharples, L., & Macionis, N. (2003). *Food tourism around the world: Development, management and markets*. Amsterdam: Elsevier Ltd.

Camprubí, R., & Coromina, L. (2016). La influencia de las fuentes de información en la formación de la imagen turística. *PASOS. Revista de Turismo y Patrimonio Cultural*, *14*(4), 781–796.

Cannon Hunter, W., Chung, N., Gretzel, U., & Koo, C. (2015). Constructivist Research in Smart Tourism. *Asia Pacific Journal of Information Systems*, *25*(1), 105–120. doi:10.14329/apjis.2015.25.1.105

Cano Fuentes, M. (2006). Las estrategias de promoción exteriror del turismo deportivo y naturaleza español por parte del instituto de turismo de España. *Estudios Turísticos*, *169-170*, 39–49.

Cantallops, A. S., & Salvi, F. (2014). New consumer behavior: A review of research on eWOM and hotels. *International Journal of Hospitality Management*, *36*, 41–51. doi:10.1016/j.ijhm.2013.08.007

Cantoni, L., Kalbaska, N., & Inversini, A. (2009). E-learning in tourism and hospitality: A map. *Journal of Hospitality, Leisure, Sports and Tourism Education (Pre-2012), 8*(2), 148.

Cantoni, V., Lombardi, L., Porta, M., & Setti, A. (2016). Interactive, Tangible and Multi-sensory Technology for a Cultural Heritage Exhibition: The Battle of Pavia. In S. Margenov, G. Angelova, & G. Agre (Eds.), *Innovative Approaches and Solutions in Advanced Intelligent Systems* (pp. 77–94). Cham: Springer International Publishing. doi:10.1007/978-3-319-32207-0_6

CanTur - Sociedad Regional Cántabra de Promoción Turística (2015). *Green Spain – The Spirit of the North Press Kit*. Author.

Cardoso, A., & Almeida, L. (2005). O Caminho Português de Santiago. Editora Lucerna, 1.ª edição, Cascais.

Caro, J. L., Luque, A., & Zayas, B. (2015). Nuevas tecnologías para la interpretación y promoción de los recursos turísticos culturales. *Pasos. Revista de Turismo Y Patrimonio Cultural, 13*(4), 931-945.

Carrozzino, M., Tecchia, F., & Bergamasco, M. (2009). Urban procedural modeling for real-time rendering. *Proceedings of the 3rd ISPRS International Workshop 3D-ARCH.*

Carter, R. W., & Bramley, R. (2002). Defining heritage values and significance for improved resource management: An application to Australian tourism. *International Journal of Heritage Studies*, *8*(3), 175–199. doi:10.1080/13527250220000/18895

Carvalho, J., & Raposo, R. (2014). A adoção de media sociais como estratégias comunicacionais por museus: aplicações e tendências. In B. Passarelli, A. M. da Silva, & F. Ramos (Eds.), E-Infocomunicação: Estratégias e Aplicações (4th ed.; pp. 329–348). São Paulo: Senac.

Carvalho, R. (2014). A literature review of the role of cultural capital in creative tourism. In *Contemporary Issues in Tourism & Management Studies TMS Conference Series 2014* (pp. 17-28). University of the Algarve, School of Management, Hospitality and Tourism.

Carvalho, R., Costa, C., & Ferreira, A. M. (2015). *Community based tourism festivals in the Médio Tejo Region, Portugal – A potential for the specialized cultural consumption of Creative Tourism.* Paper presented at IV International Congress on tourism – Tourism in the 21st Century, Management School of Polytechnic Institute of Cávado e Ave, Guimarães.

Carvalho, R., Costa, C., & Ferreira, A. M. (2016). *Turismo Criativo – Uma leitura contemporânea de capital cultural.* Communication presented at the PDT Meeting, University of Aveiro.

Carvão, S. (2009). *Tendências do turismo internacional. Revista Científica EXEDRA*. Escola Superior de Educação de Coimbra. Nº temático - Turismo e Patrimônio. pp. 17-32. Portugal. Retrieved February 01, 2017, from http://www.exedrajournal.com/docs/S-tur/02-Sandra-Carvao-32.pdf

Case, A. (2015). *Calm technology: principles and patterns for non-intrusive design*. Sebastopol, CA: O'Reilly Media, Inc.

Casella, G., & Coelho, M. (2013). Augmented heritage: situating augmented reality mobile apps in cultural heritage communication. *Proceedings of the International Conference on Information Systems and Design of Communication*, 138-140. doi:10.1145/2503859.2503883

Castellani, A. P., Ministeri, G., Rotoloni, M., Vangelista, L., & Zorzi, M. (2012). Interoperable and globally interconnected smart grid using ipv6 and 6lowpan. *2012 IEEE International Conference on Communications (ICC)*, 6473–6478.

Castells, M. (2002). *A sociedade em rede*. Lisboa: Fundação Calouste Gulbenkian.

Catchoom. (2016). Retrieved: Nov. 16, 2016 from http://catchoom.com/

Categories for the Description of Works of Art (CDWA) (Getty Research Institute). (2014, March 25). Retrieved from http://www.getty.edu/research/publications/electronic_publications/cdwa/

Catherwood, D. W., & Van Kirk, R. L. (1992). *The Complete Guide to Special Event Management: Business Insights, Financial Advice, and Successful Strategies from Ernst & Young, Advisors to the Olympics, the Emmy Awards and the PGA Tour*. New York: John Wiley & Sons.

Cattell, R. (2011). Scalable SQL and NoSQL data stores. *SIGMOD Record*, *39*(4), 12–27. doi:10.1145/1978915.1978919

CDN Media. (2016). *Google translate word Lens*. Retrieved April, 3rd, 2015, from http://cdn-media-2.lifehack.org/wp-content/files/2015/04/google-translate-word-lens.jpg

Çeltek, E. (2016). *Augmented Reality Advertisements in Tourism Marketing. In Mobile Computing and Wireless Networks: Concepts, Methodologies, Tools, and Applications* (pp. 1082–1102). Hershey, PA: IGI Global.

Cerezo-Medina, A., & Guevara-Plaza, A. (2015). Necesidades formativas tecnológicas en turismo. Estudio de caso de Andalucía. *PASOS. Revista de Turismo y Patrimonio Cultural*, *13*(4), 913–929.

Cerutti, S., & Piva, E. (2016). The role of tourists' feedback in the enhancement of religious tourism destination. *International Journal of Religious Tourism and Pilgrimage*, *4*(3), 6–16.

Cesar, P. A. B., & Tronca, B. (2016). Ruins of the Jesuit - Guaranis Missions of São Miguel Arcanjo: An Overview on the UNESCO World Heritage in Brazil. In Tourism and History World Heritage: Case Studies of Ibero-American Space, Interdisciplinary. Centre of Social Sciences (CICS-NOVA).

Cetica, M., Marras, L., Materazzi, M., & Poggi, P. (2007). Tecniche di imaging multispettrale. In M. Martini, A. Castellano, & E. Sibi-lia (Eds.), Elementi di archeometria. Metodi fisici per i beni culturali (pp. 231–252). Academic Press.

CEUD. (2016). Retrieved: Nov. 16, 2016 from http://goo.gl/fUHPj6

Chabries, D. M., Booras, S. W., & Bearman, G. H. (2003). Imaging the past: Recent applications of multispectral imaging technology to deciphering manuscripts. *Antiquity*, *77*(296), 359–372. doi:10.1017/S0003598X00092346

Chaffey, D., Ellis-Chadwick, F., Mayer, R., & Johnston, K. (2006). *Internet Marketing: Strategy, Implementation and Practice. Practice* (Vol. 3). Upper Saddle River, NJ: Prentice-Hall, Inc.

Challis, K. (2006). Airborne laser altimetry in alluviated landscapes. *Archaeological Prospection*, *13*(2), 103–127. doi:10.1002/arp.272

Chalmers, A., Roussos, I., & Ledda, P. (2006). Authentic illumination of archaeological site reconstructions. In *Conference on Colour in Graphics, Imaging, and Vision* (Vol. 2006, pp. 431–434). Society for Imaging Science and Technology.

Chanda, S. (2013). The special visitor: Each and every one of us. *ICOFOM Study Series*, (42), 83–96. Retrieved from http://network.icom.museum/fileadmin/user_upload/minisites/icofom/pdf/ISS_42__2013_Rio_red.pdf

Chandel, S. S., Sharma, V., & Marwah, B. M. (2016). Review of energy efficient features in vernacular architecture for improving indoor thermal comfort conditions. *Renewable & Sustainable Energy Reviews*, *65*, 459–477. doi:10.1016/j.rser.2016.07.038

Chane, C., Schütze, R., Boochs, F., & Marzani, F. (2013). Registration of 3D and Multispectral Data for the Study of Cultural Heritage Surfaces. *Sensors (Basel, Switzerland)*, *13*(1), 1004–1020. doi:10.3390/s130101004 PMID:23322103

Chang, Y. L., Hou, H. T., Pan, C. Y., Sung, Y. T., & Chang, K. E. (2015). Apply an Augmented Reality in a Mobile Guidance to Increase Sense of Place for Heritage Places. *Journal of Educational Technology & Society*, *18*(2), 166–178.

Chan, M., Estève, D., Fourniols, J.-Y., Escriba, C., & Campo, E. (2012). Smart wearable systems: Current status and future challenges. *Artificial Intelligence in Medicine*, *56*(3), 137–156. doi:10.1016/j.artmed.2012.09.003 PMID:23122689

Chan, S., & Cope, A. (2015). Strategies against Architecture: Interactive Media and Transformative Technology at the Cooper Hewitt, Smithsonian Design Museum. *Curator*, *58*(3), 352–368. doi:10.1111/cura.12118

Charara, S. (2016). *Hussein Chalayan has turned emotion sensing into a thing of beauty: Biometric wearables at the Design Museum's new Fear and Love exhibition* [online article]. Retrieved December 7, 2016, from http://www.wareable.com/wearable-tech/hussein-chalayan-emotions-design-museum-3603

Charara, S. (2016). Virtual reality versus augmented reality: Which is the future?. Wearable blog, London.

Char-lee, J. M., Ritchie, B. W., Ruhanen, L. M., & Moyle, B. D. (2014). An institutional assessment of three local government-level tourism destinations at different stages of the transformation process. *Tourism Management*, *41*, 107–118. doi:10.1016/j.tourman.2013.09.007

Charles, S. (2011). O individualismo paradoxal – Introdução ao pensamento de Gilles Lipovetsky. In Os Tempos Hipermodernos. Lisboa, Portugal: Edições 70.

Chelini, M. (2012). Novas tecnologias para...novas (?) expografias. *Revista Museologia & Interdisciplinaridade, 1*(2), 59–71. Retrieved from http://seer.bce.unb.br/index.php/museologia/article/view/7904

Chen, D., Brown, J., & Khan, J. Y. (2014). Performance analysis of a distributed 6lowpan network for the smart grid applications. *Intelligent Sensors, Sensor Networks and Information Processing (ISSNIP), 2014 IEEE Ninth International Conference on*, 1–6.

Chen, C. F., & Chen, F. S. (2010). Experience quality, perceived value, satisfaction and behavioral intentions for heritage tourists. *Tourism Management, 31*(1), 29–35. doi:10.1016/j.tourman.2009.02.008

Chen, C.-F., & Phou, S. (2013). A closer look at destination: Image, personality, relationship and loyalty. *Tourism Management, 36*, 269–278. doi:10.1016/j.tourman.2012.11.015

Cheng, K. H., & Tsai, C. C. (2013). Affordances of augmented reality in science learning: Suggestions for future research. *Journal of Science Education and Technology, 22*(4), 449–462. doi:10.1007/s10956-012-9405-9

Chen, W. (2014). Historical Oslo on a handheld device–a mobile augmented reality application. *Procedia Computer Science, 35*, 979–985. doi:10.1016/j.procs.2014.08.180

Cheung, M. Y., Luo, C., Sia, C. L., & Chen, H. (2009). Credibility of electronic word-of-mouth: Informational and normative determinants of on-line consumer recommendations. *International Journal of Electronic Commerce, 13*(4), 9–38. doi:10.2753/JEC1086-4415130402

Chiu, D. K. W., & Leung, H. (2005). Towards ubiquitous tourist service coordination and integration. In *Proceedings of the 7th international conference on Electronic commerce - ICEC '05*. New York: ACM Press. doi:10.1145/1089551.1089656

Cho, Y., & Fesenmaier, D. R. (2001). A new paradigm for tourism and electronic commerce: Experience marketing using the virtual tour. *Tourism Distribution Channels: Practices, Issues and Transformation*, 351-370.

Choay, F. (2000). *A alegoria do patrimônio.* Edições 70.

Choi, S., Lee, W., Youn, J. H., Moore, D., & Schuette, M. (2015). An energy-efficient neighbor discovery protocol for 6lowpan smart grid applications. Wireless Communications and Networking Conference Workshops (WCNCW), 2015 IEEE, 52–57.

Chou, D., & Chou, A. (2007). Analysis of a new information systems outsourcing practice: Software-as-a-service business model. *International Journal Information Systems Change Management, 2*(4), 392–405. doi:10.1504/IJISCM.2007.017385

Chow, S.-K., & Chan, K.-L. (2009). Reconstruction of photorealistic 3D model of ceramic artefacts for interactive virtual exhibition. *Journal of Cultural Heritage, 10*(2), 161–173. doi:10.1016/j.culher.2008.08.011

Christou, C., Angus, C., Loscos, C., Dettori, A., & Roussou, M. (2006). A versatile large-scale multimodal VR system for cultural heritage visualization. *Proceedings of the ACM symposium on Virtual reality software and technology.* doi:10.1145/1180495.1180523

Chun, R. (2016). *The SFMOMA's New App Will Forever Change How You Enjoy Museums* [online article]. Retrieved October 29, 2016, from https://www.wired.com/2016/05/sfmoma-audio-tour-app/

Chung, J. Y., & Buhalis, D. (2008). A study of online travel community and Web 2.0: Factors affecting participation and attitude. *Proceedings Enter, 2008*, 267–278.

Chung, N., Han, H., & Joun, Y. (2015). Tourists intention to visit a destination: The role of augmented reality (AR) application for a heritage site. *Computers in Human Behavior*, *50*, 588–599. doi:10.1016/j.chb.2015.02.068

Chung, N., & Lee, H. (2016). Sharing economy in geotag: What are the travelers goals sharing their locations by using geotags in social network sites during the tour?. *International Journal of Tourism Cities*, *2*(2), 125–136. doi:10.1108/IJTC-08-2015-0022

Chung, N., Lee, S., & Han, H. (2015). Understanding communication types on travel information sharing in social media: A transactive memory systems perspective. *Telematics and Informatics*, *32*(4), 564–575. doi:10.1016/j.tele.2015.02.002

Ciampi, M., Leccese, F., & Tuoni, G. (2003). Ventilated facades energy performance in summer cooling of buildings. *Solar Energy*, *75*(6), 491–502. doi:10.1016/j.solener.2003.09.010

CIMI. (2001). *Guide to best practice: Dublin Core version 1.1*. Consortium for the Computer Interchange of Museum Information, CIMI Consortium.

Classen, C. (2007). Museum manners: The sensory life of the early museum. *Journal of Social History*, *40*(4), 895–914. doi:10.1353/jsh.2007.0089

Cleveland Museum of Art. (2013). *About Gallery One*. Retrieved from http://www.clevelandart.org/gallery-one/about

Clough, G. W. (2014). *How Will 3-D Printing Change the Smithsonian?* [online article]. Retrieved December 5, 2016, from http://www.smithsonianmag.com/smithsonian-institution/how-will-3d-printing-change-the-smithsonian-180949426/?no-ist

CNBC. (2016). *Virtual reality devices could transform the tourism experience*. Retrieved January, 8th, 2016, from http://www.cnbc.com/2016/01/08/virtual-reality-devices-could-transform-the-tourism-experience.html

Coburn, E., Light, R., McKenna, G., Stein, R., & Vitzthum, A. (2010). *LIDO – Lightweight Information Describing Objects, version 1.0*. ICOM/CIDOC for the Data Harvesting Working Group.

Cohen, K. (2001). Monsters, Inc.: The secret behind why pixar is so good. *Animation World Magazine*, (6), 6–12.

Cohen, E. H. (2011). Educational dark tourism at an in populo site: The Holocaust Museum in Jerusalem. *Annals of Tourism Research*, *38*(1), 193–209. doi:10.1016/j.annals.2010.08.003

Cohen, E., & Avieli, N. (2004). Food in tourism: Attraction and impediment. *Annals of Tourism Research*, *31*(4), 755–778. doi:10.1016/j.annals.2004.02.003

Collins-Kreiner, N. (2010). Researching pilgrimage: Continuity and transformations. *Annals of Tourism Research*, *37*(2), 440–456. doi:10.1016/j.annals.2009.10.016

Communications of the ACM. (2009, November 5). *Virtual Cocoon Could Simulate Five Senses*. Retrieved 28 February 2017, from http://cacm.acm.org/news/26100-virtual-cocoon-could-simulate-five-senses/fulltext

Conati, C., Carenini, G., Toker, D., & Lallé, S. (2015). *Towards User-Adaptive Information Visualization*. AAAI.

Cook, D., & Das, S. (2005). *Smart environments: technologies, protocols, and applications*. Hoboken, NJ: John Wiley.

Cooke, P. N., & Lazzeretti, L. (Eds.). (2008). *Creative cities, cultural clusters and local economic development*. Edward Elgar Publishing.

Cooper, A., Reimann, R., Cronin, D., & Noessel, C. (2014). *About the face: The essentials of interaction design*. Indianapolis: Wiley.

Corine, B. (2014). *GuidiGO new storytelling platform enhances Keith Haring exhibition at the de Young Museum through Google Glass* [online article]. Retrieved September 10, 2016, from http://blog.guidigo.com/blog/guidigo-new-storytelling-platform-enhances-keith-haring-exhibition-at-the-de-young-museum-through-google-glass/

Correia, V. (2002). *Conimbriga Ruínas - Museu monográfico*. Retrieved from http://www.conimbriga.pt/portugues/ruinas0.html

Corsi, C., & Vermeulen, F. (Eds.). (2012). *Ammaia I: The Survey. A Romano-Lusitanian Townscape Revealed. Archaeological Reports Ghent University (ARGU) 8*. Ghent: Academia Press.

Costa, H., Cabrita, C., Monteiro, J., & Semião, J. (2015). *Mecanismo de Deteção de Consumos Anómalos em Redes Energéticas Inteligentes. CRC2015*, 19–20.

Council, E. U. (2003). *Council Resolution of 6 May 2003 on accessibility of cultural infrastructure and cultural activities for people with disabilities (2003/C 134/05)*. Official Journal of the European Union.

Couto, P., Magalhães, L., Melo-Pinto, P., & Gabriel, R. (2005). Caracterização do Movimento Tridimensional de Corpos Articulados. In Atas do 13o Encontro Português de Computação Gráfica. Vila Real.

Coyle, L., & Cunningham, P. (2003). Exploiting re-ranking information in a case-based personal travel assistant. *Proceedings of the 5th International Conference on Case-based Reasoning*, 11-13.

Cracolici, M. F., & Nijkamp, P. (2009). The attractiveness and competitiveness of tourist destinations: A study of Southern Italian regions. *Tourism Management*, *30*(3), 336–344. doi:10.1016/j.tourman.2008.07.006

Creative Tourism Network. (2014). Retrieved from http://www.creativetourismnetwork.org/

Crofts, N., Dionissiadou, I., Doerr, M., & Reed, P. (Eds.). (1998). *CIDOC Conceptual Reference Model - Information groups*. ICOM/CIDOC Documentation Standards Group.

Crompton, J. L. (1979). An assessment of the image of Mexico as a vacation destination and the influence of geographical location upon that image. *Journal of Travel Research*, *17*(1), 18–23. doi:10.1177/004728757901700404

Cultural Institute. (2013). *Google Art Project: Toda a Arte do Mundo na Ponta dos Seus Dedos* [online article]. Retrieved December 21, 2016, from https://www.google.com/intl/pt-BR/culturalinstitute/about/artproject/

Cunningham, P. (2016). *No more lost in translation – smart earpiece to translate foreign languages instantly for travellers*. Retrieved July 19, 2016, from http://www.lonelyplanet.com/news/2016/05/18/new-earpiece-instant-translation/

Czikk, J. (2013). *New ScopifyROM App Gives Royal Ontario Museum Visitors an Augmented Experience* [online article]. Retrieved September 15, 2016, from http://www.betakit.com/new-scopifyrom-app-gives-royal-ontario-museum-visitors-an-augmented-experience/

Da Cruz, G., Velozo, T., & Elvas Falcão Soares, A. (2011). Twitter, Youtube e innovación en la promoción turística online: Análisis de las estrategias del Ministerio de Turismo de Brasil. *Estudios y perspectivas en turismo, 20*(3), 627-642.

Dadda, A., & Ouhbi, I. (2014). A decision support system for renewable energy plant projects. *2014 International Conference on Next Generation Networks and Services (NGNS)*, 356-362. doi:10.1109/NGNS.2014.6990278

Dalbavie, J. (2014). La table interactive du musée d'Histoire Naturelle de Lille. *La Lettre de l'OCIM*, (152). 10.4000/ocim.1339

DALI Activity Group. (2001). *Digital Addressable Lighting Interface Manual*. Retrieved January 18, 2017 from goo.gl/vVJzup

Dallen, T. (1999). Participatory planning: A view of tourism in Indonesia. *Annals of Tourism Research*, *26*(2), 371–391. doi:10.1016/S0160-7383(98)00104-2

Damala, A., Van der Vaart, M., Clarke, L., Hornecker, E., Avram, G., Hub, K., & Ruthven, I. (2016). Evaluating tangible and multisensory museum visiting experiences: Lessons learned from the meSch project. *MW2016: Museums and the Web 2016*. Retrieved from http://mw2016.museumsandtheweb.com/paper/evaluating-tangible-and-multisensory-museum-visiting-experiences-lessons-learned-from-the-mesch-project/

Damala, A., Stojanovic, N., Schuchert, T., Moragues, J., Cabrera, A., & Gilleade, K. (2012). Adaptive augmented reality for cultural heritage: ARtSENSE project. *Euro-Mediterranean Conference*, 746-755. doi:10.1007/978-3-642-34234-9_79

Datta, P., Bigham, G., Zou, Z., & Hill, G. (2015). A global study of heritage site ecology, proclivity and loyalty. *Journal of Hospitality and Tourism Management*, *25*, 19–29. doi:10.1016/j.jhtm.2014.12.002

Davis, F. D. (1989). Perceived usefulness, perceived ease of use and user acceptance of information technology. *Management Information Systems Quarterly*, *13*(3), 319–339. doi:10.2307/249008

de Boer, V., Wielemaker, J., van Gent, J., Oosterbroek, M., Hildebrand, M., Isaac, A., & Schreiber, G. et al. (2013). Amsterdam Museum Linked Open Data. *Semantic Web – Interoperability, Usability, Applicability*, *4*(3), 237–243.

De Castro, S. (2009). *Micoturismo: Enquadramento Estratégico em Áreas Protegidas* (Unpublished Master Dissertation). Universidad Técnica de Lisboa, Portugal.

De Frutos, P., Martínez, F., & Esteban, S. (2012). Edible wild mushroom tourism as a source of income and employment in rural areas. The case of Castilla y León. *Forest Systems*, *21*(1), 81–98. doi:10.5424/fs/2112211-02545

de Heras Ciechomski, P., Schertenleib, S., Maïm, J., & Thalmann, D. (2005). *Reviving the Roman Odeon of Aphrodisias: Dynamic Animation and Variety Control of Crowds in Virtual Heritage*. Retrieved from http://infoscience.epfl.ch/record/99010

De La Rosa, B. M. (2003). Nuevos turistas en busca de un nuevo producto: El patrimonio cultural. *Pasos. Revista de Turismo y Cultura*, *1*(2), 157–159.

De Rojas, C., & Camarero, C. (2008). Visitors experience, mood and satisfaction in a heritage context: Evidence from an interpretation center. *Tourism Management*, *29*(3), 525–537. doi:10.1016/j.tourman.2007.06.004

Debevec, P. (2003). Image-based techniques for digitizing environments and artifacts. In *3-D Digital Imaging and Modeling, 2003. 3DIM 2003. Proceedings. Fourth International Conference on* (pp. 234–241). IEEE. doi:10.1109/IM.2003.1240255

Debevec, P. (1996). *Modeling e Rendering Architecture from Photographs*. Berkeley, CA: University of California. doi:10.1145/237170.237191

Debut, V., Carvalho, M., Figueiredo, E., Antunes, J., & Silva, R. (2016). The sound of bronze: Virtual resurrection of a broken medieval bell. *Journal of Cultural Heritage*, *19*, 544–554. doi:10.1016/j.culher.2015.09.007

Deliyiannis, I., & Papaioannou, G. (2014). Augmented Reality For Archaeological Environments On Mobile Devices: A Novel Open Framework. *Mediterranean Archaeology and Archaeometry*, *14*(4), 1–10.

Demo, P. (1995). *Metodologia científica em ciências sociais*. São Paulo, SP: Atlas.

Dennis, K., & Urry, J. (2009). *After the car* (1st ed.). Cambridge, UK: Polity Press.

Department for Transport. (2002). *Inclusive mobility*. London: DfT.

Desvallées, A., & Mairesse, F. (2010). Key Concepts of Museology. Paris: Armand Colin. Retrieved from http://icom.museum/fileadmin/user_upload/pdf/Key_Concepts_of_Museology/Museologie_Anglais_BD.pdf

Devlin, K., & Chalmers, A. (2001). Realistic visualisation of the pompeii frescoes. In *Proceedings of the 1st international conference on Computer graphics, virtual reality and visualisation* (pp. 43–48). ACM.

Díaz-Andreu, M. (2013). Ethics and archaeological tourism in Latin America. *International Journal of Historical Archaeology, 17*(2), 225–244. doi:10.1007/s10761-013-0218-1

Díaz-Andreu, M. (2014). Turismo y arqueología. Una mirada histórica a una relación silenciada. []. Elsevier.]. *Anales de Antropologia, 48*(2), 9–39. doi:10.1016/S0185-1225(14)70242-5

Díaz, M., Martín, C., & Rubio, B. (2016). State-of-the-art, challenges, and open issues in the integration of Internet of things and cloud computing. *Journal of Network and Computer Applications, 67*, 99–117. doi:10.1016/j.jnca.2016.01.010

Dibble, T. (2015). *Technology is changging travel.* Retrieved July 18, 2015, from https://www.screenpilot.com/2015/03/wearables-wanderlust-how-technology-is-changing-travel/

Die Welt. (2016). *„Wir haben kein einziges Bett mehr frei".* Retrieved May 21, 2016, from http://www.welt.de/153592079

Digital Binocular Station. (2016). *The digital binocular station.* Retrieved January, 9th, 2016, from http://www.digital-binocularstation.com/

Dijkshoorn, C., Jongma, L., van Ossenbruggen, J., Schreiber, G., ter Weele, W., & Wielemaker, J. (2016). *The Rijksmuseum Collection as Linked Data. Semantic Web – Interoperability, Usability, Applicability.*

Dijkshoorn, C., van Ossenbruggen, J., Aroyo, L., & Schreiber, G. (2014), INVENiT: Exploring cultural heritage collections while adding annotations. *Proceedings of the 3rd International Conference on Intelligent Exploration of Semantic Data (IESD'14)*, 1279.

Dikaiakou, M., Efthymiou, A., & Chrysanthou, Y. (2003). Modelling the Walled City of Nicosia. In *Proceedings of the 4th International Conference on Virtual Reality, Archaeology and Intelligent Cultural Heritage* (pp. 61–70). Aire-la-Ville, Switzerland: Eurographics Association. https://doi.org/10.2312/VAST/VAST03/061-070

Doljenkova, V. (2015). *Beacons: Exploring Location-Based Technology in Museums* [online article]. Retrieved December 6, 2016, from http://www.metmuseum.org/about-the-museum/museum-departments/office-of-the-director/digital-media-department/digital-underground/2015/beacons

Dong, B., Cao, C., & Lee, S. E. (2005). Applying support vector machines to predict building energy consumption in tropical region. *Energy and Building, 37*(5), 545–553. doi:10.1016/j.enbuild.2004.09.009

Dore, C., & Murphy, M. (2012). Integration of Historic BIM (HBIM) and 3D GIS for Recording and Managing Cultural Heritage Sites. *Proceedings of the 18th International Conference on Virtual Systems and Multimedia (VSMM)*, 369–376.

Dos Santos, R. J., & Antoninni, B. O. (2004). La gastronomía típica de la Isla de Santa Catarina (Brasil). *Estudios y Perspectivas en Turismo, 13*, 89–110.

Douek, J. (2013). Music and emotion: A composers perspective. *Frontiers in Systems Neuroscience, 7*, 82. doi:10.3389/fnsys.2013.00082 PMID:24348344

Dreamworks Animation. (1998, September 7). Retrieved 1 May 2015, from http://www.dreamworksanimation.com/

Driving Mode functionality. (2017). *Google Maps será capaz de descobrir sozinho para onde o utilizador vai*. Retrieved: January 12, 2017, from http://exameinformatica.sapo.pt/noticias/software/2016-01-13-Google-Maps-sera-capaz-de-descobrir-sozinho-para-onde-o-utilizador-vai?utm_source=newsletter&utm_medium=mail&utm_campaign=newsletter&utm_content=2016-01-14

DSTATIS Statistisches Bundesamt. (2016). *Bevölkerung nach Geschlecht und Staatsangehörigkeit*. Retrieved May 21, 2016 from https://www.destatis.de/DE/ZahlenFakten/GesellschaftStaat/Bevoelkerung/Bevoelkerungsstand/Tabellen/Zensus_Geschlecht_Staatsangehoerigkeit.html

du Louvre, M., & Printing, D. N. (2010). *Diplomacy and Sèvres Porcelain, Prestige and the French art of living in the 18th century* [press release]. Retrieved October 5, 2016, from http://www.museumlab.eu/press/pdf/Louvre-DNPMuseumLab_7_PressRelease_EN.pdf

du Louvre, M., & Printing, D. N. (2012). *El niño azul, Goya and Spanish Painting in the Louvre: Louvre-DNP Museum Lab Ninth presentation in Tokyo* [press release]. Retrieved September 14, 2016, from http://www.museumlab.eu/press/pdf/Louvre-DNPMuseumLab_9_PressRelease_EN.pdf

Dylla, K., Frischer, B., Mueller, P., Ulmer, A., & Haegler, S. (2010). Rome Reborn 2.0: A Case Study of Virtual City Reconstruction Using Procedural Modeling Techniques. *CAA 2009. Making History Interactive*, 62-66.

Dylla, K., Frischer, B., Müller, P., Ulmer, A., & Haegler, S. (2010). Rome Reborn 2.0: A Case Study of Virtual City Reconstruction Using Procedural Modeling Techniques. In *37th Proceedings of the CAA Conference* (pp. 62–66). EG.

Eastman, C., Teicholz, P., Sacks, R., & Liston, K. (2011). *BIM Handbook – A Guide to Building Information Modeling for Owners, Managers, Designers, Engineers, and Contractors* (2nd ed.). Hoboken, NJ: John Wiley & Sons, Inc.

Echelon. (2009). *Introduction to the LonWorks® Platform, revision 2, Echelon*. Retrieved January 18, 2017, from goo.gl/iYnoHl

Echeverria, B. (2010). For whom does language death toll? Cautionary notes from the Basque case. *Linguistics and Education*, *21*(3), 197–209. doi:10.1016/j.linged.2009.10.001

Echtner, C. M., & Ritchie, J. R. B. (1991). The Meaning and Measurement of Destination Image. *The Journal of Tourism Studies*, *14*(1), 37–48.

Echtner, C. M., & Ritchie, J. R. B. (1993). The Measurement of Destination Image: An Emperical Assessment. *Journal of Travel Research*, *31*(4), 3–13. doi:10.1177/004728759303100402

Edelsbrunner, J., Havemann, S., Sourin, A., & Fellner, D. W. (2016). Procedural Modeling of Round Building Geometry. In *2016 International Conference on Cyberworlds (CW)* (pp. 81–88). https://doi.org/10.1109/CW.2016.19

EDUCAUSE. (2008). 7 Things You Should Know About Multi-Touch Interfaces. *EDUCAUSE Learning Inititative (ELI)*. Retrieved from http://www.educause.edu/ELI/7ThingsYouShouldKnowAboutMulti/162960

EF. (2015). *Europeana for Education and Learning*. Den Haag: Policy Recommendations. Europeana Foundation.

Egger, R., & Buhalis, D. (2008). *eTourism Case studies: Management & Marketing issues in eTourism*. Butterworth Heinemann Oxford.

Egon, F. (2003). *Wick and fuel information for Egan Bronze Oil Lamps*. Retrieved 23 January 2012, from http://www.eganbronze.com/Pages/wicksfuel.html

Ejemplo de Mealhada–Portugal, U. (2007). La importancia de la gastronomía en el Turismo. *Estudios y Perspectivas en Turismo*, *16*, 261–282.

Ekici, B. B., & Aksoy, U. T. (2009). Prediction of building energy consumption by using artificial neural networks. *Advances in Engineering Software*, *40*(5), 356–362. doi:10.1016/j.advengsoft.2008.05.003

Electric, S. (2012). *iEM3100 series / iEM3200 series Energy Meters, User Manual*. Retrieved January 18, 2017 from https://goo.gl/PcdE2E

Electric, S. (2013). *PowerLogic communication devices EGX100 Ethernet gateway Technical data sheet, EGX300 Integrated gateway-server*. Retrieved January 18, 2017 from https://goo.gl/JDNrGx

Electronic Arts. (1998, July 6). *Need For Speed (NFS)*. Retrieved 1 May 2015, from http://www.needforspeed.com/

Elwood, S. A. (2010). Embedding Ubiquitous Technologies. In J. Symonds (Ed.), Ubiquitous and Pervasive Computing: Concepts, Methodologies, Tools, and Applications (pp. 511–519). Hershey, PA: IGI Global. doi:10.4018/978-1-60566-960-1.ch033

Emoncms. (2017). *Emoncms Platform*. Retrieved January 17, 2017, from emoncms.org

Engelberger, J. F. (1982). Robotics in practice: Future capabilities. *Electronic Servicing & Technology Magazine.*

English Heritage. (2004). *Easy access to historic buildings*. Swindon, UK: EH.

English Heritage. (2005). *Easy access to historic landscapes*. Swindon, UK: EH.

EnOcean GmbH. (2016). *EnOcean Standard ESP3 Specification V1.30*. Retrieved January 18, 2017 from https://goo.gl/JLTxou

EnPROVE. (2013). *Energy Consumption Prediction with Building Usage Measurements for Software Based Decision Support*. Retrieved January 17, 2017, from www.enprove.eu

Ercek, R., Viviers, D., & Warzée, N. (2010). 3D reconstruction and digitalization of an archeological site, Itanos, Crete. *Virtual Archaeology Review*, *1*(1). 10.4995/var.2010.4794

Erenoglu, R. C., Akcay, O., & Erenoglu, O. (2017). An UAS-assisted multi-sensor approach for 3D modeling and reconstruction of cultural heritage site. *Journal of Cultural Heritage*. doi:10.1016/j.culher.2017.02.007

Estêvão, J. V., Carneiro, M. J., & Teixeira, L. (2014). The Evolving Value of eTourism for Suppliers and Visitors. In J. Gamon (Ed.), *Handbook of Research on Enterprise 2.0: Technological, Social and Organizational Dimensions* (pp. 486–510). Hershey, PA: Business Science Reference. doi:10.4018/978-1-4666-4373-4.ch026

Estimote. (2016). *Estimote: Create magical experiences in the physical world*. Retrieved: Nov. 16, 2016 from http://estimote.com/

ETE. (2016). *Keys to unlocking digital heritage for use in education*. Europeana Taskforce for Education.

Etro, F. (2009). The economic impact of cloud computing on business creation, employment and output in Europe. *Review Business and Economics*, *54*(2), 179–208.

Euromonitor. (2014). *Online Travel Intermediaries: A Fast Changing Competitive Landscape*. Retrieved July 29, 2016, from http://www.slovenia.info/pictures/TB_board/atachments_1/2014/Online_Travel_Intermediaries_A_Fast_Changing_Competitive_Landscape_19150.pdf

Europe Press. (2013 May 24). El proyecto 'Micosylva+' estima en 65 millones de euros el valor medio generado por la micología en CyL. EP Castilla y León. *Europa Press*. Retrieved from: http://www.europapress.es/castilla-y-leon/noticia-proyecto-micosylva-estima-65-millones-euros-valor-medio-generado-micologia-cyl-20130524173020.html

European Commission (EC). (2014). Transnational Cultural Tourism Products and Tourism and Accessibility for all – Call for Proposals. EC.

European Commission, Institute for Energy and Transport. (2006). *Solar radiation and PV maps – Europe*. Retrieved January 17, 2017, from http://goo.gl/wIiPed

European Commission. (2016). *CULT-COOP-09-2017*. Retrieved 3 January 2017, from https://ec.europa.eu/research/participants/portal/desktop/en/opportunities/h2020/topics/cult-coop-09-2017.html

European Parliament, Council on the Energy Performance of Buildings. (2010). Directive 2010/31/EU of the European Parliament, (OJ L153 18.6.2010), 19 May 2010.

Europeana Collections. (2017). *Europeana Collections*. Retrieved 03 January, 2017, from http://www.europeana.eu/

EWB. (2016). *Europe Without Barriers*. Retrieved: Nov. 16, 2016 from http://goo.gl/sqlJrE

Ezenagu, N., & Iwuagwu, C. (2016). The role of cultural resources in Tourism development in Awka. *African Journal of Hospitality. Tourism and Leisure*, *5*(2), 1–12.

Facebook. (2015). *Company Info | Facebook Newsroom*. Retrieved October 10, 2015, from http://newsroom.fb.com/company-info/

Fai, S., Graham, K., Duckworth, T., Wood, N., & Attar, R. (2011). Building Information Modeling and heritage documentation. *Proceedings of the XXIII International CIPA Symposium*, 43–48.

Faktenkontor Gmb, H. (2016). *Social Media-Atlas 2015/2016*. Retrieved March, 21, from http://social-media-atlas.faktenkontor.de/2015/nutzung-einzelner-kanaele.php

Falk, J. (2009). *Identity and the museum visit experience*. Walnut Creek, CA: Left Coast Press.

Falk, J. H., & Dierking, L. D. (2013). *The Museum Experience Revisited*. Walnut Creek: Left Coast Press.

Faugeras, O. (1993). *Three-dimensional computer vision: a geometric viewpoint*. MIT Press.

FCo. (2016). *Gestão de Coleções*. Retrieved from http://www.museuchapelaria.cm-sjm.pt/

FeelReal. (2016). Retrieved: Dec. 6, 2016 from http://feelreal.com/

Fernandes Galhanone, R., Marques, J. A., Toledo, G. L., & Mazzon, J. A. (2010). Turismo de lujo e internet: Oportunidades para las agencias de viajes. *Estudios y perspectivas en turismo, 19*(6), 888-908.

Ferreira Lopes, S. D. (2011). Destination image: Origins, Developments and Implications. *PASOS. Revista de Tourismo y Patrimonio Cultural*, *9*(2), 305–315.

Fertier, A. (2003). EUCREA International: Policy, objectives and programme of action. In *Access to culture and sports for people with disabilities conference proceedings*. Hellenic Ministry of Culture.

Fesenmaier, D. R., Wöber, K. W., & Werthner, H. (Eds.). (2006). *Destination recommendation systems: Behavioral foundations and applications*. Cambridge, UK: CAB International. doi:10.1079/9780851990231.0000

Fields, K. (2002). Demand for the gastronomy tourism product: motivational factors. In Tourism and gastronomy (pp. 36-50). London: Routledge.

Figat, J., Kornuta, T., & Kasprzak, W. (2014). Performance evaluation of binary descriptors of local features. In *Proceedings International Conference on Computer Vision and Graphics* (pp. 187-194). Springer International Publishing. doi:10.1007/978-3-319-11331-9_23

Figueiredo, M. J. G., Gomes, J., Gomes, C., & Lopes, J. (2014). Augmented reality tools and learning practice in mobile-learning. In C. Stephanidis & M. Antona (Eds.), Lecture Notes in Computer Science: Vol. 8514. *Universal Access in Human-Computer Interaction. Universal Access to Information and Knowledge* (pp. 301–312). Springer International Publishing. doi:10.1007/978-3-319-07440-5_28

Filieri, R., & Mcleay, F. (2013). E-WOM and Accommodation: An Analysis of the Factors That Influence Travelers Adoption of Information from Online Reviews. *Journal of Travel Research*, *53*(1), 44–57. doi:10.1177/0047287513481274

Fine Arts Museums of San Francisco. (2015). *FAMSF Improves Museum Access with Beam Device* [online article]. Retrieved December 15, 2016, from https://www.famsf.org/about/technology/beam

Finkenzeller, D., Bender, J., & Schmitt, A. (2005). *Feature-based decomposition of façades*. Proc. Virtual Concept.

Fino, E. R., Martín-Gutiérrez, J., Fernández, M. D. M., & Davara, E. A. (2013). Interactive Tourist Guide: Connecting Web 2.0, Augmented Reality and QR Codes. *Procedia Computer Science*, *25*, 338–344. doi:10.1016/j.procs.2013.11.040

Fiore, A., Mainetti, L., Manco, L., & Marra, P. (2014). Augmented reality for allowing time navigation in cultural tourism experiences: a case study. *International Conference on Augmented and Virtual Reality*, 296-301. doi:10.1007/978-3-319-13969-2_22

Fischer, C., & Kakoulli, I. (2006). Multispectral and hyperspectral imaging technologies in conservation: Current research and potential applications. *Reviews in Conservation*, *7*, 3–16.

Fitzmaurice, G. W., Ishii, H., & Buxton, W. A. S. (1995). Bricks: Laying the Foundations for Graspable User Interfaces. In *Proceedings of the SIGCHI Conference on Human Factors in Computing Systems* (pp. 442–449). New York: ACM Press/Addison-Wesley Publishing Co. http://doi.org/ doi:10.1145/223904.223964

FlatBuffers. (2017). Retrieved: Jan. 6, 2017 from https://google.github.io/flatbuffers/

Flavián, C., & Fandos, C. (Eds.). (2011). Turismo gastronómico: estrategias de marketing y experiencias de éxito. Zaragoza: Prensas Universitarias de Zaragoza.

Fodness, D., & Murray, B. (1997). Tourist information search. *Annals of Tourism Research*, *24*(3), 503–523. doi:10.1016/S0160-7383(97)00009-1

Forbes, R. J. (1966). *Studies in Ancient Technology* (Vol. 6). Holanda.

Fotis, J., Buhalis, D., & Rossides, N. (2011). Social media impact on holiday travel: The case of the Russian and the FSU markets. *International Journal of Online Marketing*, *1*(4), 1–19. doi:10.4018/ijom.2011100101

Fotis, J., Buhalis, D., & Rossides, N. (2012). *Social media use and impact during the holiday travel planning process* (pp. 13–24). Springer-Verlag. doi:10.1007/978-3-7091-1142-0_2

Fox, R. (2007). Reinventing the gastronomic identity of Croatian tourist destinations. *International Journal of Hospitality Management*, *3*(3), 546–559. doi:10.1016/j.ijhm.2006.03.001

Frazen, B. V. (2003). *Jesuítas portugueses e espanhóis no sul do Brasil e Paraguai coloniais*. São Leopoldo, RS: EdUnisinos.

FRBR. (2015). *FRBR object-oriented definition and mapping from FRBRER, FRAD and FRSAD (version 2.1)*. International Working Group on FRBR and CIDOC CRM Harmonization.

Freeman, A., Adams Becker, S., Cummins, M., McKelroy, E., Giesinger, C., & Yuhnke, B. (2016). *NMC Horizon Report: 2016 Museum Edition*. Austin, TX: The New Media Consortium. doi:10.1111/j.2151-6952.2010.00064.x

Frischer, B. (2009, May 15). *Rome Reborn*. Retrieved 29 January 2017, from http://romereborn.frischerconsulting.com/

Frost & Sullivan. (2008). *Market demands for hosted UC services*. Frost & Sullivan.

Funari, P. P. A., Manzato, F., & Alfonso, L. P. (2013). Tourism and archaeology in Brazil: Postmodern epistemology in two case studies. *International Journal of Historical Archaeology*, *17*(2), 261–274. doi:10.1007/s10761-013-0219-0

Fundación de la Innovación. (2011). *Cloud computing. La tercera ola de las tecnologías de la información*. Bankinter.

Gagliano, A., Nocera, F., & Aneli, S. (2016). Thermodynamic analysis of ventilated façades under different wind conditions in summer period. *Energy and Building*, *122*, 131–139. doi:10.1016/j.enbuild.2016.04.035

Gaitatzes, A., Christopoulos, D., & Roussou, M. (2001). Reviving the past: cultural heritage meets virtual reality. *Proceedings of the 2001 conference on Virtual reality, archeology, and cultural heritage*. doi:10.1145/584993.585011

Gajos, K. Z., Wobbrock, J. O., & Weld, D. S. (2008). Improving the performance of motor-impaired users with automatically-generated, ability-based interfaces. In *Proceedings of the SIGCHI conference on Human Factors in Computing Systems* (pp. 1257-1266). ACM. doi:10.1145/1357054.1357250

Gajos, K., & Weld, D. S. (2004). SUPPLE: automatically generating user interfaces. In *Proceedings of the 9th international conference on Intelligent user interfaces* (pp. 93-100). ACM.

Gallarza, M. G., Saura, I. G., & Garcia, H. C. (2002). Destination image: Towards a conceptual framework. *Annals of Tourism Research*, *29*(1), 56–78. doi:10.1016/S0160-7383(01)00031-7

Ganapathy, S. (2013). Design guidelines for mobile augmented reality: User experience. Human Factors in Augmented Reality Environments. In Human Factors in Augmented Reality Environment. Springer.

Garagnani, S., & Manferdini, A. (2013). Parametric Accuracy: Building information Modeling Process Applied to the Cultural Heritage Preservation. International Archives of the Photogrammetry, Remote Sensing and Spatial Information Sciences.

Garau, C. (2014). From territory to smartphone: Smart fruition of cultural heritage for dynamic tourism development. *Planning Practice and Research*, *29*(3), 238–255. doi:10.1080/02697459.2014.929837

Garau, C. (2015). Perspectives on Cultural and Sustainable Rural Tourism in a Smart Region: The Case Study of Marmilla in Sardinia (Italy). *Sustainability*, *7*(6), 6412–6434. doi:10.3390/su7066412

Garcia, A., Arbelaitz, O., Linaza, M. T., Vansteenwegen, P., & Souffriau, W. (2010). Personalized tourist route generation. In *International Conference on Web Engineering* (pp. 486-497). Springer Berlin Heidelberg.

García, J. J. (2016). Estrategias de las empresas turísticas a través de dispositivos móviles. AECA. *Revista de la Asociación Española de Contabilidad y Administración de Empresas*, *113*, 16–20.

Garrido Carretero, F. (2013). The virtual reconstruction of the andalusian palace of Onda (Castellón): Architecture and Territory. *Virtual Archaeology Review*, *4*(9). 10.4995/var.2013.4245

Gartner, W. C. (1994). Image formation process. *Journal of Travel & Tourism Marketing*, *2*(2-3), 191–216. doi:10.1300/J073v02n02_12

Gasdia, M. & Rheem, C. (2012). *Mobile Hits the Mainstream: Leisure and Business Traveler Trends*. PhoCusWright.

Gąsiorek, A. (2015). *Beacon-Enabled Google Glass at Museums: "It's Not Some Distant Future. It's Already Happening"* [online article]. Retrieved December 2, 2016, from https://kontakt.io/blog/beacon-enabled-google-glass-at-museums/

Gaspar, B. (2014). *Sigillvm portvgaliae*. Retrieved from http://portugal-sigillvm.net/

Gatti, L. F. (2008). Theodor W. Adorno: Indústria cultural e crítica da cultura. In *Curso livre de teoria crítica*. Campinas, SP: Papirus.

Gavalas, D., Konstantopoulos, C., Mastakas, K., & Pantziou, G. (2014). Mobile recommender systems in tourism. *Journal of Network and Computer Applications*, *39*, 319–333. doi:10.1016/j.jnca.2013.04.006

Geertz, C. (2004). Religion as a cultural system. In *The interpretation of cultures: selected essays* (pp. 87–125). Fontana Press.

Georgopoulos, A. (2014). 3D virtual reconstruction of archaeological monuments. *Mediterranean Archaeology and Archaeometry*, *14*(4), 155–164.

Germann Molz, J. (2012). *Travel connections: Tourism, technology, and togetherness in a mobile world.* Abingdon, UK: Routledge.

Gervautz, M., & Schmalstieg, D. (2012). Anywhere interfaces using handheld Augmented Reality. *Computer*, *45*(July), 26–31. doi:10.1109/MC.2012.72

Geser, G., & Niccolucci, F. (2012). Virtual museums, digital reference collections and e-science environments. *Uncommon Culture, 3*(5/6), 12–37. Retrieved from http://firstmonday.org/ojs/index.php/UC/article/view/4714

Giddens, A. (2002). *As consequências da modernidade*. Lisboa, Portugal: Celta Editora.

Gil Soldevilla, S., Palao Errando, J. A., & Marzal Felici, J. J. (2014). Brands as New Forms of Religiosity: The Case of the World of Red Bull. *Trípodos,* (35), 57-74

Gilbert, S. (2016). Please turn on your phone in the museum: Cultural institutions learn to love selfies and social media. *Atlantic (Boston, Mass.)*, *3*, 32–33.

Gnome. (2016). *User Interface Guidelines for Supporting Accessibility*. Retrieved: Nov. 16, 2016 from https://goo.gl/xGAH6f

Gokarakonda, S., & Kumar, A. (2016). Passive Architectural Design Index applied to vernacular and passive buildings. *The International Journal of Environmental Studies*, *73*(4), 563–572. doi:10.1080/00207233.2016.1178982

Gómez, M. M., & Rubio, F. R. (1999). Turismo cultural: el caso de Sevilla. *Cuadernos de turismo*, *4*, 33-50.

Gonçalves, A. (2003). *O Forum Flaviano de Conimbriga*. Retrieved 26 January 2012, from http://lsm.dei.uc.pt/forum/

Gonçalves, A. J. M. (2002). Reconstrução de ambientes históricos utilizando o VRML: o caso do Fórum Flaviano de Conimbriga. Tese (Mestrado em Engenharia Informática). Departamento de Engenharia Informática, Universidade de Coimbra.

Gonçalves, A., Magalhães, L., Moura, J., & Chalmers, A. (2008). Accurate modelling of roman lamps in conimbriga using high dynamic range. In *Proceedings of the 9th International conference on Virtual Reality, Archaeology and Cultural Heritage* (pp. 101–108). Eurographics Association.

Gonçalves, C. (2014). *Gestão da Manutenção em Edifícios: Modelos para uma abordagem LARG (Lean, Agile, Resilient e Green)*. Tese de Doutoramento em Engenharia Industrial. Universidade Nova de Lisboa, Faculdade de Ciências e Tecnologia.

Gonzáles Gonzáles, M., Rodríguez Banga, E., Campillo Díaz, F., Méndez Pazó, F., Rodríguez Liñares, L., & Iglesias Iglesias, G. (2008). Specific features of the Galician language and implications for speech technology development. *Speech Communication*, *50*(11-12), 874–887. doi:10.1016/j.specom.2008.02.004

Gonzales, M. L. (2012). Cloud Computing y su aplicación fuera del campo de la Informática. *Revista de Información, Tecnología y Sociedad*, 66.

Gonzàlez, F., Villarejo, L., Miralbell, O., & Gomis, J. M. (2012). How to use mobile technology and augmented reality to enhance collaborative learning on cultural and natural heritage? An e-learning experience. *New Trends on Global Education Conference*, 1-5.

González, M. V. (2009). Gestión turística del patrimonio cultural: enfoques para un desarrollo sostenible del turismo cultural. *Cuadernos de turismo*, (23), 237-254.

González, M. V. (2009). Gestión turística del patrimonio cultural: enfoques para un desarrollo sostenible del turismo cultural. *Cuadernos de turismo*, *23*, 237-254.

Goodman, L. (1961). Snowball Sampling. *Annals of Mathematical Statistics*, *32*(1), 148–170. doi:10.1214/aoms/1177705148

Google and IPSOS OTX MediaCT. (2011). *The Mobile Movement Understanding Smartphone Users*. Think Mobile with Google. Retrieved October 20, 2015, from https://ssl.gstatic.com/think/docs/the-mobile-movement_research-studies.pdf

Görz, G., Schiemann, B., & Oischinger, M. (2008). An implementation of the CIDOC Conceptual Reference Model (4.2.4) in OWL-DL. CIDOC 2008, Athens, Greece.

Gouveia, F., & Lira, S. (2008). An Information Model for Virtual Museums. The case of an Ecomuseum. In K. Robering (Ed.), *Information Technology for the Virtual Museum. Museology and the Semantic Web* (pp. 103–111). London: LIT-Verlag Münster.

Gower, S. M. (2010). Trunyan: Where the dead lie. *Jakarta Post*. Retrieved April 22, 2010, from http://www.thejakartapost.com/news/2010/04/22/trunyan-where-dead-lie.html

Graham, L. (2016). *Virtual reality devices could transform the tourism experience*. CNBC.

Grance, T., & Mell, P. (2008). *Perspectives on cloud computing and standards*. NIST, Information Technology.

Granero-Montagud, L., Portalés, C., Pastor-Carbonell, B., Ribes-Gómez, E., Gutiérrez-Lucas, A., Tornari, V., . . . Dietz, C. (2013a). *Deterioration estimation of paintings by means of combined 3D and hyperspectral data analysis*. Paper presented at the SPIE - Optics for Arts, Architecture, and Archaeology IV. doi:10.1117/12.2020336

Granero-Montagud, L., Portalés, C., Pastor-Carbonell, B., Ribes-Gómez, E., Gutiérrez-Lucas, A., Tornari, V., . . . Dietz, C. (2013b). *SYDDARTA: new methodology for digitization of deterioration estimation in paintings*. Paper presented at the SPIE - Optics for Arts, Architecture, and Archaeology IV. doi:10.1117/12.2020333

Greer, M. (2009). *Software as a service inflection point: Using cloud computing to achieve business agility*. New York: Global Authors Publishers.

Gretzel, U. & Yoo, K. H. (2008). Use and impact of online travel reviews. *Information and communication technologies in tourism 2008*, 35-46.

Gretzel, U., Fesenmaier, D. R., Lee, Y. J. & Tussyadiah, I. (2010). 11 Narrating travel experiences: the role of new media. *Tourist experience: Contemporary perspectives*, 171.

Gretzel, U., Yoo, K. H., & Purifoy, M. (2007). *Online travel review study: Role and impact of online travel reviews*. Laboratory for Inteligent Systems in Tourism, Texas A&M University.

Gretzel, U. (2011). Intelligent systems in tourism: A social science perspective. *Annals of Tourism Research*, *38*(3), 757–779. doi:10.1016/j.annals.2011.04.014

Gretzel, U., Sigala, M., Xiang, Z., & Koo, C. (2015). Smart tourism: Foundations and developments. *Electronic Markets, 25*(3), 179–188. doi:10.1007/s12525-015-0196-8

Gretzel, U., Werthner, H., Koo, C., & Lamsfus, C. (2015). Conceptual foundations for understanding smart tourism ecosystems. *Computers in Human Behavior, 50*, 558–563. doi:10.1016/j.chb.2015.03.043

Greuter, S., Parker, J., Stewart, N., & Leach, G. (2003). Real-time Procedural Generation of `Pseudo Infinite' Cities. In *Proceedings of the 1st International Conference on Computer Graphics and Interactive Techniques in Australasia and South East Asia*. New York: ACM. https://doi.org/10.1145/604471.604490

Grilo, A., & Tavares, L. (2008). *Building Information Model e a Competitividade do sector da Construção*. Lisboa: OPET – Observatório de Prospectiva da Engenharia e da Tecnologia.

Grimshaw, D. (1993). *Bringing GIS into Bussines Geoinformation*. London: Longman.

Grossmann, E., & Santos-Victor, J. (2005). Least-squares 3D reconstruction from one or more views and geometric clues. *Computer Vision and Image Understanding, 99*(2), 151–174. doi:10.1016/j.cviu.2005.01.002

Grossman, R. (2009). The case for cloud computing. *IT Professional, 11*(2), 23–27. doi:10.1109/MITP.2009.40

Groves, R. M., Portalés, C., & Ribes-Gómez, E. (2014). *Assessment of Mechanical and Chemical Deterioration of Artworks*. Paper presented at the International Conference on Ageing of Materials & Structures (AMS), Delft, The Netherlands.

Guarnieri, A., Remondino, F., & Vettore, A. (2006). Digital photogrammetry and TLS data fusion applied to Cultural Heritage 3D modeling. *International Archives of Photogrammetry, Remote Sensing and Spatial Information Sciences. ISPRS Commission V Symposium.*

Guasch-Portas, V., & Soler-Fuensanta, J. R. (2014). Cloud Computing, turismo y protección de datos. *Revista de Análisis Turístico, 17*, 61–68.

Guedes, A. S., & Jiménez, M. I. M. (2015). Spatial patterns of cultural tourism in Portugal. *Tourism Management Perspectives, 16*, 107–115. doi:10.1016/j.tmp.2015.07.010

Guerra, J., Pinto, M., & Beato, C. (2015). Virtual Reality-Shows A new vision for tourism and heritage. *European Scientific Journal, 11*(9), 49–54.

Guidi, G., Russo, M., & Angheleddu, D. (2014). 3D Survey and virtual reconstruction of archeological sites. *Digital Applications in Archaeology and Cultural Heritage, 1*(2), 55–69. doi:10.1016/j.daach.2014.01.001

Guimarães, F., Figueiredo, M. J. G., & Rodrigues, J. I. (2015). Realidade Aumentada e Transmedia Storytelling em Museus e Património Cultural: Artefacto Digital I-Lugar. *Proceedings of 7th International Conference on Digital Arts*, 259-263.

Gunn, C. (1988). *Vacationcapes: Design tourist regions*. New York: Van Nostrand Reinhold.

Gunn, C. (1994). The emergence of effective tourism planning and development. In A. Seaton, L. Jenkins, R. Woods, P. Dieke, M. Bennett, L. MacLellan, & R. Smith (Eds.), *Tourism The State of the Art* (pp. 10–19). Chichester, UK: John Wiley & Sons.

Gunn, C. A. (1988). *Vacationscape: Designing tourist regions*. New York: Van Nostrand Reinhold.

Gupta, P., Seetharaman, A., & Raj, J. R. (2013). The usage and adoption of cloud computing by small and medium businesses. *International Journal of Information Management, 33*(5), 861–874. doi:10.1016/j.ijinfomgt.2013.07.001

Guttentag, D. A. (2010). Virtual reality: Applications and implications for tourism. *Tourism Management, 31*(5), 637-651. https://doi.org/10.1016/j.tourman.2009.07.003

Guttentag, D. A. (2010). Virtual Reality: Applications and Implications for Tourism. *Tourism Management, 31*(5), 637–651. doi:10.1016/j.tourman.2009.07.003

Guzmán-López, T., & Jesus, M. M. (2011). Turismo, cultura y gastronomía. Una aproximación a las rutas culinarias. *Encontros Científicos-Tourism & Management Studies*, (1), 915-922.

Hackeling, G. (2014). *Mastering machine learning with scikit-learn: apply effective learning algorithms to real-world problems using scikit-learn*. Birmingham, UK: Packt Publishing Ltd.

Hahn, E., Bose, P., & Whitehead, A. (2006). Lazy Generation of Building Interiors in Realtime. In *Electrical and Computer Engineering, 2006. CCECE '06. Canadian Conference on* (pp. 2441–2444). https://doi.org/10.1109/CCECE.2006.277767

Haines-Young, R., Bunce, R., & Parr, T. (1994). Countryside Information System: An information system for environmental policy development and appraisal. *Geographical Systems, 1*(4), 329–345.

Hall, S. (2013). *Creating strong cross media concepts for museum exhibitions*. Umeå Universitet. Retrieved from http://umu.diva-portal.org/smash/record.jsf?pid=diva2:630513

Halpenny, E. A., Salenieks, T., Song, L. D., Van Winkle, C., & MacKay, K. (2013). Albertan festivals' Adoption of Social Media and Mobile Digital Technology. In *TTRA Canada Annual Conference 2013 Academic papers*. Ottawa: TTRA Canada Chapter.

Hancock, M. (2015). Museums and 3D Printing: More Than a Workshop Novelty, Connecting to Collections and the Classroom. *Bulletin of the Association for Information Science and Technology, 42*(1), 32–35. doi:10.1002/BUL2.2015.1720420110

Han, D., Jung, T., & Gibson, A. (2014). Dublin AR: Implementing Augmented Reality (AR) in Tourism. In Z. Xiang & I. Tussyadiah (Eds.), *Information and Communication Technologies in Tourism* (pp. 511–523). Wien: Springer International Publishing.

Handayani, B. (2016). The Paradox of Authenticity and its Implications for Contemporary and 'Bizarre'. *Tourism Campaigns.*

Hannam, K., Butler, G., & Morris, C. (2014). Developments and key issues in tourism mobilities. *Annals of Tourism Research, 44*, 171–185. doi:10.1016/j.annals.2013.09.010

Happa, J., Williams, M., Turley, G., Earl, G., Dubla, P., Beale, G., & Chalmers, A. et al. (2009). Virtual relighting of a roman statue head from herculaneum: a case study. In *Proceedings of the 6th International Conference on Computer Graphics, Virtual Reality, Visualisation and Interaction in Africa* (pp. 5–12). ACM. doi:10.1145/1503454.1503456

Harris, T., Weiner, D., Warner, T., & Levin, R. (1996). Pursuing social goals through participatory GIS: Redressing South Africa's historical political ecology. In J. Pickles (Ed.), *Ground Truth: The Social Implications of GIS* (pp. 196–222). Guildford: Guildford Press.

Hartmann, R. (2014). Dark tourism, thanatourism, and dissonance in heritage tourism management: New directions in contemporary tourism research. *Journal of Heritage Tourism, 9*(2), 166–182. doi:10.1080/1743873X.2013.807266

Haslhofer, B., & Klas, W. (2010). A Survey of Techniques for Achieving Metadata Interoperability. *ACM Computing Surveys, 42*(2), 1–37. doi:10.1145/1667062.1667064

Hastie, T., Tibshirani, R., & Friedman, J. H. (2009). The elements of statistical learning: data mining, inference, and prediction: with 200 full-color illustrations. In Linear Methods for Regression (pp. 43-94). New York: Springer.

Haugstvedt, A.-C., & Krogstie, J. (2012). *Mobile augmented reality for cultural heritage: A technology acceptance study*. Paper presented at the Mixed and Augmented Reality (ISMAR), 2012 IEEE International Symposium on. doi:10.1109/ISMAR.2012.6402563

Hauschild, T. (1964). *Der Kultbau neben dem römischen Ruinenkomplex bei Estoi in der Provinz Lusitania*. Berlin (TU).

Hauschild, T. (1984/88). O edifício de culto do complexo das ruínas romanas perto de Estoi, na provincia da Lusitânia. Arqueologia e História, 10(1-2), 123-150.

Hauschild, T., & Teichner, F. (2002). Milreu – Ruínas. Lisboa: IPPAR (Colecção "Roteiros da Arqueologia Portuguesa", 9).

Ha, Y. W., Kim, J., Libaque-Saenz, C. F., Chang, Y., & Park, M. C. (2015). Use and gratifications of mobile SNSs: Facebook and KakaoTalk in Korea. *Telematics and Informatics*, *32*(3), 425–438. doi:10.1016/j.tele.2014.10.006

Hays, S., Page, S. J., & Buhalis, D. (2013). Social media as a destination marketing tool: Its use by national tourism organisations. *Current Issues in Tourism*, *16*(3), 211–239. doi:10.1080/13683500.2012.662215

He, Y., Gao, M., & Shang, J. (2013). A Virtual Reconstruction Methodology for Archaeological Heritage in East Asia – Practical Experience from the Re-relic Program in China. *Virtual Archaeology Review*, *4*(9). 10.4995/var.2013.4253

Heart, T., & Pliskin, N. (2002). Renting restaurant applications from application service providers. *International Journal of Hospitality Information Technology*, *2*(2), 45–61. doi:10.3727/153373402803617764

Heath, C., & Vom Lehn, D. (2010). Interactivity and Collaboration: new forms of participation in museums, galleries and science centres. In Museums in a digital age (pp. 266–280). JOUR, Routledge.

Hecht, B., Schöning, J., Erickson, T., & Priedhorsky, R. (2011). Geographic Human-Computer Interaction. In *CHI '11 Extended Abstracts on Human Factors in Computing Systems*. Vancouver: AMC Press. doi:10.1145/1979742.1979532

Hedstrom, M., & King, J. L. (2003). *On the LAM: Library, archive, and museum collections in the creation and maintenance of knowledge communities*. Organization for Economic Cooperation and Development. Retrieved January 10, 2017, from http://www.oecd.org/edu/innovation-education/32126054.pdf

Heidelberg, B. A. W. (2015). Managing ghosts: Exploring local government involvement in dark tourism. *Journal of Heritage Tourism*, *10*(1), 74–90. doi:10.1080/1743873X.2014.953538

Heitmann, S. (2011). Authenticity in Tourism. In *Research themes for Tourism* (pp. 45–58). CAB International.

Hellenic Ministry of Culture. (2017). *Respecting the rights of the disable people: Access by lift to the top of the Acropolis*. Retrieved April 26, 2017, from http://www.yppo.gr/files/g_423.pdf

Hennessey, S., Yun, D., & MacDonald, R. M. (2014). Segmenting and profiling the cultural tourism market for an Island destination. *International Journal of Management and Marketing Research*, *7*(1), 15–28.

Henry, A. (1987). *Consumer behavior and marketing action*. Boston: Academic Press.

Herbert, D. (2001). Literary places, tourism and the heritage experience. *Annals of Tourism Research*, *28*(2), 312–333. doi:10.1016/S0160-7383(00)00048-7

Herlocker, J. L., Konstan, J. A., & Riedl, J. (2000). Explaining collaborative filtering recommendations. In *Proceedings of the 2000 ACM conference on Computer supported cooperative work* (pp. 241-250). ACM.

Hernández, J. M. G., de la Calle Vaquero, M., & García, M. D. C. M. (2015). Cultura y patrimonio en las prácticas turísticas de la población madrileña. *International Journal of Scientific Management and Tourism*, *1*(4), 97–124.

Hewitt, C. (2016). *The New Cooper Hewitt Experience* [website]. Retrieved November 1, 2016, from http://www.cooperhewitt.org/new-experience/

Hglund, J., Ilic, D., Karnouskos, S., Sauter, R., & da Silva, P. G. (2012). Using a 6lowpan smart meter mesh network for event-driven monitoring of power quality. *Smart Grid Communications (SmartGridComm), 2012 IEEE Third International Conference on*, 448–453.

Hill, J., Ford, W. R., & Farreras, I. G. (2015). Real conversations with artificial intelligence: A comparison between human–human online conversations and human–chatbot conversations. *Computers in Human Behavior*, *49*, 245–250. doi:10.1016/j.chb.2015.02.026

Hjalager, A. M. (2010). A review of innovation research in tourism. *Tourism Management*, *31*(1), 1–12. doi:10.1016/j.tourman.2009.08.012

HMS. (2016). *Srbija 1914 / Augmented Reality Exhibition at Historical Museum of Serbia, Belgrade*. Retrieved: Nov. 16, 2016 from https://vimeo.com/126699550

Hobsbawm, E., & Ranger, T. (1984). A invenção das Tradições. São Paulo, SP: Paz e terra.

Ho, C. I., Lin, M. H., & Chen, H. M. (2012). Web users behavioural patterns of tourism information search: From online to offline. *Tourism Management*, *33*(6), 1468–1482. doi:10.1016/j.tourman.2012.01.016

Hochmeister, M., Gretzel, U., & Werthner, H. (2013). *Destination expertise in online travel communities*. Springer Berlin Heidelberg.

Hohl, M. (2009). Calm Technologies 2.0: Visualising Social Data as an Experience in Physical Space. *Parsons Journal for Information Mapping*, *1*(3), 1–7.

Hohmann, B., Havemann, S., Krispel, U., & Fellner, D. (2010). A GML shape grammar for semantically enriched 3D building models. *Computers & Graphics*, *34*(4), 322–334. doi:10.1016/j.cag.2010.05.007

Holdgaard, N. (2011). The Use of Social Media in the Danish Museum Landscape. In Trant & D. Bearman (Eds.), *Museums and the Web 2011: Proceedings*. Toronto: Archives & Museum Informatics. Retrieved from http://www.museumsandtheweb.com/mw2011/papers/the_use_of_social_media_in_the_danish_museum_l

Holmes, K. (2015). *The Environment Is Your Playground in an Interactive 3D Ecosystem* [online article]. Retrieved October 15, 2016, from http://thecreatorsproject.vice.com/blog/the-environment-is-your-playground-in-an-interactive-3d-ecosystem

Holt-Lunstad, J., Smith, T. B., & Layton, J. B. (2010). Social relationships and mortality risk: A meta-analytic review. *PLoS Medicine*, *7*(7), 859. doi:10.1371/journal.pmed.1000316 PMID:20668659

Hooper, G., & Lennon, J. (2016). *Dark Tourism: practice and interpretation*. Abingdon, UK: Routledge.

Horrigan, J. B. (2014). *Use of cloud computing applications and services*. Retrieved December, 2016, from Pew Internet 2016: http://www.pewinternet.org/Reports/2008/Use-of-Cloud-Computing-Applications-and-Services/Data-Memo.aspx

Hosteltur. (2017). *Transformación digital: Cloud Computing*. Retrieved from https://www.hosteltur.com/comunidad/nota/018691_transformacion-digital-cloud-computing.html

Hsu, C. H. C., & Huang, S. (2012). An extension of the theory of planned behavior model for tourists. *Journal of Hospitality & Tourism Research (Washington, D.C.)*, *36*(3), 390–417. doi:10.1177/1096348010390817

Hsu, C. L., & Lin, J. C. (2008). Acceptance of blog usage: The roles of technology acceptance, social influence and knowledge sharing motivation. *Information & Management*, *45*(1), 65–74. doi:10.1016/j.im.2007.11.001

Hsu, F. M., Lin, Y. T., & Ho, T. K. (2012). Design and implementation of an intelligent recommendation system for tourist attractions: The integration of EBM model, Bayesian network and Google Maps. *Expert Systems with Applications*, *39*(3), 3257–3264. doi:10.1016/j.eswa.2011.09.013

Huang, Z., Hui, P., Peylo, C., & Chatzopoulos, D. (2013). *Mobile augmented reality survey: A bottom-up approach.* arXiv preprint arXiv:1309.4413

Huang, X. K., Yuan, J. Z., & Shi, M. Y. (2012). Condition and key issues analysis on the smarter tourism construction in China. In *Multimedia and signal processing* (pp. 444–450). Springer Berlin Heidelberg.

Huang, Y., & Bian, L. (2009). A Bayesian network and analytic hierarchy process based personalized recommendations for tourist attractions over the Internet. *Expert Systems with Applications*, *36*(1), 933–943. doi:10.1016/j.eswa.2007.10.019

Hudson, G., Reed, P., & Lea, T. (2017). *Emoncms: GitHub repository*. Retrieved January 17, 2017, from http://github.com/emoncms

Hudson, S., Huang, L., Roth, M. S., & Madden, T. J. (2016). The influence of social media interactions on consumer–brand relationships: A three-country study of brand perceptions and marketing behaviors. *International Journal of Research in Marketing*, *33*(1), 27–41. doi:10.1016/j.ijresmar.2015.06.004

Hughes, G., & Schirmer, D. (1994). Interactive multimedia, public participation and environmental assessment. *The Town Planning Review*, *65*(4), 399–414. doi:10.3828/tpr.65.4.n7220465t3813122

Hughes, H., & Allen, D. (2005). Cultural tourism in Central and Eastern Europe: The views of induced image formation agents. *Tourism Management*, *26*(2), 173–183. doi:10.1016/j.tourman.2003.08.021

Huh, H. J., Kim, T., & Law, R. (2009). A comparasion of competing theoretical models for understanding acceptance behavior of information systems in upscale hotels. *International Journal of Hospitality Management*, *28*(1), 717–724. doi:10.1016/j.ijhm.2008.06.004

Hui, L., Hung, F. Y., Chien, Y. L., Tsai, W. T., & Shie, J. J. (2014). Mobile Augmented Reality of Tourism-Yilan Hot Spring. *Ubi-Media Computing and Workshops (UMEDIA), 7th International Conference*, 209-214.

Hunt, J. D. (1975). Image as a factor in tourism development. *Journal of Travel Research*, *13*(3), 1–7. doi:10.1177/004728757501300301

Husain, W., Dih, L. Y., Yen, H. F., & Jothi, N. (2012). MyTourGuide. com: a framework of a location-based services for tourism industry. In *Computer & Information Science (ICCIS), 2012 International Conference* (*Vol. 1*, pp. 184-189). IEEE.

Hutchinson, C. W., & Castilon, K. (2009). Navigating the next-generation application architecture. *IT Professional*, *1*(2), 18–22.

Hwang, K. (2008). Massively distributed systems: From grids and P2P to clouds. *International Conference on Grid and Pervasive Computing*, 5036, 1.

Hyvönen, E. (2007). Semantic Portals for Cultural Heritage. In Handbook on Ontologies. Springer Verlag.

Hyvönen, E., Mäkelä, E., Kauppinen, T., Alm, O., Kurki, J., Ruotsalo, T.,..., Nyberg, K. (2009). CultureSampo — Finnish Culture on the Semantic Web 2.0: Thematic Perspectives for the End-user. *Proceedings of Museums and the Web 2009.*

Hyvönen, E. (2012). Publishing and Using Cultural Heritage Linked Data on the Semantic Web. In J. Hendler & Y. Ding (Eds.), *Synthesis Lectures on Semantic Web: Theory and Technology*. Palo Alto, CA: Morgan & Claypool. doi:10.2200/S00452ED1V01Y201210WBE003

Hyvönen, E., Tuominen, J., Alonen, M., & Mäkelä, E. (2014). *Linked Data Finland: A 7-star model and platform for publishing and re-using linked datasets. The Semantic Web: ESWC 2014 Satellite Events, Revised Selected Papers.* Springer Verlag.

Ibarra, J. G. (2001). Análisis de la oferta de turismo cultural en España. *Estudios turísticos*, 15-40.

Ibermuseus. (2016). *Anunciamos os resultados do 7º Prêmio de Educação e Museus* [press release]. Retrieved December 20, 2016, from http://www.ibermuseus.org/acao-educativa/conheca-os-projetos-vencedores-do-7o-premio-ibero-americano-de-educacao-e-museus/

ICOM. (1995). *Graphic Data Mode*. ICOM/CIDOC Data Model Working Group.

ICOM. (2005). *Definition of the CIDOC Conceptual Reference Model, Version 4.2* (N. Crofts, M. Doerr, T. Gill, S. Stead, & M. Stiff, Eds.). ICOM/CIDOC CRM Special Interest Group.

ICOM. (2011). *ICOM recommendation on Linked Open Data for museums* (N. Crofts, M. Doerr, & M. Nyman, Eds.). ICOM/CIDOC CRM Special Interest Group.

IEEE. (2011). *IEEE standard for ubiquitous green community control network protocol.* IEEE-SA board of governors, IEEE Std, 2011, 10, 016–5997.

IEEE. (2013). IEEE Adoption of Smart Energy Profile 2.0 Application Protocol Standard. *IEEE Std, 2030*, 1–348.

IET Instituto de Estudios Turísticos. (2015). *Turistas extranjeros: ¿DE DÓNDE VIENEN?*. Sociedad Regional Cántabra de Promoción Turística.

IETF. (2014). *The Constrained Application Protocol (CoAP)*. IETF RFC 7252. Retrieved January 18, 2017 from https://tools.ietf.org/html/rfc7252

Imposa, S. (2010). Infrared thermography and Georadar techniques applied to the Sala delle Nicchie (Niches Hall) of Palazzo Pitti, Florence (Italy). *Journal of Cultural Heritage*, *11*(3), 259–264. doi:10.1016/j.culher.2009.04.005

Inakage, M. (1990). A simple model of flames. In *CG International'90* (pp. 71–81). Springer.

Inamo Restaurant. (2016). *Interactive Menu*. Retrieved, August, 3rd, 2016, from http://www.inamo-restaurant.com

INEGI. (2017). Retrieved from: www.inegi.con.mx

InformationWeek. (2016). *InformationWeek:10 Fantastic iPhone, Android Apps For Museum Visits*. Retrieved: Nov. 16, 2016 from https://goo.gl/rYnhm2

Institute of Museum and Library. (2015). *Opening the World of Museums and Libraries to Visually Impaired Visitors* [online article]. Retrieved December 19, 2016, from https://www.imls.gov/news-events/project-profiles/opening-world-museums-and-libraries-visually-impaired-visitors

Instituto Nacional de Estadística (INE). (2016). Retrieved March 2, 2016 from http://www.ine.es/

Instituto Nacional de Estadística. (2016). *Statistics of Tourist Movements at Borders (FRONTUR) Total year 2015. International tourist arrivals by country of residence.* Author.

Internet World Stats. (2015). *Internet Usage Statistics. The Internet Big Picture*. Retrieved October 10, 2015, from http://www.internetworldstats.com/stats.htm

Inversini, A., & Cantoni, L. (2011). Towards online content classification in understanding tourism destinations information competition and reputation. *International Journal of Internet Marketing and Advertising*, *6*(3), 282–299. doi:10.1504/IJIMA.2011.038240

Ioannidis, Ch., & Vozikis, K. Th. (2007). *Application of a GIS for the accessibility of archaeological sites by visitors with disability and visitors with reduced mobility. XXI International CIPA Symposium*, Athens, Greece.

Isaac, A., Clayphan, R., & Haslhofer, R. (2012). EUROPEANA: moving to linked open data. Information Standards Quarterly, 24(2-3).

Ishii, H., & Ullmer, B. (1997). Tangible Bits: Towards Seamless Interfaces Between People, Bits and Atoms. In *Proceedings of the ACM SIGCHI Conference on Human Factors in Computing Systems* (pp. 234–241). New York: ACM. doi:10.1145/258549.258715

ISO. (2014). *Information and documentation — A reference ontology for the interchange of cultural heritage information. ISO 21127:2014*. Geneva, Switzerland: International Organization for Standardization.

Israel, K. (2011). *Informação e tecnologia nos museus interativos do contemporâneo*. Universidade de São Paulo. Retrieved from http://www.usp.br/celacc/ojs/index.php/blacc/article/view/285

Ivars Baidal, J. A. (2004). Tourism Planning in Spain – Evolution and Perspectives. *Annals of Tourism Research, 31*(2), 313–333. doi:10.1016/j.annals.2003.12.001

Jarosz, W., Donner, C., Zwicker, M., & Jensen, H. W. (2008). Radiance caching for participating media. *ACM Transactions on Graphics, 27*(1), 7. doi:10.1145/1330511.1330518

Javornik, A. (2016). *The Mainstreaming of Augmented Reality: A Brief History*. Harvard Business Review.

Jebbit. (2015). *3 Ways that Wearables are Transforming Marketing Interactions*. Retrieved May 29, 2016, from https://www.jebbit.com/blog/3-ways-wearables-transforming-marketing-interactions/

Jeffman, T.M.W. (2013). Redes socias segmentadas: Socialidade, consumo e segmentação na era digital. *Artigo submetido ao NT 1 Sociabilidade, novas tecnologias e práticas internacionais do SIMSOCIAL 2013*. Performances Interacionais e Mediações Sociotécnicas Salvador - 10 e 11 de outubro de 2013.

Jeffman, T.M.W. (2014). Literatura que cabe na tela: Uma análise da cultura participativa, consumo e conexões nos booktubers. *VII Encontro Nacional de Estudos do Consumo, III Encontro Luso-Brasileiro de Estudos do Consumo, I Encontro Latino-Americano de Estudos do Consumo. Mercados Contestados – As novas fronteiras da moral, da ética, da religião e da lei. 24, 25 e 26 de setembro de 2014*, Pontifícia Universidade Católica do Rio de Janeiro (Puc-Rio).

Jenkins, O. H. (1999). Understanding and Measuring Tourist Destination Images. *International Journal of Tourism Research, 1*(1), 1–15. doi:10.1002/(SICI)1522-1970(199901/02)1:1<1::AID-JTR143>3.0.CO;2-L

Jensen, J., & Becker, R. (2015). *Shedding New Light on the Past: The Potential for Short Wave Ultraviolet Photography in Archaeology*. Paper presented at the 80th Annual Meeting of the Society for American Archaeology, San Francisco, CA.

Jensen, H. W., & Christensen, P. H. (1998). Efficient simulation of light transport in scenes with participating media using photon maps. In *Proceedings of the 25th annual conference on Computer graphics and interactive techniques* (pp. 311–320). ACM.

Jensen, H. W., Durand, F., Dorsey, J., Stark, M. M., Shirley, P., & Premože, S. (2001). A physically-based night sky model. In *Proceedings of the 28th annual conference on Computer graphics and interactive techniques* (pp. 399–408). ACM.

Jiang, J., Gretzel, U., & Law, R. (2010). Do negative experiences always lead to dissatisfaction? Testing attribution theory in the context of online travel reviews. *Information and communication technologies in tourism 2010*, 297-308.

Jiménez Fernández-Palacios, B., Morabito, D., & Remondino, F. (2016). Access to complex reality-based 3D models using virtual reality solutions. *Journal of Cultural Heritage*.

Jiménez Fernández-Palacios, B., Nex, F., Rizzi, A., & Remondino, F. (2015). ARCube—The augmented reality cube for archaeology. *Archaeometry*, *57*(S1), 250–262. doi:10.1111/arcm.12120

Jímenez, A., Thomé-Ortiz, H., & Burrola, C. (2016). Biocultural heritage, mycological tourism and ethnoknowledge. *El periplo sustentable*, *30*, 180-205.

Johansson, B. (2004). *Exploring application service provision*. Springer.

Johnson, L., Adams, S., & Witchey, H. (2011). *The NMC Horizon Report: 2011 Museum Edition*. Retrieved from http://www.nmc.org/pdf/2011-horizon-report-museum.pdf

Johnson, L., Becker, S., Estrada, V., & Freeman, A. (2015). *NMC Horizon Report: 2015 Higher Education Edition*. Austin, TX: The New Me; http://doi.org/ISBN

Johnston, T. (2013). Mark Twain and The Innocents Abroad: Illuminating the tourist gaze on death. *International Journal of Culture and Hospitality Research.*, *7*(3), 199–213. doi:10.1108/IJCTHR-05-2012-0036

Jovicic, D. (2016). Cultural tourism in the context of relations between mass and alternative tourism. *Current Issues in Tourism*, *19*(6), 605–612. doi:10.1080/13683500.2014.932759

Jung, T., tom Dieck, M. C., Lee, H., & Chung, N. (2016). Effects of Virtual Reality and Augmented Reality on Visitor Experiences in Museum. In A. Inversini & R. Schegg (Eds.), *Information and Communication Technologies in Tourism 2016: Proceedings of the International Conference* (pp. 621–635). Cham: Springer International Publishing. doi:10.1007/978-3-319-28231-2_45

Jung, T.H. & Han, D.I. (2014). Augmented Reality (AR) in Urban Heritage Tourism. *e-Review of Tourism Research*, *5*, 1-8.

Jung, T., Chung, N., & Leue, M. C. (2015). The determinants of recommendations to use augmented reality technologies: The case of a Korean theme park. *Tourism Management*, *49*, 75–86. doi:10.1016/j.tourman.2015.02.013

Júnior, F. H. (2000). Centralidade em São Paulo: trajetória, conflitos e negociação na metrópole. São Paulo, SP: Cortes e Edusp.

Junta de Andalucia. (2012). *Cloud computing aplicado a los sectores de la agroindustria, eficiencia energética, industrias culturales y turismo*. Edita Consejería de Economía Junta de Andalucía.

Kabassi, K. (2010). Personalizing recommendations for tourists. *Telematics and Informatics*, *27*(1), 51–66. doi:10.1016/j.tele.2009.05.003

Kaminski, J., Benson, A. M., & Arnold, D. (2013). *Contemporary Issues in Cultural Heritage Tourism*. Routledge.

Kampel, M., Mara, H., & Sablatnig, R. (2006). Automated investigation of archaeological vessels. In *Signal Processing Conference, 2006 14th European* (pp. 1–5). IEEE.

Kang, B., Brewer, K. P., & Bai, B. (2007). Biometrics for Hospitality and Tourism: A New Wave of Information Technology. *Hospitality Review*, *25*(1), 1–9.

Kang, E. J., Scott, N., Lee, T. J., & Ballantyne, R. (2012). Benefits of visiting a 'dark tourismsite: The case of the Jeju April 3rd Peace Park, Korea. *Tourism Management*, *33*(2), 257–265. doi:10.1016/j.tourman.2011.03.004

Kaplan, A., & Haenlein, M. (2010). Users of the world, unite! The challenges and opportunities of Social Media. *Business Horizons*, *53*(1), 59–68. doi:10.1016/j.bushor.2009.09.003

Karaman, S., Bagdanov, A. D., Landucci, L., DAmico, G., Ferracani, A., Pezzatini, D., & Del Bimbo, A. (2016). Personalized multimedia content delivery on an interactive table by passive observation of museum visitors. *Multimedia Tools and Applications*, *75*(7), 3787–3811. doi:10.1007/s11042-014-2192-y

Karlsson, S. (2005). The Social and the Cultural Capital of a Place and their Influence on the Production of Tourism – A Theoretical Reflection based on an Illustrative Case Study. *Scandinavian Journal of Hospitality and Tourism*, *5*(2), 102–115. doi:10.1080/15022250510014408

Kebir, N., & Maaroufi, M. (2016). Decision-support model for battery energy storage system inclusion in grid-connected PV systems for medium voltage applications. *2016 IEEE International Conference on Renewable Energy Research and Applications (ICRERA)*, 897-902. doi:10.1109/ICRERA.2016.7884465

Keesing, R. M. (1974). Theories of culture. *Annual Review of Anthropology*, *3*(1), 73–97. doi:10.1146/annurev.an.03.100174.000445

Kelly, H. (2016). *This museum wants the Apple Watch to be your tour guide* [online article]. Retrieved December 7, 2016, from http://money.cnn.com/2016/03/31/technology/apple-watch-de-young-museum/

Kenderdine, S., & Hart, T. (2014). *mARChive: Sculpting Museum Victoria' s Collections* [online article]. Retrieved November 29, 2016, from http://mw2014.museumsandtheweb.com/paper/marchive-sculpting-museum-victorias-collections/

Kenderdine, S. (2013). Pure Land: Inhabiting the Mogao Caves at Dunhuang. *Curator: The Museum Journal*, *56*(2), 199–218. doi:10.1111/cura.12020

Kennedy-Eden, H., & Gretzel, U. (2012). A taxonomy of mobile applications in tourism. *E-review of Tourism Research*, *10*(2), 47–50.

Khajeh-Hosseini, A., Greenwood, D., Smith, J., & Sommerville, I. (2012). The cloud adoption toolkit: Supporting cloud adoption decisions in the enterprise. *Software, Practice & Experience*, *42*(4), 447–465. doi:10.1002/spe.1072

Khan, S. (2014). Word play in destination marketing: An analysis of country tourism slogans. *TEAM Journal of Hospitality and Tourism*, *11*(1), 27–39.

Kidd, J., Ntalla, I., & Lyons, W. (2011). Multi-touch interfaces in museum spaces: reporting preliminary findings on the nature of interaction. *Proceedings of the International Conference Re-Thinking Technology in Museums 2011: Emerging Experiences*. Retrieved from http://www.idc.ul.ie/techmuseums11/paper/paper1.pdf

Kim, A., & Johnson, K. (2016). Power of consumers using Social Media: Examining the influences of brand-related user-generated content on Facebook. *Computers in Human Behavior*, *58*, 98–108. doi:10.1016/j.chb.2015.12.047

Kim, M. H., Harvey, T. A., Kittle, D. S., Rushmeier, H., Dorsey, J., Prum, R. O., & Brady, D. J. (2012). 3D imaging spectroscopy for measuring hyperspectral patterns on solid objects. *ACM Transactions on Graphics*, *31*(4), 1–11. doi:10.1145/2185520.2185534

Kim, Y. G., & Kim, W. J. (2014). Implementation of augmented reality system for smartphone advertisements. *International Journal of Multimedia and Ubiquitous Engineering*, *9*(2), 385–392. doi:10.14257/ijmue.2014.9.2.39

Kiourt, C., Koutsoudis, A., & Pavlidis, G. (2016). DynaMus: A fully dynamic 3D virtual Museum framework. *Journal of Cultural Heritage*, *22*, 984–991. doi:10.1016/j.culher.2016.06.007

Králová, A., & Pavlíčeka, A. (2015). Development of Social Media Strategies in Tourism Destination. *Procedia: Social and Behavioral Sciences*, *175*, 358–366. doi:10.1016/j.sbspro.2015.01.1211

Kirner, C., & Silva, K. A. C. (2010). *Vantagens educacionais no uso de jogos em Realidade Aumentada*. Renote. *Revista Novas Tecnologias na Educação*, *8*(3), 10–15.

Kivela, J. Y., & Crotts, J. (2006). Tourism and gastronomy: Gastronomys influence on how tourists experience a destination. *Journal of Hospitality & Tourism Research (Washington, D.C.)*, *3*(3), 354–377. doi:10.1177/1096348006286797

KNX. (2017). *KNX Specifications*. Retrieved January 18, 2017 from https://goo.gl/ENqlWB

Koo, C., Shin, S., Kim, K., Kim, C., & Chung, N. (2013). Smart Tourism of the Korea: A Case Study. PACIS, 1-38.

Kops, L. (2013). *Improving a travel recommender service by segmentation and personalization* (Master's degree dissertation). University of Twente.

Korgaonkar, P., Silverblatt, R., & Girard, T. (2006). Online retailing, product classifications, and consumer preferences. *Internet Research*, *16*(3), 267–288. doi:10.1108/10662240610673691

Korstanje, M. E., & Skoll, G. (2015). From Disasters to Religiosity: Republica de Cromañon, Buenos Aires, Argentina. In Religious tourism and pilgrimage management: An international perspective. CABI. doi:10.1079/9781780645230.0267

Korstanje, M. E. (2016). *The Rise of Thana Capitalism and Tourism*. Abingdon, UK: Routledge.

Korstanje, M. E., & George, B. (2015). Dark Tourism: Revisiting Some Philosophical Issues. *E-review of Tourism Research*, *12*(12), 127–136.

Korstanje, M. E., & George, B. (Eds.). (2017). *Virtual Traumaescape and exploring the roots of dark tourism*. Hershey, PA: IGI Global.

Kotler, P., & Armstrong, G. (2010). *Principles of marketing*. Pearson Education.

Kotler, P., Bowen, J., & Makens, J. (2014). *Marketing for hospitality and tourism* (6th ed.). Pearson Education Limited.

Kounavis, C. D., Kasimati, A. E., & Zamani, E. D. (2012). Enhancing the tourism experience through mobile augmented reality: Challenges and prospects. *International Journal of Engineering Business Management*, *4*, 1–6. doi:10.5772/51644

Kourouthanassis, P., Boletsis, C., Bardaki, C., & Chasanidou, D. (2015). Tourists responses to mobile augmented reality travel guides: The role of emotions on adoption behavior. *Pervasive and Mobile Computing*, *18*, 71–87. doi:10.1016/j.pmcj.2014.08.009

Koutsourakis, P., Simon, L., Teboul, O., Tziritas, G., & Paragios, N. (2009). Single view reconstruction using shape grammars for urban environments. In *Computer Vision, 2009 IEEE 12th International Conference on* (pp. 1795–1802). IEEE. doi:10.1109/ICCV.2009.5459400

Kovačević, D. (2014). *Record edition of the best major European Festival*. Retrieved May 29, 2016, from http://vojvodinahouse.eu/uploads/images/bilteni/Vojvodina%20World%204.pdf

Kovács, P. T., Rozinaj, G., Murray, N., Sulema, Y., & Rybárová, R. (2015). *Application of immersive technologies for education: state of the art*. Paper presented at the 2015 International Conference on Interactive Mobile Communication Technologies and Learning (IMCL), Thessaloniki, Greece. doi:10.1109/IMCTL.2015.7359604

Kovalenko, O., Mrabet, Y., Schouten, K., & Sejdovic, S. (2015). Linked Data in Action: Personalized Museum Tours on Mobile Devices. *Proceedings of the ESWC2015 Developers Workshop*.

Kralisch, A., Eisend, M., & Berendt, B. (2005). Impact of culture on website navigation behaviour. *Proceeding of the 11th International Conference on Human-Computer Interaction*.

Krentzman, A. R. (2013). *What Is Spirituality?*. Retrieved July 10, 2013, from http://www.takingcharge.csh.umn.edu/enhance-yourwellbeing/purpose/spirituality/what-spirituality

Krevelen, D. W. F., & Poelman, R. (2010). A Survey of Augmented Reality Technologies, Applications and Limitations. *The International Journal of Virtual Reality*, *9*(2), 1–20.

Kudan. (2016). *Kudan Computer Vision*. Retrieved: Nov. 16, 2016 from https://www.kudan.eu/

Kugel, S. (2011). Travel Lessons From the World of Academia *The New York Times*. Retrieved December 6, 2011, from http://frugaltraveler.blogs.nytimes.com/2011/12/06/travel-lessons-from-the-world-of-academia/?login=facebook

Kunst, J. (1994). *Indonesian music and dance: traditional music and its interaction with the West*. Royal Tropical Institute.

Kurogi, T., Nakayama, M., Sato, K., Kamuro, S., Fernando, C. L., Furukawa, M., . . . Tachi, S. (2013). Haptic transmission system to recognize differences in surface textures of objects for telexistence. In 2013 IEEE Virtual Reality (VR) (pp. 137-138). IEEE. doi:10.1109/VR.2013.6549400

Kuvan, Y. (2005). The use of forests for the purpose of tourism: The case of Belek Tourism Center in Turkey. *Journal of Environmental Management*, *75*(3), 263–274. doi:10.1016/j.jenvman.2005.01.003 PMID:15829368

Kysela, J., & Štorková, P. (2015). Using augmented reality as a medium for teaching history and tourism. *Procedia: Social and Behavioral Sciences*, *174*, 926–931. doi:10.1016/j.sbspro.2015.01.713

Lam, X. N., Vu, T., Le, T. D., & Duong, A. D. (2008). Addressing cold-start problem in recommendation systems. In *Proceedings of the 2nd international conference on Ubiquitous information management and communication* (pp. 208-211). ACM.

Lancha, J., & Oliveira, C. (2013). *Corpus dos mosaicos romanos de Portugal / Corpus des mosaïques romaines du Portugal: II, Conventus pacensis: 2, Algarve Este*. Faro: Universidade do Algarve.

Lash, S., & Urry, J. (1998). Economias de signos y espacio: sobre el capitalismo de la posorganización. Buenos Aires, CF: Amorrortu, 1998.

Law, R., Buhalis, D., & Cobanoglu, C. (2014). Progress on information and communication technologies in hospitality and tourism. *International Journal of Contemporary Hospitality Management*, *26*(5), 727–750. doi:10.1108/IJCHM-08-2013-0367

Lawson, F., & Baud Bovy, M. (1977). *Tourism and recreational management*. London: CBI Pub. Co.

Layar. (2016). Retrieved: Nov. 16, 2016 from https://www.layar.com/

Lázaro, A. (2008). El aprovechamiento micológico como vía de desarrollo rural en España: Las facetas comercial y recreativa. *Anales de Geografía*, *28*, 111–136.

Le Bœuf, P., Sinclair, P., Martinez, K., Lewis, P., Aitken, G., & Lahanier, C. (2005). Using an ontology for interoperability and browsing of museum, library and archive information. *International Council of Museums 14th Triennial Meeting*. The Hague: ICOM Committee for Conservation.

Leavitt, N. (2009). Is cloud computing really ready for prime time? *IEEE Computer Society Issue*, *42*(1), 15–20. doi:10.1109/MC.2009.20

Leawo. (2016). *Yelp app*. Retrieved October, 18th, 2016, from http://www.leawo.com/

Leblanc, L., Houle, J., & Poulin, P. (2011). Component-based Modeling of Complete Buildings. In *Proceedings of Graphics Interface 2011* (pp. 87–94). Ontario, Canada: Canadian Human-Computer Communications Society. Retrieved from http://dl.acm.org/citation.cfm?id=1992917.1992932

Lebres, F. (2011). *Reconstrução fidedigna da vila velha no séc. XIII. Universidade de Trás-os-Montes e Alto Douro.* Vila Real.

Lee, H., Chung, N. & Jung, T. (2015). Examining the cultural differences in acceptance of mobile augmented reality: Comparison of South Korea and Ireland. *Information and Communication Technologies in Tourism*, 477-491.

Lee, K., Lee, H.R. & Ham, S. (2013). The effects of presence induced by smartphone applications on tourism: Application to cultural heritage attractions. *Information and Communication Technologies in Tourism*, 59-72.

Lee, S. S., Boshnakova, D., & Goldblatt, J. (2016). *The 21st Century Meeting and Event Technologies Powerful Tools for Better Planning, Marketing, and Evaluation.* Waretown: Apple Academic Press.

Lee, H., & Kwon, J. (2010). Combining Context-Awareness with Wearable Computing for Emotion-based Contents Service. *International Journal of Advanced Science & Technology*, *22*, 13–24.

Lee, L., Pavlov, N., & Animation, D. (2008). Procedural fracturing and debris generation for Kung-Fu Panda. In *ACM SIGGRAPH 2008 talks* (p. 59). ACM. doi:10.1145/1401032.1401108

Lee, S. W., Lim, C. H., & Salleh, E. I. B. (2016). Reflective thermal insulation systems in building: A review on radiant barrier and reflective insulation. *Renewable & Sustainable Energy Reviews*, *65*, 643–661. doi:10.1016/j.rser.2016.07.002

Lee, T. Y., & Crompton, J. (1992). Measuring novelty seeking in tourism. *Annals of Tourism Research*, *4*(4), 732–737. doi:10.1016/0160-7383(92)90064-V

Lee, W., Xiong, L., & Hu, C. (2012). The effect of Facebook users arousal and valence on intention to go to the festival: Applying an extension of the technology acceptance model. *International Journal of Hospitality Management*, *31*(3), 819–827. doi:10.1016/j.ijhm.2011.09.018

Lei, F., & Hu, P. (2009). A baseline model for office building energy consumption in hot summer and cold winter region. *International Conference on Management and Service Science (MASS'09)*, Beijing, China. doi:10.1109/ICMSS.2009.5301031

Lennon, J. J., & Foley, M. (2000). *Dark tourism.* London: Cengage Learning EMEA.

Lerma, J. L., Cabrelles, M., & Portalés, C. (2011). Multitemporal thermal analysis to detect moisture on a building façade. *Construction & Building Materials*, *25*(5), 2190–2197. doi:10.1016/j.conbuildmat.2010.10.007

Lerones, P. M., Fernández, J. L., Gil, Á. M., Gómez-García-Bermejo, J., & Casanova, E. Z. (2010). A practical approach to making accurate 3D layouts of interesting cultural heritage sites through digital models. *Journal of Cultural Heritage*, *11*(1), 1–9. doi:10.1016/j.culher.2009.02.007

Lester, J., & Scarles, C. (2013). *Mediating the Tourist Experience. From Brochures to Virtual Encounters.* Routledge Taylor and Francis Group.

Leung, D., Law, R., van Hoof, H., & Buhalis, D. (2013). Social Media in Tourism and Hospitality: A Literature Review. *Journal of Travel & Tourism Marketing*, *30*(1-2), 1–2, 3–22. doi:10.1080/10548408.2013.750919

Levent, N., & Pascual-Leone, A. (2014). *The multisensory museum: cross-disciplinary perspectives on touch, sound, smell, memory and space.* Rowman & Littlefield.

Lewis, R., & Séquin, C. (1998). Generation of 3D building models from 2D architectural plans. *Computer Aided Design*, *30*(10), 765–779. doi:10.1016/S0010-4485(98)00031-1

Lexhagen, M., Nysveen, H., & Hem, L. E. (2005). Festival coordination: An exploratory study on intention to use mobile devices for coordination of a festival. *Event Management*, *9*(3), 133–146. doi:10.3727/152599505774791167

Li, H., & Qian, Z. (2016). Archaeological heritage tourism in China: The case of the Daming Palace from the tourists' perspective. *Journal of Heritage Tourism*, 1-14.

Liang, H. (2012). Advances in multispectral and hyperspectral imaging for archaeology and art conservation. *Applied Physics. A, Materials Science & Processing*, *106*(2), 309–323. doi:10.1007/s00339-011-6689-1

Liarokapis, F., Brujic-Okretic, V., & Papakonstantinou, S. (2006). Exploring Urban Environments Using Virtual and Augmented Reality. Journal of Virtual Reality and Broadcasting, 3(5).

Library of Congress. (2017, May 18). *Metadata object Description Schema*. Retrieved from http://www.loc.gov/standards/mods/

LifeSaver. (2013). *Context Sensitive Monitoring of Energy Consumption to Support Energy Savings and Emissions Trading in Industry*. Retrieved January 17, 2017, from www.lifesaver-fp7.eu

Lijun, M., Chan, W., & Tse, T. (2008). A tale of clouds: Paradigm comparisons and some thoughts on research issues. *IEEE Asia-Pacific Services Computing Conference*, 468.

Lillegraven, T. N., & Wolden, A. C. (2010). *Design of a bayesian recommender system for tourists presenting a solution to the cold-start user problem* (Master's degree dissertation). Institutt for datateknikk og informasjonsvitenskap, Trondheim.

Li, M., Wu, B., & Cai, L. (2008). Tourism development of World Heritage Sites in China: A geographic perspective. *Tourism Management*, *29*(2), 308–319. doi:10.1016/j.tourman.2007.03.013

Lin, A., & Chen, N. (2012). Cloud computing as an innovation: Perception, attitude, and adoption. *International Journal of Information Management*, *32*(6), 533–540. doi:10.1016/j.ijinfomgt.2012.04.001

Linaza, M.T., Gutierrez, A. & García, A. (2013). Pervasive augmented reality games to experience tourism destinations. *Information and Communication Technologies in Tourism*, 497-509.

Lin, C. H., & Kuo, B. Z. L. (2016). The behavioral consequences of tourist experience. *Tourism Management Perspectives*, *18*, 84–91. doi:10.1016/j.tmp.2015.12.017

Lindenmayer, A. (1968). Mathematical models for cellular interactions in development I. Filaments with one-sided inputs. *Journal of Theoretical Biology*, *18*(3), 280–299. doi:10.1016/0022-5193(68)90079-9 PMID:5659071

Lindgaard, G., Fernandes, G., Dudek, C., & Brown, J. (2006). Attention web designers: You have 50 milliseconds to make a good first impression! *Behaviour & Information Technology*, *25*(2), 115–126. doi:10.1080/01449290500330448

Lipovestky. (2007). *A era do vazio: ensaios sobre o individualismo contemporâneo*. Lisboa, Portugal: Relógio d'Agua.

Lipovetsky, G., & Charles, S. (2011). *Os Tempos Hipermodernos*. Lisboa, Portugal: Edições 70.

Lira, J., López, P., & Rodríguez, A. (2005). Detection of Mayas archaeological sites using high resolution radar images. *International Journal of Remote Sensing*, *26*(6), 1245–1260. doi:10.1080/01431160512331326512

Litvin, S. W., Goldsmith, R. E., & Pan, B. (2008). Electronic word-of-mouth in hospitality and tourism management. *Tourism Management*, *29*(3), 458–468. doi:10.1016/j.tourman.2007.05.011

Liu, Y., Xu, C., Pan, Z., & Pan, Y. (2006). Semantic modeling for ancient architecture of digital heritage. *Computers & Graphics*, *30*(5), 800–814. doi:10.1016/j.cag.2006.07.008

Liu, Y., Xu, C., Zhang, Q., & Pan, Y. (2008). The Smart Architect: Scalable Ontology-Based Modeling of Ancient Chinese Architectures. *IEEE Intelligent Systems*, *23*(1), 49–56. doi:10.1109/MIS.2008.16

Liu, Y., Zheng, X., Tang, F., & Chen, X. (2014). Ontology design with a granular approach. *Expert Systems with Applications*, *41*(10), 4867–4877. doi:10.1016/j.eswa.2014.02.019

Li, W. H. A., & Fu, H. (2012). Augmented reflection of reality. *Proc. ACM SIGGRAPH 2012 Emerging Technologies*. doi:10.1145/2343456.2343459

Li, Y. (2000). Geographical consciousness and tourism experience. *Annals of Tourism Research*, *27*(4), 863–883. doi:10.1016/S0160-7383(99)00112-7

Llodrà-Riera, I., Martínez-Ruiz, M. P., Jiménez-Zarco, A. I., & Izquierdo-Yusta, A. (2015). A multidimensional analysis of the information sources construct and its relevance for destination image formation. *Tourism Management*, *48*, 319–328. doi:10.1016/j.tourman.2014.11.012

Lohmann, G., & Netto, A. P. (2017). *Tourism theory - Concepts, models and systems*. London, UK: CABI. doi:10.1079/9781780647159.0000

London Charter. (2009). Retrieved 14 November 2016, from http://www.londoncharter.org/fileadmin/templates/main/docs/london_charter_2_1_en.pdf

Lonely Planet. (2016). *Virtual reality and new technologies increasingly a part of the travel industry*. Retrieved, April, 30th, 2016, from http://www.lonelyplanet.com/news/2016/04/11/travel-tourism-virtual-reality/

Lopes, R., Tim, T., Smelik, R. M., Jan de Kraker, K., & Bidarra, R. (2010). A Constrained Growth Method for Procedural Floor Plan Generation. In *GAMEON'10*. Retrieved from http://graphics.tudelft.nl/~rafa/myPapers/bidarra.GAMEON10.pdf

López-Guzmán, T. J., & Sánchez-Cañizares, S. M. (2008). La creación de productos turísticos utilizando rutas enológicas. *Pasos. Revista de Turismo y Patrimonio Cultural*, *2*, 159–171.

López-Guzmán, T., & Sánchez Cañizares, S. M. (2012). La gastronomía como motivación para viajar. Un estudio sobre el turismo culinario en Córdoba. *Guía de Estilo para Autores*, *10*, 575.

Lopez-Menchero, V. M., & Grande, A. (2011). The principles of the Seville Charter. In *XXIIIrd International CIPA Symposium* (*Vol. 2011*, pp. 2–6). Prague, Czech Republic: Academic Press.

Lord, B., & Piacente, M. (2014). *Manual of Museum Exhibitions*. Rowman & Littlefield.

Louvre. (2016). *Louvre Website* [website]. Retrieved December 21, 2016, from http://www.louvre.fr/en/homepage

Lu, C.-W., Li, S.-C., & Wu, Q. (2011). Interconnecting zigbee and 6lowpan wireless sensor networks for smart grid applications. *Sensing Technology (ICST), 2011 Fifth International Conference on*, 267–272.

Lu, J., Wu, D., Mao, M., Wang, W., & Zhang, G. (2015). Recommender system application developments: A survey. *Decision Support Systems*, *74*, 12–32. doi:10.1016/j.dss.2015.03.008

Lynch, M. F., Duinker, P. N., Sheehan, L. R., & Chute, J. E. (2011). The demand for Mikmaw cultural tourism: Tourist perspectives. *Tourism Management*, *32*(5), 977–986. doi:10.1016/j.tourman.2010.08.009

Lyotard, J. F. (1989). *A condição pós-moderna*. Lisboa, Portugal: Editora Gradiva.

Machado, M. (2016). *General format.* Retrieved February 02, 2017, from www.unisinos.br/noticias/universidade/a-historia-dos-sete-povos-na-palma-da-sua-mao

Maciel, M. (2006). *Vitrúvio - Tratado De Arquitetura.* Ist Press.

MacLeod, N. (2006). Cultural Tourism: Aspects of Authenticity and Commodification. In M. Smith & K. Robinson (Eds.), *Cultural Tourism in a Changing World. Politics, participation and (re)presentation.* Cleveland, OH: Channel View Publications.

Mad Pixel Factory. (2014). *Second Canvas: The Second Screen for Art.* Retrieved November 30, 2016, from http://www.secondcanvas.net/

Madden, L. (2011). *Professional Augmented Reality Browsers for smartphones: Programming for junaio, Layar, and Wikitude.* Chichester, UK: John Wiley & Sons, Ltd.

Magalhães, J., & Mattoso, J. (Eds.). (1993). História de Portugal: Vol. 2. A Monarquia Feudal. Círculo de Leitores, Lisboa.

Magalhaes, L. G., Sousa, J. J., Bento, R., Adao, T., Pereira, F., Filipe, V., & Peres, E. (2014). Proposal of an Information System for an Adaptive Mixed Reality System for Archaeological Sites. *Procedia Technology, 16*, 499–507. https://doi.org/10.1016/j.protcy.2014.10.117

Magnenat-Thalmann, N., & Papagiannakis, G. (2010). Recreating Daily life in Pompeii. *Virtual Archaeology Review, 1*(2), 19–23. doi:10.4995/var.2010.4679

Magoulès, F., Zhao, H., & Elizondo, D. (2013). Development of an RDP neural network for building energy consumption fault detection and diagnosis. *Energy and Building, 62*, 133–138. doi:10.1016/j.enbuild.2013.02.050

Maguire, J. S., & Mathews, J. (2010). Cultural intermediaries and the media. *Social Compass, 4*(7), 405–416. doi:10.1111/j.1751-9020.2010.00285.x

Maguire, J. S., & Mathews, J. (2012). Are we all cultural intermediaries now? An introduction to cultural intermediaries in context. *European Journal of Cultural Studies, 15*(5), 551–562. doi:10.1177/1367549412445762

Mahjoub, M., Mdhaffar, A., Halima, R., & Jmaiel, M. A. (2011). Comparative study of the current cloud computing technologies and offers. *2011 First International Symposium on Network Cloud Computing and Applications (NCCA)*, 131-134. doi:10.1109/NCCA.2011.28

Maicas, J. M., & Viñals, M. J. (2016). Edeta 360° Virtual Tour for visiting the heritage of Lliria (Spain). *Proceedings of the Archaeologica 2.0. 8th International Congres on Archaeology, Computer Graphics, Cultural Heritage and Innovation.*

Mak, A. H. N., Lumbers, M., Eves, A., & Chang, R. C. Y. (2012a). Factors influencing tourist food consumption. *International Journal of Hospitality Management, 3*(3), 928–936. doi:10.1016/j.ijhm.2011.10.012

Mäkelä, E., & Hyvönen, E. (2014). SPARQL SAHA, a Configurable Linked Data Editor and Browser as a Service. In Lecture Notes in Computer Science: Vol. 8798. The Semantic Web: ESWC 2014 Satellite Events (pp. 434-438). Springer Verlag.

Mäkelä, E., Hyvönen, E. & Ruotsalo, T. (2011). How to deal with massively heterogeneous cultural heritage data – lessons learned in CultureSampo. *Semantic Web – Interoperability, Usability, Applicability.*

Mäkilä, T., Helle, S., Viinikkala, L., Lehtonen, T., Arimaa, J. P., Heimo, O., & Pönni, V. et al. (2013). The Futuristic History project: recreating history with augmented reality solutions. *Proceedings of NODEM*, 165-170.

Makzan. (2010). *Flash Multiplayer Virtual Worlds.* Olton, UK: Packt Publishing, Ltd.

Malinowski, B. (1926). *Myth in primitive psychology*. London: Norton.

Malzbender, T., Gelb, D., & Wolters, H. (2001). Polynomial texture maps. In *Proceedings of the 28th annual conference on Computer graphics and interactive techniques* (pp. 519–528). ACM.

Manes, G. (2001). The Tetherless Tourist: Ambient Intelligence in Travel & Tourism. *Information Technology & Tourism*, *5*(4), 211–220. doi:10.3727/109830503108751144

Manguinhas, H., Freire, N., Isaac, A., Stiller, J., Charles, V., Soroa, A., . . . Alexiev, V. (2016). Exploring Comparative Evaluation of Semantic Enrichment Tools for Cultural Heritage Metadata. In N. Fuhr, L. Kovács, T. Risse & W. Nejdl (Eds.), *Research and Advanced Technology for Digital Libraries: 20th International Conference on Theory and Practice of Digital Libraries, TPDL 2016 Proceedings* (pp. 266-278). Cham: Springer International Publishing. doi:10.1007/978-3-319-43997-6_21

Månsson, M. (2011). Mediatized tourism. *Annals of Tourism Research*, *38*(4), 1634–1652. doi:10.1016/j.annals.2011.02.008

Marangunić, N., & Granić, A. (2015). Technology acceptance model: A literature review from 1986 to 2013. *Universal Access in the Information Society*, *14*(1), 81–95. doi:10.1007/s10209-014-0348-1

Marconi, M., & Lakatos, E. (2010). Fundamentos da metodologia científica: Técnicas de pesquisa (7th ed.). Atlas, São Paulo.

Margaris, D., Vassilakis, C., & Georgiadis, P. (2017). Knowledge-Based Leisure Time Recommendations in Social Networks. In *Current Trends on Knowledge-Based Systems* (pp. 23–48). Springer International Publishing. doi:10.1007/978-3-319-51905-0_2

Mariaca, R., Silva, L., & Castaños, C. (2001). Proceso de recolección y comercialización de hongos comestibles silvestres en el Valle de Toluca, México. *Ciencia Ergo Sum*, *8*(1), 30–40.

Mariani, M., Di Felice, M., & Mura, M. (2016). Facebook as a destination marketing tool: Evidence from Italian regional Destination Management Organizations. *Tourism Management*, *54*, 321–343. doi:10.1016/j.tourman.2015.12.008

Márquez-González, C., & Caro, H. (2017). World Heritage Cities of Spain: eWOM as an element of tourism development. *PASOS: Revista de Turismo y Patrimonio Cultural*, *15*(2), 437–457.

Marrero Rodríguez, J. R., & Abdul-Jalbar, B. (2012). Turismo cultural y planificación del viaje: un estudio de caso. *Tourism & Management Studies*, (8), 41-47.

Marsland, S. (2015). *Machine learning: An algorithmic perspective*. CRC Press.

Marson, F., & Musse, S. R. (2010). Automatic real-time generation of floor plans based on squarified treemaps algorithm. *Int. J. Comput. Games Technol., 2010*, 7:1–7:10. https://doi.org/10.1155/2010/624817

Martin, J. (2005). Algorithmic beauty of buildings methods for procedural building generation. *Computer Science Honors Theses*, 4.

Martínez-Graña, A. M., Goy, J. L., & Cimarra, C. A. (2013). A virtual tour of geological heritage: Valourising geodiversity using Google Earth and QR code. *Computers & Geosciences*, *61*, 83–93. doi:10.1016/j.cageo.2013.07.020

Martínez, H., Skournetou, D., Hyppölä, J., Laukkanen, S., & Heikkilä, A. (2014). Drivers and bottlenecks in the adoption of augmented reality applications. *Journal of Multimedia Theory and Application*, *1*, 27–44.

Martinez, K., Cupitt, J., Saunders, D., & Pillay, R. (2002). Ten years of art imaging research. *Proceedings of the IEEE*, *90*(1), 28–41. doi:10.1109/5.982403

Martínez-Peña, F., Gómez, R., Ortega, P., Cabezón, A., Francés, D., Sevillano, J., & Aldea, J. (2009). *MICODATA: Sistema de Información Geográfica sobre la producción, aprovechamiento y ordenación del recurso micológico en Castilla y León.* Paper presented at 5to. Congreso Forestal Español. Montes y Sociedad: Saber qué hacer, Ávila, Spain.

Martín, H. S., & Bosque, I. A. R. (2008). Exploring the cognitive-affective nature of destination image and the role of psychological factos in its formation. *Tourism Management, 29*(2), 263–277. doi:10.1016/j.tourman.2007.03.012

Mathur, P., & Nishchal, N. (2010). Cloud computing: New challenge to the entire computer industry. *2010 1st International Conference on Parallel Distributed and Grid Computing PDGC*, 223-228.

Matsukura, H., Yoneda, T., & Ishida, H. (2013). Smelling screen: Development and evaluation of an olfactory display system for presenting a virtual odor source. *IEEE Transactions on Visualization and Computer Graphics, 19*(4), 606–615. doi:10.1109/TVCG.2013.40 PMID:23428445

McCabe, S. (2014). Towards a better theory of tourism experience? A response to Gnoth and Matteucci. *International Journal of Culture. Tourism and Hospitality Research, 8*(2). doi:10.1108/IJCTHR-04-2014-0026

McCluskey, M. (2016). *Holocaust Museum Asks Guests to Stop Playing Pokémon Go There.* Retrieved November 17, 2016, from http://search.ebscohost.com/login.aspx?direct=true&site=eds-live&db=heh&AN=116804468

McGregor, I., & Holmes, J. G. (1999). How storytelling shapes memory and impressions of relationship events over time. *Journal of Personality and Social Psychology, 76*(3), 403–419. doi:10.1037/0022-3514.76.3.403

McKercher, B., Cros, H. D., & McKercher, R. B. (2002). *Cultural tourism: The partnership between tourism and cultural heritage management.* New York: Haworth Hospitality Press.

McKercher, B., Ho, P. S., & du Cros, H. (2005). Relationship between tourism and cultural heritage management: Evidence from Hong Kong. *Tourism Management, 26*(4), 539–548. doi:10.1016/j.tourman.2004.02.018

McMullan, T. (2015). *Shake up the gallery: how iPads are changing the way we visit museums* [online article]. Retrieved October 15, 2016, from http://www.alphr.com/apple/1001182/shake-up-the-gallery-how-ipads-are-changing-the-way-we-visit-museums

Melek, Z., & Keyser, J. (2002). Interactive simulation of fire. In *Computer Graphics and Applications, 2002. Proceedings. 10th Pacific Conference on* (pp. 431–432). IEEE. doi:10.1109/PCCGA.2002.1167889

Melián González, S., Bulchand Gidumal, J., & González López-Valcárcel, B. (2010). La participación de los clientes en sitios web de valoración de servicios turísticos. El caso de Tripadvisor. *Revista de Análisis Turístico, 10*, 17–22.

Mendes-Filho, L., & Santos Dantas De Carvalho, M. (2014). Factores que influyen en el uso del contenido generado por el usuario en Internet: Un Estudio Preliminar Con Viajeros Brasileños. *Estudios Y Perspectivas en Turismo, 23*(3), 607-625.

Menezes, U. T. B. (1999). Os 'usos culturais' da cultura: contribuição para uma abordagem crítica das práticas e políticas culturais. In *Turismo: espaço paisagem e cultura* (pp. 88–99). São Paulo, SP: Hucitec.

Mercator European Research Centre on Multilingualism and Language Learning. (2008). *Basque: The Basque language in education in Spain* (2nd ed.). Author.

Mercuri, F., Orazi, N., Zammit, U., Paoloni, S., Marinelli, M., & Valentini, P. P. (2011). *Thermographic analysis of cultural heritage: recent applications and perspectives.* Paper presented at the Matter and Materials in/for Cultural Heritage, Craiova, Romania.

Merrell, P., Schkufza, E., & Koltun, V. (2010). Computer-generated residential building layouts. *ACM Trans. Graph., 29*(6), 181:1–181:12. https://doi.org/10.1145/1882261.1866203

Mestanza, J. G., & Revilla, R. G. (2016). Cultural tourism in Malaga. Museums challenge. *International Journal of Scientific Management and Tourism*, *2*(3), 121–135.

Metallinou, A., Wollmer, M., Katsamanis, A., Eyben, F., Schuller, B., & Narayanan, S. (2012). Context-sensitive learning for enhanced audiovisual emotion classification. *IEEE Transactions on Affective Computing*, *3*(2), 184–198. doi:10.1109/T-AFFC.2011.40

Middleton, V. T., Fyall, A., Morgan, M., & Ranchhod, A. (2009). *Marketing in travel and tourism*. Routledge.

Miguélez Fernández, L. (2013). *Tour virtual por la red de museos de Gijón*. Master, Univeridad de Oviedo.

Mihajlović, I. (2014). ICT and New Trends in Consumer Behaviour – New Experiential knowledge, Opportunities or Challenges for Intermediaries. *Journal of Marketing Management*, *2*(1), 43–64.

Miles, W. F. S. (2002). Auschwitz: Museum interpretation and darker tourism. *Annals of Tourism Research*, *29*(4), 1175–1178. doi:10.1016/S0160-7383(02)00054-3

Milgram, P., & Kishino, F. (1994). A taxonomy of mixed reality visual displays. *IEICE Transactions on Information and Systems*, *77*(12), 1321–1329.

Milgram, P., Takemura, H., Utsumi, A., & Kishino, F. (1994). *Augmented reality: a class of displays on the reality-virtuality continuum*. Telemanipulator and Telepresence Technologies.

Millán, M. G., & Agudo, E. M. (2010). El turismo gastronómico y las Denominaciones de Origen en el sur de España: Oleoturismo. Un estudio de caso. *Pasos. Revista de Turismo y Patrimonio Cultural*, *1*, 91–112.

Miller, M. (2008). *Cloud computing: Web-based applications that change the way you work and collaborate online*. QUE Publishing.

Milošević, Ž. (2016). *Dušan Kovačević: Promoting CoMuntry's Image and Economic Contribution*. Retrieved October 29, 2016, from http://www.diplomacyandcommerce.rs/dusan-kovacevic-promoting-countrys-image-and-economic-contribution/

Ministry of the Presidency (2014). *Spain Today 2014*. NIPO (official publication identification number): 002-14-032-0.

Ministry of the Presidency. (2015). *Spain Today 2015*. Retrieved March 19, 2016, from http://www.lamoncloa.gob.es/lang/en/espana/spaintoday2015/Paginas/index.aspx

Mirahmadi, M., & Shami, A. (2012). *A Novel Algorithm for Real-time Procedural Generation of Building Floor Plans*. CoRR, abs/1211.5842

Modbus. (2006). *MODBUS over Serial Line Specification and Implementation Guide V1.02, December 20*. Retrieved January 18, 2017, from http://www.modbus.org/docs/Modbus_over_serial_line_V1_02.pdf

Modbus. (2012). *MODBUS Application Protocol Specification V1.1b3, April 26*. Retrieved January 18, 2017, from http://www.modbus.org/docs/Modbus_Application_Protocol_V1_1b3.pdf

Mogollón, J. M. H., Di Clemente, E., & Guzmán, T. J. L. G. (2015). El turismo gastronómico como experiencia cultural. El caso práctico de la ciudad de Cáceres (España). *Boletín de la Asociación de Geógrafos Españoles*, (68), 407-428.

Molina, S. (2016). Turismo creativo. *Turismo: Estudos & Práticas*, *5*(1), 205-223.

Molina, S. (2003). *O Pós-Turismo*. São Paulo, Brasil: Aleph.

Molina, S. (2003). *O pós-turismo*. São Paulo, SP: Aleph.

Molz, J. G. (2007). Eating difference: The cosmopolitan mobilities of culinary tourism. *Space and Culture*, *10*(1), 77–93. doi:10.1177/1206331206296383

Momoh, J. (2012). *Smart grid: Fundamentals of design and analysis* (Vol. 63). John Wiley & Sons. doi:10.1002/9781118156117

Monteiro, J., Eduardo, J., Cardoso, P. J. S., & Semião, J. (2014). A Distributed Load Scheduling Mechanism for Micro Grids. *IEEE International Conference on Smart Grid Communications (IEEESmartGridComm)*. doi:10.1109/SmartGridComm.2014.7007659

Monteiro, J., Cardoso, P. J. S., Serra, R., & Fernandes, L. (2014). Evaluation of the Human Factor in the Scheduling of Smart Appliances in Smart Grids. *16th International Conference on Human-Computer Interaction*. doi:10.1007/978-3-319-07446-7_52

Morency, L. P., Mihalcea, R., & Doshi, P. (2011). Towards multimodal sentiment analysis: Harvesting opinions from the web. In *Proceedings of the 13th International Conference on Multimodal Interfaces* (pp. 169-176). ACM. doi:10.1145/2070481.2070509

Morgan, J. (2012). The multisensory museum. *Glasnik Etnografskog Instituta*, *60*(1), 65–77. doi:10.2298/GEI1201065M

Mortara, M., Catalano, C. E., Bellotti, F., Fiucci, G., Houry-Panchetti, M., & Petridis, P. (2014). Learning cultural heritage by serious games. *Journal of Cultural Heritage*, *15*(3), 318–325. doi:10.1016/j.culher.2013.04.004

Morton, E. (2014). Leave me be beneath a tree: trunyan cemetery in Bali. *Slate*. Retrieved October 23, 2014, from http://www.slate.com/blogs/atlas_obscura/2014/10/23/trunyan_cemetery_with the taru_menyan_tree_in_bali_indonesia.html

Moscardo, G. M., & Ballantyne, R. (2008). Interpreation and attractions. In A. Fyall, B. Garrod, A. Leask, & S. Wanhill (Eds.), *Managing visitor attractions: New directions (pp. 237-252)*. Oxford, UK: Butterworth-Heinemann. doi:10.1016/B978-0-7506-8545-0.50022-8

Mulholland, P., Wolff, A., Kilfeather, E., & McCarthy, E. (2014). *Using event spaces, setting and theme to assist the interpretation and development of museum stories. Proceedings of Knowledge Engineering and Knowledge Management, EKAW 2014, Linköping, Sweden* (pp. 320–332). Springer.

Müller, P., Vereenooghe, T., Wonka, P., Paap, I., & Van Gool, L. (2006a). Procedural 3D Reconstruction of Puuc Buildings in Xkipché. In *Eurographics Symposium on Virtual Reality, Archaeology and Cultural Heritage (VAST)* (pp. 139–146). EG.

Müller, P., Wonka, P., Haegler, S., Ulmer, A., & Van Gool, L. (2006b). Procedural modeling of buildings. *ACM Transactions on Graphics*, *25*(3), 614–623. doi:10.1145/1141911.1141931

Müller, P., Zeng, G., Wonka, P., & Van Gool, L. (2007). Image-based procedural modeling of facades. *ACM Transactions on Graphics*, *26*(3), 85. doi:10.1145/1276377.1276484

Munar, A. M., & Jacobsen, J. K. S. (2013). Trust and involvement in tourism social media and web-based travel information sources. *Scandinavian Journal of Hospitality and Tourism*, *13*(1), 1–19. doi:10.1080/15022250.2013.764511

Munar, A. M., & Jacobsen, J. K. S. (2014). Motivations for sharing tourism experiences through social media. *Tourism Management*, *43*, 46–54. doi:10.1016/j.tourman.2014.01.012

Muntean, R., Hennessy, K., Antle, A., Rowley, S., Wilson, J., Matkin, B., … Wakkary, R. (2015). ʔeləw̓k̓w – Belongings: A Tangible Interface for Intangible Cultural Heritage. In Electronic Visualisation and the Arts (EVA 2015) (pp. 360–366). doi:<ALIGNMENT.qj></ALIGNMENT>10.14236/ewic/eva2015.41

Murphy, A. (2015). *Accessibility in museums: creating a barrier-free cultural landscape* [online article]. Retrieved December 5, 2016, from http://advisor.museumsandheritage.com/features/accessibility-in-museums-creating-a-barrier-free-cultural-landscape/

Murphy, M., McGoverna, E., & Pavia, S. (2011). Historic Building Information Modeling – Adding Intelligence to Laser and Image Based Surveys. *4th ISPRS International Workshop "3D Virtual Reconstruction and Visualization of Complex Architectures"*.

Murphy, M., & Pavia, S. (2009). Historic Building information modelling (HBIM). *Structural Survey: Journal of Building Pathology and Refurbishment*, *27*(4), 311–327. doi:10.1108/02630800910985108

Murty, M. N., & Devi, V. S. (2011). *Nearest Neighbour Based Classifiers. Pattern recognition: an algorithmic approach.* London: Springer.

Museo del Prado. (2015). *Hoy toca el Prado* [online article]. Retrieved September 10, 2016, from https://www.museodelprado.es/actualidad/exposicion/hoy-toca-el-prado/29c8c453-ac66-4102-88bd-e6e1d5036ffa

Museum of Science and Industry. (2016). *Exhibit Science Storms: Wonder Is All Natural* [website]. Retrieved November 22, 2016, from http://www.msichicago.org/explore/whats-here/exhibits/science-storms/the-exhibit/fire/fire-and-water/

Museum, N. (2016). *Pipilotti Rist: Pixel Forest.* Retrieved November 29, 2016, from http://www.newmuseum.org/exhibitions/view/pipilotti-rist-pixel-forest

Musialski, P., & Wimmer, M. (2013). Inverse-procedural Methods for Urban Models. In *Proceedings of the Eurographics Workshop on Urban Data Modelling and Visualisation* (pp. 31–32). Aire-la-Ville, Switzerland: Eurographics Association. https://doi.org/10.2312/UDMV/UDMV13/031-032

MWCM. (2016). *Multitouch wall Cleveland Museum.* Retrieved: Nov. 16, 2016 from https://goo.gl/kI2oCh

Nadarajan, M., & Kirubakaran, V. (2016). Simulation tools for residential buildings-A review on concepts and technologies. *Journal of Engineering and Applied Sciences (Asian Research Publishing Network)*, *11*(5), 2998–3007.

Nakamura, S. (2009). Overcoming the Language Barrier with Speech Translation Technology. *NISTEP Quarterly Review*, *31*, 35–49.

Naniopoulos, A., & Marki, E. (2003). Accessibility and Comprehensibility of Monuments and Archaeological Sites for people with Restricted Mobility. A Preliminary Investigation for the Application of a Methodology on Sites of the 9th Ephorate of Byzantine Antiquities. In *Access to culture and sports for people with disabilities conference proceedings.* Hellenic Ministry of Culture.

Naniopoulos, A., & Nalmpantis D. (2004). *An overview of: Problems, suggestions and good practices concerning the situation in Greece.* Maple project deliverable. Thessaloniki: AUTh.

Naniopoulos, A., Antonopoulos, C., Karadedos, G., Polychroniou, I., Tsalis, P., Genitsaris, E., . . . Palantzas, G. (2011a). Handbook of basic principles for the realization of accessibility improvements in Monumental spaces. PROSPELASIS project Deliverable. Thessaloniki: AUTh.

Naniopoulos, A., Giannakos, C., Xenakis, C., Papanikolaou, E., Kalliagra, S., Kourbeti, C., Tselegidis, I., & Digbasbani, A., (2010a). *Proposal of functional alternative solutions in pre-study level for selected Monuments/spaces.* PROSPELASIS project Deliverable. Thessaloniki: AUTh.

Naniopoulos, A., Giannakos, C., Xenakis, C., Papanikolaou, E., Kalliagra, S., Sakantamis, K., … Karagiorgos, F. (2011b). *Proposal of functional solutions in final study level for selected Monuments/spaces.* PROSPELASIS project Deliverable. Thessaloniki: AUTh.

Naniopoulos, A., Papanikolaou, E., Kalliagra, S., Tsalis, P., Palantzas, G., Nalmpantis, D., Genitsaris, E., Kyriakopoulos, N., & Tokmakidis, P. (2010b). *Evaluation and mapping of the existing situation in selected Monuments/spaces.* PROSPELASIS project Deliverable. Thessaloniki: AUTh.

Narciso, D., Pádua, L., Adão, T., Peres, E., & Magalhães, L. (2015). MixAR Mobile Prototype: Visualizing Virtually Reconstructed Ancient Structures In Situ. *Procedia Computer Science, 64*, 852–861. https://doi.org/10.1016/j.procs.2015.08.638

Narumi, T., Kajinami, T., Nishizaka, S., Tanikawa, T., & Hirose, M. (2011). Pseudo-gustatory display system based on cross-modal integration of vision, olfaction and gustation. In *Virtual Reality Conference (VR)*, 2011 *IEEE* (pp. 127-130). IEEE. doi:10.1109/VR.2011.5759450

National Disability Authority of Ireland (NDA). (2011). *Code of practice on accessible heritage sites*. Dublin: NDA.

National Museums Scotland. (2013). *National Museums Scotland looks to grab new audiences with digital game of territories* [press release]. Retrieved December 1, 2016, from http://www.capturethemuseum.com/press/

Natural History Museum. (2015). *Explore virtual reality with David Attenborough's First Life* [online article]. Retrieved December 5, 2016, from http://www.nhm.ac.uk/about-us/news/2015/june/dive-back-in-time-with-david-attenborough-s-first-life.html

Navarro, S., Seguí, A. E., Portalés, C., Lerma, J. L., Akasheh, T., & Haddad, N. (2009). *Integration of tls data and non-metric imagery to improve photo models and recording-a case study on djin block no. 9, petra (jordan).* Paper presented at the Virtual Systems and Multimedia.

Negruşa, A. L., Toader, V., Sofică, A., Tutunea, M. F., & Rus, R. V. (2015). Exploring gamification techniques and applications for sustainable tourism. *Sustainability, 7*(8), 11160–11189. doi:10.3390/su70811160

Nelson, P. (1970). Information and consumer behavior. *Journal of Political Economy, 78*(2), 311–329. doi:10.1086/259630

Neo, H.-F., Rasiah, D., Tong, D. Y. K., & Teo, C.-C. (2014). Biometric technology and privacy: A perspective from tourist satisfaction. *Information Technology & Tourism, 14*(3), 219–237. doi:10.1007/s40558-014-0014-8

Netto, V. M. (2014). *Cidade e sociedade: as tramas da prática e seus espaços*. Porto Alegre, RS: Sulinas.

Neuhofer, B., Buhalis, D., & Ladkin, A. (2013). Experiences, Cocreation and Technology: A conceptual Approach to Enhance Tourism. Tourism and Global Change: On the Edge of something big. *CAUTHE 2013 Conference Proceedings.*

Neuhofer, B., Buhalis, D., & Ladkin, A. (2012). Conceptualizing Technology enhanced destination experiences. *Journal of Destination Marketing & Management, 1*(1-2), 36–46. doi:10.1016/j.jdmm.2012.08.001

Neuhofer, B., Buhalis, D., & Ladkin, A. (2014). A typology of technology enhanced tourism experiences. *International Journal of Tourism Research, 16*(4), 340–350. doi:10.1002/jtr.1958

Neuhofer, B., Buhalis, D., & Ladkin, A. (2015). Smart technologies for personalized experiences: A case study in the hospitality domain. *Electronic Markets, 25*(3), 243–254. doi:10.1007/s12525-015-0182-1

Neumüller, M., Reichinger, A., Rist, F., & Kern, C. (2014). 3D Printing for Cultural Heritage: Preservation, Accessibility, Research and Education. In M. Ioannides & E. Quak (Eds.), 3D Research Challenges in Cultural Heritage: A Roadmap in Digital Heritage Preservation (pp. 119–134). Berlin: Springer Berlin Heidelberg. doi:<ALIGNMENT.qj></ALIGNMENT>10.1007/978-3-662-44630-0_9

Neves, A., Magalhães, A., & Lourenço, F. (2007). *Oferta educativa e formativa em Turismo: Articulação com o mercado de emprego*. Lisboa, Portugal: Gráfica Europan, Lda.

Neves-Silva, R. (2012). *Decision Support Systems for Energy Efficiency*. "Portugal — Caminhos da Excelência em Ciência e Tecnologia", Fundação Calouste Gulbenkian. Retrieved January 17, 2017, from http://ciencia2012.fct.pt/files/ciencia2012_RuiNevesSilva.pdf

Nikiforova, B. (2013). Social media in travel, tourism and hospitality: Theory, practice and cases. *Journal of Tourism History*, *5*(1), 99–101. doi:10.1080/1755182X.2012.758973

Nilsson, T., Blackwell, A., Hogsden, C., & Scruton, D. (2016). Ghosts! A Location-Based Bluetooth LE Mobile Game for Museum Exploration. In L. Joyce & B. Quinn (Eds.), Mapping the Digital: Cultures and Territories of Play (pp. 129–138). Oxford, UK: Inter-Disciplinary Press. Retrieved from http://arxiv.org/abs/1607.05654

Nisheva-Pavlova, M., Spyratos, S., & Stanchev, P. (2014), *Museum Collections and the Semantic Web. Fourth International Conference on Digital Presentation and Preservation of Cultural and Scientific Heritage*, Veliko Tarnovo, Bulgaria.

Nishino, K., & Ikeuchi, K. (2002). Robust Simultaneous Registration of Multiple Range Images. *5th Asian Conf. Computer Vision*, 454–461.

NIST. (2011). *The NIST Definition of Cloud Computing*. Retrieved November, 2016, from NIST - National Institute of Standards and Technology: http://nvlpubs.nist.gov/nistpubs/Legacy/SP/nistspecialpublication800-145.pdf

Nofuente, K. (2016). *Virtual Reality and The Future of Museum Tours: Using Oculus Rift to Dream with Disney and Dalí* [online article]. Retrieved December 1, 2016, from http://www.techtimes.com/articles/127404/20160127/virtual-reality-future-museum-tours-using-oculus-rift-dream-with-disney-dali.htm

Noh, Z., Sunar, M., & Pan, Z. (2009). *A Review on Augmented Reality for Virtual Heritage System. Learning by Playing. In Game-based Education System Design and Development. Springer*. doi:10.1007/978-3-642-03364-3_7

Nomad Agency. (2016). *Beacon Analytics at Maritime Museum* [online article]. Retrieved December 6, 2016, from http://www.nomadagency.com.au/portfolio-item/beacon-analytics-at-maritime-museum/

Nyaupane, G. P., Timothy, D. J., & Poudel, S. (2015). Understanding Tourists in Religious Destinations: A Social Distance Perspective. *Tourism Management*, *48*, 343–353. doi:10.1016/j.tourman.2014.12.009

O'Connor, P. (2011). *An Analysis of the use of Facebook by International Hotel Chains (Comunicação apresentada no International Council on Hotel, Restaurant and Institucional Education – CHRIE)*. Denver, CO: Conference.

Oakes, E. (2007). *Encyclopedia of World Scientist*. Infobase Publishing.

OASIS. (2012). *Energy Interoperation Version 1.0*. Retrieved January 18, 2017 from https://goo.gl/4To3QZ

OASIS. (2014). *MQTT Version 3.1.1. OASIS Standard*. Retrieved January 18, 2017 from https://goo.gl/VCBTTT

OBrien, H. L., & Toms, E. G. (2008). What is user engagement? A conceptual framework for defining user engagement with technology. *Journal of the American Society for Information Science and Technology*, *59*(6), 938–955. doi:10.1002/asi.20801

OConnor, P., & Frew, A. J. (2002). The future of hotel electronic distribution: Expert and industry perspectives. *The Cornell Hotel and Restaurant Administration Quarterly*, *43*(3), 33–45. doi:10.1016/S0010-8804(02)80016-7

OECD. (2014). *Tourism and the Creative Economy, OECD Studies on Tourism*. OECD Publishing. 10.1787/9789264207875-en

OECD. (2016). *OECD Tourism Trends and Policies 2016*. OECD Publishing. 10.1787/tour-2016-en

Oficina del Peregrino. (2016). *Estadísticas oficiales.* Retrieved November, 13th, 2017, from https://oficinadelperegrino.com/estadisticas/

Oghuma, A. P., Libaque-Saenz, C. F., Wong, S. F., & Chang, Y. (2016). An Expectation-Confirmation Model Of Continuance Intention To Use Mobile Instant Messaging. *Telematics and Informatics, 33*(1), 34–47. doi:10.1016/j.tele.2015.05.006

Oh, H., Fiore, A. M., & Jeoung, M. (2007). Measuring Experience Economy Concepts: Tourism Applications. *Journal of Travel Research, 46*(2), 119–132. doi:10.1177/0047287507304039

Ohlman, B., Eriksson, A., & Rembarz, R. (2009). What networking of information can do for cloud computing. 18th IEEE International Workshops on Enabling Technologies: Infrastructures for Collaborative Enterprises WETICE '09, 78-83. doi:10.1109/WETICE.2009.27

Okerlund, J., Segreto, E., Grote, C., Westendorf, L., Scholze, A., Littrell, R., & Shaer, O. (2016). SynFlo: A Tangible Museum Exhibit for Exploring Bio - Design. *Proceedings of the TEI '16: Tenth International Conference on Tangible, Embedded, and Embodied Interaction*, 141–149. doi:10.1145/2839462.2839488

Olesen, A. R. (2016). For the sake of technology? The role of technology views in funding and designing digital museum communication. *Museum Management and Curatorship, 31*(3), 283–298. 10.1080/09647775.2016.1163643

Olins, W. (2014). *Brand new: The shape of brands to come.* Thames & Hudson.

Olivares, D.E., et al. (2014). Trends in Microgrid Control. *IEEE Transactions on Smart Grid, 5*(4), 1905-1919.

Oliveira, M. (2013). *Royal Ontario Museum ScopifyROM App Adds Interactivity to Exhibits* [online article]. Retrieved November 30, 2016, from http://www.huffingtonpost.ca/2013/10/02/royal-ontario-museum-app_n_4031715.html

Oliveira, S. (2007). La importancia de la Gastronomia en el turismo. *Estudios y Perspectivas en Turismo, 16*, 261–282.

Oliver, A., Neila, F. J., & García, A. (2011). PCM inclusion in gypsum boards for thermal energy storage through latent heat: Thermal characterization with DSC. *Informes de la Construccion, 63*(522), 61–70. doi:10.3989/ic.09.039

Olsson, T., Lagerstam, E., Kärkkäinen, T., & Väänänen-Vainio-Mattila, K. (2013). Expected user experience of mobile augmented reality services: A user study in the context of shopping centres. *Personal and Ubiquitous Computing, 17*(2), 287–304. doi:10.1007/s00779-011-0494-x

ONTSI. (2012). *El estudio cloud computing. Retos y oportunidades.* Madrid: Ministerio de Industria.

Open Archives Initiative. (2014, August 14). *ORE Specifications and User Guides - Table of Contents.* Retrieved from http://www.openarchives.org/ore/1.0/toc

OpenADR Alliance. (2014). *OpenADR 2.0 profile specification, a profile.* Retrieved January 18, 2017 from www.openadr.org/specification

Organismo Autonomo Parques Nacionales. (2014). *Amplicacion del Parque Nacional Picos de Europa en 2.467,59 ha.* Author.

Pacifico, D., & Vogel, M. (2012). Archaeological sites, modern communities, and tourism. *Annals of Tourism Research, 39*(3), 1588–1611. doi:10.1016/j.annals.2012.04.002

Padoan, R., Steemers, T. A. G., Klein, M. E., Aalderink, B. J., & Bruin, G. d. (2008). *Quantitative Hyperspectral Imaging of Historical Documents: Technique and Applications.* Paper presented at the 9th International Conference on NDT of Art, Jerusalem, Israel.

Pádua, L., Adão, T., Narciso, D., Cunha, A., Magalhães, L., & Peres, E. (2015). Towards Modern Cost-effective and Lightweight Augmented Reality Setups. *International Journal of Web Portals*, *7*(2), 33–59. doi:10.4018/IJWP.2015040103

Pal, B. (2015). Heritage Tourism and Bishnupur "The City of Archaeological Monuments". *Asian Journal of Multidisciplinary Studies*, *3*(10). Retrieved from http://ajms.co.in/sites/ajms2015/index.php/ajms/issue/view/31/showToc

Palmisano, C., Tuzhilin, A., & Gorgoglione, M. (2008). Using context to improve predictive modeling of customers in personalization applications. *IEEE Transactions on Knowledge and Data Engineering*, *20*(11), 1535–1549. doi:10.1109/TKDE.2008.110

Palomar-Vazquez, J., & Viñals-Blasco, M. J. (2016). *Exploring Three-js library possibilities for the dissemination of cultural heritage projects*. doi: 10.4995/var.2016.5834

Palomar-Vazquez, J., Baselga, S., Viñals-Blasco, M.-J., García-Sales, C., & Sancho-Espinós, I. (2017). Application of a combination of digital image processing and 3D visualization of graffiti in heritage conservation. *Journal of Archaeological Science: Reports*, *12*, 32–42. doi:10.1016/j.jasrep.2017.01.021

Palos, P. R., & Correia, M. B. (2016b). The paradigm of the cloud and web accessibility and its consequences in Europe. In *7th International Conference on Software Development and Technologies for Enhancing Accessibility and Fighting Info-exclusion DSAI 2016*. Vila Real, Portugal: ACM. doi:10.1145/3019943.3019995

Palos, P.R., & Correia, M.B. (2016a). La actitud de los recursos humanos de las organizaciones ante la complejidad de las aplicaciones SaaS. *Dos Algarves: A Multidisciplinary e-Journal*, 87-103. doi:10.18089/DAMeJ.2016.28.6

Palos, P. R., & Aguayo-Camacho, M. (2016). Los cambios organizacionales y la nube en el entorno turístico: Estudio de caso. *International Journal of World of Tourism*, *3*(5), 33–42.

Pamart, A., Guillon, O., Faraci, S., Gattet, E., Genevois, M., Vallet, J. M., & De Luca, L. (2017). Multispectral photogrammetric data acquisition and processing forwall paintings studies. *Int. Arch. Photogramm. Remote Sens. Spatial Inf. Sci.*, *XLII-2*(W3), 559–566. doi:10.5194/isprs-archives-XLII-2-W3-559-2017

Pang, A. S.-K. (2013). *The distraction addiction: getting the information you need and the communication you want without enraging your family, annoying your colleagues, and destroying your soul*. New York: Little Brown and Company.

Pantoja, J., Docampo, J., Martín, A., Maturana, R., & Navalón, C. (2016). *The new Prado Museum website: A (semantic) challenge*. MW2016 Museums and the Web 2016. Retrieved January 10, 2017, from http://mw2016.museumsandtheweb.com/paper/the-new-prado-museum-website-a-semantic-challenge/

Papagiannakis, G., Ponder, M., Molet, T., Kshirsagar, S., Cordier, F., Magnenat-thalmann, N., & Thalmann, D. (2002). LIFEPLUS: Revival of life in ancient Pompeii. *Proceedings of the 8th International Conference on Virtual Systems and Multimedia (VSMM '02)*, 25–27.

Parish, Y. I., & Müller, P. (2001). Procedural modeling of cities. In *Proceedings of the 28th annual conference on Computer graphics and interactive techniques* (pp. 301–308). ACM.

Park, J.-Y., & Jang, S. (2013). Confused by too many choices? Choice overload in tourism. *Tourism Management*, *35*, 1–12. doi:10.1016/j.tourman.2012.05.004

Park, M., Lim, K., Seo, M., Jung, S., & Lee, K. (2014). Spatial augmented reality for product appearance design evaluation. *Journal of Computational Design and Engineering*, *2*(1), 38–46. doi:10.1016/j.jcde.2014.11.004

Parra-López, E., Bulchand-Gidumal, J., Gutiérrez-Taño, D., & Díaz-Armas, R. (2011). Intentions to use social media in organizing and taking vacation trips. *Computers in Human Behavior*, *27*(2), 640–654. doi:10.1016/j.chb.2010.05.022

Paton, N. W., Al-Qaimari, G., & Doan, K. (1994). On interface objects in Object-Oriented Databases. *12th British National Conference on Databases*. Springer-Verlag.

Pauwels, P., Verstraeten, R., De Meyer, R., & Van Campenhout, J. (2008). Architectural Information Modeling For Virtual Heritage Application. *Proceedings of the 14th International Conference on Virtual Systems and Multimedia*, 18–23.

Pearce, P. L. (1982). Perceived changes in holiday destinations. *Annals of Tourism Research*, *9*(2), 145–164. doi:10.1016/0160-7383(82)90044-5

Pearlson, K., & Saunders, C. (2009). *Strategic management of information systems* (4th ed.). Hoboken, NJ: Wiley.

Peeters, P., Dijkmans, C., Mitas, O., Strous, B., & Vinkensteijn, J. (2015). *Research for Tran Committee: Tourism and the sharing economy: challenges and opportunities for the EU.* Brussels: European Parliament. Retrieved from http://www.europarl.europa.eu/RegData/etudes/STUD/2015/563411/IPOL_STU(2015)563411_EN.pdf

Peña Serna, S., Schmedt, H., Ritz, M., & Stork, A. (2012). *Interactive Semantic Enrichment of 3D Cultural Heritage Collections.* Paper presented at the The 13th International Symposium on Virtual Reality, Archaeology and Cultural Heritage VAST, Brighton, UK.

Pendit, U. C., Zaibon, S. B., & Bakar, J. A. A. (2014). Mobile Augmented Reality for Enjoyable Informal Learning in Cultural Heritage Site. *International Journal of Computers and Applications*, *92*(14), 19–26. doi:10.5120/16077-5286

Pendrana, M. (2014). Location-based services and tourism: Possible implications for destination. *Current Issues in Tourism*, *17*(9), 753–762. doi:10.1080/13683500.2013.868411

Peng, C., Chen, B.-Y., & Tsai, C.-H. (2010). Integrated Google Maps and smooth street view videos for route planning. In *2010 International Computer Symposium (ICS2010).* Tainan: IEEE. doi:10.1109/COMPSYM.2010.5685494

Pesonen, J., & Horster, E. (2012). Near field communication technology in tourism. *Tourism Management Perspectives*, *4*, 11–18. doi:10.1016/j.tmp.2012.04.001

Phillips, W. J., Wolfe, K., Hodur, N., & Leistritz, F. L. (2013). Tourist word of mouth and revisit intentions to rural tourism destinations: A case of North Dakota, USA. *International Journal of Tourism Research*, *15*(1), 93–104. doi:10.1002/jtr.879

Philokyprou, M., Michael, A., Malaktou, E., & Savvides, A. (2017). Environmentally responsive design in Eastern Mediterranean. The case of vernacular architecture in the coastal, lowland and mountainous regions of Cyprus. *Building and Environment*, *111*, 91–109. doi:10.1016/j.buildenv.2016.10.010

Picard, M. (1997). Cultural tourism, nation-building, and regional culture: The making of a Balinese identity. *Tourism, ethnicity, and the state in Asian and Pacific societies*, 181-214.

Picard, M. (1990). Cultural Tourism in Bali: Cultural Performances as Tourist Attraction. *Indonesia*, *49*, 37–74. doi:10.2307/3351053

Picard, M. (2008). Balinese identity as tourist attraction from cultural tourism(pariwisata budaya) toBali erect(ajeg Bali). *Tourist Studies*, *8*(2), 155–173. doi:10.1177/1468797608099246

Pike, S., & Page, S. (2014). Destination Marketing Organizations and destination marketing: A narrative analysis of the literature. *Tourism Management*, *41*, 202–227. doi:10.1016/j.tourman.2013.09.009

Pike, S., & Ryan, C. (2004). Destination Positioning Analysis through a Comparsion of Cognitive, Affective and Conative Perceptions. *Journal of Travel Research*, *42*(4), 333–342. doi:10.1177/0047287504263029

Pine, J., & Gilmore, J. (1999). *The experience economy.* Boston: Harvard Business School Press.

Pine, J., & Gilmore, J. (1999). Welcome to the Experience Economy. *Harvard Business Review*, 97–105. PMID:10181589

Pires, J., & Cruz, A. J. (2007). Techniques of thermal analysis applied to the study of cultural heritage. *Journal of Thermal Analysis and Calorimetry*, *87*(2), 411–415. doi:10.1007/s10973-004-6775-0

Pixar. (1990, December 20). Retrieved 1 May 2015, from http://www.pixar.com/

Pletinckx, D. (2008). Interpretation Management: How to Make Sustainable Visualisations of the Past. *EPOCH Conference on Open Digital Cultural Heritage Systems.*

Podoshen, J. S. (2013). Dark tourism motivations: Simulation, emotional contagion and topographic comparison. *Tourism Management*, *35*, 263–271. doi:10.1016/j.tourman.2012.08.002

Pollefeys, M. (1999). *Self-calibration and metric 3D reconstruction from uncalibrated image sequences* (PhD thesis). ESAT-PSI, KU Leuven.

Pollefeys, M., Van Gool, L., Akkermans, I., De Becker, D., & Demuynck, K. (2001). A guided tour to virtual Sagalassos. In *Proceedings of the 2001 conference on Virtual reality, archeology, and cultural heritage* (pp. 213–218). ACM. doi:10.1145/584993.585027

Pölmann, A. (2013). Intercultural Capital: Toward the Conceptualization, Operationalization, and Empirical Investigation of a Rising Marker of Sociocultural Distinction. *SAGE Open*, 3. Retrieved July 7, 2016, from http://sgo.sagepub.com/content/3/2/2158244013486117.full

Pölmann, A. (2016). Habitus, reflexivity, and the realization of intercultural capital: The (unfulfilled) potential of intercultural education. *Cogent Social Sciences*, *2*, 1–12.

Poon, A. (1993). *Tourism, technology and competitive strategies*. Wallingford: CABI.

Poria, Y. (2007). Establishing cooperation between Israel and Poland to save Auschwitz Concentration Camp: Globalising the responsibility for the Massacre. *International Journal of Tourism Policy*, *1*(1), 45–57. doi:10.1504/IJTP.2007.013897

Poria, Y., Butler, R., & Airey, D. (2003). The core of heritage tourism. *Annals of Tourism Research*, *30*(1), 238–254. doi:10.1016/S0160-7383(02)00064-6

Poria, Y., Reichel, A., & Biran, A. (2006). Heritage site management: Motivations and expectations. *Annals of Tourism Research*, *33*(1), 162–178. doi:10.1016/j.annals.2005.08.001

Portalés Ricart, C., Giner Martínez, F., & Sanmartín Piquer, F. (2005). *Back to the 70's*. Paper presented at the ACM SIGCHI International Conference on Advances in Computer Entertainment Technology, Valencia, Spain.

Portalés, C., Alonso-Monasterio, P., & Viñals, M. J. (2016, 5-7 September). *A new methodology for the 3D photorealistic virtual reconstruction of the archaeological site "Castellet de Bernabé" (Llíria, Spain)*. Paper presented at the ARQUEOLÓGICA 2.0 - 8° Congreso Internacional, Documentación 3D avanzada, modelado y reconstrucción de objetos patrimoniales, monumentos y sitios, Valencia.

Portalés, C., Alonso-Monasterio, P., & Viñals, M. J. (2017). 3D virtual reconstruction and visualisation of the archaeological site "Castellet de Bernabé" (Llíria, Spain). *Virtual Archeaology Review, 8*(16).

Portalés, C., Lerma, J. L., & Pérez, C. (2009). Photogrammetry and augmented reality for cultural heritage applications. *The Photogrammetric Record*, *24*(128), 316–331. doi:10.1111/j.1477-9730.2009.00549.x

Portalés, C., Viñals, M. J., Alonso-Monasterio, P., & Morant, M. (2010). AR-Immersive Cinema at the Aula Natura Visitors Center. *IEEE MultiMedia*, *17*(4), 8–15. doi:10.1109/MMUL.2010.72

Potion. (2010). *Memory Pool*. Retrieved from http://www.potiondesign.com/project/memorypool/

Prahalad, C. K., & Ramaswamy, V. (2003). The new frontier of experience innovation. *MIT. Sloan Management Review*, *44*(4), 12–18.

Prahalad, C. K., & Ramaswamy, V. (2004). Co- creation experiences: The next practice in value creation. *Journal of Interactive Marketing*, *18*(3), 5–14. doi:10.1002/dir.20015

Preetham, A. J., Shirley, P., & Smits, B. (1999). A practical analytic model for daylight. In *Proceedings of the 26th annual conference on Computer graphics and interactive techniques* (pp. 91–100). ACM Press/Addison-Wesley Publishing Co.

Prieur, A., & Savage, M. (2013). Emerging Forms of Cultural Capital. *European Societies, 15*(2), 246-267. DOI: 566_ 58010.1080/14616696.2012.748930

Prieur, A., Rosenlund, L., & Skjott-Larsen, J. (2008). Cultural Capital Today: A Case Study from Denmark. *Poetics*, *36*(1), 45–71. doi:10.1016/j.poetic.2008.02.008

Prieur, A., & Savage, M. (2011). Updating cultural capital theory: A discussion based on studies in Denmark and in Britain. *Poetics*, *39*(6), 566–580. doi:10.1016/j.poetic.2011.09.002

Priskin, J. (2001). Assessment of natural resources for nature based tourism: The case of Central Coast Region of Western Australia. *Tourism Management*, *22*(6), 637–648. doi:10.1016/S0261-5177(01)00039-5

Priuer, A. (2013). Contemporary Cultural Capital: Two New Tendencies; Emerging Cultural Capital and New Forms of Distinction. *Workshop, LSE.*

PROSPELASIS Team. (2012). *D7: Interventions realized in selected Monuments*. PROSPELASIS project Deliverable. Thessaloniki: AUTh.

Provincial Diputation of Cuenca. (2015). *Memoria anual 2015 del parque arqueológico de Segóbriga*. Salelices, Cuenca. Retrieved March 2, 2016 from https://www.dipucuenca.es/noticias/-/publicador/el-parque-arqueologico-de-segobriga-cerro-2015-con-casi-50-000-visitantes-un-5-34-mas-que-en-2014

Prweb. (2016). *Digital frontiers media uses augmented reality to market St. Pete/Clearwater tourism with miles media*. Retrieved May, 1st, 2016, from http://www.prweb.com/releases/2011/03/prweb5141134.htm

Qualcomm. (2016). *Invisible Museum*. Retrieved: Nov. 16, 2016 from https://goo.gl/aS0NKh

Quattrini, R., Pierdicca, R., Frontoni, E., & Barcaglioni, R. (2016). Virtual Reconstruction of Lost Architectures: from the Tls Survey to AR Visualization. *XXIII ISPRS Congress*.

Raczkowski, J. (1996). Visual simulation and animation of a laminar candle flame. *International conference on image processing and computer graphics*.

Rae, J., & Edwards, L. (2016). Virtual reality at the British Museum: What is the value of virtual reality environments for learning by children and young people, schools, and families?. *MW2016: Museums and the Web 2016*. Retrieved from http://mw2016.museumsandtheweb.com/paper/virtual-reality-at-the-british-museum-what-is-the-value-of-virtual-reality-environments-for-learning-by-children-and-young-people-schools-and-families/

Rafael, L. (2015). "Monitorização de indicadores (2014)". In *Relatório de Atividades 2014*. Faro: Direção Regional de Cultura do Algarve. Retrieved October 14, 2016, from http://www.cultalg.pt/pt/drca/instrumentos-de-gestao

Rahim, S., Khan, S. A., Javaid, N., Shaheen, N., Iqbal, Z., & Rehman, G. (2015). Towards multiple knapsack problem approach for home energy management in smart grid. In *Network-Based Information Systems (NBiS), 2015 18th International Conference on* (pp. 48-52). IEEE. doi:10.1109/NBiS.2015.11

Raine, R. (2013). A dark tourist spectrum. *International Journal of Culture, Tourism and hospitality Research, 7*(3), 242-256.

Rakshit, R., & Ogneva-Himmelberger, Y. (2008). Application of Virtual Globes in Education. *Geography Compass, 2*(6), 1995–2010. doi:10.1111/j.1749-8198.2008.00165.x

Ramos, C., Henriques, C., & Lanquar, R. (2016). Augmented Reality for Smart Tourism in Religious Heritage Itineraries: Tourism Experiences in the Technological Age. In J. Rodrigues, P. Cardoso, J. Monteiro, & M. Figueiredo (Eds.), *Handbook of Research on Human-Computer Interfaces, Developments, and Applications* (pp. 250–278). Hershey, PA: IGI Global. doi:10.4018/978-1-5225-0435-1.ch010

Ranasinghe, N., Nakatsu, R., Nii, H., & Gopalakrishnakone, P. (2012). Tongue mounted interface for digitally actuating the sense of taste. In *Wearable Computers (ISWC), 2012 16th International Symposium on* (pp. 80-87). IEEE. doi:10.1109/ISWC.2012.16

Ranasinghe, N., Cheok, A. D., Fernando, O. N. N., Nii, H., & Ponnampalam, G. (2011). Electronic taste stimulation. In *Proceedings of the 13th international conference on Ubiquitous computing* (pp. 561-562). ACM.

Ratten, V. (2013). Cloud computing: A social cognitive perspective of ethics, entrepreneurship, technology marketing, computer self-efficacy and outcome expectancy on behavioural intentions. *Australasian Marketing Journal, 21*(3), 137–146. doi:10.1016/j.ausmj.2013.02.008

Rátz, T. (2016, May 29). 'Be global, go local' – Innovation and creativity in the development of alternative guiding services in Budapest. *Journal of Tourism and Cultural Change*, 1-14.

Rau-Chaplin, A., MacKay-Lyons, B., & Spierenburg, P. (1996). The LaHave House Project: Towards and Automated Architectural Design Service. In *Proceedings of the International Conference on Computer Aided Design (CADEX-96)* (pp. 62–66). IEEE.

Reed, P. A. (1995). *CIDOC Relational Data Model. A Guide*. ICOM/CIDOC.

Reeves, W. T. (1983). Particle systems—a technique for modeling a class of fuzzy objects. [TOG]. *ACM Transactions on Graphics, 2*(2), 91–108. doi:10.1145/357318.357320

Reffat, R. M., & Nofal, E. M. (2013). Effective Communication with Cultural heritage using Virtual Technologies. *International Archives of the Photogrammetry. Remote Sensing and Spatial Information Sciences, XL-5*(W2), 519–524.

Reilly, P. (1990). Towards a virtual archaeology. In *Computer Applications in Archaeology* (pp. 133–139). Oxford, UK: British Archaeological Reports.

Reilly, P., & Rahtz, S. (1992). Introduction: archaelogy and the information age. In *Archaeology and the information age: a global perspective* (pp. 1–28). London, UK: Routledge. doi:10.4324/9780203168349_chapter_1

Reinecke, K., & Bernstein, A. (2013). Knowing What a User Likes: A Design Science Approach to Interfaces that Automatically Adapt to Culture. *Management Information Systems Quarterly, 37*(2), 427–453.

Reisinger, Y. (2009). *International Tourism Cultures and Behavior*. Elsevier Inc.

Reyes-García, V., Huanca, T., Vadez, V., Leonard, W., & Wilkie, D. (2006). Cultural, Practical, and Economic Value of Wild Plants: A Quantitative Study in the Bolivian Amazon. *Economic Botany, 60*(1).

RGEU. (2008). *Regulamento Geral das Edificações Urbanas, Decreto n.º 38382*. RGEU.

Ribeiro, A. P. (2015). *Paradoxos da "oferta cultural". In Políticas culturais para o desenvolvimento*. Conferência ARTEMREDE.

Ricci, F. (2002). Travel recommender systems. *IEEE Intelligent Systems*, *17*(6), 55–57.

Richards, G. (2001). El desarrollo del turismo cultural en Europa. *Estudios turísticos*, 3-14.

Richards, G. (2002). Gastronomy: An essential ingredient in tourism production and consumption. *Tourism and Gastronomy, 11*, 2-20.

Richards, G. (2012). *Tourism, Creativity and Creative industries*. Paper presented at the Conference Creativity and Creative Industries in Challenging Times, NHTV Breda.

Richards, G. (2013). *Creating relational tourism trough exchange*. Paper present at the ATLAS Annual Conference, Malta.

Richards, G. (2014). *The challenge of creative tourism.* Working draft. February 2014.

Richards, G. (2014). *Tourism trends: The convergence of culture and tourism.* Academy for Leisure NHTV University of Applied Sciences. Retrieved January 10, 2017, from https://www.academia.edu/9491857/Tourism_trends_The_convergence_of_culture_and_ tourism

Richards, G. (2016). Co-designing experiences with consumers: the case of creative tourism. Input for a workshop on experience design, Tromsø.

Richards, G. (1996). *Cultural tourism in Europe*. Wallingford: CAB International.

Richards, G. (2011). Creativity and Tourism - The state of the Art. *Annals of Tourism Research*, *38*(4), 1225–1252. doi:10.1016/j.annals.2011.07.008

Richards, G., & Raymond, C. (2000). Creative Tourism. *Atlas News*, *23*, 16–20.

Richards, G., & Wilson, J. (2006). Developing creativity in tourist experiences: A solution to the serial reproduction of culture?. *Tourism Management*, *27*(6), 1408–141. doi:10.1016/j.tourman.2005.06.002

Richards, G., & Wilson, J. (2007). Tourism development trajectories: from culture to creativity? In G. Richards & J. Wilson (Eds.), *Tourism, creativity e development* (pp. 1–33). Routledge.

Richards, L. (2015). *Handling qualitative data: A practical guide*. London: Sage.

Richards-Risseto, H., Remondino, F., Agugiaro, G., Robertsson, J., Schwerin, J., & Girardi, G. (2012). Kinect and 3D GIS in Archaeology. *18th International Conference on Virtual Systems and Multimedia (VSMM)*. Doi:10.1109/VSMM.2012.6365942

Rickly, J. M., & McCabe, S. (2017). Authenticidad para Turismo Diseño y experiencia. In Design Science in Tourism (pp. 55-68). Springer International Publishing.

Ricoeur, P. (1978). *O conflito das interpretações: ensaio de hermenêutica*. Rio de Janeiro, RJ: Imago.

Ricolfe, J. S. C., Merino, B. R., Marzo, S. V., Ferrandis, M. T. R., & Rodríguez, C. M. (2008). Actitud hacia la gastronomía local de los turistas: Dimensiones y segmentación de mercado. *PASOS. Revista de Turismo y Patrimonio Cultural*, *6*(2es), 189–198.

Ridel, B., Reuter, P., Laviole, J., Mellado, N., Couture, N., & Granier, X. (2014). The Revealing Flashlight: Interactive spatial augmented reality for detail exploration of cultural heritage artifacts. *Journal on Computing and Cultural Heritage*, *7*(2), 6. doi:10.1145/2611376

Rieder, B. (2013). *Studying Facebook via data extraction*. In *Proceedings of the 5th Annual ACM Web Science Conference on - WebSci '13* (pp. 346–355). New York: ACM Press. doi:10.1145/2464464.2464475

Rihova, I. (2013). *Customer-to-customer co-creation of value in the context of festivals* (Doctoral Dissertation). Available from Eprints Bournemouth University. Retrieved December 2, 2016, from http://eprints.bournemouth.ac.uk/21072/

Rinde, L. (2008). *Procedural Generation of Indoor Environments*. Charmers University of Technology.

Ripoll Perelló, S., Bayarri, V., Latova, J., Herrera, J. A., Benavides, M., & Tenrero, H. P. (2014). El proyecto de investigación: Elaboración de un Sistema Gestor para la protección, puesta en valor y divulgación de Arte Rupestre y Estaciones Prehistóricas. *Revista Segovia Histórica (SgH)*, 25-40.

Ritzer, G. (1995). *The McDonaldization of society*. London: Sage.

Rizzo, L. S., Rizzo, R. G., & Trono, A. (2013). Religious Itineraries as the Driving Forces behind Sustainable Local Development in the Veneto? Towards a Proposal for Promoting an Unusual and Often "Subliminal" Form of Heritage: Sanctuaries and Minor Churches. *Almatourism-Journal of Tourism, Culture and Territorial Development*, *4*(7), 59–92.

Robinson, G. (1992). Geographical Information Systems (GIS) and planning in Scotland: The RLUIS project and andvances in GIS. *Scottish Geographical Magazine*, *108*(1), 22–28. doi:10.1080/00369229218736838

Roche, K. (2011). *Pro IOS 5 Augmented Reality*. New York: Apress. doi:10.1007/978-1-4302-3913-0

Rockstar. (1998, November 30). *Grand Theft Auto: The Official Site*. Retrieved 1 May 2015, from http://www.rockstargames.com/grandtheftauto/

Roden, C. (2003). *Local food and culture in Local Food & Tourism International Conference: Larnaka, Cyprus 9-11 November 2000* (OMT, Coord.). Madrid: World Tourism Organization.

Rodrigues, N., Magalhaes, L. G., Moura, J. P., & Chalmers, A. (2008). *Automatic Reconstruction of Virtual Heritage Sites*. Paper presented at the International Symposium on Virtual Reality, Archaeology and Intelligent Cultural Heritage.

Rodrigues, N., Magalhães, L., Moura, J., & Chalmers, A. (2014). Reconstruction and generation of virtual heritage sites. *Digital Applications in Archaeology and Cultural Heritage*, *1*(3–4), 92–102. https://doi.org/10.1016/j.daach.2014.06.003

Rodrigues, J. M. F., Lessa, J., Gregório, M., Ramos, C., & Cardoso, P. J. S. (2016). *An Initial Framework for a Museum Application for Senior Citizens. In Proceedings Software Development and Technologies for Enhancing Accessibility and Fighting Info-exclusion* (pp. 414–421). ACM. doi:10.1145/3019943.3020002

Rodrigues, J. M. F., Pereira, J. A. R., Sardo, J. D. P., Freitas, M. A. G., Cardoso, P. J. S., Gomes, M., & Bica, P. (2017) Adaptive Card Design UI Implementation for an Augmented Reality Museum Application. *11th Int. Conf. on Universal Access in Human-Computer Interaction, integrated in the 19th Int. Conf. on Human-Computer Interaction.*

Rodrigues, N. (2010). *Rule-based Generation of virtual traversable architectural-period houses*. University of Trás-os-Montes e Alto Douro.

Rodrigues, N. C. S. (2005). *Visualização de superfícies dinâmicas*. Lisboa: N. C. S. R.

Rodrigues, N., Dionísio, M., Gonçalves, A., Magalhães, L. G., Moura, J. P., & Chalmers, A. (2008a). Incorporating Legal Rules on Procedural House Generation. In *Proceedings of the 24th Spring Conference on Computer Graphics* (pp. 59–66). New York: ACM. https://doi.org/10.1145/1921264.1921279

Rodrigues, N., Dionísio, M., Gonçalves, A., & Magalhães, L. M. G., & P, M. J. (2008b). Rule-based Generation of Houses. *Computer Graphics & Geometry*, *10*(2), 49–65.

Rodrigues, N., Magalhães, L. G., Moura, J. P., & Chalmers, A. (2008c). Automatic reconstruction of virtual heritage sites. In *Proceedings of the 9th International conference on Virtual Reality, Archaeology and Cultural Heritage* (pp. 39–46). Eurographics Association.

Rodrigues, N., Magalhães, L., Moura, J., Chalmers, A., Santos, F., & Morgado, L. (2010). ArchHouseGenerator - A Framework for House Generation. *Journal of Virtual Worlds Research*, *2*(5). Retrieved from https://journals.tdl.org/jvwr/index.php/jvwr/article/view/846

Rodríguez-Rodríguez, L., Jiménez-Sánchez, M., Domínguez-Cuesta, M. J., & Aranburu, A. (2015). Research history on glacial geomorphology and geochronology of the Cantabrian Mountains, north Iberia (4342°N/42°W). *Quaternary International*, *364*, 6–21. doi:10.1016/j.quaint.2014.06.007

Rodzi, N. I. M., Zaki, S. A., & Subli, S. M. H. S. (2013). Between tourism and intangible cultural heritage. *Procedia: Social and Behavioral Sciences*, *85*, 411–420. doi:10.1016/j.sbspro.2013.08.370

Roeva, O., Fidanova, S., & Paprzycki, M. (2013). Influence of the population size on the genetic algorithm performance in case of cultivation process modelling. In *Proc. Federated Conf. on Computer Science and Information Systems (FedCSIS)*. IEEE.

Rogers, E. (1995). *Diffusion of innovations* (4th ed.). New York: Free Press.

Røine, P. C. (2010). *Tourist application for android. Specialisation project. Department of Computer and Information Science, Norwegian University of Science and Technology*. NTNU.

Roque, V., & Raposo, R. (2013). *Os Media Sociais como uma Ferramenta de Comunicação e Marketing no Turismo: uma análise das atividades online dos principais atores portugueses*. Academic Press.

Rosen, E. (2008). *Buzz Marketing de Boca em Boca*. Cascais: Gestãoplus.

Rota do Românico. (2014). *O território da Rota do Românico*. Retrieved from http://www.rotadoromanico.com/vPT/Paginas/Homepage.aspx

Rota do Românico. (2016). *Aplicativo da rota do Românico*. Retrieved May, 15th, 2016, from http://www.rotadoromanico.com/vPT/Paginas/Homepage.aspx

Rot, E., Mikinac, K., & Bogdan, S. (2014). General Characteristics of Religious Tourism in Croatia. *UTMS Journal of Economics*, *5*(1), 79–87.

Roussos, I., & Chalmers, A. (2003). High fidelity lighting of knossos. In *Proceedings of the 4th International conference on Virtual Reality, Archaeology and Intelligent Cultural Heritage* (pp. 195–202). Eurographics Association.

Roussou, M. (2008). *The components of engagement in virtual heritage environments*. Paper presented at the New heritage: beyond Verisimilitude. Conference on Cultural heritage and New Media, Hong Kong.

Rowen, C., & Koetter, F. (2006). Cidade Colagem. *Cosac Naify*, *2006*, 293–321.

Royal National Institute for the Blind. (1995). *Building sight*. London: JMU.

Rubinstein, P. (2015). *The Use of Technology to Enhance Music Festivals*. Retrieved May 29, 2016, from http://www.youredm.com/2015/03/07/the-use-of-technology-to-enhance-music-festivals

Rublee, E., Rabaud, V., Konolige, K., & Bradski, G. (2011). ORB: An efficient alternative to SIFT or SURF. In *Proceedings of the International Conference on Computer Vision* (pp. 2564-2571). IEEE. doi:10.1109/ICCV.2011.6126544

Ruiz Zapatero, G. (1998). Fragmentos del pasado: La presentación de sitios arqueológicos y la función social de la arqueología. *Treballs d'Arqueologia*, *5*, 7–34.

Ruiz Zapatero, G. (2013). La divulgación arqueológica: Las ideologías ocultas. *Cuadernos de Prehistoria y Arqueología de la Universidad de Granada*, *19*, 11–36.

Russel, J., Ward, L., & Pratt, G. (1981). Affective quality attributed to environments: A factor analytic study. *Environment and Behavior*, *13*, 259–288.

Russo, A. P., & Borg, J. (2002). Planning considerations for cultural tourism: A case study of four European cities. *Tourism Management*, *23*(6), 631–637. doi:10.1016/S0261-5177(02)00027-4

Ryu, M. H., Kim, S., & Lee, E. (2009). Understanding the factors affecting online elderly users participation in video UCC services. *Computers in Human Behavior*, *25*(3), 619–632. doi:10.1016/j.chb.2008.08.013

Saffer, D. (2006). *Designing for Interaction: Creating Innovative Applications and Devices*. Berkley, CA: New Riders.

Salgado Criado, J., Bujarski, L., & Merten, R. (2013). *European Online Travel Overview* (9th ed.). Phocuswright.

Salvi, J., Fernandez, S., Pribanic, T., & Llado, X. (2010). A state of the art in structured light patterns for surface profilometry. *Pattern Recognition*, *43*(8), 2666–2680. doi:10.1016/j.patcog.2010.03.004

Sánchez-Cañizares, S., & López-Guzmán, T. (2011). Gastronomy as a tourism resource: Profile of the culinary tourist. *Current Issues in Tourism*, *3*, 229–245.

Sansoni, G., Trebeschi, M., & Docchio, F. (2009). State-of-The-Art and Applications of 3D Imaging Sensors in Industry, Cultural Heritage, Medicine, and Criminal Investigation. *Sensors (Basel, Switzerland)*, *9*(1), 568–601. doi:10.3390/s90100568 PMID:22389618

Santos, M. (1997). Metamorfoses do espaço habitado (4th ed.). São Paulo, SP: Hucitec.

Santos, M. (2008). Técnica, espaço, tempo: Globalização e meio técnico-científico e informacional (5th ed.). São Paulo, SP: EdUSP.

Santos, M. L. E. V. (1972). Arqueologia romana do Algarve (vol. 2). Lisboa: Associação dos Arqueólogos Portugueses.

Santos, D. S., Dionísio, M., Rodrigues, N., & Pereira, A. (2011). Efficient Creation of 3D Models from Buildings Floor Plans. *International Journal of Interactive Worlds*, *2011*, 1–30. doi:10.5171/2011.897069

Santos, M. J. C., & Meléndez, A. P. (2016). The role of satisfaction in cultural activities word-of-mouth. A case study in the Picasso Museum of Málaga (Spain). *Tourism and Management Studies*, *12*(1), 145–152. doi:10.18089/tms.2016.12115

Sarikprueck, P., Lee, W., Kulvanitchaiyanunt, A., Chen, V. C., & Rosenberger, J. (2014). Novel hybrid market price forecasting method with data clustering techniques for EV charging station application. *2014 IEEE Industry Application Society Annual Meeting*. doi:10.1109/IAS.2014.6978374

Sassen, S. (2010). *Sociologia da globalização*. Porto Alegre: Artmed.

Schatzki, T. (2001). Introduction: Practice Theory. In The Practice Turn in Contemporary Theory (pp. 10-23). London: Routledge.

Schatzki, T. (2002). *The site of the social: a philosophical account of the constitution of social and change*. University Park, PA: The Pennsylvania State University Press.

Schiaffino, S., & Amandi, A. (2009). Building an expert travel agent as a software agent. *Expert Systems with Applications*, *36*(2), 1291–1299. doi:10.1016/j.eswa.2007.11.032

Schiavoni, S., DAlessandro, F., Bianchi, F., & Asdrubali, F. (2016). Insulation materials for the building sector: A review and comparative analysis. *Renewable & Sustainable Energy Reviews*, *62*, 988–1011. doi:10.1016/j.rser.2016.05.045

Schieder, T., Adukaite, A., & Cantoni, L. (2014). Mobile Apps Devoted to UNESCO World Heritage Sites: A Map. In Z. Xiang & I. Tussyadiah (Eds.), *Information and Communication Technologies in Tourism 2014* (pp. 17–31). Springer.

Schlüter, R. G. (2003). *Gastronomia e turismo*. São Paulo: Editora Aleph.

Schmalstieg, D., & Höllerer, T. (2016). *Augmented Reality: Principles and Practice*. Boston: Addison-Wesley Professional. doi:10.1145/2897826.2927365

Schmidt-Belz, B., Nick, A., Poslad, S., & Zipf, A. (2002). Personalized and location-based mobile tourism services. *Workshop on "Mobile Tourism Support Systems" in conjunction with Mobile HCI.*

Schreiber, G., Amin, A., Aroyo, L., van Assem, M., de Boer, V., Hardman, L., & Wielinga, B. et al. (2008). Semantic annotation and search of cultural-heritage collections: The MultimediaN E-Culture demonstrator. *Web Semantics: Science, Services, and Agents on the World Wide Web*, *6*(4), 243–249. doi:10.1016/j.websem.2008.08.001

Schuller, B. W. (2015). Modelling User Affect and Sentiment in Intelligent User Interfaces: A Tutorial Overview. In *Proceedings of the 20th International Conference on Intelligent User Interfaces* (pp. 443-446). ACM. doi:10.1145/2678025.2716265

Schuster, E. (2015). *How do you envision 3D printing finding a place in science centers and museums? Do you already use or have plans for 3D printing?* [online article]. Retrieved December 4, 2016, from http://www.astc.org/astc-dimensions/how-do-you-envision-3d-printing-finding-a-place-in-science-centers-and-museums-do-you-already-use-or-have-plans-for-3d-printing/

Scianna, A., Gristina, S., & Paliaga, S. (2014). Experimental BIM Applications in Archeology: A Wok-Flow. Lecture Notes in Computer Science, 8740, 490-498. Doi:10.1007/978-3-319-13695-0_48

Scitovsky, T. (1992). *The Joyless Economy: The Psychology of Human Satisfaction* (revised edition). Oxford, UK: Oxford University Press.

Seaton, A. (2009). Purposeful otherness: Approaches to the management of thanatourism. *The darker side of travel: The theory and practice of dark tourism*, 75-108.

Seaton, A. V. & Lennon, J. J. (2004). Thanatourism in the early 21st century: Moral panics, ulterior motives and alterior desires. *New horizons in tourism: Strange experiences and stranger practices*, 63-82.

SEGITTUR. (2012). *Informe y conclusiones think-tank de turismo del transporte*. Retrieved from https://es.slideshare.net/Turismoas/informe-conclusiones-think-tank-del-transporte

Segittur. (2016). *Ministerio de Energia,Turismo y Agenda Digital*. Segitur Turismo e Innovación. Retrieved from http://www.segittur.es/es/inicio/index.html

Seo, B. K., Kim, K., & Park, J. I. (2010, November). Augmented reality-based on-site tour guide: a study in Gyeongbokgung. *Asian Conference on Computer Vision*, 276-285.

Setton, M. G. C. (2005, January/April). Um novo capital cultural: Pré disposições e disposições à cultura informal nos segmentos com baixa escolaridade. *Educ. Soc. Campinas*, *26*(90), 77–105. doi:10.1590/S0101-73302005000100004

SFMOMA. (2016). *The New SFMOMA Announces Transformed Digital Strategy: Supported by Bloomberg Philanthropies, SFMOMA Puts Mobile at the Forefront*. Press release, San Francisco Museum of Modern Art. Retrieved from https://s3-us-west-2.amazonaws.com/sfmomamedia/media/press-releases/downloads/SFMOMA_Digital_Engagement_Press_Release_5_2_2016.pdf

Shackley, M. (2001). Potential futures for Robben Island: Shrine, museum or theme park? *International Journal of Heritage Studies*, *7*(4), 355–363. doi:10.1080/13581650120105552

Shaer, O., & Hornecker, E. (2010). Tangible User Interfaces: Past, Present, and Future Directions. *Foundations and Trends in Human-Computer Interaction*, *3*(1–2), 1–137. doi:10.1561/1100000026

Shah, H., Warwick, K., Vallverdú, J., & Wu, D. (2016). Can Machines Talk? Comparison Of Eliza With Modern Dialogue Systems. *Computers in Human Behavior, 58*, 278–295. doi:10.1016/j.chb.2016.01.004

Sharpley, R., & Stone, P. R. (2009). Life, death and dark tourism: future research directions and concluding comments. *The darker side of travel: The theory and practice of dark tourism*, 247-251.

Sharpley, R., & Stone, P. R. (Eds.). (2009). The darker side of travel: The theory and practice of dark tourism. Channel View Publications.

Sharpley, R., & Stone, P. R. (2009a). (Re)presenting the macabre: interpretation, kitschification and authenticity. In R. Sharpley & P. R. Stone (Eds.), *The darker side of travel (pp. 110-128)*. Bristol, UK: Channel View.

Shirt, G. (2011). Cultural Tourism and Accessibility. In P. Robinson, S. Heitmann, & S. Dieke (Eds.), *Research Themes for Tourism* (pp. 160–175). Cabi International.

SIGA. (2012). *Diverse Beliefs: Tourism of Faith Religious tourism gains ground*. FICCI and YES BANK Ltd. Retrieved January 26, 2017, from http://ficci.in/spdocument/20207/diverse-beliefs-tourism-of-faith.pdf

Sigala, M., Christou, E., & Gretzel, U. (Eds.). (2012). *Social media in travel, tourism and hospitality: Theory, practice and cases*. Ashgate Publishing, Ltd.

Signorini, M. (2009). Plants and traditional knowledge: An ethnobotanical investigation on Monte Ortobene (Nuoro, Sardinia). *Journal of Ethnobiology and Ethnomedicine, 5*(6), 1–14. PMID:19208227

Silberberg, T. (1995). Cultural tourism and business opportunities for museums and heritage sites. *Tourism Management, 16*(5), 361–365. doi:10.1016/0261-5177(95)00039-Q

Silva, F. (2004). *A Quadratura do Circulo. Desenvolvimento, Sustentabilidade, Criação de valor, Emancipação*. Lisboa, Portugal: Editora Caminho.

Silva, M. M., & Mendes Filho, L. (2014). Intenção de Uso de Comentários de Viagem Online na Escolha de um Meio de Hospedagem: Fatores Influenciadores. *Revista Brasileira De Pesquisa em Turismo, 8*(3), 419–434. doi:10.7784/rbtur.v8i3.805

Silva, P. B., & Coelho, A. (2011). Procedural Modeling for Realistic Virtual Worlds Development. *Journal of Virtual Worlds Research, 4*(1). Retrieved from https://journals.tdl.org/jvwr/index.php/jvwr/article/view/2109

Simon, C., Huxhagen, U., Mansouri, A., Heritage, A., Boochs, F., & Marzani, F. (2010). *Integration of high resolution spatial and spectral data acquisition systems to provide complementary datasets for cultural heritage applications*. Paper presented at the IS&T/SPIE Electronic Imaging meeting. doi:10.1117/12.838891

Siotto, E., Dellepiane, M., Callieri, M., Scopigno, R., Gratziu, C., Moscato, A., & Palleschi, V. et al. (2015). A multidisciplinary approach for the study and the virtual reconstruction of the ancient polychromy of Roman sarcophagi. *Journal of Cultural Heritage, 16*(3), 307–314. doi:10.1016/j.culher.2014.05.011

Skavronskaya, L., Scott, N., Moyle, B., Le, D., Hadinejad, A., Zhang, R., Gardiner, A., Coghlan, A. & Shakeela, A. (2017). Cognitive psychology and tourism research: state of the art. *Tourism Review, 72*(2).

Skevakis, G., Konstantinos Makris, K., Arapi, P., & Christodoulakis, S. (2013), Elevating Natural History Museums' Cultural Collections to the Linked Data Cloud. *Proceedings of the 3rd International Workshop on Semantic Digital Archives (SDA 2013)*.

SM. (2016). *Science Museum - atmosphere gallery*. Retrieved: Nov. 16, 2016 from https://vimeo.com/20789653

SmartClasses. (2016). *Smart Classes: Data Structures*. Retrieved: Nov. 16, 2016 from http://btechsmartclass.com/DS/U3_T1.html

Smith, R. (2016). *"Pipilotti Rist: Pixel Forest," Deep in the Wilds of Video* [Art & Design Article [online]]. Retrieved November 29, 2016, from http://www.nytimes.com/2016/10/28/arts/design/pipilotti-rist-pixel-forest-deep-in-the-wilds-of-video.html

Smith, M. K., & Robinson, M. (2006). *Cultural tourism in a changing world. Politics, participation and (re)presentation*. Cleveland, OH: Channel View Publications.

Smith, S. L. J. (1994). The Tourism Product. *Annals of Tourism Research*, *21*(3), 582–594.

Smithsonian Institution. (2012). *New Technology Resurrects Ancient Chinese Cave at Smithsonian's Sackler Gallery: "Pure Land" Digital Installation Brings Buddhist Treasures to Washington, D.C.* [press release]. Retrieved November 28, 2016, from http://www.asia.si.edu/press/2012/sackler-25-digital-cave-release.asp

Smithsonian Institution. (2016). *Smithsonian Releases High-Resolution 3-D Model of Apollo 11 Command Module to Explore and Print* [online article]. Retrieved December 5, 2016, from http://newsdesk.si.edu/releases/smithsonian-releases-high-resolution-3-d-model-apollo-11-command-module-explore-and-print

Sodhi, R., Poupyrev, I., Glisson, M., & Israr, A. (2013). AIREAL: Interactive tactile experiences in free air. *ACM Transactions on Graphics*, *32*(4), 134. doi:10.1145/2461912.2462007

Sosinski, B. (2011). *Cloud computing bible*. Hoboken, NJ: Wiley & Sons.

Sparks, B., & Pan, G. W. (2009). Chinese outbound tourists: Understanding their attitudes, constraints and use of information sources. *Tourism Management*, *30*(4), 483–494. doi:10.1016/j.tourman.2008.10.014

SPARQL Working Group. (2008, January 15). *SPARQL Query Language for RDF*. Retrieved from https://www.w3.org/TR/rdf-sparql-query/

Spectrum. (2011). InDawson, A., & Hillhouse, S. (Eds.), *SPECTRUM 4.0. The UK Museum Collections Management Standard*. The Collections Trust.

Spiliotis, E., Marinakis, V., Doukas, H., & Psarras, J. (2016). Integrating a decision support system with smart grid infrastructures and ICT solutions towards energy cost reduction: An action plan to optimally schedule the operation of heating and electricity systems. *2016 7th International Conference on Information, Intelligence, Systems & Applications (IISA)*, 1-6.

Sreeni, K., Priyadarshini, K., Praseedha, A., & Chaudhuri, S. (2012). *Haptic rendering of cultural heritage objects at different scales*. Paper presented at the International Conference on Human Haptic Sensing and Touch Enabled Computer Applications. doi:10.1007/978-3-642-31401-8_45

Staab, S., Werthner, H., Ricci, F., Zipf, A., Gretzel, U., Fesenmaier, D. R., & Knoblock, C. (2002). Intelligent systems for tourism. *IEEE Intelligent Systems*, *17*(6), 53–64. doi:10.1109/MIS.2002.1134362

Stake, R. (1994). Case Studies. In N. Denzin & Y. Lincoln (Eds.), *Handbook of Qualitative Research* (pp. 236–247). Thousand Oaks, CA: Sage Publications.

Stankov, U., Jovanović, T., & Dragićević, V. (2014). Facebook Travel Related Usage Patterns of Tourism Students. In *SINTEZA 2014 Impact of Internet on Business activities in Serbia and Worldwide*. Belgrade: Singidunum Univeristy. doi:10.15308/sinteza-2014-743-749

Steichen, B., Conati, C., & Carenini, G. (2014). Inferring Visualization Task Properties, User Performance, and User Cognitive Abilities from Eye Gaze Data. *ACM Transactions on Interactive Intelligent Systems*, *4*(2), 11. doi:10.1145/2633043

Stepaniuk, K. (2015). The relation between destination image and Social Media user engagement – theoretical approach. *Procedia: Social and Behavioral Sciences*, *213*, 616–621. doi:10.1016/j.sbspro.2015.11.459

Stepchenkova, S., & Morrison, A. M. (2008). Russia's destination image among American pleasure travelers: Revisiting Echtner and Ritchie. *Tourism Management*, *29*(3), 548–560. doi:10.1016/j.tourman.2007.06.003

Stone, P. (2012). *Dark tourism as 'mortality capital': The case of Ground Zero and the significant other dead*. Academic Press.

Stone, P. (2006). A dark tourism spectrum: Towards a typology of death and macabre related tourist sites, attractions and exhibitions. Tourism: An Interdisciplinary. *International Journal (Toronto, Ont.)*, *54*(2), 145–160.

Stone, P. (2011). Dark tourism: Towards a new post-disciplinary research agenda. *International Journal of Tourism Anthropology*, *1*(3-4), 318–332. doi:10.1504/IJTA.2011.043713

Stone, P. R. (2012a). Dark tourism as 'mortality capital': The case of Ground Zero and the significant other dead. In R. Sharpley & P. R. Stone (Eds.), *The contemporary tourist experience: Concepts and consequences* (pp. 30–45). Abingdon, UK: Routledge.

Stone, P. R. (2012b). Dark tourism and significant other death: Towards a model of mortality mediation. *Annals of Tourism Research*, *39*(3), 1565–1587. doi:10.1016/j.annals.2012.04.007

Stone, P., & Sharpley, R. (2008). Consuming dark tourism: A thanatological perspective. *Annals of Tourism Research*, *35*(2), 574–595. doi:10.1016/j.annals.2008.02.003

Strauss, P. (2008). *Mini Augmented Reality Ads Hit Newstands*. Chicago: Technabob.

Stuart, G., & Fleming, P. D. (2014). *Smart energy performance indicators for live historical and normative feedback systems*. Frankfurt: Improving Energy Efficiency in Commercial Buildings (IEECB).

Stumbo, N. J., Wang, Y., & Pegg, S. (2011). Issues of Access: What Matters to People with Disabilities as They Seek Leisure Experiences. *World Leisure Journal*, *53*(2), 91–103. doi:10.1080/04419057.2011.580549

Styliania, S., Fotisb, L., Kostasa, K., & Petrosa, P. (2009). Virtual museums, a survey and some issues for consideration. *Journal of Cultural Heritage*, *10*(4), 520–528. doi:10.1016/j.culher.2009.03.003

Subirats, E. (1989). *A cultura como espetáculo*. São Paulo, SP: Nobel.

Sundstedt, V., Chalmers, A., & Martinez, P. (2004). High fidelity reconstruction of the ancient Egyptian temple of Kalabsha. In *Proceedings of the 3rd international conference on Computer graphics, virtual reality, visualisation and interaction in Africa* (pp. 107–113). ACM. doi:10.1145/1029949.1029970

Su, Y. W., & Lin, H. L. (2014). Analysis of international tourist arrivals worldwide: The role of world heritage sites. *Tourism Management*, *40*, 46–58. doi:10.1016/j.tourman.2013.04.005

Szekely, P., Knoblock, C., Yang, F., Zhu, X., Fink, E., Allen, R., & Goodlander, G. (2013). Connecting the Smithsonian American Art Museum to the Linked Data Cloud. In *Lecture Notes in Computer Science: Vol. 7882. The Semantic Web: Semantics and Big Data: 10th International Conference, ESWC 2013*. Springer Verlag. doi:10.1007/978-3-642-38288-8_40

Tang, X.-X. (Ed.). (2012). *Virtual Reality - Human Computer Interaction*. InTech.

Tan, M., & Teo, T. (1998). Factors influencing the adoption of the internet. *International Journal of Electronic Commerce*, *2*(3), 5–18. doi:10.1080/10864415.1998.11518312

Taño, D. G., Gidumal, J. B., Armas, R. J. D., & López, E. P. (2013). Antecedentes del Uso de los Medios Sociales por el Turista: Motivación, Oportunidad Y Capacidad. *Cuadernos De Turismo*, (31), 153-173.

Tasci, A. D., & Gartner, W. C. (2007). Destination image and its functional relationships. *Journal of Travel Research*, *45*(4), 413–425. doi:10.1177/0047287507299569

Tavares, E., & Dalto, R. (1999). *Missões Jesuítico Guaranis*. São Leopoldo, RS: Unisinos.

Tech Museum of Innovation. (2014). *Body Metrics* [website]. Retrieved December 7, 2016, from https://www.thetech.org/plan-your-visit/galleries/bodymetrics

Teichner, F. (2008). Zwischen Land und Meer – Entre tierra y mar. *Studien zur Architektur und Wirt-schaftsweise ländlicher Siedlungen im Süden der römischen Provinz Lusitanien. Stvdia Lvsitana,* 3.

Teichner, F. (2011-2012). La producción de aceite y vino en la villa romana de Milreu (Estói): El éxito del modelo catoniano en la Lusitania. *AnMurcia*, *27-28*, 471–484.

Tepavčević, B., & Stojaković, V. (2013). Procedural modeling in architecture based on statistical and fuzzy inference. *Automation in Construction*, *35*, 329–337. doi:10.1016/j.autcon.2013.05.015

The Freedom Trail Foundation. (2015). *Explore the trail*. Retrieved August 2, 2016, from http://www.thefreedomtrail.org/freedom-trail/

The Japan News. (2016). Fingerprints to be tested as "currency". *The Japan News*. Retrieved from http://the-japan-news.com

Thingspeak. (2017). *Thingspeak platform*. Retrieved January 17, 2017, from thingspeak.com

Thomé-Ortiz, H. (2015). Turismo micológico, una nueva mirada al bosque. *Ciencia y Desarrollo*, *41*, 14–19.

Thompson, C. J. (2000). Postmodern Consumer Goals Made Easy. In *The Why of Consumption: Contemporary Perspectives on Consumer Motives, Goals, and Desires* (pp. 118-137). New York: Routledge. Retrieved January 6, 2016, from https://www.researchgate.net/publication/292726261_Postmodern_consumer_goals_made_easy

Thompson, C. J., & Arnould, E. J. (1998). Narrative analysis of a marketing relationship: The consumers perspective. *Psychology and Marketing*, *15*(3), 195–214. doi:10.1002/(SICI)1520-6793(199805)15:3<195::AID-MAR1>3.0.CO;2-5

Thornton, G. (2016). *Emerging clouds in hotel technology - Spotlight on cloud-based PMS*. Retrieved January, 2017, from Grant Thornton - An instinct for growth: http://www.grantthornton.co.uk/globalassets/1.-member-firms/united-kingdom/pdf/publication/2016/emerging-clouds-in-hotel-technology.pdf

Tian, F., Xu, F., & Fu, J. (2013). Augmented reality technology overview for tourism app development. *2013 International Conference on Machine Learning and Cybernetics*, *4,* 1483-1489. doi:10.1109/ICMLC.2013.6890839

TIC. (2015). *Centre for Tourism, Innovation and Culture (TIC)*. Retrieved January 26, 2017, from http://www.sdu.dk/en/Om_SDU/Institutter_centre/C_Tik.aspx

Tigu, G., Cristache, S. E., Mahika, E. C., & Totan, L. (2014). Analysis of the cultural tourism trends and perspectives in Romania. *ESSACHESS – Journal for Communication Studies, 7*(1), 191-208.

Tilden, F. (1957). Interpreting our heritage (4th ed.). The University of North Carolina Press.

Timothy, D. J., & Boyd, S. W. (2003). *Heritage Tourism*. New York: Prentice Hall.

Timothy, D. J., & Olsen, D. H. (Eds.). (2006). *Tourism, Religion and Spiritual Journeys*. London: Routledge.

Tokmakidis, K. (2011). *The process of creating haptic models*. Presentation in the frame of the 4th PROSPELASIS Seminar "Maintenance and Management of accessibility improvement interventions", Thessaloniki, Greece.

Tom Dieck, M. C., & Jung, T. (2015). A theoretical model of mobile augmented reality acceptance in urban heritage tourism. *Current Issues in Tourism*, 1–21. doi:10.1080/13683500.2015.1070801

Torres Bernier, E. (2003). Del turista que se alimenta al turista que busca comida. In *Gastronomía y Turismo. Cultura al Plato* (pp. 305–316). Buenos Aires: CIET.

Torres, J. (2011). *Empresas en la nube. Ventajas y retos del cloud computing*. Barcelona: Libros de Cabecera.

Toselli, C. (2006). Algunas reflexiones sobre el turismo cultural. *Pasos. Revista de turismo y patrimonio cultural, 4*(2), 175-182.

Tournaki, S., Frangou, M., Tsoutsos, T., Morell, R., Guerrero, I., Urosevic, Z., & Claridge, N. et al. (2016). *Towards Nearly Zero Energy Hotels Technical Analysis and Recommendations. 5th International Conference on Renewable Energy Sources and Energy Efficiency*, Nicosia, Cyprus.

Trescak, T., Esteva, M., & Rodriguez, I. (2010). A Virtual World Grammar for automatic generation of virtual worlds. *The Visual Computer*, *26*(6–8), 521–531. doi:10.1007/s00371-010-0473-7

Triggs, B., McLauchlan, P. F., Hartley, R. I., & Fitzgibbon, A. W. (1999). Bundle adjustment—a modern synthesis. In *International workshop on vision algorithms* (pp. 298–372). Springer.

Trinchão Andrade, B., Mazetto Mendes, C., de Oliveira Santos Jr, J., Pereira Bellon, O. R., & Silva, L. (2012). 3D preserving xviii century barroque masterpiece: Challenges and results on the digital preservation of Aleijadinhos sculpture of the Prophet Joel. *Journal of Cultural Heritage*, *13*(2), 210–214. doi:10.1016/j.culher.2011.05.003

TripAdvisor APP. (2017). *TripAdvisor.* Retrieved: January 12, 2017, from https://play.google.com/store/apps/details?id=com.tripadvisor.tripadvisor&hl=pt_PT

TripAdvisor. (2015). Retrieved from https://www.tripadvisor.com.my/Attraction_Review-g294225-d2628462-Reviews-Trunyan_Cemetery-Indonesia.html

Tripoto Travel App. Plan Trips. (2017). *Tripoto Travel App: Plan Trips.* Retrieved: January 12, 2017, from https://play.google.com/store/apps/details?id=com.tripoto

Tristán, R. M. (2014). *Investigadores revelan el arte rupestre 'invisible' en las cuevas de la meseta (FOTOS)*. Retrieved 27 April, 2017, from http://www.huffingtonpost.es/2014/06/15/arte-rupestre-invisible-_n_5492612.html

Tsalis, P., & Naniopoulos, A. (2008). *Needs of people with disabilities in tourist activities. MEDRA Project deliverable.* Toroslar Municipality.

Tscheu, F., & Buhalis, D. (2016). Augmented Reality at Cultural Heritage sites. In A. Inversini & R. Schegg (Eds.), *Information and Communication Technologies in Tourism 2016 ENTER* (pp. 607–619). Springer. doi:10.1007/978-3-319-28231-2_44

Tseng, C., Wu, B., Morrison, A. M., Zhang, J., & Chen, Y. C. (2015). Travel blogs on China as a destination image formation agent: A qualitative analysis using Leximancer. *Tourism Management*, *46*, 347–358. doi:10.1016/j.tourman.2014.07.012

TURESPAÑA. (2016). *Travelling in Spain.* Retrieved February 26, 2016, from http://www.spain.info/en/informacionpractica/transportes/reportajes/viajar_por_espana_1.html

Turismo de Barcelos. (2014). *Impacto económico do Caminho Português de Santiago no concelho de Barcelos. Relatório interno não publicado.* Câmara Municipal de Barcelos, Barcelos.

Turismo de Portugal. (2011). Plano Estratégico Nacional do Turismo versão 2.0. Turismo de Portugal, I.P., Lisboa.

Turismo de Portugal. (2014). Turismo 2020: cinco princípios para uma ambição. Turismo de Portugal, I.P., Lisboa.

Tussyadiah, I. (2013). Expectation of Travel Experiences with Wearable Computing Devices. In *Information and Communication Technologies in Tourism 2014* (pp. 539–552). Cham: Springer International Publishing. doi:10.1007/978-3-319-03973-2_39

Tutenel, T., Smelik, R. M., Lopes, R., de Kraker, K. J., & Bidarra, R. (2011). Generating Consistent Buildings: A Semantic Approach for Integrating Procedural Techniques. *Computational Intelligence and AI in Games, IEEE Transactions on, 3*(3), 274–288. https://doi.org/10.1109/TCIAIG.2011.2162842

TWSJ. (2016). *The Wall Street Journal: Best Apps for Visiting Museums*. Retrieved: Nov. 16, 2016 from https://goo.gl/cPTyP9

Tzanelli, R. (2016). *Thanatourism and Cinematic Representations of Risk: Screening the End of Tourism*. Abingdon, UK: Routledge.

UCL Faculty of the Built Environment. (2016). Augmented Urban Reality. The Bartlett Space Syntax Laboratory, The Bartlett School of Architecture, London.

UN Committee on the Rights of Persons with Disabilities. (2013). *General comment on Article 9: Accessibility*. Retrieved April 24, 2017, from www.ohchr.org/HRBodies/CRPD/GC/DGCArticle9.doc

Undeen, D. (2013). *3D Scanning, Hacking, and Printing in Art Museums, for the Masses* [online article]. Retrieved November 4, 2016, from http://www.metmuseum.org/about-the-museum/museum-departments/office-of-the-director/digital-media-department/digital-underground/posts/2013/3d-printing

UNESCO. (1982). *Mexico City declaration on cultural policies*. World Conference on Cultural Policies, Mexico City, Mexico.

UNESCO. (1996). *Our Creative Diversity, report of the World Commission on Culture and Development*. Paris: UNESCO.

UNESCO. (2001). *UNESCO Universal Declaration on Cultural Diversity a vision a conceptual platform a pool of ideas for implementation a new paradigma*. UNESCO. Retrieved January 26, 2017, from http://unesdoc.unesco.org/images/0012/001271/127162e.pdf

UNESCO. (2015). Retrieved March 2, 2016, from http://www.unesco.org/

UNESCO. (2016). *Routes of Santiago de Compostela: Camino Francés and Routes of Northern Spain*. Retrieved October,14th, 2016, from http://whc.unesco.org/en/list/669

United Nations. (1993). *United Nations General Assembly Rules on the Equalization of Opportunities for Persons with Disabilities Resolution 48/96*. Author.

Unity. (2016). *Unity 3D*. Retrieved: Nov. 16, 2016 from https://unity3d.com/pt

University of New Mexico. (2016). *Thomas Caudell Biography*. Retrieved May, 15th, 2016, from http://ceet.unm.edu/about/people/thomas-caudell.html

UNWTO & UNEP. (2008). *Climate Change and Tourism, Responding to Global Challenges*. Madrid: World Tourism Organization and United Nations Environment Programme.

UNWTO. (2011). *Religious Tourism in Asia and the Pacific*. Retrieved January 26, 2017, from http://cf.cdn.unwto.org/sites/all/files/pdf/110325_religious_tourism_excerpt.pdf

UNWTO. (2014). *Tourism can protect and promote religious heritage.* Press Release. Retrieved January 26, 2017, from http://media.unwto.org/press-release/2014-12-10/tourism-can-protect-and-promote-religious-heritage

UNWTO. (2016). *Conference on Religious Heritage and Tourism: How to increase religious heritage tourism in a changing society*. Cultural Heritage Agency of the Netherlands and UNWTO. Retrieved January 26, 2017, from http://europe.unwto.org/event/conference-religious-heritage-and-tourism-how-increase-religious-heritage-tourism-changing-soc

UNWTO/UNESCO. (2015). *World Conference on Tourism and Culture, Building and Partnership, Siem Reip* – 2015. Author.

Urmann, D. (2012). *7 Ways Social Travel Sites are Engaging Users*. Retrieved April 16, 2017, from https://www.socialfresh.com/travel-social-media-tools/

Urry, J. (2002). *The Tourist Gaze* (2nd ed.). London, UK: Sage.

Urry, J. (2002). *The tourist gaze*. London: Sage Publications.

Uzzell, D. L. (1989). The hot interpretation of war and conflict. In D. L. Uzzell (Ed.), *Heritage interpretation (pp. 33-47)*. Bristol, UK: Belhaven Press.

Uzzell, D. L., & Ballantyne, R. (1998). Heritage that hurts: interpretation in a postmodern world. In D. L. Uzzell & R. Ballantyne (Eds.), *Contemporary issues in heritage & environmental interpretation (pp. 152-171)*. London: The Stationary Office.

Vachirasricirikul, S., & Ngamroo, I. (2014). Robust LFC in a smart grid with wind power penetration by coordinated V2G control and frequency controller. *IEEE Transactions on Smart Grid*, *5*(1), 371–380. doi:10.1109/TSG.2013.2264921

Vainstein, N., Kuflik, T., & Lanir, J. (2016). Towards Using Mobile, Head-Worn Displays in Cultural Heritage: User Requirements and a Research Agenda. In *Proceedings of the 21st International Conference on Intelligent User Interfaces* (pp. 327-331). ACM. doi:10.1145/2856767.2856802

Valtolina, S., Franzoni, S., Mazzoleni, P., & Bertino, E. (2005). Dissemination of cultural heritage content through virtual reality and multimedia techniques: A case study. *Multimedia Modelling Conference, Proceedings of the 11th International*, 214-221. doi:10.1109/MMMC.2005.36

VAM. (2016). *Interactive IPAD Museum Catalog*. Retrieved: Nov. 16, 2016 from https://vimeo.com/31821923

Van Krevelen, D., & Poelman, R. (2010). A survey of augmented reality technologies, applications and limitations. *Int. J. of Virtual Reality*, *9*(2), 1.

VanGo Yourself. (2016). *Recreate Artworks with Your Friends* [website]. Retrieved December 21, 2016, from http://vangoyourself.com/

Vaquero, L. M., Rodero-Merino, L., Cáceres, J., & Lindner, M. (2009). A break in the clouds: Towards a cloud definition. *Computer Communication Review*, *39*(1), 50–55. doi:10.1145/1496091.1496100

Vavliakis, K. N., Karagiannis, G. T., & Mitkas, P. A. (2012). *Semantic Web in Cultural Heritage after 2020.* Paper presented at the workshop, "What will the Semantic Web look like 10 years from now?", held in concunction with the 11th International Semantic Web Conference 2012, Boston, MA.

Vaz, R., Fernandes, P., & Veiga, A. (2016). Proposal of a Tangible User Interface to Enhance Accessibility in Geological Exhibitions and the Experience of Museum Visitors. *Procedia Computer Science, 100*, 832–839.

Vecchio, P., Mele, F., De Paolis, L. T., Epicoco, I., Mancini, M., & Aloisio, G. (2015). Cloud computing and augmented reality for cultural heritage. LNCS, 9254, 51–60. doi:10.1007/978-3-319-22888-4_5

Veiga, A. (2013). *Gestão de Projetos de Museus e Exposições*. Belo Horizonte: C/Arte.

Vela, M. R., & Tarrés, C. S. (2005). El turismo rural-cultural: un modelo de gestión del marketing turístico a nivel local basado en la medida de la imagen del destino. *Cuadernos de turismo*, *16*, 197-222.

Venkatesh, V., Morris, M. G., Davis, G. B., & Davis, F. D. (2003). User acceptance of information technology: Toward a unified view. *Management Information Systems Quarterly*, *25*(3), 425–478.

Venkatesh, V., Thong, J. Y., & Xu, X. (2012). Consumer acceptance and use of information technology: Extending the unified theory of acceptance and use of technology. *Management Information Systems Quarterly*, *36*(1), 157–178.

Venturi, R., & Brown, D. S. (2006). Uma significação para os estacionamentos dos supermercados. A&P ou Aprendendo com Las Vegas. In *Uma nova agenda para a arquitetura: antologia teórica 1965-1995* (pp. 337–354). Cosac Naify.

Verhoeven, G. (2008). Imaging the invisible using modified digital still cameras for straightforward and low-cost archaeological near-infrared photography. *Journal of Archaeological Science*, *35*(12), 3087–3100. doi:10.1016/j.jas.2008.06.012

Versichele, M., Neutens, T., Delafontaine, M., & Van de Weghe, N. (2012). The use of Bluetooth for analysing spatiotemporal dynamics of human movement at mass events: A case study of the Ghent Festivities. *Applied Geography (Sevenoaks, England)*, *32*(2), 208–220. doi:10.1016/j.apgeog.2011.05.011

Vert, S., & Vasiu, R. (2014). Relevant aspects for the integration of linked data in mobile augmented reality applications for tourism. *International Conference on Information and Software Technologies*, 334-345. doi:10.1007/978-3-319-11958-8_27

Viagem, Z. H. (2014). *General format*. Retrieved February 02, 2017, from http://zh.clicrbs.com.br/rs/vida-e-estilo/viagem/noticia/2016/04/espetaculo-som-e-luz-nas-ruinas-de-sao-miguel-arcanjo-ganha-nova-roupagem-a-partir-desta-sexta-5788650.html

Vidal, C., & Muñoz, G. (2015). Métodos avanzados para el análisis y documentación de la arqueología y la arquitectura maya: los “mascarones” de Chiloé y La Blanca. In C. Vidal & G. Muñoz (Eds.), *Artistic Expressions in Maya Architecture: Analysis and Documentation Techniques* (pp. 75–90). Oxford, UK: Archaeopress.

Viglia, G., Minazzi, R., & Buhalis, D. (2016). The influence of e-word-of-mouth on hotel occupancy rate. *International Journal of Contemporary Hospitality Management*, *28*(9), 2035–2051. doi:10.1108/IJCHM-05-2015-0238

Villarrubia, G., De Paz, J. F., De La Prieta, F., & Bajo, J. (2014). Hybrid indoor location system for museum tourist routes in augmented reality. *Information Fusion (FUSION), 17th International Conference*, 1-8.

Vinha, I. (2004). *Gastronomia. Atracção turística primária (Estudo de caso os “domingos gastronómicos”)*. Tesis de Licenciatura, Universidade de Aveiro.

Vlachopoulou, M., Chin, G., Fuller, J., & Lu, S. (2014). Aggregated residential load modeling using dynamic Bayesian networks. *Smart Grid Communications (SmartGridComm), IEEE International Conference on*, 818-823. doi:10.1109/SmartGridComm.2014.7007749

Vlahakis, V., Ioannidis, N., Karigiannis, J., Tsotros, M., Gounaris, M., Stricker, D., & Almeida, L. et al. (2002). Archeoguide: An Augmented Reality Guide for Archaeological Sites. *IEEE Computer Graphics and Applications*, *22*(5), 52–60. doi:10.1109/MCG.2002.1028726

Voas, J., & Zhang, J. (2009). Cloud computing: New wine or just a new bottle? *IT Professional*, *11*(2), 15–17. doi:10.1109/MITP.2009.23

Vuforia. (2016). *Vuforia*. Retrieved: Nov. 16, 2016 from https://www.vuforia.com/

W3C. (2009, August 18). *SKOS Simple Knowledge Organization System Primer*. Retrieved from https://www.w3.org/TR/skos-primer/

W3C. (2013, December 11). *OWL*. Retrieved from https://www.w3.org/OWL/

W3C. (2014, June 24). *RDF 1.1 Primer*. Retrieved from https://www.w3.org/TR/rdf11-primer/

Waisman, M. (2013). *O interior da história*. São Paulo, SP: Perspectiva.

Walle, A. H., & Asgary, N. (2015). Archaeological tourism in the Middle East: A community-based resource management model. *Middle East Journal of Management*, *2*(1), 36–52. doi:10.1504/MEJM.2015.069008

Wall, G., & Mathieson, A. (2006). *Tourism: Change, Impacts, and Opportunities*. New York: Prentice Hall.

Walmsley, D. Y., & Young, M. (1998). Evaluative images and tourism: The use of personal constructs to describe the structure of destination images. *Journal of Travel Research*, *36*(3), 65–69. doi:10.1177/004728759803600307

Walter, T. (2009). Dark tourism: mediating between the dead and the living. In *The Darker Side of Travel: The Theory and Practice of Dark Tourism. Aspects of Tourism* (pp. 39–55). Bristol, UK: Channel View Publications.

Wang, C., Chow, S., Wang, Q., Ren, K., & Lou, W. (2013). Privacy-preserving public auditing for secure cloud storage. *IEEE Transactions on Computers*, *62*(2), 362–375. doi:10.1109/TC.2011.245

Wang, D., & Xiang, Z. (2012). The New Landscape of Travel: A Comprehensive Analysis of Smartphone Apps. In M. Fuchs, F. Ricci, & L. Cantoni (Eds.), *Information and Communication Technologies in Tourism 2012* (pp. 308–319). Vienna: Springer Vienna. doi:10.1007/978-3-7091-1142-0_27

Wang, N. (1999). Rethinking authenticity in tourism experience. *Annals of Tourism Research*, *26*(2), 349–370. doi:10.1016/S0160-7383(98)00103-0

Wang, P. (2012). A Personalized Collaborative Recommendation Approach Based on Clustering of Customers. In D. Yang (Ed.), *International Conference on Applied Physics and Industrial Engineering 2012, Pt B* (Vol. 24, pp. 812-816). doi:10.1016/j.phpro.2012.02.121

Wang, X., Li, X. R., Zhen, F., & Zhang, J. (2016). How smart is your tourist attraction?: Measuring tourist preferences of smart tourism attractions via a FCEM-AHP and IPA approach. *Tourism Management*, *54*, 309–320. doi:10.1016/j.tourman.2015.12.003

Wang, Y., & Fesenmaier, D. R. (2004). Towards Understanding Members› General Participation In An Active Contribution To An Online Travel Community. *Tourism Management*, *25*(6), 709–722. doi:10.1016/j.tourman.2003.09.011

Wang, Y., Stash, N., Aroyo, L., Gorgels, P., Rutledge, L., & Schreiber, G. (2008). Recommendations based on semantically enriched museum collections. *Web Semantics: Science, Services, and Agents on the World Wide Web*, *6*(6), 283–290. doi:10.1016/j.websem.2008.09.002

Wang, Y., Stash, N., Hollink, L., & Schreiber, G. (2009). Using Semantic Relations for Content-based Recommender Systems in Cultural Heritage. *Proceedings of the 2009 International Conference on Ontology and Semantic Web Patterns (WOP'09)*, 516.

Wang, Z., Zhu, W., Cui, P., Sun, L., & Yang, S. (2013). Social Media Recommendation. In N. Ramzan, R. van Zwol, J.-S. Lee, K. Clüver, & X.-S. Hua (Eds.), *Social Media Retrieval* (pp. 23–42). London: Springer - Verlang. doi:10.1007/978-1-4471-4555-4_2

Ward, T. (2012). *Augmented Reality using Appcelerator Titanium Starter*. Birmingham, UK: Packt Publishing Ltd.

Wasan, P. (2014). Sustainable Technology in Hospitality Industry. In V. Jauhari (Ed.), Managing Sustainability in the Hospitality and Tourism Industry Paradigms and Directions for the Future (pp. 101–135). Boca Raton, FL: CRC Press.

Watanabe, A. (2012). *Inside 'world's first augmented reality hotel*. The Australian Journal.

Watson, B., Muller, P., Wonka, P., Sexton, C., Veryovka, O., & Fuller, A. (2008). Procedural Urban Modeling in Practice. *Computer Graphics and Applications, IEEE, 28*(3), 18–26. https://doi.org/10.1109/MCG.2008.58

Webel, S., Olbrich, M., Franke, T., & Keil, J. (2013). *Immersive experience of current and ancient reconstructed cultural attractions*. Paper presented at the Digital Heritage International Congress (DigitalHeritage). doi:10.1109/DigitalHeritage.2013.6743766

Weber, J. (2008). Cloud Computing. *Times Online*. Retrieved October 21, 2016, from http://www.fba.unlp.edu.ar/tic/archivos/Q09.pdf

Weber, J. (2014). Augmented Reality Gaming: A new Paradigm for Tourist Experience. Information and communication technologies in tourism. *Information and Communication Technologies in Tourism, eProceedings of the ENTER 2014*.

Weiser, M., Gold, R., & Brown, J. S. (1999). The origins of ubiquitous computing research at PARC in the late 1980s. *IBM Systems Journal, 38*(4), 693–696. doi:10.1147/sj.384.0693

Wessels, S., Ruther, H., Bhurtha, R., & Schröeder, R. (2014). *Design and creation of a 3D Virtual Tour of the world heritage site of Petra, Jordan*. Paper presented at the AfricaGeo.

White, L., & Frew, E. (2013). *Dark Tourism: Place and identity: managing and interpreting dark places*. London: Routledge.

Whittle, C. G., & Jones, C. R. (2013). User perceptions of energy consumption in university buildings: A University of Sheffield case study. *Journal of Sustainability Education, 5*. Retrieved January 17, 2017, from https://goo.gl/5HGN1K

Wichels, S. (2014). *Nuevos desafíos en Relaciones Públicas 2.0: La creciente influencia de las plataformas de online review en Turismo*. Academic Press.

Wikitude. (2016). *Wikitude, see more*. Retrieved: Nov. 16, 2016 from http://www.wikitude.com/

Wilkinson, P. F. (2010). Review of "The darker side of travel: The theory and practice of dark tourism", by Sharpley & Stone. *e-Review of Tourism Research, 8*(1).

Williams, R. (2014). *Second canvas: the art of apps* [online article]. Retrieved November 30, 2016, from http://www.telegraph.co.uk/technology/apple/10804445/Second-canvas-the-art-of-apps.html

Williams, N., Inversini, A., Buhalis, D., & Ferdinand, N. (2017). Destination eWOM drivers and characteristics. *Annals of Tourism Research, 64*, 87–101. doi:10.1016/j.annals.2017.02.007

Williams, P., Paul, J., & Hainsworth, D. (1996). Keeping track of what really counts: Tourism resource inventory systems in British Columbia, Canada. In L. Harrison & W. Husbands (Eds.), *Practicing Responsible Tourism: International Case Studies in Tourism Planning, Policy & Development* (pp. 404–421). New York, NY: J. Wiley & Sons.

Will, L. (2012). The ISO 25964 Data Model for the Structure of an Information Retrieval Thesaurus. *Bulletin of the American Society for Information Science and Technology, 38*(4), 48–51. doi:10.1002/bult.2012.1720380413

Willson, G. B., McIntosh, A. J., & Zahra, A. L. (2013). Tourism and spirituality: A phenomenological analysis. *Annals of Tourism Research*, *42*, 150–168. doi:10.1016/j.annals.2013.01.016

Wind, S. (2011). Open source cloud computing management platforms: Introduction, comparison, and recommendations for implementation. *IEEE Conference on Open Systems ICOS*, 175-179. doi:10.1109/ICOS.2011.6079245

Winkler, G., Meisenbach, C., Hable, M., & Meier, P. (2001). Intelligent energy management of electrical power systems with distributed feeding on the basis of forecasts of demand and generation. In *16th International Conference and Exhibition on Electricity Distribution. Part 1: Contributions*. CIRED. doi:10.1049/cp:20010857

Witten, I. H., Frank, E., Hall, M. A., & Pal, C. J. (2016). *Data Mining: Practical machine learning tools and techniques*. Morgan Kaufmann.

Wojciechowski, R., Walczak, K., White, M., & Cellary, W. (2004). *Building virtual and augmented reality museum exhibitions*. Paper presented at the ninth international conference on 3D Web technology. doi:10.1145/985040.985060

Wonka, P., Wimmer, M., Sillion, F., & Ribarsky, W. (2003). Instant Architecture. In *ACM SIGGRAPH 2003 Papers* (pp. 669–677). San Diego, CA: ACM. doi:10.1145/1201775.882324

World Health Organization. (2016). *Disability and health* [online article]. Retrieved December 5, 2016, from http://www.who.int/mediacentre/factsheets/fs352/en/

World Tourism Organization. (2016). Retrieved March 2, 2016, from http://www2.unwto.org/

WTO. (1980). Manila Declaration on World Tourism. *World Tourism Conference*.

WTO. (1985). *Tourism bill of rights and tourist code*. General Assembly of the World Tourism Organization, Sofia, Bulgaria.

Wu, J., & Lu, X. (2013). Effects of extrinsic and intrinsic motivators on using utilitarian, hedonic, and dual-purposed information systems: A meta-analysis. *Journal of the Association for Information Systems*, *14*(3), 153.

Xiang, Z., & Gretzel, U. (2010). Role of social media in online travel information search. *Tourism Management*, *31*(2), 179–188. doi:10.1016/j.tourman.2009.02.016

Xifra, J., & Chias, J. (2008). *Las Relaciones Públicas y el Marketing*. Barcelona: UOC.

Xin, M., & Levina, N. (2008). Software-as-a service model: Elaborating client-side adoption factors. *International Conference on Information Systems ICIS*. doi:10.2139/ssrn.1319488

Xu, Y. (2011). Literature review on web application gamification and analytics. Honolulu, HI: Academic Press.

Xu, F., Weber, J., & Buhalis, D. (2013). Gamification in tourism. In *Information and Communication Technologies in Tourism 2014* (pp. 525–537). New York, NY: Springer International Publishing. doi:10.1007/978-3-319-03973-2_38

Yamada, T., Yokoyama, S., Tanikawa, T., Hirota, K., & Hirose, M. (2006). Wearable olfactory display: Using odor in outdoor environment. In *IEEE Virtual Reality Conference (VR 2006)* (pp. 199-206). IEEE. doi:10.1109/VR.2006.147

Yamamoto, G. T. (2009). *Mobilized Marketing and the Consumer: Technological Developments and Challenges*. Hershey, PA: Business Science Reference.

Yamamoto, K., & Fujita, S. (2017). A Dynamic Real-Time Navigation System for Urban Tourists. In *Planning Support Science for Smarter Urban Futures* (pp. 167–184). Springer International Publishing. doi:10.1007/978-3-319-57819-4_10

Yanagida, Y. (2012). A survey of olfactory displays: Making and delivering scents. In Sensors, 2012 IEEE (pp. 1-4). IEEE.

Yang, C. H., Lin, H. L., & Han, C. C. (2010). Analysis of international tourist arrivals in China: The role of World Heritage Sites. *Tourism Management, 31*(6), 827–837. doi:10.1016/j.tourman.2009.08.008

Yastikli, N. (2007). Documentation of cultural heritage using digital photogrammetry and laser scanning. *Journal of Cultural Heritage*, *8*(4), 423–427. doi:10.1016/j.culher.2007.06.003

Yázigi, E. (2001). *A alma do lugar: turismo, planejamento e cotidiano*. São Paulo, SP: Contexto.

Yeoman, I. (2013). A futurists thoughts on consumer trends shaping future festivals and events. *International Journal of Event and Festival Management*, *4*(3), 249–260. doi:10.1108/IJEFM-06-2013-0017

Yin, R. (2009). *Case Study Research: Design and Methods*. Thousand Oaks, CA: Sage Publications.

Yong, L., Mingmin, Z., Yunliang, J., & Haiying, Z. (2012). Improving procedural modeling with semantics in digital architectural heritage. *Computers & Graphics*, *36*(3), 178–184. doi:10.1016/j.cag.2012.01.003

Yoo, K. H., & Gretzel, U. (2011). Creating more credible and persuasive recommender systems: The influence of source characteristics on recommender system evaluations. In Recommender systems handbook (pp. 455-477). Springer US.

Yoo, K. H., Lee, Y., Gretzel, U., & Fesenmaier, D. R. (2009). Trust in travel-related consumer generated media. *Information and communication technologies in tourism 2009*, 49-59.

Yoo, K. H., & Gretzel, U. (2008). What motivates consumers to write online travel reviews? *Information Technology and Tourism*, *10*(4), 283–295. doi:10.3727/109830508788403114

Yoo, K. H., & Gretzel, U. (2010). Antecedents and impacts of trust in travel-related consumer-generated media. *Information Technology and Tourism*, *12*(2), 139–152. doi:10.3727/109830510X12887971002701

Yovcheva, Z., Buhalis, D. & Gatzidis, C., (2012). Smartphone augmented reality applications for tourism. *e-Review of Tourism Research*, *10*(2), 63-66.

Yovcheva, Z., Buhalis, D., & Gatzidis, C. (2013a). Engineering augmented tourism experiences. In L. Cantoni & Z. Xiang (Eds.), *Information and communication technologies in tourism* (pp. 24–35). Springer Berlin Heidelberg.

Yovcheva, Z., Buhalis, D., Gatzidis, C., & van Elzakker, C. P. (2014). Empirical Evaluation of Smartphone Augmented Reality Browsers in an Urban Tourism Destination Context. *International Journal of Mobile Human Computer Interaction*, *6*(2), 10–31. doi:10.4018/ijmhci.2014040102

Yovcheva, Z., Buhalis, D., Gatzidis, C., & van Elzakker, C. P. J. M. (2013b). Proposing a design framework for smartphone AR browsers used in unfamiliar urban tourism destinations. *Designing Mobile Augmented Reality Workshop.*

Yu, C. C., & Chang, H. P. (2009). Personalized location-based recommendation services for tour planning in mobile tourism applications. In *International Conference on Electronic Commerce and Web Technologies* (pp. 38-49). Springer Berlin Heidelberg. doi:10.1007/978-3-642-03964-5_5

Yuan, Z., Bi, T., Muntean, G. M., & Ghinea, G. (2015). Perceived synchronization of multisemedia services. *IEEE Transactions on Multimedia*, *17*(7), 957–966. doi:10.1109/TMM.2015.2431915

Yuen, S., Yaoyuneyong, G., & Johnson, E. (2011). Augmented Reality: An overview and five directions for AR in Education. *Journal of Educational Technology Development and Exchange*, *4*(1), 119–140. doi:10.18785/jetde.0401.10

Zeng, B., & Gerritsen, R. (2014). What do we know about social media in tourism? A review. *Tourism Management Perspectives*, *10*, 27–36. doi:10.1016/j.tmp.2014.01.001

Zevi, A. (1992). Saber ver a arquitetura (3rd ed.). São Paulo, SP: Martins Fontes.

Zhang, Y., & Wang, J. (2015). Probabilistic solar power forecasting based on k-nearest neighbor and kernel density estimator. 2015 IEEE Power & Energy Society General Meeting, 1-5.

Zhang, Q., Cheng, L., & Boutaba, R. (2010). Cloud computing: State-of-the-art and research challenges. *Journal of Internet Service Application*, *1*(1), 7–18. doi:10.1007/s13174-010-0007-6

Zhang, W., & Watts, S. A. (2008). Capitalizing on content: Information adoption in two online communities. *Journal of the Association for Information Systems*, *9*(2), 73.

Zhang, Y., & Cole, S. T. (2016). Dimensions of lodging guest satisfaction among guests with mobility challenges: A mixed-method analysis of web-based texts. *Tourism Management*, *53*, 13–27. doi:10.1016/j.tourman.2015.09.001

Zhao, L., Lu, Y., Zhang, L., & Chau, P. Y. (2012). Assessing the effects of service quality and justice on customer satisfaction and the continuance intention of mobile value-added services: An empirical test of a multidimensional model. *Decision Support Systems*, *52*(3), 645–656. doi:10.1016/j.dss.2011.10.022

Zheng, W., Liao, Z., & Qin, J. (2017). Using a four-step heuristic algorithm to design personalized day tour route within a tourist attraction. *Tourism Management*, *62*, 335–349. doi:10.1016/j.tourman.2017.05.006

Zhou, X., Xu, C., & Kimmons, B. (2015). Detecting tourism destinations using scalable geospatial analysis based on cloud computing platform. *Computers, Environment and Urban Systems*, *54*, 144–153. doi:10.1016/j.compenvurbsys.2015.07.006

Ziulkoski, C. (2013). *General format*. Retrieved February 02, 2017, from http://www.karolinaziulkoski.com/Museum-Without-Walls

About the Contributors

João Rodrigues graduated in Electrical Engineering in 1993, he got his M.Sc. in Computer Systems Engineering in 1998 and Ph.D. Electronics and Computer Engineering in 2008 from University of the Algarve, Portugal. He is Adjunct Professor at Instituto Superior de Engenharia, also in the University of the Algarve, where he lectures Computer Science and Computer Vision since 1994. He is member of associative laboratory LARSyS (ISR-Lisbon), CIAC and the Associations APRP, IAPR and ARTECH. He participated in 15 financed scientific projects, and he is co-author more than 150 scientific publications. His major research interests lies on computer and human vision, assistive technologies and human-computer interaction.

Célia M. Q. Ramos graduated in Computer Engineering from the University of Coimbra, obtained her Master in Electrical and Computers Engineering from the Higher Technical Institute, Lisbon University, and the PhD in Econometrics in the University of the Algarve (UALG), Faculty of Economics, Portugal. She is Adjunct Professor at School for Management, Hospitality and Tourism, also in the UALG, where she lectures computer science. Areas of research and special interest include conception and development of information systems, tourism information systems, big data, etourism, econometric modeling and panel-data models. Célia Ramos has published in the fields of information systems and tourism, namely, she has authored a book, two book chapters, conference papers and journal articles. At the level of applied research, she has participated in several funded projects.

Pedro Cardoso holds a PhD in the field of Operational Research from the University of Seville (Spain), a Master in Computational Mathematics from the University of Minho (Portugal) and a Degree in Mathematics - Computer Science from the University of Coimbra (Portugal). He teaches Computer Science and Mathematics at the Instituto Superior de Engenharia of the Universidade do Algarve (UAlg) and is member of LARSys/UAlg. He has high knowledge in the fields of databases, algorithms and data structures, and Operational Research. Over the past few years has been involved in 7 national and international scientific and development projects and is the co-author of about 50 scientific publications.

Cláudia Henriques has a PhD in Economics (Algarve University, 2002), thesis under the subject of "Management and Planning of Sustainable Tourism in cities and historic city quarters. The case of Lisbon". She is lecturer of Tourism Economics, Cultural and Creative Sector and Tourism Planning and Managing at Algarve University (ESGHT_UALG) from 1993 until today. Her Research interests are in Cultural Tourism, Tourism Planning and Management; Cultural and Tourism Policies and Cultural heritage (Historic Centres). She is member of CIEO (Centre for Spatial and Organizational Dynamics).

* * *

Telmo Adão attained his PhD in Computer Science at the University of Trás-os-Montes and Alto Douro, where he developed a procedural modelling methodology for the production of coarse traversable buildings composed by arbitrary shapes. During his journey as a researcher, he developed work not only in computer graphics but also in context-aware advertising, accessibility for blind people, usability for children, computer vision applied to the elderly, augmented reality in cultural heritage and human-computer interfaces for persons with disability. Currently, he is working in hyperspectral remote sensing for disease detection in agroforestry. Machine learning is also in his range of interests.

Dora Agapito holds a PhD in Tourism, a master in Marketing, and a bachelor degree in Communication Sciences. She is Assistant Professor at the Faculty of Economics of University of Algarve, Portugal, and an active member of the scientific committees for the Master of Tourist Organizations Management and the Master of Communication Design for Tourism and Culture in the same institution. Her research and publication interests are in tourism marketing, sensory tourist experiences, rural tourist experiences, sensory marketing, and social marketing. She is a member of the Research Centre for Spatial and Organizational Dynamics (CIEO).

Juan Miguel Alcántara-Pilar is Associate Professor of Marketing at University of Granada (Spain) at the Faculty of Education, Economy and Technology of Ceuta. His areas of specialization are marketing online, cross-cultural marketing, language effect on consumer behavior and behaviors in multi-racial communities. He has published several books as co-author on these matters (Springer, IGI Global). He has also published various peer-reviewed papers in prestigious journals such as Cross Cultural Management: An International Journal, International Journal of Advertising, European Research on Management and Business Economics and Computers in Human Behavior, among others. He has participated in prestigious international congress (EMAC, ICORIA, Academy of Marketing).

Pau Alonso-Monasterio is PhD by the Universitat Politècnica de València, where she has been developing her career as a researcher in tourism management of natural and cultural heritage sites, through more than 20 research and development international projects (ENPI, Interreg, Euromed Heritage, Azahar, etc.). She also has been combining her role as researcher with teaching in grade and postgraduate courses at university. Dr. Alonso-Monasterio is specialized in designing maps for visitors in areas with natural and cultural heritage, having published, among others, maps in World Heritage Sites such as Petra Archaeological Park (Jordan) and the Maya Site of Copán (Honduras), and in natural protected areas such as the Albufera Natural Park (Valencia, Spain), as well as thematic maps like the edited for Ramsar Convention 'Mediterranean Wetlands Cultural Landscapes'. She has contributed in Ramsar COP exhibitions, and has been member of the design team in the Visitors Center of Tous Dam (Turia River, Spain), the Visitor Center of Gandia Marsh (Spain) and the Visitor Center of Ghar el Melh (Tunis).

Julia Altmman is an Architecture Student at the University of Caxias do Sul. Scholarships student FAPERGS.

Tanja Armenski, PhD, is an Assistant Professor at the Department of Geography, Tourism and Hotel Management, Faculty of Sciences, University of Novi Sad, Serbia. Her research areas are destination competitiveness, consumer behaviour, cross-cultural studies and applied statistics. She has been a Departmental coordinator for international student mobility as well as the participant in the several projects of national and international importance. Tanja is currently in the Editorial Board of the Academica Turistica Journal and a member of the Canadian Association of Geographers and the Statistical Society of Canada.

João Pedro Bernardes is graduate in History (Variant in Archaeology) by the University of Coimbra (1985) and post-graduate (M Phil in1996, PhD in 2002), with a dissertation about the Roman Settlement in Leiria region (Portugal). He teached disciplines of Archaeology and Ancient History at the University of Azores. Since 1997 he teaches at University of Algarve disciplines as History of the Classical Culture and Classical Archaeology, where he is associate professor. He was director of the Department of History, Archaeology and Cultural Heritage of the University of Algarve. He directed archaeological excavations in the country, but over all in the region of Leiria and Algarve. He made missions of research in the German Archaeological Institute of Rome, in the Center Pierre Paris of the University of Bordéus III, or in the archaeological Institute of Southampton University. He was member of the National commission of evaluation of the research projects submitted for the National Plan of Archaeological Works in the year of 2005. He was member of History and archaeology board of Phd and Pos-doc grants evaluation for the Fundação para a Ciência e Tecnologia (Portuguese Foundation for the Science ant Technology - FCT). Currently, he is a member of the Panel for the evaluation of Multiannual Projects of Archaeology submitted to the Portuguese Ministry of culture. He has published papers in national and international journals, proceedings of scientific meetings and books, most of all on Roman Archaeology. He has developed and coordinated National Research Projects financed by the Portuguese Institutions programs and he was the project leader (coordinator) of the international project "Roman Mosaics of Andalusia and Algarve - MOSUDHIS" (program INTERREG III), and he was the principal investigator of the Portuguese partner of the projects "El mundo funerario romano en el sudoeste europeo – MORSUDE (i2Tep Programme) and "CROSUDHIS: Ciudades romanas del suroeste de Hispania" (Poctep Programme). Recently he coordinated a study entitled "Cultural Heritage and Territory" about the Portuguese Cultural Heritage Classified ordered by Government of Portugal (Secretary of State for Culture), under Portuguese Studies plan for the culture of the European strategic framework 2014-2020.

Rui Carvalho is a PhD Tourism Student at the University of Aveiro, Portugal. He completed his degree in Cultural and Tourism Management and MSc degree in Development of Cultural Tourism Products at the Polytechnic Institute of Tomar, Portugal. He is also a Member of the research unit on Competitiveness, Governance and Public Policies (GOVCOPP) of the University of Aveiro and is a Tourism Teacher at the Vocational School of Torres Novas, Portugal. His research interests include cultural and creative tourism, creative experiences, co-creation, tourism events, tourism consumption in postmodernity, sociology and anthropology in tourism and epistemology of tourism.

Sergio Casas has a degree in Computer Science and also a degree in Telecommunications Engineering - Telematics Specialty. He received his PhD in Computational Mathematics at the University of Valencia in 2014. He works as a post-doctoral researcher in the Robotics Institute of the University of Valencia, where he is also a part-time professor at the School of Engineering (ETSE).

Pedro César is an Architect and urban planner, Prof. Dr. at the University of Caxias do Sul - PPGTURH.

Marija Cimbaljević is PhD candidate at the Faculty of Science, University of Novi Sad. She received her MSc degree in tourism from the University of Novi Sad in 2014. Her research interests lie in the area of tourism and particularly area of smart tourism. Further, her research interests include information technology and geographic information systems (GIS). She is currently engaged as an teaching assistant at the Faculty of Sciences, Department of Geography, Tourism and Hotel Management in Novi Sad, Serbia.

Marisol B. Correia is a professor in the Information Technologies and Systems scientific area of the School of Management, Hospitality and Tourism of the University of Algarve and she is a member collaborator of the Centre for Management Studies of IST of the University of Lisbon. She holds a PhD in Electronics and Computer Engineering from the University of the Algarve, a masters in Electronics and Computer Engineering from the University of Lisbon and 5-year undergraduate degree in Informatics Engineering from the University of Coimbra. She is a scientific reviewer for some international journals and conferences and she participated in I&DT projects. She has presented papers at international conferences and has published scientific papers in several journals. Her current research interests include Information Technologies applied to Hospitality, Management, Tourism and Marketing, Cloud Computing, Websites Evaluation, Web Semantic, Business Intelligence and Evolutionary Computation.

Carlos Costa, PhD, is Full Professor at the University of Aveiro. He holds a Doctorate in Tourism from the University of Surrey (UK) and a degree in Regional and Urban Planning from the University of Aveiro. He is the Director of the Department of Tourism, Editor of the Tourism & Development Magazine, and Head of the Tourism research group of the Research Unit on Governance, Competitiveness and Public Policy (GOVCOPP). He is also the Technical-Scientific Director of the spin-off tourism company 'idtour-unique solutions'.

J. M. Cotos is Professor at Santiago de Compostela University (Spain) Researcher at IT Research Center (CITIUS, http://citius.usc.es).

Paula Odete Fernandes graduated in Business Administration, received MSc Degree in Management and a PhD in Economics and Management (2005). She is currently a Coordinator Professor of the Department of Economics and Management at the Polytechnic Institute of Bragança (IPB) -Portugal. She teaches several courses in the area of Management, since 1992. She is researcher and Scientific Coordinator of UNIAG (Applied Management Research Unit), and researcher of NECE (UBI). She participated in 8 international projects I&D and has more than 160 publications in peer-reviewed journals, book chapters and proceedings, and has several communications at international scientific conferences. She serves as a member of Program Board and Organizing Committees for some Scientific Committees of International Conferences and has collaborated as reviewer with several journals.

Ana Maria Ferreira, PhD, Associate Professor at the University of Évora, Portugal. Received his doctorate in tourism from the University of Aveiro. She has a degree in History and a MSc Degree in Art History from the Universidade Nova de Lisboa. She is a member of the Interdisciplinary Center of History, Culture and Societies (CIDEHUS), University of Évora. In addition to being a member of several scientific boards of scientific journals, she is a regional coordinator of the CREATOUR Research Project - Developing creative tourism destinations in small towns and rural areas. Among her research interests are: Tourism, Culture and Urban and Rural Regeneration, Cultural districts and clusters of tourist attractions. Colocation; Cultural and creative industries. Creative tourism companies, Cultural Tourism and Creative Tourism, Creative tourism experiences, Co-creation, Interorganizational Networks and Copetition.

Mauro Figueiredo has a PhD in computer science from the University of Salford, Manchester, in 2005. He was teacher at University of Coimbra from 1989 until 1996. Since 1996 he is at the Algarve University where he is adjunct professor. His research interests are in the use of information technologies for education, e-learning, b-learning, games and augmented reality. His PhD students are currently working with ebooks and augmented reality tools for e-learning. He is author of more than seventy international journal and conferences articles, book chapters and books and he collaborated and participated in different National projects. He is the international coordinator of the Erasmus+ project MILAGE: Interactive Mathematics by implementing a Blended-Learning model with Augmented Reality and Game books. He has several papers best awards. He already organized several international conferences. Most of the research is conducted at Univ. Algarve, at CIMA (Center of Marine and Environmental Research) and CIAC (Center for the Arts and Communication Research). CV: http://w3.ualg.pt/~mfiguei/cvmfuk.pdf ORCID: http://orcid.org/0000-0001-9394-4868.

Marco Freitas is a detail-oriented professional with more than five years of experience as a software developer since he graduated at the University of the Algarve in 2008, in Electric and Electronic Engineering. Skilled at programming in C# and operating in Visual Studio he also has two programming certifications in Java 7. He is capable of explaining complex software issues in easy-to-understand terms and has a problem solving creative approach. Follows standards, adheres to procedures, calculates risks and weighs all sides of a problem. As a team member, he is loyal and committed to his organization. open-minded, thorough and dependable person. He is introverted but friendly, relaxed, easygoing and funny when he feels comfortable around others. Likes to help, listen to music, read books and go to the cinema. Enjoys learning, traveling and trying new foods.

Alexandra Gonçalves is Regional Director of Culture of the Algarve since December 2013. Adjoint Professor at the University of the Algarve/School of Management, Hospitality and Tourism since 1997. Master in Cultural and Heritage Management and Doctor in Tourism.

César Gonçalves has a degree in Mechanical Engineering, Master in Industrial Engineering, with research focused on reliability and failure rate analysis and a PhD in Industrial Engineering with research in the maintenance performance measurement. He is a professor in mechanical engineering course at the Instituto Superior de Engenharia of Universidade do Algarve, in the subjects of Maintenance Management, Reliability, Drawing, Mechanical Technology, CAD and CAM. His research interests are maintenance management, BIM and augmented reality. He was a speaker in congresses and conferences focusing in maintenance issues namely connected with buildings. He is also author of international journals papers.

Feliz Gouveia graduated in Electrotechnical Engineering from the University of Porto in 1986. Earned a PhD in Computer Systems from the Université de Technologie de Compiègne in 1992. Participated in research and development projects for the European Space Agency and several european companies in the areas of knowledge management and object-oriented databases. From 1996 is associate professor at University Fernando Pessoa, Porto, where he participated in European projects in the area of elearning and presence research.

Bintang Handayani, SIK., M.Si., MBA., Ph.D., is a Senior Researcher at President University, Indonesia. Her work scrutinises personification and impression management of a nation and its market offerings in consumer cultures. It tackles nation-brand images (NBI), Tourism and Hospitality attributes, Dark Sites phenomenon, Nation's Positioning, Place Attachment from Socio-cultural and Post-modern perspectives, coupled with Communication & Media studies.

Nuria Huete Alcocer is an Assistant Professor of Econometrics since October 2013 in the area of Spanish and International Economics, Econometrics, History, and Economic Institutions at the Faculty of Economics and Business, Albacete, University of Castilla-La Mancha. Research interests include: Tourism Marketing and Quantitative Methods in Economics and Business Tourism.

Serkan Kılıç, born in 1981, graduated in Business Administration in Bursa, Turkey. He received the Master degree and the PhD degree from the Uludağ University. He is currently working as an Assistant Prof. in the Department of Business Administration at Uludağ University in Turkey. He teaches marketing and innovation related courses at Uludağ University. His research interests are marketing, retailing, branding, consumer behavior and innovation. Dr. Kılıç has written three books named as Private labels in Retailing, Innovation Management and New Product Innovation. He has many published articles in different journals. He has also worked on internationalization and generation related projects as an academician and project manager.

Maximiliano Korstanje is editor in chief of International Journal of Safety and Security in Tourism (UP Argentina) and International Journal of Cyber Warfare and Terrorism (IGI-GlobalUS). Besides being Senior Researchers in the Department of Economics at University of Palermo, Argentina, he is a global affiliate of Tourism Crisis Management Institute (University of Florida US), Centre for Ethnicity and Racism Studies (University of Leeds), The Forge (University of Lancaster and University of Leeds UK) and The International Society for Philosopher, hosted in Sheffield UK. With more than 700 published papers and 25 books, Korstanje was awarded as Outstanding Reviewer 2012. International Journal of Disaster Resilience in the Built Environment. University of Salford, UK, Outstanding Reviewer 2013, Journal of Place Management and Development, Institute of Place, Manchester Metropolitan University, UK and Reviewer Certificate of Acknowledgement 2014, International Journal of Contemporary Hospitality Management (IJCHM), University of Central Florida, US. Now he co-edits almost 10 specialized journals in such themes as human rights, mobility, tourism and terrorism. Korstanje is subject to biographical records for Marquis Who`s Who in the World since 2009. He had nominated to 5 honorary doctorates for his contribution in the study of the effects of terrorism in tourism. In 2015 he was awarded as Visiting Research Fellow at School of Sociology and Social Policy, University of Leeds, UK and the University of La Habana Cuba. In 2017 is elected as Foreign Faculty Member of AMIT, Mexican Academy in the study of Tourism, which is the most prominent institutions dedicated to tourism research in Mexico.

Víctor-Raúl López Ruiz is Professor of Econometrics at Castilla-La Mancha University. His fields of research are Intellectual Capital Measurement, International Growth, Regional Economy and Models Applied to Management. He is the author of several working papers, books and documents on these topics. He has taught international courses on Intellectual Capital and has also been awarded several research prizes. Further information available at http://victorraullopez.blogspot.com/.

Luís Gonzaga Magalhães has a BSc and MSc in Informatics from the University of Minho and a PhD in Computer Science from the University of Trás-os-Montes e Alto Douro. Currently, he is an Assistant Professor with Habilitation at University of Minho. Recently, he assumed the role of Scientific Coordinator of the Computer Vision, Interaction and Graphics unit at the Computer Graphics Centre. He is also a Senior Researcher at ALGORITMI Centre. He is author or co-author of more than 70 scientific publications on international journals and conference proceedings. His research interests include the use of Computer Vision, Augmented Reality, Computer Graphics, and more recently on the use of procedural modeling techniques. He is or was a research member in projects related to Expeditious Modeling of Virtual Environments, Immersive 3D Environments, Virtual Environments for Education, Virtual Heritage and High Dynamic Range Imaging. More recently was the scientific leader of a I&DT project with the industry which aimed to develop a mixed reality system for cultural and entertainment industries.

María Pilar Martínez-Ruiz, PhD, is Associate Professor of Marketing at Marketing Department, University of Castilla-La Mancha (Spain). Visiting Professor at University of Edinburgh (UK) and University of Plymouth (UK). Her research interests fall in the areas of consumer behaviour, retailing, marketing communications, tourism, innovation and ICT. Professor Martínez-Ruiz has published several articles in different high standing international Journals, such as Tourism Management, Service Industries Journal, Service Business, European Journal of Marketing, Journal of Retailing and Consumer Services, Journal of the Operational Research Society, International Journal of Market Research, Total Quality Management and Business Excellence, Decision Support Systems and Electronic Commerce, European Journal of Operational Research, among others. She was co-track chair of the Pricing and Retailing Track at the 2012 AMA Summer Marketing Educators' Conference. She is author of several chapters and books on these areas, and serve as a reviewer and associated editor of several international journals.

Sergio Gómez Melgar is a researcher and associate professor at the University of Huelva, specializing in energy efficiency in buildings. Sergio is the responsable researcher of the Energy Efficiency project at TEP192 Control and Robotics Research Group in the University of Huelva. This research pertains to instrumentation and data analysis for improving energy efficiency in buildings and cities, with specific application in passive design for energy efficiency, monitoring and control, and integration of renewable energy in buildings and cities. Sergio Gomez Melgar is also LAR Architecture's CEO. In his leadership position at the firm, he has designed more than 600,000 sq. feet of buildings of diverse typologies including residential, educational, social, healthcare, administrative and physical rehabilitation facilities for both private and publics sector clients. Some of his constructed works such as Zaranda House and Engineers University School in Huelva, have received international energy efficiency awards (Viena 2012, Gijon 2013 and Dublin 2014).

Jânio Monteiro graduated in Electrical and Computers Engineering in 1995 from the University of Porto, and later concluded a Master and PhD degrees respectively in 2003 and 2010, also in Electrical and Computer Engineering from Instituto Superior Técnico, Technical University of Lisbon. Since 2003, he is a member INESC-ID Lisbon. He participated in four European R&TD projects funded by the European Commission, and six national projects, with local companies, coordinating two of them. He is one of the editors of one book and of more than four dozen publications, including journal papers, publications in scientific conferences, book chapters and national patents. His main areas of interest involve communication networks, smart grids, sensor networks, human-machine interfaces and Internet of Things. He is currently an Assistant Professor of the Electrical Engineering Department of Instituto Superior de Engenharia, University of the Algarve where he teaches several courses related with "Computer Networks", "Sensor Networks" and "Smart Grids".

António Mortal is Assistant Professor in Mechanical Engineering Department of University of Algarve / ISE. Since 1992 he has taught subjects related to the energy, renewable energy and energy efficiency in undergraduate and graduate level. He also develops consultant and research activities in this area. Currently his main line of activity is related with energy in buildings, HVAC systems, energy audits, indoor air quality and with the application of the EPBD directive in Portugal. He also has experience using modelling tools for energy simulation in buildings as DesignBuilder software. He has experience in organizational coordination and leadership, actually he is the head of the Engineering School (ISE/UALG). He has more than 20 articles in scientific conferences.

Aristotelis Naniopoulos is a professor in Transport Systems at the Faculty of Engineering, Aristotle University of Thessaloniki (AUTh). He is currently Director of the Transport Systems Research Group (www.tsrg.gr) and the Laboratory of Urban and Regional Planning and Development (UREDLab) of AUTh. He graduated the same school from both the departments of Surveying Engineering (1976) and the Architecture Engineering (1981) from where he holds the two corresponding degrees. He pursued postgraduate studies in Operational Research at Cranfield Institute of Technology of U.K (1976), where he obtained the M.Sc. Degree. He also obtained the Ph.D. degree in Transport (1988). Prof. Naniopoulos has participated in more than 50 national and international projects, having acted as a coordinator in many of them.

Sergey Nogin completed the B.Sc. in Electrical and Electronics Engineering in 2015, from ISE, University of Algarve. He is now a student of the M.Sc. degree of the same institution.

Miguel Otón is a Professor at Santiago de Compostela University.

Erkan Özdemir received the Master degree and the PhD degree from the Uludağ University in Turkey. He is currently working as an Assoc. Prof. in the Department of Business Administration at Uludağ University in Turkey. He teaches marketing management, sales management, marketing strategies courses at Uludağ University. His research interests are marketing, consumer behavior, high-tech marketing and innovation. Dr. Özdemir has written three books named as Marketing Strategies to Women Consumers,

Marketing Ethics, Marketing of High-Tech Products and Services. He has many published articles in different journals. He also served as an assistant researcher at Uludağ University Technology Transfer Office Project supported by The Scientific and Technological Research Council of Turkey (TÜBİTAK) between 2014 and 2015 and has been in charge of business development and entrepreneurship department at Uludağ University Technology Transfer Office.

Pedro Palos has a PhD in Business Economics from the University of Seville, Bachelor in Information Systems Engineering and Bachelor in Research and Market Techniques. More than 20 years working in companies of the sector of Information Technology in different management positions. He is Associate Professor in the Department of Business Management and Sociology (Marketing and Research and Markets Area), teaching at the Faculty of Business Studies and Tourism of the University of Extremadura (Spain). He has participated with various lectures, courses and articles in various congresses and programs on digital economy, entrepreneurship and management both nationally and internationally, being his research lines Digital Marketing and Information Systems. He is a member of the UEx MARKETUR Research Group Research Group.

Vanja Pavluković is Associate Professor of Tourism at the University of Novi Sad Faculty of Sciences, Department of Geography, Tourism and Hotel Management. Her research interests focus on destination competitiveness, business travel and tourism, travel agency and tour operator management and event management. She has also published various peer-reviewed papers in international journals such as Current Issues in Tourism, International Journal of Tourism Research, Acta Oeconomica, European Journal of Tourism Research and Tourism and Hospitality Management.

João Pereira received his Bachelor's Degree in Electrical and Electronic Engineering in 2012 and is now finishing his Master also in Electrical and Electronic Engineering at University of the Algarve. He is a Researcher in the Associative Laboratory LARSyS (ISR-LX) and in the University of the Algarve. His major interests lie on programming, learning and exploring new frameworks.

Emanuel Peres is an assistant professor at Trás-os-Montes e Alto Douro University (UTAD) in Portugal. He has been lecturing in areas such as web development, electronics, power electronics, telecommunications and computer networks since 2003. He is an integrated researcher at the Technology and Science Associate Laboratory (INESC-TEC) and his research focuses on combining sensing networks, in-field processing units and mesh communication networks to develop data acquisition systems which enable decision support tools for precision agriculture. Human–Machine interaction, namely augmented reality systems, new interfaces and mobile devices, in areas such as education, agriculture and tourism, is also an area of interest. From 2010 onwards he has been involved in management positions at UTAD. He is an Editor-in-Chief of the International Journal of Web Portals (IJWP) since January 2016. As a member of UTAD's Urban Eco-Efficiency Unit, he is currently involved in several research projects mainly related with the application of UAV in agriculture and forestry.

José Peyroteo completed a B.Sc. degree in Electrical and Electronics Engineering in 2015, from ISE, University of Algarve. He is a currently a student of the M.Sc. degree of the same institution.

Patrícia Pinto holds a PhD in applied statistics to economics and business. She is Professor at the Faculty of Economics, University of Algarve, and an active member of board of the PhD program in Tourism in the same institution. Her current research interests are in applied statistics and modeling in the areas of integrated quality management in tourism destinations, events management, tourism destinations image, branding, marketing strategies, customer satisfaction, and environment behavior. She is a member of the Research Centre for Spatial and Organizational Dynamics (CIEO).

Cristina Portales Ricart is MSc. in Geodesy and Cartography from the Universidad Politécnica de Valencia and MSc. in Surveying and Geoinformation from Technische Universität Wien (2003). Research fellow at the Mixed Reality Laboratory of the University of Nottingham (2005) and at the Interaction and Entertainment Research Centre of the Nanyang University of Singapore (2006), both in the area of computer vision. In 2008 she received the Ph.D. degree by the UPV. From 2011-2012 she worked at AIDO (Industrial Association of Optics, Colour and Imaging), where she was primarily involved in technical management of the FP7 funded project SYDDARTA. In 2012 she received the Juan de la Cierva post-doctoral grant by the Spanish Ministry to join IRTIC (Research Institute of Robotics and Information and Communication Technologies), where she continued researching in accurate 3D reconstruction. Her current research interests are focused on geometric calibration, image processing, 3D reconstruction, multispectral imaging, augmented reality and human-computer-interaction.

José Rodrigues is adjunct professor teaching at the Geomatics Node of the Department of Civil Engineering, and he's also a researcher at the Marine and Environmental Research Center (CIMA). He graduated in Mathematics from the University of Lisbon, Portugal, and obtained his PhD degree in Computational Geometry from the University of Seville, Spain. His research interests are in Computational Geometry, Geographic Information Systems and Web3D. Over the years he taught courses in the Geomatics field such as geographical informations systems, mathematical cartography, photogrammetry, GIS programming and 3D Data Acquisition and Modelling, at undergraduate and graduate level. He is board member of the Scientific Commission of the Master in Geomatics. Since 2015, he is Vice Director of the Engineering Institute of the University of Algarve.

Carlos Santos concluded the B.Sc. Degree (five-year program) in Mechanical Engineering, from University of Algarve, in 1997. In 2013 he also concluded a Master of Science degree in Energy and Building Air Conditioning, from University of Algarve.

João D. P. Sardo was born in Faro, Portugal in 1989. He graduated in electrical and electronics engineering in 2011 and received the post-graduation in 2013, both from the University of the Algarve. In 2011 he co-founded eLab Hackerspace, a community oriented laboratory. An electronics, digital fabrication and open source enthusiast.

Till Maximilian Schuh holds a master in Tourism Economics and Regional Development and a bachelor in Sustainable Business Management. His master thesis was developed under the theme of tourism destination image and it was presented in several international conferences. His research and publication interests are in tourism marketing, sustainable tourism and rural tourism. Since August 2016, he works at the Thomas Cook AG in Oberursel, Germany as a business assistant.

Jorge Semião received the B.Sc. (five-year program), the M.Sc. and the Ph.D. degrees in electrical engineering from Instituto Superior Técnico, Technical University of Lisbon, Portugal, respectively in 1996, 2001 and 2010, with specialization in Electronic and Computer Systems, and Microelectronics. He joined University of the Algarve in 1997, and he is currently an Assistant Professor and the Director of the Electrical Engineering Department of Instituto Superior de Engenharia, University of the Algarve, in Faro, Portugal. He is also a senior researcher in the Quality, Test and Co-Design of HW/SW Systems research group of Instituto de Engenharia de Sistemas e Computadores R&D in Lisbon (INESC-ID), Portugal. His research interests include CMOS aging, dynamic voltage and frequency scaling, reliability, fault-tolerance and fault-detection. He participated in several research projects, and he is the author and co-author of over 80 scientific articles published, three national patents and three patents still under patent pending.

Caroline Silva is an architecture student at the University of Caxias do Sul.

Uglješa Stankov is Associate Professor of Tourism at the University of Novi Sad Faculty of Sciences, Department of Geography, Tourism and Hotel Management. His main research interests are IT applications in tourism, e-marketing and geoinfromation technologies. For this purpose, he actively cooperates with the researchers and professional organizations and participates in several international projects. He has also published various peer-reviewed papers in international journals such as Acta Oeconomica, Open Geosciences, European Journal of Tourism Research and Tourism and Hospitality Management.

Humberto Thomé-Ortiz is a doctor in Rural Sciences by the Autonomous University of Chapingo. Full time faculty at the Institute for Agricultural and Rural Sciences (ICAR) of the Autonomous University of the State of Mexico. Member of the National System of Researchers, Level I. His research areas are Local Agro-food Systems, Territorial Development, and Agro-food Tourism. He is principal investigator of the Project "Agro-food tourism in the State of Mexico and its perspectives for rural development" funded by the Mexican National Council for Science and Technology. His most recent publication is "Native maizes in feminised campesino strategies in the face of climate change".

Michele Trentin is a Master Student in Tourism and Hospitality from the University of Caxias do Sul (UCS).

Bruna Tronca is an architect graduated from the University of Caxias do Sul (UCS), Master Student in Tourism and Hospitality, Scholarships student CAPES.

Panagiotis Tsalis is a civil engineer specialized in accessibility issues. His PhD thesis concerns the development of a standard for the assessment and improvement of accessibility for persons with restricted mobility at municipal level. Dr. Tsalis has participated in various European and national research projects concerning accessibility of people with disabilities and people with restricted mobility in general. Furthermore, he has participated in several conferences and scientific publications with papers and presentations on this particular subject, and has given lectures on accessibility issues at the Aristotle University of Thessaloniki and the University of Thessaly. Finally, he has acted as instructor on accessibility issues for the Greek National Confederation of Persons with Disability.

Roberto Ivo Fernandes Vaz graduated in Electronic and Telecommunications Engineering (2012) at University of Aveiro – Portugal, and has an MSc Degree in Interactive Multimedia Communication (2014) by the same University. Currently, he's a Ph.D. student at UT Austin|Portugal Digital Media Doctoral Program. He participated in one international project I&D in Brazil (between the Federal University of Minas Gerais and the MM Gerdau Museum), has experience designing museographic projects and researches in the areas of human-computer interaction, digital media, interaction design, technology in museums and technological accessibility.

Ana Veiga graduated in Architecture and Urbanism (Federal University of Minas Gerais – UFMG, 2001), specialized in Construction Technology and Productivity (UFMG, 2002), M. A. in Architecture and Urbanism (UFMG, 2005) and D.Sc. in Image Art and Technology (UFMG – School of Fine Arts, 2012), with her thesis published as a book: "Gestão de projetos de museus e exposições" (Museums and Exhibits Project Management) by Editora C/Arte, FAPEMIG, 2013. Professor at the Federal University of Minas Gerais (UFMG), Department of Technology at the School of Architecture. Experience, projects and research in the following subject areas: Project Management Software Applications, Telework, Web (web design, web writing, UX, SEO, WordPress), Cultural Writing, Museums and Exhibits, Drawing and Scientific Illustration. Coordinator of the GRAFT research group and its virtual laboratory (LavGRAFT). Member of UNIC (Brazilian National Union of Scientific Illustrators).

María José Viñals is full Professor at the Higher School of Architecture in the Universitat Politècnica de València (UPV), Spain. She took a MA and a PhD in Geography at the Universitat de València-Estudi General (Spain). Dr. Viñals was the Director of the UPV International Office (2005-09) and director of the Spanish Wetland Centre (Fundación Biodiversidad, Spanish Ministry of Environment) during four years. Her field of expertise focuses on Natural and Cultural Heritage Planning and Management, Public Use and Conservation of Natural Protected Areas and Heritage Sites, Tourism and Heritage Interpretation. She usually teaches in undergraduate and graduate Environmental Sciences, Tourism and Architecture studies. Furthermore, she has been the director of several professional masters and courses in Spain and other countries (Italy, Portugal, Morocco, Tunisia, Australia, Nicaragua, Argentina, Uruguay, Jordan, Ecuador, Honduras, etc.). She has mentored and supervised the research work over a hundred of graduate students and has directed eight doctoral theses. Dr. Viñals has led interdisciplinary teams, that have conducted research in various aspects of protected areas and world heritage sites, particularly addressing issues related to the outdoor recreation planning and managing, and natural and cultural tourism resources. She has been also consultant to the Spanish Ministry of Environment, International Spanish Agency for Cooperation and Development (AECID), to the International Ramsar Convention on Wetlands, UNESCO Word Heritage Centre, to the UN World Tourism Organization, and advisor to World Wildlife Fund (WWF). Dr. Viñals has published more than a hundred fifty international research works (papers, books, conference papers, book chapters, etc.) devoted particularly to heritage and tourism management. Currently, she is an evaluator of the National Agency for Assessment and Accreditation (ANECA) of the Spanish Ministry of Education.

Index

M

N

P

Q

R

S

T

U

V

W

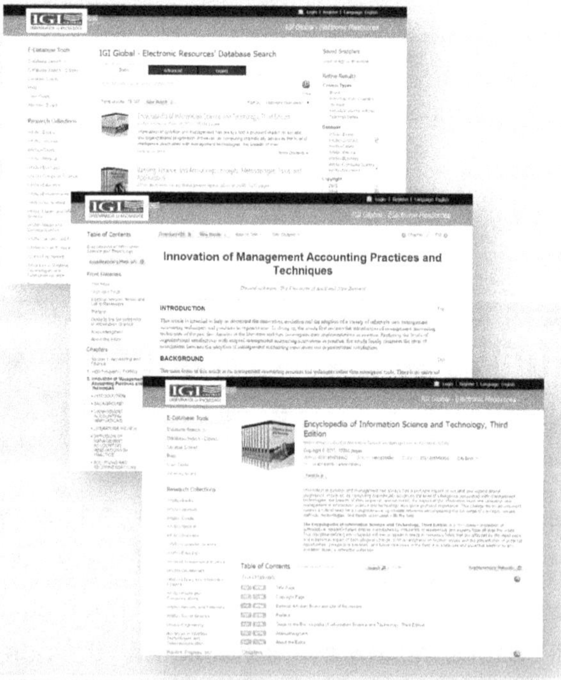
IGI Global - Electronic Resources' Database Search
Innovation of Management Accounting Practices and Techniques
INTRODUCTION
BACKGROUND
Encyclopedia of Information Science and Technology, Third Edition
Table of Contents

www.ingramcontent.com/pod-product-compliance
Lightning Source LLC
LaVergne TN
LVHW080406011026
849161LV00009B/2357